The Cultural History Reader

The Cultural History Reader is the first volume to collect together the distinctive contributions made by cultural historians across the spectrum of historiographical methods. It offers a unique view into the insights to be gained from examining how cultural factors have shaped people's experiences of the world and guided their actions.

Featuring eleven thematic sections, covering everything from childhood to technology and war to popular culture, this book bridges disparate themes, periods, nationalities and religions to present detailed analyses of a variety of cultural responses and interpretations in diverse historical contexts. Peter McCaffery and Ben Marsden use their wealth of experience in teaching and researching cultural history to identify key topics and to provide the most telling extracts, illustrating how different social and cultural factors intersect and link together to give a richer picture of the past in all its surprising complexity. They also provide authoritative and clearly written introductions that contextualize each section and show the ways in which the themes have been handled by different cultural historians.

The book provides a detailed and accessible introduction to cultural history as a discipline, outlining how it has developed since the eighteenth century and where it differs from related disciplines such as sociology, anthropology and archaeology. *The Cultural History Reader* is a perfect resource for all students of cultural history and all those interested in how focusing on cultural factors has shaped our understanding of the past.

Peter McCaffery taught Sociology and Cultural History in the University of Aberdeen. His publications include *Midwifery and the Medicalization of Childbirth,* edited with Edwin van Teijlingen, George Lowis and Maureen Porter (2000). He is interested in problems of inter-disciplinary collaboration, both in research and in professional practice.

Ben Marsden is Director of the Centre for the History and Philosophy of Science, Technology and Medicine at the University of Aberdeen. He has been involved in the teaching of cultural history, especially of science and technology, since 1992. His books include *Watt's Perfect Engine: Steam and the Age of Invention* (2002), *Engineering Empires: A Cultural History of Technology in Nineteenth-Century Britain* with Crosbie Smith (2005), and *Uncommon Contexts: Encounters between Science and Literature, 1800–1914* edited with Ralph O'Connor and Hazel Hutchison (2013).

Routledge Readers in History

The Decolonization Reader
Edited by James Le Sueur

The Enlightenment: A Sourcebook and Reader
Edited by Olga Gomez, Francesca Greensides and Paul Hyland

The European Women's History Reader
Edited by Christine Collette and Fiona Montgomery

The Fascism Reader
Edited by Aristotle A. Kallis

The Feminist History Reader
Edited by Sue Morgan

The Global History of Childhood Reader
Edited by Heidi Morrison

The Global History Reader
Edited by Bruce Mazlish and Akira Iriye

The History and Narrative Reader
Edited by Geoffrey Roberts

The History of Sexuality in Europe Reader
Edited by Anna Clark

The History On Film Reader
Edited by Marnie Hughes-Warrington

The Irish Women's History Reader
Edited by Alan Hayes and Diane Urquhart

The Modern Historiography Reader
Edited by Adam Budd

The Nature of History Reader
Edited by Keith Jenkins and Alun Munslow

The New Imperial Histories Reader
Edited by Stephen Howe

The Cultural History Reader

Edited by

Peter McCaffery and Ben Marsden

Routledge
Taylor & Francis Group

LONDON AND NEW YORK

First published 2014
by Routledge
2 Park Square, Milton Park, Abingdon, Oxon OX14 4RN

and by Routledge
711 Third Avenue, New York, NY 10017

Routledge is an imprint of the Taylor & Francis Group, an informa business

British Library Cataloguing in Publication Data
A catalogue record for this book is available from the British Library

Library of Congress Cataloging-in-Publication Data
The cultural history reader / edited by Peter McCaffery and Ben Marsden.
      pages cm.—(Routledge readers in history)
   Includes bibliographical references and index.
   1. Civilization—History.   2. Readers—Civilization.   I. McCaffery,
Peter Gabriel, 1935–   II. Marsden, Ben.
   CB7.C84 2013
   909—dc23   2013025669

ISBN: 978-0-415-52042-3 (hbk)
ISBN: 978-0-415-52043-0 (pbk)

Typeset in Perpetua and Bell Gothic
by RefineCatch Limited, Bungay, Suffolk

Printed and bound by CPI Group (UK) Ltd, Croydon, CR0 4YY

In memory of Joan Pittock Wesson, 1930–2012

Contents

PART VII
Childhood

PART VIII
Individualism

PART IX
Literacy and Orality

PART X
Technology

Acknowledgements

We would like to thank our students, colleagues and former colleagues in the Cultural History group, especially: Louise Bourdua, Rainer Broemer, Jennifer Carter, Leigh Clayton, David Cram, Melvin Dalgarno, Nigel Dower, Paul Dukes, David Dumville, John Dunkley, Nick Fisher, Elizabeth Hallam, David Irwin, Marius Kwint, Colin Maclaren, David Mannings, Eric Matthews, Elizabeth Neswald, Colm O'Boyle, Ralph O'Connor, Hushang Philsooph, William Scott, David Smith, Michael Spiller, Trevor Stack, Andrew Walls, Colin Whatford, Roger Williams, Philip Withington and Chris Wright – and especially Andrew Wear, for his helpful comments on parts of the manuscript for this Reader, and also Janet Mackay and Susan McCourt and colleagues on the library staff at the University of Aberdeen. Our thanks to Peter Burke for his encouragement, and to four anonymous reviewers for their comments on an early outline of plans for this book. In addition, special thanks are due to our editors at Routledge (Paul Brotherston, Laura Mothersole and Eve Setch) for their patience. Peter McCaffery would like to thank Teresa McCaffery. Ben Marsden would like to thank Rebecca Duffield.

The articles listed below have been reproduced with kind permission (some have been shortened and edited). Whilst every effort has been made to trace copyright holders, this has not been possible in all cases. Any omissions brought to our attention will be remedied in future editions.

Part I: Gender

McKeon, Michael. 'Historicizing Patriarchy: The Emergence of Gender Difference in England, 1660–1760' in *Eighteenth Century Studies* 28:3 (1995), pp. 295–303, 317–18. Copyright © 1995 by the American Society for Eighteenth-Century Studies. Reprinted with permission of The Johns Hopkins University Press.

Davidoff, Leonore and Hall, Catherine. *Family Fortunes: Men and Women of the English Middle Class 1780–1850* (second edition) (London: Routledge, 2002), pp. xiii–xxiv. Copyright © 2002 Taylor & Francis. Reproduced by permission of Taylor & Francis Books UK.

Tosh, John. *A Man's Place: Masculinity and the Middle-Class Home in Victorian England* (New Haven: Yale University Press, 1999), pp. 102–22. Copyright © 1999 John Tosh.

Part II: Commerce, Credit and Consumption

Le Goff, Jacques. *Money and the Middle Ages: An Essay in Historical Anthropology* (Cambridge: Polity, 2012), pp. 142–50. The English Edition © Polity Press 2012.

Padgett, John F. and McLean, Paul D. 'Economic credit in Renaissance Florence' in *The Journal of Modern History* 83:1 (Chicago: University of Chicago Press, 2011). Copyright © 2011 University of Chicago Press. Reproduced by permission of University of Chicago Press.

Breen, Timothy H. 'The meanings of things: interpreting the consumer economy in the eighteenth century' in Brewer, John and Porter, Roy, eds, *Consumption and the World of Goods* (London: Routledge, 1994), pp. 249–60. Copyright © 1994 Taylor & Francis. Reproduced by permission of Taylor & Francis Books UK.

Part III: Time, Space and Measurement

Woodward, David. 'Reality, Symbolism, Time and Space in Medieval World Maps' in *Annals of the Association of American Geographers* 75:4 (1985), pp. 510–21. Copyright © 1985 Taylor & Francis. Reproduced by permission of Taylor & Francis Books UK.

Glennie, Paul and Thrift, Nigel. 'The Spaces of Clock Times' in Joyce, Patrick, ed., *The Social in Question: New Bearings in History and the Social Sciences* (London: Routledge, 2002), pp. 151–74. Copyright © 2006 Taylor & Francis. Reproduced by permission of Taylor & Francis Books UK.

Alder, Ken. *The Measure of All Things: The Seven-Year Odyssey that Transformed the World* (London: Little Brown, 2004), pp. 132–42. Copyright © 2002 Ken Alder, reprinted with permission of Little, Brown Group Ltd. and Ken Alder.

Part IV: Others

Nirenberg, David. *Communities of Violence: Persecution of Minorities in the Middle Ages* (Princeton: Princeton University Press, 1996), pp. 3–7. Copyright © 1996 Princeton University Press. Reprinted with permission of Princeton University Press.

White, Richard. *The Middle Ground: Indians, Empires, and Republics in the Great Lakes Region 1650–1815* (Cambridge: Cambridge University Press, 1991), pp. 50–60. Copyright © 1991 Cambridge University Press. Reproduced with permission of Cambridge University Press.

Gombrich, Richard F. *Theravada Buddhism: A Social History from Ancient Benares to Modern Colombo* (London: Routledge, 2006), pp. 171–95. Copyright © 2006 Taylor & Francis. Reproduced by permission of Taylor & Francis Books UK.

Part V: Popular Culture

Watkins, Carl. '"Folklore" and "Popular Religion" in Britain during the Middle Ages' in *Folklore* 115:2 (2004), pp. 140–50. Copyright © 2004 The Folklore Society. Reprinted with permission of Routledge Journals; Taylor and Francis Ltd.

Thompson, Edward P. *Customs in Common* (New York: New Press, 1993), pp. 1–15. Copyright © 1993 E.P. Thompson and Merlin Press Ltd., www.merlinpress.co.uk.

Burke, Peter. 'Introduction to the Third Edition' in *Popular Culture in Early Modern Europe* (Farnham: Ashgate, 2009), pp. 7–15. Copyright © 2009 Peter Burke. Reprinted by permission of the Publishers.

Part VI: Religion

Bossy, John. 'Moral Arithmetic: Seven Sins into Ten Commandments' in Leites, Edmund, ed., *Conscience and Casuistry in Early Modern Europe* (Cambridge: Cambridge University Press, 1988), pp. 214–34. Copyright © 1988, 2002 Maison des Sciences de l'Homme and Cambridge University Press, reproduced with permission.

Brooke, John Hedley. 'Science and Religion' in Olby, Robert C., Cantor, Geoffrey N., Christie, John R.R. and Hodge, Michael J.S., eds, *Companion to the History of Modern Science* (London: Routledge, 1990), pp. 763–82. Copyright © 1990 Taylor & Francis. Reproduced by permission of Taylor & Francis Books UK.

Part VII: Childhood

Mintz, Steven. 'Children of the Covenant'. Reprinted with permission of the publisher from *Huck's Raft: A History of American Childhood*, pp. 7–12, 17–21, 30–1, Cambridge, MA: Harvard University Press. Copyright © 2004 by the President and Fellows of Harvard University Press.

Koepp, Cynthia J. 'Curiosity, science, and experiential learning in the eighteenth century' in Immel, Andrea and Witmore, Michael, eds, *Childhood and Children's Books in Early Modern Europe 1550–1800* (London: Routledge, 2005), pp. 153–80. Copyright © 2005 Taylor & Francis. Reproduced by permission of Taylor & Francis Books UK.

Brewer, John. 'Childhood revisited: the genesis of the modern toy' in *History Today* 30.12 (London, UK: Institute for Historical Research, 1980), pp. 32–9. © History Today.

Part VIII: Individualism

Martin, John Jeffries. *The Myth of Renaissance Individualism* (Basingstoke: Palgrave Macmillan, 2004), pp. 208–23. Copyright © 2004 John Jeffries Martin. Reprinted with permission of Palgrave Macmillan.

Mascuch, Michael. *Origins of the Individualist Self: Autobiography and Self-Identity in England 1591–1791* (Cambridge: Polity, 1997), pp. 71–96. Copyright © 1997 Michael Mascuch.

Kinmonth, Earl H. 'Nakamura Keiu and Samuel Smiles: a Victorian Confucian and a Confucian Victorian' in *American Historical Review* 85:3 (1980), pp. 535–56. Copyright © Oxford University Press. Reprinted with permission of Oxford University Press.

Part IX: Literacy and Orality

Clanchy, Michael T. *From Memory to Written Record: England 1066–1307* (third edition) (Malden: Wiley-Blackwell, 2012), pp. 187–8, 262–5, 295–300. © Wiley-Blackwell.

Franklin, Simon. *Writing, Society and Culture in Early Modern Rus, c. 950–1300* (Cambridge: Cambridge University Press, 2002), pp. 2–9. Copyright © 2002 Simon Franklin, published by Cambridge University Press. Reprinted with permission.

Hudson, Nicholas. 'Constructing oral tradition: the origins of the concept in Enlightenment intellectual culture' in Fox, Adam and Woolf, Daniel, eds, *The Spoken Word: Oral Culture in Britain 1500–1850* (Manchester: Manchester University Press, 2003), pp. 240–55. © Manchester University Press.

Part X: Technology

Mayr, Otto. *Authority, Liberty, and Automatic Machinery in Early Modern Europe* (Baltimore: Johns Hopkins University Press, 1986), pp. 115–21. © 1986 Otto Mayr. Reprinted with the permission of The Johns Hopkins University Press.

Macleod, Christine. *Heroes of Invention: Technology, Liberalism, and British Identity, 1750–1914* (Cambridge: Cambridge University Press, 2007), pp. 1–12. Copyright © 2007 Christine Macleod, published with permission of Cambridge University Press.

Marx, Leo. 'Technology: The Emergence of a Hazardous Concept' in *Technology and Culture* 51:3 (2010), pp. 561–77. Copyright © 2010 by the Society for the History of Technology. Adapted and reprinted with permission of The Johns Hopkins University Press.

Part XI: War

Hirsch, Adam J. 'The collision of military cultures in seventeenth-century New England' in *Journal of American History* 74.4 (1988), pp. 1187–212. Oxford University Press for the Organization of American Historians.

Smith, Leonard V. 'The "*culture de guerre*" and French historiography of the Great War of 1914–1918' in *History Compass* 5.6 (2007), pp. 1967–79. © History Compass.

Introduction to the Reader

WHAT IS CULTURAL HISTORY? In this book, we respond to that question by presenting the enquirer with diverse examples of good research. The diversity of the material presented in these pages points to the breadth of cultural history. At the same time, readers will perceive a family likeness underlying this diversity. In order to indicate what this resemblance consists of, the book starts with two introductory chapters. The present chapter addresses the question of what cultural history is now. The following one outlines how it developed historically.

Three points are made in these prefatory remarks. First, cultural history is about how people have set out to find meaning in their lives. Secondly, it is helpful to consider many different fields of activity, ranging (for example) from family life to exploration to making war, and to try to trace inter-relationships between manifestations of the quest for meaning in these various contexts. Thirdly, the terms now used to denote such fields of activity are liable to carry the seeds of misunderstanding or confusion. The very terms used in this Reader as headings for the sections into which the book is divided – words such as 'literacy', 'religion', 'technology' or 'childhood' – need to be examined with an interest in how they came into common usage, and with a certain degree of mistrust.

Cultural history involves practice and discourse on different levels. To start with, there is the practice and discourse of those being studied. The traces available to the historian attempting to reconstruct what life meant to them may consist of songs they sang, writings they read or ships they sailed in – or an immense variety of other materials.

The historian's way of using these materials, these traces, as evidence to support a certain interpretation of those people's outlook and motivation, constitutes a separate level of practice and discourse. For example, Jack Goody (1993) was curious to know what flowers have meant to people in various societies at different periods in the past. His interest in the history of gardens led him to visit gardens and to seek out images of flowers, writings on gardening and records of trade in plants. This Reader presents a number of instances of how evidence has been used by writers of cultural history in recent decades.

At another level, again, Goody's book on the culture of flowers can stimulate us to reflect on how we can more fully know the past, and how we can reconstruct the subjective element in the responses to the natural environment of people in previous generations in this or that part of the world.

Likewise, in addition to offering examples of how research into cultural history has been undertaken by its practitioners, this book is aimed at raising in the mind of its readers questions about how to achieve a better understanding of what life meant to people in the past. Hence the need for differentiating not only between (a) historical actors' quest for meaning and (b) cultural historians' quest for what that meaning was in specific contexts, but also between the detailed study of a specific topic and (c) reflection concerning the nature of the insight that cultural historians seek.

This book is concerned with all of these levels. The extracts presented can be enjoyed simply at level (a), as stories of lives led by Renaissance merchants or by samurai in rapidly industrialising Japan, and so on. But they are gathered in this book so as to illustrate level (b), namely how evidence concerning the past can be used to address questions as to the meaning people's lives held for them. Furthermore, the selection of extracts has been guided by the aim of stimulating reflection in more general terms, at level (c), on the issue of what counts as good cultural history.

Defining cultural history

How, then, may cultural history be defined? The working definition employed in this book runs as follows:

Cultural history is the study of the meanings people have found in their lives and relationships, and in the world around them, and of the processes whereby these meanings were produced, negotiated, expressed and reproduced.

Being so comprehensive in scope, cultural history is capable of being defined in a variety of ways. The definition offered here says nothing explicitly about how cultural history relates to other kinds of history, or to other academic disciplines besides history. But such questions readily arise, and they can usefully be addressed in order to make clear what it is that renders cultural history distinctive. After considering the similarities and differences between cultural history and other ways of looking at the past, it will be time to examine what may be meant by the word 'culture'.

To speak of 'cultural history' seems at first sight to be comparable to speaking of, say, economic history or military history. Economic historians specialise in looking at the ways in which people have engaged in economic activity. Military historians focus on how they made war. Thus it is tempting to say that cultural historians concern themselves with a particular sphere of life, namely culture, distinguishable from economics and warfare. But even though the word 'culture' is sometimes reserved for art, music and drama, to say that cultural history is concerned purely with artistic creation would be misleading. Cultural historians concern themselves not with one special type of activity but with the meanings people have found in whatever they did and experienced. Thus, as well as having a close affinity with obviously meaning-focused disciplines like art history, the history of religions and the study of literature and storytelling, cultural history has much to contribute to economic, political and legal history.

This leaves unanswered the question of how cultural history relates to 'plain history' – a question that has no across-the-board answer. As will emerge from the historical account to follow, cultural historians in the nineteenth century were critical of a prevailing tendency at that time for history to be identified with the study of public affairs and the workings of the State. But more recently, that degree of specialisation has tended to be rejected by professional historians. Between 'plain history' and cultural history the difference now has more to do with where the emphasis lies and what questions drive the analyses and interpretations of the historian. 'Plain history' has more to do with tracing the sequence of events and inferring patterns amongst those events. Cultural historians, on the other hand, set out to reconstruct the meanings that participants attributed to events, and how they related these events to other aspects of their lives.

When it comes to discussing the relationship between cultural history and disciplines other than history, there is widespread agreement that anthropologists have a great deal in common with cultural historians, their primary concern being with how human communities preserve or modify the traditions that give shape and meaning to their members' lives. In the interwar years, which were the early days of systematic anthropological fieldwork, it used to be the case that the stability of customs was emphasised, and there was often an assumption that one cultural milieu could be understood separately from another. However, this tendency later came in for sustained criticism, with increasing globalisation and rapid social change. Cultural historians and anthropologists alike now share a concern to avoid the danger of over-emphasising homogeneity and stability, and they have a common interest in 'agency' – the active part played by individuals in making sense of their experiences and trying to shape their own lives (Ahearn 1999). Like cultural historians, anthropologists tend to lay emphasis on the importance of symbols and rituals, and seek to relate these to mundane patterns of everyday life.

Archaeology, too, has much in common with cultural history. The methodological tools of both disciplines include the investigation of material culture to gain insight into the life-world of the people who made and used the artefacts which outlived them. Whereas archaeologists used to concentrate their research on prehistoric sites, and largely left it to others to integrate material remains with documentary evidence from periods for which there are written records, this earlier division of labour has yielded place to a recognition by both sides that careful scrutiny of artefacts and patterns of settlement can serve as a check on the possible ideological distortion in written records. For instance, the study of ancient Israel used to depend largely on evidence drawn from the scrutiny of the Hebrew scriptures, but it has now been broadened by using the results of Middle Eastern archaeology (Finkelstein and Mazar 2007).

As with archaeology, so with human geography; recent decades have seen expanded interest in the subjective aspects of life in human settlements, and of trade and other interactions between them. Geographers and cultural historians share an interest in travel-narratives and in the history of map-making. The growth of cultural geography reflects an increased interest in understanding how people have oriented themselves in the world. What has this or that human community conceived to be the 'good life'? What features of their environment have their tools, their myths and their aspirations led them to see as having relevance to their hopes of sustaining a flourishing communal life? Relevant features of an environment (be it that of a human population or of creatures of any other species) are sometimes called 'affordances' (Ingold 1992). This term can serve as one way of specifying the focus of attention which cultural historians concentrate upon when analysing historical phenomena. Because human beings have the ability to communicate in language and other symbols, their assessment of what constitute relevant features of their environment may include much more than is possible for other species.

To say that human beings seek meaning in life is to use a metaphor drawn from the sphere of language and communication. Words have meanings, as do gestures, symbols and symbolic actions like putting on a uniform. From this linguistic and symbolic core, the word 'meaning' can be extended to refer to something even more intangible. The broader sense of the word 'meaning' is linked to two ideas in particular: intention, as in 'Start as you mean to go on', and value, as in 'Your approval means a lot to me'. (For semantic analyses of the concept of meaning, see Lyons 1977, Millikan 2004 and Jackendoff 2011.) Thus, to define cultural history by its focus on the meanings that people have found in their lives is to say that it involves directing attention to what they intended and what they valued. At the same time, it also implies that unpacking symbols and accounting for their resonance is a key part of the task of a cultural historian. For these reasons, cultural history draws upon semiotics, the study of signs and signification, as well as upon linguistics. (See Darnton 1984 and Hunt 1992 for instances of history interpreted in this manner.)

On the other hand, although human motivation is one topic of research in academic psychology, historical research had until recently attracted little attention from psychologists. From the 1880s to the 1980s their aspiration to establish psychology as a branch of the natural sciences led most of them to prefer laboratory-based research, in which the behaviour of those who were the subjects of psychological experiments was largely studied in a decontextualised way – that is to say, with minimal reference to historical and social context. This made sense as a means of achieving standardisation, and has facilitated the use of sophisticated statistical methods. But by the 1990s a minority of psychologists were questioning this approach. Cultural psychology has now gained recognition as one branch of mainstream psychology. Meanwhile, cultural historians have begun to take a greater interest in the study of the emotions (Bourke 2006; Matt 2011). Thus there is currently some convergence between their interests and those of psychologists. However, research by cultural psychologists is generally intended to serve practical ends, especially in the contexts of education and of mental health (Baumeister 1991; Park and Folkman 1997; Wells 2009). The study of the past thus tends to be seen as less useful than a focus upon contemporary issues.

In sociology, too, the emphasis is often laid upon the study of societies in the present or the fairly recent past. But many sociologists aim to place their research findings within a long-term context. Hence there is considerable overlap between sociology and social history (Burke 2005a). How, then, does social history relate to cultural history? While social historians do include in their analyses the subjective factors of intentions and values, and thus meaning, they also set out to clarify the functioning of institutions, even when these are shaped by impersonal forces rather than by interpersonal relations. A characteristic concern of sociology and social history alike is with large-scale processes of structural change that develop in ways that had not been envisaged or intended. But it is the intentions that are the primary focus of interest for a cultural historian. Social history enjoyed increased popularity in the 1960s and 1970s, before being somewhat overshadowed in the 1980s by the rise of cultural history. One response has been to argue that only a combination of the two holds promise for a deeper understanding of the past, and so there is talk of socio-cultural analysis and of cultural-and-social history.

Akin to the sociology of culture, and also to the history of popular culture, is the discipline of cultural studies. This has come to be focused on the study of modern news and entertainment media, while developing a sophisticated body of theory to analyse both the production of material for circulation and the resonance it has for those to whom it is addressed. (See Smith 2011 and Hall, Evans and Nixon 2013.) Cultural studies might thus be described as a specialised genre of cultural history.

The final group of disciplines or sub-disciplines with which cultural history may be compared and contrasted includes intellectual history, philosophy and cognitive science. Again, there is an overlap, in that all three have to do with how human beings generate their interpretations of reality, and thus the meanings they are able to discern in their experience. But all three give priority to elucidating how people represent the world discursively, rather than to the practical side of life and the ways in which people's actions often reflect custom and loyalty rather than logic and conceptual thought. By contrast, practice and discourse are of equal importance for cultural historians, since both play a part in the forging of meaning. Cultural history deals with that which was taken for granted and mundane, as well as with that which was out of the ordinary and provoked conscious reflection.

How, then, is it best to relate the task of cultural history to the slippery concept of 'culture'? This is, after all, a word that in the course of time has acquired several distinct meanings. That being so, it would be unhelpful (as has already been pointed out) to define cultural history by reference to culture, as if culture were the object that it investigates. Better, instead, to ask how this one word came to be put to use in such a variety of different ways.

More will be said in the chapter that follows about how, from the mid-nineteenth century onwards, the term 'culture' came to be more and more widely employed, thanks to German and British authors such as Klemm, Tylor and Arnold. On the one hand it was used by Klemm and Tylor to refer to the way of life shared by a community, and on the other by Arnold to denote the arts. The former is 'culture' in the anthropological sense. The latter is 'culture' conceived as that which enriches human existence by lifting people out of a narrow preoccupation with transitory material self-interest.

Among those who sought, in the second half of the twentieth century, to bring together these strands in the word's range of meanings was the literary critic and academic Raymond Williams (1921–1988). On him, too, more will be said below. Here it is worthwhile to mention that he distinguished three levels of culture. The first is 'the lived culture of a particular time and place, only fully accessible to those living in that time and place'. Secondly, there is 'the recorded culture . . . from art to the most everyday facts'. Thirdly, there is 'the factor connecting lived cultures and period cultures', namely 'the culture of the selective tradition' (Williams 1961: 49).

To put this in another way, although the Victorian world has gone, it has left behind traces. From these traces people in later generations can create accounts of what Victorian life meant to those who lived at that time. Williams insisted that cultural history 'must be more than the sum of the particular histories' (of politics, of war, of trade, of music etc.), for 'it is with the relations between them, the particular forms of the whole organization, that it is especially concerned,' and therefore analysing culture involves 'the study of the relationships between the elements in a whole way of life' (1961: 46).

These quotations are drawn from a work entitled *The Long Revolution*. Williams conceived of the study of culture as a part of a complex process whereby human societies might be transformed for the better. He shared the aspiration of Victorian intellectuals like Arnold to lift people out of a myopic concern with short-term gain. But he was enough of a Marxist to hold that this aspiration could be realised only if the realities of everyday life were given due attention. His rather unusual marriage of political motivation with aesthetic sensibility made him peculiarly aware of how problematic a term 'culture' is.

Williams presented elsewhere, in *Keywords*, an account of how the meanings of 'culture' had grown more and more complex over the centuries. It is, of course, related to 'agriculture', and its seventeenth-century usage expressed the notion that in their development human beings, like plants, need to be tended and nurtured (Horowitz 1998). The botanical metaphor was gradually forgotten as the word acquired a broader range of meanings. But it is worth pointing out that it contains an ambiguity, arising from the implied reference to a gardener who is an active supplier of nutrients to the plants. The plants that benefit from this tending are to that extent playing a more passive part in the process of growth. Regardless of whether or not the metaphor of cultivation is present to the mind of the word's user, talk of 'culture' constantly raises the issue of agency versus passivity. Children are, after all, far from being passive recipients – a point well brought out in the title of a book on childhood language acquisition: *The Guided Reinvention of Language* (Lock 1980). Children have the capacity to develop differently from how their parents may have intended.

Tempting as it may be to define 'culture' as a way of referring to the constellation of formative influences on a set of people living in a given milieu, this idea turns out to be unsatisfactory when applied to specific historical processes, because it tacitly foregrounds the idea that socialisation determines outcomes. It thus tends to distract attention from the creative element in the absorption and modification of influence.

There is another problem with the word 'culture', one that has become more evident over time, as globalisation has proceeded. As was pointed out above (in the context of cultural history's affinity with anthropology), it will not do to identify a culture with the practices and outlook of a particular group. Individuals from one group have a tendency to pick up new ways of acting and thinking as they encounter members of another group. Speaking of a culture as if it were a bounded entity carries the risk of being led thereby to apply a static model of cultural phenomena, as if cultures were homogeneous and self-contained. It is better to conceive 'culture' as a shorthand way of referring to a potentially changing repertoire of possible resources for understanding the world and acting within it.

In addition to these two types of problem with the word 'culture' – its ambiguity as between activity and passivity, and its potential for suggesting a static framework – there is a third reason for being wary of the term. This is its tendency to acquire an ever wider range of meanings. The anthropologists Kroeber and Kluckhohn (1963) offered a list of 164 meanings that had been given to it. Since then, it has been adopted for their own purposes by political scientists, management theorists and primatologists, not to mention its journalistic usages. Baldwin and colleagues (2005) enumerated 313 meanings. Confusion is hard to avoid when using what is now generally recognised to be an imprecise term, just because of its many overtones. Admittedly 'culture' can still in some contexts be a useful term, meriting the careful analysis it has received from Williams (1961), Sewell (1999) and Cubitt (2007: 141–2). Without that care, the lack of precision makes it unsuitable for the purpose of trying to pin down what is distinctive about cultural history.

The interweaving of strands in cultural history

This Reader is divided into sections, each concerned with an aspect of experience. But extracts have, where possible, been chosen which are relevant to the subject matter of more than one section. For example, the extract on childhood in seventeenth-century Massachusetts, by Mintz, touches on the religious beliefs held by parents. What Thompson has to say about popular culture arises from the author's primary interest in the relationships between employers and those who work for them. When Kinmonth sketches the background to the enthusiastic reception by samurai, in the wake of the Meiji Restoration, of a Victorian treatise on self-reliance, he is shedding light on relationships between cultural traditions that are often contrasted with each other as instances of individualism, on the one hand, and a collective sense of identity on the other. And the difference described by Hirsch between Pequot notions of how to make war and the military mindset of the settlers who came into conflict with them in the 1630s had a great deal to do with technology. Specialised research on one aspect of experience needs to be complemented by knowledge about other aspects. (See Beattie and Fenton 2010 for instances where this principle is applied.) Religion should not be separated from war, nor gender relations from the economy. That principle has guided the structuring of this Reader.

By dint of prolonged familiarity with evidence relating to a particular historical milieu, researchers arrive at a sense of the interconnectedness of spheres such as gender and religion, war and work. For many historians, this is the background to the narrative they present to their readers, or to their analyses of the development of institutions. For cultural historians, it constitutes the foreground.

In cultural history, what is of primary concern is people's active engagement in the effort to make sense of what they are doing and experiencing, rather than the outcomes, such as defeat or victory in a war. This difference appears very clearly from a comparison between military history written before the 1970s and some of the more recent work on soldiering. For example, a traditional account of battles fought in the First World War, such as Terraine 1964, may indeed have much to say about what the troops endured, but even if it has, this theme will be subordinated to the aim of providing an explanation for successes and failures. After the 'cultural turn', most cultural historians of war initially concentrated attention on how civilian life had been affected (see Winter 1992). But in the twenty-first century, more and more publications about the 1914–18 war and other wars have focused on what motivated members of the armed forces, and how they tried to make sense of their experiences (Watson 2008). This reflects the growing interest in the history of emotions (Burke 2005b and 2008: 110–12), as well as the idea of 'history from below', which already guided many cultural historians in choosing a research topic.

The introductory remarks at the start of each section in this Reader will provide further examples to illustrate the connections between the various section-headings under which the extracts are distributed. But here a preliminary instance may be helpful.

In her study of parenting in England between 1760 and 1830, Bailey (2012: 3) points out that being a parent was just one aspect of a person's life, and should therefore be studied in the context of their other commitments. As an instance, Bailey points to the father recruited into the army, and the symbolic significance of his departure from home for the wars. This theme is linked to the debate among gender historians regarding the contested thesis that the years on either side of 1800 saw the spread of an ideology of 'separate spheres'. (See Vickery 1993 for a critique of this thesis.) Were mothers in this period put under greater pressure than women in earlier generations to stay at home and care for their children, leaving it to their husbands to engage with the wider world in their roles as breadwinners? If so, did this pressure stem from a religious source, with preachers now laying greater emphasis on the emotional lives of believers? Or had it more to do with industrialisation and urbanisation? In the hands of a good cultural historian, the themes of childhood, gender, war, religion, work and economic change may intersect, to the extent that each is relevant to an understanding of the set of resources and constraints affecting an individual. To gain a better insight as to how individuals could fashion a sense of personal identity within a changing environment is cultural history's ideal.

The altered meanings of significant words

There is great value in cultivating awareness of the way certain terms are used that have come to form part of everyday discourse and are readily adopted by cultural historians in sketching their agenda. In the preceding paragraph, terms like childhood, religion and work were used for spheres of cultural involvement. Yet just as the word 'culture' itself came to carry a wide range of meanings, the same applies to those terms as well. For greater clarity, it is as well to be aware that words now seen as unproblematic may well have been used differently in the past. This was what stimulated Raymond Williams to compile his 'vocabulary of culture and society' – a list of words he had found cropping up in writings and conversations about the broad range of topics that interested him. In *Keywords* he gathered together over a hundred such words, along with what he was able to find out about their derivations and the ways in which their meanings had developed, sometimes after a term had been borrowed from another language and another national context.

It is sometimes worthwhile to use evidence from non-European languages to see what latent problems there may be with familiar words. For instance, once Japan had begun to industrialise, a suitable word was needed for employees paid to do factory work. This proved to be by no means straightforward. In Tokugawa Japan, before 1868, rural labour had been viewed as the fulfilment of a social obligation. Existing words for peasant labourers thus had connotations arising from the quasi-feudal nature of rural society. They were unsuitable for use in the context of a purely contractual relationship between a capitalist firm and its factory hands. The word that now came into use for the purpose was *shokkō*. However, this label was resented by workers, who felt demeaned by it (Smith 1984; Nimura 1987). The conceptual link between work and performance of one's duty to a superior implied that hiring oneself out for paid work without regard for social obligation seemed dishonourable. Has this example any broader relevance for cultural history in general? It can serve to remind us that what may seem to be just a simple descriptive term (such as 'worker' in English) may fail to convey the evaluative moral overtones carried by a corresponding term within a different semantic framework. To illustrate the ethically neutral character that the word 'work' has in modern discourse, consider how the term 'sex-worker' has since the 1980s come to be employed in English in place of the more stigmatised word 'prostitute'. But would people in Victorian times have been willing to refer to prostitution as 'sex work'?

Acquiring a feel for the fact that the same word often connotes something different today than it did in an earlier period is an important part of the cultural historian's striving to re-create a past world where people related to one another differently and saw things differently, especially if they spoke another language. It becomes particularly necessary when the period being studied is more remote. In the lives of people in medieval Europe, for instance, there was not the separation that subsequently grew up between the religious sphere and the rest of life. Admittedly, convenience may sometimes require the use of a shorthand, as in the section headings used in this Reader. But those headings do not refer to elements suitable for being studied in isolation from each other.

To quote Raymond Williams once more, cultural history 'must be more than the sum of the particular histories.' This is what makes it interesting and exciting.

References

Ahearn, L.M. (1999) 'Agency', *Journal of Linguistic Anthropology*, 9: 12–15.

Bailey, J. (2012) *Parenting in England 1760–1830*, Oxford: Oxford University Press.

Baldwin, J.R., Faulkner, S.L., Hecht, M.L. and Lindsley, S.L. (eds) (2005) *Redefining Culture: perspectives across disciplines*, New York, NY: Routledge.

Baumeister, R.F. (1991) *Meanings of Life*, New York, NY: Guilford Press.

Beattie, C. and Fenton, K.A. (eds) (2010) *Intersections of Gender, Religion and Ethnicity in the Middle Ages*, Basingstoke: Macmillan.

Bourke, J. (2006) *Fear: a cultural history*, London: Virago.

Burke, P. (2005a) *History and Social Theory*, Cambridge: Polity.

Burke, P. (2005b) 'Is there a cultural history of the emotions?', in P. Gouk and H. Hills (eds) *Representing Emotions*, Farnham: Ashgate.

Burke, P. (2008) *What Is Cultural History?*, second edn, Cambridge: Polity.

Cubitt, G. (2007) *History and Memory*, Manchester: Manchester University Press.

Darnton, R. (1984) *The Great Cat Massacre and Other Episodes in French Cultural History*, London: Allen Lane and New York, NY: Basic Books.

Finkelstein, I. and Mazar, A. (ed. B.B. Schmidt) (2007) *The Quest for the Historical Israel*, Atlanta, GA: Society of Biblical Literature.

Goody, J. (1993) *The Culture of Flowers*, Cambridge: Cambridge University Press.

Hall, S., Evans, J. and Nixon, S. (eds) (2013) *Representation: cultural representations and signifying practices*, second edn, Thousand Oaks, CA: Sage.

Horowitz, M.C. (1998) *Seeds of Virtue and Knowledge*, Princeton, NJ: Princeton University Press.

Hunt, L. (1992) *The Family Romance of the French Revolution*, Berkeley: University of California Press.

Ingold, T. (1992) 'Culture and the perception of the environment', in E.J. Croll and D.J. Parkin (eds) *Bush Base: Forest Farm: culture, environment, and development*, London: Routledge.

Jackendoff, R.S. (2011) *A User's Guide to Thought and Meaning*, Oxford: Oxford University Press.

Kroeber, A.L. and Kluckhohn, C. (1963) *Culture: a critical review of concepts and definitions*, New York, NY: Random House (first published 1952).

Lock, A. (1980) *The Guided Reinvention of Language*, New York: Academic Press.

Lyons, J. (1977) *Semantics*, 2 vols, Cambridge: Cambridge University Press.

Matt, S.J. (2011) 'Current emotion research in history', *Emotion Review*, 3: 117–24.

Millikan, R.G. (2004) *Varieties of Meaning*, Cambridge, MA: MIT Press.

Nimura, K. (1987) 'The historical characteristics of labor relations in Japan', *Annals of the Society for the Study of Social Policy*, 31, online English translation <http://oohara. mt.tama.hosei.ac.jp/nk/English/eg-hischarjlr.html>.

Park, C.L. and Folkman, S. (1997) 'Meaning in the context of stress and coping', *Review of General Psychology*, 1: 115–44.

Sewell, W.H., Jr. (1999) 'The concept(s) of culture', in V.E. Bonnell and L. Hunt (eds) *Beyond the Cultural Turn*, Berkeley, CA: University of California Press.

Smith, P. (ed.) (2011) *The Renewal of Cultural Studies*, Philadelphia, PA: Temple University Press.

Smith, T.C. (1984) 'The right to benevolence: dignity and Japanese workers, 1890–1920', *Comparative Studies in Society and History*, 26: 587–613, at 589–90.

Terraine, J. (1964) *The Western Front, 1914–1918*, London: Hutchinson.

Vickery, A. (1993) 'Golden Age to separate spheres? A review of the categories and chronology of English women's history', *Historical Journal*, 36: 383–414.

Watson, A. (2008) *Enduring the Great War: combat, morale and collapse in the German and British Armies 1914–1918*, Cambridge: Cambridge University Press.

Wells, C.G. (2009) *The Meaning-Makers*, Bristol: Multilingual Matters.

Williams, R. (1961) *The Long Revolution*, London: Chatto & Windus.

Williams, R. (1983) *Keywords: a vocabulary of culture and society*, second edn, London: Fontana.

Winter, J.M. (1992) 'Catastrophe and culture: recent trends in the historiography of the First World War', *Journal of Modern History*, 64: 525–32.

Histories of Cultural History

> Cultural history is a curious kind of history: to the question "What is it?" there
> seems to be no easy answer. Theoretical definitions turn out to be practically
> appalling, and when one attempts a functional definition of the art, made up from
> the works of cultural historians themselves, one can go mad. (Colie 1964: 607)

Directions and definitions

'CULTURAL HISTORY' has many histories. It has become common to chart the
'emergence' of this field, as exciting as it is perplexing, from a great variety of intellectual
and practical sources. Narrating that 'emergence' requires multiple acts of retrospective
reconstruction. For the last forty years or so, we might say that 'cultural history' has been the
sum total of the work that self-defined cultural historians have pursued. The methods and
sources of 'cultural history', according to this empirical approach, would simply be those used
by this community. But if we are to seek origins in earlier periods, and to suggest boundaries in
the present, we cannot avoid labelling certain studies as 'cultural history' which were not
so described when they were written. Are we, then, 'trying to catch a cloud in a butterfly
net' (Burke 1991: 6)? The emergence of cultural history and its antecedents (amongst
them ethnography and anthropology, folklore studies, literary history and philology, art
history, history of ideas, social and labour history, historical sociology) over this longer
period may be charted in a 'positive' manner: particular techniques have been clarified or
adopted, from the mainstream of history and from other disciplines, particular topics have
come under the historian's gaze, and particular kinds of sources have begun to be used. The
emergence of the field may also be charted if not in a 'negative' mode then in a reactive one,
as 'cultural history' has defined itself, at least in the past, against other disciplines, like
political history.

One of the core challenges in trying to chart a course for past cultural history relates to
these contrasting perspectives: has 'cultural history' been a set of histories of culture or cultures, or has 'cultural history' been a way, or collections of ways, of doing history in a 'cultural'
manner? In either case, it should help if we try to understand the past and present meanings of

the word 'culture', in popular and in academic discourse. Yet that notoriously slippery word has had, and still does have, numerous conflicting and overlapping meanings (Williams 1983: 87–93; Sewell 1999; Eagleton 2000). The same is true of the related words *culture* in French and *Kultur* in German. Indeed, cultural history, *histoire culturelle* and *Kulturgeschichte* have been, and are being, practised differently in different countries, across continents, and in numerous languages (including, but by no means limited to, English, French and German). We may not be able to identify 'national traditions' of cultural history – especially where cultural history has been eclectic, heterogeneous in its products and only rarely formally institutionalised – but in practice cultural history has taken distinct forms in diverse arenas, its flavour often a response to ambient circumstances and agendas (see Chartier 2009 for a global perspective, Rogge 2011 for Europe, Jordanova 2011 for Britain, Arcangeli 2011 for a synthesis of traditions).

If we choose to start with the idea that 'cultural history' has been the history of culture, we might begin by exploring the meanings of the term 'culture' – famously described by Raymond Williams (1921–1988) as 'one of the two or three most complicated words in the English language' (Williams 1983: 87). Here we need one eye on the present and one on the past. We need to accept present-day diversity in usage whilst also understanding the concept's rich history: who has used 'culture', and related terms like 'cultivation' and 'civilisation', in English and other languages, for what purposes – and in connection with which disciplines (Bénéton 1975)? We might also ask, cautiously, who has written about 'culture' (or rather, one or more of its connotations) even before the word came into general use? Rather than settling on a single definition, we can accept the range of meanings as indicative of intense debate, at least since the Enlightenment, about the proper relationship between three core aspects of 'culture': general human development (intellectual, spiritual or aesthetic), particular ways of life (of a people, or period), and the works and practices of art and intellect (music, literature, painting, theatre, film and so forth).

The phrase 'culture of' was originally associated with the tending or 'cultivation' of the soil in agriculture and then, by extension, to the process of human 'upbringing' (Horowitz 1998). Later scholars began to refer to 'the culture', in the sense of educational cultivation, 'of the mind', 'of the understanding', or even 'of the arts' (intellectual, or even practical). By familiarity, it became possible to use 'culture' as an independent noun to indicate a social process, or stage, of development – or the achievement of a cultivated, educated, state. By the eighteenth century, when the *philosophes* of the French Enlightenment wanted educational provision for the masses, the word 'culture' on its own came to mean the development of that which is latent in human beings. The meanings of the French *culture* thus followed patterns similar to that of the English 'culture' – shifting from the 'culture of' something specific to 'culture' in general as an independent noun. *Cultur* or, later, *Kultur*, which was common in Germany from the 1780s, stood sometimes for the idea of 'civilization', in the sense of a progressive process of human development – even though, as we see below, scholars from the Romantic period onwards insisted that there was a plurality of local human 'cultures' rather than the linear development of a single Western standard; they began to use 'culture' as a term capturing humanity's more spiritual, emotional and imaginative characteristics in distinction to the increasingly materialistic, technological and even imperial connotations of 'civilisation' (Burke 1991: 20; Bowden 2009). Especially from the twentieth century, however, anthropologists and archaeologists came to associate 'culture' with artefacts and material things. Just as the word 'culture' has struggled to capture the changing relationship between intellectual and artefactual products, so have cultural historians returned, again and again, to the question of how – if at all – symbolic representations and material conditions are connected (Williams 1983: 87–93). That final theme runs constantly through the histories of cultural history sketched below.

The old cultural history and *Kulturgeschichte*

We may begin to understand the complex meanings of the word 'culture', but to find a starting point for 'cultural history' is almost as problematic as locating a beginning for the discipline of 'history'. 'Cultural history' has often been attached to the writing of histories of 'culture' howsoever defined; but that merely reminds us that a major source for cultural history has been the wider and constantly changing discipline of history itself. 'History' has been practised in many different ways; but 'cultural history' is especially indebted to those forms which have moved beyond constitutional history, politics and diplomacy amongst powerful elites, and the military encounters that have disrupted such power-broking. Cultural history, in its many manifestations, has tended to be a counter to those kinds of history that have focused on the powerful at the expense of the weak or marginal, on diplomatic action at the expense of everyday life, and on disruptive activities, like war, at the expense of human routines.

Where, precisely, can we locate an 'old cultural history' that moved beyond politics, narrowly conceived (Kelley 1996)? To find examples of cultural history even before the word 'culture' was used in the senses current from the late eighteenth century takes some mental agility, and it is undertaken at the risk of inventing origins – but it has been attempted. Peter Burke has no trouble in finding, in most cases long before 1800, histories of: language, literature and genres; artists, art and music; religious doctrines (especially heresies); philosophers and philosophy; disciplines; modes of thought or 'what was generally believed'; and even 'culture' in the then new sense of a combination of arts (possibly in synchronised advance). Into the eighteenth century, claims about the 'genius', 'spirit', 'temper' or 'humour' of a particular age or nation were not at all uncommon (Burke 1991). The *philosophe* and one-time king's historiographer Voltaire (1694–1778) wrote critically of history-writing of the 'kings-and-battles' type, recommending instead an *histoire des moeurs* (history of manners, or customs). Voltaire's *Essay on the Manners and Spirit of Nations* (1756) was much read in eighteenth-century Europe although it attracted scathing criticism, initially for its universalising pretensions and later for its judgmental aspects. Voltaire wanted an exemplary and modern history of the progress of the human mind (Force 2009). Those wanting to move beyond politics, however, accepted that power, custom and the conditions of society could not easily be separated. Giambattista Vico (1688–1744) had been trained in law and his *New Science* (1725; 1744; 1999) elaborated a history of civil society up to the present or, more precisely, a 'history of the ideas, the customs, the deeds of mankind': the social action he there described was, he insisted, an essential attribute of humanity (Mali 2012). Scottish Enlightenment figures, notably Adam Ferguson (1723–1816), wrote histories of society which they saw as natural histories of man, collectively, in 'his' social state (Heath and Merolle (eds) 2007).

Many eighteenth-century historians were wedded, like Voltaire, to a belief in 'progress' which served to unify the history of mankind. The concept of 'civilisation' in the eighteenth century was contrasted with 'barbaric', 'savage' or otherwise 'rude' ways of life: 'civilisation' as a process and as a label indicated humanity's rise from a primitive state to polite society, the cultivation of the arts and the exercise of reason. A history of 'civilisation' thus usually charted, and assumed, continuous progress and a correspondence between material and intellectual evolution (Gilbert 1960: 40–41). Such a history, though, raised various questions: civilisations were numerous, they sometimes declined or even died, and the hoped-for cultural unity was hard to find – unless it was selectively imposed. Did manners, virtue and the sciences really advance together? The Romantic philosopher Johann Gottfried Herder (1744–1803), another founder of cultural history, attacked the claim of the universal historians that 'civilisation', as the self-development of humanity, was a linear process leading to a superior eighteenth-century European culture: since different climates demonstrably led to different arts, there could be no absolute scale against which the excellence of culture could be measured. He thus wrote about 'the specific and variable cultures [plural] of social and economic groups within a nation': as a counter to the 'mechanical' (rational, industrial) and linear view of 'civilisation', Herder's approach emphasised the non-material aspects of humanity's development within diverse traditions, or folk-culture (Williams 1983: 89). Reviewing philologist Christian Adolph Klotz's *Genius saeculi*, Herder translated the title as *Zeitgeist*: this 'spirit of the times', or of the age, indicated a shared cultural climate, of a group in a particular time, that climate extending to intellectual, political, artistic, or moral dimensions (Barnard 2003).

The idea of a unity of culture, or national 'spirit', combined with progress according to a divine plan, is represented in the philosophy of history associated with the idealist G.W.F. Hegel (1770–1831). Hegel adopted the idea of a unity of cultural expression by nations or groups, coherent with the idea of a *Zeitgeist*. At the same time he proposed a progressive and dynamic unfolding of civilisation in a universal narrative. The history of mankind was the history of God gradually creating Himself and the universe, the divine spirit progressing to a higher plane, and civilisation rising. In this view, assorted forms of cultural expression at a particular time and in a particular place were manifestations of an underlying principle; different cultures, in time and place, were necessary stages in the process of unfolding. For Hegel, there was at any given point a particular national spirit to be observed in a society, impressing a common stamp on diverse endeavours including religion, politics, law, custom, science and art; the progressive national spirit was, allegedly, best expressed in condensed and cryptic form through a period's fine art (Gombrich 1969: 7–9, 14) – the paintings of Rembrandt, the sculpture of Michelangelo. However, the ideas of unfolding, whether inevitable or not, and of the implied superiority of particular 'cultures', would later discomfort commentators, especially those outside German traditions of history and philosophy. Admittedly, 'the history of culture as such, the history of all the aspects of life as it was lived in the past, could never be undertaken without some ordering principle, some centre from which the panorama can be surveyed' (Gombrich 1969: 25). Yet Hegel's idea was (so Gombrich claimed) 'exegetical', or at best heuristic, rather than observational. He and his followers worked to show historical events demonstrating what they already believed to be the case: cultural unity, patterns unfolding, and progression.

The German historian Leopold von Ranke (1795–1886) objected to this kind of ideas-driven history. In his studies of international politics he instead emphasised the use of primary sources and favoured painstaking and, in theory, objective narrative history. His first expertise was in philology and translation and he wanted, in a new professional history, to borrow traditional techniques from those disciplines – especially the use of a wide range of sources, including the mundane. Ranke's history was not without a meta-narrative: he expected to see the Divine hand at work in human affairs; and he wanted more than a dry and selective accumulation of facts and opinions. Although his own studies tended to emphasise politics and the state, he did not, like Voltaire and some of the Scottish history-writers, want to use history to judge past events and provide future instruction. Rather, as he wrote in the preface to his *History of the Latin and Teutonic Peoples*, he wanted to show 'what actually [i.e., essentially] happened' (*wie es eigentlich gewesen*), by appreciating and recording the facts. Although he allowed the historian to go some little way beyond the mere facts, in interpretative acts that discerned general essences and patterns (like the action of the hand of God), Ranke was critical of the grand sweeps and big ideas of 'philosophical history' (represented especially by Hegel). He gave more emphasis to human agency and particularity, which he thought was lost in such master narratives of unfolding civilisation. Ranke's 'document-based narrative political history' tended to marginalise the histories of 'civilisation' typical of late eighteenth-century Europe and beyond. But more vehement attempts even than Ranke's to strip judgment, interpretation, and a sense of unity from history could lead to a sense of historical chaos (Burke 1991: 19; Iggers and Powell 1990; Ranke, ed. Iggers, 2010).

Nineteenth-century forms of cultural history steered an uneasy path between quasi-Hegelian approaches where the 'spirit of the age', illustrated in locally integrated cultural expression, represented the stages of humanity's pre-ordained progress and Rankean narratives, dominated by the particular facts and contingencies revealed in primary sources. One especially important figure in Germany was the ethnologist Gustav F. Klemm (1802–67) who tried to synthesise Enlightenment notions of universal progress with his own contemporary experiences of museology, liberal politics, and social and technological change as Europe industrialised. From the 1840s, Klemm started to use *Kultur* in a way close to the 'civilisation' of the eighteenth-century's universal histories of humanity. The term *Geschichte der Kultur* ('history of culture') had been used in print by the 1790s, but Klemm's *Allgemeine Kulturgeschichte der Menschheit* (1843–52), or *General Cultural History of Mankind*, had a distinctive message: it traced a linear process of human development from original savagery to the (cultural) pinnacle of European freedom, with that process driven by the interactions of race and culture; within that overarching perspective he also used culture in Herder's ethnographic sense as a complete 'way of life' (Williams 1983: 90; Burke 1991: 7; Manias 2012).

The Swiss historian Jacob Burckhardt (1818–97), author of *Die Cultur der Renaissance in Italien* (1860), advocated another variety of *Kulturgeschichte* and for this he has been adopted, more so than Klemm, as a founder of modern cultural history (Gilbert 1960, 1986 and 1990; Grosse 1999). Unlike the eighteenth-century figures discussed above, Burckhardt was quite consciously a cultural historian. Although he avoided debates about historical method his dislikes were clear: some historians' scientific pretensions; the rational and teleological history associated with Hegel; political, diplomatic and military history, which he thought at best incomplete; and unstructured narrative history, which he found inadequate. In his student days he had been encouraged, by professors of ancient history and philology, to take into account customs, religion, the sciences, art, politics and language – as manifested in written and material remains. The cultural history that he later developed was similarly wide in scope, described general conditions rather than particularities, favoured enduring rather than accidental elements, and hoped to capture the characteristic features of the past. He wanted to extend the range of acceptable sources to include anything from literary works to monuments, his ambition being to reveal the modes of humanity's thought and the manner of its achievements (in literature and art) in any particular age. Although Burckhardt did examine the general and material conditions of politics and society, he did not see them as rigid determinants of culture but rather as, at most, temporary inspirations for the intellectual or artistic activity that was his real interest. Unsurprisingly, he tended to study periods in which fine art was at its high-point (Gilbert 1960: 42–6).

In *Die Cultur* he investigated the Renaissance through the medium of its fine art, exemplary literature and high thought. He used what in retrospect is an 'interdisciplinary' approach, discerning links between apparently diverse features of 'culture' or what we might now call cultural practice. For him, the Renaissance was an epoch with a culture that was 'developed' and therefore unified. He looked for and found parallels to coordinate the facts manifested in philosophy, architecture and other elements of culture; and he could never entirely rid himself from the sense that a cultural 'spirit' was evolving, embodied in successive national spirits (Gombrich 1969:14–15, 21, 24). Burckhardt's work, like Klemm's and indeed like most historians', reflected contemporary concerns. He was particularly worried that civilisation, in the material form of industrialisation and in the challenge of democracy, might actually 'endanger cultural life', rather than guaranteeing intellectual, spiritual or artistic progress (Gilbert 1860: 44). Culture, with all its novelty and freedom, must always be studied, elucidated and defended – for it was culture's role, historically and in his present day, to criticise the dominant forces of state and religion. Culture had a kind of catalytic capacity to modify and destroy older forms as new ones came into being; and history preserved those cultural standards which were otherwise threatened by modern life (Gilbert 1960: 46–8). It was useful, then, for Burckhardt to see, on the one hand, the diverse aspects of Renaissance culture as unified, and on the other hand, as manifestations of the critical creativity of the 'individual'. Burckhardt's Renaissance man became a self-conscious individual, turning from the inwardness of the Middle Ages to the promises of the external world; in art, general facial types were replaced by individuals, true to life (Gombrich 1969: 17, 20; and see our section 'Individualism').

To insist on a 'reason' for the unity of a culture, and to represent that reason as social, economic, or political, has run the risk of 'reducing' the cultural to those spheres. Yet merely to assert the unity of a developed culture (assuming such connections between cultural forms) without claiming a particular 'model' for or agency of connection has appeared to detractors, perhaps understandably, to be little more than a leap of faith. In this trouble we can see, perhaps, the origins of the often-repeated claim that cultural history lacks a unifying subject (cultural historians look at everything) or its own unifying methodology (since under any single conventional social, political, or linguistic model, the distinctness of cultural history collapses by a process of reduction). Imitating exemplars (like Burckhardt's) or using a multiplicity of models drawn from different areas of scholarship – the entrenched 'disciplines' which have developed after Burckhardt's day – lays the cultural historian open to charges of hero-worship, inconsistency or dilettantism. (For a statement of the paradox see Gilbert 1960: 40.) Cultural historians – in asserting parallels between things taken to be distinct – might seem inspired, mysteriously equipped to discern, interpret and describe some unifying atmosphere; but from a disciplinary perspective they are in danger of being caricatured as vague or transgressive. How would Burckhardt's immediate successors respond to such concerns?

Responses and reactions to *Kulturgeschichte*

Burckhardt's work was quickly translated, notably into English as *The Civilization of the Period of the Renaissance in Italy* (1878), its new title further reflecting the overlapping meanings of 'culture' and 'civilisation' in the late nineteenth century. The book, which is often presented as foundational for modern 'cultural history', was certainly more widely read than his other works (Gossman 2002). In different ways, varieties of *Kulturgeschichte* from Klemm to Burckhardt were appropriated and naturalised in new national and scholarly contexts. In this section, we consider Matthew Arnold's influential discussion of culture and its functions, a discussion which echoed Burckhardt's political concerns. E.B. Tylor (1832–1917), also in Britain, followed Klemm's approach, and saw an inclusive theory of a culture's development as a path to reform. The career of the statistician Karl Pearson (1857–1936) shows how widespread the reading and re-crafting of *Kulturgeschichte* might be. Karl Lamprecht (1856–1915) and Wilhelm Dilthey (1833–1911) indicate other paths for cultural history as it encountered other sciences. We close this section with a discussion of Burckhardt's disciple, the Dutch historian Johan Huizinga (1872–1945), and some of the questions left unanswered by his form of cultural history.

The reading of Burckhardt's seminal study, art historian Ernst Gombrich (1909–2001) claimed, was a 'passport to *Bildung,* to "culture" in the Victorian sense of the term' (Gombrich 1969: 18). By the 'Victorian sense', Gombrich meant 'culture' as defined in the complex utterances of the poet, literary critic and inspector of schools Matthew Arnold (1822–88). In his *Culture and Anarchy: an essay in political and social criticism* (1869), Arnold characterised culture as 'a pursuit of our total perfection by means of getting to know . . . the best which has been thought and said' (Arnold 1869: viii; Collini 1993; Garnett 2009). 'Culture' here combined two senses: humanity's continuing intellectual and spiritual development; and exemplary works of art and intellect (Williams 1983: 90). That second sense, 'culture' as fine art, canonical literature, and philosophical thought, especially as produced in classical Greece and Rome, was, Arnold was well aware, high-minded – not least because it provided the means by which to criticise 'stock notions and habits', however conventional, traditional, or popular. Arnold picked out features of this 'high culture' which were similar to those favoured by Burckhardt, and he defended them against his own contemporaries who disparaged a smattering of Greek and Latin as a mere social adornment having little relevance to modern society. Arnold wanted to spread culture 'amongst the benighted' as 'sweetness and light'. For him, 'culture' was not 'book-ish, pedantic, and futile'; rather it was 'the great help out of our present difficulties' (Arnold 1869: viii).

What difficulties did he have in mind? Arnold hoped that exemplary and permanent past culture, standing separate from the transitory interests of state, religion or commerce, would, by somewhat mysterious means, unify a society fragmented and endangered by the extension of the franchise. Echoing Thomas Carlyle's 'Signs of the Times' (1829), Arnold issued a trenchant critique of the division of contemporary society according to those political, religious and commercial interests he disparaged as 'mechanical'. He feared that society was in danger of further fragmentation, and indeed cultural dilution, with the emergence of 'mass' cultural activity, typified by cheap reading matter, gaudy spectacle, and unchallenging theatre: the pursuits of the many rather than the elite; the traditional routines and rituals of individuals and communities, rather than 'higher' forms that might be aspired to. As with many such aspirational exemplars, Arnold's culture was largely defined as a series of negations – negating, that is, partial, transitory, local, 'low' or 'interested' forms in a kind of secular replacement for absolute moral values – at a time when Arnold recognised the shaking of a traditional reliance on (Christian) religious values to stabilise and integrate British, and perhaps European, society.

Adopting Arnold's views, a cultural history would be a socially valuable historical analysis of those products, especially literary, of fine classical artistic inspiration. There was little incentive to deal with the habits of the masses, or the rituals of the everyday, which for Arnold hardly counted as culture at all. That fact was ironic, given contemporary developments stimulated by German *Kulturgeschichte* and having a lasting impact on archaeology, anthropology and ethnography. The first chapter of Victorian reformer and anthropologist Edward Burnett Tylor's *Primitive Culture* (1871) asserted: 'Culture, or civilization, taken in its broad, ethnographic sense, is that complex whole which includes knowledge, belief, art, morals, law, custom, and any other capabilities and habits acquired by man as a member of society'. In this inclusive, relative to Arnold at least, low-brow view of culture Tylor borrowed from the ethnography of Gustav Klemm (Manias 2012). Rather than looking for the permanent 'best' in past cultures, Tylor saw a progression of transitory human societies in which, for example, specific religious practices were cultural vestiges, lingering in societies for which they were once suited but which no longer had any direct 'use' for them.

Tylor's work illustrates a number of key features central to anthropological approaches in cultural history, notably 'material culture', folk culture, and studies of the 'Other' in non-European contexts. As Keeper of the University of Oxford's Museum of Natural History, Tylor was passionately concerned with the ways in which what we would now call 'material culture' (Harvey 2009) could inform historical, and anthropological, practice. Following Tylor, the term 'cultural history' was often explicitly used by archaeologists, anthropologists and ethnographers in the context of material remains and especially, for the first group, the artefacts of pre-history. Such objects might have symbolic resonance or religious and cosmological significance, providing clues to systems of 'high' values; but in pottery, jewellery, tools, or clothing, they could equally be the material expressions of the gradations and structures of everyday, secular and mundane life – especially for peoples chronologically or geographically distant from contemporary Europe or North America. Studies of 'folk culture', nations and 'nationalism', and cultural 'groups' recognised (and still recognise: Bourdieu 1990) that factors making a group cohesive need not be imposed from above by elite and powerful voices of 'high culture'. Culture, as acquired 'habits', customs or *mores*, might be held in common, by the many rather than the few. Lastly, ethnographically inspired studies of local cultures re-invigorated the kinds of historical accounts of the 'Other' that had been undertaken from the Enlightenment onwards (Pagden 1982). How might an ethnographer or historian of one particular culture describe or represent that of another (Abulafia 2008)? Would encounters with, and attempts to represent, 'Other' cultures reflect the agendas of those doing the representing? Might they at the same time lead to the advocates and enactors of a culture, perhaps under review or threat, being encouraged to systematise their understanding, or representations, of their own culture (see our section 'Others')?

Karl Pearson illustrates another local appropriation of European cultural history. During the early 1880s, before his appointment as a mathematics professor in London, Pearson explored the possibilities of German styles of cultural history in a British context (Porter 2004: 91–124). Although he studied and worked in Britain, Pearson was interested in the development of the Germanic peoples, especially in the medieval and Reformation periods, in part to understand the formation of his own culture. He saw their progress as independent of external influence, and, like Klemm and Tylor, was interested in folk rituals and myths – seeing, also, institutions now considered vestigial as once having been socially fruitful. Pearson was less concerned with Burckhardt's work on elites and more with those studies, often targeted on popular audiences, which focused on the customs and practices of the everyday. In the 1840s, Karl Dietrich Hüllmann (1765–1846) had argued for a history taking in all humanity, concentrating on urban life, and exploring such matters as 'guilds, festivals, dress, family life, drink, and crime' (Porter 2004: 97). Through cultural history, which did not have the dominance in Britain of quasi-scientific (essentially positivist) Rankean political history, this future statistician Pearson emphasised the importance not of Thomas Carlyle's 'heroes', those inspired individuals who drove history forward, but of collective numerically significant humanity.

A literal translation of the German *Kulturgeschichte* simply as 'cultural history' fails, then, to specify the multiple ambitions of *Kulturgeschichte* in Germany or elsewhere: undermining purely political history, entertaining popular audiences, questioning bureaucratic centralisation – or documenting the progressive and at times imperialist history of 'civilisation'. Just after Pearson's foray into cultural history, Karl G. Lamprecht's huge *Deutsche Geschichte* (12 vols., 1891–1901) appeared (Chickering 1993). Lamprecht found an explicit, and controversial, guarantee of the cultural 'unity' of particular periods, not in Hegelian spirit or in Marxist material conditions, but by 'linking cultural history to a record of progress through stages, following an economic logic and a broadly Darwinian model of competition amongst social forms' (Porter 2004: 97). There were scientific laws governing world history and civilisation's progress. Every culture-epoch had its 'common psychological attitude'. These psychological states were causally connected and they followed in sequence, in an evolutionary process echoing Darwin's. A science of progressive social psychology 'explained' historical development (Gilbert 1960: 53). Wilhelm Dilthey likewise claimed that a shared psychology, as he understood it, underwrote the 'structural unity of culture', especially when a culture was at its height and at its most integrated (Gombrich 1969: 26).

Burckhardt's chief intellectual heir in the early twentieth century was the Dutch scholar, Johan Huizinga. Another outsider to the historical discipline, he trained first as a philologist. He shared the dislikes of many earlier cultural historians. Political history was not for him. He objected, too, to Rankean historical forms which filtered out anecdote, individual intentions, and even 'exemplary' biography. Huizinga was not a Marxist for whom consciousness and 'culture' (considered as art, literature and thought) were secondary, constrained or even determined by the dominant forces and relations of production. The political and economic, rather than being determinants of culture in history, were, for Huizinga, disconnected from it. His chief work, *The*

Waning of the Middle Ages (1919), like Burckhardt's magnum opus, was an exemplar of 'cultural history' in practice rather than a set of theoretical prescriptions (Huizinga 1919; Colie 1964). His chief sources were art and literature and his chief concerns were to discover the modes of thinking and of feeling (for example, about love and death). Like Burckhardt he saw culture as unified. As well as the elite cultural productions favoured by Burckhardt (and Arnold), he did examine too the customs of everyday life shared by the ordinary mass of individuals, echoing the work of Enlightenment historians and more recent ethnographers like Klemm and Tylor. When Huizinga studied customs, folklore and 'forms of life', he did so only as he perceived them to be connected with the integrated life of his chosen period (Gilbert 1960: 49): that is, he was not looking for distinct cultural variants for distinct classes. Where Burckhardt had celebrated spontaneity, Huizinga took as the subject of cultural history what was 'common and typical' in the reactions of past people to their experiences; the aim of the cultural historian was to find and describe the forms, structures and functions of social phenomena (Gilbert 1960: 49–50). A later interest for him was 'play', something he insisted was central to past human cultures (Anchor 1978).

If there were questions left unanswered, they were shared by other cultural historians: how were cultural epochs to be defined, how did the aspects of developed cultures become unified, and how might a culture arise or change? Ernst Gombrich controversially insisted in the late 1960s that '*Kulturgeschichte* has been built, knowingly and unknowingly, on Hegelian foundations which have crumbled' (Gombrich 1969: 6). Gombrich was Director of the Warburg Institute which had been founded by Aby Warburg (1866–1929), a student of Lamprecht and an admirer of Burckhardt. In his view, Huizinga had needed an overarching theory and thus had tended to re-interpret the style of the artists he examined so as to fit with what he knew of their ambient culture; he simply assumed that 'the art of an age must be shown to express the same spirit that is expressed by its literature and life' (Gombrich 1969: 29). He looked for cultural unity to interpret – and, unsurprisingly, he found it. If a culture was 'unified', how had it become so – or was unity merely in the eye of the beholder? Unity of culture, and separateness from conventional causal agents (the social, the political), tended to imply (or rely upon) stability. Were cultural historians only capable of documenting *static* cultural forms, and unable to determine causes for culture's genesis, change, or demise? A further question was what political responsibility did the cultural historian have? How might a historical discipline reacting against the dominance of politics formalise the relationship of 'culture' to political and social forms and show its relevance to them – without being subsumed within them. In a rare act of reflection within the extended historical community, Huizinga attempted to answer some of these questions in his essay on 'The task of cultural history' (Huizinga 1929/1960). Huizinga's antipathy to the political in his history spread to his posture in life: but it was a position which he found impossible to sustain as he lived through the turmoil of mid-twentieth-century Europe (Colie 1964). It became unconvincing, then, to insist that politics, including political ideology, did not matter.

Can we find or impose a linear trajectory for 'cultural history', when 'culture' and 'civilisation' have been given many meanings, in many languages? And with the increasing professionalisation of academic disciplines (from history and the history of art, through English literature and philology, to archaeology, anthropology and folk-lore studies), where can the interdisciplinary endeavour be situated in this ever more crowded space? If in the eighteenth and early nineteenth centuries the absence, in much historical writing, of explicit theorising about the relationship of 'culture' to the social, anthropological, psychological, political, economic, artistic and literary realms was not seen as a serious omission, work by Klemm, Burckhardt, Tylor, Lamprecht and others, and in parallel work within those emerging disciplines, did increasingly raise that question. Such discussions have continued to disrupt cultural history's sporadic ambitions for univocal coherent disciplinary integrity.

Twentieth-century alternatives: Structures and ideas

In the Anglophone world, the phrase 'cultural history' began to appear prominently in the titles of monographs published in the 1910s. There was little consensus about what precisely it meant. C.J.H. Hayes (1917) made the 'cultural history' of a region, modern Europe, distinct from but supplementary to its 'political history'; D. Mishew (1919) sketched the 'cultural history' of an ethnic group, the Bulgarians; H.L. Gordon's biography of Rabbi Elijah Gordon illuminated the 'cultural and political history' of the Jews in Russia (Gordon 1926). For the Haeckelian 'monist' and popular science author Adolf Heilborn (1873–1941), women had a history that was both 'natural and cultural' (Heilborn 1927) – evolutionary studies of their physiology were rightly complemented by a *Kulturgeschichte* taking in their 'soul' and social development. In the early 1930s, the polymathic philosopher-journalist Egon Friedell (1878–1938) organised his vast 'cultural history' of the modern age by relating a sequence of political events to artistic or intellectual movements: Enlightenment and revolution; Romanticism and liberalism; Imperialism and impressionism (Friedell 1930–3). In contrast, through the 1930s the publisher Cresset issued a series of 'short cultural histories' celebrating the distinct civilisations of non-Western countries including Japan (1931), Russia (1931), China (1935) and India (1937) (for example, Sansom 1931). These examples, taken with Huizinga's work, confirm the popularity of cultural history in the first decades of the twentieth century. They also confirm a proliferation of methods and foci, as cultural historians continued their encounter with the social sciences, pondered the value of present-centred history, and re-considered how best to account for 'ideas' in history.

From the late 1920s, one group of scholars in France began to take a radical anti-individualist and newly 'scientific' approach to history. Thanks to its explicit reflections on historical methodology and its well-known exemplars, this *École des Annales* ('Annales school') has had a considerable influence on the definition and gravitational centre of 'cultural history' and has been widely emulated (Stoianovich 1976; Burke 1990). The key figures in the early days were Marc Bloch (1886–1944), author of works on French 'rural history', feudal society, and historiography (Bloch 1954), and Lucien Febvre (1878–1956), who trained in philology, geography and studies of the environment. In 1929 Bloch and Febvre launched the *Annales d'histoire économique et sociale*. The journal was particularly active after 1946, when it assumed the name *Annales: economies, sociétés, civilisations*. Whether or not the Annales school had a single 'paradigm' has been debated (Hunt 1989: 2) but there were certainly shared attitudes and patterns. Bloch and Febvre wanted a history not about individuals (elites, power-brokers or 'heroes') but about multitudes – 'about people, about rhythms of life, work, death'; one which would be impersonal, concerned with deep structures, and charting long-term trends; one which tackled the whole of Europe but, after the First World War, avoided nation, militarism, and regional identity; it was to be a 'scientific history', not because it claimed like Rankean history to be constructed upon objective facts, but because it relied upon the sciences of economics, demography and geography; it was to be a history of structures rather than events, and of problems rather than periods (Rubin 2002: 82; Fink 1989: 128–65). Barely interested in the disruptions, particularities and elite conversations of politics, diplomacy and war, they deployed statistical techniques to track the commonalities of peoples *en masse*. Febvre wrote of an *histoire totale* ('total history') which incorporated geographical, environmental and economic factors – one in which 'different spheres of action are always interlocked, inseparable' (Rubin 2002: 82). With this approach to cultural history, the particular actions of individuals mattered little in comparison to the statistically demonstrated grand sweep of history.

Historians' political orientations have often been coded within their methodologies – in their choices of subject and approach. Cultural historians, like historians in general, continued to be concerned with the messages that history might deliver about the present, the past, and the relationship between them. In 1931, for example, Herbert Butterfield (1900–1979) published *The Whig Interpretation of History* (see Ashplant and Wilson 1988; Wilson and Ashplant 1988), where he remarked how scholars aligned to the British Whig party and its Liberal successors had constructed moralising and teleological histories in which social and political, rather than cultural or civilising, achievements accumulated until their present day. This was history with a message, not in the sense of choosing an exemplary earlier culture to study and celebrate, but rather, diachronically, a movement towards an allegedly enlightened present. Butterfield's immediate target was a group of politically motivated historians; but his study had broader ramifications, proposing, as it did, that history ought not to be written in a linear fashion with a view to the present, but rather in open acceptance of all its contingent diversity. Butterfield's study echoed earlier critiques of linear progressive universal history and also, in his relativism, he was akin to anthropologically inspired cultural histories.

Reinforced by Butterfield's work, especially within disciplines like history of science, historians have tended to emphasise non- or anti-whiggish approaches which avoid teleological narratives, which do not judge the past according to present views, and, by extension, do not consider the non-Western world (and its cultures) as 'inferior' in terms of Western values deemed 'superior'. In such 'relativist' approaches, which assign priority to no absolute standard of judgment, many earlier 'functions' of history and cultural history are lost. The past is no longer a theatre of exemplary 'cultures' played out for present emulation, or even the source of evidence of the inexorable unfolding of civilisation. Even the history of scientific ideas, undertaken in the nineteenth century by figures like William Whewell (1794–1866) to provide guidance on how best to do future science, loses its apparent 'progressive' tendency (Whewell 1840). Indeed, statements about past 'progress' themselves become open to historical interrogation and deconstruction, rather than being 'matters of fact'. In the spirit of Raymond Williams, historians asked: what different things did 'progress' mean and what functions did ideologies of progress serve? What, indeed, was the history of the 'idea of progress'(Pollard 1971; Williams 1983: 243–5; Spadafora 1990)?

Early cultural historians had treated 'thought', or 'ideas', as one aspect of a unified culture – without paying much attention to questions of origins or autonomy of ideas. In the first generations of the Annales school, 'total history', the structures of the *longue durée*, and the combined economic, social, geographic and environmental preoccupations left 'ideas', as part of transient culture, a poor second or third. A complementary approach to the Annales historians, looking at the history of fields with an 'intellectual' dimension, came in a new discipline called by A.O. Lovejoy (1873–1962) the 'history of ideas': ideas from science, philosophy, politics, social theory, aesthetics and a host of other disciplines. A *Journal for the History of Ideas* was first published in 1940. Historians juxtaposing and comparing 'ideas' asked whether they should also study the origins and development of 'ideas'. Should 'ideas' be treated independently of the contexts within which they were 'discovered', expressed, or disseminated – or should they be studied, at least in part, as products, reflections, or even crystallisations of cultural, social or economic contexts? A common strategy, in the early days of the 'history of ideas', was to study 'ideas' as part of (high) culture but as only loosely connected to social and economic contexts.

The key journal for the history of scientific thought, *Isis* (founded in 1913), described itself from the start as an 'international review devoted to the history of science and its cultural influences' – the chief concerns being the influence of science on culture, or the relationship of scientific ideas to other aspects of high intellectual culture. When history of science was done in this way, 'scientific ideas' (Newtonian laws, Darwinian evolution) were periodically 'discovered' (often by 'great minds') but thereafter developed according to an 'internal' dynamic, independent of 'external' (economic, social, even institutional) factors. But from the 1930s, there were alternative perspectives, from Marxist historians and from sociologists. The Marxist physicist Boris Hessen (1893–1936) argued that Newton's work served to augment the power of his bourgeois class. In 1941, the sociologically informed historian Robert Merton (1910–2003) considered 'external' factors, and especially 'institutions', reframing scientific societies as well-functioning liberal democracies. More controversially, Merton extended the work of sociologist Max Weber (1864–1920), a self-confessed connoisseur of the universal history of culture, and a methodological innovator who thought carefully about the inter-relationship between ideas and material interests. Weber's claim about the relationship between a 'Protestant ethic' and the 'spirit' of capitalism is well-known. Merton argued that Puritan religious attitudes had stimulated early modern scientific endeavour, in its more utilitarian manifestations (Merton 1973; Weber 2002). Debates about the 'Merton thesis' continue to this day. Even with the tools of the sociologist, these 'internal' and 'external' perspectives, in science and other areas, were hard to articulate with each other.

In later decades, 'history of ideas' has been superseded by 'intellectual history'. Although still primarily concerned with 'the consciously expressed ideas of original thinkers' (Burke 2012: 8), intellectual history pays far greater attention to the processes whereby ideas have been generated, expressed, disseminated or appropriated in diverse contexts – so much so, indeed, that the distinguished historian William J. Bouwsma has suggested replacing the term 'intellectual history' with 'cultural history', to avoid the impression that only above the 'baser aspects of living' there exists some fine 'intellectual activity', the study of which is itself 'exalted' (Brett in Canadine 2002: 113–14, quoting Bouwsma 2000).

In search of cultural history: Unity and discipline

By the late 1950s and early 1960s 'cultural history' had achieved some success, in terms of studies undertaken and books sold, but in some important senses, it was a victim of that success. Multiple approaches to cultural history had been explored, by exemplary case study (Burckhardt, Huizinga), in creative extensions of German *Kulturgeschichte*, in programmatic statements (Annales school), and in a proliferation of specialist fields (history of ideas). But the boundaries between 'history' and these many varieties of 'cultural history' had always been permeable. Fertile aspects of cultural approaches were adopted by historians not specifically designating themselves 'cultural', and not always concerned to engage too deeply with abstruse foundations in sociology, anthropology, psychology or literary studies. It is not surprising, then, that a number of soul-searching articles on the state of 'cultural history' appeared from the later 1950s to the early 1960s. These took for granted the existence of cultural history, pondered its origins and present state, and at the same time voiced concerns about its future, especially as a potentially autonomous discipline in the academy.

In the 1950s Jacques Barzun (1907–2012), a scholar of Romanticism who staked a claim for the cultural unity of the Romantic age, promoted a genre of cultural history which encompassed the history of 'thought and society' but stood apart from two existing disciplines: 'intellectual history' was for him too concerned with the logic of ideas; cultural anthropology had too wide a definition of culture – as anything from pots and pans to religion (Barzun 1956: 387, 392). In a lecture delivered in 1954 he had begun with the possibly ironic claim: 'Every reader today understands the meaning of the term Cultural History'. Barzun settled on culture as the 'literature and the temper of recent times'. As for cultural history, its acceptance was recent. Two decades earlier it had meant little to any but the historical professionals, who preferred their history as past politics, and for them, as a translation of *Kulturgeschichte*, it carried a 'taint of fraud': it was unable to shake off Hegelian essences, the *Zeitgeist* and the 'spirit of the age' (Barzun 1956: 388). Marxist history had provided an alternative, in which ideas were manifestations of underlying economic forces, yet the recognition that nearly identical capitalist systems had been accompanied by clearly different cultures questioned that approach – and led to a renewed interest in 'habits, assumptions, and beliefs', not considered to be determined by material circumstance (Barzun 1956: 389). With growing concern for the rise and fall of whole cultures, exemplified in Spengler's *Decline of the West* (1918), Barzun could claim that 'anyone who thinks at all is something of a cultural historian', concerned less with economic base and environment and more with cultural forces, crises, trends and contexts (Barzun 1956: 390).

So far so good. But Barzun admitted that, even if 'we all more or less take cultural history for granted' (Barzun 1956: 392), that was not to say that all understood it in the same way, or that it faced no problems. To be of any value, cultural history needed to embrace 'ideas' and 'art'; but the former were indefinite as historical agents, and the latter appeared distant from the main currents of history. For the historian, culture needed to be more than simply the things of the mind or the highbrow – it needed to take in what he rather vaguely designated 'background' and 'underpinning'. How, then, could cultural history be justified, in subject matter and also in method? One professional issue was the tension between the cultural historian's desire to unite philosophy, history and the arts in past societies and the undoubted contemporary fragmentation of scholarship through disciplinary specialisation (Barzun 1956: 391). The cultural historian needed to steer a difficult path between total description and circumscribed narrative, never knowing in advance which particular facts were required to render a narrative intelligible. Thus, 'the cultural historian selects his material not by fixed rule but by the *esprit de finesse* that Pascal speaks of, the gift, namely, of seeing a quantity of fine points in a given relation without ever being able to demonstrate it'. He can show but not prove, persuade but not convince, assessing connectedness and strength of influence in cultural life which is, unlike the political or the economic, 'intricate and emotionally complex' (Barzun 1956: 393–4). The cultural historian must, it seems, make intuitive leaps to find and elaborate connections between the assorted cultural phenomena he or she explores.

Although Barzun recognised that a lack of 'scientific' demonstration, the prominence of interpretation and an affinity with high ideas might be seen as weaknesses, he tried to respond by claiming that culture 'has continuity' and thus the 'cultural historian ... deals ... with the modifications, the combinations, the rearrangements of ideas, feelings and sensations familiar to all who lead a conscious existence'. As for high ideas, they became the commonplaces of the many and were thus worthy of study. Cultural history parted company from history of ideas and intellectual history narrowly defined, since to dwell on the internal logic of ideas was to lose touch with history: neatness indicated the historian had gone too far; instead the cultural historian relished 'the intelligible disorder of history'. Despite this relishing of complexity, Barzun nevertheless continued to insist on 'the internal unity of cultural periods', claiming that the family likeness, common feel and texture, or shared 'style' found in various manifestations by the cultural historian was not (*pace* Hegel) the product of some single cause but rather an indication that cultural forms provided unified answers to shared problems of the age (Barzun 1956: 397–9). But to say that culture was a set of answers to shared problems raised as many questions as it answered.

Writing in 1960, Felix Gilbert (1905–1991) doubted if there was a 'clearly defined and delimited' area of 'cultural history'. Two rather familiar claims constituted the field's 'double face': all history already was or should become cultural history, so there was no need for a separate area of cultural history; or, a lack of agreed methods meant that cultural history was not a recognised discipline and was unlikely to be accepted as such. As we might guess, Gilbert considered the big problem in defining the field – as a 'history of culture', with the meaning of 'culture' to be elucidated – to stem from the way in which the chief connotations of 'culture' and 'civilisation' had switched and blurred through the eighteenth, nineteenth and twentieth centuries. He pointed out that in different languages and at different times, both terms had meant: the material and technological aspects of everyday human activity (an archaeological or anthropological perspective on 'culture' in the nineteenth century); or the 'higher' forms of achievement in artistic and intellectual fields allegedly indicative of Western superiority (an eighteenth-century view of 'civilisation', but more often termed 'culture' in the nineteenth century). The first meaning failed to capture the full scope of contemporary 'cultural history'; the latter perspective was in danger of giving 'cultural history' a bad name in a more relativistic age. Moreover, in Germany, 'civilisation' had been associated with the material, and 'culture' with aspirations, ideals and artistic self-expression – causing still further confusion (Gilbert 1960: 40–41). Care in defining 'culture' was unlikely to help 'cultural history' understand and respect its boundaries.

One indication, nevertheless, of that perceived 'success' of cultural history was the way in which historians began to look again at certain founding figures. In 1964 R.L. Colie looked back on Huizinga and chose to emphasise his subtle shift in focus away from Burckhardt's (and Arnold's) preoccupation with the 'high' culture of art, literature and thought towards what we would now dub the 'ordinary', although not quite the comprehensive patterns of the everyday laid out by the Annales historians. In this account, Huizinga had been concerned with what persists in a culture rather than with the transitory happenings of politics, diplomacy and war which tend to promote change, or provide evidence of it. Colie emphasised Huizinga's studied anti-political stance: the historian had insisted there was more to history than political events or trends; but a weakness in this approach, according to some readers, was that his failure to consider the political and economic meant he had little of significance to say about the relationship, so fundamental from a Marxist perspective, between the economic 'base' and its cultural manifestations. Had the decades since Huizinga left these key problems unaddressed, with cultural historians choosing simply to explore, rather than to seek solid methodological foundations?

In a lecture tellingly entitled *In Search of Cultural History* (1967), partly inspired by George Nadel, editor of the *History and Theory* journal founded in 1960 as a repository for discussions of styles, methods and innovations in historical writing, the distinguished art historian Ernst Gombrich talked of 'different ways of life, different systems of reference, different scales of value – in short different cultures' (Gombrich 1969: 2). Gombrich claimed that the revered father figures of cultural history had either retained Hegelian approaches in original or secularized form, or had implied the existence at various times of a unified culture, the aspects of which were the product of a single cause, be it material, psychological, or of some other form. Gombrich seriously doubted whether 'all aspects of culture can be traced back to one key cause' (Gombrich 1969: 30). A belief in the 'existence of an independent supra-individual collective spirit' had for him 'blocked the emergence of a true cultural history' (Gombrich 1969: 36). To find its new path, cultural history should return to individuals, not collectives, and to fragments, not unities. Gombrich was even wary of structures and patterns. He thus distanced himself not only from the neo-Hegelians that seemed to haunt him but also from the Annales school. He advised the contextual study of 'the individual human being', not as typical of a major period, but as progenitor of a movement, or, more interestingly, as respondents to a new style (Gombrich 1969: 37, 39; for a critique see Arcangeli 2011: 20–21). Elite individuals were once again in fashion, albeit briefly, despite the Annales historians and the efforts of Lawrence Stone, who advocated detailed collective biographical portraits (prosopographies) of figures, whether or not distinguished, that would shed light on interests shared amongst groups (Stone 1971; Shapin and Thackray 1974).

Despite all the talk of success, Leonard B. Meyer's review of *In Search of Cultural History* took Gombrich's message to be that the subject had 'come upon evil days', since few wanted to explain the interactions between aspects of a unified culture, most now repudiated Hegelian foundations and their varieties, and even the less directly Hegelian but still holistic approaches to culture and cultural change of Marx, Lamprecht, Dilthey and Huizinga were out of fashion. Although Gombrich had cleared 'the stables of cultural history of the feculence of the sacred cows of Hegelian holism', he was 'suggestive and sketchy rather than specific and systematic' about cultural history's future (Meyer 1970: 397–8). In retrospect, one of Gombrich's more fruitful positive claims was that historians might explore individual responses to stylistic movements: what we might now call creative 'appropriations', allowing both for the agency of the individual and the persistence of cultural forms. For Meyer, though, Gombrich's advocacy of cultural history as a kind of 'cultivated humanism' was inadequate, even quaint, as a fresh agenda. Meyer insisted that historians do inevitably engage in a patterning of events; Gombrich's acceptance of fragmentation would only lead to a redefinition of cultural history as 'a collection of individual investigations of quite distinct historical continuities'. But if the aspects of the history of a culture could not be related in a way that was coherent and intelligible, 'then what has been thought of as cultural history would seem to be a doubtful enterprise at best'. Meyer insisted: 'it is ... the goal of cultural history not only to explain the histories of ... styles, movements, institutions, and the like ... but to relate these to one another and to account for their intricate interaction in some coherent and consistent way' (Meyer 1970: 399). Was there scope, in other words, for a theoretically convincing history of unified 'culture', or should cultural historians strike out on another path?

Labour, class, literature: Ware, Thompson and Williams

To understand how cultural historians tried to resolve these paradoxes we need to scroll back and explore various approaches taken by historians and literary scholars on either side of the Atlantic. A particularly intriguing figure was Caroline F. Ware (1899–1990), who edited *The Cultural Approach to History* (1940) for the American Historical Association. In Ware's early career she had briefly studied anthropology, had written about the experiences of the industrial working classes and had been fascinated by the 'frontier thesis' of her teacher Frederick Jackson Turner (1861–1932): Turner had examined geography, environment, economy, and society all together as interconnected forces shaping the United States, the lives of the common people, and national values. Ware's project of 1940 integrated these elements, whilst also rethinking the purpose of history after a long period of war, depression and unemployment. It was a response to the prevalent fact-obsessed 'scientific' history (with its focus on political and intellectual elites). It was also a so-called 'new history' in the United States which (like the Annales school) paid greater attention to social and economic forces, but was seen by its critics as unfocused, because of its range. Ware proposed (perhaps inadvertently echoing Febvre) a history of 'total culture': a complete discussion of the social fabric, lives, thoughts and reactions, not just of dominant groups but of ordinary men and women (including ethnic groups), especially in mechanised industry and in urban areas. These workers were the new frontiersmen. Borrowing from Marx, Ware saw mentality as a social product, performing a social function. History would be written from the 'bottom up' (Fitzpatrick 1991; on attempts to bring mechanism and industry within the cultural fold, see also our section 'Technology').

Although the relationship to Ware's work is unclear, scholars in Britain also began to think of new ways of studying the 'culture' of the industrial classes. In the 1950s and 1960s members of the so-called New Left espoused an anti-determinist variant of Marxist analysis, rejecting Marx's proposed subordination of culture to material causation. As we have seen, that subordination had seemed to reduce the scope for an analysis of culture, in history, independent of the social and economic. These authors were sensitive to the work of Antonio Gramsci (1891–1937). His posthumously published *Prison Notebooks* saw 'culture' present within the working classes as their creation rather than being an imposition by the bourgeois from above. Gramsci ascribed to 'subaltern' or intermediate cultural groups greater autonomy than, for example, Marx had allowed (Hoare and Nowell (eds) 1971). In this context, two scholars of particular interest to the cultural historian are E.P. Thompson (1924–1993) and Raymond Williams.

Thompson's work began within British 'social history', but it was increasingly relevant to studies of culture. Marxist historians and early members of the Annales school had prepared scholars for a new 'social history' which was more strongly, and more explicitly, influenced by sociological and economic theory and practices than the ethnology and anthropology that had been linked to *Kulturgeschichte* and its offshoots. The Social History Society and the journal *Social History* were both founded in 1976. Even apparently unpromising areas like history of science and medicine had their 'social' turn: claims that 'external' or institutional approaches to the history of science and medicine were defunct turned out to be wildly exaggerated (Hall 1963; Shapin 1992). The history of medicine, especially in the work of Roy Porter (1946– 2002), moved away from elite theorising to socio-economic studies of the multitudes of producers and consumers of medicine (Porter 1997). Much of this work had been influenced, more or less directly, by E.P. Thompson.

Thompson's monumental study of the making of the English working class saw culture attached to classes, rather than nations, and culture defined, in part, through class conflict (Thompson 1963 and 1991, discussed in our 'Popular culture' section). Thompson rejected unreconstructed Marxist conceptions of base and superstructure, developing instead a language of 'cultural and moral mediations'. Class consciousness was not socially determined. It emerged with the creative and active handling of practical experiences in cultural terms, especially by embodying them in 'traditions, value-systems, and institutional forms' (Hunt 1989: 4 quoting Thompson 1963: 10; on traditions and their invention see Hobsbawm and Ranger (eds) 1983). Thompson's object was to recover the 'culture of plebeian life' (Jordanova 2011: 67). This 'history from below', like Ware's history from the 'bottom up', gave voice to the 'masses', to the hitherto neglected, to the inarticulate, and to the marginalised. It had echoes in Marxist historian George Rudé's studies of the Parisian crowd in the French Revolution (Rudé 1959, 1964), and in the 'oral history' which especially from the 1970s captured the voices of rarely recorded groups (Thompson, P. 2000). Also relevant to cultural historians is E.P. Thompson's much-cited study of work-discipline and the changing practical experience in workers' lives of 'factory time' (Thompson 1967) (see our section 'Space, Time and Measurement').

Working in parallel with Thompson was the Marxist literary critic, Raymond Williams. He was acutely conscious, and proud, of his working-class origins in Wales. Returning to study at Cambridge at the end of the Second World War, Williams was struck by the rapidly shifting meanings of 'culture', and of a whole vocabulary of related words indicating complex links between values and social interests. 'Culture' especially appeared to him to connect areas – art, society, class, industry – normally seen as distinct. In the 1940s, however, two older meanings (as a kind of social superiority; as creative writing, painting, and acting) had given way to two newer meanings: a set of values associated with the critical study of literature (adopted via Arnold and, more recently, the literary critic F.R. Leavis); and a particular way of life (in an anthropological sense) (Williams 1983: 12–14). Williams read T.S. Eliot's *Notes Towards the Definition of Culture*, which admitted (1948: 31) that in its broadest sense culture embraced 'all the characteristic activities and interests of a people', from the dog races, via Wensleydale cheese, to the music of Elgar. For Eliot, the culture of society as a whole was a healthy accumulation of those many connected but locally distinct cultures he deemed proper to the peoples of different classes (or groups). He insisted that religion and an 'organic' class system were essential conditions for the survival of culture (Eliot 1948: 15). Unsurprisingly, Williams 'grasped but could not accept' Eliot's idea, and instead developed his own views in *Culture and Society, 1780–1950* (1958a).

The book traversed literary history from Edmund Burke, via Charles Dickens, to George Orwell, to show how economic conditions formed the reality grasped through the imagination. Scholars and librarians variously classified it as 'cultural history, historical semantics, history of ideas, social criticism, literary history and sociology' (Williams 1983: 13). Impossible to pigeon-hole, but true to its original inspiration, *Culture and Society* charted the historical, not merely intellectual, relationship between those 'keywords' that had intrigued Williams. If he favoured one of the many meanings of 'culture', it was certainly not Arnold's: that culture was a recipe for moral perfection and social cohesion through the study of the exemplary. Although he was writing about literary works, he preferred the all-encompassing anthropological definition that culture concerned a 'whole way of life' (for the whole of society). In a now famous phrase, he asserted simply that 'culture is ordinary' (Williams 1958). Williams's literary studies thus involved questions of literacy, mass reading, and the expression and consumption of ideas by communities going far beyond the traditional elites.

Williams's *Keywords: a vocabulary of culture and society* (1976; revised 1983) had begun life as a projected appendix to *Culture and Society*; dropped from the book, it saw the light of day, much expanded, nearly twenty years later. Cultural historians had long been concerned to trace the shifting meanings of words in a 'historicist' manner: noting the traps laid by the terms 'genius' and 'individualism', Barzun had called in 1956 for the 'closest attention to words, making sure that [the cultural historian] does not betray them any more than they betray him' (Barzun 1956: 401; and see our section 'Individualism'). To the modern reader, *Keywords* looks like a set of hypertext pages: although it is printed as a conventional book with a linear arrangement, the dense interconnections between the entries encourage sampling and shifts from concept to concept. When he revised *Keywords* in 1983, adding 'genius', 'Western', 'technology' and other terms, Williams relied on advice from correspondents across the disciplines including Peter Burke (see below). Others have updated the work as *New Keywords* (Williams 1983: 27; Bennett *et al.* 2005; and see our section 'Technology').

A 'new history' encounters theory: Burke and Darnton

As Thompson and Williams explored the meaning of working-class 'culture' and literacy, in the 1950s and 1960s Fernand Braudel (1902–1985) and his successors were pointing the Annales school in new directions. From the 1920s Braudel had tackled geographically or intellectually vast topics: the Mediterranean world in the reign of Philip II; capitalism and 'material life' (or 'material civilisation'); and French 'identity'. Braudel wanted to reveal the structures of the 'everyday life' of groups like the working poor (Braudel 1949, 1967, 1981, 1988). He considered history at three levels: long-term trends (the *longue durée*), dominated by geography; the medium-term, focusing upon social life; and, last and least important, the particular event, associated with the individual or with politics (Hunt 1989: 3). A third generation of the Annales school, following Braudel, included Emmanuel Le Roy Ladurie, whose 'total regional history' discussed regions of France. Geography and the long-term were present but less dominant than in Braudel; medium term events (processes stretching over periods of decades) and their interactions were still considered more important than political and intellectual life (Hunt 1989: 3). This third generation also included the medievalist Philippe Ariès (1914–1984) (Hutton 2004), who famously claimed that the apparently universal notion of 'childhood' had been discovered in one particular historical period (Ariès 1960/62; see our section 'Childhood'). Ariès's writings on death (Ariès 1977/83) have helped to establish the cultural historian's study of generations and life-stages, including old age.

Another key figure in this period was the French medievalist Jacques Le Goff (see Le Goff 1980; and our section 'Commerce, Credit and Consumption'). He encouraged the Annales historians to try to discover the 'ideas commensurate with the demographic rhythms and the agrarian patterns' they had earlier studied. Were there similarly slow-moving, widely dispersed 'mental structures', and 'representations and rituals' which corresponded to their former preoccupations (Rubin 2002: 82)? The answer, for a fourth-generation Annales school, was yes. In 1978, Le Goff, Roger Chartier and Jacques Revel published a manifesto for a *nouvelle histoire* or (another) 'new history' (Le Goff *et al.* 1978). The 'new history', and its subsequent elaborations, was easiest to define by what it was not: it rejected grand narratives of events, a narrow focus on political elites, the view from above seen through the actions of 'great men', claims that it was possible to recover individuals' 'motivations' and 'intentions', the purported objectivity of history (bequeathed by Ranke's followers), and the idea that history was the domain of a delimited group of professionals (Burke 2001). Borrowing from anthropology and literary theory, the new history would emphasise the history of 'representations' (in textual and other forms) and, in order to find a place for 'ideas' or something like them, the history of *mentalités* (mentalities). Febvre had earlier talked about an *outillage mental* (or mental toolkit) through which people constructed their world; the new *mentalités* likewise were mental structures, not determined by the social and material, but rather themselves constituting social reality; going beyond linguistic equipment and conceptual frameworks, they took in psychological elements (states of perception and feeling) and the structure of popular beliefs. These *mentalités* or *représentations collectives* concerned such matters as 'death, childhood, sexuality, kinship, purgatory and the hereafter' (Rubin 2002: 82; Hunt 1989: 6–7; Burke 1997a; and Brett in Cannadine 2002: 124–7). 'Intellectual history', filling a void left by the Annalistes' earlier lack of interest in ideas, had tended to focus on original 'thinkers' and on explicit and conscious reason; the history of *mentalités*, however, 'finds room for everyone's ideas', for unconscious assumptions, and for imagination (Burke 2012: 8).

In various respects the work of Michel Foucault (1926–1984) and Hayden White supported and extended the history of *mentalités* and encouraged the turn towards 'culture'. Foucault undermined the Marxist's or neo-Marxist's claim that 'culture' was determined, or directly influenced, by material social context. Furthermore, for Foucault no objects or concepts were straightforwardly 'natural': all were discursive. Power was to be located in discourse, and it might be found in the most unlikely places, from feelings to medical observations to academic disciplines (Hunt 1989: 9). Many of Foucault's specific claims (on the history of sexuality, or madness) have been disputed. But he has had a lasting impact on methods and attitudes. Foucault offered scholars the perspective of a 'history embodied': his focus on such spaces as prisons and asylums indicated how human bodies, conceived in certain times and places as controlled, marginal or deviant, manifested the exercise of power (to discipline, incarcerate or 'cure') and especially showed knowledge to be, at any time or place, the 'representation of con-vention as nature' (Rubin 2002: 83). The criminal or insane body was controlled, in space, but also defined, by constructed knowledge. Paradoxically, Foucault's invitation to re-conceive forms of knowledge (scientific or social) not as 'natural', there to be discovered or rationally established, but rather as temporary conventions constructed in the exercise of forms of power – that invitation endangered many of the intellectual disciplines, including anthropology, through which culture had been interrogated. Intellectual system-building was, then, just another exercise of power to be unmasked. In literary studies around this time, Hayden White issued a wake-up call to historians of all types, asking them to consider the diverse rhetorical and discursive strategies deployed by their heroes in historical writing. What forms of plot, character and narrative had these earlier historians preferred and elaborated? White's contro-versial work made it hard for subsequent historians to forget the literary tropes and narrative structures of their forebears and to fail to reflect on their own norms of writing (White 1978).

Trenchant critiques of history and innovations within it have often come from figures immersed in the methods of other disciplines – like philology, psychology, art history or literary studies. Peter Burke and Robert Darnton drew inspiration from the social sciences (Pallares-Burke 2002: 129–57 (Burke), 158–83 (Darnton); Burke 2005). Burke first studied the Renaissance, its 'sense of the past', and its social and cultural forms (Burke 1967, 1969, 1972). Since the late 1970s, he has worked innovatively on 'popular culture' in early modern Europe (Burke 1978/1994/2009), occasionally in dialogue with E.P. Thompson (see our section 'Popular culture'). Burke was fascinated by the Annales school, helping to spread its work in English translation and writing its history (Burke 1990). E.H. Carr (1892–1982) had called for a 'socially oriented history' in 1961 (Carr 1961), and Burke was one of those who systematically addressed what history might learn from social, anthropological and cultural theory (Burke 2005). It is not unreasonable to suggest that the continued encounter between 'history' and 'theory' is what makes cultural history distinctive.

Darnton's studies of the French Revolution (Darnton 1980) illustrate the ever closer connections between anthropology and cultural history in practice. In the nineteenth and early twentieth century, anthropology was a significant element in German-style *Kulturgeschichte*. In the second half of the twentieth century, these encounters were vigorously renewed. Keith Thomas explicitly discussed what history might learn from anthropology (Thomas 1963). In his *Religion and the Decline of Magic* (1971), which focused upon the surprisingly alien 'systems of belief' of the early modern populace, he admitted a particular debt to social anthropologists of witchcraft in modern Africa (Thomas 1971: ix; Pallares-Burke 2002: 80–105). Anthropology has subsequently provided a toolkit for cultural historians studying 'public events and collective experiences rich with symbolic meaning', hoping to enter into conversation with past peoples, seeking to 'learn' a past culture as if it were a language, and exploring rituals rich in symbolic value. Historians early learnt from anthropologists by adopting the binary demarcations of pure/polluted and sacred/profane discussed by Mary Douglas but, as real historical situations turned out to be more messy, they turned to Clifford Geertz (1926–2006) (Rubin 2002: 86). One of the most successful was Darnton.

Every historian applies selection criteria when choosing what to study: whilst Whig historians used to cherry-pick the past for 'foreshadowings' of familiar modern achievements, cultural historians, from Klemm, through Tylor, to Darnton, have looked at 'the irrational, the eccentric and the bizarre', to foster tolerance as well as understanding of cultural difference (Evans in Cannadine 2002: 9). Social anthropology has provided the tools for getting to grips with unfamiliar beliefs, and for indicating that a ritual might be the point of departure for investigating 'all aspects of life' (Rubin 2002: 86). Seeing the past as a 'foreign country', and a strange one at that, to be explored using techniques drawn from the social sciences, Darnton echoed Carr, Thomas and even Gombrich, whose cultural historian was a 'broadminded traveller' to 'foreign lands' (Gombrich 1969: 42).

In his discussion of the meaning of the bizarre 'Great Cat Massacre' (Darnton 1984, 1986), Darnton adopted the techniques of cultural anthropologist Geertz, with whom he had taught at Princeton in the 1970s. Geertz's *The Interpretation of Cultures* (1973) was decisive for Darnton and subsequently it has been inspirational for historians of diverse periods and geographies (Hunt 1989: 12). Geertz defined culture as 'an historically transmitted pattern of meanings embodied in symbols, a system of inherited conceptions expressed in symbolic forms by means of which men communicate, perpetuate, and develop their knowledge about and attitudes towards life' (Geertz 1973). Particularly important to Darnton was Geertz's practice of 'thick description' (1973), in which a ritual was carefully unfolded rather than necessarily 'explained'. Geertz's discussion of the Balinese cock-fight has remained the locus classicus for cultural historians curious to learn from anthropology (Geertz 1972). In Geertz's mode of interpretation, individual expression took place 'within a general idiom', cultural meanings were 'inscribed' if not as actual texts then, metaphorically, like texts to be 'read' by historians equipped with the skills of literary interpretation (Hunt 1989: 12–13).

But from the mid-1980s, Chartier criticised Geertz, and the historians who followed his approaches, for accepting too readily the independent existence of coherent symbolic systems: Chartier proposed, instead, that in practice cultural forms were used, adopted or 'appropriated' by individuals and groups in different ways (Chartier 1985; and see LaCapra 1988). The disproportionate influence of one anthropologist, Geertz, and the relative failure of cultural historians to learn from others has been remarked upon by Jordanova (2011: 66), Rubin and Mandler. Rubin wryly comments that since the 1980s the anthropologists and ethnographers have had their own crisis of meaning, with early works questioned by some of the post-colonial, feminist and deconstructive meanings unleashed especially after Foucault (2002: 87–8). Mandler urges cultural historians to look again to social scientists for better theories of meaning rather than relying upon the outdated prestige of 'almost randomly chosen' theorists of earlier periods (Mandler 2004: 113).

There are parallels between Darnton's work and studies in a sociologically re-oriented history of science. Undertaken especially from the late 1970s and in the 1980s, these studies in the history of science focused on controversial, open-ended, hard-to-comprehend situations precisely because they were revealing of that which was often submerged, hidden, or unarticulated. To the historian, that which is strange is arguably more striking, and more visible – if not necessarily easy to decipher. In times of controversy, however, tacit assumptions tend to be stated explicitly, opened up, and questioned, thus revealing aspects of a culture normally hidden because routine and accepted. Darnton's work has also, however, led to its own controversy, especially about the active role taken by historians seeking to emulate him as interpreters of the past, against ideas (from Ranke, or, in a different way, from the earlier *Annalistes*) of allegedly neutral and objective historians merely 'recovering' 'what actually/ essentially happened'. In one sense, rather than seeking a kind of insulation from Hayden White's claims about the sometimes unacknowledged literary craft of the historian, Darnton seems to have embraced and acknowledged that creative role (see Sewell 1997).

Studies of France, including the French Renaissance, Enlightenment and Revolution, have proved fertile for cultural historians. One influential work is Natalie Zemon Davis's *The Return of Martin Guerre* (1983), a case study of sixteenth-century peasant identity focusing upon an impostor arriving in a village in the Pyrenees. The book grew out of Davis's consultancy work on Daniel Vigne's film *Le retour de Martin Guerre* (Pallares-Burke 2002: 50–79). Like Darnton and Burke, Davis deployed anthropological and literary techniques – but she too has been criticised by empirically oriented historians for her interpretative speculations. Davis's *Martin Guerre* has an Italian counterpart in Carlo Ginzburg's *The Cheese and the Worms* (1980), an account of the radical ideas, not of an elite figure, but of the 'ordinary' miller Menocchio. (On Ginzburg's historical practice, see Pallares-Burke 2002: 184–211.) His 'autodidactism' and his beliefs about the big questions of the day were the products of fashioning, or appropriation, from existing cultural resources (Rubin 2002: 81). He illustrates the freedom of individuals to shape identities, rather than being constrained by a monolithic 'culture' (see our section 'Individualism').

The growth of the historical profession, and of allied disciplines, in the final quarter of the twentieth century has been accompanied by fragmentation and the emergence of specialist interest groups crossing and criticising established intellectual boundaries. In line with the push towards 'history from below', social and cultural historians have moved further from political history to the 'social composition and daily life of workers, servants, women, ethnic groups' (Hunt 1989: 2). Rubin suggests that we should understand this, in Foucault's terms, as a series of historical ventures working to uncover the past operation of power based on representing biological and other forms of difference, especially in gender and race, as somehow given by

Nature. (See Rubin 2002: 84; for a recent contribution to the debates on gender see Wahrman 2008.) There has been an explosion of studies of minority, marginal, peripheral, disadvantaged, low-status or disempowered groups – the working classes, women, non-whites, religious dissenters, children and, more recently, the 'disabled' (see our sections 'Gender', 'Others', 'Religion'). A later trend has been for studies of such disadvantaged groups to be displaced by studies of the relationships between differently empowered groups, or for the study of powerful groups by methods originally developed to study the disempowered. Studies of 'women in history' have been supplemented, even displaced, by studies of gender relations and, more recently, 'masculinities' (Tosh 2005); studies of ethnic minorities have counterparts in studies of 'whiteness' (Hale 1998); postcolonial studies restore historical agency to those once portrayed as merely subjected to imperialist ambitions (Young 2001).

A 'new cultural history': Hunt and Chartier

Cultural history has been enriched by many of these approaches but this enrichment has also motivated scholars, especially since the late 1980s, to take stock of 'cultural history', to attempt to delineate and invigorate it, or, later, simply to wonder at its proliferating 'varieties'. In 1989 Lynn Hunt sought to capture a 'new cultural history' (Hunt 1989) which had been emerging since the mid-1970s in a reaction to pre-existing historical forms: social history, even when focused on cultural processes, might still see 'culture' as socially determined by material conditions; for the earlier Annales historians, 'culture', at least in the form of ideas, came a poor second or even third to long-term structures. The history of *mentalités* attempted to restore autonomy and independence to culture by denying its roots in the social – yet that form of history had been accused of lack of focus, whilst also suffering from its over-reliance on the favoured quantitative approaches of the Annales school. Hunt was wary that cultural history might become incoherent, and degenerate into the pursuit of new, fashionable topics: an 'endless search for new cultural practices to describe, whether carnivals, cat massacres, or impotence trials' (Hunt 1989: 9). How, then, were scholars to produce a history of culture when so much work had been done precisely to shake off a set of theoretical assumptions about culture's relationship to the social world (Hunt 1989:10)?

This 'new cultural history' turned out to be light on sociologising, despite the origins of earlier forms of cultural history in a rapprochement between history and sociology, and heavy in what were to be the new key disciplines: anthropology and literary theory, especially where they could be allied. Hunt particularly pointed to the historical studies of Darnton and Davis, which emphasised the search for meanings and advocated the 'reading' of cultural phenomena as 'texts', whether or not they were manifest in literary form. This new cultural history, attracted by the social anthropology of Victor Turner, Mary Douglas and others, explored rituals, carnivals, and rites of passage. In this tradition, Davis's *Society and Culture in Early Modern France* (1975) fostered an interest in 'community', the values of which might be perpetuated by festive life or ritualized violence (Hunt 1989: 11; see also Anderson 1983).

Recruited to this programme was Chartier, co-creator but also critic of the *mentalités* approach, who more recently had become interested in the ways historical actors differently appropriated available cultural materials or practices (Hunt 1989: 13–15). There was less emphasis on community (culture held in common) and more on creative difference (the selective appropriation of cultural goods). Here, Chartier was influenced, as we have seen, by Geertz (and Darnton) but also by Pierre Bourdieu (1930–2002), whose complex notion of *habitus* referred to 'patterns of representation, classification and judgment incorporated by each individual' (Chartier 2009: 11; Bourdieu 1977). Having dispatched the idea that culture was merely a reflection of social reality, Chartier argued against a parallel cultural reductionism, insisting that rituals and other symbolic actions do not simply reflect some pre-existent and coherent communal meaning. Instead, actors deployed varying strategies, discernible in texts which were authored, published or read (1988). Chartier, then, reflects in historical practice a 'cultural turn' – stimulated by White, Geertz, Foucault, and Bourdieu – which, in Rubin's neat formulation, treats as its fundamentals 'the conditions of communication, the terms of representation, the interaction between structures of meaning – narratives, discourses – and the ways in which individuals and groups use them and thus express themselves': the historian following this 'cultural turn' asks not so much 'How it really was' but rather 'How was it for him, or her, or them?' (Rubin 2002: 81).

Chartier provides an instance of the shift by historians of culture towards a sophisticated use of literary techniques. In practice, cultural historians following this linguistic turn consider 'texts, print and readings': the production, construction, and writing of texts; their dissemination in print; their reception, or appropriation, by readers capable of subverting intended messages (Chartier 1987, 1989). The history of the book, the newspaper, and print in general thus becomes an integral part of cultural history. Scholars want to uncover how a text 'works' as well as what it 'means' (see also our section 'Literacy and Orality'). By what processes have intellectual products been fashioned? How have ideas been constructed, disseminated, and changed by audiences active in the construction of meanings?

The crucial link between anthropological and literary approaches in the new cultural history is 'the use of language as metaphor. Symbolic actions . . . are framed as texts to be read or languages to be decoded' (Hunt 1989: 16–17). Gender too, understood 'as a system of cultural representation', following Joan Scott in her *Gender and the Politics of History* (1988), was to be 'at the forefront of the new cultural history' (Hunt 1989: 18–19; see also our section 'Gender'). Scott linked gender history with the analysis of discourse. Davis took into account literary theory and studies of reading, for example in her *Fiction in the Archives* (1987), where documents were to be treated as 'fictions', or rather, narratives told by historical actors, valued by them for particular reasons – not least because they built coherence into the anarchy of experience (Hunt 1989: 19). On the one hand, historical actors are concerned with representation: 'practices, whether economic or cultural, depend on the representations individuals use to make sense of their world' (Hunt 1989: 19). The new cultural history is concerned, in its case studies, with the 'mechanics of representation' (Hunt 1989: 20); but historians too should be aware of their narrative choices. Hunt's own introduction to the 'new cultural history' came in the form of the 'perpetual romance, the quest without end, the ironic doubling back over territory'. Finally, and in summary, the new cultural history should be characterised by its rejection of master-narratives and social theories, and their replacement by an open-minded 'close examination – of texts, of pictures, and of actions' (Hunt 1989: 21–2).

Cultural history now

Claims for the 'new cultural history' were ambitious but they were fragmented, and attempts to establish a new centre of gravity for 'cultural history' have not been altogether successful, so great was the number of satellites in orbit. In the 1960s Gombrich had asserted that historical styles rely upon 'techniques': the cultural historian lacked an academic voice 'because he does not represent a [single] technique, a discipline' (Gombrich 1969: 46). Hunt's programme, drawing in diverse techniques from literary theory and social and cultural anthropology, had not established that single methodological orthodoxy that might give cultural history a clear disciplinary voice (see also Chartier 2003). Thus, when Peter Burke took stock of 'cultural history' in the 1990s, he prescribed neither methods nor content, instead erecting a 'big tent' populated with exotic *Varieties of Cultural History* (1997). Burke enthused about new or revived objects of study, like 'dreams', 'chivalry', the language of 'gesture' and 'social memory' – with its associated field 'commemoration' (see Green 2008: chapters 5 and 6; Confino 2011; Abir-Am and Elliot (eds) 1999; and our section 'Technology' for 'heroes of invention'). He might also have mentioned attempts by cultural historians to reconstruct past 'passions', 'feelings' and 'emotions' (Bourke 2006) from understandably slim historical traces – or, more easily, to discuss the formal written discourse representing the meanings of the 'comic' and of 'laughter' (Burke 1997; Skinner 2004). Curiously, the unwillingness to restrict methods or topics in cultural history has not hindered its survival. Rather the opposite. In 2002, responding to the question 'what is history now', Cannadine asserted: 'now cultural history seems to be in the ascendant', thanks to its receptivity to anthropology, to the 'very large claims about the terrain of the past which it encompasses', and to the 'shift in interest from explanation to understanding' (Cannadine 2002: x). In the same collection, Richard Evans refers to the demise of grand narratives, of teleology and of socially and economically conditioned historical writing, and their replacement with a cultural history that emphasises identity, consciousness, mentality and the individual human being – including 'history's obscure, the losers and bystanders' (Evans in Cannadine 2002: 8–9).

The last decade has seen significant changes in the institutional representation of cultural history and intense debate about its current and future state. In 2004 the journal *Social History* was renamed *Cultural and Social History*. Recognising that British cultural history has an unusually close association with what has in Britain been called 'social history', Jordanova noted that for this new journal, culture is 'seen as a product of social practice'; but more than that, she speculated that here cultural history 'stands more securely for an array of values, such as epistemological sophistication, than social history does' – and also signals a wider range of sources (including visual, material, and even musical), a kinship with other disciplines, a willingness to work in a more explicitly conceptualised way, and an openness to interdisciplinary work (Jordanova 2011: 71–2). Paradoxically, Peter Mandler's contribution to the first issue identified 'The problem with cultural history' (Mandler 2004). Cultural historians, more interested in the language play of 'representations' than in formal 'discipline', social structures and quantities, are enamoured of theory but diffident in theoretical debates. Where, then, is the 'community of rational discourse, or argument based on common standards of evidence, evaluation and explanation'? Without the formulation of arguments that can actually be tested, how can cultural history speak effectively to neighbouring disciplines and wider publics (Mandler 2004: 94–5)?

Mandler proposes that cultural historians borrow 'more honestly and systematically' from a wider range of current intellectual frameworks, rather than recycling those which had borne fruit in the past (Mandler 2004: 96). He identifies not one but three core problems. The first, tagged as 'whose discourse?' and illustrated by discussions of 'race', asserts that cultural historians need to abandon simple ideas of 'influence' – especially of figures considered 'canonical' – and instead discover empirically the reach or 'throw' of the discourses they identify, accepting the multiplicity of interpretations made by contemporaries (Mandler 2004: 97–8). The second problem concerns the relationship of 'representations' with, for example, socio-economic 'realities'. What does it meant to say that 'Modernism' in art history and the supposed economic dynamism associated with 'modernity' correlate? There seems to be no reason that avant-garde art should reflect the conservative perspectives of a wider culture (Mandler 2004: 103–8). We can no longer make a nineteenth-century assumption that there is a unity of culture, most vividly expressed in high art. Scepticism and nuance are required. The third problem concerns the construction of cultural meaning: 'national identity' has frequently been constructed by historians in reference to a range of 'Others'; yet social anthropologists long ago moved on to different ways of seeing the construction of collective identity (Mandler 2004: 109–12).

For these three problems, there are three solutions – or at least pointers towards future practice. First, value those who document the production, mechanisms of diffusion, and reception of meaning through texts, as in James A. Secord's study of the nineteenth-century evolutionary best-seller *Vestiges* and its many readers (Secord 2000; Frasca-Spada and Jardine 2000; for the cultural history of science see Dear 1995). Second, pay more attention to the relationship of the mixture of categories with which cultural historians deal – or, put another way, to the crossing of genres amongst the texts cultural historians examine. Mandler here echoes Rubin: 'To deal with culture is thus to deal by definition with the mixing of categories' (Rubin 2002: 90). Mandler's exemplar, again chosen from the cultural history of science, is Alison Winter's study of 'Mesmerism' (animal magnetism) and its representations in modes as diverse as politics and music (Winter 1998). Third, get a better theory of meaning, by re-engaging with recent work in the social sciences, including that by psychologists and economists (Mandler 2004: 113–16).

It is still too early to see whether Mandler's claims have been heeded within a new 'cultural and social history'. What we can say is that in 2007, a group of cultural historians (including David F. Smith and the editors of this volume) organised a 'Varieties of Cultural History' conference at the University of Aberdeen to stimulate further discussion of the state and future of the field. The conference culminated with a call for a new society dedicated to the subject. The International Society for Cultural History (ISCH) was formally created in 2008. In her discussion of British cultural history delivered at one of the early meetings of ISCH, Jordanova admitted the difficulty of defining 'culture' normatively for those attempting a 'history of culture', and of distilling the meaning of cultural history empirically by looking at what cultural historians have done and do. She did suggest, however, that 'cultural history privileges the capacity of human beings to generate ideas, ways of life, meanings, objects, images and sounds, texts and so on' (Jordanova 2011: 64) – only to admit that other fields, many of them represented in literature and geography departments rather than in history, also specialised in those areas. Jordanova sees the field in Britain as informally recognisable (by readers and publishers), defined by contrast (as against economic, political, diplomatic, demographic, and social history) and, more positively, characterised, at least, by methodological innovation and a greater willingness to engage with (critical) theory by comparison with other forms of history (Jordanova 2011: 65). Perhaps she is right to assert that 'cultural history is the activity that places what happens between the ears at centre stage, and develops its practices and principal analytical modes accordingly' (Jordanova 2011: 76).

Jordanova cautions against proposing a narrow definition of cultural history, as does Chartier, who has spoken of the risk of 'imposing a definition too narrow and orthodox to respectably convey the diversity of the objects and approaches that characterize the practice of cultural historians' (Chartier 2009: 10). Chartier does, however, suggest that cultural history should be understood as 'constructed' on some fundamental issues, amongst which these three are essential: the relationship between popular and elite culture; the link between 'collective representations and unique productions'; and the 'relationships between discourse and practice, language and experience'. Together these may provide cultural history with a 'theoretical and methodological consistency' whilst, at the same time, challenging historians' convictions: 'facts' are replaced by actors' representations; the 'intrinsic' meanings of disembodied ideas are modalised through historicity, materiality, and appropriation; quantification gives way to anthropological analyses of 'conscious strategies and unrecognized constraints' (Chartier 2009: 15–16).

Burke's newest discussion of the 'strengths and weaknesses' of cultural history had been aired at the Aberdeen meeting (2007) and, appropriately enough, opened the first issue of the journal *Cultural History*, established in association with the ISCH (Burke 2012). According to Burke, the current popularity of cultural history is reflected in the introductions to the subject published from 2000 in many languages, and in the vast range of 'cultural histories' of topics from tea to terrorism (Burke 2012: 1). Disciplines from geography to psychology now have their 'cultural' sub-disciplines, reflecting a shift in academia away from the social to the cultural (Burke 2012: 2). But cultural historians should consider their subject's potential weaknesses. Success makes it harder for cultural history to define itself in opposition to previously dominant forms (politics, events, institutions, the economic). These have been drawn into cultural history – and we now speak of 'political rituals, Cold War culture' (Rubin 2002: 80) and even 'cultures of warfare' (Krimmer and Simpson (eds) 2011, and our section 'War'). Has all history become, in these various ways, cultural history – making 'cultural history' redundant? At the same time, the long-lamented vagueness of the concept of culture, threatening a disintegration of meanings of cultural history, has led scholars to look 'beyond the cultural turn' (Bonnell and Hunt 1999; Burke 2012: 3). A second problem is that the 'cultural turn' has been one of many, including the linguistic, visual, material, narrative, and 'practical' turn – competing, inconsistent, and none completely replacing an 'old cultural history' of art and literature in society (Burke 2012: 4). To Burke's list we might also add, most recently, a 'global turn' in cultural history (Poirrier 2008; Chartier 2009). Burke also ponders the problem, and equally the opportunity, of seeing culture, metaphorically, as a 'language' or 'text' that scholars can 'read' – when, following Chartier and others, it will always be necessary to appreciate the appropriation of the 'script' in varied, creative, subsequent 'performances' (Burke 2012: 4–5).

Another lingering issue, like that of the multiplicity of meanings assigned to 'culture', is that of 'explanation' and causality in cultural history. If simplistic economic, social, or political explanations are considered inadequate, is it any better to claim, in a cultural reductionist manner, that any individual acts in a particular way 'because of his culture'? (For an earlier discussion of causality in the writing of cultural history, see Weingartner 1968.) Burke's final problem is what he calls 'constructionism', in which 'nations, social classes or genders' are cultural or discursive constructions, reflecting the free agency of individuals to shape their lives from existing materials, rather than being determined or constrained by the social. Cultural historians must continually ask who is doing the construction, how that construction is constrained, and from what materials new entities are constructed, when active agents, rather than starting from nothing, engage in continuous reconstruction from available materials and motifs (Burke 2012: 6–7). Burke suggests, finally, that scholars should explore a 'cultural history of intellectual practices' which takes account of the ways in which ideas are received in and adapted to local contexts, especially as they are translated between varied human cultures (Burke 2012: 9; for a parallel proposal that 'mediation' is key to cultural history, see Jordanova 2011: 76). In this formulation, much of cultural history is an account of those cultural 'encounters' which are often revealing of normally tacit views, values and practices (see our section 'Others').

So: is it the case, as we sometimes hear, that 'we are all cultural historians now'? Could it be that the most easily reproducible elements of earlier forms of cultural history have been incorporated, perhaps in diluted form and stripped of their most imposing sociological or anthropological inspirations, into the everyday practice of historians who would *not* feel any particular need to designate themselves as 'cultural'? Judging from the experience of the last fifty years, and thinking of Colie's critique of cultural history, there is no particular reason to believe that an end is in sight to the critics' dissatisfaction, whether it be on the grounds that cultural history is too narrow and theoretical to be of use, or that it is so diverse in perspectives as to be ill-defined.

Our main concern above has been to trace movements within history and other disciplines that have variously been appropriated by, or adopted into, forms of cultural history from the eighteenth century to the present day. In this survey we have mentioned both movements and figures closely associated with campaigns to define, promote and enrich cultural history in its many forms. Twenty-first century students of cultural history can refer to studies which indicate the diverse national forms assumed by cultural history (Chartier 2009; Rogge 2011); and they can benefit from a growing number of introductory works, in English and other languages, aimed at capturing the meanings and practices of contemporary cultural history – and also its histories (Ashplant and Smyth 2001; Burke 2004/2008; Green 2008; Arcangeli 2011; and in French, Ory 2004; Poirrier 2004). Students might follow the advice – about focus as much about method – offered by Burke, Chartier or Mandler. As to the future of cultural history, though: 'what will happen is anyone's guess' (Jordanova 2011: 73).

References

Abir-Am, P. and Elliot, C.A. (eds) (1999) *Commemorative Practices in Science* (*Osiris*, Vol. 14), Chicago: University of Chicago Press.

Abulafia, D. (2008) *The Discovery of Mankind: Atlantic encounters in the Age of Columbus*, New Haven, CT: Yale University Press.

Anchor, R. (1978) 'History and play: Johan Huizinga and his critics', *History and Theory*, 17: 63–93.

Anderson, B. (1983, 2nd edn 1991) *Imagined Communities: reflections on the origin and spread of nationalism*, London: Verso.

Arcangeli, A. (2011) *Cultural History: a concise introduction*, London: Routledge.

Ariès, P. (1960) *L'Enfant et la vie familiale sous l'Ancien Régime*, trans. R. Baldick (1962) *Centuries of Childhood: a social history of family life*, London: Jonathan Cape.

Ariès, P. (1977) *L'Homme devant la mort*, trans. H. Weaver (1983) *The Hour of Our Death*, Harmondsworth: Penguin.

Arnold, M. (1869) *Culture and Anarchy: an essay in political and social criticism*, London: Smith, Elder; online at <http://www.gutenberg.org/ebooks/4212>.

Arnold, M. (1993) *Culture and Anarchy: and other writings by Matthew Arnold*, ed. S. Collini, Cambridge: Cambridge University Press.

Arnold, M. (2009) *Culture and Anarchy by Matthew Arnold*, ed. J. Garnett, Oxford: Oxford University Press.

Ashplant, T.G. and Smyth, G. (eds) (2001) *Explorations in Cultural History*, London: Pluto Press.

Ashplant, T.G. and Wilson, A. (1988) 'Present-centred history and the problem of historical knowledge', *The Historical Journal*, 31: 253–74.

Barnard, F.M. (2003) *Herder on Nationality, Humanity, and History*, Montreal: McGill-Queen's University Press.

Barzun, J. (1956) 'Cultural history as a synthesis', in F. Stern (ed.) *The Varieties of History: from Voltaire to the present*, London: Meridian Books.

Bénéton, P. (1975) *Histoire de mots: culture et civilisation*, Paris: Presses de la Fondation Nationale des Sciences Politiques.

Bennett, T., Grossberg, L. and Morris, M. (2005) *New Keywords: a revised vocabulary of culture and society*, Oxford: Blackwell.

Bloch, M.L.B. (1954) *The Historian's Craft*, trans. P. Putnam, Manchester: Manchester University Press.

Bonnell, V.E. and Hunt, L. (eds) (1999) *Beyond the Cultural Turn: new directions in the study of society and culture*, Berkeley, CA: University of California Press.

Bourdieu, P. (1977) *Outline of a Theory of Practice*, trans. R. Nice, Cambridge: Cambridge University Press.

Bourdieu, Pierre (1990) *The Logic of Practice*, trans. R. Nice, Cambridge: Polity Press.

Bourke, J. (2006) *Fear: a cultural history*, London: Virago.

Bouwsma, W.J. (2000) *The Waning of the Renaissance 1550–1640*, New Haven, CT: Yale University Press.

Bowden, B. (2009) *Civilization: the evolution of an imperial idea*, Chicago: University of Chicago Press.

Braudel, F. (1949) *La Méditerranée et le monde méditerranéan à l'époque de Philippe II*, Paris: Colin.

Braudel, F. (1967) *Civilisation matérielle, économie et capitalisme, XVe-XVIIIe siècle*, Paris: Colin.

Braudel, F. (1980) 'The history of civilizations', in Braudel, *On History*, Chicago: University of Chicago Press.

Braudel, F. (1981) *The Structures of Everyday Life: the limits of the possible*, trans. S. Richards, London: Collins.

Braudel, F. (1988) *The Identity of France*, trans. S. Reynolds, London: Collins.

Brett, A. (2002) 'What is intellectual history now?', in D. Cannadine (ed.) *What Is History Now?*, Basingstoke: Palgrave Macmillan.

Burckhardt, J. (1860) *Die Cultur der Renaissance in Italien: ein Versuch*, Basel: Schweighauser, trans. from the 3rd German edn S.G.C. Middlemore (1878) *The Civilization of the Period of the Renaissance in Italy*, London: Kegan Paul.

Burke, P. (1967) *The Renaissance*, London: Longmans.

Burke, P. (1969) *The Renaissance Sense of the Past*, London: Arnold.

Burke, P. (1972) 'The historians: the discovery of social and cultural history', in Burke, *Culture and Society in Renaissance Italy, 1420–1540*, London: Batsford.

Burke, P. (1978) *Popular Culture in Early Modern Europe*, London: Temple Smith.

Burke, P. (1990) *The French Historical Revolution: the Annales school, 1929–89*, Stanford, CA: Stanford University Press.

Burke, P. (1991) 'Reflections on the origins of cultural history', in J.H. Pittock and A. Wear (eds) *Interpretation and Cultural History*, Basingstoke: Macmillan.

Burke, P. (1994) *Popular Culture in Early Modern Europe*, 2nd edition, Aldershot: Scolar Press.

Burke, P. (1997) *Varieties of Cultural History*, Ithaca, NY: Cornell University Press.

Burke, P. (1997a) 'Strengths and weaknesses of the history of mentalities', in Burke, *Varieties of Cultural History*, Cambridge: Polity Press.

Burke, P. (ed.) (2001) *New Perspectives on Historical Writing*, 2nd edn, Cambridge: Polity Press.

Burke, P. (2005) *History and Social Theory*, 2nd edn, Cambridge: Polity Press.

Burke, P. (2004; revised edn 2008) *What is Cultural History?*, Cambridge: Polity Press.

Burke, P. (2009) *Popular Culture in Early Modern Europe*, 3rd edition, Aldershot: Ashgate.

Burke, P. (2012) 'Strengths and weaknesses of cultural history', *Cultural History*, 1: 1–13.

Butterfield, H. (1931) *The Whig Interpretation of History*, London: G. Bell.

Cannadine, D. (ed.) (2002) *What is History Now?*, Basingstoke: Palgrave Macmillan.

Carr, E.H. (1961) *What is History?*, London: Macmillan.

Chartier, R. (1985) 'Texts, symbols, and Frenchness', *Journal of Modern History*, 57: 682–95.

Chartier, R. (1987) *The Cultural Uses of Print in Early Modern France*, Princeton, NJ: Princeton University Press.

Chartier, R. (1988) *Cultural History: between practices and representations*, Cambridge: Polity Press.

Chartier, R. (1989) 'Texts, printing, readings', in L. Hunt (ed.) *The New Cultural History*, Berkeley, CA: University of California Press.

Chartier, R. (2003) 'La nouvelle histoire culturelle existe-t-elle?', *Cahiers du Centre de Recherches Historiques*, 31: 13–24.

Chartier, R. (2009) 'Cultural history between tradition and globalization', *Penn History Review*, 16: 9–16.

Chickering, R. (1993) *Karl Lamprecht: a German academic life (1856–1915)*, Atlantic Highlands, NJ: Humanities Press.

Colie, R.L. (1964) 'Johan Huizinga and the task of cultural history', *American Historical Review*, 69: 607–30.

Collini, S. (ed.) (1993) *Culture and Anarchy: and other writings by Matthew Arnold*, Cambridge: Cambridge University Press.

Confino, A. (2011) 'History and memory', in A. Schneider and D. Woolf (eds) *The Oxford History of Historical Writing, vol. 5: historical writing since 1945*, Oxford: Oxford University Press.

Darnton, R. (1980) 'Intellectual and cultural history', in M. Kammen (ed.) *The Past Before Us: contemporary historical writing in the United States*, Ithaca, NY: Cornell University Press.

Darnton, R. (1984) *The Great Cat Massacre and Other Episodes in French Cultural History*, New York: Basic Books.

Darnton, R. (1986) 'The symbolic element in history', *Journal of Modern History*, 58: 218–34.

Davis, N.Z. (1975) *Society and Culture in Early Modern France: eight essays*, London: Duckworth.

Davis, N.Z. (1983) *The Return of Martin Guerre*, Cambridge, MA: Harvard University Press.

Davis, N.Z. (1987) *Fiction in the Archives: pardon tales and their tellers in sixteenth-century France*, Stanford, CA: Stanford University Press.

Dear, P. (1995) 'Cultural history of science: an overview with reflections', *Science, Technology & Human Values*, 20: 150–70.

Eagleton, T. (2000) *The Idea of Culture*, Malden, MA: Blackwell.

Eliot, T.S. (1948) *Notes Towards the Definition of Culture*, London: Faber and Faber.

Fink, C. (1989) *Marc Bloch: a life in history*, Cambridge: Cambridge University Press.

Fitzpatrick, E. (1991) 'Caroline F. Ware and the cultural approach to history', *American Quarterly*, 43: 173–98.

Force, P. (2009) 'Voltaire and the necessity of modern history', *Modern Intellectual History*, 6: 457–84.

Frasca-Spada, M. and Jardine, N. (eds) (2000) *Books and the Sciences in History*, Cambridge: Cambridge University Press.

Friedell, E. (1930–3) *A Cultural History of the Modern Age: the crisis of the European soul from the Black Death to the World War*, trans. C.F. Atkinson, 3 vols., New York: Knopf.

Garnett, J. (ed.) (2009) *Culture and Anarchy by Matthew Arnold*, Oxford: Oxford University Press.

Geertz, C. (1972) 'Deep play: notes on the Balinese cockfight', *Daedalus*, 101: 1–37; reprinted in his (1973) *The Interpretation of Cultures: selected essays*, New York: Basic Books.

Geertz, C. (1973) 'Thick description: toward an interpretive theory of culture', in *The Interpretation of Cultures: selected essays*, New York: Basic Books.

Gilbert, F. (1960) 'Cultural history and its problems', *Comité International des Sciences Historiques: Rapports*, 40–58.

Gilbert, F. (1986) 'Jacob Burckhardt's student years: the road to cultural history', *Journal of the History of Ideas*, 47: 249–74.

Gilbert, F. (1990) *History: politics or culture? Reflections on Ranke and Burckhardt*, Princeton: Princeton University Press.

Ginzburg, C. (1980) *The Cheese and the Worms: the cosmos of a sixteenth-century miller*, trans. J. and A. Tedeschi, Baltimore, MD: Johns Hopkins University Press.

Gombrich, E.H. (1969) *In Search of Cultural History: the Philip Maurice Deneke Lecture 1967*, Oxford: Clarendon Press.

Gordon, H.L. (1926) *Rabbi Elijah Gordon: his life and works. A chapter in the cultural and political history of the Jews in Russia*, New York: Bloch.

Gossman, L. (2002) 'Jacob Burckhardt: Cold War liberal', *Journal of Modern History*, 74: 538–72.

Green, A. (2008) *Cultural History*, Basingstoke: Palgrave Macmillan.

Grosse, J. (1999) 'Reading history: on Jacob Burckhardt as source-reader', *Journal of the History of Ideas*, 60: 525–47.

Hacking, I. (1999) *The Social Construction of What?*, Cambridge, MA: Harvard University Press.

Hale, G.E. (1998) *Making Whiteness: the culture of segregation in the South, 1890–1940*, New York: Pantheon Books.

Hall, A.R. (1963) 'Merton revisited, or science and society in the seventeenth century', *History of Science*, 2: 1–16.

Harvey, K. (ed.) (2009) *History and Material Culture: a student's guide to approaching alternative sources*, London: Routledge.

Hayes, C.J.H. (1917) *A Political and Cultural History of Modern Europe*, New York: Macmillan.

Heath, E. and Merolle, V. (eds) (2007) *Adam Ferguson: history, progress and human nature*, London: Pickering & Chatto.

Heilborn, A. (1927) *The Opposite Sexes: a study of woman's natural and cultural history*, trans. J.E. Pryde-Hughes, London: Methuen.

Hoare, Q. and Nowell, G. (eds) (1971) *Selections from the Prison Notebooks of Antonio Gramsci*, London: Lawrence & Wishart.

Hobsbawm, E. and Ranger, T. (eds) (1983) *The Invention of Tradition*, Cambridge: Cambridge University Press.

Horowitz, M.C. (1998) *Seeds of Virtue and Knowledge*, Princeton, NJ: Princeton University Press.

Huizinga, J. (1919) *Herfsttij der Middeleeuwen*, Haarlem: H.D. Tjeenk Willink; abridged trans. F. Hopman (1924) *The Waning of the Middle Ages: a study of the forms of life, thought and art in France and the Netherlands in the XIVth and XVth centuries*, London: Edward Arnold; also trans. in full R.J. Payton and U. Mammitzsch (1996) *The Autumn of the Middle Ages*, Chicago: University of Chicago Press.

Huizinga, J. (1929) 'The task of cultural history', in Huizinga (1960) *Men and Ideas: history, the Middle Ages, the Renaissance*, trans. J.S. Holmes, London: Eyre & Spottiswoode.

Hunt, L. (ed.) (1989) *The New Cultural History*, Berkeley, CA: University of California Press.

Hutton, P.H. (2004) *Philippe Ariès and the Politics of French Cultural History*, Amherst, MA: University of Massachusetts Press.

Iggers, G. and Powell, J.M. (eds) (1990) *Leopold von Ranke and the Shaping of the Historical Discipline*, Syracuse, NY: Syracuse University Press.

Jordanova, L. (2011) 'The practice of cultural history in Britain', in J. Rogge (ed.) *Cultural History in Europe: institutions, themes, perspectives*, Bielefeld: Transcript.

Kelley, D.R. (1996) 'The old cultural history', *History of the Human Sciences*, 9: 101–26.

Krimmer, E. and Simpson, P.A. (2011) *Enlightened War: German theories and cultures of warfare from Frederick the Great to Clausewitz*, Rochester, NY: Camden House.

LaCapra, D. (1988) 'Chartier, Darnton, and the great symbol massacre', *Journal of Modern History*, 60: 95–112.

Le Goff, J. (1980) *Time, Work and Culture in the Middle Ages,* trans. A. Goldhammer, Chicago: University of Chicago Press.

Le Goff, J., Chartier, R. and Revel, J. (eds) (1978) *La Nouvelle Histoire,* Paris: Retz.

Mali, J. (2012) *The Legacy of Vico in Modern Cultural History,* Cambridge: Cambridge University Press.

Mandler, P. (2004) 'The problem with cultural history', *Cultural and Social History,* 1: 94–117.

Manias, C. (2012) 'The growth of race and culture in nineteenth-century Germany: Gustav Klemm and the Universal History of Humanity', *Modern Intellectual History,* 9: 1–31.

Merton, R. (1973) 'The normative structure of science', in *The Sociology of Science: theoretical and empirical investigations,* Chicago: University of Chicago Press.

Meyer, L.B. (1970) '*In Search of Cultural History:* by E.H. Gombrich', *History and Theory,* 9: 397–9.

Mishew, D. (1919) *The Bulgarians in the Past: pages from Bulgarian cultural history,* Lausanne: Librairie Centrale des Nationalités.

Ory, P. (2004) *L'Histoire culturelle,* Paris: Presses Universitaires de France.

Pagden, A. (1982) *The Fall of Natural Man: the American Indian and the origins of comparative ethnology,* Cambridge: Cambridge University Press.

Pallares-Burke, M. (2002) *The New History: confessions and conversations,* Cambridge: Polity Press.

Pittock, J.H. and Wear, A. (eds) (1991) *Interpretation and Cultural History,* Houndmills: Macmillan.

Poirrier, P. (2004) *Les Enjeux de l'histoire culturelle,* Paris: Seuil.

Poirrier, P. (ed.) (2008) *L'Histoire culturelle: un 'tournant mondial' de l'historiographie?,* Dijon: Editions Universitaires de Dijon.

Pollard, S.P. (1971) *The Idea of Progress: history and society,* Harmondsworth: Penguin.

Porter, R. (1997) *The Greatest Benefit to Mankind: a medical history of humanity from antiquity to the present,* London: HarperCollins.

Porter, T.M. (2004) *Karl Pearson: the scientific life in a statistical age,* Princeton and Oxford: Princeton University Press.

Ranke, L. von (2010) *The Theory and Practice of History,* ed. G. Iggers, London: Routledge.

Rogge, J. (ed.) (2011) *Cultural History in Europe: institutions, themes, perspectives,* Bielefeld: Transcript.

Rubin, M. (2002) 'What is cultural history now?', in D. Cannadine (ed.) *What is History Now?,* Basingstoke: Palgrave Macmillan.

Rudé, G. (1959) *The Crowd in the French Revolution,* Oxford: Clarendon Press.

Rudé, G. (1964) *The Crowd in History: a study of popular disturbances in France and England 1730–1848,* New York: Wiley.

Sansom, G.B. (1931) *Japan: a short cultural history,* London: Cresset.

Scott, J.W. (1988) *Gender and the Politics of History,* New York: Columbia University Press.

Secord, J.A. (2000) *Victorian Sensation: the extraordinary publication, reception, and secret authorship of Vestiges of the Natural History of Creation,* Chicago: University of Chicago Press.

Sewell, W.H. Jr (1997) 'Geertz, cultural systems, and history: from synchrony to transformation', *Representations,* 59: 35–55.

Sewell, W.H. Jr (1999) 'The concept(s) of culture', in V.E. Bonnell and L. Hunt (eds) *Beyond the Cultural Turn: New Directions in the Study of Society and Culture,* Berkeley, CA: University of California Press.

Shapin, S. (1992) 'Discipline and bounding: the history and sociology of science as seen through the externalism-internalism debate', *History of Science,* 30: 333–69.

Shapin, S. and Thackray, A. (1974) 'Prosopography as a research tool in history of science: the British scientific community 1700–1900', *History of Science*, 12: 1–28.

Skinner, Q. (2004) 'Hobbes and the classical theory of laughter', in T. Sorrell and L. Foisneau (eds) *Leviathan after 350 Years*, Oxford: Clarendon Press.

Spadafora, D. (1990) *The Idea of Progress in Eighteenth-Century Britain*, New Haven, CT: Yale University Press.

Stoianovich, T. (1976) *French Historical Method: the Annales paradigm*, Ithaca, NY: Cornell University Press.

Stone, L. (1971) 'Prosopography', *Daedalus*, 100: 46–71.

Thomas, K. (1963) 'History and anthropology', *Past & Present*, 24: 3–24.

Thomas, K. (1971) *Religion and the Decline of Magic: studies in popular beliefs in sixteenth and seventeenth century England*, London: Weidenfeld and Nicolson.

Thompson, E.P. (1963) *The Making of the English Working Class*, London: Victor Gollancz.

Thompson, E.P. (1967) 'Time, work-discipline, and industrial capitalism', *Past & Present*, 38: 56–97.

Thompson, E.P. (1991) *Customs in Common*, London: Merlin Press.

Thompson, P. (2000) *The Voice of the Past: oral history*, 3rd edition, New York: Oxford University Press.

Tosh, J. (2005) *Manliness and Masculinities in Nineteenth-century Britain: essays on gender, family and empire*, Harlow: Pearson Longman.

Tylor, E.B. (1871) *Primitive Culture*, London: John Murray.

Vico, G. (1999) *New Science: principles of the new science concerning the common nature of nations*, trans. D. Marsh, introd. A. Grafton, Harmondsworth: Penguin.

Wahrman, D. (2008) 'Change and the corporeal in seventeenth- and eighteenth-century gender history: or, can cultural history be rigorous?', *Gender & History*, 20: 584–602.

Ware, C.F. (ed.) (1940) *The Cultural Approach to History*, New York: Columbia University Press.

Weber, M. (2002) *The Protestant Ethic and the 'Spirit' of Capitalism and Other Writings*, ed. and trans P. Baehr and G.C. Wells, London: Penguin.

Weingartner, R.H. (1968) 'Some philosophic comments on cultural history', *History and Theory*, 7: 38–59.

Whewell, W. (1840) *The Philosophy of the Inductive Sciences: founded upon their history*, London: J.W. Parker.

White, H. (1978) *Tropics of Discourse: essays in cultural criticism*, Baltimore: Johns Hopkins University Press.

Williams, R. (1958) 'Culture is ordinary', reprinted in Williams (1989) *Resources of Hope: culture, democracy, socialism*, London: Verso.

Williams, R. (1958a) *Culture and Society, 1780–1950*, London: Chatto & Windus.

Williams, R. (1961) 'The analysis of culture', in *The Long Revolution*, London: Chatto & Windus.

Williams, R. (1976) *Keywords: a vocabulary of culture and society*, New York: Oxford University Press; revised edition (1983) London: Flamingo.

Williams, R. (1981) *Culture*, London: Fontana.

Wilson, A. and Ashplant, T.G. (1988) 'Whig history and present-centred history', *The Historical Journal*, 33: 1–16.

Winter, A. (1998) *Mesmerized: powers of mind in Victorian Britain*, Chicago: University of Chicago Press.

Young, R.J.C. (2001) *Postcolonialism: an historical introduction*, Malden, MA: Blackwell.

PART I

Gender

Introduction

GENDER IDENTITIES AND RELATIONSHIPS have long been interwoven with other aspects of people's efforts at finding meaning in their lives – for instance, in relation to childhood, religion, literacy and war. Being so closely bound up with much else in people's lives, the form taken by gender relations has necessarily varied at different times in the past and in different social environments, reflecting changes in the patterns of accommodation between men's roles and those of women. And yet, because the male–female dichotomy readily appears to be a biological given, roles that are assigned on the basis of gender have often seemed unalterable rather than time-bound. To show how they have varied is a prime task for cultural historians, though one that can be tackled in different ways. Wahrman (2004) claims to have dated a major change in British people's perceptions of gender to the last two decades of the eighteenth century. Others would emphasise long-term continuity, although allowing for change. Systematic obstacles to women's chances of achieving individual autonomy can be shown to have persisted through many centuries, even though the nature of these obstacles has varied. Precisely because male dominance rested on the interlocking effects of customs in many cultural spheres, it continued from the Middle Ages to the nineteenth century, despite significant changes that altered its more obvious manifestations.

Male dominance was underpinned ideologically in seventeenth-century Europe by a presumption that women's alleged moral deficiencies (Mendelson and Crawford 1998) needed to be held in check by familial subordination to men, just as potentially deviant political subjects needed to be governed by a hierarchical system of control (Weil 1999). Some responses to this ideology in Britain's North American colonies at this time are discussed in Norton (1996 and 2011). A less ostensibly hierarchical ideology gradually came to displace this in the eighteenth century, in a cultural context increasingly concerned with sensibility (Fletcher 1995; Wahrman 2008). Writings by Enlightenment authors on the physical differences between male and female bodies were worded in such a way as to imply a self-evident need for men to be protectors of 'the weaker sex' (Jordanova 1989). By the nineteenth century, the exclusion of middle-class women from opportunities for earning their own living was being justified by feminine vulnerability.

The theme of relations between spouses has often been closely bound up with that of gendered work roles and spheres of activity. Women in some social contexts would normally marry only after having already been economically active, perhaps for many years. Marrying at a later age meant greater freedom in choosing a spouse. In such a cultural environment, a wife's degree of autonomy vis-à-vis her husband tended to be greater (Maynes and Waltner 2001; De Moor and Zanden 2010). It is important to note this possibility, so as to counteract the impression that in the past women were never free agents, but moved from being under the control of their parents to being subject to their husbands. In an oft-quoted article (Scott 1986 – see also Scott 2008 and Butler 2011), it was argued that gender historians should not only document the power imbalances in society at large but also recognise women's active responses to the possibilities available to them, even in roles defined as subordinate. Thus, Capp (2003) links the generally lower level of literacy among women with the fact that many women's life-circumstances facilitated an oral culture, in which social solidarity was highly valued and skill in story-telling was appreciated – a skill exercised by mothers for the benefit of young children, as well as in adult company. The wish to balance attention to instances of male dominance with recognition of women's agency has generated much discussion in recent decades around the theme of domesticity as opposed to involvement in the marketplace and politics. Davidoff (2003) is among those who have suggested that by the early nineteenth century it had come to be widely – though by no means universally – accepted that men and women of the middle class should live in 'separate spheres', with men taking care of the public sphere, and women's activity being confined to domestic concerns. (But see Vickery 1993 and Abrams 2008 for criticisms of this narrative.)

In the first reading below, McKeon recommends reserving the term 'patriarchy' for the Enlightenment period and the nineteenth century. In distinguishing between patriarchy and patriarchalism, he is seeking to persuade his readers to avoid thinking of patriarchy as if it were a timeless phenomenon – and to be alert to the history of the concepts they use. In McKeon's view, earlier patterns of male dominance were instances of patriarchalism. Its various forms included the political ideology advocated in the seventeenth century by Sir Robert Filmer, in his posthumously published *Patriarcha* (Filmer 1949). McKeon moves on from considering issues of terminology to arguing that two types of pressure were at work in bringing about this gradual transition. One was economic. The other had to do with changing attitudes to knowledge, and a tendency to attribute differences between men and women to Nature. McKeon (2005) later elaborated his thesis in book-form: see Cody (2008) for the broader context of his work.

The second reading, by Davidoff and Hall, has particular relevance to questions about the notion of 'separate spheres'. It gives the authors' responses to criticisms of their widely read study of changing gender relations, first published in 1987 with the subtitle *Men and Women of the Middle Class in England, 1780–1850*. Their book argued that these seven decades had seen a radical cultural change: middle class families had sought to distinguish themselves, both from the working class and from the aristocracy, by their espousal of high moral values expressed through the husband's hard work and his wife's devotion to the upbringing of their children. As Vickery (1993) had pointed out, one flaw in the argument lies in the absence of equally detailed evidence concerning the preceding period.

The third of this section's readings, by Tosh, relates early Victorian notions of gender to the experience of middle-class boys in Britain, as well as to that of their sisters and their mothers. It is focused on the decades from 1830 to 1860, which in this author's view coincided with the heyday of masculine domesticity as an ideal, and a little beyond. In the book it comes from, he argues that from the 1870s onwards this ideal lost some of its attractiveness, with Britain's increasing involvement in imperial expansion. But during those decades, home was not just a woman's place – it was a man's place too. Yet it was also in the home that a son's path in life must diverge from that considered appropriate for a daughter. Unlike his sister, the boy needed to differentiate himself from the feminine values represented by his mother. Yet as an adult and a father he would be expected to cherish his home life and his family. Tosh's findings invite comparison with those of Frank (1998) on the Northern USA.

References

Abrams, L. (2008) 'The "unseamed picture": conflicting narratives of women in the modern European past', *Gender & History*, 20: 628–43.

Butler, J. (2011) 'Speaking up and talking back: Joan Scott's critical feminism', in J. Butler and E. Weed (eds) *The Question of Gender: Joan W. Scott's critical feminism*, Bloomington, IN: Indiana University Press.

Capp, B.S. (2003) *When Gossips Meet: women, family and neighbourhood in early modern England*, Oxford: Oxford University Press.

Cody, L.F. (2008) review of McKeon 2005, *Journal of Social History*, 41: 1051–3.

Davidoff, L. (2003) 'Gender and the "Great Divide": public and private in British gender history', *Journal of Women's History*, 15: 11–27.

De Moor, T. and Zanden, J.L. van (2010) 'Girl power: the European marriage pattern and labour markets in the North Sea region in the late medieval and early modern period', *Economic History Review*, 63: 1–33.

Fletcher, A. (1995) *Gender, Sex, and Subordination in England, 1500–1800*, New Haven, CT: Yale University Press.

Filmer, R. ([1685] 1949) *Patriarcha and other political works*, ed. P. Laslett, Oxford: Blackwell.

Frank, S.M. (1998) *Life with Father: parenthood and masculinity in the nineteenth-century American North*, Baltimore, MD: Johns Hopkins University Press.

Jordanova, L. (1989) *Sexual Visions: images of gender in science and medicine between the eighteenth and twentieth century*, London: Harvester Wheatsheaf.

Maynes, M.J. and Waltner, A.B. (2001) 'Women's life-cycle transitions in world-historical perspective: comparing marriage in China and Europe', *Journal of Women's History*, 12: 11–21.

McKeon, M. (2005) *The Secret History of Domesticity*, Baltimore, MD: Johns Hopkins University Press.

Mendelson, S. and Crawford, P. (1998) *Women in Early Modern England, 1550–1720*, Oxford: Oxford University Press.

Norton, M.B. (1996) *Founding Mothers and Fathers: gendered power and the forming of American society*, New York, NY: Knopf.

Norton, M.B. (2011) *Separated by their Sex: women in public and private in the colonial Atlantic world*, Ithaca, NY: Cornell University Press.

Scott, J.W. (1986) 'Gender: a useful category of historical analysis', *American Historical Review*, 91: 1053–75.

Scott, J.W. (2008) 'Unanswered questions', *American Historical Review*, 113: 1422–30.

Vickery, A. (1993) 'Golden Age to separate spheres? A review of the categories and chronology of English women's history', *Historical Journal*, 36: 383–414.

Wahrman, D. (2004) *The Making of the Modern Self: identity and culture in eighteenth-century England*, New Haven, CT: Yale University Press.

Wahrman, D. (2008) 'Change and the corporeal in seventeenth- and eighteenth-century gender history: or, can cultural history be rigorous?', *Gender & History*, 20: 584–602.

Weil, R.J. (1999) *Political Passions: gender, the family, and political argument in England, 1680–1714*, Manchester: Manchester University Press.

Chapter 1

Michael McKeon

HISTORICIZING PATRIARCHY: THE EMERGENCE OF GENDER DIFFERENCE IN ENGLAND, 1660–1760

T HE POWERFUL APPEAL of the category "patriarchy" depends upon, but also is limited by, its implicit claim to a comprehensive application. In recent years it is the limitation of the term that has seemed most visible. In naming the persistent experience of male dominance—across cultures, across historical periods—patriarchy operates on a level of abstract reference that appears to posit an implausibly universal human nature and that, by seeming to explain everything, in the end explains very little. Some have urged the replacement of "patriarchy" by categories more concretely reflective of contextual variation. But any effort at historical or cultural specification requires a universalizing backdrop of the sort asserted by "patriarchy" to render its object intelligible as the singular instance of a general phenomenon.

In the following essay I aim to argue a broad thesis about how and why the modern system of gender difference was established during the English Restoration and eighteenth century. In making this argument I hope to exemplify how patriarchy may be historicized: how the history of male dominance may be understood to entail a general continuity complicated by specific and divergent discontinuities. Central to my thesis will be the view that to historicize patriarchy requires, among other things, an inquiry into the relationship between the modern systems of sexuality—of sex and gender difference—and class. Much of my argument will be based on evidence drawn from recent research into early modern political theory, marriage law, agrarian change, the conceptual history of sexuality, and the social history of homosexuality. It should go without saying that the entire argument is deeply indebted to the work on gender and patriarchy undertaken by feminist studies over the past two decades.

Some recent research substantiates and sophisticates received wisdom; some of it propounds new lines of thought. My procedure will be to use both kinds of research to formulate and develop a hypothesis that conceives gender difference within the context of the early modern divisions of labor and knowledge. I will conclude with a brief discussion of the demands involved in trying to account for historical change of the sort posited in the notion of an early modern "division," change that is both monolithic in its broadest scope and diversely ramified in its human applications.[1]

I

There is some value in employing the term "patriarchalism" to refer to the traditional regime that is replaced by the modern conception of gender difference. Although specifically associated with Sir Robert Filmer's theory of royal absolutism, "patriarchalism" also takes in, more inclusively, the set of ideas and social practices entailed in the analogy between the family and the state.[2] The patriarchal analogy works because it is based on a hierarchical notion of authority that is implicitly analogical: as in the microcosm, so in the macrocosm. In premodern England this analogy was "traditional" in the sense that it was entertained and acted upon as a tacit and unexamined article of belief—a way of giving to political arrangements the apparently integral and natural legitimacy of family arrangements. Puritan thought and the onset of political crisis in the seventeenth century forced this tacit knowledge to become explicit. Now the analogy between familial and political order had to be rationalized, and people were obliged to concretize both terms and acknowledge what was problematic in the comparison. The apparent integrity of patriarchal authority in the family was found in fact to consist of several distinct authorities—that of the father, the husband, and the master—whose compound complexity deviated from the simplicity of the model of absolute royal prerogative.[3] In this sense, Filmer marks not the triumphant ascendancy of patriarchal thought, but its demise as tacit knowledge, the fact that it is in crisis. He wrote his *Patriarcha* on the eve of warfare between royalists and parliamentarians in 1642; it was published in 1680 and again in 1685, when the Exclusion Crisis renewed that conflict in other terms.[4]

This is not to say, however, that Filmer's opponents were immediately prepared to reject the analogy. In 1644, the parliamentarian Henry Parker argued that because arbitrary power does not rule the family, therefore it is not to be endured in the state: "And who now hath any competent share of reason, can suppose, that if God and nature have been so careful to provide for liberty in Families, and in particulars; that Man would introduce, or ought to endure slavery, when it is introduced upon whole States and Generalities?"[5] In 1700, twelve years after the absolutist James II had been deposed, the feminist Mary Astell reversed Parker's question: "if absolute Sovereignty be not necessary in a State, how comes it to be so in a Family? Or if in a Family why not in a State; since no reason can be alleged for the one that will not hold more strongly for the other?"[6] Although Filmer, Parker, and Astell disagree on the question of whether the family and the state are institutions grounded in absolute authority, they agree on the continued plausibility of the analogy between family and state. And yet the more the nature and terms of the analogy were subjected to self-conscious examination, the more inevitably its force was undermined. In his *Second Treatise of Government* (printed in 1690), John Locke took the next decisive step by arguing that "the Power of a *Magistrate* over a Subject, may be distinguished from that of a *Father* over his Children, a *Master* over his Servant, a *Husband* over his Wife, and a *Lord* over his Slave."[7] Locke's famous argument formalized, in terms of a liberal political theory, a two-part development whose cultural significance was far-reaching. First, it articulated the growing conviction that the world of the family and that of the state were regulated by fundamentally different—respectively customary and contractual—principles. Second, by restricting female identity to that of wife and mother, roles whose customary authority in the broad domain of kinship was now gradually limited to the circumscribed domain of the household, it conceived the contractual affairs of the polity as an exclusively male preserve.[8]

The foundering of patriarchalist political theory at the end of the seventeenth century can be explained by reference to political developments, in particular to the succession crisis that dominated Restoration politics. Monarchal succession is based on a model of dynastic inheritance. Increasing suspicion of the heir to the House of Stuarts—James,

Duke of York—culminated in the failed effort to exclude him from the royal succession, and in his successful deposition soon after he acceded to the throne in 1685. In the Hanoverian Settlement of 1689, England's rulers agreed that dynastic inheritance, and the patriarchalist principles on which it is based, may be overruled by pressing considerations. By implication, the interests of political subjects are not necessarily best served by the system of patrilineage.[9] But the Hanoverian Settlement and the demise of patriarchalist political theory cannot be understood simply as a matter of constitutional politics. They also represent one outcome of a more general, early modern disenchantment with aristocratic ideology. For present purposes, aristocratic ideology can be summarized as the set of related beliefs that birth makes worth, that the interests of the family are identified with those of its head, and that among the gentry, honor and property are to be transmitted patrimonially and primogeniturally, through the male line. The attack on these beliefs took many forms. It was even argued that honor of birth has nothing to do with internal virtue and competence—hence the depravity, corruption, and incompetence of male aristocrats. By this way of thinking, the aristocratic family subjugates its members to the unjust tyranny of patriarchal power and the rule of primogeniture.[10]

Restoration and early eighteenth-century innovations in marriage law have an evident relevance to this widespread outcry against the monolithic injustice of the aristocratic family. The device of the "strict settlement" effectively discriminated the several family interests. It reinforced the patrimonial rights of the eldest son but strictly limited his powers of alienation; it attended to the bride's jointure should she be widowed; and it guaranteed provisions for daughters and younger sons. Thus the strict settlement separated out elements "which, by the less scrupulous and self-conscious consensus of aristocratic ideology, were less problematically comprehended within the general category of 'family.'"[11] In a similar fashion, Restoration innovations in marriage settlements and separate maintenance contracts brought to fruition a long-term development of doctrines permitting married women to possess separate property. We have seen that the contractual assumptions of liberal political theory had no real application to the civil rights of eighteenth-century women. As Susan Staves has shown, however, contemporary legal thinking went some distance toward applying contractual logic to the status of married women. After flourishing for the better part of a century, these legal devices were countered through an effort to reassert the common law principle that husbands and wives are one person—that husbands absorb most of their wives' property on marriage and logically cannot contract with them thereafter. But although this effort to restrict married women's separate property was in many ways successful, over the longer term the separability of married women's property interests from those of their husbands became an article of English marriage law.[12]

II

Thus far my argument concerning the death of patriarchalism has pursued what might be called a double separation. The family is increasingly distinguished from the state, while the component members of the family are increasingly distinguished from each other. If we pursue this phenomenon beyond the evidence of political, social, and legal ideology we arrive at the testimony of socioeconomic change. What we have learned to call the separation of the public from the domestic sphere is materially grounded in the capitalist transformation of the English countryside. To put this another way, the emergence of modern patriarchy, and its system of gender difference, cannot be understood apart from the emergence of the modern division of labor and class formation. Although the complexity of the capitalist transformation of the countryside militates against precise chronology, it obviously both predates my period and continues thereafter. Nevertheless, some crucial features of the change may be associated with the years from 1660 to 1760.

In the last few years, the pioneering research of Alice Clark and Ivy Pinchbeck has been both corrected and confirmed by feminist historians interested in the nature of women's work in early modern England.[13] At the beginning of the sixteenth century, economic production was dominated by what historians have variously called the domestic system, the domestic economy, and the family economy—a system in which the household was the major unit of production. Attempts to generalize about how this domestic economy was undermined in early modern England are frustrated by crucial variations in households based on differences in region and social status. Still, it can be said that in 1500, all women were also housewives, involved in production both for the subsistence of the household and, often, for market.[14] The domestic economy operated according to a schematic sexual division of labor—between female "inside" work and male "outside" work—that was in practice rather flexible and scarcely operative on smaller holdings. In such an economy, husbands exercised the authority of the head of a household that was organized as an integrated working partnership.[15]

The breakdown of the domestic economy, and the concomitant withdrawal of women from work deemed economically productive, was most immediately the result of capitalist innovation. The flexibility of traditional work relations depended on customary arrangements that capitalist improvement rendered unprofitable. Enclosure and the consolidation of large estates increasingly denied to lesser farmers the subsistence conditions on which their households had depended. The loss of commons rights—not only grazing, but gathering fuel and gleaning harvest leavings—deprived women in particular of customary labor. When farmers lost access to land, their wives lost the means to keep a cow and practice dairying, a common form of women's work. As a result, outside work traditionally available to women simply disappeared at the lower social strata. At the higher social strata, increased sensitivity to price levels and market demand marginalized dairying in favor of more profitable production, or transformed it into a commercial activity under the control of hired managers.[16]

What happened to that portion of the agrarian economy not organized through the household? Over the course of the eighteenth century, there was a general decrease in the agricultural employment of women, and work patterns for men and women outside the household diverged in a number of ways. Increasingly, female employment was concentrated in spring activities like dairying and calving, while male labor was specialized in the fall harvesting of cereal crops, which required heavier technology. Especially in the latter half of the century, moreover, male real wages rose as female real wages declined. By limiting quasi-independent domestic production, capitalist improvement exerted pressure on what was increasingly understood as "the labor market," so as to throw women into competition with men. This was especially true in the fall, when the vulnerability of laborers in cereal production to structural unemployment put a premium on the availability of non-harvesting jobs. That men tended to prevail in this competition was both a cause and a consequence of developing conceptions of familial income as primarily male income.[17]

At the higher social levels, the differential process of class formation led women (and men) who aspired to a proto-"bourgeois" gentility to value idleness in women. In such households, women's work was increasingly oriented toward female accomplishments, while cheap wage labor did what was once the inside work of wives. In more modest households, husbands and wives turned increasingly to wage labor, seeking work outside the home. Both lost thereby the traditional liberty to define the tasks entailed in their work. But laboring women, as we have seen, were also losing the opportunity for this kind of employment as well. The decrease of female employment in the latter half of the eighteenth century is closely correlated with a rise in fertility, whose principal causes are a fall in the age of women at first marriage and a rise in the number of women who married. It seems plausible to connect these developments: "as female employment became more precarious and lowly paid, there were obvious motives to marry younger as defense against the unemployment which was increasingly the lot of women." Even as the incidence of marriage increased, however, wives were losing the flexibility once enjoyed in household labor, which was in the process of becoming "housework," the exclusive domain of women and increasingly denigrated as unproductive.[18] The process is reflected in contemporary religious teaching. Seventeenth-century Puritan divines relegated housework to the category of "private callings," and some argued that what one did as a housewife had no bearing on salvation.[19]

So, by the middle of the eighteenth century, the distinction between "inside" and "outside" work, based upon a flexible sexual division of labor, had gone a long way—at least in the higher social orders—toward ossifying into the familiar, culturally ramified opposition between the domestic and the public realms.[20] The completion of this ideological process in the following century would entail not only a further rigidification and universalization of the division across class lines, but also a revaluation of domestic work as not so much lesser as different: economically unproductive, but charged with the office of spiritual cultivation and maternal nurture. This must be supplemented, however, by two caveats. First, it should be clear that male domination and the subordination of women are constants in this long-term process. What changes is the form patriarchy takes under different historical circumstances. Second, the modern ideology of separate spheres has a cultural authority whose force doesn't require demonstration. Nonetheless, it is important to recognize that the ideology systematizes and superintends a social practice whose complex variability belies the stark simplicity of the model.

My argument has been that the long-term and uneven shift from patriarchalism to modern patriarchy entailed a separation out of elements which had formerly been tacitly understood and experienced as parts of an integral whole—the cosmos, the social order, the family, economic production. This schematic distinction between "traditional" and "modern" ways of organizing experience may also be expressed as the difference between a "vertical" hierarchy of interlocking rungs and a "horizontal" differentiation of discrete interests. In the seventeenth century, the language of "interest" began to discriminate not only among private family members but also among private political, social, and economic agents over against the public interest of the sovereign power.[21] In the eighteenth century, the leveling of status hierarchy took shape in the emergence of the language and assumptions of "class," which is sanctioned not by vertical bonds of affiliation and interdependence but by shared interests and by horizontal solidarity over against other classes.[22] I want to suggest in what follows that the process of differentiation entailed in the rise of modern patriarchy can be illuminated by juxtaposing it with these contemporaneous developments—that the early modern emergence of class is one crucial element in the historicization of patriarchy.

III

The foregoing evidence suggests that the form of modern patriarchy depends upon the structural separation of the genders: that the emergence of modern patriarchy is coextensive with the emergence of gender difference, which is therefore historically specific to the modern era. I will pursue this thesis by drawing on a related body of research. It is now commonly understood that the discourse of sexuality coalesced during the eighteenth century, when the relatively unitary focus on sex in matrimonial relations subdivided into a multiple focus on different kinds of sexuality.[23] With the aid of Thomas Laqueur, we may gain access to this same territory by recognizing that it was also only in the eighteenth century that female bodies ceased to be seen as aberrant versions of a unitary male body, and were viewed instead as physically and naturally different.[24] Like the other, contemporaneous, transformations I've already discussed, this one was neither sudden nor comprehensive.[25] Even within the medical profession, class difference ensured that the alteration in attitudes and practices was gradual, uneven, and in a real sense incomplete.[26]

Nevertheless, the change was real and deeply consequential. And although biological research that substantiated the modern view was a decisive factor, the change depended first of all on a shift in scientific ideology. As in the patriarchalist analogy between the family and the state, traditional science was predicated on a hierarchical view of kinds of bodies as interlocking, analogical microcosms of a greater macrocosm.[27] In this view, there is only one sex, and sex is a sociological rather than an ontological category. Men and women exist on a continuum whose basic discriminants are social rank, cultural role, and legal entitlements, not organic identity. Embodied sexuality was relatively elastic and fluid. "Nature" was not conceived as a physiological bedrock stabilizing sexual personality; and the distinction between the biologically grounded category "sex" and the socially constructed category "gender" was therefore largely unintelligible.[28]

In the later seventeenth and eighteenth centuries, England acquired the modern wisdom that there are not one but two sexes; that they are biologically distinct and therefore incommensurable; and that they are defined not by behavior, which is variable, but by nature, which is not.[29] The evidence reinforces the schematic pattern already observed in other areas: from a totality differentiated by matters of degree there emerges, toward the end of the seventeenth century, the imperative to distinguish and divide differences of kind. It is a change from a system in which the tacitly acknowledged difference between men and women is experienced as inseparably interwoven with sociocultural factors, to one in which the difference between men and women, although complex and problematic, is nonetheless understood as what renders the system systematic. To be sure, the assertion of sexual difference remains constant despite this crucial transformation.[30] The transformation is nonetheless crucial. For it is "in the nature of" the modern, materialist criterion of the "natural" to distinguish between autonomous phenomena with a definitive empiricism that is absent in pre-modern thought, where the hierarchical differentiation between macrocosm and microcosm posits, by definition, an essential thread of metaphysical continuity.

In one sense, of course, it would be absurd to claim that it is only now that gender difference is established in English culture. Many would say, for example, that the biological assymetry of childbirth has always ensured gendered differences in behavior.[31] I want to suggest, however, that only with the modern system of sexuality—of sex and gender difference—is "gender" sufficiently separated out as a category from "sex" (from that which it defines itself against) to take on the familiar, differential function it performs in modern culture. This is a double function. In the modern system of sexuality, the category "gender" works to discriminate not only socialized behavior from natural fact, but also masculinity from femininity. Now, there is an evident tension between these two functions. On the one hand, the discrimination of gender from sex opens up a broad if indeterminate range within which "sexual" behavior resists an absolute and dichotomizing categorization because it is socially relative and variable, undetermined by the laws of natural difference. It is as though the traditional, sociocultural embeddedness of the difference between men and women were now separated out and concentrated as an explicit and inescapable principle of social construction. On the other hand, this movement inevitably entails the corollary concentration and empowerment of the natural. In fact, the determinant authority of the natural in modern culture derives precisely from its unprecedented separability from the sociocultural, which henceforth always stands at risk of a naturalizing takeover. This sort of takeover can be seen in the paradoxical way modern usage tends to discriminate between masculine and feminine "gender" so as to bracket the radical effect of its implicit distinction between culture and nature, treating gender difference as a strictly dyadic, experientially articulated and socially mediated expression of sexual difference rather than as ontologically distinct from it. I think this tension is inherent in the modern system of sexuality, which promotes a rigid, "naturalistic" differentiation of "genders" even as it expressly promulgates "gender" as a category whose social character precludes such differentiation.

Of course, the slippage from the counternatural to the naturalized conception of gender can be avoided. Yet because the modern conceptualization and analysis of gender difference is authorized by the discovery of a fundamental sexual difference—because the early modern "emergence of gender difference" is therefore also the emergence of sexual difference—gender is inseparable from and coextensive with sex. When we make the gender argument, we tend to presume a sexual dispensation that will, by the very demands of the argument, evade meticulous examination. This can be seen with unusual clarity in the way Bernard Mandeville, in 1723, unmasks as an acculturation the apparent naturalness of female modesty:

> The Lessons of [modesty], like those of *Grammar*, are taught us long before we have occasion for, or understand the Usefulness of them . . . A Girl who is modestly educated, may, before she is two Years old, begin to observe how careful the Women, she converses with, are of covering themselves before Men; and the same caution being inculcated to her by Precept, as well as Example, it is very probable that at Six she'll be ashamed of shewing her Leg, without knowing any Reason why such an Act is blameable, or what the Tendency of it is. . . .
>
> This strict Reservedness is to be comply'd with by all young Women, especially Virgins, if they value the Esteem of the polite and knowing World; Men may take greater Liberty, because in them the Appetite is more violent and ungovernable. Had equal Harshness of Discipline been imposed upon both, neither of them could have made the first Advances, and Propagation must have stood still among all the Fashionable People: which being far from the Politician's Aim, it was advisable to ease and indulge the Sex that suffer'd most by the Severity, and make the Rules abate of their Rigour, where the Passion was the strongest, and the Burthen of a strict Restraint would have been the most intolerable. . . .
>
> The Multitude will hardly believe the excessive Force of Education, and in the difference of Modesty between Men and Women ascribe that to Nature, which is altogether owing to early Instruction . . . It is Shame and Education that contains [sic] the Seeds of all Politeness . . .[32]

In Mandeville's argument, the developing notion of a naturally based difference between male and female sexual appetites provides the necessary foundation for the brilliant analysis of the gendered—that is, the acculturated—quality of behavior and of the virtues with which it's associated. The brilliance of the analysis is characteristic of an age that may justly be seen as witnessing the birth of the sociological imagination, which demystifies what appears given by recognizing it as, not natural, but social or cultural. What must be recognized as well, however, is the flip side of this insight: its dependence on a knowledge of what is *truly* given, without which the demystification loses all coherence. At the most abstract level, the Enlightenment defamiliarization of the natural depends on the fundamental principle of empirical epistemology, the insistence that knowledge requires the self-conscious detachment of the subject from its object of knowledge. In this way, the empiricist insistence on a radical separation of subject from object enacts its wholesale repudiation of tacit knowledge. The separation isolates what is known from the familiar and customary matrix of its intelligibility. Yet in the same gesture, it also preserves that matrix itself—the province of the knowing subject—as immune to such skeptical analysis.[33]. . . .

Notes

MICHAEL MCKEON teaches English literature at Rutgers University. He is the author of *Politics and Poetry in Restoration England* (1975) and *Origins of the English Novel* (1987). He is currently working on a study of eighteenth-century British pastoralism. This essay will be part of a collection of studies in the early modern division of knowledge in England.

1   I am grateful to my colleagues Elin Diamond, Annie Janowitz, Cora Kaplan, and Carolyn Williams for helping me think about aspects of this argument.

2   On the currency of the analogy in early modern English thought, see Gordon J. Schochet, *Patriarchalism in Political Thought: The Authoritarian Family and Political Speculation and Attitudes Especially in Seventeenth-Century England* (New York: Basic Books, 1975); Susan D. Amussen, *An Ordered Society: Gender and Class in Early Modern England* (Oxford: Blackwell, 1988), chapter 2.

3   See Amussen, *Ordered Society*, 38–39, 57.

4   See Schochet, *Patriarchalism*, 116.

5   Henry Parker, *Jus Populi . . .* (London, 1644), 42, quoted in Amussen, *Ordered Society*, 58.

6   *Some Reflections Upon Marriage* (London, 1700), 28–29.

7   *Two Treatises of Government*, ed. Peter Laslett, 2nd ed. (Cambridge: Cambridge Univ. Press, 1967), 286.

8   For a lucid discussion of these matters see Ruth Perry, "Mary Astell and the Feminist Critique of Possessive Individualism," *Eighteenth–Century Studies*, 23, (1990): 444–57.

9   See Michael McKeon, *The Origins of the English Novel, 1600–1740* (Baltimore: Johns Hopkins Univ. Press, 1987), 181–82.

10 See generally McKeon, *Origins*, chapter 4.

11 McKeon, *Origins*, p. 154.

12 See Susan Staves, *Married Women's Separate Property in England, 1660–1833* (Cambridge: Harvard Univ. Press, 1990), 1–5, 178–95.

13 Alice Clark, *Working Life of Women in the Seventeenth Century* (London: Routledge, 1919); Ivy Pinchbeck, *Women Workers and the Industrial Revolution, 1750–1850* (1930: London: Virago, 1981).

14 See Susan Cahn, *Industry of Devotion: The Transformation of Women's Work in England, 1500–1660* (New York: Columbia Univ. Press, 1987), 33.

15 See Cahn, *Industry*, 46, 80–81, 89–90; Amussen, *Ordered Society*, 43, 68–69; Bridget Hill, *Women, Work, and Sexual Politics in Eighteenth–Century England* (Oxford: Blackwell, 1989), 35.

16 Hill, *Women*, 36–37, 50–51; Cahn, *Industry*, 38–39; K.D.M. Snell, *Annals of the Laboring Poor: Social Change and Agrarian England, 1660–1900* (Cambridge: Cambridge Univ. Press, 1985), 22, 62. See Deborah Valenze, "The Art of Women and the Business of Men: Women's Work and the Dairy Industry c. 1740–1840," *Past & Present*, no. 130 (1991): 142–69.

17 See Snell, *Annals*, 21–22, 37, 45, 51, 58–62, 157–58. Snell's data come entirely from the south of England.

18 See Hill, *Women*, 47–48, 49–50; Cahn, *Industry*, 43–44, 47, 99, 120, 158; Snell, *Annals*, 53, n. 36, 215–18, 311–12, 348–49 (quotation, 348). On the rise in fertility see generally E.A. Wrigley, "The Growth of Population in Eighteenth-Century England: a Conundrum Resolved," in *People, Cities, and Wealth: The Transformation of Traditional Society* (Oxford: Blackwell, 1987), 215–41.

19 See Cahn, *Industry*, 71.

20 Ibid., 22, 157–58.

21 See J.A.W. Gunn, *Politics and the Public Interest in the Seventeenth Century* (London: Routledge, 1969).

22 See Harold Perkin, *Origins of Modern English Society* (London: Routledge, 1969), 176–77.

23 See Michel Foucault, *The History of Sexuality*, vol. I, trans. Robert Hurley (New York: Vintage, 1990), 33, 37–39.

24 See Thomas Laqueur, *Making Sex: Body and Gender from the Greeks to Freud* (Cambridge: Harvard Univ. Press, 1990), 5–6.

25   See Ivan Illich, *Gender* (New York: Pantheon, 1982), chapters I and VI; Sander Gilman, *Sexuality: An Illustrated History* (New York: John Wiley, 1989), 4, 8, 168, 173, 174. Both these formulations of the nature of the change in how gender was conceived also differ substantially from that of Laqueur.

26   See review of Laqueur by Michael Mason in *London Review of Books*, 12, no. 21 (November 8, 1990), 16–17.

27   See Laqueur; *Making Sex*, 10–11, 148, 153.

28   Ibid., 124–25, 128, 135, 142.

29   Ibid., 136, 148, 154. Stephen Jay Gould has confirmed Laqueur's thesis as consonant with a more general early modern alteration in attitudes toward causality and meaning: see *New York Review of Books*, 38, no. 11 (June 13, 1991), 11–13.

30   See Katharine Park and Robert A. Nye's instructively critical review of Laqueur's book in *The New Republic*, 204, no. 7 (February 18, 1991), 53–57.

31   But see Salvatore Cucchiari, who posits a bisexual "pregender" society in which there is no basic correlation between childbearing in the sense of childbirth and in the sense of childcare: "The Gender Revolution and the Transition from Bisexual Horde to Patrilocal Band: the Origins of Gender Hierarchy," in Sherry B. Ortner and Harriet Whitehead, eds., *Sexual Meanings: The Cultural Construction of Gender and Sexuality* (Cambridge: Cambridge Univ. Press, 1981), 31–79.

32   *The Fable of the Bees*, ed. F.B. Kaye (Oxford: Clarendon Press, 1924), Remark (C.), I, 69–72.

33   For a highly suggestive discussion, within the twentieth-century context, of these and other issues with which I am concerned, see Eve Kosofsky Sedgwick, *Epistemology of the Closet* (Berkeley: Univ. of California Press, 1990), Introduction (allowing for inevitable differences in the meanings attached to the crucial terms "gender," "sex," and "sexuality").

Chapter 2

Leonore Davidoff and Catherine Hall

INTRODUCTION TO THE SECOND EDITION OF *FAMILY FORTUNES*

'You cannot step twice into the same river;
for other waters are ever flowing on to you'

(Heraclitus)

GOING INTO A MAJOR LONDON book shop shortly after *Family Fortunes* was first published, we found the staff puzzled about where it should be displayed. It was not the usual economic and social history volume; and if it was shelved under women's history, what about the word 'men' in the title? This confusion underlines the difficulty of placing a study which has attempted to cross conceptual, as well as, disciplinary boundaries.

The book was conceived and written at a time when sweeping questions could still be posed and the results painted on a broad canvas. The decade and a half which has passed since its first publication has seen major changes. Rather than attempting to revise the original text, in this essay we have thought about the book's reception and its place in both scholarship and wider social events in the intervening years.

The initial uncertainty which greeted our analysis has continued. While the influence of *Family Fortunes* has been extensive, it remains controversial. We are seen as revisionists in relation to class analysis.[1] We become part of the orthodoxy in some versions of women's history.[2] And we are combined with the traditionalists in a reinterpretation of modern British historiography.[3]

These contradictory readings are not surprising. The practice of history is a complex and messy business; and whether or not we care to admit the fact, 'it is always informed by suppositions and judgements'.[4] When we began our study in the early 1980s, we were acutely aware of how social and cultural categories were constructed, particularly the categories of 'woman' and 'man', 'femininity' and 'masculinity'. We believed that the early nineteenth century in England was a time of heightened fear about both social and economic chaos and the perils of daily life. Partly as a reaction, among the middle strata at this period there was an especial fascination with carving up their world into discrete categories and classes. These preoccupations show in the forms of nascent science, the filters of evangelical religion, the intense grading of social and economic groups, particularly men and women.

We felt that the only way to trace the shifts in middle-class society and gender relations was to look in detail at local communities and particular individuals. At the time we began, the 'post modern' emphasis on close-grained analysis at the micro level was just beginning. While we do consider some texts in detail, our work also uses a wider and eclectic sweep of sources.[5] The evolution of many modern organisations and institutions – scientific, legal, economic, domestic, cultural, even the development of the physical landscape – are an integral part of our story.

The book

Based on a study of middle-class individuals, families and organisations in two localities – the rural counties of Suffolk and Essex and the industrial/commercial town of Birmingham – *Family Fortunes* is in three parts. The first is about the mental and spiritual worlds of provincial middle-class men and women, the second about the economic and material activities which provided their livelihoods, the third about their daily lives, family and kinship relationships, homes and gardens, and the public activities with which they engaged.

We felt that our subject demanded local and bounded studies, because, as David Sabean has argued, 'when interest is centred on how consciousness is formed in social intercourse . . . then "particular, concrete contexts" become the locus of serious work'. The focus of study then becomes 'activities, structures, processes and logics that simply are not visible outside the local context'.[6] This did not, however, mean giving up on 'the big picture' for we also aimed at saying something more general about the relationship of gender and class in this period. While *Family Fortunes* concentrated on selected localities, we used a comprehensive – although not definitive – range of sources aimed at painting our local areas from every aspect.

The first part of the book focuses on two major waves of domestic ideology: the first in the 1790s and 1800s, which was associated with evangelical religion; the second in the 1830s and 1840s, which was more secular in its emphasis. Women, we argue, were from the start central to the effort to imagine a particular – and for some a new – pattern of family life, whether it was Hannah More, after her evangelical conversion, instructing her readers about the proper spheres of men and women, or Mrs. Sarah Stickney Ellis in the 1840s arguing for female satisfaction through selflessness.

By the latter decade, the expectation was that middle-class women should not be gainfully employed and many were able to retreat to a domesticated life in their suburban villas and gardens. These homes were seen as providing a bedrock of morality in an unstable and dangerous world. For John Claudius Loudon, influential architect, designer and land-scape gardener, and one of the key arbiters of middle-class taste in mid-century, 'the body of the contained and domesticated woman', 'like the plant in the pot' was the guarantee of social virtue (pp. 191–2).

Part Two concerns the centrality of the family enterprise to all economic activity in this period and the extent to which commercial and professional practises were built on familial lines. The aim of *the establishment*, a critical concept for these men and women was, above all, to maintain the family, educate children, provide for dependants and live a religious life. The establishment included both production and consumption in its daily activities. It might be an iron foundry or a farm, a medical practice or a clerical household; it was possible to have an establishment without an enterprise.

Rich new opportunities were opening up for men in the world of commerce, manufac-turing and the professions. Manliness and occupational position came to be more intimately linked, particularly occupations which gave independence from immediate patronage.

The increasingly elaborated world of the market had few spaces for women of the middling ranks. Provincial Corn Exchanges, banking houses and attorneys' offices were not sites for 'ladies' and their marginalisation from gainful employment in public places meant that 'private' activities such as writing, having lodgers or taking in pupils were crucial to their survival. By the mid-nineteenth century, *work*, when it meant gainful employment, was becoming a problematic activity for a particular group of middle-class women; significantly 'work' in their vocabulary usually meant sewing for the family, preferably embroidery. The work of reproduction, however, as the particular responsibility of women, continued to be critical to the establishment: women produced and serviced people. There were myriad ways in which men depended on the capital, labour and contacts of their wives and other female relatives to support and maintain both family businesses and establishments.

Part Three deals with the making of the family, the home and garden, and the public world dominated by middle-class men. By the second quarter of the nineteenth century, 'family' was coming to be understood in a more circumscribed way, while childhood came to be more demarcated from other stages of life. The separation of home from work was a long and never completed process, yet the development of the villa and the suburb in the 1830s marked the translation of particular ideas about family life into concrete form, as in the bricks and mortar of Birmingham's new suburb of Edgbaston. In the innumerable societies and organisations established in this period, the Botanical Societies with their gardens, the philanthropic ventures, the more directly commercial and political endeavours, and the assumption that men would occupy the positions of power and leadership within them was rarely challenged.

Yet, as we conclude, contradictions flowed from this for both men and women. From the outset, some women had contested these restrictions. Ann Taylor may have defended the 'smaller but more perfect circle' of the private in the early nineteenth century but this was increasingly challenged by her daughters' and granddaughters' generations as they encountered the constraint of 'a world more rigidly divided into separate spheres' (p. 453). 'The mid century common-sense division into a public world of politics and market activity and the private sphere now contained in the suburban villa set the framework for the feminism of John Stuart Mill' (p. 454).

Family Fortunes is a story of exclusion and contestation, of boundaries which could never fully be fixed, yet had to be dismantled. Central to our argument is the language of public and private spheres, a language which comes from the tracts, poems, letters and diaries of the men and women whose stories we were telling. But that language was already carrying a heavy conceptual baggage, one which we perhaps did not fully recognise at the time of writing. We attempted 'to reconstitute the world as middle-class people saw it' (p. 28), a claim which it was possible to make with a degree of confidence in the 1980s, before post-structuralist understanding of language had made this more problematic.

Even then, however, our intention was always to move beyond the public/private divide and show how 'autonomous' male actors were embedded in families, how 'dependent' women provided the contacts and capital, not to speak of the hidden labour and personnel, which made countless enterprises possible: 'Public was not really public and private not really private despite the potent imagery of "separate spheres"' (p. 33). Both were constructions with specific meanings which had to be understood as products of a particular historical time.

We fleshed out these arguments, demonstrating in numerous instances the crossings of the boundaries, both in their imagined and material forms: the energetic women who claimed the right to vote in church meetings or speak in public; the armies of women who as domestic servants were employed in the so-called private sphere of the home; the independent women who utilised the language of their distinctive sphere to make claims for themselves. All provide examples of the possibilities of transgression. Similarly the men who failed to provide for their wives and children, who were in danger of being defined both by themselves and others as 'mice rather than men' (p. 229), underlined the fragility of both the particular construction of manliness which was so precious to serious Christians of this period, and the inefficacy of 'separate spheres' when questions of familial survival became pressing. Harriet Martineau, for example, could never have engaged in a writing life if the family business had not collapsed.

'Separate spheres', we argued, became the common-sense of the middle class, albeit a common-sense that was always fractured. Something significant changed at the end of the eighteenth century; there was a historic break and a realigned gender order emerged, more characteristic of modern times, associated with the development of modern capitalism and urbanisation. This is not to suggest that there were no continuities. Nor that ideas of 'separate spheres' were invented in the 1780s. Rather, existing expectations about the proper roles of men and women were re-worked with a significantly different emphasis.[7] Between 1780–1850 enterprise, family, home, masculinity and femininity were re-drawn, negotiated, reformed and reinstalled. *Family Fortunes* is, in other words, a book about the making of selves: in that sense it prefigured attention to issues around identity.

Family Fortunes has been read by some as the narrative of the triumph of 'separate spheres', the confinement of women to the domestic sphere and their exclusion from the public world.[8] Undoubtedly there are elements of that story present; the structure of the book may contribute to this reading. However, the intention behind the three-part division was that each part should be conceptualised as carrying equal weight: here was no simple story of the ideological as an effect of the material or vice versa. Rather, we were arguing for a multifaceted notion of causation and change.

The narrative begins with the evangelical revival and the articulation of topical ideologies of manliness and femininity, shifting conceptions of the family and its relation to 'the world' in the heady decades of the French Revolution: these ideologies are given a dynamic power in transforming patterns of life in families and households amongst the 'middling sorts'. The book ends with the beginnings of the deconstruction of 'separate spheres' partially, at least, through nascent feminism. The feminism of the mid to late nineteenth century was built on a sense of grievance and it was women's sense of their exclusion from the public sphere and its consequences which led to their demand for entry to education, the professions and citizenship rights.

In a review essay published just after *Family Fortunes* came out, Linda Kerber reflected on the use of 'separate spheres' as a trope by U.S. feminist historians. She treats 'separate spheres' as a metaphor, one which permeated contemporary language and enabled historians to select what to study and how to think about it. The origins, she argues, lie in the 1960s with Betty Friedan's classic text, *The Feminine Mystique*, reflecting middle-class women's angst about their relation to home and work. At a more theoretical level there was the influence of Marxism on feminism, particularly Engels on the privatisation of the household. The great power of the Marxist interpretation was that it both described the separation and offered an explanation of the way in which this served the interests of the dominant classes. Separate spheres were seen as due neither to cultural accident nor to biological determinism, but as 'social constructions camouflaging social and economic service, a service whose benefits were unequally shared'. This form of analysis provided a route out of the Whiggish account of inexorable progress culminating in the granting of female suffrage.

In Kerber's depiction the first phase of the usage of 'separate spheres' in the 1960s and early 1970s was associated with ideas of subordination, victimisation and the deteriorating status of women, a phase also associated with use of prescriptive sources detailing the way women *should* live. The second phase (post 1975) is associated with the idea of a rich women's culture, built on their separate world. This was then used to analyse the ways in which the language of 'separate spheres' was utilised to develop feminist claims. In a third phase, in the 1980s, feminist historians were determined to embed women's experience in the larger course of human history, to attend to relations between the sexes, to look at and consciously criticise these paradoxical, rhetorical constructions. *Family Fortunes* was an English version of this moment.[9]

Kerber concludes that 'from the historiographer's perspective "separate spheres" was at least in part a strategy that enabled historians to move the history of women out of the realm of the trivial and anecdotal and into the realm of analytic social history'.[10] This was critical to our strategy, for we were arguing that the ideas and practices associated with 'separate spheres' played a significant part in defining a distinctive middle-class culture. The book was to be an intervention not in *women's* history alone but in history *per se*.

In *Family Fortunes*, the concept of class was a critical element in the process of historical change. This drew on the twin legacies of Marx and Weber alongside the British historiography of the nineteenth century. In linking questions of gender formation to questions of capitalism and class we were also firmly in the tradition of British feminist historiography. Alice Clark had provided a classic account of the transformation which the development of modern forms of capitalism brought to women's lives from the seventeenth century.[11] Ivy Pinchbeck's *Women Workers in the Industrial Revolution* took issue with Clark's argument and provided a more optimistic reading, but never doubted some articulation between new economic forms and changing patterns of family life and women's work.[12]

In focusing on questions of class and culture we were exploring the ways in which classes defined themselves in antagonism to other classes, as E.P. Thompson argued in *The Making of the English Working Class*.[13] In our case, the intensely religious provincial middle-class men and women of Birmingham and East Anglia whose lives we attempted to map out, placed themselves in opposition to an indolent and dissolute aristocracy, and a potentially subversive working class. One of the most compelling strands binding the disparate elements of this middle class was the commitment to an imperative moral code within a revised domestic world, a precursor to the Heavenly Home. The evangelical revival, in which the home was central, made 'the religious idiom the cultural norm for the middle class' (p. 25).

Definitions of manliness and femininity were key categories to the construction of this moral order. What emerged, therefore, was 'a gendered concept of class' (p. 30). In linking the story of class to the story of gender we were insisting on the centrality of forms of masculinity and femininity, home and family, to the main stream narratives of national history.[14] Such claims were inevitably markers of a particular historiographical moment.

How does *Family Fortunes* look a decade and a half after it appeared? Where does the original argument take us now? In this essay we are not attempting to review all the new relevant literature. Rather, we examine a number of areas which have a bearing on issues with which the book was engaged.

Disciplines, divisions and the questions historians ask

Family Fortunes was always understood to take an interdisciplinary approach. The resulting protean nature of the book was both enriching and limiting. With such an all-embracing method, claims could be made which are no longer in keeping with much of the current historical focus on variation, even down to differences within local areas. While giving full recognition to that heterogeneity, we would still argue, as Pamela Sharpe has for women's history, that 'the appreciation that women's experiences were diverse does not render all explanatory frameworks barren'.[15]

Even at the time, we faced an academic scene carved into divisions which, if anything has grown more rigid. Certain questions are assigned to one subject and can thus legitimately be ignored by another.[16] Subjects are also given a hierarchical weighting in terms of their 'hardness' and 'softness'. This binary is reinforced by the feeling that the higher the level of abstraction, the more significant. It is the topics 'that are most divorced from blood, sweat and tears that have the highest prestige'.[17] More than this, the arguably gendered nature of these hierarchies rumbles below the surface. The more abstract and the more scientific the vocabulary, the more masculine – and important – it seems.

Within the discipline of history, similar divisions occur, each field having its smaller circles, its own specialised journals and conferences. Quantitative method (cliometrics) and historical demography which can deliver 'hard facts' held a privileged position in the 1960s and 1970s. In the 1970s and 1980s it was social history and the influence of Marxism which dominated much that was innovative in British history. In the 1990s the critique of grand narratives and the emphasis on language and post structural forms of analysis has brought cultural history to the forefront.

Women's history has made some impact on these divisions; for example, studies of women's work now have a firm place within economic history. Historical demographers have become aware of more sophisticated understandings of motivation and agency rather than just concentrating on structures and rates expressed statistically. The field of family history is now quite fragmented as attention has turned towards meaning and language relevant to individual actors, not least because of the attention to gender issues. But there has been a price to pay for the continued barriers between these sub-fields.

Women's history often remains distinct from family history and both are separate from demographic history. Later development of the history of sexuality, followed by lesbian and gay history, while exciting, necessary contributions have increased fragmentation and a narrowing of disciplinary practice.[18] Sealing off each new area has increased the battle for legitimacy with more traditional historians. And we should not take for granted that the sentiments of the late Regius Professor of History from Cambridge have completely disappeared. He expressed 'doubts about much of [the] work on children, women and marriage; sometimes it does not seem overwhelmingly central to one's concerns. Much social history has a charming quality of timelessness. The facts of birth, copulation and death do not alter much through the ages'.[19]

Not only is the focus of research chosen, but the way questions are ultimately framed is often a product of present day concerns. Texts and their reception are located in political arguments and claims to power, although this may be unrecognised. As Jane Flax has put it, 'like all writing, my own must have political and unconscious motives and meanings exceeding my intent. So do the various readings and appropriations of it.'[20]

Past historical studies are littered with controversies directly related to issues current at the time and experienced by many within their own lifetimes.[21] In the 1950s and 1960s it was the salience of the labour movement and working-class integration in British society which encouraged the standard of living debate and growth of labour history; in the 1970s and 1980s the burning question of why the British economy had 'failed' helped to promote the search for the elusive entrepreneurial ideal and its putative rejection by the taking on of aristocratic life styles.[22] It also contributed to the vigorously debated question of whether or not there had been an 'industrial revolution' and if so when. *Family Fortunes* had its own concerns prompted from within the women's movement. Was there such an entity as 'the family'? Historically what was the extent and nature of women's work? How was the gender order related to the distribution and control of income, property and other resources? Was domesticity a modern phenomenon?

Periodisation

Any of these themes invites the inevitable question of continuity or change. This perennial issue can be read as a more sophisticated version of the lay question, 'was it better or worse then'? But, baldly put, are we here asking productive questions?[23] The more we know of the lives of both men and women, the more we are aware of continuities across generations. Yet disjunctions and dislocations are also critical and allow us to mark significant change.[24] Historians need to divide up the past into discrete periods to make it manageable. We search for 'turning points' depending on the phenomena that engage us.[25] However, the objects of social and cultural history often do not have key events on which to hang our narrative.

Change is gradual and uneven. Above all, change permeates lives of uneven lengths which overlap each other in generations. In this book, at the beginning of our period the people active in the communities we study were born in the mid-eighteenth century while at the end they were products of the 1810s and 1820s. Bearing in mind that religious, cultural, social and political values are often formed during adolescence, a particularly influential cohort in our story came to adulthood during the radicalising period of the French Revolution. It was their generation which would play a leading role through the first half of the nineteenth century.

While the nineteenth century dominated the historiography of the 1960s and 1970s the growth of interest in the eighteenth century has meant that we now have a much better understanding of the social and cultural continuities of the 'long eighteenth century'.[26] Nevertheless, if attention is paid to generational change, rather than taking a decade by decade snapshot approach, it may be argued that both beliefs and practices, for example around domesticity, which have been found in earlier periods, had become more widespread by the early nineteenth century. By that time more people among the expanded middle classes had greater resources to practise the domestic ideal. This points to a danger with the cultural historian's use of a few selected texts. Finding some examples of domesticity in earlier periods is not enough to make general claims about change *or* continuity.[27]

It is now clear that various manifestations of 'separate spheres' and differentiated gender roles were part of early modern society. Thus Michael McKeon and Anthony Fletcher both argue that 'modern patriarchy' was in place by the mid to late eighteenth century.[28] And now we know much more of the eighteenth century 'middling sort'. New work on consumption has brought those middling people into a different perspective as we have grasped the diversity of their tastes, the elaboration of a consumer culture and the relation between that commercial world and urban politics.[29]

Both Margaret Hunt and John Smail emphasise the distinctive nature of this middling group, with their concentration on business and their ambivalence towards upper-class mores. Much of Hunt's story for this earlier period is remarkably similar to the one we tell. She found a central concern with the family, prudential morality and the dignity of work. The families she studied were concerned to make their boys into successful businessmen and to train girls along narrower paths. Here, too, the majority of trading women operated on a small scale. Her critique of the harmonious picture of family life which we presented underpins her own argument, that 'family conflict may be just as important as the inter-group conflicts (such as class conflict) have dominated the social history of the period'.[30] Certainly the absence of court records in *Family Fortunes* played a part in constructing a story which emphasised those families which stayed together and survived.[31] On the other hand, as Amy

Erickson has noted, the heavy emphasis on the use of court records by early modern historians may have given us too much focus on dysfunctional families.[32]

For Amanda Vickery, however, nothing significantly changed at the end of the eighteenth century. Women were able to go on making inroads into an expanded public culture and the recourse by moralists to prescriptive discussion of the proper roles of women was a reaction to those incursions.[33] Yet there is a paradox here. For she also argues that whenever resources permit, women will be removed from productive labour and confined to the home, a practice going back to the Romans, if not before.[34] Other eighteenth-century historians think that an important shift did occur around the end of their period, though opinions differ as to why: The French Revolution, republicanism and feminism often loom large, alongside the evangelical revival. Norma Clarke, for example, sees much richer possibilities open to women writers in the 1770s than in the decades which followed, when their independent intellectual life became increasingly problematic.[35]

Dror Wahrman's ambitious project on the making of the modern self gives sex and gender its own dynamic in the narrative, marking one of the important theoretical shifts of the 1990s. Understandings of gender, he argues, 'might well have a logic or dynamic of their own . . . not necessarily reducible to those of the unequal structures of power in which these categories are deployed'. He takes the position that sex was given, gender was a field of play and performance[36] (although, note, this distinction between sex and gender has recently been queried).[37] Even a woman such as Hannah More could triumph in transgressing the boundaries of masculinity and femininity in the 1770s.

By the 1790s, however, this had changed and gender categories were now widely expected to mirror the presumed rigidity and stability of sexual ones. Transgressing gender boundaries was no longer acceptable. The playful More of the 1770s became the prim architect of the 'separate spheres' of the 1790s. In this account the American war – that virtual civil war, when cousins fought cousins and Anglo-Saxon Protestants fought each other – is given a significance in disturbing the boundaries of identity, and producing a 'gender panic' which resulted in a narrowing of possibilities. Such an emphasis on the instability of identities and their unsettled and ambivalent character owes much to contemporary critical theory.[38]

Anna Clark agrees that by the 1790s, the gains which elite women had made in politics had been lost and their capacity to speak as public intellectuals diminished to defenders of feminine virtue. But in the 1820s and 1830s, she argues, middle-class women were able to make use of the elaborated domestic ideal to develop their associational life. It was not until the 1830s and 1840s, as *Family Fortunes* argues, that gainful employment for ladies was widely denounced. Meanwhile, as Clark has demonstrated, radicals in the 1830s adopted the notion of domesticity in a bid to secure the privileges of separate spheres for working-class women. At the same time the claims made by women radicals impelled middle-class moralists to assert domesticity more strenuously.[39]

This then is an uneven and fractured history which continues into succeeding decades. Our original supposition that the development of feminism in the mid-1850s marked a break with a particular mapping of public and private space seems to be borne out in recent work by cultural historians. Thus Judith Walkowitz and Lynda Nead have both emphasised the new visual pleasures which middle-class women were able to enjoy in the late nineteenth-century metropolis while Lynne Walker has laid out the ways in which London feminists in the second half of the nineteenth century changed the nature of domesticity to include their work and established women's clubs and housing.[40]

As Deborah Cherry comments: 'walking purposefully or wandering, trudging backwards and forwards, working and shopping: all these activities required a redefinition of the middle-class feminine body in a redefinition of city spaces'.[41] Yet Patricia Hollis' depiction of the ways in which women used their separate sphere as the basis for a claim to be in local government and Lisa Tickner's analysis of the ways in which even the fiercest of suffragettes used 'separate spheres' ideology to advance the movement suggests the continued utility of these constantly shifting categories through to the early twentieth century.[42]

Similarly, James Hammerton's study of conflict in nineteenth-century married life argues that it was in the second half of the nineteenth century, just as middle-class marriage became established as the bastion of privacy and domesticity, that it was increasingly subjected to public scrutiny and regulation. His study starts, he suggests, where *Family Fortunes* ended.[43] John Tosh's chronology is similar. In *A Man's Place*, the major study of middle-class masculinity in the nineteenth century, he sees domesticity as marking the predominant version of manliness between 1830–1870. This was a time when the early modern form of masculinity as reputation seems to have shifted via forces such as romanticism and the stress on the individual, to a more interiorised sense of personal identity.[44] From the 1860s, however, the undermining of orthodox religious belief and its associations with the unsettling of the domestic order opened the way for a flight from domesticity. A new taste for the single life and a reluctance to marry went alongside new forms of sexual antagonism and a celebration of homosocial activities.[45]

A recent discussion of the usefulness of the 'separate spheres' paradigm has argued that the significance of continuities can be overdone. There are important moments when breaks do occur. In the words of Anne Summers: 'A reinstatement of the concept of "separate spheres" is not a matter of scholastic disputation but part of the attempt to comprehend the history of modernity'. Late eighteenth-century Enlightenment liberal intellectualism, she suggests, did open doors for women, but those doors closed with the onset of new forms of professionalism and the growth of more bureaucratic institutions. Similarly, urbanisation and the increasing numbers of middle-class families who could afford for women not to work took place in the context of an ideal of 'women's mission' which empowered women to challenge the wider society from within their roles as daughters, sisters, wives and mothers.[46]

Women, politics and the public

A number of authors have clarified the ways in which elite women, in particular, were able to engage in aspects of political life and contest any simple definitions of men's and women's spheres. Much of this research has focused on the eighteenth century and on aristocratic and gentry women. The activities of Georgiana, Duchess of Devonshire, have been much cited in this context. In the celebrated Westminster election of 1784, she extended the forms of female participation, bringing much calumny upon her head in the process.[47] So sharp were the criticisms of the Duchess that she was never able to engage on the same scale with another contested election and her efforts were mercilessly pilloried in the press.

Somewhat less ambitious and high-profile women, however, continued to flaunt the colours of their political friends, organise dinners and private meetings, canvass on behalf of fathers, husbands and brothers. Elaine Chalus has shown how eighteenth-century politics was part of the world in which women lived. Balls, dinners and visits could always be occasions to discuss political as well as other matters.[48] As Kathryn Gleadle and Sarah Richardson suggest, the fears expressed across a wide variety of genres between the mid-eighteenth and the mid-nineteenth centuries, indicate that contemporaries were well aware of the potential which women had to express forms of authority. While women did not have the same opportunities as men, they conclude, 'we should also recognise that the barriers against their activities were not as inflexible as has been commonly assumed'.[49]

In the eighteenth century women could hold the vote in their own names in some burgage and freeholder boroughs, and their testimony was heard in disputed election cases which came under the scrutiny of the House of Commons. Their writing, publishing and exercise of patronage were all aspects of their widespread engagement with the world of politics.[50] The by now legendary activities of the Yorkshire Tory landowner and lesbian, Anne Laster, are instructive here. In the years immediately following the formal exclusion of women from the franchise in 1832, she was to be found canvassing with great energy, putting heavy pressure on her tenants to vote for her favoured Tory, contributing money to his election fund, wearing the colours, and identifying herself fully with the struggle to defeat the hated Whigs in Halifax. 'After the 1832 Reform Act', as Jill Liddington argues, 'the formal political rights enjoyed by some women may have declined relative to the rights of their enfranchised male tenants; but the power of property ensured they could now exercise very real political leverage over a larger proportion of these tenants'.[51]

Middle-class women's activities were also burgeoning, as many historians have noted. The concentration by cultural, social and economic historians of the eighteenth century on consumption has elaborated our picture of the build-up of material goods, the innovations in food, clothing, furniture and household decoration – much of it garnered from British excursions abroad. This allowed for more choice and more creative use of materials of all kinds – from cloth to garden plants.[52] Both the meanings of these forms of consumption and the motivation for such display has occasioned controversy, as has the question as to when, and among whom consumption began to oust production from living spaces. We now know, too, more about the extension of women's domestic activities through charity work and philanthropy, often within a religious framework. Visiting the poor and sick, teaching in Sunday schools and other venues, fund raising, making use of their position as consumers to exercise influence over tradesmen: all these were well established activities of eighteenth-century middling and lesser gentry women.[53]

Critical to this recent work is an expanded notion of *the political* which rightly takes attention away from high politics and insists on the significance of other levels of activity. Family, as Katherine Lynch notes, needs to be put back into politics and the public sphere. Civil society included the family as well as voluntary associations.[54] Some women could shine in salons, debating societies, book clubs and even female coffee houses, enjoying the conversation beloved by polite society.[55]

As Linda Colley suggests in *Britons*, women were also making a place for themselves as patriots, utilising the conditions of war to unsettle the boundaries between the masculine and the feminine. Whether organising collections of money and clothing, making flags and banners, or marching in celebration of peace 'these female patriots were staking out a civic role for themselves'.[56] Similarly, Kathleen Wilson argues that the American War gave women many opportunities to act as patriots, not only in England but as they travelled with the army in the Americas, enacting their imperial as well as their national roles.[57] These were significant expansions of the terrain of female action, offering women many opportunities to engage in the new public culture of eighteenth-century England.

Yet important questions remain about the relation between presence, influence and power. Anne Lister could not vote herself and her pressure on her tenants did not always have the desired effects.[58] Formal political and institutional power remained the preserve of a small group of men, and while women could cajole, persuade and negotiate, there were many spaces in which they had no place. These were the kind of exclusions which fuelled the feminism of the 1850s.

Thus we now have a diverse and contradictory story of women's more public life. Unfortunately the relationship of men and masculinity in moulding those realms beyond the domestic which we investigated in our final chapter, remains mainly unexamined.

Why should this be? To understand this it is necessary to turn to a more conceptual level.

Public and private: Conceptions and usage

The division of social life into public and private domains has recently caught the intellectual imagination and stimulated lively empirical as well as theoretical debate.[59] Yet these concepts remain in a tangle of various usage in part because of their 'metaphorical richness'.[60] Public and private, like so much of Western culture, are binary categories. Like all dualisms, one category necessitates the other.[61] In this sense they act as self fulfilling prophecies, disguising the hierarchical, power relationship between the two terms.[62] While there has been some disquiet with binary divisions on analytic as well as empirical grounds, the public and private division still forms a central locus for historians, particularly its sub-species, the 'separate spheres' paradigm which we have been discussing.[63]

It is useful to look at the derivation of these terms. Public has had a myriad of meanings over its long history.[64] The public includes the whole community, open to general observation and accessible to all. Note, however, this 'all' means those persons who are legally or properly qualified (OED). Here we already have a qualifier which excludes a variety of people who are not considered *persons*, a category which became the focus of contention in nineteenth-century discussions of slavery, race and the status of women.

Further, it is often unrecognised that all these categories carry implicit gender connotations. In general discussions of the public and civil society, a nod may be given to 'the bourgeois family' but it is then left unexplored.[65] Nor has there been much conceptual investigation of the links between the public and forms of masculinity. The key relationship of the male public actor to family and household remains muted. John Tosh, an exception to this neglect, notes that for men the relationship between domesticated masculinity and other forms of homosociality was inherently full of tension. He emphasises that it is a mis-reading of separate spheres to see such tensions as aberrant.[66]

The Latin roots of the word *private* go back to deprive, mutating into withdrawn or concealed. These meanings tally with modern usage of private as the personal or something of one's very own. The intimate and hidden aspect of private also shows up in our euphemism for genitalia as private parts or the enclosed place for getting rid of bodily wastes, previously known as a 'privy'.[67] These meanings coalesce around the early modern concept of private property. Where public connotes democratic access, private implies hierarchy where 'I can do what I like with my own'. That rhetoric of absolute private property rights has been extremely powerful but, in fact, absolute rights were never practicable and carried a moral element of restraint.[68] As we shall see, these rights and restraints were divided unequally between different individuals and groups, including men and women.

The division between public and private is closely related to the binaries of individual/society and civilised/natural.[69] The image of the individual shifted depending on time and place. Even for the eighteenth- and nineteenth-century middle classes there were variant individualities within Evangelicalism, romanticism and political economy. But at the core is a sense of a separate, solitary, autonomous human being – a being who is a free spirit, a detached single agent, 'as opposed to Society and Family' (OED).

Such images subliminally attached to the individual are, above all, masculine. The individual and the feminine sit uneasily together at best.[70] As the concept developed, to be an individual it was necessary to both command a unit of domestic economy (note, not necessarily a family in the modern sense) and at the same time 'command effective market capacity . . . even if the property concerned was only in one's own capacity to labour'.[71]

To effectively carry out these tasks, the masculine individual was placed in an abstract realm of pure reason, honouring mind over body – and even soul. Hegel long ago recognised the underlying effort involved in such a masculinity divorced from its own materiality and the role played by private property in balancing that tension: 'the body defines the self which requires personal property in order to objectify itself'.[72]

It can be argued that the essence of femininity in the nineteenth century was its location in the body – in Victorian language women were 'the Sex'. In the last analysis, then, bodies, their surroundings and their potentialities lay at the foundation of law, civil society and the state. Women, like children, were (and to an extent still are) defined by relationships to others. Throughout the modern period the angst and isolation of pure masculine individualism has been staunched by private relationships: the Mother, the Wife (the Mistress) who hovers in the background ready with warm milk, and a warm bed, if not a warm body.[73]

These categories also become part of what we call Nature and the way the natural is understood. Recent historical work on the sixteenth to eighteenth centuries in particular has charted the development of 'Nature', so often seen as feminine, which presupposes the 'man-made', or social. It easily follows that the family, as a natural unit, is then within the private. As Ludmilla Jordanova has written of this period, the family became the place where the individual and Nature met.[74] . . .

Notes

1   Richard Price, 'Historiography, Narrative and the Nineteenth Century', *Journal of British Studies*, Vol 35, 1996

2   Amanda Vickery, 'From Golden Age to Separate Spheres? A Review of the Categories and Chronology of English Women's History' *Historical Journal*, Vol 36, No 2, 1993; Penelope Lane, 'Women, Property and Inheritance: Wealth Creation and Income in Small English Towns, 1750–1835'; Jon Stobart and Alastair Owens, *Urban Fortunes: Property and Inheritance in the Town 1700–1900* (Ashgate, 2000)

3   Miles Taylor, 'The Beginnings of Modern British Social History', *History Workshop Journal*, No 43, 1997

4   Ludmilla Jordanova, *History in Practice*, Edward Arnold, London, 2000, p. 113

5   '. . . in history, despite trying to stay "within the text", social reality is always in play', Michele Barrett, 'Words and Things: Materialism and Method in Contemporary Feminist Analysis', Michele Barrett and Ann Phillips, eds, *Destabilising Theory: Contemporary Feminist Debates* (Polity Press, 1992) p. 210; Helen Longino, 'Feminist Standpoint Theory and the Problem of Knowledge', *Signs: Journal of Women in Culture and Society*, Vol 19, No 1, 1993; Kathleen Canning, 'Feminist History After the Linguistic Turn: Historicising Discourse and Experience', *Signs: Journal of Women in Culture and Society*, Vol 19, No 2, 1994

6   David Sabean, *Property, Production and Family in Neckerhausen 1700–1870* (Cambridge University Press, 1990) pp. 11 & 37

7   John Tosh warns against 'ambitious models of change' for the place of gender in history. 'The Old Adam and the new man: emerging themes in the history of English masculinities 1750–1850', in Tim Hitchcock and Michele Cohen, eds, *English Masculinities: 1660–1800* (Longman, 1999) p. 237

8   See particularly Amanda Vickery, 'From Golden Age to Separate Spheres?' and Linda Colley, *Britons: Forging the Nation 1707–1837* (Yale University Press, 1992)

9   For a detailed and perceptive placing of *Family Fortunes*, see Judith Newton, 'Family Fortunes: History and Literature in Materialist-Feminist Work', *Radical History Review*, No 43, 1989 reprinted in her *Starting Over: Feminism and the Politics of Cultural Critique* (University of Michigan Press, Ann Arbor, 1994)

10   Linda Kerber, 'Separate Spheres, Female World, Woman's Place: the rhetoric of women's history', *Journal of American History*, Vol 75, No 1, 1988

11   Alice Clark, *Working Life of Women in the Seventeenth Century* 1st pub. 1919, new edition with introduction by Amy Erickson (Routledge, 1992)

12   Ivy Pinchbeck, *Women Workers and the Industrial Revolution 1750–1850* (Frank Cass, 1969)

13   E.P. Thompson, *The Making of the English Working Class* (Gollancz, 1963)
14   At this time it was not considered problematic to conceptualise national history as outside the global, the continental or the colonial. It was the debates over nation and empire which surfaced in the 1980s which began to shift historiographical paradigms. See the introduction to Catherine Flail, Keith McClelland and Jane Rendall, *Defining the Victorian Nation, Class, Race, Gender and the Reform Act of 1867* (Cambridge University Press, 2000). Questions of gender and class in relation to race in this period, drawing on the discussion in *Family Fortunes*, have been taken up by, for example, Mrinalini Sinha, *Colonial Masculinities. The 'Manly' Englishman and the 'Effeminate' Bengali* (Manchester University Press, 1995); E.M. Collingham, *Imperial Bodies: The Physical Experience of the Raj, c.1800–1947* (Polity Press, 2001); and Catherine Hall, *Civilising Subjects. Metropole and Colony in the English Imagination 1830–1867* (Polity Press, 2002)
15   Pamela Sharpe, ed. *Women's Work: The English Experience 1650–1914* (Edward Arnold, 1998) p. 208
16   Michele Barrett, 'Words and Things', p. 212
17   Arthur Stinchcombe, 'The Origins of Sociology as a Discipline', *Acta Sociologica*, Vol 27, No. 1, 1984, p. 52
18   Jane Flax, *Disputed Subject: Essays on Psychoanalysis, Politics and Philosophy* (Routledge, 1993) p. 58
19   G.R. Elton, *Return to Essentials: Some Reflections on the Present State of Historical Study* (Cambridge University Press, 1991), pp. 117–118
20   Jane Flax, *Disputed Subjects*, p. 21
21   James Epstein, 'Victorian Subjects: Introduction', special issue, *Journal of British Studies*, Vol 34, No 3, 1995, p. 295
22   Martin Wiener, *English Culture and the Decline of the Industrial Spirit, 1880–1980* (Cambridge University Press, 1981); W.D. Rubinstein, *Capitalism, Culture and Decline in Britain 1750–1990* (Routledge, 1993), summary in F.M.L. Thompson, *Gentrification and the Enterprise Culture: Britain 1780–1980* (Oxford University Press, 2000)
23   In women's history, for example, as Pamela Sharpe points out, both tend to suggest women's impotency to deal with their situation, continuity implying forces of subordination too powerful to be overturned, whereas change is unilinear – the position of women is seen as worsening as a result of industrialisation. Pamela Sharpe, 'Continuity and Change: Women's History and Economic History in Britain', *Economic History Review*, Vol LVIII, No 2, 1995
24   See Judith Bennett 'Women's History: A Study in Change and Continuity', *Women's History Review*, 1993, Vol 2, No 2 and debate with Bridget Hill; Judith Bennett, 'Confronting Continuity', *Journal of Women's History*, Vol 9, No 3, 1997; John Tosh, 'The Old Adam and the New Man'
25   Ludmilla Jordanova, *History in Practice*, p. 116
26   Richard Price, 'Historiography, Narrative and the 19th Century'
27   For the expansion in numbers and proportion able to sustain a middle-class life style see John Rule, *Albion's People: English Society 1714–1815* (Longmans, 1992)
28   Michael McKeon, 'Historicizing Patriarchy: the Emergence of Gender Difference in England, 1660–1760', *Eighteenth-Century Studies* XXVIII 1995, p. 295; Anthony Fletcher, *Gender, Sex and Subordination in England, 1500–1800* (Yale University Press, 1995)
29   Peter Earle, *The Making of the English Middle Class: Business, Social and Family Life in London 1660–1730* (University of California Press, 1989); John Smail, *The Origins of Middle Class Culture: Halifax, Yorkshire, 1660–1780* (Cornell University Press, 1994); Margaret Hunt, *The Middling Sort: Commerce, Gender and the Family in England 1680–1780* (University of California Press, 1996); Kathleen Wilson, *The Sense of the People: Politics, Culture and Imperialism in England, 1715–1785* (Cambridge University Press, 1998)
30   Hunt, *The Middling Sort*, p. 8
31   James A. Hammerton's book does much to redress this harmonious picture: *Cruelty and Companionship: Conflict in Nineteenth-Century Married Life* (Routledge, 1992)
32   Personal communication, 15/12/01
33   Amanda Vickery, 'From Golden Age to Separate Spheres?'
34   Anna Clark, 'Review of Amanda Vickery's *Gentleman's Daughter: Women's Lives in Georgian England*', September 1998, 'Reviews in History' ed. David Cannadine, Institute of Historical Research, University of London, <http//:www.history.ac.uk/reviews/ihr/anna.html>
35   Norma Clarke, *Dr. Johnson's Women* (Hambledon, 2000) and personal communication, 15/12/01
36   Dror Wahrman, *'Percy's Prologue*: from Gender Play to Gender Panic in Eighteenth Century England', *Past and Present*, No 159, 1998; Dror Wahrman, 'Gender in Translation: How the English Wrote Their Juvenal 1644–1815', *Representations*, Vol 65, Winter, 1999

37   Miriam Fraser, 'What is the Matter of Feminist Criticism', *Economy and Society*, Vol 31, No 4, 2002 (seen in manuscript by kind permission of the author)

38   From a very extensive literature see Judith Butler, *Gender Trouble: Feminism and the Subversion of Identity* (Routledge, 1990); Judith Butler, *Bodies that Matter: On the Discursive Limits of Sex* (Routledge, 1993); Stuart Hall and Paul de Gay (eds) *Questions of Cultural Identity* (Sage, 1996)

39   Anna Clark, 'Separate Spheres Revisited: Aristocratic and Middle-Class Women in Politics, 1760–1840', unpublished ms. 1999. We are grateful to Anna Clark for allowing us to read this piece. Anna Clark, review essay, 'Gender and Politics in the Long Eighteenth Century, *History Workshop Journal* 48, Autumn 1999, pp. 252–7; Anna Clark, *The Struggle for the Breeches: Gender and the Making of the British Working Class* (Rivers Oram, 1995); K.D. Reynolds, *Aristocratic Women and Political Society in Victorian Britain* (Clarendon Press, 1998); Clare Midgley, *Women Against Slavery: The British Campaigns 1780–1870* (Routledge, 1992); Alex Tyrrell and Paul Pickering in *The People's Bread: A History of the Anti-Corn Law League* (Leicester University Press, 2000) argue that 'the ideology of separate spheres had a profound hold on the imagination of the Victorian bourgeoisie and negotiating this ideology was a central middle-class concern', p. 123

40   Judith R. Walkowitz, *City of Dreadful Delight: Narratives of Sexual Danger in Late Victorian London* (Virago, 1992); Lynda Nead, *Victorian Babylon: People, Streets and Images in Nineteenth-Century London* (Yale University Press, 2000); Lynne Walker, 'Home and Away: The Feminist Remapping of Public and Private Space in Victorian London' in (eds) I. Borden, J. Kerr and J. Rendall with A. Pivaro, *The Unknown City: Contesting Architecture and Social Space* (MIT Press, 2001); Erica Rappaport, *Shopping for Pleasure: Women in the Making of London's West End* (Princeton University Press, 2000)

41   Deborah Cherry, *Beyond the Frame: Feminism and Visual Culture, Britain 1850–1900* (Routledge, 2000), p. 31. Art historians have made much use of the new work on space and place being done by historical and cultural geographers, work in which *Family Fortunes* is frequently cited. For example, Alan Lester, *Imperial Networks in Nineteenth-century South Africa and Britain* (Routledge, 2001)

42   Patricia Hollis, *Ladies Elect: Women in English Local Government, 1865–1914* (Clarendon Press, 1987); Lisa Tickner, *The Spectacle of Women: Imagery of the Suffrage Campaign 1907–14* (Chatto and Windus, 1987)

43   James Hammerton, *Cruelty and Companionship*

44   John Tosh, *A Man's Place: Masculinity and the Middle Class Home in Victorian England* (Yale University Press, 1999); John Tosh, 'The old Adam and the new man'

45   John Tosh, *A Man's Place*; John Gillis, *A World of Their Own Making: Myth, Ritual and the Quest for Family Values* (Oxford University Press, 1997); M. Jeanne Peterson's *Family, Love and Work in the Lives of Victorian Gentlewomen* (Indiana University Press, 1989) is the most significant example of a study which argues that the nineteenth century saw *no* key changes in the patterns of gentlewomen's lives and that rank remained throughout this period a more important marker of inequality than gender. Gentlewomen had careers, she argues, as partners of their husbands, and most of them were entirely satisfied with this. For a review of some of the studies of Victorian women see Judith S. Lewis, 'Separate Spheres: Threat or Promise?' *Journal of British Studies*, Vol 30, 1991

46   Anne Summers, 'Common Sense About Separate Spheres', *Female Lives, Moral States: Women, Religion and Public Life in Britain 1800–1930* (Threshold Press, 2000) p. 5

47   Amanda Foreman, *Georgiana, Duchess of Devonshire* (HarperCollins, 1999)

48   Elaine Chalus, '"That Epidemical Madness": Women and Electoral Politics in the Late Eighteenth Century' in Hannah Barker and Elaine Chalus, eds, *Gender in Eighteenth Century England: Roles, Representations and Responsibilities* (Longman, 1977)

49   Kathryn Gleadle and Sarah Richardson, eds, 'Introduction', *Women in British Politics, 1760–1860: The Power of the Petticoat* (Macmillan, 2000) p. 8; a similar point has emerged in relation to religious practice. See Beverly M. Kienzle and Pamela Walker, *Women Preachers and Prophets Through Two Millennia of Christianity* (University of California Press, 1998)

50   Elaine Chalus, 'Women, Electoral Privilege and Practice in the Eighteenth Century', in Gleadle and Richardson eds, *Women in British Politics*

51   Jill Liddington ed., *Female Fortune, Land, Gender and Authority: The Anne Lister Diaries and Other Writings 1833–1836* (Rivers Oram, 1998) p. xvii

52   John Brewer and Roy Porter, eds, *Consumption and the World of Goods* (Routledge, 1993)

53   Margaret Hunt, *The Middling Sort*; Amanda Vickery, *The Gentleman's Daughter: Women's Lives in Georgian England* (Yale University Press, 1998)

54   Katherine A. Lynch, 'The Family and the History of Public Tale', *Journal of Interdisciplinary History* Vol. XXIV, No. 4, 1999; see also Jane Rendall, 'Women and the Public Sphere', *Gender and History*, Vol 11, No 3, 1999

55   Amanda Vickery, *The Gentleman's Daughter*
56   Linda Colley, *Britons*, p. 281
57   Kathleen Wilson, *The Island Race: Englishness, Empire and Gender in the Eighteenth Century* (Routledge, 2002)
58   Jill Liddington, *Female Fortune*
59   The discussion of 'the public' was stimulated by the introduction of Habermas's study of civil society to the English speaking world. For Habermas and his followers the public has often been confined to the political sphere, the relationship of civil society, formal polities and the state, thus neglecting the economy as a developing public arena. Jurgen Habermas, *The Structural Transformation of the Public Sphere: An Inquiry into a Category of Bourgeois Society* (MIT Press, 1989); see critique: Craig Calhoun, ed. *Habermas and the Public Sphere* (MIT Press, 1992) especially article by Nancy Fraser; Anne Summers, 'Introduction', *Female Lives, Moral States*; Leonore Davidoff, 'Regarding Some "Old Husband's Tales": Public and Private in Feminist History', *Worlds Between: Historical Perspectives on Gender and Class* (Polity Press, 1995)
60   Ludmilla Jordanova, 'Naturalising the Family', *Nature Displayed: Gender, Science and Medicine 1760–1820* (Longman, 1999)
61   Others would be: subject/object; reason/nature; mind/body; independence/dependence; individual/society; masculine/feminine. See Anna Yeatman, 'A Feminist Theory of Social Differentiation', Linda Nicholson, ed., *Feminism/Postmodernism* (Routledge, 1990), p. 288
62   In sociology known as 'functionalism' which also leads to 'false universality', Elizabeth Minnich, *Transforming Knowledge* (Temple University Press, 1990), Chapter 5
63   Further developed in Susan Reverby and Dorothy Helley, 'Introduction', *Gendered Domains: Rethinking the Public and Private in Women's History* (Cornell University Press, 1992); Jane Rendall, 'Women and the Public Sphere'. For a critique see Lawrence Klein, 'Gender and the Public/Private Distinction in the 18th Century: Some Questions About Evidence and Analytic Procedure', *Eighteenth Century Studies*, Vol 29, No 1, 1995
64   Lawrence Klein, Appendix, pp. 105ff
65   Geoff Eley, 'Nations, Publics and Political Cultures: Placing Habermas in the 19th Century', N. Dirks, G. Eley and S. Ortner, eds, *Culture/Power/History: A Reader in Contemporary Social Theory* (Princeton University Press, 1994)
66   John Tosh, 'The old Adam', p. 229
67   Raymond Williams, *Keywords: A Vocabulary of Culture and Society* (Fontana, 1976), p. 204. The English government with its monarchy still in place, has *private members* legislation in the House of Commons and the *Privy Council*, originally the body by which the king's most secret business was conducted
68   John Brewer and Susan Staves, eds, 'Introduction', *Early Modern Conceptions of Property* (Routledge, 1995), p. 17
69   It is significant that the OED gives one meaning of public as 'all civilized nations'
70   For further discussion see Chapter 2: 'Conceptualising the Family' in L. Davidoff, M. Doolittle, J. Fink and K. Holden, *The Family Story: Blood, Contract and Intimacy, 1830–1960* (Addison, Wesley, Longman, 1999)
71   Anna Yeatman, 'A Feminist Theory of Social Differentiation', p. 287
72   From Hegel's *Principles of the Philosophy of Right*, 1821, quoted in Michelle Perrot, *A History of Private Life*, Vol 14 (Harvard University Press, 1990) p. 100
73   For a discussion of psychoanalytic interpretations within a feminist critique, see Jessica Benjamin, *The Bonds of Love: Psychoanalysis, Feminism and the Problem of Domination* (Pantheon Books, 1988)
74   Ludmilla Jordanova, 'Naturalising the Family', p. 179

Chapter 3

John Tosh

BOYS INTO MEN

I recommence my diary under rather different cares than those on which I last wrote. I have at length obtained the grand object of my wishes, the anticipated deliverance from & compensation for all the passing annoyances to which I was subject at Manchester. I am in London.

EDWARD HERFORD WAS 19 YEARS of age and beginning the final stages of his training as an attorney when he wrote this entry in his diary in February 1835. The pent-up frustration of submitting to the indignities of parental discipline, and the excitement of living away from home for the first time, mark this out as the reflection of a youngster on the threshold of manhood. Edward's father, John Herford, was a prosperous Unitarian liquor merchant, with firm views about how his sons should conduct themselves under his roof. They were expected to make do with a meagre allowance, to be in bed by 10.30 p.m., and to defer to their father's conventional liberal opinions. Edward bridled at all these restrictions. He fumed at his father's parsimony; he sealed the door to his bedroom in order to stay up late undetected; and he reacted indignantly to his father's complacent claim to be the friend and companion of his children. Most significant of all, he challenged his father's declared principles, first by announcing that he would be a *radical* lawyer, and later by abandoning Unitarianism in order to become a High Church Anglican.[1]

There is something almost timeless about this story of filial rebellion, as though the compulsion of sons to level with their fathers bridges the gulf between our own day and the 1830s. Edward's awareness that he entered into quarrels with his father as much 'for the sake of contradiction' as from principle strikes a particularly modern note. But there are three less familiar aspects which should give us pause. First, Edward's radicalism may have caused offence, but his choice of the law as a profession was what his father had insisted on. Edward had been compelled to abandon his original ambition to be a surgeon – an assertion of patriarchal authority for which in the longer term he was profoundly grateful. Secondly, Edward's arrival in London in 1835 did not signal the end of his confinement under the parental roof. Four years later, when his training was over and he returned to Manchester to take up a legal appointment, he was back in his father's house, still chafing at 'the most unaccountable ill feeling & intolerably arbitrary conduct of my father', and he appears to have remained there until his marriage. Lastly, one figure was conspicuously absent from the story – Edward's mother. She had died when he was 16. A mother's mediating influence was conventionally looked to for a softening of the tension between a father and a son entering manhood – a piece of common wisdom which is certainly borne out in this instance.[2] Then as now, the passage of boys to manhood was deeply marked by their parents, but parental roles were different. Fathers exercised much more authority over their sons' choice of profession or business than they do today, while mothers – often justifiably – were credited with immense moral and emotional influence. And the power of each parent was immeasurably increased by the convention that – unless study or employment took them far afield – sons lived at home for as long as they remained unmarried.

The progress of the middle-class boy from infancy to manhood was marked by a sequence of well-defined stages. First came the acknowledgement, at the age of six or so, that he was not only a child but a *male* child and therefore entitled to wear breeches or trousers. The modern reader is still pulled up short by photographs of the infant Robert Baden-Powell or Robert Louis Stevenson in what to us is girls' dress. Every middle-class boy wore petticoats during his earliest years, just like his sisters. There is in fact good reason for our surprise. In many ways petticoats for boys were a conservative residue of the past, rather than an accurate indicator of Victorian attitudes to gender. Prevailing conceptions of a deep divide between the sexes were founded on a theory of *natural* or biological difference. Logically this extended to children and should have encouraged markers of sexual difference from birth. This may be the reason why relatively little was made of breeching – the moment when a boy put away his petticoats, usually at about the age of six. There are comparatively few references to breeching in the family documents of the time. The emphasis is less on the ritual than on its consequences. Phil Holt, aged six, was described by his father as 'looking very sturdy & well – he strutts about in his knickerbockers and speaks in a deep important voice and gives himself such airs that he constantly makes us laugh'.[3] In the Early Modern period, on the other hand, breeching had been a great event, marked by ceremonial dressing and often the donning of a sword.[4] It corresponded with a view of gender as an identity acquired over time. The Victorians also thought of masculinity – and to a lesser extent femininity – as something which developed over an extended period, but they had a surer sense of innate sexual difference. Breeching meant less to them than to their forebears. And it mattered not so much for its symbolic importance as its practical consequences.

Once out of petticoats boys' horizons expanded. Greater freedom of movement allowed them to spend more time out of doors, to engage in rough-and-tumble, and to team up with other boys. Above all, breeching heralded the start of school. Nursery lessons alongside their sisters came to an end. Few boys were educated at home after the age of six or seven. Earlier in the century the more fastidious parents, like those of Tom Macaulay or John Ruskin, sometimes kept their sons out of school on the grounds of religious scruples or class sensitivity. William Cobbett had asked how boys were ever to 'learn to talk and act like men' if they were confined to the society of boys during their school hours. But home education became increasingly rare during Victoria's reign. By 1872 J.R. Seeley's belief that educating boys alongside their peers retarded rather than advanced them was distinctly eccentric.[5] The complaints of Evangelical writers that school taught boys to despise the weak and to scoff at their sisters went largely unheeded.[6]

The majority view was that school prepared boys for the wide world in a way which home tuition could not match. At a practical level the foundations for an occupation were laid there. These included not only the relevant academic subjects, but a training in mental discipline. The engineer Joshua Murgatroyd told his 13-year-old son that boys were better equipped to succeed at business if they had learned 'to fix their thoughts on what their mind ought to be engaged with' – something which school was best fitted to teach.[7] There was

Fig. 3.1 Robert Baden-Powell, aged three, 1860.

also the long-held belief that school was an indispensable introduction to the company of males. It taught a boy to rub shoulders with his peers, to experience competition, and to bend to public authority. In smaller schools, like the private boarding establishments run by the clergy, a boy whose father was distant or dead could sometimes find in his teacher a surrogate parent. That consolation was much less likely in a public school, where the emphasis was on learning to 'shift for oneself' in conditions which sometimes approached brute anarchy. In the 1830s public school was far from being the typical education of middle-class boys, apart from the sons of the clergy. But as the number and standing of the public schools rose, the very distinctive masculine socialization which they offered became the defining experience of the upper middle class.[8]

Except for the tiny minority destined for university, most middle-class boys ended their formal education in their mid-teens. Training for a business or profession now began. At an age when many of them had scarcely entered puberty, boys began to keep long hours at work, surrounded by people much older than themselves. There was little concept of adolescence in the modern sense of an extended transition between childhood and adulthood. Parents, employers and teachers were often intent on forcing their charges through the remaining stages to manhood as quickly as possible – a distinctive feature of English upbringing much noted by foreign observers.[9] In the past the transition had not been so abrupt. When work was located in the home, children could be acculturated to it gradually from an early age. But as work became separated from home, a more formal induction was indicated, sometimes coinciding with full membership of a Dissenting congregation or first communion in the Church of England.[10] The young man would be ceremonially introduced to the workplace and his first position, say as a clerk or a junior buyer. But most fathers were denied the satisfaction of bringing their sons into their own line of business. The majority of young men had to be placed elsewhere. Sometimes this was by means of a formal apprenticeship, as in medicine or engineering. In business and commerce the aspirant was just as likely to find himself taken on in a menial capacity without the security of apprenticeship, in the hope of working up to a more lucrative and responsible position. . . .

The greatest challenge was reserved for those boys who moved to a strange town and had to fend for themselves. The preferred solution was to have the boy live either with his employer or with a kinsman. . . . But for many this kind of extension of family living was not available. James Watts – a future mayor of Manchester – came to London in the 1820s and shared accommodation with another Manchester lad. He found that London was creating 'a desire in me that I never felt before for business', but neither the place nor the people were congenial to his pious outlook on life. 'The young men here are no company to me – they go of a Sunday to Places of all kinds of amusement. . . . Let me flee from them.' He survived homesickness and moral scruples to return home and enter business in Manchester.[11] The apprentices whose company James Watts shunned were certainly testing the boundaries of respectable conduct, yet they enacted only a pale reflection of the tearaway, rumbustious behaviour for which apprentices had been notorious in previous centuries. In fact the more decorous behaviour of apprentices by this time is a striking indication of the popular reformation of manners which Francis Place traced over the first decades of the nineteenth century. Social concern about apprentices was now focused not so much on the threat they posed to order as on their welfare. The temperance societies directed much of their activity at young men. The Young Men's Christian Association, founded by Nonconformists in 1844, was intended to provide social and reading facilities in the towns for apprentices and shop assistants who lacked the amenities of a regular home.[12] . . .

Endlessly played out in thousands of cases, there is an easy predictability about this process of ascent to manhood. How boys become men takes on the appearance of the natural, or at the very least becomes the social norm. Yet the reality for individuals was anything but routine. Becoming a man involved detaching oneself from the home and its feminine comforts. It required a level of material success in the wider world which was so often represented in threatening and alienating terms. And it depended on the recognition of manhood by one's peers in an atmosphere which had as much to do with competition as camaraderie. Attaining manhood could not therefore be blandly described as a natural process, or a matter of filling one's allotted niche. It made more sense to represent it as a period of conflict, challenge and exertion. The Victorians were little disposed to underestimate the difficulties. The pronounced individualism which marked their thinking about morality and society led them rather to play up the challenges posed by the attainment of manhood. In a pamphlet entitled *How Men Are Made* (1859), the popular Baptist writer William Landels declared that men 'do not simply grow'; they are made 'not by passively yielding to an internal pressure, but by the putting forth of an internal force which resists and masters, if it cannot change, the outward'. In a later reworking of the theme he added, 'that man was never worth anything who simply *grew* into a man by passive growth, as the acorn grows into the oak'.[13] As a Nonconformist minister Landels naturally emphasized a *moral* activism which was not to everyone's taste; but the embattled individualism reflected a very widespread experience.

So too did the stress on personal qualities. Boys became men not only by jumping through a succession of hoops, but by cultivating the essential manly attributes – in a word *manliness*. Energy, will, straightforwardness and courage were the key requirements. Sometimes there was an implied claim to natural endowment; more often a manly bearing was taken to be the outcome of self-improvement and self-discipline. This aspect was explicit in what was for the Victorians the key attribute of manliness – independence. The term meant more than freedom from patronage (its principal association in the eighteenth century); it suggested autonomy of action and opinion. Edward Herford reflected on the meaning of the word in his diary. For him it meant 'not vulgar low-born independence, but [a] tolerable opinion of yourself hidden under a very modest demeanour, and not the least sense of shame or fear of doing that which is not morally wrong'.[14] Independence could only be acquired at the cost of competitive relations with one's peers. This was a recurrent theme of paternal homilies. The Liverpool cotton broker and politician Robert Holt habitually wrote in these terms to his eldest son, Richard: 'You must fight for your places [in class] as we have to do in the Town Council'.[15] . . . .

Not surprisingly, the Evangelicals set out to clean up physical manliness, like other expressions of popular mores. Their reformed version, vigorously promoted by virtually all the churches during the Victorian period, set a new moral standard. The fatal flaw in the traditional notion of manliness from the Evangelical standpoint was that it was built on *reputation* and therefore involved playing to the worldly standards of one's peers. Instead of this dangerous chimera the Evangelicals substituted *character* – the inner moral resources of a man which should determine his dealings with the world. 'Manliness is superiority and power certainly,' Isaac Taylor conceded in his *Advice to the Teens* (1820); 'but it is power and superiority of character, not of vociferation'.[16] The traditional vocabulary of manliness – words like 'sturdy', 'vigorous' and 'robust' – was redefined to include a moral as well as a physical dimension; this was particularly true of 'courage', now interpreted to mean standing up for what is true and right, rather than showing physical guts. Character was formed by two areas of experience, moralized work and moralized home. Work acquired almost hallowed authority. Manly energy was to be focused not on anti-social self-assertion, but on occupation or 'calling'. The material reward for living by the work ethic was not only personal wealth, but true freedom from dependence or patronage. At the same time the Evangelicals aimed to destroy the sexual licence of the old physical manliness by anchoring masculine energies in the home. Under the new dispensation, to be manly meant not only maintaining and protecting a household; it demanded an attention to domestic relationships as well. Wife, children and servants all required a man's care and time, summed up in the picture of the paterfamilias conducting family prayers or sharing blameless amusements with his family at the fireside.[17]

The Evangelical intervention throws into high relief one of the central dilemmas of manhood in the nineteenth century – its relation to domesticity. In essentials the dilemma is a perennial one. Becoming a man means leaving women behind – or at least the women who have provided nurture in childhood. It entails renouncing the comforts of the hearth in favour of the rigours of an all-male public atmosphere. And, once a new household has been established, sustaining one's manhood depends on a pattern of life which is proof against any suspicion of petticoat government or unduly softened manners. These tensions had surfaced in the eighteenth century. Moralists like James Fordyce were very conscious of the difficulty of striking the right balance between the enervating allure of women's company and the boorishness of men's. The pamphleteer who spoke in 1779 of 'that dangerous parent' was referring not to the arbitrary or violent father, but the emasculating mother. Men were given to doubting their own or each other's manliness because of too great a fondness for home. Among the wealthy one of the recommendations of the Grand Tour was that it served to break the hold of domesticated femininity and instil masculine self-reliance in the young traveller.[18]

So there was nothing new about the tension between manliness and domesticity. But for those young men who were touched by Evangelical influence, the contradiction was intensified by the novel idea that domesticity was a *defining* attribute of manliness – and this at a time when home was associated ever more closely with women, and femininity was counterposed ever more sharply to masculinity. The Evangelical programme not only accepted a prominent role for women in the upbringing of boys, but commended it. As Mary Sewell remarked, boys needed 'the affections trained and developed to make good domestic men', and this required 'good, intelligent women'.[19] . . . . For a boy brought up in an Evangelical family, home was also likely to be the scene of his conversion, and the feminine associations of this experience were hard to ignore; the abject acknowledgement of powerlessness and dependence which the convert must make was no doubt temporary, but it was alarmingly close to common stereotypes of womanly behaviour. However cautious we have learned to be about applying a simple model of separate spheres to real life, home was the women's sphere in a more emphatic sense in the nineteenth century than ever before, and boys grew up in a correspondingly more feminine atmosphere.

In Evangelical discourse the pivotal figure in a boy's upbringing was of course his mother. Some doubts were voiced. The Congregationalist minister John Angell James conceded that boys who became too dependent on the comforts of home might become 'pitiable spectacles of querulous effeminacy and helpless imbecility'. But the general drift of Evangelical teaching was to turn the received wisdom about the dangers of a mother's influence on its head. By the 1830s she was widely credited with the dominant moral influence over her son. She was considered better qualified to impart spiritual truths to him, notwithstanding her husband's formal role in family prayers. And her influence was supposed to hold him to a virtuous path even from beyond the grave.[20] When the attorney John Taylor's mother died in 1845, he prayed before her corpse that 'I might be enabled to resist and overcome the habits of drinking and smoking, and the company of gay and foolish companions with whom I much associated'.[21] Evangelicals were clear that a mother's responsibility extended to the manliness of her son. Thomas Binney went so far as to call her 'the father of the child'. 'Women are not to be men in character, ambition, pursuit or achievement: but they are to be *more*; they are to be the *makers* of men.'[22] . . .

The vaunting of moral motherhood also begged the important question of how much influence was exercised by the father over his sons. Evangelicals like Sarah Ellis might write him out of the script, but the father was a crucial presiding figure, not only because he set boundaries and tried to enforce them, but because at a deeper level he had a personal stake in his son's attainment of masculinity. . . . Posterity is often thought of as a consideration which weighs most heavily on men of position and power. It was the head of a large business or the owner of an estate who was likely to be most preoccupied by questions of inheritance. In that sense posterity mattered little to the majority of men in the middle class. But the transmission of masculine attributes and masculine status to the next generation was a matter of keen concern to every man who had male offspring, and it mattered all the more if he had little else to leave behind him. Sons have traditionally been seen as threatening the father with displacement and oblivion: that fantasy underlies the classic nineteenth-century accounts by sons of their upbringing, as well as Freud's theory of Oedipal conflict. But sons also hold out the prospect of symbolic immortality, reproducing the name, the attributes and sometimes the occupation of the father. That prospect was all the more alluring at a time when the facts of demography made it unlikely that a father would live to see all his offspring in full possession of their adult status. In preparing sons for their place in a man's world the father's own manhood was at stake, mortgaged to the future.[23] . . . .

Fatherhood was no more an unchanging construct than motherhood was. The nature of men's stake in the masculinity of the next generation shifted in the course of the Victorian era. One of the most significant changes was the steady decline of occupational endowment. The father no longer had the same power to set up his son for life. From the 1850s onwards places in the public service were increasingly filled by competitive examination, and entry into the professions was coming to depend on regulated training instead of apprenticeship or patronage. The days when a trusted official like James Mill could ease his son John Stuart Mill into a junior appointment (and a lifetime's career) at India House were over. Middle-class fathers were obliged to think less about trade or family contacts and more about education. The passport to a good career was now a carefully laid academic knowledge which would carry a boy over a succession of hurdles leading to a professional qualification. Middle-class employment diversified and became more bureaucratized, reflecting the impersonal quality of urban industrial society which weighed on so many Victorians. . . .

Uncertainty about the prospects of achieving masculine independence placed an even greater emphasis on personal qualities. Fathers might regret the decline in their power of endowment, but this only intensified their concern about the other aspect of a father's traditional duty to his son – to train him in manliness. To the Victorians this seemed a more difficult task than ever before. They believed that the economic discipline of the market-place was placing entirely new stresses on the individual, at a time when the traditional props of social hierarchy and revealed religion were also beginning to crumble. For a young man embarking on adult life in these challenging circumstances self-government was the key. A resilient, self-reliant character, able to rub shoulders with all sorts and to handle any situation, was an absolute prerequisite – and one not easily ensured by even the most responsible parent. The precise emphasis varied according to the balance of moral and material considerations. The Anglican vicar John Breay reflected in 1838:

> I can truly say that the older my children grow, the more difficulty do I find in the discharge of parental duties. The best mode of attempting the formation of character occupies much of my thoughts. With respect to the girls, the path appears to me comparatively clear; but the boys, who must eventually mix with a variety of characters, occasion me much anxiety.[24]

Breay was most exercised by the sexual dangers his sons faced. Other fathers pitched their anxieties at a more worldly level and worried about how resilient their sons would be when exposed to the full blast of competitive individualism.

This is the context in which to interpret one of the most significant shifts in the culture of manliness in the nineteenth century – the rise of the public school.[25]. . . For most parents, the appeal of the public schools was founded on two enduring preoccupations: in place of patronage and personal contacts they offered an academic preparation for university and for entry into the professions; and in complete contrast to the atmosphere of home and family they offered a crash course in manliness.[26]

Home and boarding school are always experienced in polarized terms, but how the difference between them was understood by bourgeois Victorians tells us a lot about their transition from boyhood to manhood. The most telling characteristic of the public school is that it was effectively a men-only sphere. Not only were women excluded from the school body or the teaching staff; they were effectively banned as points of emotional reference. Family photographs were frowned upon, as were fabrics and china which smacked of the feminine. No boy who valued his reputation would speak of mother or sisters. In *Tom Brown's Schooldays* (1857) Tom takes a robust attitude towards his delicate protégé Arthur: 'his blundering schoolboy reasoning made him think that Arthur would be softened and less manly for thinking of home'. . . . It was observed that back at home boys became more formal with their mothers, more distant from their fathers, and more callous towards their sisters – tendencies which prepared boys better for the all-male society of the public sphere than for their future roles as husbands and fathers.[27]

Freed of female distraction, the schools could get on with their real job of instilling manliness. . . . What counted were the time-honoured attributes of sturdy manliness which long predated the Evangelical offensive. The key was independence. Learning to 'shift for yourself', to be resilient, to rub shoulders with your peers, to stand out from the crowd if need be – these qualities were an essential preparation for life, including public life. The training process could begin very young. Christopher Oxley Parker was just nine when he was sent to preparatory school in 1863. 'I was very much pleased with you today', his father wrote. 'Considering that it was your first separation from home you behaved manfully. I could plainly see that your heart was full but you bore yourself bravely through, and a little overflow at the last was only to be expected'.[28] The touch was sensitive, but the message clear – and other fathers were less understanding. The promotion of 'independence and manliness of character' was singled out as a prime virtue of public school life by the Clarendon Commissioners in 1864.[29] It was closely associated in the minds of Victorian fathers with physical toughness, especially endurance. The schools were known to be lacking in the barest comforts and sometimes dangerous to health; they also lived by the rule of the jungle, and acts of gross cruelty were periodically reported. But within limits this was the kind of regime which middle-class fathers wanted for their sons. What had been good enough for the landed class for generations was good enough for them. They looked to the confident, resilient and self-contained products of the school and worried little about how this was achieved. Like Edward Thring of Uppingham School, they believed that 'the learning to be responsible, and independent, to bear pain, to play games, to drop rank, and wealth, and home luxury, is a priceless boon'.[30]

As a statement about gender the Victorian public school phenomenon is clear enough. It was an admission on the part of middle-class fathers that they could not prepare their sons for the adult world as they had done in the past. They could not deal from their own resources with the new, more impersonal conditions of professional and business life, and they recognized that in a society which valued maternal influence so highly the odds were heavily stacked against an effective manly training at home. Manliness was best instilled by proxy, under the care of a surrogate father who could set to work without the distractions of home comfort and feminine charm. . . .

Notes

1   Edward Herford, Diary, 5 February 1835, 2 April 1832, 23 April 1832, 30 June 1834, Manchester Central Reference Library, MS 923.4/H32. I have also drawn on an unpublished paper on Edward Herford by John Seed.

2   Edward Herford, Diary, 30 June 1834, 7 April 1832 and 28 January 1839; Sarah Ellis, *The Mothers of England*, London, 1843, pp. 305–6.

3   Robert Holt to Richard Holt, 31 May 1882, Holt Papers, Liverpool Record Office DUR 14/1.

4   Anthony Fletcher, *Gender, Sex and Subordination in England, 1500–1800*, London, 1995, p. 297.

5   William Cobbett, *Advice to Young Men*, 1830, repr. London, 1926, p. 292; J.R. Seeley, *Lectures and Essays*, London, 1870, pp. 269–70; J.R. Seeley to Edith Seeley (sister), 2 April 1872, Seeley Papers, London University Library.

6   E.g. Sarah Lewis, *Woman's Mission*, 7th edn, London, 1840, p. 32.

7   Thomas T. Spicer, *Masculine Education*, London, 1855, p. 14; Joshua Murgatroyd to Thomas Murgatroyd, 12 August 1868, Murgatroyd Papers, Manchester Central Reference Library M478/15/1.

8   Amongst a large and uneven literature, see especially David Newsome, *Godliness and Good Learning*, London, 1961, and J.R. de S. Honey, *Tom Brown's Universe: the Development of the Victorian Public School*, London, 1977.

9   Ludwig Wiese, *German Letters on English Education*, trans. W.D. Arnold, London, 1854, pp. 46–52; Hippolyte Taine, *Notes on England*, trans. E. Hyams, London, 1957, p. 206.

10   Leonore Davidoff and Catherine Hall, *Family Fortunes: Men and Women of the English Middle Class, 1780–1850*, London, 1987, p. 344.

11   James Watts to mother, and James Watts to Harriet Rigby, both undated, Watts Papers, Manchester Central Reference Library C/1/1.

12   Mary Thale (ed.), *The Autobiography of Francis Place*, Cambridge, 1972; Clyde Binfield, *George Williams and the YMCA*, London, 1973.

13   William Landels, *How Men Are Made*, London, 1859, pp. 8–9, and *True Manhood: Its Nature, Foundation and Development*, London, 1861, p. 43.

14   Edward Herford, Diary, 9 July 1832.

15   Robert Holt to Richard Holt, 1 November 1883, Holt Papers, 920 DUR/I4/I.

16   Isaac Taylor, *Advice to the Teens: or Practical Helps towards the Formation of One's Own Character*, 3rd edn, London, 1820, p. 93.

17   See generally Davidoff and Hall, *Family Fortunes*; Marjorie Morgan, *Manners, Morals and Class in England, 1774–1858*, London, 1994, esp. p. 64.

18   Margaret Hunt, 'English Urban Families in Trade, 1660–1800: the Culture of Early Modern Capitalism', Ph.D. thesis, New York University, 1986, pp. 246–76; Fletcher, *Gender, Sex and Subordination*; Anon., *Female Government*, 1779, quoted in Paul Langford, *A Polite and Commercial People: England, 1727–1783*, Oxford, 1989, p. 606. Michèle Cohen, 'The Grand Tour: Constructing the English Gentleman in Eighteenth-Century France', *History of Education* 21 (1992), pp. 241–57.

19   Mary Sewell, quoted in Mary Bayly, *The Life and Letters of Mrs Sewell*, London, 1889, p. 117.

20   John Angell James, 'The Young Man from Home' (1839), repr. in *Works*, London, 1860, vol. 5, p. 423; Ellis, *Mothers of England*, pp. 37, 305–6.

21   John Taylor, *The Autobiography of a Lancashire Lawyer*, Bolton, 1883, pp. 129–30.

22   Thomas Binney, *Address on the Subject of Middle Class Female Education* (1873), quoted in Davidoff and Hall, *Family Fortunes*, p. 116.

23   For some stimulating reflections on this theme, see Bruce Mazlish, *James and John Stuart Mill: Father and Son in the Nineteenth Century*, London, 1975, esp. p. 33.

24   Revd John Breay, quoted in Davidoff and Hall, *Family Fortunes*, pp. 332–3.

25   The literature on the other kinds of school patronized by middle-class families is frustratingly inadequate. School histories tend to be less fully documented, and there are fewer surviving collections of letters home (partly because of the large number of day schools).

26   J.A. Banks, *Prosperity and Parenthood*, London, 1954, pp. 228–9. The best studies of the public school during the period of transition are Newsome, *Godliness and Good Learning* and Honey, *Tom Brown's Universe*.

27   Thomas Hughes, *Tom Brown's Schooldays*, 1857, repr. Oxford, 1989, p. 237; Leslie Stephen, 'Thoughts of an Outsider: Public Schools', *Cornhill Magazine* 27 (1873), p. 286; Peter Cominos, 'Late Victorian Sexual Respectability and the Social System', *International Review of Social History* 8 (1963), p. 26.

28   John Oxley Parker to Christopher Oxley Parker, 2 February 1863, in J. Oxley Parker, *The Oxley Parker Papers*, Colchester, 1964, pp. 241–2.

29   Quoted in John Chandos, *Boys Together: English Public Schools, 1800–1864*, London, 1984, p. 329.

30   George R. Parkin, *Edward Thring*, London 1898, vol.2, pp. 195–6.

PART II

Commerce, Credit and Consumption

Introduction

TO GAIN A BETTER SENSE of how people in the past found meaning in their lives, it helps to pay attention to what they valued and how their actions expressed their values. Acquiring commodities is one way in which people have shown what they valued. Moreover, at times when specific types of commercial activity have attracted disapproval, the cultural values at stake have become more explicit. Slave-trading and campaigns against it (Walvin 1996) provide examples.

In some historical contexts, commerce itself was viewed askance. The medieval clergy generally regarded commerce as morally dubious – and this was a period when the church was powerful. The church's distrust centred particularly on merchants whose transactions involved lending money at interest, since this might render them guilty of the sin of usury (Le Goff 1988; Favier 1998). From the twelfth century onwards, when trade was increasingly conducted between parties who used different currencies and lived under different rulers, the calculation of exchange-rates might serve to hide the charging of interest. (Banking and commerce were not at that time two separate occupations.) Le Goff (1984) suggests it was partly in response to the morally ambiguous role of merchant usurers that preachers began devoting sermons to the doctrine of Purgatory as an intermediate stage after death, during which sinners who were partly good and partly bad would suffer and be purified before entering heaven. As for literature on the day-to-day experience of commerce in this period, Spufford (2002) provides a varied picture, illustrated by contemporary artists, of the place of merchants in medieval culture. Works by Jardine (1996) and Welch (2005), likewise lavishly illustrated, concentrate on the tastes of Renaissance merchants and their customers. Traditionally, rulers and nobles displayed wealth by acquiring luxuries. But as the prosperity and status of merchants rose, notably in the Italian city-states in the fifteenth century, they too engaged in conspicuous consumption.

In the first reading below, Le Goff addresses the question of how the authority enjoyed by the clergy affected medieval people's attitudes towards money, and their understanding of commercial relationships. Writing over fifty years after his first publication (Le Goff 1956) on merchants and bankers in the Middle Ages, he expresses his conviction that the medieval world was profoundly different from the capitalist world that took shape in later centuries. Financial dealings were understood concretely, in terms of relations between one person and another. These relations were judged in moral terms, by reference to the religious ideal of loving one's neighbour. For Le Goff, real insight into the commercial culture of the Middle Ages is incompatible with the anachronistic assumption that 'money' was understood then as it is now.

How does this approach square with the research of Padgett and McLean, authors of the next reading, on Renaissance merchants? They were writing primarily for economic historians. But that discipline, too, had sought to learn from anthropology. So they follow their statistical analysis of Florentine tax returns from 1427 (not included in this abridgement) with a discussion of the mentality expressed in the letters exchanged between Renaissance merchants conducting business in Europe's major financial centres. They emphasise that the market dealings which are the subject-matter of the letters were far from being governed by any concept of arm's length, impersonal calculation and cut-throat competition. Rather, these were 'personalistic markets' (p. 43). The individuals operating in them often invoked interpersonal concepts like friendship, honour and trust.

As merchants transported goods across greater and greater distances in the early modern world, a vocabulary developed for speaking of trust as the basis for confidence in the fulfilment of contractual obligations. The concept of 'credit' became central. Muldrew (1998) points out that a household's credit became a 'cultural currency'. A similar point is made by Sandberg (2010) in relation to the French aristocracy and their concern for reputation as an underpinning for their financial investments. The mid-seventeenth century, with an inadequate supply of coinage in circulation in England, saw speculation that alchemy might provide a remedy (Wennerlind 2003). In the 1690s, in the absence of a solution along these lines, paper currency supplemented the supply of coins, thus raising to the level of a national preoccupation the issues of trust raised by small-scale private borrowing (Hoppit 1990). 'Bills of credit' was the phrase used to refer to the paper money issued in Massachusetts in 1690 (Baker 2005) and subsequently by other American colonies. Both in Britain and in North America, argument raged about whether the growth of credit should be seen as a morally pernicious development or as its opposite: an incentive for good commercial behaviour, encouraging people to be reliable and to make the most of available opportunities for wealth-creation.

The third reading begins with an anecdote set in rural Pennsylvania in 1744. Breen thus stimulates reflection on what wealth-creation requires, namely the existence of consumers anxious to acquire the commodities being produced and marketed. 'Consumption' and 'demand' should not be thought of as timeless phenomena. They depend upon the consumer's attributing to what is purchased a meaning that varies according to the cultural context. In the context of colonial North America, what it meant to acquire consumer goods was bound up with the fact that purchasers were participating in a rising tide of prosperity. A fine carpet thus became something more than a luxury. It served as tangible evidence that its owners were no longer just scraping by. They could afford a better standard of living than their parents and grandparents. Breen subsequently (2004) developed his thesis that the mid-century economic boom contributed to the collective self-confidence expressed not long afterwards in the American Revolution.

With the exception of Sombart (1913/1967), earlier generations of historians had set themselves to explain the growth in productive forces. Breen is among the many historians (Agnew 1993; Roche 2000; Berg 2005) who in recent decades have focused on the long-term growth in consumption. Did the previous lack of historical research on consumption reflect the stereotype of the female consumer, prone to extravagant expenditure on luxuries?

Discussions of the gender dimension to the history of consumption can be found in Auslander 1996, Roberts 1998 and Kuchta 2002. Shepard (2000) draws attention to links between gender and credit in an earlier period.

References

Agnew, J.-C. (1993) 'Coming up for air: consumer culture in historical perspective', in J. Brewer and R. Porter (eds) *Consumption and the World of Goods*, London: Routledge.

Auslander, L. (1996) 'The gendering of consumer practices in nineteenth-century France', in V. De Grazia (ed.) *The Sex of Things: gender and consumption in historical perspective*, Berkeley, CA: University of California Press.

Baker, J.J. (2005) *Securing the Commonwealth: debt, speculation, and writing in the making of early America*, Baltimore, MD: Johns Hopkins University Press.

Berg, M. (2005) *Luxury and Pleasure in Eighteenth-Century Britain*, Oxford: Oxford University Press.

Breen, T.H. (2004) *The Marketplace of Revolution: how consumer politics shaped American independence*, Oxford: Oxford University Press.

Favier, J. ([1987] 1998) *Gold and Spices: the rise of commerce in the Middle Ages*, trans. C. Higgit, New York, NY: Holmes and Meier.

Hoppit, J. (1990) 'Attitudes to credit in Britain, 1680–1790', *The Historical Journal*, 33: 305–22.

Jardine, L. (1996) *Worldly Goods: a new history of the Renaissance*, Basingstoke: Macmillan.

Kuchta, D. (2002) *The Three-Piece Suit and Modern Masculinity: England, 1550–1850*, Berkeley, CA: California University Press.

Le Goff, J. (1956) *Marchands et Banquiers du Moyen Âge*, Paris: Presses Universitaires de France, Que Sais-je? N°. 699.

Le Goff, J. ([1980] 1984) *The Birth of Purgatory*, trans. A. Goldhammer, Chicago, IL: University of Chicago Press.

Le Goff, J. ([1986] 1988) *Your Money or Your Life: economy and religion in the Middle Ages*, trans. P. Ranum, New York: Zone Books.

Muldrew, C. (1998) *The Economy of Obligation: the culture of credit and social relations in early modern Europe*, Basingstoke: Macmillan.

Roberts, M.L. (1998) 'Gender, consumption and commodity culture', *American Historical Review*, 103: 817–44.

Roche, D. ([1997] 2000) *A History of Everyday Things: the birth of consumption in France, 1600–1800*, trans. B. Pearce, Cambridge: Cambridge University Press.

Sandberg, B. (2010) *Warrior Pursuits: noble culture and civil conflict in early modern France*, Baltimore, MD: Johns Hopkins University Press.

Shepard, A. (2000) 'Manhood, credit and patriarchy in early modern England c. 1580–1640', *Past & Present*, 167: 75–106.

Sombart, W. ([1913] 1967) *Luxury and Capitalism*, ed. P. Siegelman, trans. W.R. Dittmar, Ann Arbor, MI: Michigan University Press.

Spufford, P. (2002) *Power and Profit: the merchant in medieval Europe*, London: Thames & Hudson.

Walvin, J. (1996) *Questioning Slavery*, London: Routledge.

Welch, E. (2005) *Shopping in the Renaissance: consumer cultures in Italy 1400–1600*, New Haven, CT: Yale University Press.

Wennerlind, C. (2003) 'Credit-money as the Philosopher's Stone: alchemy and the coinage problem in seventeenth-century England', in M. Schabas and N. De Marchi (eds) (2003) *Oeconomies in the Age of Newton*, Durham, NC: Duke University Press (Annual Supplement to *History of Political Economy*, volume 35).

Chapter 4

Jacques Le Goff

CAPITALISM OR *CARITAS*? AND CONCLUSION TO *MONEY* AND THE MIDDLE AGES

A medieval absence: capitalism

THREE MAJOR THINKERS offered definitions of capitalism in the nineteenth and twentieth centuries. Their views have recently been discussed in a book of great interest by Philippe Norel.[1] Norel claims that, for Braudel, capitalism was very different from a market economy. It was a product of the emergence and increasing power of a group of merchants whose success was essentially based on provisioning the large towns in the face of the constraints of the political authorities. It was not so much a system of economic organization as a state of mind and a body of practices for bypassing regulation. For Braudel, the phenomenon had appeared by the twelfth century, at least in the Italian cities, and by the thirteenth century in Paris. Everything I have so far said in this book shows that I do not believe in the reality of this medieval capitalism.

For Karl Marx, still according to Norel, capitalism was a true mode of production. Its historical appearance came when the bourgeoisie and the nobility appropriated the modes of production. For Marx, though capitalist relations of production emerged very gradually between the twelfth and the fifteenth centuries, they were only truly established in the sixteenth and seventeenth centuries. For me, this view has at least the advantage of excluding the Middle Ages from capitalism. The third scholar discussed by Norel is Max Weber. In the early twentieth century, Weber defined capitalism as an organization of the economy aimed at the profit that could be made through the prior accumulation of a sufficient mass of capital. He believed that this system appeared in the sixteenth century, and became solidly established between the sixteenth and the nineteenth centuries. As is well known, Weber added a thesis which has been much debated, that of the influence exerted by the Protestant Reformation on, if not the birth, at least the growth of capitalism. The crux here for me in this argument is that it makes it impossible to speak of capitalism before the sixteenth century. We need to add to these three theses that of an American historian with close ties with Braudel, Immanuel Wallerstein. For Wallerstein, capitalism was linked to what Braudel called a world economy, and he saw Europe as joining a world economy around 1450, which makes this also the date of the birth of capitalism.

What are for me the essential components of capitalism which were not present in medieval Europe? The first is a sufficient and regular supply either of precious metals, making it possible to mint coins, or of paper money, as had already been achieved by the Chinese. As we have seen, the Middle Ages was several times on the brink of monetary famine, and this was still the case at the end of the fifteenth century. As is well known, Christopher Columbus among others, and perhaps first in his almost mystical conception of this El Dorado, for him Indian though in reality American, saw a land of gold that would satisfy the appetite of Christendom. The discovery of America meant the regular transfer to Europe of large quantities of precious metals, gold and silver, regulated in Europe by the Casa de Contratación in Seville in the sixteenth century. It was only then that this first demand of capitalism was met.

A second precondition for the introduction of capitalism was the formation of a single market, in place of the multiplicity of markets which had fragmented the use of currencies, imperfectly regulated by the fairs and the Lombards. This happened only in the sixteenth century, and has still, for that matter, not been wholly achieved, through a succession of globalizations. The third component, which I see as decisive, is the appearance of an institution which failed to take root in Antwerp in the fifteenth century, but which was finally established in 1609 in Amsterdam, that is, the Stock Exchange.

The importance of *caritas*

I will now return to the historians who have denied the existence of capitalism, even of a pre-capitalism, in the Middle Ages, with whose ideas I largely agree, who look at the notion of value in the Middle Ages quite differently. I believe that we should accord a crucial role in this system to the notion of *caritas,* and that if we wish to define a type of economy to which we can relate the medieval monetary economy, we need to turn to the sphere of the gift.

Among medievalists, it is Anita Guerreau-Jalabert who seems to me to have best explained the importance of *caritas* and of the gift in western medieval society.[2] She argues that this society was dominated by religion and the Church, here agreeing with Polanyi, who emphasized that there was no such thing as an independent economy in the Middle Ages, but that it was imbricated into a whole dominated by religion. Money was not, therefore, an economic entity in the medieval West; its nature and its use were governed by other considerations. Guerreau-Jalabert notes that the god who dominated medieval society, according to the Epistle of John (5, 4, 8 and 16), was *caritas,* and that 'charity appears as the yardstick by which the quality of the Christian was measured. To act against charity was to act against God and sins against charity, it follows, were among the most serious.' It is easier to understand, seen from this perspective, why the practice in which money played an essential role, usury, was condemned as one of the worst of sins. She also explains that charity was not simply the supreme virtue for Christians. It was also the supreme 'western social value', which she demonstrates by quotations from Peter Lombard and Thomas Aquinas. Charity also, she adds, encompassed love and friendship, but though friendship, love, *caritas* and peace existed in ancient Rome, and still exist today, the realities encompassed by these words in the Middle Ages were not at all the same. They were 'different social logics', each of which had its own coherence. *Caritas* in general and money in particular, limited in the Middle Ages to coin, are, in the eyes of historians, associated within one same economic process. I repeat: the error of modern historians with regard to 'money' in the Middle Ages springs from their failure to pay attention to anachronism. *Caritas* was the essential social link between medieval man and God, and between all men in the Middle Ages. The point is several times made by Thomas Aquinas: 'Charity is the mother of all the virtues, inasmuch as it informs all the virtues' (*Summa theologica*, 1–2 q. 62, a.4).[3]

What sort of economy was it? Anita Guerreau-Jalabert clearly and convincingly shows that it was a form of gift economy, and that, in the social model of Christianity, 'the supreme gift is that of God's love for Man which puts Charity in hearts'. It is hardly surprising, therefore, that for her, as I have tried to show above, the essential act by which the use of money was justified in the Middle Ages was almsgiving. As almsgiving generally happened through the intermediary and under the control of the Church, we see once again the preponderance of the Church in the functioning of medieval society, including in the use of money. The spread of money in the Middle Ages should thus be seen as an extension of the gift. Jacques Chiffoleau has observed that an increase in commercial transactions and in the use of money at the end of the Middle Ages went together with an increase in voluntary gifts, which far exceeded the fiscal levies imposed by earthly powers.[4] Guerreau-Jalabert has returned, therefore, to the ideas of Polanyi: rather than speak of the economic thought of, for example, the scholastics, which did not exist, we should locate trade and material wealth firmly 'within a value system that was always subject to *caritas*'.

Alain Guerreau has shown that this shift of perspective with regard to monetary values also applied to the fixing of prices.[5] The 'just price', which reflected the ideas of the Church in this sphere, had three characteristics. The first was that it was defined locally, as was observed, for example, in the thirteenth century by the theologian Alexander of Hales. The just price was the price that was customary in a given place. The second characteristic was the stable nature, in keeping with the common good, of the prices used in transactions. It was, Guerreau observes, 'the exact opposite of what is usually understood by the notion of competition and the free play of supply and demand'. The third characteristic is the reference to *caritas*. Guerreau emphasizes that, in all the great theologians of the thirteenth century, William of Auvergne, Bonaventure and Thomas Aquinas, the notion of just price, which relates back to *justicia,* was, like it, based on *caritas.*

Together, these considerations mean that it is impossible to speak of capitalism, or even pre-capitalism, in the Middle Ages before the end of the fifteenth century. It was only in the sixteenth century that elements which would characterize capitalism appeared: the abundance of precious metals from America from the sixteenth century and the appearance of a lasting stock exchange, that is, according to the *Dictionnaire culturel*, 'an organized public market where transactions in values, commodities or services were carried out'.[6]

Elsewhere in this same dictionary, however, Alain Rey correctly notes that 'there was a radical change in western Europe towards the end of the eighteenth century', and he quotes an illuminating passage from an Enlightenment author, Guillaume-Thomas Raynal, in his *Philosophical History* of 1770 (III, 1). In other words, in spite of the important innovations of the sixteenth and seventeenth centuries, as I tried to show generally in a book with the title *A Long Middle Ages*,[7] we may also speak of 'a Long Middle Ages' in the case of the sphere we today refer to as money, one which lasted until the eighteenth century, which was also when the concept of economy first appeared.

I would like to observe here that, sometimes taken to extremes, even to excess, the ideas I have just expressed, and by which I am largely persuaded, appear in a work of great originality by a contemporary Spanish anthropologist, Bartolomé Clavero, published in Milan in 1991, and in French translation, with a preface which I contributed, in 1996.[8] This is a work which has caused much ink to flow. Clavero is primarily concerned with the period from the sixteenth to the eighteenth centuries but his book has an important introduction devoted to the Middle Ages as starting point for the discussion of medieval usury. For Clavero, all the historians of medieval usury and of its mental and practical environment have been on the wrong track. They have started from the contemporary world, and its phenomena, conceptions and vocabulary, and transported them to the Middle Ages, where they were unknown, did not operate and explain nothing. Their judgement has been clouded by anachronism, and in particular by the fascination of capitalism, fatal endpoint of economic thinking and practice, which, like a magnet, attracts medieval attitudes to what we call the economy. Clavero draws on various economists; first, as I do myself, on Polanyi, but also on Bernard Groethuysen, E. P. Thompson and, in part, on Max Weber. Just as, for Clavero, the economy did not exist in the Middle Ages, so the law was not of overriding importance for the social order. Before it came charity, friendship, that is, 'mutual goodwill', and justice, but charity preceded justice. In the feudal world, the concept of benefit was first of all canonical, and over time became bank-related, but the bank, in the Middle Ages, was no more than a 'frontier practice'. The *antidora,* a word which in Greek meant benefit, signified the 'counter-gift', which came from the Bible and defined the relations between human society and God. Clavero explicitly says that 'the economy did not exist', but qualified this by adding 'but only an economy of charity'. In this system, the only event that can be compared with those of today is bankruptcy, and in fact most of the establishments that have been called banks in the Middle Ages failed. As for money, or rather moneys, 'currency was put at the service of the transmission of goods which was an expression of charity.' For me, what is probably most interesting in the work of Clavero is the criticism of most of our contemporaries, historians included, who are incapable of recognizing that the men of the past were different from us. An essential lesson from the study of money in the Middle Ages is the disastrous role of anachronism in historiography.

It has been a great pleasure to find the core of my ideas in the works of a contemporary economist who seeks to show that 'the Middle Ages could not be the age of the lift-off of capitalism,' adding: 'It was only in 1609, in Holland, that the drawing up of a balance sheet was required by Stevin, the first economist to be concerned with this type of rationalization'.[9]

Conclusion

According to Karl Polanyi, the economy had no specificity in western society until the eighteenth century. It was, he said, embedded in what he called the labyrinth of social relations.[10] I believe this observation to be equally true of the conceptions of the Middle Ages, which did not include the notion of economy, other than in the sense of domestic economy inherited from Aristotle, and I have tried in this book to show that this was true of money too. Money is notoriously difficult to define. As I indicated in my introduction, Albert Rigaudière has neatly demonstrated that the notion of money always eludes those who try to define it. The principal dictionaries bear witness to the difficulty of providing a precise definition: '[any sort of money] and by extension what this money represents: capital, funds, fortune, specie, cash, takings, resources, wealth, not counting colloquial expressions such as bread, dough, dosh . . .' (*Le Petit Robert,* 2003 edition).

This absence of a medieval notion of money has to be seen in conjunction with the absence not only of a specific economic sphere, but also of economic theses or theories. Historians who attribute an economic thought to scholastic theologians or to the mendicant orders, particularly the Franciscans, are guilty of anachronism. As a general rule, in most areas of individual or collective existence, medieval people behaved in ways that make them alien to us and which mean that contemporary historians need to turn to anthropology to inform their interpretations. This medieval 'exoticism' is particularly visible in the sphere of money. We have to substitute, for the general idea we have of it today, the medieval reality of many moneys, the minting, use and circulation of which expanded considerably in this period. It is difficult for us to appreciate the scale of this in the absence of adequate numerical sources from before the fourteenth century, and we are often ignorant of whether the money indicated in a source is metal coin or money of account.

The rise of money, especially from the twelfth century, during what Marc Bloch called the second feudal age, also permeated the institutions and practices we call feudalism. To oppose money and feudalism is to defy historical reality. The growth of money went together with the development of the whole of medieval social life. Though it was associated with the towns, money also circulated widely in the countryside. It benefited from the growth of trade, which is one of the reasons for the importance of the Italians in this sphere, including in northern Europe. The increasing use of money in the Middle Ages was also associated with the formation of princely and royal administrations, whose need for funds led to the creation, with varying degrees of success, of a range of taxes paid in cash. The greater presence of money in the Middle Ages took the form of a proliferation of currencies and it was only at a late stage, from the fourteenth century, and to a limited degree, that the use of these currencies was replaced by other means of exchange and of payment, such as the bill of exchange or the annuity. Further, even if the practice seems to have been less common at the end of the Middle Ages, types of thesaurization persisted, not only in the form of ingots but also and predominantly in the form of treasure and gold and silver objects.

It is also clear that, in parallel with a certain social and spiritual promotion of the merchant, the management of money benefited from a shift in the ideas and practices of the Church which, it seems, wished to assist the people of the Middle Ages in their desire to safeguard both their money and their lives, that is, both their earthly wealth and their eternal salvation. Given that, even in the absence of specific conceptions, a sphere like that of the economy existed outside any consciousness of it on the part of the clergy and the laity, or rather lack of consciousness of it, I remain inclined to locate the use of money in the Middle Ages within a gift economy, money sharing in the general subordination of human beings to the grace of God. Two conceptions seem to me to have dominated the use of money in the Middle Ages in earthly practice: the search for justice, most notably found in the theory of the just price, and the spiritual requirement expressed by *caritas*.

It may be true that the medieval Church, in the course of time, was induced to rehabilitate those who handled money, if only on certain conditions, and that in the late fourteenth and the fifteenth centuries, within a restricted elite consisting of those we call the pre-humanists, wealth – and particularly wealth in money – was restored to respectability. It remains the case that, though it may have ceased to be accursed and infernal, money remained suspect throughout the Middle Ages. Lastly, I feel I need to spell out, like many famous historians before me, that capitalism was not born in the Middle Ages, and that the Middle Ages was not even a pre-capitalist age: the shortage of precious metals and the fragmentation of markets prevented the necessary preconditions from being realized. It was only in the period between the sixteenth and the eighteenth centuries that there took place the 'great revolution' which Paolo Prodi wrongly situated, as I have tried to show, in the Middle Ages.[11] In the Middle Ages, money, like economic power, had not liberated itself from the global value systems of the Christian religion and society. The creativity of the Middle Ages lay elsewhere.

Notes

1   Philippe Norel, *L'Histoire économique globale* (Paris: Seuil, 2009).

2   Anita Guerreau-Jalabert, *'Spiritus* et *caritas.* Le baptême dans la société médiévale', in F. Héritier-Augé and E. Copet-Rougier (eds), *La Parenté spirituelle* (Paris: Ed. des Archives contemporaines, 1995), pp. 133–203; Anita Guerreau-Jalabert, *'Caritas* y don en la sociedad medieval occidental', *Hispania. Revista Espanola de historia,* 60/1/204 (2000): 27–62.

3   See Hélène Pétré, *Caritas. Etude sur le vocabulaire latin de la charité chrétienne* (Louvain: 1948).

4   Jacques Chiffoleau, *La Comptabilité de l'au-delà. Les hommes, la mort et la religion dans la région d'Avignon à la fin du Moyen Age (vers 1320–vers 1408)* (Ecole française de Rome, 1980).

5   Alain Guerreau, 'Avant le marché, les marchés: en Europe XIIIe–XVIIIe siècles, notes critiques', *Annales ESC* (2001): 1129–75.

6   *Dictionnaire culturel* (Le Robert, 2005), vol. 1, p. 1056.

7   Jacques Le Goff, *Un long Moyen Age* (Paris: Tallandier, 2004).

8   Bartolomé Clavero, *Antidota. Antropologia católica de la economia moderna* (Milan: Giuffre, 1991), trans. French as *La Grâce du don. Anthropologie catholique de l'économie moderne,* with a preface by Jacques Le Goff (Paris: Albin Michel, 1996).

9   Philippe Norel, *L'Invention du marché. Une histoire économique de la mondialisation* (Paris: Seuil, 2004). In a later book (*L'Histoire économique globale* (Paris: Seuil, 2009), which I have already used for the definitions of capitalism, Norel thought he could detect the first forms of capitalism in the form of an agrarian capitalism in sixteenth-century England, which would be the basis of the industrialization by which capitalism spread in the eighteenth century, when what Marx called the 'primitive accumulation of capital' began to appear.

10   Karl Polanyi and Conrad M. Arensberg (eds), *Trade and Market in the Early Empires* (New York: Free Press, 1956).

11   Paolo Prodi, *Settimo non rubare. Furto e mercato nella storia dell'Occidente* (Bologna: 2009).

Chapter 5

John F. Padgett and Paul D. McLean

ECONOMIC CREDIT IN RENAISSANCE FLORENCE

Introduction

WHAT WERE THE SOCIAL and institutional factors that led to, and reinforced, the precocious emergence of Florentine commercial capitalism, especially in the domain of international merchant banking?[1] The dominant stream of answers emphasized by economic historians focuses on the invention in late medieval and Renaissance Italy of a variety of innovative business techniques—bills of exchange, double-entry bookkeeping, partnership contracts, commercial courts. If these impressive organizational inventions are interpreted as facets of a broader rise of efficient impersonal markets, then a tension emerges in Florentine, and indeed in European, historiography between economic historians and the research of social and political historians who emphasize the deeply personalistic—mainly familial and clientelistic—character of social relationships of the period. Were impressive early capitalist business techniques really signs of a teleological breakthrough of the market from its traditional social shackles, as the master narrative of modernization would have it? Or instead were economic relations in the market embedded in, and hence reflective of, the surrounding social and political networks of the time, as anthropologically oriented historians have argued?[2] If evidence can be found in support of both propositions, then how are we to reconcile these seemingly contradictory interpretations?

In this article, we address these historical questions through both a statistical analysis of Florentine commercial credit in the early Quattrocento and a documentary study of business correspondence from the same time. Our conclusion will be that commercial credits among Florentine companies were indeed highly correlated with a wide range of noneconomic, social relationships among the partners of these companies. . . .

Because of these correlations between social and economic ties, Florentine economic credit was built on the social models of friendship and gift-giving reciprocity. . . . Reputations cleared markets, as much as did prices.

We develop this thesis about the structure and operation of the Renaissance Florentine economy through the following steps. After describing our comprehensive quantitative data on commercial credit from the 1427 tax census (*catasto*), we document the magnitude of reliance on commercial credit among Renaissance Florentine companies in various industries and markets. Next, we analyze these commercial credits statistically, in order to measure correlations between business credits and various social and political relations among the partners of companies. Finally, we examine a sample of business letters from the period in order to illustrate the cultural *mentalité* through which the behaviors measured by our statistics were produced. Florentine businessmen's frequent use of the language of friendship (*amicizia*) and honor (*onore*) in their letters to one another illustrates both how deeply the language of social obligation infused their economic relations and how business credit expanded the range of application of such mental models well beyond their family and neighborhood origins. . . .

Florentine businessmen were not just businessmen. They were also fathers, brothers, neighbors, in-laws, republican officeholders, factional fighters, humanists, and patrons of the arts. The colloquialism "Renaissance man" reflects the Florentine social reality that the intellectual, economic, and political activities of its elite merchant republicans were remarkably diverse.[3] Among their many activities, the pursuit of business did not necessarily assume first place in their career ambitions or in their biographies. The average period during which a Florentine banker was actually doing banking was only 8.2 years.[4] Success in business often was a stepping stone toward other elite activities, like becoming a city councilor, an ambassador, a *rentier*, or an art patron.[5] Cosimo de' Medici was not unique in this regard. In such a social context, "there is scant reason to expect that Renaissance economic exchanges, occurring within dense and multi-textured social networks, lack broader cultural meanings shared by other Renaissance exchange systems: gift giving, hospitality, the exchange of greetings, or the exchange of women."[6] The strategic implication of this dense social-network overlap is that "single actions [such as the granting of business credit] are moves in many games at once."[7]

Renaissance Florence was not a large city by modern standards—in 1427 there were only 37,246 residents.[8] Thus, most Florentine businessmen knew much about one another, both in business and outside of business, if only through reputation. Even were a Florentine businessman to desire to withdraw from the inquiring eyes of the social networks around him,[9] reputation and the subsequent flow of business credit and business opportunities would compel him not to, or else he would fail in his business. . . .

The Italian word *onore* means both "honor" and "political office," reflecting the historical reality in Italian republics that to be elected to a public office was conceived to be an honor, bespeaking respect from one's fellow citizens. Office holding in the Florentine republic was not a matter for professional politicians. Many normal "amateur," but respected and articulate, citizens were elected to serve short stints in Florentine public office, taking temporary and unpaid time out from their normal business or other pursuits. . . .[10]

One common criticism of personalistic markets is that they are inherently self-limiting in extensibility and scale compared to impersonal markets. This criticism has less force when discussing topologically open-ended social networks, like porous elites, than it does when discussing topologically closed and fragmented social networks, like families. Florentine merchant-banking credit markets were very personalistic. Yet they radiated geographically all over Europe and brokered much of Europe's international trade, without reliable judicial support. The organizational secret of the Florentines in their markets was their blending of multiple social networks into dense but socially open merchant-republican elites. Members of these overlapping elites reciprocally offered commercial credit to one another and to their clients, not as competitors but as honorable Renaissance men. Using gossip, ostracism, and reputation to discipline their wide extension of credit to one another, such men "kept everyone in line" through the same dense and multitextured social networks that had created them in the first place.

Business letters and the *mentalité* of credit

We close with a textual analysis of business letters from the general time period covered by this article, in order to illustrate the discursive framings and the cognitive *mentalité* of the Florentine businessmen who produced the commercial-credit behavior documented above. Statistical and textual evidence provide complementary perspectives on the phenomenon of commercial credit, we believe, as long as care is taken to align them. Textual evidence provides insight into the psychology of businessmen from a distant culture, at the risk of a tiny and perhaps unrepresentative sample. Statistical evidence measures the behaviors of the entire population of Florentine businessmen, at the cost of loss of detail about individuals. Even with perfect data, there is no guarantee that these two perspectives will yield the same answers. Not all talk translates into action, and not all actions are self-conscious. Consistent answers or not, we believe that juxtaposing diverse evidentiary perspectives deepens our understanding of Florentine commercial credit.

Because of the importance of relational credits in our statistical analysis, we focus on letters between *corrispondenti*—that is, between legally autonomous companies that had extensive and recurrent two-way business with one another.[11] Primarily, we examine published business letters to and from the Francesco Datini company in Milan and unpublished business letters to and from the Andrea de' Bardi company in Florence.[12] Within this small sample of letters, we highlight Florentine businessmen's use of the language of friendship (*amicizia*) and of honor (*onore*) in discussing deals with one another.

An important theoretical point in our discussion will be the two-way causality between language and social relations. On the one hand, linguistic expressions reference "real" social relationships and obligations in the writers' past experience. On the other hand, Florentine linguistic tropes and learned cognitive models, like "family" (*famiglia*) and "friends" (*amici*), were extended far beyond their objective referents as businessmen sought to frame and interpret one anothers' market actions in such terms. This loose coupling or ambiguity between Florentine language and objective reality enabled both the creative construction of new social relationships and the creative construction of lies.[13] On the whole, the benefits of the former apparently outweighed the costs of the latter. Linguistic ambiguity was the medium through which economic and social logics bled into each other.

Here are two examples of *corrispondenti* relations between companies, in Florentine businessmen's own words:

> Of the affairs you still have to complete here, point yourself still towards Pisa with my company there, and also write often to me in Bruges, because I am going to live there, and in three days I am leaving here to go there. With the grace of God I will stay there a little while, and if there is anything I can do for you, write to me of it and I will do it, for you and for your whole company, as if it were for myself alone.[14]
>
> Anything that comes to you for us, you may commit to Paris or London, if it be to your own [company] there, to ours in Barcelona, in Lucca to Bartolomeo Belbani & co, and in Venice to the Medici: continue in this way if no one instructs you otherwise. We do not wish you to lend [*credere*] our money, nor the money of our company to any Venetian or Lombard, nor to Antonio Quarti & co, nor to Niccolaio Tonghi, nor to Filippo Rapondi or others that might bring business to you from Dino Rapondi of Paris. Follow these instructions, and with the others [with whom you correspond] do as you wish and as if it were for yourself, having always due regard to lending well and, again, not to get yourself too indebted with anyone, and especially with Diamante degli Alberti & co.[15]

Within very explicitly stated constraints, partners in *corrispondenti* relationships each offered to do whatever the other requested and was authorized to take discretionary action on behalf of the other, taking advantage of local opportunities. The accounting methods for keeping tabs on these discretionary actions were the paired *conti correnti* and *conti di esercizio* discussed above. An example of the mechanics of this is as follows: correspondent A would take discretionary action on behalf of correspondent B, charging B's current account in A's book and recording therein A's actions taken and B's financial commitments.[16] This was really A giving credit to B since this was B's account money but A's disposable cash being used. Typically B would do likewise for A, thereby paying back the "loan" not with cash but with reciprocated discretionary actions. If all went well, which it did not always, each side actively made money for the other.

The word "to lend" in these and other Renaissance business letters is *credere*, which normally means "to believe" or "to believe in."[17] The language of medieval and Renaissance Italian expresses the idea that to offer someone credit typically meant having confidence in them, not only financially but also morally. "To give credit" and "to believe in someone" were essentially the same idea. Having credit was a sign that others trusted you to record your debts accurately, regard them seriously, and pay them promptly. It was also a sign that you were a person of character and honor, in more domains than just the economic.

Amicizia

While fifteenth-century Florentine business letters overwhelmingly focus on the day-to-day details of transactions, spelling them out monotonously and repetitiously, it is also true that they are inflected sufficiently often with the rhetorics of friendship and fictive kinship to see these framings as constitutive of commercial interaction. This is how Andrea Bardi could directly link the terms *merchantivolmente* (in a merchantlike way) and *amichevolmente* (in a friendly way) in a letter concerning the resolution of a *differenza* to the Orlandini company in Bruges on March 26, 1405.[18] Consider the following additional examples:

> Your offer we accept like dear friends [*chari amici*], and we see that by your Tommaso you have written concerning our condition and company: this he did as a worthy [*valente*] person and out of courtesy. . . . And although you have many friends here who serve you, nonetheless we offer ourselves to all of your pleasures and, wanting advice concerning one thing or another, tell us and I will do it willingly [*faròllo volentieri*].[19]
>
> As much as you offer to do with love in this matter, all of it we have observed, and we thank you for it, and we are certain you would do even more; and if anything occurs in Avignon or here that needs to be done, we will commit ourselves to you loyally [*con fidanza*], advising you of it first. . . . As for us, you may do with us as you would with your own, and we will do all we can. Thus we have told your Tommaso and prayed him to have such confidence in us as one could with you.[20]
>
> I will take confidence with you as I believe I may, and I would like that this confidence remain between us.[21]

In part, the language in these passages may reflect important concerns of the theologians who elaborated the Church's usury doctrine and whose ideas appeared in the confessional guidebooks consulted by the laity.[22] Here, we have in mind specifically the idea that the economy was constituted by a community of the faithful linked together in love and the theologians' emphasis on the importance of a completely, unconditionally free will for an economic transaction to be considered legitimate.[23] But the language also recalls the language of patronage letters. The final sentence of the Borromei letter is a common concluding element of much correspondence, but it appears with particular regularity in patronage-related letters in which writers assure recipients of their loyalty to one another.[24] *Amicizia* was not a word that had a single, clear-cut meaning: it could be understood in religious, political, economic, or even humanistic inflections, depending on the context.[25]

Florentines saw no contradiction between friendship and making money.[26] One purpose of helping one another was to make money, but one purpose of making money was to make friends, through generosity in gifts.[27] Profit and friendship were paired concepts in the Florentine understanding because both were facets of the same social-exchange mentality of constructing one another through reciprocity. A businessman from a later period phrased the idea as follows:

> With regard to Galilei and company, I see that there is no more need of blandishments for in truth they do things like gentlemen. The letter which I have from them now is so full, so much to the point, and so agreeable that I feel under a permanent bond of obligation to them. . . . Maintain close relations with them and we over here will always perform our part duly as we do every day; of this you and they will be the judge.[28]

Interpreting business relations as friends occurred not only when business was going well but also when business turned sour:

> We want only what is owed to us. May it please you also to want to do thus, and truly, for in good faith not a little have we discussed this dispute between us. May you or yours also wish to settle it as is done between friends. And so let it please you that not having sent these letters [i.e., business correspondence germane to the dispute] to [your office in] Florence, to send them without further delay.[29]
>
> I am advised by many letters that Basciano [da Pessina] is not there. You will have spoken with him about these blessed accounts that, by his shortcomings, are not settled, and truly it is a great wrong; this is not the friendship [*amicizia*] and brotherhood [*fratelanza*] that I had with him, and he has not done well in clamming up with me [*pigliare gozzo*], and I don't know why. . . . And I must observe that when he made accounts with me in Avignon, that amounted to 40,000 pounds or so, there was not even a penny missing, we had such a great relationship, so that one could go so far as to say that if I owed him 1000 florins, I would approach him and say to him how I considered him more than a brother, and I still do. And despite what he has done to me, I will never forget the love and brotherhood that was between him and me.[30]

The ambiguous meanings of *amizicia*, or even of *amore*, were in no way precise enough to imply what exactly to do in markets. Invoking *amicizia* in business was instead an attempt to negotiate empathetic understanding of one anothers' interests. Words by themselves could not enforce reliable economic behavior. For that, the social anchoring of language in actual families and in actual neighborhoods, with third-party observers and enforcers, was useful. But ambiguities in shared language were essential for the creative relational extension and groping of Renaissance businessmen beyond the limits of their social inheritance. The language of *amicizia* was an important first step in this Florentine relational extension from family and neighborhood into markets. By itself, however, that dyadic trope was not sufficient for scaling up into large, far-reaching, and highly connected credit networks.

Onore

Like *amicizia*, the word *onore* did not have a single unambiguous meaning in Renaissance Florence. As was evident in our statistics, the republican conception of *onore* as public office or service to the state was alive and well in the Florence of 1427. But medieval conceptions of *onore* as ancient lineage or as martial glory had hardly vanished. And sober guildsmen's conceptions of *onore* as thrift, discipline, and hard work maintained their appeal, especially among new men. Newer conceptions of *onore* as patronage, in the senses of liberality and *magnificenza* so prominent in the Medici regime soon to come, were starting to gain traction. These alternative meanings of *onore* and nobility were put into contrast with each other in the humanist dialogues of the time.[31] To the extent that the inflection was on the republican conception of *onore*, service to the community was highlighted, with commercial credit flowing in recognition of that.

Regardless of precise inflection, business-letter discussions of honor came up most often in times of economic trouble. Thus, for example, in a dispute concerning a thousand florins missing because of the actions of a certain Michele, Andrea de' Bardi wrote to both Antonio di Sandro Cittadini and Domenico Pazzi in May 1405 that they should take action "for the honor of said Michele."[32] And in a letter of March 31, 1404, Bardi wrote to Alberto Aldobrandini in Paris urging him to settle a particular deal because it redounded to both his honor (*onore*) and his advantage (*utile*).[33] In the same letter quoted above about the deadbeat Basciano, Datini went on to assert that "I would come back a thousand miles to do my duty towards him and every other good affair; and it concerns his honor not to do likewise to me, even if I did not merit it."[34]

In this context, complimenting people about their honor might gain overtones of a veiled threat about loss of that honor:

> Dearest friend, . . . When I was there I spoke to you many times about the money that you owe to the heirs of your partner Antonio di Tuccio Manetti. And now Andrea di Buonaventura has arrived there, who comes there for this reason and for other business of his, and he has begged me that I write to you concerning this matter, and that I pray of you that you should wish to act towards him as the worthy man that you are. And I am quite certain it need not be said to you, that you will pay your debt to him in this matter, both out of duty, and also to lighten the burden on your heart. And I pray of you that you should wish to do this for them like the worthy man that you are.[35]

Indeed the question of honor was always tied, overtly or covertly, to the issue of reputation (*fama*). *Fama* typically refers to other merchants' collective evaluation of one's character. Gossip—either orally or through letters—was the mechanism through which such collective evaluations were made. Such gossip could help you:

> I, Andrea, have received letters from Ciandrello. I have told him so much about you, and that you have done him such honor, that if something pertained to you alone it would suffice [to obtain his help]. And if it were not already the case that I were obligated [*obrighato*] to you in every respect, now I am [obligated to you] that much more, and I thank you.[36]

Or such gossip could hurt you:

> We have heard via letters from Montpelier that this Guglielmo Pigniolo has lost
> the confidence [of others: *avea perduto la fede*]. We do not know if this is true.
> These times are too dangerous. Tell us what you hear of it, and similarly how the
> affairs of the Bocci are proceeding, having seen these fail and how many evils
> have come this year to merchants.[37]

Tommaso Spinelli provides a clear example of the link between merchant gossip and
personal anxiety about honor. In a letter to his friend Gherardo Maffei about the setbacks
he received as a papal banker, Spinelli referred to his honor—as Jacks and Caferro put it, the
banker's most precious commodity—half a dozen times, sometimes in salvific terms.
He wrote that the Pope "has found out the truth and has recognized that I did my duty, and
he has endorsed me as a faithful man and a good merchant, and it is clear that I have done
the greatest service to the Church of God for a long time, and thus he absolves me and
imposes silence on whosoever would speak to the contrary." The last part of the absolution
pleased him the most, as it would clear his name "in the presence of merchants, and I greatly
desire this strictly for honor's sake. . . . I will have lost my [goods], but I will at least have
conserved my honor." All of this was driven by Tommaso's strong desire to leave the Pope's
employ with a good reputation for himself (*ch'io lassi buona fama di me*).[38]

The establishment and measurement of honor through gossip among businessmen was
important to the discipline of Florentine markets. But in social exchange there is also the
deeper idea of making one another through gifts. "For Paolo da Certaldo, 'a man without a
friend is like a body without a soul' and 'a man who loses his friends is worse than dead.'"[39]
This was no mere metaphor in Renaissance Florentine markets. Because credit was the
lifeblood of Florentine business, fellow businessmen made you by extending credit and
business to you, and they could destroy you by withdrawing that from you. Social exchange,
friends, and reputation were not peripheral to markets; they were the discipline that made
personalistic markets work.

Republican elections to the Priorate did not eliminate this process of intense gossip
among merchants about one another's honor. Rather they built on it by measuring and certi-
fying gossip about character into a public status observable by all. Election to the Priorate was
not an automatic guarantee of one's economic creditworthiness. But it was an institutional-
ized signal that even someone not known directly by you might be worth taking a business
chance on. Thereby, cliquish personal networks based on private *amicizia* opened out into
elitist personal networks based on public *onore*.

Our emphasis on the blending of economic, social, and political logics in commercial
credit is reinforced by the widespread presence of the same language of *raccomandazione* in
both business and patronage letters.[40] By *raccomandazione*, Florentines did not simply mean
being recommended to others, and certainly not only being recommended to others for specific tasks or opportunities. *Raccomandazione* was equally, but more profoundly, a plea for
recognition. To be in a circle of *raccomandazione* yielded material benefits, but it also signified
one's membership in a community of people who promised to act responsibly and support-
ively toward one another, in a manner similar to obligational claims to honor. To deny the
need for *raccomandazione* was not to deny its value but to uphold the certainty of its being
offered. This is the cultural meaning behind Bartolomeo Rustichi's assertion to the Datini
company in Genoa that "we do not recommend to you very much our own affairs: it does not
seem to us necessary, but we consider you will undertake them employing such diligence as
were they your own; and this we remind you, and pray of you and we will do the same for
you."[41] Businessmen in markets and politicians in state offices did not do the same things in

Renaissance Florence, but they communicated in similar ways. This is not altogether surprising since there was so much dual-role overlap between these two sets of actors. Despite the potential for divergence across the two sets of evidence, in fact, our statistical and textual analyses came to similar conclusions. . . .

Undoubtedly, the organization of financial markets varies a great deal across cases and across spatial, temporal, and cultural contexts. Neoclassical economic theory eviscerates this variation. The neoclassical approach, influential in economic history, is constructed on the assumption of impersonal markets—choices are made on the basis of goods and their prices, not on the basis of the identities of the persons transacting. But as we have shown, Renaissance Florentine markets did not operate like this, especially in the most technically advanced sectors of the Florentine economy. . . .

Notes

1   For an overview, see Raymond de Roover, "The Organization of Trade," in *The Cambridge Economic History of Europe*, vol. 3, *Organization and Policies in the Middle Ages* (Cambridge, 1963), 42–118. See also Richard A. Goldthwaite, *The Economy of Renaissance Florence* (Baltimore, 2009).

2   See, e.g., Karl Polanyi, "The Economy as an Instituted Process," in *Trade and Markets in the Early Empires*, ed. Karl Polanyi, Conrad M. Arensberg, and Harry W. Pearson (Glencoe, IL, 1957), 243–69; and Mark Granovetter, "Economic Action and Social Structure: The Problem of Embeddedness," *American Journal of Sociology* 91 (1985): 481–510.

3   Vespasiano da Bisticci, *Renaissance Princes, Popes and Prelates: The Vespasiano Memoirs; Lives of Illustrious Men of the XVth Century* (New York, [ca. 1480] 1963).

4   Data are compiled from the annual guild censuses of banks from 1340 to 1399 contained in Archivio di Stato di Firenze (hereafter ASF), *Arte del Cambio* 11, 14.

5   Lauro Martines, *The Social World of the Florentine Humanists, 1390–1460* (Princeton, NJ, 1963); Richard A. Goldthwaite, *Private Wealth in Renaissance Florence* (Princeton, NJ, 1968); Francis William Kent, *Household and Lineage in Renaissance Florence* (Princeton, NJ, 1977); Gene Brucker, *The Civic World of Early Renaissance Florence* (Princeton, NJ, 1977); Michael Baxandall, *Painting and Experience in Fifteenth-Century Italy* (Oxford, 1988); John F. Padgett and Christopher K. Ansell, "Robust Action and the Rise of the Medici, 1400–1434." *American Journal of Sociology* 98 (1993): 1259–1319; Philip Jacks and William Caferro, *The Spinelli of Florence: Fortunes of a Renaissance Merchant Family* (University Park, PA, 2001).

6   Ronald E. Weissman, *Ritual Brotherhood in Renaissance Florence* (New York, 1982), 35.

7   Padgett and Ansell, "Robust Action and the Rise of the Medici," 1263.

8   David Herlihy and Christiane Klapisch-Zuber, *Tuscans and Their Families: a Study of the Florentine Catasto of 1427* (New Haven, CT, 1985), 56.

9   As Francesco Datini, the "merchant of Prato," would have liked to have done: Iris Origo, *The Merchant of Prato: Daily Life in a Medieval Italian City* (New York, 1957), 82–83; Richard C. Trexler, *Public Life in Renaissance Florence* (Ithaca, NY, 1980), 134.

10 For the nine-person Priorate or city council, elected tours of duty were for two months, during which time councilors lived in the *Palazzo Vecchio*, or city hall, leaving their business to be run by others. . . . See John M. Najemy, *Corporatism and Consensus in Florentine Electoral Politics, 1280–1400* (Chapel Hill, NC, 1982); and Nicolai Rubinstein, *The Government of Florence under the Medici, 1434 to 1494* (Oxford, 1964).

11 Because of our focus on reciprocal *corrispondenti*, the extensive theoretical literature in economics on asymmetric principals and agents is not really relevant. That is more relevant to employers and employees or to home-office partners and overseas branch managers.

12 On Datini, see Luciana Frangioni, ed., *Milano fine trecento: il carteggio milanese dell'Archivio Datini di Prato* (Florence, 1994). On Bardi, see ASF, [*Archivio*] *Mediceo avanti il Principato* (hereafter *MAP*) 84, 87, 94. . . .

13 For Florentine examples, see Padgett and Ansell, "Robust Action and the Rise of the Medici," on the "robust action" of Cosimo de' Medici; Paul D. McLean, *The Art of the Network* (Durham, NC, 2007), esp. 1–34; and Ronald Weissman, "The Importance of Being Ambiguous: Social Relations, Individualism, and Identity in Renaissance Florence," in *Urban Life in the Renaissance*, ed. Susan Zimmerman and Ronald Weissman (Dover, DE, 1989), 269–80. Weissman (*Ritual Brotherhood in*

Renaissance Florence, 1–42), on "Judas the Florentine," cogently discusses the dark side of the credit behavior analyzed here. Lying and cheating, while no doubt existing (and documented here), were not common enough to destroy the system.

14   Frangioni, *Milano fine trecento*, letter 657: Manno di ser Iacomo & Co. in Milan to the Datini company in Barcelona, March 24, 1397. This and subsequent translations are by McLean.

15   ASF, *MAP* 87, fol. 341r: Andrea Bardi to the Orlandini in Bruges, April 6, 1405. Note that prohibited trade is specified more in terms of people than in terms of types of transactions. See also Andrea Bardi's letter to Domenico and Poldeo Pazzi in Paris, March 27, 1405 (ibid., fol. 352r), where he instructs them to honor bills of exchange for any amount with the Tornabuoni of Bruges, the Medici of Venice, and the Bardi companies of Barcelona and Florence, but imposes limits of 500 or 1,000 florins on exchanges involving certain other companies: the Sacchi, Antonio Grisolfi, Zanobi di Taddeo Gaddi of Venice, Guglielmo del Pontico of Lucca, and so on. Instructions written in 1441 for Gerozzo de' Pilli, the Medici's partner in London (ASF, *MAP* 94, fol. 214ff.; see also Florence Edler de Roover, "Andrea Banchi, Florentine Silk Manufacturer and Merchant in the Fifteenth Century," *Studies in Medieval and Renaissance History* 3 (1966): 223–85, 91) remain substantially the same as those written around 1400.

16   The expression "pay it and post it to our account" (*pagate e ponete a nostro conto*) became a common feature of business correspondence in the 1390s. The earliest example we found in Datini's Milan correspondence appears in late 1383 (Frangioni, *Milano fine trecento*, letter 334). A variant of the expression appears in a letter of March 1387 from Lemo and Ghiselo and partners of Milan to the Datini company in Pisa (ibid., letter 137), the first occurrence we find between companies not tied by a shared partner.

17   Florence Edler, *A Glossary of Mediaeval Terms of Business* (Cambridge, 1934), 34.

18   ASF, *MAP* 87, fol. 339r.

19   Frangioni, *Milano fine trecento*, letter 751: Giovanni Borromei to Datini and his company in Barcelona, April 1400.

20   Ibid., letter 606: Manno di ser Iacomo & Co. in Milan to the Datini company in Barcelona, December 16, 1396.

21   ASF, *MAP* 87, fol. 353r: Francesco Bardi to Francesco Mannini in Bruges, June 5, 1405.

22   For recent scholarship on the topic of usury, see Odd Langholm, *The Legacy of Scholasticism in Economic Thought: Antecedents of Choice and Power* (Cambridge, 1998); . . . . Lawrin D. Armstrong, *Usury and Public Debt in Early Renaissance Florence: Lorenzo Ridolfi on the Monte Commune* (Toronto, 2003).

23   See Langholm, *Legacy of Scholasticism in Economic Thought*, 61 ff.

24   See McLean, *Art of the Network*, esp. chap. 4.

25   Leon Battista Alberti wrote an extended debate on the various contemporary meanings of the idea of *amicizia*: see *The Albertis of Florence: Leon Battista Alberti's Della Familia*, ed. and trans. Guido A. Guarino (Lewisburg, PA, [ca. 1433] 1971), bk. 4.

26   As Weissman, *Ritual Brotherhood in Renaissance Florence*, 40, puts it, "It is useful to remember that although personal relations in the Renaissance were often accompanied by demonstrations of strong affection, it was the perception of moral obligation, not the modern criterion of psychological intimacy, that distinguished relations between friends from relations between strangers. And Florentines could be cold and calculating in their acquisition and cultivation of personal relations."

27   Alberti, *Albertis of Florence*, 263–73; Weissman, *Ritual Brotherhood in Renaissance Florence*, 36–41, gives many quotations to support this.

28   Gertrude Richards, *Florentine Merchants in the Age of the Medici: Letters and Documents from the Selfridge Collection of Medici Manuscripts* (Cambridge, 1932), 85: Giovanni Maringhi to ser Niccolo Michelozzi, May 4, 1501.

29   ASF, *MAP* 87, fol. 339r: Andrea de' Bardi to the Orlandini company in Bruges, March 26, 1405. In practically identical terms, Bardi also wrote to the Baldesi company in Bruges that "we have wanted, and still want, to settle this dispute as one must do between friends" (ibid., fol. 346r: July 6, 1405). And several times in the same letter he claimed to have acted toward them "with love and faith, as one must do between friends." According to another letter he wrote the same day to the Orlandini (ibid., fol. 347v), he believed that between friends "one may be more forthright in speech" and remarked that "we hold it dear that you have spoken from your heart at length."

30   Frangioni, *Milano fine trecento*, appendix, letter 8: Francesco Datini to Tieri di Benci in Avignon, August 4, 1392.

31   See Alberti, *Albertis of Florence*; McLean, *Art of the Network*, chap. 3; and Albert Rabil, *Knowledge, Goodness, and Power: The Debate over Nobility among Quattrocento Italian Humanists* (Binghamton, NY, 1991).

32   ASB, *MAP* 87, fols. 343r and 343v. Honor, he noted elsewhere, required that *corrispondenti* look out for one another's salvation (*salvezza*) as well as their own (fol. 345v).

33   Ibid., fol. 335v.

34   Frangioni, *Milano fine trecento*, appendix, letter 8: Francesco Datini to Tieri di Benci in Avignon, August 4, 1392.

35   Ibid., appendix, letter 18: Tommaso di ser Giovanni to Lorenzo di Tingo, May 28, 1400.

36   ASF, *MAP* 87, fol. 337r: letter of October 1, 1404, from Andrea de' Bardi to Orlandini company in Bruges. Honor typically communicated both an obligatory, internalized commitment and an expectation of assistance by others—a duality succinctly expressed by Bardi in a letter to Simone and Iacopo Covoni in the fall of 1404 (ibid., fol. 337v). Here, he both expressed his obligation to them (*in su quello vi si scrisse esserne voi obrighato*) and urged them to honor their obligation to him: "as long as we both shall live I am certain you will do your duty."

37   Ibid., fol. 340r: Andrea de' Bardi to Lorenzo di Dinozzo & Co. in Avignon, April 4, 1405.

38   See Jacks and Caferro, *Spinelli of Florence*, 75–76, 303–4. On the notion of *fama* in general, see Thelma Fenster and Daniel Lord Smail, eds., *"Fama": The Politics of Talk and Reputation in Medieval Europe* (Ithaca, NY, 2003).

39   Weissman, *Ritual Brotherhood in Renaissance Florence*, 28.

40   See McLean, *Art of the Network*, chap. 6.

41   Federigo Melis, ed., *Documenti per la storia economia dei secoli XII–XVI* (Florence, 1972), doc. 10: October 1395.

Chapter 6

Timothy H. Breen

THE MEANINGS OF THINGS: INTERPRETING THE CONSUMER ECONOMY IN THE EIGHTEENTH CENTURY

T HE SEARCH FOR THE 'MEANINGS OF THINGS' – a marvellous phrase suggested by a recent book of similar title – begins at Curtis's, a small tavern located in rural Pennsylvania.[1] It was here in Newcastle – at 'the sign of the Indian King' – that Dr Alexander Hamilton took his breakfast on the morning of 5 June 1744. The Scottish physician was just setting out on a long journey that before the summer's end would take him from Baltimore to New England and back again. Hamilton had no doubts that he was a proper gentleman – at least, by colonial American standards – and as he made his way from village to village, he greeted social peers with easy affability, inferiors with studied condescension. Hamilton recorded the more curious, witty exchanges in a journal published later as *Hamilton's Itinerarium*.

William Morison, a fellow traveller and land speculator returning to Philadelphia, would just as soon have avoided breakfast that morning. Hamilton described the curious scene. Morison, he observed, was 'a very rough-spun, forward, clownish blade, much addicted to swearing, [and] at the same time desirous to pass for a gentleman'. The doctor humoured Morison's pretensions. Not so the woman who ran Curtis's Tavern. Seeing a stranger 'in a greasy jacket and breeches, and a dirty worsted cap, and withal a heavy forward, clownish air and behaviour', she assumed Morison must be 'some ploughman or carman, and so presented him with some scraps of cold veal' and a cup of 'damned washy tea'.

The provocation proved too much for Morison to bear, especially since it occurred in front of the polished Dr Hamilton. '"Damn him",' Morison spluttered, ' "if it wa'n't [sic] out of respect to the gentleman in company . . . he would throw her cold scraps out at [of?] the window and break her table all to pieces, should it cost him 100 pounds for damages."' Morison pulled off the offending 'worsted cap', clapped a 'linen' one on his head, and announced defiantly, '"Now . . . I'm upon the borders of Pennsylvania and must look like a gentleman".'

After departing the tavern, Morison remained defensive, and in a final attempt to impress the Scotsman, he announced that tho' he seemed to be but a plain, homely fellow, yet he would have us know that he was able to afford better than many that went finer; he had good linen in his bags, a pair of silver buckles, silver clasps, and gold sleeve buttons, two Holland shirts and some neat nightcaps, and that his little woman at home drank tea twice a day.[2]

As told by Hamilton, Morison's tale illustrates aspects of the social and cultural history of eighteenth-century consumption that historians all too frequently take for granted. Morison's humiliation reminds us that consumer goods possessed no intrinsic meanings. Things, in this case buttons and caps, shirts and tea, acquired significance only as they were woven into a complex cultural conversation about the structure of colonial society. They were the stuff of claims and counter-claims, of self-representation among people who understood the language of Holland shirts and neat nightcaps.[3]

What we are witnessing in the tavern is the generation of cultural meanings. Consumers like Morison were also producers. The two activities – consuming and producing – were inevitably linked, aspects of a single cultural process, for as soon as a consumer acquired an object, he or she immediately produced an interpretation of that object, a story that gave it special significance.

It is misleading, therefore, to portray eighteenth-century consumers as passive beings. To be sure, the historical literature sometimes gives the impression that colonial Americans were self-sufficient agrarians, people of a pre-capitalist turn of mind who despite heroic efforts found themselves overwhelmed by the intrusive forces of a commercial economy. From this perspective the colonial American consumer becomes a victim, an unwilling or unenthusiastic participant in an expanding Atlantic market.[4]

This familiar interpretation rests, I believe, on a fundamental misunderstanding of the relation between consumption and production. It privileges the work place as the ultimate source of values, of social attitudes and of interests and passions. But surely consumption – the very act of appropriating the goods of the market place – generates meanings as central to the constitution of social reality as are those customarily associated with labour. This is what Roger Chartier, the French cultural historian, seems to have suggested when he wrote – alas, in awkward prose –

> Defined as 'another production,' cultural consumption . . . can thus escape the passivity traditionally attributed to it. Reading, viewing and listening are . . . so many intellectual attitudes which, far from subjecting consumers to the omnipotence of the ideological or aesthetic message that supposedly conditions them, make possible reappropriation, redirection, defiance, or resistance.[5]

In a word, Chartier compels us to reject the notion that early modern consumers were merely soft wax tablets upon which a dominant or hegemonic culture, however defined, freely inscribed its own ideology.

The conversation at Curtis's Tavern raises – for me, at least – a second significant issue. The event involved strangers. Indeed, two of the central figures in this exchange were travellers, men on the move in a society that at mid-century was just beginning to open out, to extend its imaginative horizons beyond the traditional, narrowly bounded communities of an earlier period and to consider the possibility of forming new, larger collectivities, communities of persons who had experienced the 'new birth', who had served in the armies that fought the wars of empire, and who had participated in an exciting Anglo-American market. The roads of eighteenth-century America carried peddlers, itinerants and soldiers, all representatives of an increasingly fluid society that was in the process of radical reorganization.[6]

My point is that consumer historians should situate Morison's Holland shirts and silver buckles in their proper historical context. We are searching for eighteenth-century meanings, and although it has sometimes been tempting to regard 'consumption' as a general, essentially timeless category of analysis, in other words, as a ubiquitous and unfortunate aspect of modern capitalism, this anachronistic perspective misses the creative specificity of particular societies. The challenge of an eighteenth-century world of goods was its unprecedented size and fluidity, its openness, its myriad opportunities for individual choice that subverted traditional assumptions and problematized customary social relations.[7]

In making these general remarks I am not denigrating a growing body of scholarship that analyses consumer behaviour in early modern America. Much of this work is of high quality. It helps us map out a world of goods and to state with increasing confidence what sorts of colonial Americans were most likely to have purchased various British manufactures.[8]

Still, at the risk of sounding unappreciative, I confess certain uneasiness about the current direction of the field. Closely argued studies seldom rise above the particular. They reveal to us objects that happened to have been listed in probate inventories; in other words, they show us decontextualized things that have lost their meanings, that no longer tell us stories about the creative possibilities of possession, about the process of self-fashioning, or about the personal joys and disappointments that we sense must also have been a product of that eighteenth-century commercial world.[9]

To ask so much from the artefacts of another age is perhaps unreasonable. In all but a few cases, the private associations that gave particular objects special meanings have been lost. Nevertheless, while accepting such constraints, I want to explore the relation between consumer behaviour in eighteenth-century America and the development of larger systems of meanings, to connect market experiences to political ideology and to analyse more fully how ordinary men and women crafted social identities within a rapidly expanding consumer economy.[10] Considerations of this sort raise challenging questions about representations of power and gender.

From this essentially hermeneutic perspective, the study of early modern consumption focuses properly on the intersection of the social and intellectual. The current literature has not systematically explored these connections because, as I have already suggested, it operates largely within an analytic framework that privileges production over consumption, exports over imports and that seems uncomfortable with the notion that broad popular participation in a consumer market could possibly have helped generate radical political ideology.

I

A study linking consumer experience to political ideology begins appropriately with the market itself. Although much about consumer behaviour in eighteenth-century America remains obscure, one can with reasonable confidence hazard several generalizations. First, while the consumption of British goods rose steadily over the course of the entire century, the pace picked up dramatically after 1740. It is the *speed* of the transformation that immediately catches our eye. British Customs Office records – a complete listing of all goods exported from Great Britain to the American colonies during the eighteenth century – reveal that the per capita consumption of British manufactures actually grew at a faster rate than did the population itself. This was an impressive achievement since the American population was doubling every twenty-five years.[11]

In other words, consumer goods flooded the American market. The pace of economic life seemed to be accelerating. Men and women alive at mid-century enjoyed access to a range of goods that their fathers and mothers could not possibly have possessed, and it is not surprising to discover eighteenth-century observers commenting directly on this extraordinary commercial activity. Contemporaries were clearly conscious of a rapidly changing material culture. A Virginian like John Wayles recounted in 1766 that only a generation earlier the planters had lived modestly, spending only a few pounds on imported manufactures. But now, he explained, 'nothing are so common as Turkey or Wilton Carpetts'.[12] And William Eddis, an Englishman who resided briefly in Baltimore, concluded that consumer demand explained the highly visible transformation of the American frontier. 'To supply the real and imaginary necessities' of those who had transformed 'uncultivated tracts' into 'flourishing establishments', Eddis explained,

> store keepers . . . were encouraged. . . . Warehouses were accordingly erected and woolens, linens, and implements of husbandry were first presented to the view of a laborious planter. As wealth and population increased, wants were created, and many considerable demands, in consequence, took place for the various elegancies as well as the necessaries of life.[13]

The quickening of the consumer market touched the lives of quite ordinary men and women. To be sure, wealthy colonists purchased finer goods than did their less affluent neighbours. But more significant was the fact that almost everyone could – and did – acquire British manufactures. It was a market from which few were excluded. All one needed was money, and sometimes not even that. Easy credit offered throughout the colonies allowed rural farmers and urban artisans to obtain a few yards of coloured cloth, a piece of ribbon, a teapot, little metal items; in other words, one of the tantalizingly small objects included in what eighteenth-century shippers labelled simply as 'parcels of sundries'. After examining hundreds of Massachusetts inventories, Gloria Main claimed to have found persuasive evidence of 'a radically altered life-style among the modestly propertied'.[14] Research carried out in other colonies points to the same conclusion. Even native Americans were caught up in the sudden swirl of fashion. Dr Alexander Hamilton, who as we have already seen, possessed a sharp eye for dress, reported that the Mohawk sachems in Boston 'had all laced hats, and some of them laced matchcoats and ruffled shirts'. These splendid Indians, he thought, appeared 'à la mode François'.[15]

And to all this widespread consumer activity – people of various classes and backgrounds, women as well as men, purchasing ever more goods after 1740 – we must add a third element, choice. Each year the market presented people with more possibilities. Individuals were encouraged to select from among different grades and colours. The language of consumption became increasingly complex, forcing everyone to distinguish with ever greater precision exactly what they wanted.[16] Again, many examples of this explosion of consumer choice could be offered. Let me cite a single case. In 1758 Mary Alexander, a leading New York merchant, ordered from her British supplier David Barclay and Sons eighteen cups and saucers, fourteen coffee cups and ninety-six salad dishes. Alexander soon received a letter from Barclay's begging her to provide more detail. She should describe what she desired 'by round or long common Dishes for Meat, Soup Dishes, or deep Sallad or Pudding Dishes, [for] otherwise [we are] at a Loss to know what' to ship to America.[17] It is clear from the advertising of the eighteenth century that consumers learned quickly. They made demands upon merchants, merchants upon wholesalers, and wholesalers upon British suppliers. Americans wanted the latest styles, and not as an angry George Washington complained in a note sent to his London merchant in 1760, '[of] Articles . . . that could [only] have been used by our Forefathers in the days of yore'.[18]

Even what might be labelled the criminal element of colonial America developed a discerning eye for new British imports. In 1750 John Morrison – no relation to the William Morison who we encountered at Curtis's Tavern – organized a gang of thieves that terrorized Philadelphia. Morrison, a 24-year-old Irishman who had originally migrated to Pennsylvania as an indentured servant, peddled 'Limes and Onions from House to House', and he used his conversations with customers to observe 'how the Windows and Doors were fastened'. Morrison and his accomplices burgled homes and shops, stealing from 'Mr. R—d's House . . . two Silk Gowns, two other Gowns, three fine Aprons, a Tea Chest, some Cambrick Hankerchiefs and other Things, which one of his Companions carried to New York for Sale'. An anonymous pamphlet listed in the manner of a contemporary journal advertisement the other goods that the gang had robbed – a lexicon whose very complexity reveals a growing sensitivity to the possibilities of an expanding consumer market – tea kettles, wearing linen, silver spoons, coats and hats, table cloths, iron boxes, a coffee mill, a pewter basin, a pair of stays, a calico gown, a necklace, a silk waistcoat, a scarlet long cloak, a camblet cloak, a blue cloth jacket, a pair of black silk stockings and two pairs of pumps. The consumer market had created its own criminal class. 'For what Trifles', the author of this piece lectured, 'did this poor Wretch continually hazard his Life!'[19]

By mid-century these 'trifles' had thus become part of a new visual landscape.[20] Colonists could view the imported manufactures on display in urban stores and in rural shops; they purchased them in the countryside from peddlers and factors. Indeed, they could hardly control their curiosity about a range of goods that allowed them to present themselves as more beautiful, as more important or as more cosmopolitan. A single example of consumer eagerness must suffice. Dr Hamilton noted in his journal that he and his slave reached Newport, Rhode Island

> betwixt seven and eight at night, a thick fog having risen, so that I could scarce find the town. When within a quarter of a mile of it my man, upon account of the portmanteau, was in the dark taken for a peddler by some people in the street, whom I heard coming about him and inquiring what he had got to sell.[21]

These particular consumers anticipated perhaps that Hamilton's 'man' was carrying the kinds of goods that they had seen advertised in colonial newspapers in an increasingly elaborate language of textures, brands and colours. What we are witnessing here is the sudden incorporation into a colonial imagination of an unprecedented quantity of consumer goods. Their very presence in daily life compelled creative responses and active appropriations.

Ordinary Americans suddenly found themselves able to shape new identities, to fashion themselves in exciting ways. That was certainly the message of a pamphlet published in Philadelphia in 1772 under the title *The Miraculous Power of Clothes and the Dignity of Tailors, being an Essay on the Words, Clothes Makes Men*. 'Dunces', the author instructed, 'are they who persuade themselves and others, that nothing but true merit, the love of country, honesty, and, in short, nothing but virtue, can make us happy and truly famous.' But such a view was naive. Imported cloth obviously held the key to success in this consumer society. As the essay explained, 'Clothes alone effect that which virtue, honesty, merit, and love for our country, in vain try to perform.' If the world was a stage, then the 'simple good man' had better acquire the latest styles. There were many choices, of course. The narrator discovered the splendid possibilities while visiting a local tailor's shop, where he 'found [the craftsman] amidst a chaos of velvet, brocade, and other rich stuffs, out of which he created illustrious personages, graces, honours, and other worthies'. The tailor had just cut out a divine and 'was not a little vexed that the velvet would not reach to form completely the right reverend belly'. Workers busily shaped other social identities. 'Over the chair hung two excellencies without sleeves. . . . On the bench lay a great many young beaux, most amiable young gentlemen and sighing lovers, who seemed to wait impatiently for their formation and the evolution of their beings.' The tour of the shop concluded at the door where the author encountered 'two apprentices who had not yet capacity for other work, [and therefore] sat . . . exercising themselves upon the suit of a poet'.[22]

II

No one would treat descriptions of this sort as objective accounts. We are dealing here with perceptions, with cultural readings, with attempts by people of different background and experience not only to interpret the eighteenth-century consumer economy, but also their place within it. This is the point at which social and intellectual history intersect. Real experiences as consumers sparked the production of meanings. These meanings were, of course, highly charged with political implications, for it was through the contest over the meanings of consumption that colonists challenged or defended the traditional social order. For almost everyone the meanings of things raised perplexing questions about gender and equality.

Historians have generally concentrated upon the critique of consumption. It is true that unprecedented consumer activity sparked a shrill, highly moralistic response. By the middle of the eighteenth century that discourse could claim an impressive genealogy. Some statements that appeared in colonial American newspapers and pamphlets sounded as if they had been lifted directly from religious and republican sources that Europeans had been reading for a very long time. But borrowing in itself does not tell us much about the production of meanings. To draw again on Chartier: 'The ways in which an individual or a group appropriates an intellectual theme or a cultural form are more important than the statistical distribution of that theme or form.'[23] The history of the meanings of consumption moves properly from the sociological to the intellectual, from the experiential to the ideological.[24]

With such stipulations in mind, we might pay closer attention to what colonial writers were actually saying about whom. They began predictably enough by describing consumption as addictive, dangerous and volatile. Small, seemingly innocent purchases, they warned, could lead to the destruction of the consumer. Behind every transaction hovered the spectre of luxury. In a typical admonition from this period, Philopatriae reminded the readers of the *Boston Gazette,* 'Luxury makes her Appearance in a Manner so engaging, so easily she deceives us under the show of Politeness and Generosity, that we are not aware of Danger, 'till we feel the fatal Poison.'[25] According to another American writer, 'Thus luxury proceeds from one to another; and the baneful contagion spreads at last to the very dregs of the people.'[26]

Because of their high visibility, clothes presented the most troubling challenge to traditional hierarchy. Cloth was the major British import for the entire eighteenth century, and the bright stripes and colourful prints, especially the lighter weight textiles, were quickly transformed into garments. Indeed, dress was the most sensitive index to fashion.[27] 'We run into . . . Extremes as to Dress', complained the *Boston Gazette,* 'so that there is scarce any Distinction between Persons of great Fortune and People of ordinary rank.' Another writer insisted in an essay on the merits of setting up a central market in Boston that

> They that are poorer . . . should and must give way to the Rich. Who but they
> ordinarily should buy the dearest and best of the kind? . . . Now and then we

that are poorer may taste of the best too and be thankful. But we should be willing to live low, where God has set us, and having food and raiment (tho' not so much of it as some, nor of so fine a sort), let us be therewith content.[28]

This observer was whistling in the dark. The poor and the middling sorts did in fact purchase fine raiment. And their failure to stay in their proper place nearly drove the Reverend Jonathan Mayhew to distraction. Mayhew, of course, usually appears in colonial histories as a spokesman for radical country politics. He created a minor controversy by celebrating the anniversary of the execution of Charles I. But when he commented on dress, Mayhew fervently defended a divinely sanctioned social order. He pointed out in his *Christian Sobriety* that 'not only the custom of all civilized nations in all ages, but [also] the holy scriptures themselves, warrant some distinctions of dress in persons, answerable to the differences in their stations and circumstances in life'.

The young people of Boston, however, challenged these social and moral conventions, for 'instead of being content with such clothing as is suitable to their degree and circumstances, to their own or to their parents' worldly estate, they aspire after what is far beyond either'. Their clothing, thought Mayhew, was 'wholly disproportionate to their rank and circumstance'. And he concluded – as did many of his contemporaries –

> By this means those good ends which might otherwise be answered in society, by the distinction of dress, are in a great measure defeated; for this confounds all ranks, destroys due subordination, and even inverts the natural order of things, by settling poor people of low degree above the rich, and those that are on high.[29]

During the seventeenth century, Governor John Winthrop had grumbled about 'due subordination'. The legislature of the Puritan commonwealth had even enacted sumptuary laws to make certain that the poor would not confound the social order.[30] It is not clear whether such statutes ever had much effect on actual behaviour, but in Mayhew's time sumptuary laws were out of the question. There were too many consumers purchasing too many yards of brightly coloured cloth. William Tennent, a revivalist not usually regarded an historian of popular manners, understood better than did Mayhew the egalitarian thrust of the consumer economy. 'Formerly Vices were described by the Classes of Mankind to which they belonged', explained the famed evangelist, 'but we find they have spread themselves so universally among all Ranks in the British Empire, that we can no longer describe them in that manner.' Vices, Tennent readily admitted, prevailed

> in a great Degree, in the dissolute Reign of *Charles* the Second, but they were confined chiefly to the Channel of the Court. The middle and lower Classes of People, and the Inhabitants of Villages and Country Places continued Strangers to them. But this cannot be said of the present Generation. Our common and Country People seem to vie with the first Classes of Mankind in Vices, which were formerly peculiar to them alone.

Although Tennent may have been correct about the democratization of sin, neither he nor Mayhew – no, not even the entire American clergy – could turn back the consumer clock.[31]

Within this particular moral critique, women did not fare very well, and colonial writers –almost all of them anonymous scribblers – regularly blamed women for consumer excess. They became symbols of threatening economic change. The association of women with luxury, of course, had a long history, and as we have already observed, colonial American commentators certainly borrowed from this heavily engendered moral rhetoric. Indeed, 'luxury' was usually described as a 'she', as effeminate, soft and weak.

Even as we pick up echoes of an older moral tradition, however, we still must account for the extraordinary shrillness of the attack on these particular women. Their acquisition of British imports, their inability to resist the temptations of the market place and their selfish unconcern for hard-working husbands became nearly obsessional themes in the colonial press. 'Are there not too many Wives', one writer asked the readers of the *Boston Gazette* in 1747,

> even among our lower Sort of People, so nice & delicate that they cannot think of any Thing but Velvet & Scarlet to guard them from the Inclemencies of the Winter Air? – Look into the Families of some of these vain Things, and you shall see Poverty enough – Let these precious Help-mates seriously reflect on their Husbands' Conditions – their business failing – their Credit sinking – their little Estates (if any is left) reduced almost to nothing thro' their Extravagancies – When will they leave their Scarlet Cloaks – their Velvet Hoods – their foreign gaudy Dress, and put on humble Homespun, which best becomes them![32]

What soon becomes clear from these diatribes is that colonial writers had in mind *real* women, wives and mothers, female merchants and peddlers, women who welcomed British imports because they knew all too well how difficult and tedious the production of 'homespun' goods actually was. This writing also suggests that the consumer market may have been a source of female empowerment. Some women certainly rejected a moralistic, usually republican discourse that described them as inherently weaker than men.[33] On 24 July 1732 the *Pennsylvania Gazette* published 'Celia Single's' sarcastic observation: 'I have several times in your Paper seen severe Reflections upon us Women, for Idleness and Extravagance, but I do not remember to have once seen any such Animadversions upon the Men.' And 'Senex' noted in the *Pennsylvania Packet,*

> If the fair sex are thought worthy of blame for their extravagancies in dress, what shall we say to our young gentlemen in their Macaroni coats, hats and shoes. . . .
> I doubt whether a woman would not have thought it less punishment to suffer death, than to be exposed to the multitude in the ridiculous dress of a modern beau.[34]

The acquisition of goods by women in this economy was an assertive act, a declaration of agency, and male writers found these aggressive expressions of personal independence intimidating. 'Simplicius Honestus' confessed to the readers of a Philadelphia journal that his 'lady friend' had been acting very strangely:

> I lately saw her hair raised up into a fantastic pyramid, which, instead of giving majesty to her charms (as I suppose some mischievous body had persuaded her) disfigured them by a certain air of fierceness, unnatural to her gentle countenance. I would advise her, then, to throw off this whimsical conceit, or I shall conclude that she is giving up the possession of a sincere heart . . . for the vain, coquettish pleasures of making conquests.[35]

Another Philadelphia suitor claimed to have broken off his courtship because the lady's 'absurdity in dress . . . [had] so metamorphosed [her], so horribly disfigured [her], that I am very glad I had not proceeded so far as to declare myself to her'.[36]

The liberal interpretation that I am developing is most emphatically not a form of consumer reductionism. Major social transformations seldom have single causes, and that which occurred in eighteenth-century America does not appear an exception. In politics as well as religion, ordinary men and women were encouraged to make choices from among contending possibilities, to break out of traditional communities and patterns of behaviour, to rely upon their own reason in making decisions, in a word, to reconceptualize the entire social order. Isaac Backus, the famous Baptist leader, stated the general point succinctly in 1768, 'The common people claim as good right to judge and act for themselves in matters of religion as civil rulers or the learned clergy.'[37] So too did the author of an anti-excise pamphlet published in Boston in 1754. He reminded 'Men of common Capacity' that if they did not find the behaviour of their elected representatives acceptable, they now 'have an Opportunity of chuse better Men'.[38] Popular participation in these various activities created reinforcing expectations. If change was indeed inverting 'the natural order of things', then the offenders were 'fanatics' and 'enthusiasts' in religion, demanding freemen in politics and of course, aggressive consumers, both men and women, in the market place.

All these unprecedented and unsettling activities were related to what Jürgen Habermas has labelled the 'bourgeois public sphere'. By that he referred to the creation in the eighteenth century of an imagined public space, a new collectivity of reasoning individuals who spoke in a powerful, critical voice known as public opinion. Those who claimed to speak for the 'public' and who appealed to the public judgement through pamphlets and newspapers challenged the exercise of arbitrary authority. In the name of the 'public', they demanded rights. Habermas was centrally concerned with politics, but it seems to me that his insights could be extended to a 'bourgeois public sphere' that included a broader public, one that imagined that it shared the experience of the 'new birth', that assumed that it had the right to select political representatives and that came to believe that it had as good a claim on the goods of the market place as did any group, no matter how privileged by tradition.[39]

In other words, returning to the focus of this chapter, the meanings of things in eighteenth-century America were bound up with a new, aggressive sense of individual rights based on informed choice. Situated in this manner, consumption was – as I have argued with reference to women – a source of empowerment. The very act of appropriating goods generated meanings. This is what the author of a 1754 pamphlet entitled *The Good of the Community Impartially Considered* reminded his readers during the so-called Excise Controversy:

> Every Man has a *natural Right* to enjoy the fruit of his own Labour, both as to the *Conveniencies,* and *Comforts,* as well as *Necessaries* of Life, *natural Liberty* is the same with one Man, as another; and unless in the Enjoyment of these Things they hurt the Community, the Poor ought to be *allow'd* to use them as freely as the Rich. – But such is the Perversity of human Nature, that when a Man arises to any tolerable Degree of Fortune, he begins to think all below him were made for his Service, and that they have no Right to any Thing, but what is despised & refused by him. We could very well be contented with this, if these Gentlemen would but let us enjoy such Things as we were able to purchase, *freely;* or with the same Freedom they are allow'd to do it: I am sure we Work as hard as they do for it; therefore, I cannot see why we have not as good a *natural Right* to them as they have.[40]

What we are hearing here owed almost nothing to a classic republican discourse which until very recently has dominated our understanding of political ideology in eighteenth-century America. Thanks largely to the work of Joyce Appleby, we have grown suspicious of the hegemonic claims that historians have made for civic humanism.[41] There is no doubt that the members of an educated colonial elite found the classic rhetoric of civic humanism congenial; it was a discourse that helped them situate themselves within an expanding commercial empire. But for all its shrill warnings about power and corruption, its distrust of the market place, its demands for heroic self-sacrifice and Roman simplicity, its insistence on a form of virtue that only propertied freemen could possibly possess and its appeal to 'manly' values, republicanism remained an exclusive, backward-looking ideology that bore only a tenuous relation to the social and economic experience of those consumers who in the market place had found a source of independence, rights and dignity. Republicanism and liberalism were rival representations, locked in a struggle to control and to channel eighteenth-century capitalism. We should see them as different modes of accommodation to economic change, and although these two discourses briefly came together on the eve of the revolution, American consumers continued to consume, to make choices and to resist any group or institution that challenged their right to do so. It is to this powerful discourse – and not to republicanism – that we should look for the sources of a radical, egalitarian tradition.

Let me close with a quotation from a dialogue that that 'forward, clownish blade' William Morison would undoubtedly have appreciated. It originally appeared in 1736 in the *South-Carolina Gazette*. A woman has entered a small shop, and every time she inquires about the cost of a certain object, the proprietor delivers a gratuitous sermon about the vanity of such goods. Finally, a little out of patience, the woman declares, 'Yes, Sir, but I did not ask you the Virtues of it, I ask'd you the Price.'[42]

Notes

1   See Mihaly Czikszentmihalyi and Eugene Rochberg-Halton, *The Meaning of Things: Domestic Symbols and the Self* (Cambridge, 1981). The essay that I prepared for the William Andrews Clark Memorial Library Lecture Series is part of a larger study that will explore the relation between an expanding eighteenth-century Anglo-American consumer economy and the development of various political ideologies, particularly republicanism and liberalism. Sections of this project which have been published or presented as conference papers provide full bibliographic references to a huge secondary literature and are cited in the notes below.

2   Alexander Hamilton, *Itinerarium. Being a Narrative of a Journey . . . From May to September, 1744,* ed. Albert Bushnell Hart (St Louis, 1907), 13–17.

3   T. H. Breen, '"Baubles of Britain": the American and consumer revolutions of the eighteenth century', *Past and Present,* cxix (1988), 73–104; idem, 'The meaning of "likeness": American portrait painting in an eighteenth-century consumer society', *Word and Image,* vi (Oct.–Dec. 1990), 325–50.

4   T. H. Breen, 'An empire of goods: the Anglicization of colonial America, 1690–1776', *Journal of British Studies,* xxv (1986), 467–99.

5   Roger Chartier, *Cultural History: Between Practices and Representation,* tr. Lydia G. Cochrane (Ithaca, 1988), 41.

6   Breen, 'Preliminary thoughts on writing a history of choice in eighteenth-century America', paper presented at 'Eighteenth-century politics and culture' conference, Göttingen University, 20 May 1988. Also see Frank Lambert, 'Pedlar in divinity: George Whitefield and the Great Awakening, 1737–1745', *Journal of American History,* lxxvii (Dec. 1990), 812–37.

7   The best general discussion of these topics remains Neil McKendrick, John Brewer and J. H. Plumb, *The Birth of a Consumer Society: The Commercialization of Eighteenth-Century England* (Bloomington, 1982).

8   A useful introduction to the recent literature can be found in 'Forum: toward a history of the standard of living in British North America', *William and Mary Quarterly,* 3rd series, xlv (1988), 116–70. Also Winifred B. Rothenberg, 'The bound Prometheus', *Reviews in American History,* xv (1987), 628–37.

9   See Albert O. Hirschman, *Shifting Involvements: Private Interest and Public Action* (Princeton, 1982).

10   The connection between ideology and experience is explored in T. H. Breen, 'Slavery in a polite society: Virginia's colonial planters and the challenge of commercial capitalism', paper presented at 'Recreating the world of the Virginia plantation, 1750–1829' conference, Charlottesville, Virginia, 31 May 1990.

11   Breen, 'Baubles of Britain', 73–87.

12   John Hemphill, 'John Wayles rates his neighbors', *Virginia Magazine of History and Biography,* lxvi (1958), 305.

13   William Eddis, *Letters from America,* ed. Aubrey C. Land (Cambridge, Mass., 1969), 51–2.

14   Gloria L. Main, 'The standard of living in southern New England, 1640–1773', *William and Mary Quarterly,* 3rd series, xlv (1988), 129.

15   Hamilton, *Itinerarium,* 137–8. The fullest discussion of the accommodation and resistance of native American cultures to the European consumer economy is James Axtell, *The Invasion Within: The Contest of Cultures in Colonial North America* (New York, 1985), 131–78.

16   Breen, 'Baubles of Britain', 79–87.

17   Cited in Patricia Cleary, 'She merchants of colonial America: women and commerce on the eve of revolution' (Northwestern University, Ph.D. thesis, 1984), ch. 4.

18   *The Writings of George Washington,* ed. John C. Fitzpatrick, 39 vols (Washington, DC, 1931), vol. 2,350; George Washington to Robert Cary and Co., 28 Sept. 1760.

19   *Account of the Robberies Committed by John Morrison. And his Accomplices, in and Near Philadelphia, 1750: Together with the Manner of their being discover'd, their Behaviour on their Tryalls, in the Prison after Sentence, and then at the Place of Execution* (Philadelphia, 1751), 2–10.

20   Dell Upton provides a valuable introduction to this topic in 'New views of the Virginia landscape', *Virginia Magazine of History and Biography,* xcvi (1988), 403–70. Also, William M. Kelso and Rachel Most (eds), *Earth Patterns: Essays in Landscape Archaeology* (Charlottesville, 1990).

21   Hamilton, *Itinerarium,* 184.

22   *The Miraculous Power of Clothes, and Dignity of the Taylors Being an Essay on the Words, Clothes Makes Men* (Philadelphia, 1772), 3–11.

23   Chartier, *Cultural History,* 5. Also see Albert O. Hirschman, *Shifting Involvements: Private Interest and Public Action* (Princeton, 1982), 46–61; and John Sekora, *Luxury: The Concept in Western Thought, from Eden to Smollett* (Baltimore, 1977).

24   Breen, 'Slavery in a polite society'.

25   *Boston Gazette,* 17 November 1747.

26   ibid., 18 January 1773.

27   Breen, 'Meaning of "likeness"'.

28   *Boston Gazette,* 26 February 1733; ibid., 7 January 1765.

29   Jonathan Mayhew, *Christian Sobriety . . . Preached with a Special View to the Benefit of the Young Men* (Boston, 1763), 151–5, 197–9.

30   See Stephen Foster, *Their Solitary Way: The Puritan Social Ethic in the First Century of Settlement in New England* (New Haven, Conn., 1971), 9–64.

31   William Tennent, *An Address, Occasioned by the Late Invasion of the Liberties of the American Colonies by the British Parliament* (Philadelphia, 1774), 13–16.

32   *Boston Gazette,* 17 November 1747.

33   ibid., 24 July 1732.

34   *Pennsylvania Packet,* 23 November 1772.

35   ibid.

36   ibid., 6 November 1772.

37   Cited in William G. McLoughlin, *New England Dissent, 1630–1833: The Baptists and the Separation of Church and State,* 2 vols (Cambridge, Mass., 1971), vol. 1, 327. Also see Breen, 'Thoughts on history of choice'.

38   *The Review* (Boston, 1754), 8.

39   Jürgen Habermas, *The Structural Transformation of the Public Sphere: An Inquiry into a Category of Bourgeois Society,* tr. Thomas Burger (Cambridge, Mass., 1989). Also see T. H. Breen, 'Retrieving common sense: rights, liberties and the religious public sphere in late eighteenth-century America', in Josephine F. Pacheco (ed.), *To Secure the Blessings of Liberty: Rights in American History* (forthcoming).

40   *The Good of the Community Impartially Considered* (Boston, 1754), 18–19.

41   Joyce Appleby, *Capitalism and a New Social Order: The Republican Vision of the 1790s* (New York, 1984); idem, 'Republicanism and ideology', *American Quarterly,* xxxvii (1985), 461–73; James T. Kloppenberg, 'The virtues of liberalism: Christianity, republicanism, and ethics in early American political discourse', *Journal of American History,* lxxiii (1987), 9–33; idem, 'The creation of the American Republic, 1776–1787: a symposium of views and reviews', *William and Mary Quarterly,* 3rd series, xliv (1987), 550–640.

42   *South-Carolina Gazette,* 17 January 1736.

PART III

Time, Space and Measurement

Introduction

ACCOUNTING FOR TIME and for distance might at first seem to be universal practices, reflecting the natural world rather than cultural variation. In fact, histories of measurement practices have revealed much about past cultures. Even the protracted negotiation and imposition of international standards of space, time and other physical fundamentals has not reduced the idiosyncrasies of people's subjective experience of time and place (Kern 1983). Measurement practices have often, perhaps always, encoded values (Wise 1995), reflecting local agendas and power relations even as they made claims to universality. William Thomson (later Lord Kelvin) famously observed that natural philosophers (our physicists) could have only a 'meagre and unsatisfactory' knowledge of anything they were unable to measure (Thomson 1889; see Gooday 2004 and Smith and Wise 1989 for context). This proposition has been extended to knowledge in general, as if only what can be counted matters.

This section is concerned, then, with the cultural significance of counting, measuring and calculating – and recording and communicating the results. The powerful have propagated such practices increasingly but even in the West, where their adoption has been most profound, voices of resistance can be heard. Medieval reactions against the mechanical measurement of time, although rare, include that of the Welsh poet who cursed the newly invented clock (Mayr 1986). Crosby (1997) surveys techniques of measurement developed in many areas of Western life before the seventeenth century, but he has been criticised for triumphalism (Hart 2000). Western political dominance and imperialism have been facilitated through quantification, but Western cultural historians should be wary of ethnocentrism. In the spread of industrial capitalism, especially from the early nineteenth century, technologies for measuring space and time played an important part, for some engendering efficiency, for others displacing valued traditional practices (Harvey 1989).

The topics touched on in this introduction are diverse: clocks, maps, exploration, management of labour, standardisation, perspective in art, musical notation, accountancy, demography, statistics and psychometrics. All involve the use of visual displays, on paper or in other ways, to represent aspects of the world, generally for the sake of planning ahead for coordinated activities. The phrase 'the grid mentality' captures a characteristic feature of this way of structuring experience and its representation. Edgerton (1975) uses that phrase to denote something that underlay developments in the Florentine Renaissance. Artists depicting three-dimensional scenes tried to achieve an illusion of depth. Planners and architects laid out buildings and streets in rectangular patterns. Cartographers used projection-techniques to draw maps to scale, so that the distance from one place to another could be read off. Law (1986) and Latour (1987) have analysed the processes whereby information of many different kinds was assembled to plan successive voyages of exploration. As navigators found ocean routes further and further from their European starting points, they compiled naval charts showing coastlines and offshore hazards. Each completed voyage brought back further knowledge which was incorporated in subsequent planning. Latour uses the phrase 'centres of calculation' to denote the agencies that accumulated these findings and used them in an iterative process intended to facilitate ever more effective imperial control.

The development of a grid mentality was a part of the rediscovery of the cultures of the ancient Greco-Roman world. Greek manuscripts brought to Italy from a Byzantium threatened with military defeat included Ptolemy's *Geography*, which came to Florence in 1400. Although the mapping of the earth's surface by latitude and longitude had classical precedents, the invention of mechanical devices to register the passage of time did not. That occurred unrecorded in about 1300. The hour itself was redefined when reliance on clock-time spread. In the ancient world and for much of the Middle Ages its length had varied with the seasons, as it was the twelfth part of the interval between sunrise and sunset (Dohrn-van Rossum 1996). But with machinery came the standard hour. In the late eighteenth century, in factory-based systems of production, employers used the measurement and dissemination of time to exercise tighter control over the pace of work (Thompson 1967). By the mid-nineteenth century, advocates of the railway system implemented another kind of standardisation. To avoid the time-variation between places situated far apart on an East-West axis, legislators required the use of Greenwich time throughout the British Isles, and in the USA a system of time-zones was established. In the 1880s, governments agreed to apply a similar system on a global scale (Kern 1983). Meanwhile, managers adopted time-and-motion studies and Taylor's Scientific Management as ways of forcing factory workers on assembly-lines to function like machines (Rabinbach 1992).

Kern (1983) shows that from the 1880s to World War I, the sense of living in a world so dominated by system and calculation evoked a reaction in writers and artists. Freud, Proust, Bergson and Joyce explored how the standardised flow of abstract time failed to match the varying speed of its passage as subjectively experienced. Cubism in early twentieth-century art amounted to a rejection of the 'rules' of perspective painting. Motion pictures enabled film-makers to exploit flash-backs and alternation between simultaneous sequences of events in different locations. Einstein's relativity theories undermined trust in the absolute space and time of the Newtonian universe. Kern sees all these innovations as responses to the apparent constriction imposed by the standardised time-space grid.

A clock-face is a visual display showing elapsed time. Maps and globes display geographical information visually. Musical notation, developed in the early Middle Ages (Lawson 2010; Treitler 2003) was a novel means of representing sounds in a visible format, introduced for the sake of enabling younger monks to master the repertoire of chants used year by year more quickly than had been possible when learning by ear. In this sense it was a form of literacy. Though not measurement in a numerical sense, it encouraged awareness of the numerically designated ratios associated in ancient Greek theorising with musical harmony. The art of keeping systematic accounts was also a form of literacy, useful as a way to see quickly whether or not a business was prospering. As with perspective in painting, this skill began to be cultivated in Renaissance Italy. Weber (1922/2002) believed it to be a uniquely Western practice but

Goody (1996, 1997) contests that ethnocentric view. In the eighteenth and nineteenth centuries, agricultural improvers and writers of political economy began collecting statistics about farming, commerce and demography on an ever larger scale and displaying this information in a rapidly assimilated form in order to guide the formulation of public policy (De Bruyn 2004; Porter 1986; 2004). By the early twentieth century, health reformers and educationalists were applying statistical analysis to data concerning children's height, physical health and IQ test scores (Brown 1992; Turmel 2008).

Our first reading, by Woodward, considers the intention behind medieval representations of the world that showed no regard for the consistency of scale later introduced with the rediscovery of latitude and longitude in the fifteenth century. It is questionable whether 'map' is the appropriate translation of the Latin word *mappa* in this context, since the main purpose of these *mappaemundi* was to illustrate sacred history rather than to guide travellers. Studies amplifying Woodward's argument include Edson (2010), Harvey (1996), Kline (2001) and Westrem (2001). The origin of the myth that medieval people imagined the earth to be flat is explored in Russell (1991).

Glennie and Thrift offer a critique of the claim made by Thompson (1967) that it was in the early period of factory-production that people began to pay constant attention to clock-time. They discuss how people have experienced time during the centuries since the invention of mechanical clocks. The authors argue that there have been different ways of experiencing clock-time and that people in different contexts have used clocks and watches for different purposes (Styles 2008). But different practices of time-keeping have coexisted and meshed with each other. To trace this meshing, it is important to establish when it was that reference to clock-time became widespread. They construct a richer account of the history of clock-time than any 'grand narrative' can provide.

Alder's book, from which our third extract is taken, tells how France came to adopt the metre and the litre as standard units, and why the abolition of the old measures was resisted. (In England too there was popular resentment when measures of volume traditional in one locality were replaced by a standard that seemed alien: see Sheldon *et al.* 1996.) The trust between buyers and sellers required for commerce to thrive had under the *ancien régime* been underpinned by the confidence people had in local customs that varied from one community to another. Local measures were enforced by local officials. To use them meant participating in a way of life shared by people known to each other through ongoing face-to-face relationships. The new weights and measures adopted by politicians in Paris derived from an abstract mentality that failed to engage with these local loyalties to tradition. This is why they were resisted.

References

Brown, J. (1992) *The Definition of a Profession: the authority of metaphor in the history of intelligence testing 1890–1930*, Princeton: Princeton University Press.

Crosby, A.W. (1997) *The Measure of Reality: quantification and Western society 1250–1600*, Cambridge: Cambridge University Press.

De Bruyn, F. (2004) 'From Georgic poetry to statistics and graphs: eighteenth-century representations and the "State" of British society', *Yale Journal of Criticism*, 17: 107–39.

Dohrn-van Rossum, G. (1996) *History of the Hour: clocks and modern temporal orders*, Chicago: University of Chicago Press.

Edgerton, S.Y., Jr. (1975) *The Renaissance Rediscovery of Linear Perspective*, New York, NY: Basic Books.

Edson, E. (2010) 'The medieval world view: contemplating the *mappamundi*', *History Compass*, 8: 503–17.

Gooday, G. (2004) *The Morals of Measurement: accuracy, irony and trust in late Victorian electrical practice*, Cambridge: Cambridge University Press.

Goody, J. (1996) *The East in the West*, Cambridge: Cambridge University Press.

Goody, J. (1997) 'The East in the West', *European Journal of Sociology*, 38: 171–84.

Hart, R. (2000) 'The great explanandum', *American Historical Review*, 105: 486–93.

Harvey, D. (1989) *The Condition of Postmodernity: an enquiry into the origins of cultural change*, Oxford: Blackwell.

Harvey, P.D.A. (1996) *Mappa Mundi: the Hereford world map*, Toronto: University of Toronto Press.

Kern, S. (1983) *The Culture of Time and Space, 1880–1918*, Cambridge, MA: Harvard University Press.

Kline, N.R. (2001) *Maps of Medieval Thought: the Hereford paradigm*, Woodbridge: Boydell Press.

Latour, B. (1987) 'Centres of calculation', in *Science in Action: how to follow scientists and engineers through society*, Cambridge, MA: Harvard University Press.

Law, J. (1986) 'On the methods of long-distance control: vessels, navigation and the Portuguese route to India', in Law (ed.) *Power, Action and Belief*, London: Routledge.

Lawson, F.R.S. (2010) 'Rethinking the orality-literacy paradigm in musicology', *Oral Tradition*, 25: 1–18.

Mayr, O. (1986) *Authority, Liberty and Automatic Machinery in Early Modern Europe*, Baltimore, MD: Johns Hopkins University Press.

Porter, T.M. (1986) *The Rise of Statistical Thinking, 1820–1900*, Princeton, NJ: Princeton University Press.

Porter, T.M. (2004) 'The culture of quantification and the history of public reason', *Journal of the History of Economic Thought*, 26: 165–77.

Rabinbach, A. (1992) *The Human Motor: energy, fatigue and the origins of modernity*, Berkeley, CA: University of California Press.

Russell, J.B. (1991) *Inventing the Flat Earth: Columbus and modern historians*, New York, NY: Praeger.

Sheldon, R., Randall, A., Charlesworth, A. and Walsh, D. (1996) 'Popular protest and the persistence of customary corn measures: resistance to the Winchester bushel in the English West', in A. Randall and A. Charlesworth (eds) *Markets, Market Culture and Popular Protest in Eighteenth-Century Britain and Ireland*, Liverpool: Liverpool University Press.

Smith, C. and Wise, M.N. (1989) *Energy and Empire: a biographical study of Lord Kelvin*, Cambridge: Cambridge University Press.

Styles, J. (2008) 'Time piece: working men and watches', *History Today*, 58.1: 44–50.

Thompson, E.P. (1967) 'Time, work-discipline and industrial capitalism', *Past & Present*, 38: 56–97.

Thomson, William [later Lord Kelvin] (1889) 'Electrical units of measurement', in *Popular Lectures and Addresses, vol. 1*, London: Macmillan & Co.

Treitler, L. (2003) 'The early history of music writing in the West', in Treitler, *With Voice and Pen: coming to know medieval song and how it was made*, Oxford: Oxford University Press.

Turmel, A. (2008) *A Historical Sociology of Childhood: developmental thinking, categorization and graphic visualization*, Cambridge: Cambridge University Press.

Weber, M. (1922/2002) *The Protestant Ethic and the 'Spirit' of Capitalism and other writings,* trans. P. Baehr and G.C. Wells, London: Penguin Books.

Westrem, S. (2001) *The Hereford Map: a transcription and translation of the legends with commentary,* Turnhout: Brepols.

Wise, M.N. (ed.) (1995) *The Values of Precision,* Princeton: Princeton University Press.

Chapter 7

David Woodward

REALITY, SYMBOLISM, TIME AND SPACE IN MEDIEVAL WORLD MAPS

MEDIEVAL WORLD MAPS, or *mappaemundi* as they are frequently called, form a well-defined genre of maps that have received only spasmodic attention from geographers. Some 1,100 maps, mostly in manuscript codices of the eighth to the fifteenth centuries, still survive. They are usually schematic in form, and fall into several subcategories depending on their historical origin and their graphic structure. Rooted in both the Hellenistic and Roman traditions, they were adapted by the early leaders and scholars of the Christian Church. To the extent that they embody both scriptural and classical sources, their meaning reflects the changing emphases of medieval thought.[1]

The *mappaemundi* carry levels of meaning that have been completely misunderstood. In the nineteenth century, when systematic studies of these maps first appeared, they were interpreted in light of the view that maps (to be *true* maps) were intended to show geographical reality structured according to a coordinate system, such as longitude and latitude. These nineteenth-century writers also oversimplified and underestimated medieval thinkers' understanding of the physical world; this is reflected in the frequently repeated views that most medieval scholars thought the earth was flat or that Jerusalem should be shown at its center. Some of these misunderstandings arose from a tendency to regard the culture of the Middle Ages as essentially static. *Mappaemundi* were thus gathered into only one category, the T-in-O model, so often reproduced in general histories of geography and cartography. Also contributing to this lack of understanding of medieval cartography was the apparent obliviousness to the technical and conceptual constraints on scribes and artists of the period: the media, tools, and techniques, and a failure to relate such structural concepts as perspective and projection to the mapmaking of the period.

This paper seeks to examine the validity of these commonly held views of *mappaemundi* in the light of recent reinterpretations made in art history and the history of cartography. Its aim is to show that the intention of the compilers of these maps was as much historical as geographical and that the resulting documents blended concepts of both time and space as a context for understanding the Christian life. By examining the development of such concepts as the flat earth with Jerusalem at its center, the paper also seeks to demonstrate that these maps cannot be considered as a single category spanning a thousand years of medieval history. Finally, I suggest that, in the light of these documents, our modern view of maps may need adjusting. It is now fully accepted that maps need not necessarily show only Euclidean space. Perhaps we need also to consider the idea that a map does not by its nature have to represent a cosynchronous scene but may be a many-layered cumulation of historical events as well as objects in geographical space.

Since *mappaemundi* are better understood when their variation is recognized, it is convenient to describe four main categories: tripartite, zonal, quadripartite, and transitional; typical examples of each are illustrated in Figures 7.1–4.[2] The tripartite map type consists of a disk representing the inhabited world (O), within which is a tripartite schema (T) oriented to the east with Asia taking up the upper half of the circle, Europe the lower left quarter, and Africa the lower right quarter (Fig. 7.1). The parts of the T represent the three major hydrographic features known to divide the three parts of the earth: Tanais (the Don River) dividing Europe and Asia, the Nile dividing Africa and Asia, and the Mediterranean Sea dividing Europe and Africa. The genre is rooted in a classical tradition, and it is conjectured that the earliest tripartite maps accompanied manuscripts of the *De Bello Jurgurthino* of Gaius Sallustius Crispus (Sallust) (86–34 B.C.).

The zonal category is characterized by orientation to the north or south and by the representation of the Greek *climata* in five climatic zones that follow parallels of latitude (Fig. 7.2). Its prototype is derived from the cosmographical section (ch. 5–8 of Book 2) in Macrobius's early fifth-century A.D. commentary on Cicero's *Dream of Scipio* (51 B.C.), which in turn derived its cosmography from Eratosthenes (c. 275–194 B.C.), Posidonius (c. 151–35 B.C.), Serapion of Antiochea (second or first century B.C.), Crates of Mallos (c. 168 B.C.) and, ultimately from a Pythagorean concept.

Intermediate between the tripartite and the zonal categories of *mappaemundi* is a third category, the quadripartite, which contains maps bearing the characteristics of each. Though these are not numerous, they are sufficiently distinctive and influential to warrant separate treatment. Within their circular, oval, or rectangular shapes oriented to the east, there is an

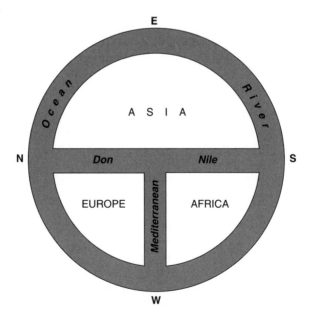

Fig. 7.1 Category 1: T-O map. Schematic drawing of the tripartite world divided among the sons of Noah. Asia represented the home of the Semitic peoples, Europe the Japhetic, and Africa the Hamitic.

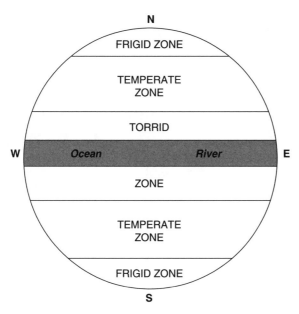

Fig. 7.2 Category 2: Zonal map. Schematic drawing of the
system of five climatic zones, derived from a model of the
ancient Greek geographers.

"ocean river" that divides the known tripartite world from the fourth part, unknown on
account of the sun's heat, but inhabited by the Antipodeans (Fig. 7.3). The maps are believed
to stem from one lost eighth-century prototype of Beatus of Liebana in his *Commentary on the
Apocalypse of St. John* in which he stressed the mandate of the Apostles to travel in all parts of
the earth to preach the Gospel.

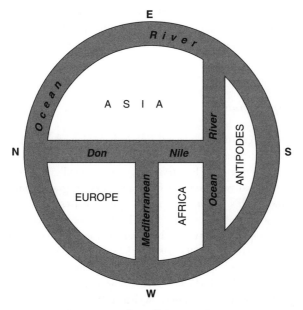

Fig. 7.3 Category 3: Quadripartite map. Schematic drawing of
the combination of the tripartite world with the fourth part—
inhabited by Antipodeans—separated by an "ocean river."

Fig. 7.4 Category 4: Transitional map. Schematic drawing of a fifteenth-century *mappamundi*. The outlines of the Mediterranean Sea are based on portolan charts, while the rest of the map retains the traditional circular frame.

The fourth category, which is transitional between the medieval and Renaissance periods, reflects the profound change in *mappaemundi* that took place in the fourteenth and fifteenth centuries. These maps differ fundamentally from the zonal or tripartite models of the late Roman world, and belong in many ways to the spirit of the Renaissance, having as their basis the configuration of the Mediterranean Sea commonly found in the portolan charts and relying in some degree on the contemporary recording of exploration, especially the Portuguese voyages to the Atlantic islands and along the west coast of Africa (Fig. 7.4).

Realism and *Mappaemundi*

From the late-nineteenth century on, several authors have viewed the *mappaemundi* primarily as bearers of locational information, a function no different from other classes of maps in the Middle Ages or any other period. The surviving corpus of medieval world maps have been seen therefore as a marked retrogression from an expected gradual improvement in the representation of the earth's features on maps. Thus Charles Beazley, in his otherwise fundamentally useful work, was able to write: "The non-scientific maps of the later Middle Ages . . . are of such complete futility . . . that a bare allusion to the monstrosities of *Hereford* and *Ebstorf* should suffice" (Beazley 1897–1906, 3:528).

A comparison between two medieval maps made within a few decades of each other lends superficial support to Beazley's view. The *mappamundi* known as the Hereford Map (c. 1290) and the earliest known dated portolan chart by Pietro Vesconte (1311) both feature the Mediterranean Sea prominently, but the positional accuracy of the Vesconte map is clearly superior to that of the Hereford Map, as Figure 7.5 demonstrates. This assessment should be modified in several significant ways, however. The first involves studying the

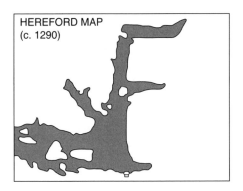 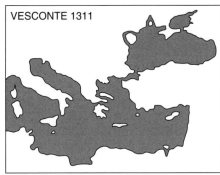

Fig. 7.5. Diagram comparing the eastern part of the Mediterranean Sea as shown on the Hereford Map (c. 1290) (left) and a portolan chart by Pietro Vesconte dated 1311 (right).

mappamundi on its own terms, according to its intended function and in the context of the scriptorium in which it was compiled. This view was forcefully expressed by John K. Wright, who developed the theme—echoed by Kimble—that the lack of geometrical accuracy in the *mappaemundi* did not necessarily warrant criticism, as this attribute was not the primary goal of this genre of map (Wright 1925, 248; Kimble 1938, 181).

We should not assume, however, that there was no interest in geographical location by the compilers of these maps but that there were certain prescribed constraints within which they had to work. The rare account of how to make a *mappamundi* by Hugh of St. Victor in his *On the Mystical Noah's Ark* provides an example of the kind of framework into which geographical information could be fitted:

> The perfect ark is circumscribed with an oblong circle, which touches each of its corners, and the space which the circumference includes represents the earth. In this space, a world map is depicted in this fashion: the front of the ark faces the east, and the rear faces the west. . . . In the apex to the east formed between the circle and the head of the ark is Paradise. . . . In the other apex, which juts out to the west, is the Last Judgment with the chosen to the right, and the reprobates to the left. In the northern corner of this apex is Hell, where the damned are thrown with the apostate spirits (Migne 1844–64. vol. 176, col. 700).

The bounding shape of the *mappamundi*, whether circular, oval, or rectangular, was thus predetermined by biblical or classical tradition. Into this space were arranged the features deemed significant for the reader. As we might expect, the scale for that part of the map of primary interest was frequently larger . . . . Matthew Paris's well-known explanation of distortion on his map of Britain demonstrates that there was a conscious awareness that scale could be conveniently adjusted within certain constraints: "if the page had allowed it, this whole island would have been longer" (Vaughan 1968, 243).

This does not mean that the importance of current geographical content was always ignored. Using the Hereford Map as an example, Crone has demonstrated that lists of place-names from written itineraries were incorporated into the map. Though its size (163 × 135 cm) clearly precluded its use as a *vade mecum* for actual journeys (for which written itineraries, pilgrim guides, and verbal directions might well have served), it is perhaps likely that the Hereford map and the other large thirteenth-century wall maps could have fulfilled a practical didactic purpose in developing the confidence or stimulating the imagination of intended travelers, for which recognizable content was desirable (Crone 1965).

For this purpose of spiritual education, however, more was required of the *mappamundi* than a modicum of current geography. The maps needed also to be imbued with the richness of the Christian historical tradition. It is thus also important to realize that the *mappaemundi* were not snapshots of the world's geography at a given point in time, but a blending of history and geography, a projection of historical events on a geographical framework. This point was made by Bevan and Phillott (1873) in a preliminary way, but a full illustration of this theme was to await the careful studies of G. R. Crone (1954, 1965), again with reference to the Hereford Map. Crone demonstrated with minute documentation that the Hereford Map was a complex blending of Greek, Roman, and Christian sources and traced its pedigree back to the late fourth and early fifth centuries A.D. As the interest in *mappaemundi* has grown in recent years—aided in part by the publication of a catalogue of these documents (Destombes 1964)—several historians and art historians have turned their attention to the maps, particularly in the context of the relationship between text and graphic images in medieval writing and painting (Ruberg 1980, 551–92). Most painters assume that the border of their work encloses a cosynchronous space, but narrative painting, in which a story is illustrated by showing several stages of a narrative side by side within the same frame, has a long history. . . . In medieval popular narrative illustrations, particularly of biblical stories, several events separated by time are portrayed in the same scene, not in sequence as in a frieze or cartoon, but placed in their appropriate positions in the scene. The chief characters thus reappear in a static landscape to express the dimension of time (Pächt 1962, 2; Hindman 1977, 38).

The *mappaemundi* are the cartographic equivalent of narrative medieval pictures. The thirteenth-century author of the Hereford Map even refers to his graphic work as a "history" on the map itself: "All who have this history. . . ." This usage is still supported by one definition of history as a "pictorial representation of an event or series of incidents," supported by the use of the word "historiated" to mean "decorated with figures" (*Oxford English Dictionary*, 1961 ed., s.v. "historiated"). This theme has been developed extensively by von den Brincken where the *mappaemundi* are seen as syncretic pictorial chronicles parallel to the textual chronicles from St. Jerome to Hartmann Schedel (von den Brincken 1968, 118). Juergen Schulz has applied this idea of the didactic moralized map to art history, focusing particularly on city views in the late-medieval period and the Renaissance.

> Cartographic historians are agreed that the main function of these maps was the representation of religious mysteries and history, rather than the recording of precise geographical facts. They never pause, however, to explain this aspect of the medieval map, which is irrelevant to their main concern, the growth of geographical knowledge. For the historian of art, by contrast, it is precisely this didactic tradition, its range in time and content, that is of primary interest (Schulz 1978, 446).

The sources of historical and geographical information on the *mappaemundi* were both classical and biblical—the commemoration of famous events and places being sometimes inseparable, with the Old Testament rather than the New more frequently represented. Though early Judaism emphasized the importance of an event's location, the earliest Christians showed little interest—with some important exceptions—in the exact location of even their most sacred events (North 1979, 76). The teachings of Christ emphasized the spiritual and not the physical world; for example, in response to the question of whether to build a shrine at Gerizim or Jerusalem, Christ's answer was to be less concerned with the location than with the motivation of the proposed action (John 4, 19–24). . . .

The early leaders of the Church, in reaction to the classical philosophers, were also anxious to point out that the knowledge of information about the earth was of strictly secondary importance to the Christian, whose mind should be on a higher spiritual plane. Thus, in characterizing a true believer, St. Augustine was able to say, "a faithful man . . . although he knows not the circles of the Great Bear, is much better than another who can weigh out the elements and number the stars and measure the skies" (Augustine 1965, 5:4).

The functions of medieval *mappaemundi* can thus be regarded as being on a different plane from those of the portolan charts or estate maps of the same period. As teaching rather than locational devices, they relied on mystical, symbolic, and allegorical imagery to a remarkable extent. The spiritual history of the Christian world, from its Creation to the Last Judgment, with a sequence of divinely planned events in between, such as the Salvation by Jesus Christ, are all carefully portrayed—in more or less detail—on the *mappaemundi*.

The threefold division of the world in the T-O maps represents the peopling of the earth in the three continents by each of Noah's sons. The families of Shem (the eldest son having the maximum share—or Asia—in the tripartite scheme), Ham (Africa), and Japheth (Europe) are often depicted or listed on these maps. This traditional division is the source for the naming of the three great groups of peoples in the Old World: the Semitic, Hamitic, and Japhetic. . . .

With all these considerations, it is inadvisable to compare the geographical accuracy of the *mappaemundi* with that of contemporary or later map types, such as the portolan charts or the great wall maps of the Renaissance. The history of cartography, like the history of science, is moving away from being primarily a search for precursors to an attempt to understand the developments in various periods on their own terms. For *mappaemundi* this means studying them not primarily as repositories of then current geographical knowledge (although a modicum of such information may sometimes be obtained from nowhere else) but as illustrated histories or moralized, didactic displays in a geographical setting. . . .

It was only after the strengthening of the idea of Jerusalem as the spiritual center, a natural outcome of the Crusades, that a noticeable shift occurred toward centering the maps on Jerusalem. This then becomes a characteristic of the fourth category, the transitional, from the end of the thirteenth century to about the mid-fifteenth century, when new discoveries extended the margins of the world map and the center moved accordingly. . . .

The Flat Earth

The question of the extent of the understanding of the earth's sphericity in the Middle Ages is confounded by several factors, summarized by several recent authors (Randles 1980; Tattersall 1981). As we have discussed, the medieval period consists of several entirely different sub-periods and it is unwise to assume that the views of a few individuals can be extended to the period as a whole. Even in the earliest period, however, despite the various difficulties of biblical interpretation, most early Church leaders held to the classical concept of the spherical earth, and Augustine specifically mentions it at least twice (Augustine 1965, 5:51). The most popular of the late Roman secular writers—Pliny, Macrobius, and Martianus Capella—also made unequivocal references to its spherical shape. It was perhaps in overreaction to these works that Severianus and Lactantius, who denied on principle that anything "pagan" could be accurate, included the spherical earth in their sweeping condemnation of the pagan writings (Jones 1934). But it must still be said that their writings were not to have the influence of the greater Church Fathers and that the importance of their views has thus probably been exaggerated on account of their controversial nature. . . .

The views of the common populace on the issue are of course barely recorded. There is some evidence from the cosmographical content of the vernacular epics and romances of the twelfth and thirteenth centuries designed for the everyday person that many thought of the earth as a disk (Tattersall 1981, 46). But the interpretation of the word "round" in these poems as either circular or spherical is fraught with confusion, and the similes of "apple" and "ball"—frequently used in these works—would seem to lend more credence to a common view of the earth's sphericity, even before 1300. . . .

Whatever the confusion about the general medieval views of the earth's shape, there is no reason to believe that the best-known form of *mappamundi,* the T-O map, with its tripartite division of the inhabited world and the surrounding ocean river, was prima facie evidence for universal medieval belief in a flat earth. . . . Despite the achievements of the thirteenth-century philosopher Roger Bacon, who had a clear idea of the value of using a systematic coordinate system to transform and inventory the positions of places and who described a systematic projection, there was no general understanding in Christian Europe of the way to represent a spherical surface on a plane until that knowledge—preserved in the *Geography* of Claudius Ptolemy—was revealed through translation at the beginning of the fifteenth century. . . .

Later Christian writers not only specifically accepted the sphericity of the earth, but provided explicit reasons for their view. Thus the Venerable Bede (672/3–735) explained that the cause of the unequal length of the days lay in the globular shape of the earth, describing it as not only "round like a shield, but also in every direction, like a playground ball" (Bede 1843–44, 210).

In the later Middle Ages, the most influential commentators agreed that the earth was spherical. The writings of Aristotle, with his elegant three-part proof of the sphericity of the earth, or the astronomical and geographical work of Ptolemy, for which the concept was essential, had found their way into the West as the channels of classical and Arabic learning became opened after the twelfth century. In the fourteenth and fifteenth centuries—despite the myth still perpetuated in some school history texts of Columbus, the common navigator, valiantly defending the idea of the globe before the learned clergy[3]—there would have remained little doubt in the mind of the medieval scholar that, in Gautier de Metz's words, "a man could go around the world as a fly makes the tour of an apple" (Caxton 1913, 52).

The limitations of the two-dimensional medium of the *mappaemundi* and the lack of a clear concept of projective geometry and perspective appear to have contributed to the belief that they represented a flat, disk-shaped earth. But since the overriding purpose of these maps—as narrative histories—was not to convey facts about the size and shape of the earth except where they bore directly on the Christian mission, they can hardly be criticized for not reflecting the philosophical thought of the time.

Conclusion

What can we learn from challenging the oft-repeated misconceptions concerning medieval world maps? In the first place, it underlines the need, now recognized by medieval historians, to evaluate the achievements of the Middle Ages on their own terms and in the context of their purpose. The function of the *mappaemundi* was primarily to provide a visual narrative of Christian history cast in a geographical framework, not to communicate geographical or cosmographical facts. They thus represent an entirely different cartographic tradition and should therefore not be ridiculed on the grounds that they appeared as retrogressions to an ever-improving literal geographical picture of the world. Nor can the disk-shaped appearance in many of these maps be taken literally to reflect a general belief in a flat earth. As we have seen, this was probably not the prevailing opinion among those (admittedly not a great number) who cared about the issue.

Second, by exaggerating the spread of time depicted within their borders, the *mappaemundi* also demonstrate that maps in general need not be seen as reflecting only spatial realities and perceptions or pictures of the earth stopped at a given moment in time. They may also consist of historical aggregations or cumulative inventories of events that occur in space. For the *mappaemundi*, this meant a curious mélange of both Christian and secular legendary history. Even the practice of placing Jerusalem at the center of the *mappaemundi* overcame the weight of the classical secular tradition only at the very end of the medieval period.

Notes

1   This paper reports preliminary research for a chapter on medieval *mappaemundi* prepared for a larger work edited by Harley and Woodward (forthcoming). Other issues involving the *mappaemundi* and full references will be found in that work. For recently published general studies, see Ruberg (1980) and Arentzen (1984).

2   There have been several attempts at classifying *mappaemundi*, as in the standard catalogue of medieval world maps edited by Destombes (1964). The classification proposed here is explained further in Harley and Woodward (forthcoming).

3   This myth was greatly expanded by Washington Irving in his biography of Columbus. See Morison (1942, 1: 117).

References

Arentzen, Jörg-Geerd. 1984. *Imago mundi cartographica. Studien zur Bildlichkeit mittelalterlicher Welt- und Ökumenekarten unter besonderer Berücksichtigung des Zusammenwirkens von Text und Bild.* Münstersche Mittelalter-Schriften 53. Munich: Wilhelm Fink Verlag.

Augustine, St. 1965. *De civitate dei of St. Augustine,* 7 vols., trans. Eva Matthews Sanford and William McAllen Green. Cambridge, Mass.: Harvard University Press.

Beazley, C. Raymond. 1897–1906. *The dawn of modern geography: A history of exploration and geographical science from the conversion of the Roman Empire to A.D. 900.* 3 vols. London: J. Murray.

Bede, the Venerable. 1843–44. *The complete works of Venerable Bede.* Vol. 6, *De temporum ratione,* trans. John Allen Giles. 12 vols. London: Whittaker and Co.

Bevan, W. L., and Phillott, H. W. 1873. *Medieval geography: An essay in illustration of the Hereford mappa mundi.* London: E. Stanford.

Caxton, William. 1913. *Mirrour of the world.* Early English Text Society, Extra Series 110. London: Kegan, Paul, Trench, Trübner and Co.

Crone, Gerald R. 1954. *The world map by Richard of Haldingham in Hereford Cathedral.* Reproductions of Early Manuscript Maps 3. London: Royal Geographical Society.

Crone Gerald R. 1965. New light on the Hereford map. *Geographical Journal* 131: 447–62.

Destombes, Marcel, ed. 1964. *Mappemondes A. D. 1200–1500: catalogue préparé par la Commission des Cartes Anciennes de l'Union Géographique Internationale.* Amsterdam: N. Israel.

Harley, J. B., and Woodward, David, eds [1987]. *The history of cartography.* Vol. 1, *Cartography in prehistoric, ancient, and medieval Europe and the Mediterranean.* Chicago: University of Chicago Press.

Hindman, Sandra. 1977. *Text and image in fifteenth-century illustrated Dutch Bibles.* Leiden: E. J. Brill.

Jones, Charles W. 1934. The flat earth. *Thought* 9: 296–307.

Kimble, George H. T. 1938. *Geography in the Middle Ages.* New York: Russell and Russell.

Migne, Jacques Paul. 1844–64. *Patrologia latina.* 221 vols. Paris.

Morison, Samuel Eliot. 1942. *Admiral of the Ocean Sea: A life of Christopher Columbus.* Boston: Little, Brown and Co.

North, Robert. 1979. *A history of biblical map making.* Beihefte zum Tübinger Atlas des Vörderen Orients, ser. B, no. 3. Wiesbaden: Ludwig Reichert Verlag.

Pächt, Otto. 1962. *The rise of pictorial narrative in twelfth-century England.* Oxford: Clarendon Press.

Randles, W. G. L. 1980. *De la terre plate au globe terrestre: Une mutation épistemologique rapide (1480–1520).* Cahiers des Annales 38. Paris: Librairie Armand Colin.

Ruberg, Uwe. 1980. Mappae Mundi des Mittelalters in Zusammenwirken von Text und Bild. In *Text und Bild: Aspekte des Zusammenwirkens zweier Kunste in Mittelalter und früher Neuzeit,* ed. Christel Meier and Uwe Ruberg. Wiesbaden: Ludwig Reichert Verlag.

Schulz, Juergen. 1978. Jacopo de' Barbari's view of Venice: Map making, city views, and moralized geography before the year 1500. *Art Bulletin* 60: 425–74.

Tattersall, Jill. 1981. Sphere or disc? Allusions to the shape of the earth in some twelfth-century and thirteenth-century vernacular French works. *Modern Language Review* 76: 31–46.

Vaughan, Richard. 1968. *Matthew Paris.* Cambridge: Cambridge University Press.

von den Brincken, Anna-Dorothee. 1968. Mappa mundi und Chronographia. *Deutsches Archiv für die Erforschung des Mittelalters* 24: 118–86.

Wright, John Kirtland. 1925. *The geographical lore of the time of the Crusades: A study in the history of medieval science and tradition in western Europe.* New York: American Geographical Society.

Chapter 8

Paul Glennie and Nigel Thrift

THE SPACES OF CLOCK TIMES

Introduction

WE STARTED TO WORK on the book that is now called *The Measured Heart* [*Shaping the Day* (Glennie and Thrift 2009)] more than ten years ago through one of those fortuitous coincidences that characterize academic life: we happened to bump into each other on the stairs and both – rather grumpily – expressed our mutual amazement at a statement made by E. P. Thompson in his then latest book – *Customs in Common* (1991) – which found Thompson arguing that since his seminal 1967 article 'Time, work-discipline and industrial capitalism', 'while interesting new work has been done on the question of time, none of it seemed to call for any major revision of my article' (viii).

We therefore decided to embark upon just such a major revision – using the interesting new work which had been done on the question of time. In this task we were aided by another fortunate coincidence. For, at about this time, a whole raft of work which had been going on in the social sciences was coming to fruition, a way of understanding the constitution of societies which we might call 'lighter touch' (see e.g. Dosse 1999; Thrift 1996, 2000). Instead of conceiving of societies as stamped out by social structures through a set of more or less formal correspondences, this way of understanding conceives of societies as loose formations of practices which are alignments of the human and nonhuman translated into particular kinds of engagement with the world. Instead of conceiving of societies as just remorseless circuits of social reproduction, this way of understanding conceives of society as a set of flickering horizons of 'experience' in a state of continual becoming without any resolution. . . .

Clock time, by its nature, is not much remarked upon. It is all but extra-archival. Witnesses are silent. Records rarely exist. In particular, we wanted to know how clocks were used in the practices of everyday life. On this aspect of clock time witnesses seemed all but mute. The extant literature surmounts this problem by a mixture of ungrounded anecdote, literary sources which are nearly all heavily rhetorical, and consequently need greater care of interpretation than they have usually received, and a few generalities gleaned from Thompson – and le Goff and Landes – which echo endlessly around, often seeming to confirm one another. To counter this tendency, we had to invest large amounts of time in work in the primary sources, of which the most important have been: probate inventories, court depositions, churchwardens, parish and borough accounts, directories, diaries and journals, newspapers, and antiquarian compilations.

In this paper, we want to problematize writing on clock times by considering some of the practices of clock time. Notice straightaway the focus on practices: we are interested less in what is meant by actions – an approach with too many humanistic resonances – than in what actions do. We are particularly interested in *everyday* practices, the accumulation of small differences upon which larger events often hang. . . .

It is received wisdom in the contemporary literature on time that time is heterogeneous, the composite effect of many different networks doing many different things to many different drums. However less attention is given to how these multiple times interdigitate, echoing backward and forward amongst each other. That they do is usually simply taken for granted. Yet our research on many of the networks that employed clocks in the period between 1300 and 1800 suggested not only that clocks were being used in many different ways – from the increasingly precise timekeeping required by the Royal Navy (driven by an ecology of devices as diverse as sandglasses, chip logs and quadrants) to the carefully judged procedures of many industries – but that these networks were also being brought together temporally in three ways. To begin with, the sheer density of clocks should not be underestimated. We estimate the number of clocks in England in c.1700 as approaching 200,000 (comprising between 3,000 and 5,000 'public' clocks on churches, town and market halls, exchanges, gates and almshouses; plus over 150,000 'private' domestic clocks and watches; plus several thousand clocks inside 'quasi-public' buildings, such as inns, alehouses, meeting rooms, workplaces, and suchlike).

Then, there were increasingly effective discourses concerning the importance of exactitude which give a boost to the cause of clock time across a number of social arenas. These values of precision, and a corresponding trust in representations of exactness, like number, become general. The values of precision took a variety of forms, from a growing trust in number; to a more general fascination with numbers and notions of numerical representation with roots as varied as science, astrology, religion and trade; and to new uses of calculation in play, as well as in 'serious' activities. . . . Clock time itself, of course, implies space – the spaces of local time, mean time, acceleration, and so on. Clock time also gains its power from its ability to coordinate and time quite different spaces. And clock time is concerned with the labour required to move from one position to another. That each hour, minute and second comes to seem as though it does not have to be negotiated but simply slides by, is the result of the density of intermediaries (Latour 1997).

In order to cope with the sameness of this variety, and the variety of this sameness, we therefore gradually distilled our thoughts into three main areas of enquiry into the history of clock time (Figure 8.1). The first of these forms of enquiry is discourses, especially of measurement and precision. The second line of enquiry is spaces, most especially urban spaces in which various networks are forced together and become tightly knit, so sharing the same times. The third line of enquiry is particular communities of practice, communities within which clock time is used in specific ways to specific ends. In turn, each of these three lines of enquiry has been passed through three different elements of clock time. First, and most obviously, there is the 'ecology of devices' (Hutchins 1995) through which discourses, spaces and communities of practice were 'timed'. These would be very varied, including not only clocks but also all manner of other timekeeping devices – sundials, pocket dials, sandglasses, bells, astrolabes, and so on. Second, there were the embodied practices which increasingly incorporated clock time. As practices as diverse as music, dance, military drill, and a host of other activities began to bow to clock time, so we are able to see clock time being literally incorporated into everyday bodily stances and gaits. Then, third, there are

	Ecology of DEVICES	Embodied PRACTICES	Timekeeping SKILLS
DISCOURSES of measurement and precision			
Urban SPACES (multiple communities)			
COMMUNITIES of practice			

Fig. 8.1 Components of this research project.

skills. We consistently looked for evidence of differential timekeeping skills in the devices, space and communities of practice we examined. Each of the skills of time is distributed in communities like a map; not everyone knows them equally or practices them equally well. This is not just a matter of experience, but of talent and aptitude. There are limits to the degree to which drills can compensate for, for example, lack of dexterity.

Practices of everyday time

In the remainder of this paper, we will try to follow through some of these points by summarizing some of the material provided in much greater length and detail in the forthcoming book. It is not our aim here to provide more than a set of indications of the arguments we make and the kinds of material that we have gathered. But we hope to communicate at least a flavour of our approach and findings by considering, first, our work on clock times in Bristol; second, how many and what kind of timekeeping devices were available; and third, the means by which various forms of clock time precision were 'translated' between communities.

Places as complexes of temporal communities

In this first section we mainly call on material from our study of clock times in Bristol from the middle ages to the late eighteenth century. Throughout the period, the city accommodated numerous overlapping sets of people using clock times in the conduct of various activities. Some of these were the sorts of activities familiar from the literature on time discipline: the conduct of Christian life, ranging from the daily timetables of the numerous mediaeval religious houses, to the timing of services and celebrations in some eighteen parish churches; the regulation of trading at markets and wharves, with rights to buy confined to household, retail customers until after a given time had been signalled, and the like; the restriction of production to set hours, either as part of protecting craft guild monopolies, or because of genuine concerns with the quality of goods produced outside daylight hours; and attempts to maintain public order through curfews, control of alehouse opening hours, and so forth.

Other uses of clock time were also disciplinary, but are much less prominent in the previous literature: clock time played an important role in both grammar and elementary schools from at least the early fifteenth century (obviously, long before E. P. Thompson's emphasis on early nineteenth century schools as initiating the inculcation of clock time amongst children). Not only was the school day organized in terms of clock time, but significant elements of education, such as translation exercises, commonly included references to clock times and daily routines, in very matter-of-fact ways. Civic and county administration was another potent source of instructions couched in clock time, affecting not only the middling householders and local elites who sat on juries, but a much broader cross-section of the (male) population for musters, and similar occasions. Likewise, the organization of festivities and recreations frequently drew on clock times. In part, there was a public order dimension to large crowd events, whether wrestling matches, baitings, hangings, or the distribution of doles on civic holidays or parish anniversaries. From around 1550, the state-organized postal service required the endorsement of official communications with the time at which it passed through the hands of postmasters en route, in Bristol as in nearly two hundred other post-towns.

However, it would be grossly misleading to tie uses of clock time to disciplinary activities *per se*. A few examples will suffice. Very many small-scale and low-key leisure or recreational activities were arranged with reference to clock times. The entertainment of friends with celebratory meals on birthdays or anniversaries provides examples, as do funerals, and so too do meetings of clubs or societies, from angling clubs to meetings of literary and philosophical societies, from clubs of bell-ringers to those comprising natives of Cork. More generally, much informal face-to-face contact was arranged in terms of clock time, whether meetings to inspect or hand over goods, to pay debts or to settle wagers. After all, we would argue, it was precisely such personal contact which had most to gain from clock time: time and coordination were important for international merchants, but it's hard to argue that clock time was any less relevant to the latter than it was to lovers arranging a tryst, or a suitor meeting his prospective in-laws. Times appear quite regularly in connection with gambling: bets on horse racing, for example, concerning the time taken to ride a given course, not simply whether one horse would beat another. Clock times also frequently appear as an element in narrating accounts of events. Such accounts take various forms. Witnesses' depositions in court cases make ready use of clock times in describing how crucial events occurred, and to some extent temporal specificity seems to have been recognized as a potential indication of careful (and credible) evidence. But clock times are also found in several different types of letters, in autobiographical and biographical writings, and other descriptions which lacked a similar pressure to provide 'objective' indications of the truth of one's account. The use of clock times in giving accounts of births and deaths was especially entrenched, and appears in various sources and circumstances, as an integral part of the practice of thinking about those vital events; the timings of funerals are among the circumstances in which the earliest uses of words like 'precisely' and 'exactly' are used to emphasize clock times (the earliest evidence here being from the mid-seventeenth century).

We term the various usages of clock times (as practices which were deemed apposite in given circumstances) by larger or smaller groups of people, 'temporal communities of practice'. Some communities we see as highly specific (e.g. astronomers, astrologers, mathematicians), others as less narrow and quite strongly applied in orientation (e.g. mariners, the military, civic officials, shipowners, shoemakers), and others as very extensive indeed (e.g. 'the urban public'). Obviously, these communities are not mutually exclusive, and a person might be part of many such communities, both because of people's multiple activities as parts of different communities of practice, and because different communities shared interests (e.g. the shared interest of astronomers and mariners in navigation). . . .

Coherence among communities of practice was contingent rather than necessary. In other words, quite different practices co-existed, over long periods, in Bristol as elsewhere. Thus reckoning in unequal hours continued through the fourteenth and early fifteenth centuries, alongside growing use of mechanical clock-derived equal hours. One irony was that unequal hours continued in use for some prosaic purposes even after several religious buildings acquired mechanical clocks and adopted equal hours reckoning. Having originally made opportunistic use of church-based time-signals, they had acquired, as it were, a life of their own, as the ways in which other activities 'had come to be done'. So in contrast to the horological literature's search for 'the sense of time' in a given time and place, as a coherent whole, our point is that there was (normally) *no such thing*. Rather there were several coexisting practices of temporal reckoning, only some of which used clocks (and might use clocks in various different ways). This proliferation of practices meant that 'the sense of time', thought of as a whole, was rather less than the sum of its parts. . . .

Documenting the everyday

Exploring our view of the everyday public 'community' as relatively sophisticated with regard to clock time is considerably impeded by the dual problems identified previously: that such things were rarely committed to writing; and that in any case very little documentation has survived. Particularly acute here, and sharply brought out by an explicitly retrogressive approach, is that the range of documented activities narrows sharply as we move back from the eighteenth century. Evidence for early uses of clock time is dominated by official documentary sources of one sort or another, and they deal overwhelmingly, and in a normative way, with regulatory activity, whether prescriptive or the product of (in a broad sense) policing. So sixteenth-century uses of clock times appear mainly in disciplinary contexts, compared with the eighteenth century, but this largely mirrors the respective ranges of source materials for those times. As a result, considerable interpretative weight rests on a relatively limited volume of exceptional types of early material.

Here we briefly illustrate one element of the multi-stranded approach set out in the first part of the paper, namely the ecology of timekeeping devices, and the density of the temporal infrastructure. We can, of course, barely scratch the surface of the topic, but it is still worth asking: just how common were mechanical clocks, other clock-time keeping devices, and the skills involved in making, maintaining and (not least) 'reading' them?

Taking the numbers and distribution of timepieces as central to an ecology of devices, it needs straightaway to be emphasized that E. P. Thompson, whilst quite correctly recognizing the lack of information then available, nevertheless massively underestimated the density of the temporal infrastructure in several ways:

> It is by no means clear how far the availability of precise clock time extended at the start of the industrial revolution. . . . there were plenty of watches and clocks around by 1800. But it is not so clear who owned them.
> (Thompson 1967: 56–97)

Thompson was sceptical that pre-industrialization labouring people, or any but the 'best-paid' artisan, could have possessed timepieces, and hence lacked access to precise clock time. But

> the situation was changing in the last decades of the century. . . . There were a lot of timepieces about in the 1790s. . . . Indeed, a general diffusion of clocks and watches is occurring (as one would expect) at the exact moment when the industrial revolution demanded a greater synchronization of labour.
> (Thompson 1967: 56–97)

On the contrary, it is now clear that a very substantial 'general diffusion of clocks' had occurred between 150 and 200 years earlier. This involved households of widely varying wealth, in both town and country. Surprisingly, given their greater cost, and the consensus view that the ownership of clocks required people already to have been socialized into the time-disciplines of factory work, clocks diffused more rapidly than many of the other 'new consumer goods' of the late seventeenth and early eighteenth centuries (Figure 8.2).

Too great an emphasis on private clocks constitutes one of the most significant defects of the horological literature as socio-cultural history. For all their later dominance, domestic clocks had not been the main sources of clock time information over the preceding centuries. That role had been filled by public clocks of various sorts. Some attention has been paid to early cathedral and palace clocks, but far more important as general timing resources were clocks in parish churches, and in town and market halls. Again, we can demonstrate this for both Bristol, and the whole of England, based on a comprehensive analysis of accounts for just over 1,000 parishes between the 1390s and the 1690s.

Bristolians did not need to own clocks to know the time. The majority of Bristol's parish churches contained clocks. . . . and, by 1640, they provided widespread coverage of the city with hour-signalling using bells. The extent to which people registered and relied upon aural time indications is evident from many anecdotal accounts of specific events, and was nicely caught by a correspondent in 1772 who . . . asserted the importance of quarter-hour bells in providing 'a constant monitor of time to all the inhabitants of the four quarters of the city' (Barry 1984). Visual signalling with dials and hands emerged only slowly. The functional orientation of visual signalling is indicated by the orientation of visible exterior dials: typically these faced towards the centre of the city and/or towards the docks.

Several secular public buildings also featured clocks, often as prominent elements of architectural design, including the Exchange, the Assembly Rooms, market halls, the Council House, and Colston's Hospital. And sundials provided both information to set clocks, and an additional source of clock time. Yet other public clocks were located *inside* public buildings, including several churches, the Exchange and the Assembly Rooms, though pictorial evidence for interiors is quite sparse. Another vital group of clocks were those in inns, taverns and alehouses. Not all licensed premises had clocks, but licensing hours made the time of

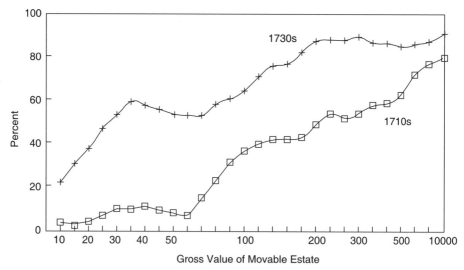

Fig. 8.2 Increasing percentage of ownership of clocks and watches in probate inventories in East Sussex in the 1710s and 1730s.

relevance to both proprietors and customers, and to the City authorities. Innkeepers' probate inventories suggest that most licensed premises had at least one clock, usually plain, in their taprooms. Though not specific to Bristol, drawings of alehouse interiors also suggest that clocks were a common feature, and so do references to clocks in plays and other literature. This matters because of the quite enormous numbers of licensed premises in Bristol, as in other port towns. . . .

The values of temporal precision

Another element that we consider at length in the book is the different uses of temporal precision found amongst different communities of practice. What counts as a valid expression of temporal precision often varied dramatically according to community of practice, as expressed in the use of specialized instruments, the means of calculation and the structure of the environment. In turn, we find that different apprehensions of precision are 'translated' between different communities of practice. The example we have chosen in this section concerns the translation between two communities of practice: one, the astronomical community, which was committed to highly accurate measurement; and the other, the navigational community, which had evolved techniques and instruments which, though often rough and ready, worked well enough in practical contexts.

Through the sixteenth and seventeenth centuries, undeniable advances in the precision of astronomical observations, in predictions of celestial movements, in mathematical techniques and auxiliary devices (such as trigonometrical and logarithmic tables), and hence in theoretical abilities to determine longitudinal positions, had been achieved by the international astronomical community. However, their very success had been based on relatively specialized methods which drew them apart from the temporal community of mariners who performed navigational tasks on board ships. The devices used by the two communities diverged. Features which had practical merits for one community offered no attraction, and perhaps even significant disadvantages, to the other, consequently inhibiting the 'travel' of precisions between them.

In particular, the priorities of abstract accuracy and practical utility varied greatly between astronomical and navigational communities. Improvements in accuracy had very different effects on communities in differing circumstances (for example, oceanic navigation imposed a need for [nearly] continuous observation in ways that land-based surveying and cartography did not). Such differences in contexts had major implications for the channelling of practices, instruments and knowledges among different temporal communities, and could create 'translation problems' among communities in which practices were diverging. In particular, new needs arose for more accurate observatory methods to be tailored for non-expert audiences (e.g. mariners, explorers on land).

Here, we highlight the two main strategies through which attempts were made to reverse the divergence of temporal communities, by considering how practices of precision were made more transferable from the highly skilled communities of master instrument makers or astronomical mathematicians in the specialized environments of their workshops, studies and observatories, towards and among more 'applied' communities of precision-users, such as navigators on ships. Making precision feasible for navigators required fundamental rearrangement of observatory networks of highly specialized people, instruments, techniques and discussion, into a form where similar results could be obtained by solitary members of ships' crews.

The first strategy was therefore to convert calculation of position from a highly complex observatory skill into a precise and explicit performative routine, in which mariners with limited mathematical skills could be drilled. Very complex and demanding procedures were restructured into reliable, learned routines consisting of many small, clear stages, using pre-printed forms and auxiliary tables. Such routines took several hours to perform, eventually producing a precisely calculated location. While overall, the navigational community was heavily 'practical' in its orientation to methods that worked in non-observatory conditions, it was not exactly de-skilled, and demonstrates how extremely complicated practices could be turned into structured performative routines. The second strategy, eventually made reliably operational towards 1800, was to reduce the skills required by absorbing as many functions as possible 'into the device'. This was the marine chronometer, a clock that needed no human intervention during a voyage, other than being looked at. In turn we can suggest that these strategies illustrate how practices were modified on their translation *between* communities of temporal practices, not just through the internal logic of developments within one particular community. . . . .

Concluding discussion

One of the most common reactions to our work is one of frustration. So we have set aside grand narratives like those of Thompson (1967), with their pleasing narrative curve through history (cf. Glennie and Thrift 1996). . . . .

Clock time skills and practices are part of more general everyday skills which historians have often tried to access. Clearly, as we have argued in this paper, this is a difficult thing to do, especially if we are not just to regard these everyday skills and practices as the recovery of folk customs, with a patina of olde worlde charm. In particular, if we are to regard these skills and practices as having important elements of improvisation and play, and therefore as one of the chief sources of renewal of social systems, then studying everyday practices and skills becomes central; everyday practices and skills are, in a sense, a motor of history.

However, we need to be careful. For when writing about these practices and skills of the past, we cannot write about a solid block of 'folkways' (Fischer 1989) or even neces-sarily a romanticized set of tactics of resistance, in de Certeau's sense. Everyday life in the past does not, cannot, add up. Four reasons come to mind. First, everyday life is *distributed,* spatially and temporally. It is not a centred object which can simply be opened to the gaze but can only be approached by moving around its spaces and times. Second, everyday life does not always work. Much of its to-and-fro consists of 'mistakes' (though, of course, what are successes and errors often become apparent only long after the original action, or are judge-ments of historians).

Third, much of everyday life is unspoken and unwritten. The rhythmic texture of gesture, glance and a sudden intake of breath, the experience of touch, sound and smell, the skilled responses to transient moments that turn out to have been crucial – this is the constantly extending horizon of banality in which everything is both ordinary and unique (see e.g. Smith 1999). But though we have known that this horizon was there, until recently our registers of communication have proved unequal to the task of representing it. Fourth, it is clearly impossible to recover all the practices of the past. Some practices will stay lost. In other words, any study of everyday life in the past must be incomplete, both because of the object being studied, and the 'documentary' means by which it can be studied. . . . .

All this said, though we might not want to close off the chains of close analysis, still we do not think we have finished where we started. As we have followed these chains, so we have come across some findings which we believe are eloquent and which we will conclude with: first, the early onset of a general awareness of clock time, as evidenced by not just the number of clocks in late mediaeval and early modern England but many other indexes as well; second, the variable nature of what counts as 'clock time', and the way in which various timekeeping technologies are continually redistributed to support that variable constitution; third, the fact that most facets of what we now call clock time had become naturalized well before the industrial revolution, and that consequently the imbrication of a sense of clock time in the general population is not an aspect of this process; fourth, the degree to which clock time is used according to activity, that in use it is a highly variable standard and this is in many ways the reason why it has been so generally adopted. . . . .

References

Barry, J. (1984) 'Social and cultural life in Bristol', Ph.D. thesis, University of Oxford.

Dosse, F. (1999) Empire of Meaning: The Humanisation of the Social Sciences, Minneapolis: University of Minnesota Press.

Fischer, D. H. (1989) Albion's Seed: Four British Folkways in North America, New York: Oxford University Press.

Glennie, P. and Thrift, N. J. (1996) 'Reworking E. P. Thompson's "Time, work-discipline and industrial capitalism"', Time and Society, 5, 275–300.

Glennie, P. and Thrift, N. J. (2009) Shaping the Day, Oxford: Oxford University Press.

Hutchins, E. (1995) Cognition in the Wild, Cambridge MA: MIT Press.

Landes, D. S. (2000) Revolution in Time, London: Viking.

Latour, B. (1997) 'Trains of thought: Piaget, formalism and the fifth dimension', Common Knowledge, 6, 170–91.

Le Goff, J. (1980) Time, Work and Culture in the Middle Ages, Chicago: University of Chicago Press.

Smith, B. R. (1999) The Acoustic World of Early Modern England, Chicago: University of Chicago Press.

Thompson, E. P. (1967) 'Time, work-discipline and industrial capitalism', Past and Present, 38, 56–97.

——(1968) The Making of the English Working Class, Harmondsworth: Penguin.

——(1991) Customs in Common, London: Merlin Press.

Thrift, N.J. (1996) Spatial Formations, London: Sage.

——(2000) 'Afterwords', Environment and Planning D: Society and Space, 18, 213–55.

Chapter 9

Ken Alder

A CALCULATING PEOPLE

There are certain ideas of uniformity which sometimes seize great minds (as they did Charlemagne's), but which invariably strike the petty. They find in them a kind of perfection which they recognize because it is impossible not to discover it; the same weights and measures in commerce, the same laws in the state, the same religion in all parts. But is uniformity always appropriate without exception?[1]

> Charles de Secondat de Montesquieu, *The Spirit of the Laws,* 1750

[This] chapter has earned Montesquieu the indulgence of all people of prejudice . . . Ideas of uniformity, of regularity, please all minds, and especially just minds . . . Uniformity of measures can only displease those lawyers who fear to see the number of lawsuits diminished, and those traders who fear a loss of profit from anything which renders commercial transactions easy and simple . . . A good law ought to be good for all men, as a true proposition [in geometry] is true for all men.[2]

> M.-J.-A.-N. Caritat de Condorcet, *Observations on 'The Spirit of the Laws',* 1793

. . . **WHEN THE DATE** for the obligatory use of the metric system arrived on 1 July 1794 the Revolutionary government had produced fewer than one thousand metre sticks and not a single French citizen was using the new system. Even the petty officials who answered to the dictatorial Committee of Public Safety were still filling out their reports in the old measures, making it impossible for the central government to monitor grain supplies. . . .

This paradox would not have been so surprising had the politicians and savants put aside their wilful disregard for the meaning of measurement in the *ancien régime* and considered the enormity of the change they were demanding. A modern system of measurement allows objects to be described in abstracted, commensurable units that relate to an absolute standard. This is true of the new metric system the French were seeking to establish, as it is of the Anglo-American non-metric measures still in use in America today. In either system a measurement stays fixed, no matter where the object is measured, or which measuring instrument is used. A metre is a metre; as a foot is a foot, a pound is a pound and a kilogram is a kilogram. . . . This form of measurement is adapted to our modern economy, in which buyers and sellers remote from one another in time and space conduct impersonal exchanges, quite certain that their measures are commensurable.

Under the *ancien régime,* by contrast, measurement was inseparable from the object being measured and the customs of the community which performed the measure-ment. These measurements were not enforced by a remote bureaucracy, but by local people answerable to their neighbours for their fairness. Far from being irrational or unnatural, this hodgepodge of measures made real sense to the peasants, artisans, shopkeepers and consumers who used them every day.

To begin with, each act of measurement in the *ancien régime* referred to a *particular* physical standard, held in local hands and safeguarded by local officials. A town's measure for the length for building materials, for instance, might derive from an iron fathom mortised into the wall of the town's markethall. The local measure for the weight of bread might derive from a master pound preserved in the guildhall of the area's bakers. The district's volume for grain might derive from a master bushel secured in the seigneur's château. And the local volume of wine might derive from a master barrel stored in the cellar of the monastery that owned the vineyard. It was the obligation of local officials – these aldermen, guildmasters, seigneurs and abbots – to enforce these standards, ensuring that exchanges made in the marketplace were fair. In return, they were entitled to extract a small fee for their services.

Not only did the physical standards differ from community to community, but the technique of measurement depended on local custom. One district measured grain heaped high in its bushel; another measured grain after it had been levelled off; still another, after the bushel had been struck to settle its contents. Even the height from which grain was poured into the receptacle was dictated by custom since contents might settle upon handling. A slight nudge might alter the amount of grain in the bushel, a difference of great concern to those who paid taxes in kind or who bought or sold foodstuffs in bulk – that is to say, the vast majority of French men and women. Similarly, the *aune* (the ell), a measure of cloth, generally equalled the width of local looms, so that a square *aune* of fabric could be appraised by folding a quick triangle. Alternatively, the shopkeeper might measure an *aune* by extending the cloth from his nose to his outstretched arm, with a complimentary thumb's worth thrown in 'for good measure'.[3] Quantity in the *ancien régime* was bound up in ritual and custom.

This meant that measurement standards were potentially open to dispute, negotiation and change – albeit with the consent of the local community. Indeed, in many places the quantity that local people called 'a bushel' had actually altered over the years as seigneurs and tenants disputed its 'true' amount (and hence the proper level of taxation and a fair price for basic foodstuffs). As such, local measures served as a living record of the shifting balance of power within the community. Outsiders, of course, did not understand these measures, but local buyers and sellers did – which suggests one of the main advantages of local diversity. They kept outsiders out. Distinctive measures protected small-town traders from big-city merchants, or at least forced the latter to pay the equivalent of a fee before they could enter the local market. Artisanal guilds took charge of their own measures so that they might define their goods in a unique way, identify interlopers and drive them out of business with ruinous lawsuits. This was as true of gunsmiths and milliners then as it is true of the computer industry today. Control over standards is control over the rules of economic life, and *ancien régime* standards were everywhere local. Yet beneath this local diversity lay the deeper meaning of measurement in the *ancien régime.*

Many *ancien régime* measures – especially those that related to the world of production – had at their origin an anthropometric meaning derived from human needs and human interests. This does not mean that they directly reflected the size of the human body, the *pied* (foot) as the size of the king's foot, or as the length of the average human foot. Rather, many *ancien régime* measures reflected the quantity of labour a person could do in a given period of time. Thus, coal in one region of France was measured in a *charge* (a 'load') equal to one-twelfth of a miner's daily output. Arable land was often measured by the *homme* ('man') or *journée* ('day') so as to designate the amount of land a peasant might plough or harvest in one day. Other units expressed the local people's evaluation of worth or quality. Thus, the size of a plot of arable land might also be measured in bushels; that is to say, a plot of land was equal to the number of bushels of grain it took to sow that field. Even in districts where land area was ostensibly measured in a unit like the *arpent,* which referred to a number of square *pieds* (feet), the dimensions of the surface area would actually vary depending on the type of field and the quality of its soil. For instance, pasture land measured in *arpents* was often divided into five distinct *degrés* based on the best use for the field. In some cases, properties described in *arpents* in the official records were in practice divided into *journées* – which could not be compared with one another on the basis of their abstract surface area.[4]

As the economic historian Witold Kula has pointed out, these anthropometric measures expressed features of primary concern to those who worked the soil or produced the goods. After all, a peasant whose plot of land was physically smaller than his neighbour's 'five-bushel' plot, but which took six bushels to sow because it was on a gentle slope and had fertile soil, might well have found that 'six bushels' expressed his stake in the land far more vividly than an abstract surface area. Moreover, these measures did not simply express the value of the land, they guided work rules and set customary limits on the labour a landlord might extract. Thus, when a foreman hired four peasants to pick a vineyard of eight *journées,* the labourers knew not to settle for less than two days' wages each; nor would they do the work with only three peasants on their gang. In this sense, the anthropometric measures of the *ancien régime* acted as a control on productivity and, indeed, masked the very idea that productivity was a value that could be measured.[5]

For just this reason some eighteenth-century landlords had begun to map their property in geometric units rather than in units of labour. They hired surveyors who could 'put all these defective [measures] in good order, so that in each district their content is regulated in either *perches, pas* or *pieds* (rods, yards, or feet)'.[6] Armed with the new square units, these landlords hoped to monitor productivity and pocket any gains. This new breed of efficiency-minded landlord-farmer was the great hope of the 'physiocrats', a group of reformers who had acquired much influence with the French royal administration and were also known as 'the economists', being the first to practise that dismal science. The physiocrats touted agricultural reform and free trade as the key to improving standards of living, and they – like economic historians ever since – have expended great effort to determine whether productivity was rising in France.[7] Unfortunately, the question is virtually unanswerable for much of France because the process of translating anthropometric measures into modern measures erases the very information that defined productivity in the *ancien régime.* When England's leading agronomist set out to assess French agriculture in the 1780s, he discovered that he could not rely on the official measures listed in the public records.

> The denomination of French measures, as the reader will see, are almost infinite and without any common standard to which they can be referred . . . The only clue tolerably general that can be in the least relied upon is drawn from the quantity of seed sown . . . [And] inquiries of this kind are not to be made in the bureaux of great cities; books and papers will not afford the information; a man must travel through the country or must always remain ignorant though surrounded by ten thousand volumes.[8]

Even the surveyors hired by 'improving' landlords were daunted by the challenge of transforming land into a factor of production expressible in square units. They warned their employers that for the actual partitioning of fields 'it is best to stick to the report of those who sow the land.'[9] That is because these anthropometric measures of land and other commodities were the outcome of centuries of protracted negotiations among artisans, peasants, traders and seigneurs. Their value had been ritualized and fixed in ways which reflected the relative bargaining power of different members of the local community. As such, *ancien régime* measures had come to express that community's sense of the proper social equilibrium. And any attempt to substitute a new kind of measurement was read as a threat to that social balance. . . .

The savants said the new measures would be 'natural' because they were based on the size of the earth. For these savants, a metric unit was natural when it could be defined *without* reference to human interests. The metre, they said, would be independent of all social negotiation or temporal change, transcending the interests of any particular community or nation. These men invoked nature as the guarantor that all people would benefit equally because no person benefited in particular. This spoke to the ideal of justice as blind. Indeed, this Enlightenment project has often been read as an attempt to displace personal relations as the foundation of the social order, and in their stead substitute a universal metric, imported from the natural sciences, by which the social world might be subject to dispassionate analysis – and schemes for improvement. But the people of the *ancien régime* also considered their measures 'natural', in that they had been built into the dimensions of the lived world and expressed their needs, their values and the history of their shared life. Their anthropometric measures sanctified man as the measure of all things, and expressed a different notion of justice, one which not only governed the domain of productive labour, but also the realm of economic exchange.[10]

The *ancien régime* was governed by a 'just price' economy in which basic foodstuffs were sold at a customary price set by the local community at a level which most of the people in that community could afford. The just price was enforced by moral sanction and ultimately by the threat of violence. The theory of this 'just price' economy had been legitimized moreover, by medieval scholastic doctrine, although this does not mean that prices were thought to be divinely sanctioned. The people of the *ancien régime* understood that production and consumption would halt if buyers and sellers were unwilling to trade. To induce production and exchange, then, the just price needed to reflect the costs of doing business, with these important caveats: that the authorities intervene in times of dearth, that locals not extort exorbitant fees from wayfarers or people in desperate need, and that sellers not conspire to rig prices.[11]

In such an economy, the diversity of weights and measures greased the wheels of commerce. In an age where bakers dared not charge more than the 'just price' for a loaf of bread for fear of precipitating a riot, bakers who wanted to preserve their livelihood when the cost of flour rose simply baked a smaller loaf. The same ruse allowed monasteries to circumvent Christian restrictions against profits by buying wine in large barrels and then selling it (for the same price) in smaller barrels. Sometimes this could lead to accusations of fraud, as when the petitioners of Notre-Dame-de-Lisque complained in 1788 that their abbot's tax collector had increased the measure of grain. More probably, he was simply trying to maintain his own revenue during a time of rapidly increasing prices.[12]

The workings of this economy were familiar to *ancien régime* officials. One government agent noted that local grain merchants profited by buying grain at one measure and selling it (for the same price) at a lesser measure. But rather than condemn this practice, he noted that it encouraged commerce in the region, since attempts to raise prices risked the wrath of the local populace. A provincial assembly warned in 1788 that 'the establishment of a uniform measure would ruin this genre of commerce, destroying at the same time an infinity of little markets which subsist only on these differences and, though of no great importance, supply the needs of nearby consumers'.[13]

In many towns, *ancien régime* officials themselves served as the 'fair mediators' who interposed themselves between buyers and sellers, setting the just price for essential foodstuffs like bread, meat, wine and beer. Indeed, superintending the economy in this way was one of the obligations of a benevolent monarch, and among the principal justifications for his rule. In setting the just price, local officials generally took market conditions into account. The price of bread, for instance, was governed by *tarifs*, numerical tables which translated the current market price of wheat into the just price for a four-pound loaf of bread of a specified quality (white bread, brown bread, second-class bread and so on). In major towns, these *tarifs* were drawn up collaboratively by aldermen and bakers who jointly estimated the cost of milling and baking bread, and outfitting a shop, while guaranteeing a modest return for the baker. These regulated prices, however, were 'sticky' in the sense that bakers could not fine-tune their prices to meet daily fluctuations in the cost of wheat. Also, bakers tended to set their prices in round numbers because of a persistent shortage of small coins. Instead of adjusting prices, bakers then altered the weight of their loaves or diluted their ingredients. Such practices were illegal, but even consumers who were aware of them generally tolerated them so long as everyone could still afford a 'pound' of bread. Equity mattered more than efficiency. Yet in times of dearth any attempt to raise prices or to 'short' bread too egregiously could spark violence. Price was not the paramount variable in the *ancien régime* economy, but merely one variable among many, including quantity, quality, the cost of production and local custom.[14]

In short, the old diversity of weights and measures, far from being irrational and unnatural, formed the backbone of the *ancien régime*'s economy. These measures did not simply define a distinct kind of economy, they defined a kind of human being. Today, we assume that the 'market' consists of the aggregate of innumerable one-on-one private exchanges, the sum total of which sets prices. We might call this the market *principle.* The *ancien régime* operated according to the idea of the market as a *place*, which one might imagine as a kind of bazaar or village fair in which buyers and sellers met in public to conduct exchanges under the watchful eye of a third party. That third party – typically an emissary of the king, a town alderman, the local seigneur or the nearby abbot – justified the taxation of these transactions by ensuring that the needy did not go hungry and the producer got a fair return for his troubles. Thus, in addition to providing peasants and artisans with a ready guide to the value of their land and labour, the weights and measures of the *ancien régime* also provided shopkeepers and consumers with some guarantee that their marketplace transactions would be fair.

In this context, the French savants' scheme to reform weights and measures was a revolutionary rupture, far more radical than the sort of translation involved in the switch from, say, Anglo-American units to the metric system. Indeed, the revolutionaries *intended* the metric system to eradicate the assumptions underlying the old just-price economy. Their goal was to make productivity the visible measure of economic progress, and to make price the paramount variable in commercial exchange. They saw the metric reform as a crucial stage in the education of modern *Homo economicus.*

Notes

1   Charles de Secondat de Montesquieu, *De l'esprit des lois* [1750], in Montesquieu, *Oeuvres complètes* (Paris: Garnier, 1875), 5, pp. 412–13.

2   Marie-Jean-Antoine-Nicolas Caritat de Condorcet, *Observations . . . dur le vingt-neuvième livre de l'Esprit des lois* [1793], in Condorcet, *Oeuvres* (Paris: Didot, 1847), 1, pp. 376–81.

3   Daryl Hafter, 'Measuring Cloth by the Elbow and Thumb: Resistance to Numbers in France of the 1780s', *Cultures of Control,* ed. Miriam Levin (Amsterdam: Harwood, 2000), pp. 69–79.

4   For an example of the regional diversity of anthropometric measures at the end of the *ancien régime,* see Jean-Baptiste Galley, *Le régime féodal dans le pays de Saint-Etienne* (Paris: Imprimerie de la Loire Républicaine, 1927), pp. 315–16, 326. For examples of anthropometric measures hidden behind seemingly abstract units, see Alfred Antoine Gandilhon, ed., *Département du Cher: Cabiers et doléances du bailliage de Bourges* (Bourges: Tardy-Pigelet, 1910), pp. 768, 770.

5   Witold Kula, *Measures and Men,* trans. R. Szreter (Princeton: Princeton University Press, 1986). The word 'anthropometric' can also mean the measurement of the human body; here, following Kula, it is used to denote measures derived from human needs. See also the prescient article by Marc Bloch, 'Le témoinage des mesures agraires', *Annales d'histoire économique et sociale* 6 (1934), pp. 280–2.

6   Galley, *Régime féodal,* p. 282.

7   For a typical claim of how the creation of uniform and abstract units of land area would improve agricultural productivity, see Bureaux de Pusy, Archives Parlementaires de 1787 à 1860, First Series (Paris: Dupont, 1875) 15 (8 May 1790), p. 440. For the most sophisticated recent treatment of agricultural productivity under the *ancien régime,* see Philip T. Hoffman. *Growth in a Traditional Society: The French Countryside, 1450–1815* (Princeton: Princeton University Press, 1996). This study, for all its quantitative virtues, tells us little about agricultural productivity outside 'modern' farms where records were kept, or about the exchanges which dominated early modern transactions. For a contrasting view, see Jean Peltre, *Recherches métrologiques sur les finages lorrains* (Lille: Atelier Reproduction des Thèses, 1977).

8   Arthur Young, *Travels during the Years 1787, 1788 and 1789* (Dublin: Gross, 1793), 2, pp. 44–6.

9   Galley, *Régime féodal,* p. 307.

10 For scientific definitions of 'natural', see Maurice Crosland, '"Nature" and Measurement in Eighteenth-Century France', *Studies on Voltaire and the Eighteenth Century* 87 (1972) pp. 277–309.

11 On the theory of the just price, see Raymond de Roover, 'The Concept of the Just Price: Theory and Economic Policy', *Journal of the History of Economic Thought* 18(1958), pp. 418–34.

12 For Notre-Damme-de-Lisque and such practices throughout *ancien régime* Europe, see Kula, *Measures and Men,* pp. 194–5.

13 Charles Porée, ed., *Département de l'Yonne, Cabiers de doléances du Bailliage de Sens* (Auxerre: Imprimerie coopérative ouvrière 'l'Universelle', 1906), pp. 177–8. For the acknowledgement by the official of the role played by metrical diversity, see Robert Vivier, 'Contribution à l'étude des anciennes mesures du département d'Indre-et-Loire', *Revue d'histoire économique et sociale* 14 (1926), pp. 180–99; 16 (1928), pp. 182–227, especially 14, p. 196.

14 On the *ancien régime* economy, see Judith Miller, *Mastering the Market: The State and Grain Trade in Northern France, 1700–1860* (Cambridge: Cambridge University Press, 1999), pp. 34–6. Also see Steven L. Kaplan, *The Bakers of Paris and the Bread Question, 1700–1775* (Durham, NC: Duke University Press, 1996). On the distinction between the market principle and the marketplace, see Steven L. Kaplan, *Provisioning Paris: Merchants and Millers in the Grain and Flour Trade during the Eighteenth Century* (Ithaca: Cornell University Press, 1984), pp. 47–8, 68–9. See also Kula, *Measures and Men,* pp. 71–8.

PART IV

Others

Introduction

WHY SHOULD PAST RELATIONS between 'us' and 'them' be considered important for cultural historians? Perhaps because constructing identity, and thereby shaping a meaning for experience, has drawn upon alleged contrasts between 'our' kind of people and those perceived and represented as different. True, the extent to which collective identity has been the main source for a sense of self has varied historically (see our 'Individualism' section). But it has been through shared cultural values that even highly original individuals have interpreted who they were, and have glimpsed what for them and theirs was the good life to be aspired to. Hence comes the pressure to affirm those cultural values by emphasising how alien are those outside the circle. The Other has been a mirror (Hartog 1988) in which to see 'ourselves'.

A cultural historian can analyse this process at two levels. At the first, it is the notion of distance or separateness that predominates in accounts of people's dealings with 'others'. The second level, tracing in detail how they managed their interaction in day-to-day practice, poses a challenge. It means being on guard against accepting then prevailing stereotypes. A nuanced approach calls for a recognition of fluid relationships, where the historian encounters blurred boundaries, borderline cases and cultural hybridity (Burke 2009). For instance, Preston (2009) describes 'symbiotic' mid-eighteenth-century land-sharing arrangements in the Mohawk Valley. There, incomers were accepted by Iroquois as neighbours, tenants and even adopted kin. Preston's detailed evidence, drawn from several locations, indicates that in some there was a flexible style of interaction and a shared communal existence between 'the Indians' and 'the settlers'. Earlier accounts, emphasising conflict, reflected the records left by the colonial hierarchy's military-minded strategic decision-makers.

We need to exercise caution in using the concept of culture, both in overviews of patterns of interaction and in nuanced case-studies. Reifying 'cultures' as merely the unchanging customs assumed to be shared by a set of people might make it easy to describe such patterns. But this simplified usage, inherited from an early stage in the concept's development, is misleading. Cultural practices and beliefs rarely come packaged in stable units. Contrasting with this caricature of culture as straitjacket (Ingold 1993) is the alternative notion of culture as a flexible repertoire of elements, continually being revised through 'cross-border' contacts. Only this more dynamic concept of culture conveys its protean character, and thus gives scope for cultural historians to recognise that all the historical actors engaged in an encounter may be able to shape and use patterns, rather than simply abide by them.

Culturally based explanations for perceived differences between the mores of different human groups continue to be contrasted with accounts couched in terms of biology, ethnicity or 'race' (Hannaford 1996; Jenkins 2008; Wade 2002). The vexed issue of how concepts of 'race' have had such ideological resonance at various times demands 'historicist' interrogation. One strategy is to examine various ways in which 'race' was deployed by learned authors. Keevak (2011) looks at its application to the inhabitants of China and Japan, supposedly differentiating them by skin-colour from 'white' people. Trautmann (1997) shows how finding linguistic similarities between Sanskrit and European languages challenged British imperial ideologies. Research by Curran (2011) on eighteenth-century comparative anatomists places their ideas in the context of the African slave trade. Kidd (2006) links 'race' to deductions drawn from Bible stories about Noah's sons Shem, Ham and Japheth – an argument that proved remarkably tenacious (Braude 1997; Whitford 2009). These examples illustrate the variety of sources that theorists of 'race' tapped into to classify human beings.

Another way of looking at how Westerners tried to pinpoint what made human populations different is adopted by Adas (1989), who asks what they thought it was that made them culturally superior. Surveying European attitudes towards the peoples of Africa, India and China from the 1600s to the mid-twentieth century, he singles out the 'machine'. Technical achievement was not at first the basis for comparisons; but its salience increased, and by the end of the nineteenth century this was what dominated European self-understanding as expressed in depictions of other 'races'.

But how did these 'others' regard those who, in large parts of the world, became their rulers? Indian historians who addressed this question in the 1980s named their enterprise 'Subaltern Studies' (Prakash 1994). It has led to a more fundamental historiographical question: how far has the writing of history by those associated with Western dominance left non-Western cultural perspectives inadequately represented (Mignolo 2012)? One resource for tackling this issue, Foucault's legacy of reflection on power/knowledge (McHoul and Grace 1995), was employed by Saïd (1995) in his study of Western discourse about 'the Orient'. Buruma and Margalit (2004) explore the history of hostile views of the West. Misperceptions were not necessarily based on enmity: MacGaffey (1994) argues that although the sixteenth-century Kongo leaders and the Portuguese appeared to arrive at a good mutual understanding, each party was interpreting the other's vocabulary as an echo of its own worldview, in what this author calls a 'dialogue of the deaf'. White (2006) would perhaps have called it a set of 'creative misunderstandings'.

'Others' can include close neighbours stigmatised as deviant (Briggs 2002) as well as far-off peoples. Neighbours have often been viewed with suspicion and at times persecuted. In the later Middle Ages Jews, heretics, 'sodomites' and lepers were objects of a hostility which Moore (2006), borrowing from the anthropological theory advanced by Douglas (1966), explains as due to a subconscious association between perceived conceptual anomaly and pollution.

In our first reading, Nirenberg asks how historians should interpret medieval episodes of violence against Jews. There is a risk that the meaning attributed to such episodes by today's historian will override the meanings they had for those involved – with particular events being subsumed under a grand narrative. (For a broader framework within which to place this type of issue, see the Introduction to this Reader.) As Nirenberg puts it, 'discourse and agency gain meaning only in relation to each other.' His work contextualises attacks on Jews by alluding to other groups attacked and by framing them within a predominant pattern of less violent coexistence. (See also Elukin 2007.)

White's book explores how the colonists in New France in the seventeenth and early eighteenth centuries found a 'middle ground' in relating to the Algonquians. It criticises earlier historians for a 'tendency to impose static categories', as though the members of each group remained as they had previously been, rather than being subtly altered by the experience of contact across cultural boundaries. This dissatisfaction leads him to seek evidence for the indigenous people's thoughts about the French as well as the colonists' views of those they called the *sauvages*. (See also White 2006.)

The extract from Gombrich's book tells the story of the arrival of Protestant missionaries in Ceylon in the early nineteenth century and the changing responses of the Buddhist monks to the newcomers' denunciations of their religion. Initially content to continue as before, they later saw that the missionaries' schools and their use of printed materials had given them a valuable advantage. Thereafter a new Buddhism developed, having some of the features of Protestantism, including a place for lay leadership. Before long, Western converts to Buddhism were arriving in the island.

References

Adas, M. (1989) *Machines as the Measure of Men: science, technology and ideologies of Western dominance*, Ithaca, NY: Cornell University Press.

Braude, B. (1997) 'The sons of Noah and the construction of ethnic and geographical identities in the medieval and early modern periods', *William and Mary Quarterly*, 54: 103–42.

Briggs, R. (2002) *Witches and Neighbours: the social and cultural context of European witchcraft*, second edition, Hoboken, NJ: Wiley-Blackwell.

Burke, P. (2009) *Cultural Hybridity*, Cambridge: Polity.

Buruma, I. and Margalit, A. (2004) *Occidentalism: the West in the eyes of its enemies*, New York, NY: Penguin Press.

Curran, A. (2011) *The Anatomy of Blackness: science and slavery in an Age of Enlightenment*, Baltimore, MD: Johns Hopkins University Press.

Douglas, M. (1966) *Purity and Danger: an analysis of the concepts of pollution and taboo*, London: Routledge.

Elukin, J.M. (2007) *Living Together, Living Apart: rethinking Jewish-Christian relations in the Middle Ages*, Princeton, NJ: Princeton University Press.

Hannaford, I. (1996) *Race: the history of an idea in the West*, Baltimore, MD: Johns Hopkins University Press.

Hartog, F. (1988) *The Mirror of Herodotus: the representation of the other in the writing of history*, trans. Janet Lloyd, Berkeley, CA: University of California Press.

Ingold, T. (1993) 'The art of translation in a continuous world', in G. Pálsson (ed.) *Beyond Boundaries: understanding, translation and anthropological discourse*, Oxford: Berg.

Jenkins, R.P. (2008) *Rethinking Ethnicity: arguments and explorations*, second edition, Thousand Oaks, CA: Sage.

Keevak, C. (2011) *Becoming Yellow: a short history of racial thinking*, Princeton, NJ: Princeton University Press.

Kidd, C. (2006) *The Forging of Races: race and scripture in the Protestant Atlantic world, 1600–2000*, Cambridge: Cambridge University Press.

MacGaffey, W. (1994) 'Dialogues of the deaf: Europeans on the Atlantic coast of Africa', in S.B. Schwartz (ed.) *Implicit Understandings: observing, reporting and reflecting on the* encounters between Europeans and other peoples in the early modern era, Cambridge: Cambridge University Press.

McHoul, A.W. and Grace, W. (eds) (1995) A Foucault Primer: discourse, power and the subject, London: Routledge.

Mignolo, W.D. (2012) Local Histories/Global Designs: coloniality, subaltern knowledges and border thinking, second edition, Princeton, NJ: Princeton University Press.

Moore, R.I. (2006) The Formation of a Persecuting Society: authority and deviance in Western Europe 950–1250, second edition, Hoboken, NJ: Wiley-Blackwell.

Prakash, G. (1994) 'Subaltern Studies as postcolonial criticism', American Historical Review, 99: 1475–90.

Preston, D.L. (2009) The Texture of Contact: European and Indian settler communities on the frontiers of Iroquoia, 1667–1783, Lincoln, NE: Nebraska University Press.

Saïd, E. (1995) Orientalism: Western representations of the Orient, second edition, Harmondsworth: Penguin.

Trautmann, T.R. (1997) Aryans and British India, Berkeley, CA: University of California Press.

Wade, P. (2002) Race, Nature and Culture: an anthropological perspective, London: Pluto Press.

White, R. (2006) 'Creative misunderstandings and new understandings', William and Mary Quarterly, 63: 9–14.

Whitford, D.M. (2009) The Curse of Ham in the Early Modern Era: the Bible and the justifications for slavery, Farnham: Ashgate.

Chapter 10

David Nirenberg*

INTRODUCTION TO *COMMUNITIES OF VIOLENCE: PERSECUTION OF MINORITIES IN THE MIDDLE AGES*

THE TRUTH OF THE DICTUM that the present shapes the past is nowhere more evident than in the effects of World War II on historical writing about European minorities.[1] Before that war and its attendant horrors, Jewish history was by and large outside the mainstream of the historical profession, written by Jews and ignored by others (as in some ways it still is).[2] When mainstream historians did touch upon the history of Jews and other minorities, it was as part of confessional history. Protestants especially wrote about medieval violence and intolerance toward minorities (heretics, Moriscos, Jews, lepers, witches) in order to claim that Catholicism had benighted Europe and made its people brutal in the period between the fall of Rome and the birth of Luther.[3] For the most part, however, the study of "Medieval Society" writ large seldom intersected with the study of its minorities.

Since the Holocaust such a position has become untenable. Few today would argue, for example, that the study of Jews and attitudes toward Jews in Germany tells us little about the formation of modern German cultural and national identities. Nor, in the wake of current attacks on Muslims in the former Yugoslavia, on "foreigners" (often Muslim) in Germany, France, and Italy, or on Jews in Russia, is it possible to argue that episodes of violence against minorities are part of a primitive European past which modern societies have left behind. The study of medieval minorities has therefore acquired a new urgency, and it has been transformed by some into a search for the roots of modern evils. "When did Europe go wrong?" is a question that has been asked more and more frequently over the past fifty years.

A frequent answer, it seems, is "in the Middle Ages." As Norman Cohn put it in his book *Warrant for Genocide*,

> As I see it, the deadliest kind of antisemitism, the kind that results in massacre and attempted genocide, has little to do with real conflicts of interest between living people, or even with racial prejudice as such. At its heart lies the belief that Jews—all Jews everywhere—form a conspiratorial body set on ruining and then dominating the rest of mankind. And this belief is simply a modernized, secularized version of the popular medieval view.[4]

The implications of Cohn's thesis are clear: the most dangerous attitudes toward minorities, or at least toward Jews, do not draw their strength from the interactions of individuals and groups within a society, but from collective beliefs, beliefs formed in the Middle Ages and transmitted to the present day.[5] Hence medievalists have written books like Cohn's *Europe's Inner Demons*, Robert Moore's *The Formation of a Persecuting Society*, and Carlo Ginzburg's *Ecstasies*[6]—books that are exercises in psychoanalysis, attempts to understand an assumed collective unconscious of modern Europeans.

There are different opinions, of course, as to when a "tolerant" European Middle Ages turned bad. Historians of Jews, Muslims, heretics, gay people, and lepers have all placed the shift at different dates, ranging from the First Crusade (which provoked a good deal of violence against European Jews) forward. Most recently Carlo Ginzburg has argued for a later date, claiming that there emerged in the first half of the fourteenth century (the period covered in the present work) an irrational fear of conspiracy which had previously been repressed in the European mentality: a belief that certain groups, whether Jews, lepers, or witches, were conspiring to destroy society. It was this irrational mentality, Ginzburg believes, that led to pogroms against the Jews, to accusations of well poisoning and ritual murder, and to the great witch hunts of the early modern period.

Regardless of their different periodizations, all these quests for the origins of European intolerance have much in common. All take the long view, seeking to establish a continuity between the hatreds of long ago and those of the here and now. This focus on the *longue durée* means that events are read less within their local contexts than according to a teleology leading, more or less explicitly, to the Holocaust Similarly, instead of emphasizing local or even individual opinions about minorities, they focus on collective images, representations, and stereotypes of the "other." The actions of groups or individuals are ignored in favor of structures of thought that are believed to govern those actions.[7] Historians therefore act as geologists, tracing the ancient processes by which collective anxieties accreted into a persecutory landscape that has changed little over the past millennium. The refutation of this widespread notion that we can best understand intolerance by stressing the fundamental continuity between collective systems of thought across historical time, or in this case across one thousand years, is an overarching goal of the present work.

The emphasis on continuity and collective systems of thought can be called "structuralist" without too much violence to that word.[8] Within the structuralist consensus in the historiography of persecution there are different methodologies. Two are especially common. The first links the rise of persecuting mentalities to other secular processes: the creation of a monetary economy or the rise of centralized monarchies, for example.[9] Exponents of this approach, such as Robert Moore, emphasize processes of historical change up to a point. They allow contingency during the gestation of intolerance, but after its birth the persecuting mentality seems to transcend particularities of time and place. The second methodology traces the pedigree of stereotypes and beliefs in order to establish the existence of a "discourse" about the "other" and fix its origins. It treats intolerance entirely as a problem in the migratory history of ideas, ignoring social, economic, political, or cultural variables. Thus Ginzburg follows the folkloric roots of the witches' Sabbath from eighth-century B.C. central Asia to Essex, England, 1645; while the author of another recent work traces the demonization and dehumanization of Jews from Alexandrian Egypt to high medieval Passion plays in order to understand "the daydreams of monks, the sermons of the preachers, the imagination of the artists, and the anxious psyche of Everyman."[10]

"Everyman" makes out badly in such works. Often "irrational," at best the receptacle of external, inherited ideologies passively and uncritically absorbed, medieval people are presented as dominated by discourse, not as active participants in its shaping. I am not arguing that negative discourses about Jews, Muslims, women, or lepers did not exist, but that any inherited discourse about minorities acquired force only when people chose to find it meaningful and useful, and was itself reshaped by these choices. Briefly, discourse and agency gain meaning only in relation to each other.[11] Even thus delimited, the notion of a "persecuting discourse" requires qualification. Such a discourse about minorities was but one of those available, and its invocation in a given situation did not ensure its success or acceptance. The choice of language was an active one, made in order to achieve something, made within contexts of conflict and structures of domination, and often contested.[12] Thus when medieval people made statements about the consequences of religious difference, they were making claims, not expressing accomplished reality, and these claims were subject to barter and negotiation before they could achieve real force in any given situation.[13] This book is about these processes of barter and negotiation, not about the creation of a "persecuting discourse."

My approach also challenges the current emphasis on the *longue durée* in the periodization of the persecution of minorities. By showing how structures are transformed by the actions and choices of people working within them, it more readily explains change over time while relying less on an appeal to the irrational. We need no longer insist on continuities of meaning in claims about minorities wherever we find continuities in form, since we can see how the meanings of existing forms are altered by the work that they are asked to do, and by the uses to which they are put. This means that we can be more critical than we have previously been about attempts to link medieval and modern mentalities, medieval ritual murder accusations and modern genocide.

The problem of periodization is central in this attempt to disrupt a now almost orthodox view of the steady march of European intolerance across the centuries. Historians have assembled that view in large part by stringing together episodes of large-scale violence against minorities. In Jewish historiography, for example, scholars have drawn a line of mounting intolerance from the Rhineland massacres of the First Crusade, through the expulsions and massacres of the thirteenth, fourteenth, and fifteenth centuries, through German ritual murder trials and Russian pogroms, to Kristallnacht and the concentration camps. The first half of the present work challenges this view by choosing two massacres (of Jews, lepers, and Muslims) used in teleological narratives and placing them within their local social, political, and cultural contexts. The more we restore to those outbreaks of violence their own particularities, the less easy it is to assimilate them to our own concerns, as homogeneity and teleology are replaced by difference and contingency. The second half presents a very different, perhaps more provocative, criticism of the teleological model. Its argument is that by focusing on moments of cataclysmic violence and reading them with post-Holocaust eyes, the teleological model has overlooked the fundamental interdependence of violence and tolerance in the Middle Ages. . . .

Notes

1 Cf. M. Bloch, *The Historian's Craft* (New York, 1953), pp. 43–47. Bloch wrote these words in hiding shortly before he himself was killed by the Nazis. I do not doubt that their articulation was itself a product of the war.

2 See G. Langmuir, "Majority History and Postbiblical Jews," in *Toward a Definition of Antisemitism* (Berkeley and Los Angeles, 1990), pp. 21–41.

3 G. G. Coulton is a salient example, most blatantly in his historical novel *The Friar's Lantern* (London, 1906). Such Protestant-Catholic polemics were particularly important in the early historiography on Muslims and Moriscos in the Iberian Peninsula.

4 *Warrant for Genocide: The Myth of the Jewish World-Conspiracy and the "Protocols of the Elders of Zion"* (New York, 1967), p. 16. A similar passage from the same work is quoted approvingly and expanded

by L. Rothkrug. "Peasant and Jew: Fears of Pollution and German Collective Perceptions." *Historical Reflections/Réflexions Historiques* 10 (1983): 59–77, here p. 60.

5   There are, of course, historians with the opposite view. B. Blumenkranz, for example, writes that "the struggle of Christianity against Judaism is not inevitable, necessary, nor essential. Rather it is a product of general conditions emerging out of internal and external politics and sociological facts. In short, it is only contingent." Such pleas for contingency have had limited influence even upon those who quote them. Thus A. Cutler and H. Cutler, whose translation of Blumenkranz was just quoted, "could not agree more with these sentiments" but proceed on the same page to argue that *"Anti-Muslimism was the primary . . .* factor in the revival of anti-Semitism during the High Middle Ages (1000–1300), the effects of which have been felt in all subsequent centuries, including our own." *The Jew as Ally of the Muslim: Medieval Roots of Anti-Semitism* (Notre Dame, IN, 1986), p. 2, quoting from *Le juif medieval au miroir de l'art chrétien* (Paris, 1966), p. 136.

6   (London, 1975); (Oxford, 1987); (New York, 1991). See also Léon Poliakov, *The Aryan Myth: A History of Racist and Nationalist Ideas in Europe* (New York, 1974); and Rothkrug's article cited above, n. 4.

7   These are, of course, relatives of very ancient dichotomies currently at the heart of theoretical debate about textual interpretation: subjectivism/objectivism, structure/agency, langue/parole, among others. Put most briefly and abstractly, the debate is over the degree of autonomy individuals have within the collective rules and institutions that structure their society. In the case of langue/parole, for example, langue refers to the background of rules by which language functions (the linguistics, so to speak), while parole refers to usage, to the ways in which individuals speak.

8   Cf. P. Anderson, *In the Tracks of Historical Materialism* (Chicago, 1984), chap. 2, "Structure and Subject," esp. pp. 44 f.

9   See, e.g., L. Little, *Religious Poverty and the Profit Economy in Medieval Europe* (Ithaca, NY, 1978), p. 42.

10   Ginzburg, *Ecstasies* (though elsewhere he provides a very elegant formulation of the problem of continuity. See his *Myths, Emblems, Clues* (London, 1986), e.g., pp. vii–xiii); M. Lazar, "The Lamb and the Scapegoat: The Dehumanization of the Jews in Medieval Propaganda Imagery," in *Anti-Semitism in Times of Crisis*, ed. S. Gilman and S. Katz (New York, 1991), pp. 38–80, here p. 39. For a very different theoretical criticism of this methodology see M. Foucault, "Nietzsche, Genealogy, History," in *Language, Counter-Memory, Practice*, ed. D. Bouchard (Ithaca, NY, 1977), pp. 139–164.

11   Here I am conflating Bourdieu's notion of "rule-governed creativity" (*Outline of a Theory of Practice* [Cambridge. 1977], pp. 15–17 and passim) with Sahlins's discussion of "historic agents" and their uses of cultural categories. See *Islands of History* (Chicago, 1985), pp. xiv, 125. A. Giddens has come to similar conclusions, albeit by different means. For the simplest exposition of his "structuration theory," see his "Hermeneutics and Social Theory," in *Hermeneutics: Questions and Prospects*, ed. G. Shapiro and A. Sica (Amherst, MA, 1984), pp. 215–231; and "Action, Subjectivity, and the Constitution of Meaning," in *The Aims of Representation: Subject/Text/History*, ed. M. Krieger (New York, 1987), pp. 159–174.

12   A point made forcefully by S. Feierman, *Peasant Intellectuals: Anthropology and History in Tanzania* (Madison, W1, 1990), esp. pp. 1–35. The same can be said of the textual records of such choices, on which see G. Prakash, *Bonded Histories: Genealogies of Labor Servitude in Colonial India* (Cambridge, 1990), p. 39; R. Williams, *Marxism and Literature* (Oxford, 1977), pp. 36–42. This abstract point has practical implications for the medievalist. Compare M. Kriegel's claim—that royal documentation is compromised by interests, while municipal documentation represents "the reality of the perception of the Jew"—with my position that we have no disinterested sources, only sources with conflicting interests. For Kriegel, see his "Un trait de psychologie sociale dans les pays méditerranéens du bas moyen age: le juif comme intouchable," *Annales: ESC* 31 (1976): 326–330, here p. 327.

13   An adaptation of L. Rosen, *Bargaining for Reality: The Construction of Social Relations in a Muslim Community* (Chicago, 1984), pp. 1–5, 47, 165–166, 180–192.

*   David Nirenberg's book *Anti-Judaism: the Western tradition* (New York: W.W. Norton, 2013) unfortunately came to our notice only after this Reader had gone to print.

Chapter 11

Richard White

THE MIDDLE GROUND: INDIANS, EMPIRES, AND REPUBLICS IN THE GREAT LAKES REGION, 1650–1815

For every time we make others part of a "reality" that we alone invent, denying their creativity by usurping the right to create, we use those people and their way of life and make them subservient to ourselves.

Roy Wagner, *The Invention of Culture*

In action, people put their concepts and categories into ostensive relations to the world. Such referential uses bring into play other determinations of the signs, besides their received sense, namely the actual world and the people concerned.

Marshall Sahlins, *Islands of History*

I

BECAUSE THE FRENCH AND ALGONQUIANS were trading partners and allies, the boundaries of the Algonquian and French worlds melted at the edges and merged. Although identifiable Frenchmen and identifiable Indians obviously continued to exist, whether a particular practice or way of doing things was French or Indian was, after a time, not so clear. This was not because individual Indians became "Frenchified" or because individual Frenchmen went native, although both might occur. Rather, it was because Algonquians who were perfectly comfortable with their status and practices as Indians and Frenchmen, confident in the lightness of French ways, nonetheless had to deal with people who shared neither their values nor their assumptions about the appropriate way of accomplishing tasks. They had to arrive at some common conception of suitable ways of acting; they had to create what I refer to as a middle ground.[1]

The creation of the middle ground involved a process of mutual invention by both the French and the Algonquians. This process passed through various stages, of which the earliest is at once the most noticed and the least interesting. It was in this initial stage that the French, for example, simply assimilated Indians into their own conceptual order. Indians became *sauvages,* and the French reduced Indian religion to devil worship and witchcraft. Algonquians, for their part, thought of the first Europeans as manitous. On both sides, new people were crammed into existing categories in a mechanical way.[2]

Literacy gave this initial stage a potency and a durability for Europeans it might otherwise have lacked. Because the French were literate, knowledge of Indians was diffused far from the site of actual contact. Such knowledge, unchallenged by actual experience with Indians, survived as a potent cultural relict. Long after it ceased to govern the actions of those who actually lived among Indians, the idea of Indians as literally *sauvages,* or wild men embodying either natural virtue or ferocity, persisted among intellectuals and statesmen in France. Assimilated into European controversies, these imaginary Indians became the Indians of Chateaubriand and Rousseau. They took on importance, but it was one detached from the continuing processes of contact between real Algonquians and real Europeans. In the *pays d'en haut* [up-country], actual Indians and whites of widely different social class and status had, for a variety of reasons, to rely on each other in order to achieve quite specific ends. It was these Frenchmen (for Frenchwomen would not appear until much later) and Algonquian men and women who created a common ground – the middle ground – on which to proceed.[3]

This process of creation resulted quite naturally from attempts to follow normal conventions of behavior in a new situation. Each side sought different goals in a different manner. French officials and merchants sought to rationalize and order what they saw as the unpredictable world of the *sauvage*; Algonquians sought, in a sense, the opposite. They wanted to change or readjust the given order by appeals for personal favor or exemption. In much the same way that they sought special power to readjust the order of the world of plants, animals, and spirits by appealing to the manitous, so they sought beneficial changes in the social world by appeals to the French. Often, in the examples that follow, when the French sought the imposition of hard-and-fast rules, the Algonquians sought the "power" that comes from knocking the order off balance, from asserting the personal, the human exception. The result of each side's attempts to apply its own cultural expectations in a new context was often change in culture itself. In trying to maintain the conventional order of its world, each group applied rules that gradually shifted to meet the exigencies of particular situations. The result of these efforts was a new set of common conventions, but these conventions served as a basis for further struggles to order or influence the world of action.[4]

The middle ground depended on the inability of both sides to gain their ends through force. The middle ground grew according to the need of people to find a means, other than force, to gain the cooperation or consent of foreigners. To succeed, those who operated on the middle ground had, of necessity, to attempt to understand the world and the reasoning of others and to assimilate enough of that reasoning to put it to their own purposes. Particularly in diplomatic councils, the middle ground was a realm of constant invention, which was just as constantly presented as convention. Under the new conventions, new purposes arose, and so the cycle continued.[5]

Perhaps the central and defining aspect of the middle ground was the willingness of those who created it to justify their own actions in terms of what they perceived to be their partner's cultural premises. Those operating in the middle ground acted for interests derived from their own culture, but they had to convince people of another culture that some mutual action was fair and legitimate. In attempting such persuasion people quite naturally sought out congruences, either perceived or actual, between the two cultures. The congruences arrived at often seemed – and, indeed, were – results of misunderstandings or accidents. Indeed, to later observers the interpretations offered by members of one society for the practices of another can appear ludicrous. This, however, does not matter. Any congruence, no matter how tenuous, can be put to work and can take on a life of its own if it is accepted by both sides. Cultural conventions do not have to be true to be effective any more than legal precedents do. They have only to be accepted.

The middle ground of the *pays d'en haut* existed on two distinct levels. It was both a product of everyday life and a product of formal diplomatic relations between distinct peoples. For historians, however, the middle ground is initially easiest to perceive as it was articulated in formal settings.[6]

In June 1695 the alliance of the Huron-Petuns, Ottawas, and French was in one of its recurrent crises. The Ottawas and Huron-Petuns, fearing that the French would make a separate peace with the Iroquois, had undertaken secret negotiations of their own with the Five Nations. These negotiations had received added impetus from English promises of trade at rates considerably below those of the French. The French commander at Michilimackinac, Antoine Laumet de La Mothe, Sieur de Cadillac, suspecting the existence of such talks but not knowing the details of them, attempted to halt the negotiations by soliciting war parties led by French partisans among the Ottawas. Though relatively few, the war parties threatened the Iroquois and thus disrupted plans for peace. The leaders of those who favored peace, particularly a Huron chief known as the Baron, sought to stop the war parties without mentioning the Huron-Petuns' negotiations with the Iroquois. To succeed, the Baron had to accomplish one of two things. He had to provide reasons acceptable both to the French and to their partisans as to why the war parties should not depart. Or, failing this, he had to alienate the pro-French Ottawas from Cadillac and the Jesuits. To achieve these ends, he convened a "grand and numerous" council of the nations of Michilimackinac to meet with one another as well as with Cadillac, the Jesuits, and "the most respectable Frenchmen of the post."[7]

The council convened to do little more than hear a story from the Baron. He told his listeners that recently there had been discovered in the country around Saginaw Bay an old man and his wife, each about a hundred years old. They had resided there ever since the expulsion of the Hurons from their own country. The old man knew and had related all that had passed in the western wars since the destruction of the Hurons and had paid particular attention to the embassies of the Iroquois to Onontio. He knew all these things because of his communications with the Master of Life who spoke directly to the old man and who sent him animals and made his fields abound with corn and pumpkins. The old man, too, knew of the present de facto truce with the Iroquois and insinuated that the first side to break it would inevitably be destroyed.[8]

The old man exhorted the Indians to be attentive to the Black Gowns and to apply themselves to prayer because, if the Master of Life "who is one in three persons, who form but one Spirit and one Will" was not obeyed, he would kill the corn as he had last year. Finally the old man had told them the eighth day should be observed by abstinence from work and should be sanctified by prayer. The dead, he said, should be given scaffold burials instead of being buried in the ground, so that they could more easily take the road to Heaven. Finally, the old man had urged that they all hearken to the voice of Onontio and follow his will. On concluding his recitation of the old man's message, the Baron offered Cadillac a present of beaver from the old man himself. Cadillac, who thought that of the whole story only the beaver was not imaginary, refused the present, "this voice being unknown to him."[9]

The Baron's story was an attempt to use and expand the middle ground so that his own interest – peace with the Iroquois – could be secured. Peace could not be protected through normal Huron cultural forms. If the matter had depended only on non-Christian Ottawas and Huron-Petuns, the Baron would not have had to resort to the story of the old man, with all its Christian and prophetic elements. If he had been addressing Indians only, the council could have been convened to consider a dream that contained the same message. Dreams, however, as the Baron realized quite well, had no legitimacy for the French who were urging their partisans to action. What did have legitimacy for them was divine revelation, and so the Baron gave them one. Baron's attempt failed because, as the chronicler of his speech huffily observed, the French only attached "belief to certain revelations and visions . . . because they are authorized." The old man was unauthorized and so proved an unsuccessful device for conveying a message in a manner that had legitimacy for Europeans.[10]

Nonetheless, the Baron's tactics were both clever and revealing. He had consciously tried to buttress the legitimacy of the old man's message by filling it with fragments of Christian doctrine (the Trinity, exhortations to prayer, attentiveness to the missionaries) and with the commands to follow the will of Onontio, the French governor. These were all items the French could hardly quarrel with. Yet the Baron also gave the message a definite Huron tinge. The prophet was an Indian who changed the Sabbath from the seventh day to the eighth. It is unlikely this was accidental. As early as 1679, the Jesuits had praised the Huron-Petuns for their particularly scrupulous observance of Sundays and feast days. The Huron-Petuns even had a special officer of the faith who gave notice of the meeting days. It would be surprising if the Baron had forgotten all this. It seems more likely that the Baron's movement of the Sabbath was intentional and that he meant it, along with the command for scaffold burials, to set the old man apart as an Indian prophet with an Indian message from the Christian God. It is unclear if the Baron seriously believed the French would accept the legitimacy of an Indian prophet, but by framing the story as he did, he created a situation in which even their rejection of the old man might serve his purposes. When Cadillac and the Jesuits rejected the old man, they rejected, too, exhortation to prayer and obedience to missionaries and Onontio. More than that, by rejecting the story, the French seemed to insinuate that God spoke directly only to whites, and not to Indians.[11]

Cadillac denounced the story as ridiculous, mocked the Baron's apparent confusion about the Sabbath, and demanded that the Indians strike the Iroquois. He left behind a troubled council. To the gathered Ottawa and Huron-Petun elders it now seemed that "the French were unwilling to listen to the voice of their pretended man of God, alleging that the Black Gowns were very desirous of being heard when they recounted stories about Paul and the anchorites of olden times; wherefore then, they asked, shall not our old man possess the same light?"[12]

The council was merely a skirmish within the larger diplomatic battle being waged over participation by the Michilimackinac Indians in the Iroquois war, but it reveals the process that formed the middle ground and made the boundaries between French and Algonquian societies so porous. To further its interests, each side had to attain cultural legitimacy in terms of the other. The Baron and Cadillac, as much as each might mangle the subtleties of the other's cultural view, had created a forum in which they could speak and understand each other. They did so by using, for their own purposes and according to their own understanding, the cultural forms of the other. The Baron appealed to a Christian tradition of prophecy and put it to Indian purposes. He sought to validate it, in Indian terms, by a gift of beaver. Cadillac, appearing in an Indian council, followed Algonquian forms and, knowing what acceptance of the gift signified, refused it. To accept the gift was to acknowledge the old man, whom the Baron would then make "talk on every occasion that he would judge favorable for his pernicious designs." He rejected an Indian adaptation of a Christian device through his own use of Algonquian-Iroquoian diplomatic forms. Both used the cultural forms of the other cleverly, if crudely. The crudeness of the Baron's Christianity or Cadillac's mastery of Indian diplomacy mattered less than the need for each to employ these foreign elements at all. They merged them into something quite different from the Algonquian, Iroquoian, and French cultures that gave them birth.

The Baron's encounter with Cadillac took place in a diplomatic forum where representatives of each culture dealt with a well-formulated body of ideas and practices. This was one aspect of the middle ground and the one in which its methods are best documented and exhibited. The middle ground itself, however, did not originate in councils and official encounters; instead, it resulted from the daily encounters of individual Indians and Frenchmen with problems and controversies that needed immediate solution. Many of these problems revolved around basic issues of sex, violence, and material exchange. The need to resolve these problems, perhaps even more than the problems of alliance, forced the middle ground into existence. But even this misstates the issue, for the distinction between official dealings and personal dealings was a hazy and confusing one in Algonquian society, where coercive mechanisms and hierarchical structures were notoriously weak.

Although French officials spoke of their relationship with the Algonquians in economic, political, and, less often, religious terms, paradoxically economic and political institutions could not control the context of contact. In the day-to-day relations of the western country, the relationships of Algonquians and Frenchmen as trading partners and allies were abstractions, pertinent, perhaps, to Indians and French as aggregates, but having little to do with actual people in face-to-face relationships. In another society, with more coercive mechanisms at an elite's disposal, personal relations between intruders such as the French and the members of the host society might be kept to a minimum and mattered little. Traders might be isolated in special quarters and granted special privileges; they might be governed by separate rules and taxed at stated rates. Isolation, however, was impossible among the Algonquians, who lacked a state with coercive institutions and in whose society obedience to authority was usually neither a social fact nor a social virtue.[13]

This weakness of political authority and lack of subordination in Algonquian society struck both the Algonquians and the French as a major difference between the two peoples. For the French this lack of subordination, not the Algonquians' state of material or technological development, was at the heart of Algonquian "savagery." The northern Indians, according to the Sieur d'Aigremont, "possess no subordination among themselves . . . being opposed to all constraint. Moreover, these peoples [have] no idea of Royal grandeur nor Majesty, nor of the powers of Superiors over inferiors."[14]

Father Membre, traveling south along the Mississippi with La Salle in 1682, clearly regarded authority as being at the heart of not only society but humanity. The Natchez and the hierarchical societies of the Mississippi were technologically like the Algonquians. They were a Stone Age people, but they were "all different from our Canada Indians in their houses, dress, manners, inclinations and customs. . . .Their chiefs possess all the authority. . . . They have their valets and officers who follow them and serve them everywhere. They distribute their favors and presents at will. In a word we generally found men there."[15]

The French did not err in noting the absence of class divisions and state and religious institutions among northern Algonquians, but they were mistaken when they took this for an absence of social order. Tradition was the storehouse of a tribal people's knowledge of themselves as a people and a guide to how they should act. As war and disease reduced populations and forced the amalgamation of previously distinct peoples, the survivors seemed to cling to their traditions. But they were like infants sucking the breasts of their dead mothers; tradition could no longer sustain them.[16]

The weakness of coercive authority among the Algonquians would have mattered less if French authority had officially reached the West. With the decline of the trade fairs, however, official French supervision of exchange became a mirage. Indians no longer traveled long distances to fortified European towns or outposts to exchange furs. Some limited exchanges of this type took place at Fort Saint Louis, in the Illinois country, and at Michilimackinac and the posts Perrot erected among the Sioux, but most trade was the work of small groups of Frenchmen traveling to Indian villages and hunting camps. Once these traders had lost their status as manitous, they were strangers without social standing in Algonquian villages. They were also wealthy strangers, with goods far in excess of their own immediate needs, who stood virtually defenseless. If they were to succeed as traders, they had to find means to protect themselves either through force or by establishing personal ties within the communities in which they traded.[17]

The French elite feared the consequences of such contact. French authorities thought that Frenchmen moving within Algonquian society would slip the net unless kept under tight control. What horrified French officials quite as much as the economic damage they believed the coureurs de bois did was the social threat they represented. According to officials, the coureurs de bois were metamorphosing into *sauvages,* that is, men beyond the control of legitimate authority. What was particularly horrifying about the "savagery" of the coureurs de bois was that they seemed to glory in it. They used their freedom to mock the men who never doubted that they were their betters. On his return to the Illinois in 1680, La Salle found that his men had not only deserted but had also demolished his fort, stolen his goods, and, in the hand of a man La Salle recognized as Le Parisien, had left scrawled on a board a parting epithet: *Nous sommes touts Sauvages* ("We are all savages").[18]

Le Parisien, of course, was no more a *sauvage* than La Salle. He merely shared with his superiors a common misunderstanding of Algonquian society as a place of license without order. It was this misperception that gave the word *sauvage* its power as a metaphor for what officials regarded as a danger and men like Le Parisien saw as an opportunity – the escape from subordination. That most coureurs de bois could fully escape the restraining hands of the state and the church was an exaggeration. Yet, in another sense, the fear of the authorities and the hope of Le Parisien were not fully misplaced. Frenchmen in the West could to a remarkable degree act independently, if only temporarily, in reaching accommodations with the Algonquians among whom they traveled and lived. They made contact a complex social process only partially under the control of church and state. In the West, this process centered on Frenchmen whom the authorities did not regard as legitimate representatives of their own society and who were actually seen as a danger to it. There was always a tension between these men and those other Frenchmen who possessed legitimate standing: men who like La Salle, came with grants from the Crown; or missionaries, like the Jesuits; or military commanders; or licensed traders. Frenchmen in the West often cooperated, but such cooperation could never be presumed. Indians thus had to establish appropriate social ties with a diverse and often quarreling group of Frenchmen.[19]

Certain of these diverse Frenchmen, in turn, posed dangers to Algonquian social order because they struck at the heart of Algonquian identity by arguing that traditional practices were not innate, but transferable from one people to another. Missionaries and Christianity, in this sense, represented a potentially subversive force that, if not assimilated into Algonquian traditions, could destroy the very identity of those who accepted it. Only in the Illinois country was this threat soon realized, and there, where the dangers of Christianity were most fully faced, the arguments of the opponents of the missionaries are revealing. The adversaries of the church based their attack partially on the argument that prayer was ineffective and baptism brought death, but they also worked from the assumption that Christianity displaced traditions central to the identity of various Illinois groups and appropriate to them. In a style of argument that foreshadowed later appeals to an "Indian way," Illinois elders contended that since identity was innate, Christianity was proper for the French; Illinois beliefs were proper for the Illinois. As a leading Peoria chief, an opponent of Christianity, phrased it:

> I shall hold a feast . . . and I shall invite all the old men and all the chiefs of bands. . . . After speaking of our medicines and of what our grandfathers and ancestors have taught us, has this man who has come from afar better medicines than we have, to make us adopt his customs? His fables are good only in his own country; we have ours, which do not make us die as his do.

Or, in the words of a Kaskaskia elder, "full of zeal for the ancient customs of the country and apprehending that his credit and that of his class [son semblable] would be diminished if their people embraced the faith":

> All ye who have hitherto hearkened to what the black gown has said to you come into my cabin. I shall likewise teach you what I learned from my grandfather, and what we should believe. Leave their myths to the people who come from afar, and let us cling to our own traditions.[20]

The operation of the middle ground must be understood within a dual context. First, there was the weakness of hierarchical controls within Algonquian villages and the frailty of any authority French officials exerted over Frenchmen in the West. Second, there was the cultural threat each society seemed to pose to the elite of the other. What this meant in practice was that both the extent and meaning of social relations between Frenchmen and Algonquians were often negotiated largely on a face-to-face level within the villages themselves, and that these relations were not what either French authorities or Algonquian elders might have preferred them to be. This does not mean that there was no official element involved, but rather that official decisions could not determine the course of actual relations.

Notes

1   The impossibility of considering any society in isolation is one of the major themes of Eric Wolf in *Europe and the People Without History* (Berkeley: University of California Press, 1982), 3–23, 385. It is also a position taken by Anthony Giddens, *A Contemporary Critique of Historical Materialism* (Berkeley: University of California Press, 1981), 23–24.

2   For concentration on European images, see Bernard Sheehan, *Savagism and Civility: Indians and Englishmen in Colonial America* (Cambridge: Cambridge University Press, 1980); Olive P. Dickason, *The Myth of the Savage and the Beginnings of French Colonialism in the Americas* (Edmonton: University of Alberta Press, 1984); Cornelius Jaenen is correct when he points out that the French lacked the power to force American Indians to acculturate. Cornelius Jaenen, *Friend and Foe: Aspects of French-Amerindian Cultural Contact in the Sixteenth and Seventeenth Centuries* (New York: Columbia University Press, 1976), 195. James Axtell's work is an exception to the usual tendency to impose static categories on Indians and whites, and Karen Kupperman disputes the extent to which cultural concepts derived from early accounts actually governed relations, Karen Ordahl Kupperman, *Settling with the Indians: The Meeting of English and Indian Cultures in America, 1580–1640* (Totowa, N.J.: Rowman & Littlefield, 1980).

3   Cornelius J. Jaenen, "Les Sauvages Ameriquains: Persistence into the Eighteenth Century of Traditional French Concepts and Constructs for Comprehending AmerIndians," *Ethnohistory* 29 (1982): 43–56.

4   A useful discussion of these processes is found in Roy Wagner, *The Invention of Culture* (Chicago: University of Chicago Press, 1081), 1–70, particularly 46–52, 87–88. Many Frenchmen of peasant backgrounds were probably closer to what Wagner calls the differentiating mode of tribal peoples than to the systematizing mode of French officials.

Attempts to get around the confining model of a basically static structure which is combined with an ephemeral history has been most thoroughly developed by Anthony Giddens, *Central Problems in Social Theory: Action, Structure and Contradiction in Social Analysis* (Berkeley: University of California Press, 1979); *Critique of Historical Materialism;* and *The Constitution of Society* (Berkeley: University of California Press, 1984). It has simultaneously emerged in anthropology, see Marshall Sahlins, *Islands of History* (Chicago: University of Chicago Press, 1985).

5   For this, see Wagner, *Invention of Culture,* 52–55.

6   The creation of the middle ground might serve as an example of what Anthony Giddens calls structuration. Giddens, *Central Problems in Social Theory,* 2–7, 69–73, 82.

7   Callières au Ministre, 20 oct. 1696, Archives Nationales, Paris [hereafter cited as AN], C11A, v.14, ff. 216–17. Narrative of . . . Occurrences . . . 1694, 1695, *Documents Relative to the Colonial History of the State of New York: procured . . . by John R. Brodhead,* ed. E. B. O'Callaghan (Albany, N.Y.: Parsons, Weed, 1853–1857) [hereafter cited as *NYCD*] 9:604–9.

8   Narrative of . . . Occurrences . . . 1694, 1695, *NYCD* 9:607.

9   *Ibid.;* it is interesting to note here that some Ottawas eventually did adopt scaffold burials, *Handbook of North American Indian,* ed. William C. Sturtevant (Washington, D.C.: Smithsonian Institution, 1978–) 15:777.

10   Narrative of . . . Occurrences . . . 1694, 1695, *NYCD* 9:607.

11   For Huron-Petuns and Sabbath, see *The Jesuit Relations and Allied Documents,* ed. Reuben Gold Thwaites (Cleveland, Ohio: Burrows Brothers, 1898) [hereafter cited as *JR*] 61:105.

12   Narrative of . . . Occurrences . . . 1694, 1695, *NYCD* 9:608. For a similar instance, see *JR* 59:223.

13   Narrative of . . . Occurrences . . . 1694, 1695, *NYCD* 9:608. For the development of trading enclaves, see Philip D. Curtin, *Cross-cultural Trade in World History* (Cambridge: Cambridge University Press, 1984), 11–12, 38, 46–49, 111–15.

14   For Sieur d'Aigremont, sec D'Aigremont to Pontchartrain, Nov. 14, 1708, *Collections of the State Historical Society of Wisconsin,* ed. Lyman C. Draper and Reuben G. Thwaites (Madison, Wis.: The Society, 1855–1911) 16:250.

15   Chrétien Le Clercq, *The First Establishment of the Faith in New France,* 2 vols. (New York: J. G. Shea, 1881), 192.

16   See Giddens, *Critique of Historical Materialism,* 93–94, 160, for a general discussion of these issues.

17   *JR* 65:239. W. J. Eccles, *The Canadian Frontier* (Albuquerque: University of New Mexico Press, 1974), 110; Champigny au Ministre, 4 nov. 1693, AN, C11A, v. 12; Memoire . . . Denonville, aoust 1688, AN, C11A, v. 10 (765–66); Callières au Ministre, 15 oct. 1694, AN, C11A, v. 15; Memoire sur le ferme . . . 10 fev. 1696, AN, C11A, v. 16; Commerce du castor . . . 1696, AN, C11A, v. 14; Milo Quaife (ed.), *The Western Country in the Seventeenth Century: The Memoirs of Lanothe Cadillac and Pierre Liette* (Chicago: Lakeside Press, 1917), 16–18. Untitled mémoire (Par tout ce qui . . .) AN, C11A, v. 17 (f. 193).

18   Duchesneau to M. de Seignelay, 10 Nov. 1679, *NYCD* 9:133–34; Denonville à Seignelay, 13 nov. 1685, AN, C11A, v.7; Champigny Memoir, 10 mai 1691, AN, C11A, v. 11; Denonville to Seignelay, Jan. 1690, *NYCD* 9:442–43. For quotation, see Relation du voyage de Cavelier de La Salle, du 22 Aout 1680 a l'automne de 1681, Pierre Margry, *Découvertes et établissements des Français . . . de l'Amérique Septentrionale 1614–1698,* 6 vols. (Paris: Maisonneuve et Cie, 1879, repr. New York, AMS Press, Inc., 1974) 2:133. On coureurs de bois, see Jaenen, *Friend and Foe,* 115; Eccles, *Canadian Frontier,* 90.

19   Louise Dechêne, in examining records of those going west between 1708 and 1717, found that of a total of 373 different individuals, 179 made just one trip and 112 made three or more. These 112 formed "l'armature du commerce interieur." The others made such voyages "une activité temporaire ou occasionnelle"; Dechêne, *Habitants et Marchands de Montréal an xvii siècle* (Paris: Libraire Plon, 1974), 219–20.

20   *JR* 64:173, 183.

Chapter 12

Richard F. Gombrich

PROTESTANT BUDDHISM IN
NINETEENTH-CENTURY CEYLON

... **DURING THE NINETEENTH CENTURY** Buddhism began to change its character. Not in the countryside or the Kandyan provinces, not as yet in a way to affect more than a very small segment of the Buddhist population. But by the end of the century quite a new kind of Buddhism had taken definite shape and begun to spread from the middle classes in Colombo. In 1892 the Anglican Bishop of Colombo published a rather well-informed book about Buddhism, in which he wrote:

> There are two Buddhisms now in Ceylon: the residuum of the old Buddhism of
> the past centuries, as it lingers in out-of-the-way places, and as it has shaped the
> habits and ways of those who are not under European influence; and a new
> revival, much more self-conscious and artificial, which aims indeed only at
> reviving what Buddhism always professed to be, but which has been influenced,
> in its estimate of that profession, very largely by Europeans.[1]

This new kind of Buddhism has been brilliantly analysed by modern scholars. Professor Bechert has called it 'Buddhist modernism'. Professor Obeyesekere 'Protestant Buddhism'. Like Dr Malalgoda, on whose fine work I draw heavily in the following account of its origins, I shall use the latter name because it has so many illuminating implications. For this movement in Theravāda Buddhism – which began in Sri Lanka but has by no means been confined to it – both originated as a protest (against Christianity) and itself reflects Protestantism. Its salient characteristic is the importance it assigns to the laity – and the correspondingly lesser importance it assigns to the Sangha. Indeed, we can begin our account of it by pointing out that the very view of Buddhist history on which this book has been based, that which identifies the fortunes of Buddhism with those of the Sangha, would be questioned by Protestant Buddhists. For they regard all adherents of a religion as equally responsible for its welfare. It is precisely because this view appears as a natural one to modern western readers, with their centuries of Protestant experience, that its novelty needs to be emphasized.

To the creation of Protestant Buddhism two kinds of influence have contributed. The primary credit must go to Protestant missionaries, and to a handful of other westerners influenced by them, antimissionary missionaries: the Theosophists. But their seed would not have fallen on fertile ground – to use the kind of image they loved – had the peace and prosperity of the nineteenth century not brought about socio-economic changes. A new Sinhalese middle class of bureaucrats, businessmen and professionals (lawyers, doctors, school-teachers, intellectuals) arose, centred on Colombo; the kind of religious individualism which had appealed to businessmen in northwest Europe from the Reformation on appealed to them too. As had happened when the Buddha first preached, the urban middle class seized the religious leadership; Buddhism for the second time began a Protestant reformation. This time, as in the European case, it was based on another effect of British rule: the use of printing, and hence the increase of reading (in this case, notably of reading English). . . .

The British missions

The great technical innovation of the missionaries, and one which was to have a profound influence, was their use of the printing press. The first Sinhala press had been established by the Dutch government of Ceylon in 1736; it was used mainly to print Christian propaganda. The second was imported for the same purpose by the Wesleyans in 1815. The Anglicans and the Baptists then each set up their own.[2] From the start, what was printed was more polemical than merely expository. With typically military metaphor, Gogerly, the manager of the Wesleyan Press, wrote in 1831, 'At present it is by means of the press our main attacks must be made upon this wretched system. . . . We must direct our efforts to pull down this stronghold of Satan.'[3] Those responsible estimated that between 1849 and 1861 1½ million tracts (in both Sinhala and English) circulated among the Ceylonese population[4] of about 3 million, of whom many could not read. . . .

Early Buddhist reactions

Theravāda Buddhists had not yet printed their scriptures, and indeed it was a long time before some monks could be persuaded of the utility of doing so. The first Buddhist press was in Colombo. Significantly, it had originally been imported by the Church Missionaries (Anglican) in 1823; they sold it off to an employee in 1855. The second was set up independently in 1862 by a Buddhist monk in Galle, the largest town in south Ceylon; he kept it going with the help of his friend King Mongkut of Siam, who himself during his monkhood had been the first Siamese to establish a printing press.[5]

Who wrote for these presses? Two monks spear-headed the Buddhist response. The Galle publications were mainly by Hikkaḍuve Sumangala (1826–1911). In Colombo, the leading Buddhist was Mohoṭṭivatte . . . Guṇānanda (1823–90). . . .

At almost the same time as the Buddhists took to printing tracts, they at last began to accept the Christian challenge to public debate. In 1864 the Anglican Seminary challenged the monks of the local temple, and were surprised – and presumably gratified – when they accepted. They were even more surprised in February 1865, when the debate took place, for nearly fifty monks, including Sumangala and Guṇānanda, turned up, and so did about two thousand Buddhist laymen. Because of disagreement on procedure, this debate finally took the form of an exchange of questions and answers in writing; and a similar event later in the year took the same form; but this was followed by a series of live public debates.[6] In almost all the major encounters Guṇānanda took the leading part on the Buddhist side. Indeed, he plausibly claimed in 1887 that over 25 years he had given over 4,000 public lectures and sermons.[7] The most important debate in which he took part was held at Pānadura, south of Colombo, in 1873, with David de Silva as his principal opponent. It took two days. On the first day the audience was estimated at 5,000, on the second day at over 10,000. This debate was a turning point. The audience was of course predominantly Buddhist and fiercely partisan; their shouts of victory echoed far and wide.[8] The missionaries realized now that they had misjudged the situation, and issued no further challenges. But to consider the debate a victory of Guṇānanda, one did not have to be present. The entire debate was published in the newspapers, both Sinhala and English, and the English version then appeared in book form. It was this book which reached Colonel Henry Steele Olcott, co-founder of the Theosophical Society, with far-reaching consequences.[9]

It is in these beginnings that the mirror-image nature of the Buddhist reaction to Protestant attacks is particularly evident. Traditionally Buddhist monks preach seated, and often holding a fan in front of their faces, in order to render the sermon as impersonal as possible. We know that Guṇānanda, at least in public debate, adopted the Christian style of preaching; he spoke standing, gesticulated, and generally acted the orator.[10] To some extent his matter too was copied from the Christians; as they questioned the historicity of his scriptures, he impugned the historicity of theirs, and so forth. . . .

The rise of the Buddhist laity

The salient characteristic of Protestant Buddhism is the enhanced importance of the laity. In 1904 Sumangala was among several prominent monks who addressed a Memorial of the Sangha of Ceylon to King Edward VII; in it they wrote 'By the laws of Buddha the laity form no part of religion. The Sangha are the only living representatives of Buddhism on earth.'[11] This slightly exaggerated statement was provoked by remarkable developments within Buddhism in the previous 30 years, some of them unintended consequences of Sumangala's own actions. It was in the field of education that the Buddhist laity first came to the fore. Monks could and did answer the missionary challenges in preaching and printing, but for the running of schools they lacked the organizational structures and probably the administrative experience. During the first fifty years of British rule the small village temple school seems to have flourished in the Low Country, but declined in the Kandyan provinces. However, these schools, with their archaic curricula and lack of English, could not compete with the Christian schools. In 1869, the year in which the Department of Public Instruction was founded, a Buddhist monk organized the opening of the first non-monastic Buddhist school in Ceylon, with a headmaster who was a convert from Christianity and had been educated at a mission school.

There is very little evidence about the extent of literacy among the Sinhalese laity before the nineteenth century. In 1821 male literacy was estimated as being 'almost as general as in England'.[12] That has been estimated for the period at just over 60 per cent.[13] It seems reasonable to suppose that even in its periods of decline the village Sangha had imparted literacy to a fair number of high-caste males. But as there was hardly any Sinhalese printing before the nineteenth century, and manuscripts were virtually confined to monasteries, even the literate can have had nothing to read: earlier lay Buddhists lived in an essentially oral culture. Schools and printing presses combined in the late nineteenth century to produce a lay reading public for the first time in Sinhalese history. For the middle classes, however, this literacy was primarily in English. This gave them access to modern knowledge and allowed them to communicate with the wider world; at the same time, it often alienated them from the traditional culture.

The danger of such alienation was apparent to active Buddhists, and they began to harness the educational revolution to their own requirements. A landmark in the history of Buddhist doctrine was the foundation of Vidyodaya Piriveṇa, a Buddhist ecclesiastical college, in 1873.[14] Already in 1864 two prominent Buddhist laymen from Colombo had written a letter to the press suggesting the establishment of a college of Buddhist studies, with £10,000 capital. The idea was novel and it took nine years to raise enough money to start Vidyodaya.[15] In this decade the institutions started by monks, notably the two presses and the non-monastic Buddhist schools just mentioned, ran into financial difficulties and collapsed. Sumangala became the principal of Vidyodaya. In this capacity he was assisted by a lay management committee which included several leading entrepreneurs, including a Colombo furniture dealer called Hewavitharanage Don Carolis, and his father-in-law Don Andris Perera.[16] Two years later, in 1875, two monks founded Vidyālaṃkāra, a similar Buddhist college.[17] Both these colleges admitted both clergy and laity. These two institutions, both in Colombo suburbs, continued for nearly a century as the leading educational institutions for Buddhist monks; they were given full University status in 1959. They have both been cradles of Protestant Buddhism, and crucial for feeding that movement back into the mainstream of Buddhism via the clergy whom they educate.

The impact of the Theosophists

Enter the Theosophists. The Theosophical Society was founded by Madame Blavatsky and Colonel Olcott in 1875 in New York; its headquarters moved to Adyar, near Madras, in 1879. In that year Bishop Copleston, the Anglican Bishop of Colombo, wrote to the Society for the Propagation of the Gospel:

> The secretary of an obscure Society – which, however, for all the Sinhalese know, may be a distinguished one – has been writing, it appears, to several Buddhist priests here, hailing them as brothers in the march of intellect, and congratulating one or two of them on the part they took so nobly against Christianity in a certain ill-judged but insignificant public controversy which took place years ago in a village called Panadura. These letters the priests have printed in a little pamphlet, along with some selections from an English book, which describes some spiritualistic performances of Buddhist priests in Thibet.[18]

The secretary was Olcott, and the English book was *Isis Unveiled*, which Madame Blavatsky had presented to Guṇānanda. In the same year the same bishop wrote: 'Buddhism as a whole is not conquered, or near it. . . . There is little doubt that Buddhism is far more vigorous in Ceylon than it was 150 years ago'.[19] . . .

A few months later, in May 1890, Blavatsky and Olcott arrived in Ceylon. They took the Three Refuges and the Five Precepts, thus formally embracing Buddhism. For the Buddhists this was a victory indeed. Olcott was a colonel and a judge; he was also an experienced organizer and fund-raiser. Moreover, as an outsider he was in a unique position to unite the different factions among Sinhalese Buddhists. Two weeks after his arrival in Ceylon he lectured at Vidyodaya on 'Theosophy and Buddhism'. His aim was to set up a branch of the Theosophical Society in Ceylon; the Sinhalese of course were more concerned with their confrontation with Christianity. In the event Olcott set up two branches, the purely Theosophical one, which never flourished and soon died, and the Buddhist Theosophical Society (BTS), which was Theosophical only in name. Buddhist Theosophy was in fact Protestant Buddhism.[20]

In 1881 Olcott published – of course in English – his *Buddhist Catechism*, which was his attempt to formulate the basic tenets to which he felt all Buddhists in the world should be able to subscribe. This document, which has gone through many editions, not all of them bearing Olcott's name, deserves to rank as a Theosophical rather than a Buddhist creed, but this is not widely realized, notably in Britain, where the connections between Theosophy and organized Buddhism have been intimate. The *Buddhist Catechism* represents the beginning of the modern world Buddhist movement. Olcott likewise devised the Buddhist flag which has been adopted by the World Fellowship of Buddhists[21] and is in widespread use today: it is composed of the five colours of the Buddha's halo. The very idea of having a Buddhist flag springs from Olcott's American background. I think that the institution of singing carols at Wesak, the traditional anniversary of the Buddha's birth, Enlightenment and death, is Olcott's answer to Christmas carols; the English ones have fallen into desuetude, but Protestant Buddhists still sing Sinhala songs at Wesak. The same analogy with Christmas underlies the flourishing modern trade in Wesak cards.

Olcott was delighted by his reception in Ceylon, and continued to visit it nearly every year until his death in 1907. The Buddhists trusted him so well that in 1884 they made him their representative to the Colonial Office with full discretion, and empowered him 'to accept and register as Buddhists persons of any nation who may make to him application to administer to them the Three Refuges and Five Precepts and to organize societies for the promotion of Buddhism'. This was written by seven monks headed by Sumangala, who till his death was chairman of the clerical division of the BTS. His traditional Buddhist ideas made him a personal rather than an ideological friend of Olcott. In 1903 Olcott wrote of the clerical division, 'I have not been able, during an intimate intercourse of twenty-two years, to arouse their zeal', and for his part Sumangala resigned from the BTS in 1905, in protest at what seemed to him Theosophy's greater identification with Hinduism, though he withdrew his resignation on Olcott's personal assurance and appeal. Relations between Olcott and Guṇānanda were worse: in 1887, shortly before his death, Guṇānanda wrote in Sinhala a kind of Buddhist catechism in answer to Olcott's, and in its preface he emphasized the need to reassert the true doctrines of Buddhism. In the same year he invited Olcott to lecture at his temple, and after Olcott's address delivered a passionate attack on Olcott and the BTS in Sinhala.[22]

Guṇānanda's attack on the BTS was probably motivated, like Sumangala's later resignation, by the spectacle of Buddhist leadership passing into lay hands; for it was the lay division of the BTS, with its local sub-divisions, which was really active and effective. This part of the BTS ran the schools which Olcott helped to found, and which were perhaps the most enduring part of his achievement in Ceylon. In 1881 he went on fund-raising tours especially to raise money for Buddhist education, and by 1889 there were 63 BTS schools and another 40 Buddhist schools (mostly with lay managers) registered with the government. BTS schools were modelled on the missionary schools, down to the cricket; education was in English, and Buddhism took the place Christianity held in the missions. Monks were not prominent as either teachers or managers of BTS schools.[23] Some of these schools became very important, and their sponsorship only changed in 1961, when the government nationalized almost all independent schools.

From now on Buddhist lay organizations proliferated, and continued to be modelled on Christian organizations. The Young Men's Buddhist Association was founded in 1898 by a Buddhist convert from Roman Catholicism; one of its aims is: 'to advance the moral, cultural, physical and social welfare of Buddhists'. In practice the YMBA has paid little attention to the Y, but developed into the most important lay Buddhist organization in Ceylon, its leadership being known nowadays as the All Ceylon Buddhist Congress.[24] It was the YMBA which set up a national network of Buddhist Sunday Schools and commissioned, printed and distributed the texts for them, till these functions were taken over in the 1960s by the government. The BTS founded two newspapers, the Sinhala one in 1880 and the

English one in 1888. In 1889 Buddhist laymen began to be involved in the administration of the Sangha's temporalities.[25] The management of Sangha property has remained a controversial topic, and the reports of the largely lay commissions which have been set up to investigate it are important documents of Protestant Buddhism.[26]

Anagārika Dharmapāla

We must return to the family of Hewavitharanage Don Carolis. His father-in-law, Don Andris Perera, was president of the Colombo branch of the lay BTS from 1883 to 1890.[27] His son, born in 1864, became the most important figure in the modern history of Buddhism. His given name was Don David Hewavitarne, but he is usually known as Anagārika Dharmapāla, a name and style which he assumed in 1881.[28] Shortly before his death in 1933 he became a monk and took a new name, but that too is little remembered. The name Dharmapāla means 'Protector of the Dhamma' – Defender of the Faith. The title *Anagārika* was an innovation. The word is Pali (and Sanskrit) and means 'homeless'; traditionally it was one of the epithets of Buddhist monks, but never a title. Dharmapāla used the term to designate a new status, to which we return below. . . .

Dharmapāla gave the layman a new place in Buddhism which went much further than organizational leadership. Traditionally lay Buddhists did not meditate; those who wished to meditate gave up the lay life. Moreover, there seems to have been very little meditation in Ceylon in the late nineteenth century. In 1890 Dharmapāla found in an old Buddhist temple a text on meditation, which he studied and ultimately caused to be published.[29] He practised meditation on the basis of this study, and thus became, so far as is known, the first Buddhist to learn meditation from a book without recourse to a master. Moreover he initiated the fashion for lay meditation, which has become so popular among the bourgeoisie of Colombo and Rangoon that few if any of them realize the untraditional nature of their activities.[30]

Lay religious activism

We come now to the heart of the Protestant Buddhist ethos. It is encapsulated in the title Anagārika. With it Dharmapāla invented a status half way between monk and layman as these roles were traditionally understood. Instead of the monk's yellow robe he wore a white robe, and he did not shave his head, but he formally undertook a life of chastity and ascetic abstention. He took the Eight Precepts. . . . Traditionally Buddhist laymen may take these vows on Buddhist holy days (*poya* days) for spells of 24 hours; and a few old people take them permanently; but Dharmapāla took them for life while still a young man. He thus made a dramatic public commitment to devoting his life to Buddhism, but without renouncing worldly – notably political – activity. By devoting his life to Buddhism Dharmapāla meant not merely, in fact not primarily, seeking his own salvation, but promoting the Sāsana, and indeed the general welfare of Buddhists as he saw it. . . .

Dharmapāla worked hard – and successfully – to inculcate into the middle classes of Colombo (it can at first hardly have amounted to more than that) some of the values of this-worldly asceticism (as Weber characterized Calvinism). Like all Protestant reformers, he preached such virtues as honesty, diligence and thrift. We have seen that these were the values that the Buddha preached to the laity. The *Advice to Sigāla*, the Buddha's most famous sermon on lay ethics, which we have discussed above, was sometimes known in Sinhala as the 'Disciplinary Code for the Laity'. Dharmapāla published a Sinhala pamphlet under precisely this title, *Gihi Vinaya*, in 1898. It has run through some 20 editions and sold about 50,000 copies. It can be said to apply Protestant values to the details of daily life, very much on the model of any late Victorian manual of etiquette. . . .

Dharmapāla accepted the western Protestant view of religion as one and the same for everybody. It would never have occurred even to his anti-Christian friends the Theosophists, with their own Protestant backgrounds, to question this assumption. So Dharmapāla saw Buddhist soteriological doctrine and activity as equally applicable to everyone. Laymen should meditate. 'Gods and priests', the stuff of communal religion, could have no place in the lives of good Buddhists. The communal religion which in fact the Sinhalese were practising must therefore be due to pernicious Hindu influence. . . .

Limited scope of Protestant Buddhism

Protestant Buddhism crystallized in the figure of Dharmapāla. For the first half of the twentieth century Ceylon remained under British rule – Independence came in 1948 – and the Sinhalese for the most part remained divided into two classes of very unequal size: a small, urbanized and largely English-educated middle class and a traditional peasantry. To these two classes corresponded the two types of Buddhism I have tried to characterize. The Sangha continued to recruit predominantly from the countryside. Those monks who progressed for their education to one of the Colombo colleges were exposed to the views of such lay intellectuals as Malalasekera and Jayatilleke; but when they returned to their village incumbencies those concerns must have seemed to most of them rarefied and remote. Many took up the traditional life of the village Sangha, their intellectual horizons perhaps having been broadened and their feelings of social responsibility somewhat enhanced. It became normal for the village monk to supervise a village Sunday school, using the course booklets and entering pupils for the examinations of the YMBA; and monks often assumed the presidency of local welfare organizations, Village Development Committees, etc. A minority of them – one would guess mainly those 'younger sons' whose prospect of succeeding to an incumbency was negligible – decided not to fit back into the traditional mould and became salaried school-teachers or found some other living away from the village; it is a safe assumption that a fair proportion of them ended by reverting to lay status. Some monks interacted with western scholars; during the period of British rule traditional learning flourished in the Sangha, producing many fine scholars.[31] However, the Sangha (in the strict sense) . . . found no new organizational forms and underwent no development which might have counterbalanced the rising tide of lay leadership. Since that tide was but dimly perceived as a problem – despite the early protest of Sumangala and his colleagues – the lack of an organized response is not surprising.

Works cited

Bechert, Heinz (1966), *Buddhismus, Staat und Gesellschaft in den Ländern des Theravāda Buddhismus*, vol. 1, Frankfurt a M and Berlin.

Copleston, R.S. (1982), *Buddhism Primitive and Present in Magadha and in Ceylon*, London and New York.

Gombrich, Richard F. (1983), 'From Monastery to Meditation Centre: Lay Meditation in Modern Sri Lanka', in Philip Denwood and Alexander Piatigorsky (ed.), *Buddhist Studies Ancient and Modern*, London, pp. 20–34.

Malalgoda, Kitsiri (1976), *Buddhism in Sinhalese Society 1750–1900*, Berkeley.

Obeyesekere, Gananath (1970), 'Religious Symbolism and Political Change in Ceylon', *Modern Ceylon Studies*, 1, 1, pp. 43–63.

Rhys Davids, T.W. (1896), 'Introduction' to *The Yogāvacara's Manual* ed. T.W. Rhys Davids, London.

Schofield, R.S. (1973), 'Dimensions of illiteracy, 1750–1850', *Explorations in Economic History*, 10, 4, pp. 437–54.

Notes

1   Copleston p. 461.
2   Above facts from Malalgoda p. 203.
3   Quoted *id.* pp. 204–5.
4   *Id.* p.205.
5   *Id.* p. 219.
6   *Id.* pp. 224–5.
7   *Id.* p.232 fn. 1.
8   *Id.* p. 226.
9   *Id.* p. 230.
10   *Id.* p. 226.
11   Quoted Bechert 1966, p. 67.
12   Quoted Malalgoda p. 176 fn. 9.
13   Schofield p. 446.
14   Malalgoda pp. 180, 240.
15   *Id.* pp. 239–40.
16   *Id.* pp. 241, 248.
17   *Id.* p. 188.
18   Quoted *id.* p. 230.
19   Quoted *id.* p. 231.
20   *Id.* pp. 242–6.
21   Bechert 1966, p. 100.
22   Malalgoda pp. 244–51.
23   *Id.* p. 250.
24   Bechert 1966, p. 52.
25   *Id.* p. 237.
26   *Id.* especially chaps. 25 (d), 26.
27   Malalgoda p. 248.
28   Biographical data on Dharmapāla from Bechert 1966, pp. 47–51; interpretation from Obeyesekere.
29   Rhys Davids 1896, p. V.
30   R.F. Gombrich 1983, pp.21–3.
31   Malalgoda p. 175.

PART V

Popular Culture

Introduction

THE PHRASE 'POPULAR CULTURE' brings to mind radically different things to cultural historians of different periods, and at first it is hard to see what those things have in common. It can refer to dances round the maypole on a village green, to television soap operas, to bear-baiting or to support for a local football team. The words suggest traditional music in a tavern rather than a symphony concert, chap-books and comics rather than textbooks and treatises. However, cultural activities like science, often associated with intellectual elites or minorities, have 'popular' forms (Cooter and Pumfrey 1994; O'Connor 2007). 'Popular culture' might be attractive and meaningful to a majority, but beyond that it is hard to specify with precision.

An increased interest in notions of 'popular culture' was a feature of the 'cultural turn' in the 1970s and 1980s. The interest derived from two main sources. First, with the study of orality (Ong 1971) came fresh awareness of cultural worlds beyond those centred on the written word. Historians wished to assimilate anthropological insights by grounding accounts of culture in the mundane practices of daily living (Burke 1977; Davis 1975), thus distinguishing cultural history from the history of ideas. Chartier (1984) pointed out the importance of tracing how cultural influences were expressed, appropriated – and thereby changed. The process of reception might give them a substantially new meaning, as with the folk religions resulting from mass conversions, which often contrasted strikingly with the religion of intellectuals (Flint 1991; Geary 1979). But in a second approach, authors influenced by Gramsci (1985) were seeking to replace crude theories of ideology with a better appreciation of the interplay between consciousness and action, especially in the behaviour of subordinate social groups (Bennett 1986; Thompson 1963, 1974; Williams 1961). Instead of attributing social changes such as growth in class-consciousness to impersonal material causes, they insisted that it comes about through the ways in which people together experience and give a collective meaning to the material circumstances of their lives. Williams contributed to the development of the discipline of Cultural Studies (Brantlinger 1990, Hall 1986 and the Introduction to this volume). Many historians aimed to write 'history from below' (Griffin 2002), showing that people in disadvantaged groups made creative choices rather than passively being ruled by those 'above' them. Initially, the phrase 'popular culture' united these two impulses, the anthropological and the political. But for reasons analysed by Harris (1995), it has come to seem problematic.

The meaning of 'popular' varies with context. 'Popular' can imply a people or populace. But who is that? 'The people' is sometimes taken to refer to a culturally homogeneous national population whose members all share, say, a certain typical sense of humour. For Browne (1984), 'popular culture' embraced 'all aspects of the world we inhabit' and was 'the culture of the times'. Yet as Browne (a founder of the Popular Culture Association) was aware, the popular culture that he portrayed as linking all Americans together was scorned by some of them, who espoused an 'elite' or 'minority' culture. Regardless of whom an author writing on 'popular culture' chooses to identify as 'the people', there is always an opposing category. But the basis for distinguishing between this elite and 'the people' varies. To give four disparate examples relating to different periods, the categories may be 'highbrow' vs 'lowbrow' (Levine 1988), 'patrician' vs 'plebeian' (Thompson 1974), 'godly' vs 'worldly' (Walsham 2008) or 'official' vs 'unofficial' (Bakhtin 1968). The diversity reflects a difference not only in the period being discussed but in how the authors choose to represent the social contexts of these divisions. Some authors envisage the social world they are writing about as composed of many groups, even when using either-or categories for convenience. Others start from a two-tier image of the dominant and the subordinate sections of society. This difference corresponds to the two kinds of reason mentioned above for being interested in this topic: the anthropological impulse and the perspective 'from below'. The trend has been to emphasise the diversity of local cultures and occupational sub-cultures, and to recognise differences based on gender (Amussen 1995).

The theme of order and disorder is a recurrent one in studies of popular culture (e.g. Ingram 1984). Accounts of medieval carnival celebrations (Bakhtin 1968; Burke 2009; Gurevich 1997; Hutton 1994; Simon 1998) describe symbolically enacted inversions of the established order and a temporary freedom from customary social constraints. The licence to mock authority at such times released pressure and showed, as Burke argues, that in this period the culture of the majority was shared by the elite, even though the reverse was not the case. However, the following centuries were marked by a tendency for elites to withdraw from their participation in the customs and thought-world of the majority. Their desire to see their subordinates subjected to greater discipline was expressed in the Reformation and the Counter-Reformation. It is by no means purely a religious concern, but reflects a pervasive tendency to render many aspects of life more systematically quantifiable, including economic activities and the understanding of the natural world. The Romantic movement in the later eighteenth century was accompanied by the rise of antiquarianism, a project of learned enquiry aimed at recording folk customs before they disappeared (Shiach 1989). Meanwhile paternalist concern for the moral welfare of the majority led to encouragement of organised games in place of sports like cock-fighting. By the late nineteenth century, the nostalgia for Merrie England expressed in early folklore studies took the form of laments over the commercialisation of working-class leisure activities – though Harvey's research (2008) shows that this had by then been under way for a century. The laments continued in the twentieth century, as in the dismissal by the literary critic F.R. Leavis of 'mass culture' as worthless (Storey 2009). Ashby (2006) gives a useful overview of the history of popular culture in the USA.

In our first reading, Watkins asks how much can be known about medieval popular religion. He outlines a recurrent problem with studies of people who were written about rather than describing their own beliefs and practices: how far have these accounts been shaped by the preoccupations of their literate authors?

Thompson expresses his concern that using the notion of culture may bias historians towards assuming that relations between rulers and ruled in eighteenth-century Britain were basically consensual. In writing *The Making of the English Working Class*, he had concluded that in this period of economic upheaval, English workers came to appreciate from their experience of collective action to claim customary rights how sharply their interests conflicted with the interests of those they served and worked for.

The reading by Burke was written thirty years after the first appearance of his widely read study of popular culture in early modern Europe. He poses searching questions concerning some of the analytical approaches adopted by historians (including Thompson) critical of his own contribution. Burke discusses meanings that authors like Muchembled have given to the word 'popular', and assesses the advantages and disadvantages of concepts, like Gramsci's 'hegemony', that others have used so as to highlight the political implications latent in a two-tier model. This leads him to consider afresh some of the problems associated with the word 'culture' and to endorse Chartier's advice to focus attention on how social groups appropriate particular cultural resources.

References

Amussen, S.D. (1995) 'The gendering of popular culture in early modern England', in T. Harris (ed.) *Popular Culture in England c.1500–1850*, Basingstoke: Macmillan.

Ashby, L. (2006) *With Amusement for All: a history of American popular culture since 1830*, Lexington, KY: University Press of Kentucky.

Bakhtin, M. (1968) *Rabelais and his World*, trans. H. Iswolsky, Bloomington, IN: Indiana University Press.

Bennett, T. (1986) 'Popular culture and "the turn to Gramsci"', in T. Bennett, C. Mercer and J. Woollacott (eds) *Popular Culture and Social Relations*, Milton Keynes: Open University Press.

Brantlinger, P. (1990) *Crusoe's Footprints: cultural studies in Britain and America*, London: Routledge.

Browne, R.B. (1984) 'Popular culture as the new humanities', *Journal of Popular Culture*, 17: 1–8.

Burke, P. (1977) 'Popular culture in seventeenth-century London', *London Journal*, 3: 143–62; revised in B. Reay (ed.) (1985) *Popular Culture in Seventeenth-Century England*, London: Routledge.

Burke, P. (2009) 'The world of carnival', in *Popular Culture in Early Modern Europe*, Farnham: Ashgate.

Chartier, R. (1984) 'Culture as appropriation: popular cultural uses in early modern France', in S.L. Kaplan (ed.) *Understanding Popular Culture: Europe from the Middle Ages to the Nineteenth Century*, Berlin: Mouton.

Cooter, R. and Pumfrey, S. (1994) 'Separate spheres and public places: reflections on the history of science popularization and science in popular culture', *History of Science*, 32: 237–67.

Davis, N.Z. (1975) *Society and Culture in Early Modern France*, Stanford, CA: Stanford University Press.

Flint, V.I.J. (1991) *The Rise of Magic in Early Medieval Europe*, Oxford: Oxford University Press.

Geary, P.J. (1979) 'The ninth-century relic trade: a response to popular piety?', in J. Obelkevich (ed.) *Religion and the People 800–1700*, Chapel Hill, NC: University of North Carolina Press.

Gramsci, A. (1985) *Selections from Cultural Writings*, ed. D. Forgacs and G. Nowell-Smith, trans. W. Boelhower, Cambridge, MA: Harvard University Press.

Griffin, E. (2002) 'Popular culture in industrializing England', *Historical Journal*, 45: 619–35.

Gurevich, A. (1997) 'Bakhtin and his theory of carnival', in J. Bremmer and H. Roodenburg (eds) *A Cultural History of Humour: from Antiquity to the present day*, Cambridge: Polity.

Hall, S. (1986) 'Popular culture and the state', in T. Bennett, C. Mercer and J. Woollacott (eds) *Popular Culture and Social Relations*, Milton Keynes: Open University Press.

Harris, T. (1995) 'Problematising popular culture', in T. Harris (ed.) *Popular Culture in England c.1500–1850*, Basingstoke: Macmillan.

Harvey, A. (2008) *The Beginnings of a Commercial Sporting Culture in Britain, 1793–1850*, Farnham: Ashgate.

Hutton, R. (1994) *The Rise and Fall of Merry England: the ritual year, 1400–1700*, Oxford: Oxford University Press.

Ingram, M. (1984) 'Ridings, rough music and the "reform of popular culture" in early modern England', *Past & Present*, 105: 79–103.

Levine, L.W. (1988) *Highbrow/Lowbrow: the emergence of cultural hierarchy in America*, Cambridge, MA: Harvard University Press.

O'Connor, R. (2007) *The Earth On Show: fossils and the poetics of popular science, 1802–1856*, Chicago, IL: University of Chicago Press.

Ong, W. (1971) 'The literate orality of popular culture today', in *Rhetoric, Romance and Technology: studies in the interaction of expression and culture*, Ithaca, NY: Cornell University Press.

Shiach, M. (1989) *Discourse on Popular Culture: class, gender, and history in cultural analysis, 1730 to the present*, Cambridge: Polity.

Simon, E. (1998) 'Carnival obscenities in German towns', in J.M. Ziolkowski (ed.) *Obscenity: social control and artistic creation in the European Middle Ages*, Leiden: Brill.

Storey, J. (ed.) (2009) *Cultural Theory and Popular Culture: a reader*, fourth edition, Harlow: Pearson/Longman.

Thompson, E.P. (1963) *The Making of the English Working Class*, London: Victor Gollancz.

Thompson, E.P. (1974) 'Patrician society, plebeian culture', *Journal of Social History*, 7: 382–405.

Walsham, A. (2008) 'The godly and popular culture', in J. Coffey and P.C.H. Lim (eds) *The Cambridge Companion to Puritanism*, Cambridge: Cambridge University Press.

Williams, R. (1961) *The Long Revolution*, London: Chatto & Windus.

Chapter 13

Carl Watkins

"FOLKLORE" AND "POPULAR RELIGION" IN BRITAIN DURING THE MIDDLE AGES

S TUDYING THE "FOLKLORE" of the Middle Ages is a frustrating enterprise. Our sources yield a harvest rich enough to whet the appetite yet still too slight to satisfy. From the early Middle Ages, law codes and penitentials depict healing rituals in which children were placed in ovens, fairies placated by casting bows and arrows into barns, and unbaptised children who were "staked" to stop them rising from the grave. From the late twelfth century onwards, *exempla* indicate that some men and women thought it unlucky to meet a priest in the street and that others were not averse to crumbling communion wafers over their crops to protect them. The twelfth and thirteenth centuries witnessed a proliferation and diversification of "historical" writing. Chroniclers increasingly found space in their narratives for tales of the wondrous: Ralph of Coggeshall told of green children found in cornfields, wild men fished from the sea and invisible spirits haunting peasant houses (Ralph of Coggeshall 1875, 117–21). On the fringe of the chronicle genre, new species of narrative also evolved that set the wondrous and fantastical at the centre rather than the edge of the historical enterprise: here Walter Map told tales of fairy women who married mortal men and stories of dead men who rose from the grave by night (Map 1983, 154–6 and 344).[1]

It is easy enough to assemble examples, but how are we to analyse them? In handling such material, three problems are immediately visible. (In a sense they are a single problem, but for the purposes of clarity it might be wise to split them at the outset.) The first is conceptual: can we speak of "folklore" in the Middle Ages and, if so, who exactly were "the folk" who used the lore? The second is evidential: the communities of medieval Europe have, because their cultures tended to be articulated by oral rather than written forms, left only the very faintest traces of beliefs and practices. These seldom survive in sufficient concentrations to allow us to describe the beliefs and practices of any single community or even a particular region. This closes down possible avenues of exploration: the opportunities for "micro-history" or "thick descriptions" are few in this period, especially in the earlier part of it (the obvious exception here is Le Roy Ladurie's *Montaillou* [1980]). A final complexity is related to the second but is methodological in character. Our scattered fragments of evidence are products of clerical pens, of a literate culture rather than of the predominantly oral culture in which beliefs were held and practices used. As such, the cultural gaps between the practitioners of oral and written culture call for thought.

This problematic trinity—a three-in-one historiographical conundrum—demands that we deploy powerful theory if we are to recreate from fragmentary remains the larger patterns of medieval belief and practice. In discussing the possibilities here, we cannot speak of "folklore" in isolation or as a given category. Rather, we need to think of the bigger picture, considering "religious culture" as an organic whole.

"Elite" religion and "folkloric" religion

One series of solutions to our problems is supplied by "popular/elite" models of medieval religion. Over the past twenty-five years, it has often been argued that religious culture in medieval Europe can best be understood in terms of social categories, that considerable gulfs existed between religions of educated elites and uneducated masses or between those of clergy and laity. Jean Delumeau, in challenging unreflective images of the Middle Ages as an "Age of Faith," questioned the comprehensiveness of the conversion process (Delumeau 1971). He argued that, although social elites may have been converted to full-blooded Christianity, the masses were only superficially Christianised and continued, beneath a veneer of official observance, to practice a protean, pagan folk-religion. This religion was articulated orally and so left few traces, occasionally preserved by the pen of elite churchmen who, more often than not, noted it for the purposes of repression. This hard-edged analysis that seemed to over-correct the older orthodoxy has been softened by later generations of scholars (Schmitt 1983; Gurevich 1988, xiii–xvi; Le Goff 1980, 1988). Jacques Le Goff and his disciples suggest that "elite/clerical" and "mass/folkloric" cultures were distinct but in a state of constant dialogue, churchmen seeking to modify the latter by a mixture of repression and reinvention (Schmitt 1976, 941–53).

In some ways this model is beguiling. In allowing us to distinguish the official Christianity of the elite from the popular religion of the folk, it provides a ring-fenced folkloric space in which we can situate accounts of green children, fairy wives and spectral knights. Yet even the more refined and nuanced approaches of Le Goff and Schmitt fail to convince fully. Criticisms of their work concentrate on the assumption that social categories such as elite/mass or clerical/lay are good predictors of religious beliefs (Delaruelle 1975; Murray 1978, 14–17, 237–41, 244–57 and 319; Brown 1981, 18–20; Brooke and Brooke 1984, 9–10 and 12–13; Rubin 1991, 7; Tellenbach 1993, 128). A cursory examination reveals that medieval society was sufficiently complex for many people to evade such classifications. Where, for instance, does the parish priest fit in? Is he a subscriber to elite or popular religion? He certainly falls into the clerical category, but how meaningful is this label? Local priests were drawn largely from the peasant communities they served and were probably afforded only rudimentary education. The difficulties multiply if we think of noble monastic converts and peasant hermits. Were their beliefs necessarily different because of their different backgrounds, or might they have shared an ascetic, world-rejecting spirituality? If we turn to praxis, we run into similar difficulties because we can find many practices that transcended social categories. Casting our eyes across the Channel for a moment, we find that the penitential handbook written around the year 1000 by Burchard of Worms, the *Corrector*, condemns those who feared to go outside before cockcrow because evil spirits were abroad (Burchard of Worms 1898, 442). This might be read as an instance of the beliefs of a literate clergyman who participated in elite culture being in tension with the folkloric beliefs of the masses. But how then do we account for Guibert of Nogent, an educated churchman of the twelfth century who was accustomed to sleep with a lamp by his bed to keep evil spirits at bay (Guibert of Nogent 1970)?

Normative and narrative sources

The temptation to categorise belief on the basis of social groups such as elite and masses, clergy and laity, literate and illiterate is born, I think, of the kinds of evidence historians have dwelt upon and the language they have absorbed from them. Much of the work of Le Goff and Schmitt has emphasised collections of sermon stories, penitential handbooks and canon law texts. Such sources have an explicit didactic project and they make a sharp contrastive distinction between Church ideals and malpractices in wider society. But have such contrasts in the normative sources been taken too much at face value? The works of a twelfth-century churchman, Gerald of Wales, offer an opportunity to test the hypothesis because here we have an author who wrote about similar issues of belief and practice in different literary genres.

Gerald, born in about 1146, was well educated and had spent time in the schools of Paris before returning to his native Wales to become archdeacon of Saint David's (Bartlett 1982, 27–57). One theme treated several times in his voluminous writings was whether laymen and women should be allowed to dance in churchyards on feast days. It emerges in his *Jewel of the Church*, a collection of instructional stories that readily betrays a school training in canon law. Here Gerald promoted a vigorous reforming agenda, attacking a wide range of abuses in the wider community. In one story, Gerald warned "that the laity ought not to engage in singing and dancing around churches and cemeteries on the feasts of saints but should devote themselves to the divine service" (Gerald of Wales 1861–91, vol. 2, 119–20). Gerald buttressed his argument with references to the Council of Toledo and the authority of the Fathers, specifically Augustine, and the view he expressed also chimed with those of countless earlier and later penitential manuals (see, for example, Morey 1937, 256). Yet Gerald's view of such dancing was not so straightforward as the *Jewel of the Church* might imply. He also visited the subject in a very different kind of writing, a narrative account of a preaching tour he had undertaken through Wales in 1188, the so-called *Journey Through Wales*. Here Gerald described how, at Saint Eluned's church in Brecon, on the feast day of the saint, all the people of the neighbourhood congregated at the Church and then danced around the churchyard, singing "traditional songs" (Gerald of Wales 1861–91, vol. 6, 32–3). Some of them fell into frenzy and began to mime work they had illicitly performed on feast days—"you might see this man imitate a cobbler, that man a tanner." Having done this, they were led to the altar, made oblations there, and "returned to themselves."

Here, it seems, we find an unofficial ritual dance serving penitential purposes in a community where Church teaching about abstaining from work on feast days was well established but where official rituals for expiating sin were not. Hence the community shaped its own redemptive strategies. More interesting for our purpose, however, is the reaction of archdeacon Gerald. Given the views expressed in his *Jewel of the Church*, we might reasonably expect him to condemn such unofficial practices. In fact, his reaction was strikingly different: "God desires not the death of a sinner, but rather that he may turn from wickedness: and so, by taking part in these festivities, many at once see and feel in their hearts the remission of their sins, and are absolved and pardoned" (Gerald of Wales 1861–91, vol. 6, 33). An archdeacon, whose theoretical role was to control and limit diversity of religious expression, was here, in practice, sympathetic to it.

What moral might we draw from this story? Normative sources may give us insights into official Christian teachings, but they do not necessarily give us straightforward access to the religious beliefs of churchmen, not even the particular churchmen who wrote them. Gerald's view of dancing in churchyards seems to change depending on which genre he is writing in. When producing an instructional work, Gerald felt constrained by canon law and the authoritative utterances of Church Fathers and Councils. But when close attention to these authorities was less urgent, as in the *Journey through Wales*, Gerald's beliefs emerged in a different shape.

This example suggests that there are risks in viewing both *exempla* and handbooks of penance through the pre-formed lenses of "popular" and "elite." Approaches to medieval religion that rely on such distinctions are problematic because they confer on "popular" or "folkloric" belief unconvincing unities, and accentuate the tensions between it and putative elite religious culture. Such readings encourage, and are encouraged by, analyses that are openly or tacitly attached to ideas of antagonistic, class-based social relations. These approaches can be restrictive. They make our evidence the product of an elite that, when faced by mass culture, was at best deeply unsympathetic, at worst hostile and uncomprehending. No one would argue that *exempla* give unproblematic access to the culture(s) of the masses, but they are often treated as if they provide quite straightforward insights into those of the clerical elite (see the critical comments in O'Neill [1986, 222]). Authors of normative sources such as handbooks of penance or sermon materials operated self-consciously within literary and theological traditions. During the process of composition, their theological and canon-legal training found forceful and articulate expression, inducing them to draw heavily on the canon of scriptural, patristic and later texts that would give their own writings authority. The act of disseminating official Christian teachings imposed such a discipline. But it does not follow that the religious and cultural values of such authors were formed solely in schools or cloister, shaped by canon law and theology alone. Their religious and cultural make-up was also moulded, to a greater or lesser extent, by other "local" cultural traditions in which they participated perhaps during childhood, through pastoral ministry in later life or even through excursions from the cloister into the world. The key question here is what happens when clerical authors are freed from the constraints of normative genres. If we read only penitentials and sermon literature the question is an unanswerable one, but if we turn to narrative writings we get a chance to observe clerical authors (sometimes the same clerical authors who produced our normative sources) in a different literary light, governed by different "rules" of genre. Hence, in thinking about evidence for medieval religious culture, it is important to consider not only who the author of that evidence is, but also the context or genre in which he was writing.

Christian conversions and pagan survivals

Contextualisation is also important in a second sense. As we have observed, sources for belief and practice in the Middle Ages are comparatively thin on the ground. This has tempted some historians to expand the geographical scope of their studies, often examining religious culture on European or still larger scales. Historians and folklorists interested in tracing "pagan survivals" from the pre-Christian into the Christian era have been especially inclined to this approach. Most recently, Carlo Ginzburg has used it to argue that the hard core of the religion of the folk was scarcely altered by Christian conversion and that we can discern fundamental continuities of belief running from antiquity through the Middle Ages into the early modern period (Ginzburg 1990). Yet there are many dangers in such a method, not least that in considering examples out of context, astonishing cultural continuities over space and time dazzle the observer and obscure fundamental differences.[2]

Such suspicions are reinforced by a closer look at the evidence from England and Scotland in the central and late Middle Ages. This reveals few compelling instances of pagan continuity. One of the strongest cases could be made for practices described in Reginald of Durham's *Book of the Wonderful Miracles of Blessed Cuthbert*. He observed how Abbot Ailred of

Rievaulx had been scandalised during a visit to Kirkcudbright, Galloway, by the ritual sacrifice of a bull performed by members of the local community (Reginald of Durham 1835, 179). On the face of it, this looks like a classic pagan animal sacrifice such as those widely condemned by ecclesiastical authorities during and immediately after the Christian conversions. Yet on closer inspection, this ritual is more complex. It was orchestrated by so-called "scholars" (or "scollofthes" according to the text) from the religious house of Kirkcudbright and, most interestingly, the bull was offered to Saint Cuthbert rather than to any pagan deity.[3] In other words, outward ritual forms that appear to be pagan were, in fact, articulating devotions to a well-established Christian saint.

The temptation here is to separate Christian from pagan, breaking the narrative of the ritual into fragments and tracing the lineage of each back through time. Yet the complexities of this account suggest that this temptation should be resisted. Rather than seeking to label each facet of the ritual as "Christian" or "pagan," we should study it as an organic whole in order to get some sense of its function and how it was understood by members of the community. Searches over great tracts of space and time for "morphologically" similar examples are unlikely to yield answers to these kinds of questions (Purkiss 2000, 7). Patrick Geary has pointed out that medieval religious culture was intimately interconnected with other dimensions of life in local communities, with agriculture, social hierarchy, family, law, politics (Geary 1994, 32–3).[4] If we accept this idea of "interconnectedness," future research might, where sources permit, look more deeply into the culture of particular localities and regions. By putting wider aspects of daily life under the historian's magnifying lens, we can get a sharper sense of the larger belief-system in which particular rituals or practices were located.

Local religious cultures

Such conjectures do not solve the problem of how religious culture in these communities should be related to that of a universal Church. To do this, we need to rethink the larger theory and move away from narrow notions of "popular" and "elite." Here a modified version of Peter Burke's model of early modern culture can help us. Burke distinguished two cultural traditions—a "great tradition" fostered through literate modes in schools and universities, and a "little tradition" that was locally various and sustained by oral means among the unlettered inhabitants of local communities (Burke 1978, 22–8). These traditions were not hermetically sealed: although the masses were essentially cut off from the "great" tradition, the elite were able to participate at will in the "little" tradition.

This model cannot be applied as it stands to medieval religious culture. It is true that substantial bodies of complex theological learning existed in monasteries and in the schools, and a great part of this never percolated into the parishes in even the most rudimentary forms. Yet the institutions of the Church did not set out to preserve the articles of religious belief in the same way that grammar schools and universities sustained Burke's elite culture. Christianity was not an exclusive tradition. Rather the reverse, monasteries, cathedral schools and, more especially, the structures of the Church at diocesan and parish level were conceived, to varying degrees, as means by which Christian belief and practice were to be spread on the world. R. I. Moore has argued that preaching and teaching, especially by the parish priest, was designed to bridge any gap that might exist between the position of the Church on one hand and belief and practice in local communities on the other (Moore 1994, 35). Such impulses served to break down cultural boundaries. There was, for example, no clear-cut distinction between oral and written cultures. The oral relations of the peasant could be, and periodically were, captured in script by chroniclers, authors of miracles collections and others. More significantly for the spread of Church teaching, versions of the "written culture" of the Church were made accessible to the peasant through recitation and preaching from the pulpit, what D. H. Green calls "diagonal channels of communication" (Green 1994, 169–72).

Such insights lead us to an adapted version of the Burke model. We can distinguish two traditions in medieval religious culture but *all* members of medieval society participated to a greater or lesser degree in *both* of them. This, essentially, is the upshot of work by W. A. Christian on sixteenth-century Spanish religion. He has stressed the "placebound" character of many beliefs and observances, and draws a distinction between "universal religion" based on sacraments, liturgy and sacred time and local religion rooted in shrines, images, saints and relics (Christian 1981a, 1981b; O'Neill 1986, 222–5). This local religion provided a range of preventive and remedial strategies ranging from processions, votive masses and invocations of special saints to searches for signs in the weather and prognosticatory lotteries, all shaped to the needs of the immediate community.

These findings can guide us when thinking about the Middle Ages. The systematic teachings of the Church can be picked out with some confidence in this period, and we can perhaps label these "official Christianity." Such teachings mingled in the localities with fluid and locally varied beliefs that did not grow directly out of the systematic teaching of the Church. These beliefs existed within the interstices of official faith and ritual and churchmen did not *necessarily* see them as pagan, unchristian, heretical or erroneous. We might be tempted to describe these beliefs as "folklore," but it might be safer to call them "unofficial beliefs" because they were not simply the property of "the folk" (a term that, I think, encourages us to see beliefs of the "masses" as easily detached from those of "elites"), but also of many educated churchmen as well. The whole notion of "the folk" and their "lore" becomes troublesome here. Although the line between official and unofficial might seem clear to us, armed with canon law tracts, sermon books and penitentials, it was probably not so clear to the inhabitants of local communities. Nor can we assume that these lines were clear-cut even for the diocesan clergy, let alone those of the parish.

None of this excludes the potential for tensions within the system of belief. Returning to a familiar example, if we re-examine the bull sacrifice at Kirkcudbright, we can begin to distinguish subscribers to different cultural values and the frictions that emerged between them. We have on one hand our author Reginald, a Benedictine monk from Durham. He was a friend of Ailred of Rievaulx, who had travelled up to Galloway to visit a Cistercian house at Dundrennan. *En route* Ailred had run into the ritual bull sacrifice performed by the "scholars" of Kirkcudbright. In this account, we find on one hand the austere spirituality of the enclosed Cistercians rooted in credal Christianity and strict obedience to their Rule; a culture in which Abbot Ailred had been deeply immersed since his early twenties. On the other hand, we find a community of independent "scholars," monks not tied to any religious order, free to practice distinctive local rituals and heavily involved in the religious life of the lay community living around them. Tensions between these two religious cultures were sharpened by ethnic distinctiveness. Walter Daniel, another Cistercian and biographer of Abbot Ailred, characterised Galloway as "a wild country where the inhabitants are like beasts and altogether barbarous" and noted how Rievaulx had "planted" the abbey of Dundrennan amidst the savagery to spread the Cistercian message (Daniel 1950, 45–6). Here then, we have a sharp encounter between the ardent official Christianity of the Cistercians and the localised, syncretistic Christianity of a community from the upland peripheries. Yet the encounter is sharp precisely because it involves the juxtaposition of especially (and unusually) concentrated forms of official and unofficial belief.

If we move away from this coincidence of extremes to Gerald of Wales and the rites in Saint Eluned's churchyard, a different picture emerges. Here we have not a senior and zealous monk in a new reforming order, but a secular clergyman, an archdeacon, responsible for pastoral care in the marches. Gerald was well acquainted with canon law and might make authoritative utterances about dancing in churchyards when writing instruction manuals, but when he met diverse practices on the ground he was more tolerant. Gerald lacked the resources to impose Church law by force. As a churchman working in the community he had to negotiate official Christian values and those of the communities he encountered. Inevitably, there must have been cultural compromise in such situations, and here we seem to see it. Gerald was interested in the core elements of the Church's reform agenda such as lay control over churches and enforcing clerical celibacy (Bartlett 1982, 29–31). Where he found novel ritual articulations of official Christian ideas, his attitude was more relaxed. Such pragmatism may also have been informed by discriminating sympathy. It is conjectural but nonetheless possible that Gerald's Cambro-Norman upbringing and career in the Marches may have soaked him in the culture of these places and hence inclined him to see these rituals in a more positive light.

This is, admittedly, slender evidence on which to base general conclusions. If, nonetheless, we pursue this line for a moment, we can perhaps still say something about method. Three things emerge here, all of which are, in one shape or form, arguments for greater contextualisation. First, we need to think of medieval religious culture as a commingling of unofficial and official belief that varies over space and time—forming not a series of cultural compartments, but a spectrum. This spectrum comprehends, albeit at the opposite ends, the beliefs of peasant and prelate alike (Van Engen 1986, 519–52; Duffy 1992). Second, it is dangerous to fence "folklore" off as a special object of study, and still more dangerous to associate the term with particular social groups. Rather we should regard the accounts that we tend to label "folklore" as facets of larger cultural systems that bind communities. Finally, we need to study accounts of belief and practice in authorial context, considering the impact of genre, authorial objectives and, perhaps most importantly, the cultural formation of the author as well as that of the community he described.

Notes

1   There are several good introductions to the penitentials (McNeill and Gamer 1938; Vögel 1978). Perhaps the most influential penitential manual was the *Corrector* of Burchard of Worms (1898) (on the light this text might shed on religious culture, see Vögel [1974]). On law codes, synodal legislation and associated material (for England) see Whitelock *et al.* (1981). For the later period see Powicke and Cheney (1964). The earliest *exempla* collections are found in continental Europe, and include Jacques de Vitry (1890) and Stephen of Bourbon (1877). A useful summary of material in early and late collections can be found in Tubach (1969) and Bremond *et al.* (1982). For the English material see Mosher (1911). The categories of source material indicated here are among the most obvious places to look for medieval "folklore" but far from exhaust the possibilities. Hagiography, church art, archaeological remains, book illumination, romance literature and even charters, cartularies and legal records can yield information. The range of possible written sources for medieval England is catalogued by Graves (1975).

2   For a sceptical discussion of pagan "continuities" see Hutton (1991). Also very useful here is Flint (1991) and Wilson (1992).

3   The early history of this house at Kirkcudbright is obscure. Cowan and Easson (1957, 50) base their entry on Reginald and add nothing new.

4   A debate in this area between Keith Thomas (1975) and Clifford Geertz (1975, 1990) is also instructive.

References cited

Bartlett, Robert. *Gerald of Wales, 1146–1223*. Oxford, 1982.

Bremond, Claude, Jacques Le Goff, and Jean-Claude Schmitt. *L'Exemplum*: *Typologie des sources du moyen âge occidental*. Turnhout, 1982.

Brooke, Christopher N. L., and Rosalind Brooke. *Popular Religion in the Middle Ages*: *Western Europe 1000–1300*. London, 1984.

Brown, Peter. *The Cult of Saints*: *Its Rise and Function in Latin Christianity*. London, 1981.

Burchard of Worms. *Corrector siue Medicus, Die Bussbücher und das kanonische Bussverfahren*, ed. H. J. Schmitz. Düsseldorf, 1898.

Burke, Peter. *Popular Culture in Early Modern Europe*. London, 1978.

Christian, William A. *Local Religion in Sixteenth-Century Spain*. Princeton, 1981a.

Christian, William A. *Apparitions in Late Medieval and Renaissance Spain*. Princeton, 1981b.

Cowan, Ian B., and David E. Easson. *Medieval Religious Houses of Scotland with an Appendix on the Houses of in the Isle of Man*. London, 1957.

Daniel, Walter. *The Life of Ailred of Rievaulx*. London, 1950.

Delaruelle, Etienne. *La Piété populaire au moyen âge*. Turin, 1975.

Delumeau, Jean. *Le Catholicisme entre Luther et Voltaire*. Paris, 1971. English translation (1977), *Catholicism between Luther and Voltaire*, London and Philadelphia.

Duffy, Eamon. *The Stripping of the Altars*: *Traditional Religion in England c.1400–1580*. New Haven, 1992.

Flint, Valerie I. J. *The Rise of Magic in Early Medieval Europe*. Oxford, 1991.

Geary, Patrick. *Living with the Dead in the Middle Ages*. Ithaca, 1994.

Geertz, Clifford. "An Anthropology of Religion and Magic I." *Journal of Interdisciplinary History* 6 (1975): 71–89.

Geertz, Clifford. "History and Anthropology." *New Literary History* 21 (1990): 321–35.

Gerald of Wales. *Gemma Ecclesiastica, Giraldi Cambrensis Opera*, ed. John S. Brewer, James F. Dimock, and George F. Warner. 8 vols. London, 1861–91.

Ginzburg, Carlo. *Ecstasies*: *Deciphering the Witches' Sabbath*. Translated by R. Rosenthal. London, 1990.

Graves, Edgar B. *A Bibliography of English History to 1485*. Oxford, 1975.

Green, Dennis H. *Medieval Listening and Reading*: *The Primary Reception of German Literature 800–1300*. Cambridge, 1994.

Guibert of Nogent. *Self and Society in Medieval France*: *Memoirs of Abbot Guibert of Nogent*. Translated by John F. Benton. New York, 1970.

Gurevich, Aron. *Medieval Popular Culture*: *Problems of Belief and Perception*. Translated by J. M. Bak and P. A. Hollingsworth. Cambridge, 1988.

Hutton, Ronald. *The Pagan Religions of the Ancient British Isles*: *Their Nature and Their Legacy*. Oxford, 1991.

Jacques de Vitry. *The Exempla or Illustrative Stories from the Sermones Vulgares of Jacques de Vitry*, ed. Thomas F. Crane. London, 1890.

Le Goff, Jacques. *Time, Work and Culture in the Middle Ages*. Translated by A. Goldhammer. Chicago, 1980.

Le Goff, Jacques. *The Medieval Imagination*. Translated by A. Goldhammer. Chicago, 1988.

Le Roy Ladurie, Emmanuel. *Montaillou*: *Cathars and Catholics in a French Village 1294–1324*. Translated by Barbara Bray. Harmondsworth, 1980.

Map, Walter. *De Nugis Curialium, The Courtiers' Trifles*, ed. and translated by M. R. James, and revised by Roger Mynors and Christopher Brooke. Oxford, 1983.

McNeill, John T., and Helena M. Gamer, eds. *Medieval Handbooks of Penance*: *A Translation of the Principal Libri Poenitentiales And Selections From Related Documents*. New York, 1938.

Moore, R. I. "Literacy and the Making of Heresy *c.*l000–*c.*1150." In *Heresy and Literacy, 1000–1530*, eds. Peter Biller and Anne Hudson. Cambridge, 1994.

Morey, Adrian. *Bartholomew of Exeter, Bishop and Canonist: A Study in the Twelfth Century.* Cambridge, 1937.

Mosher, Joseph A. *The Exemplum in the Early Religious and Didactic Literature of England.* New York, 1911.

Murray, Alexander. *Reason and Society in the Middle Ages.* Oxford, 1978.

O'Neill, M. R. "From 'Popular' to 'Local' Religion: Issues in Early Modern European History." *Religious Studies Review* 12 (1986): 222–6.

Powicke, Frederick M., and Christopher R. Cheney, eds. *Councils and Synods with Other Documents relating to the English Church II, 1205–1313.* 2 vols. Oxford, 1964.

Purkiss, Diane. *Troublesome Things: A History of Fairies and Fairy Stories.* London, 2000.

Ralph of Coggeshall. *Radulphi de Coggeshall Chronicon Anglicanum*, ed. Joseph Stevenson. London, 1875.

Reginald of Durham. *Reginaldi Monachi Dunelmensis Libellus de Admirandis Beati Cuthberti Virtutibus* ed. James Raine. Durham, 1835.

Rubin, Miri. *Corpus Christi: The Eucharist in Late Medieval Culture.* Cambridge, 1991.

Schmitt, Jean-Claude. "Religion populaire et culture folklorique." *Annales: Economies, Sociétés, Civilisations* 31 (1976): 941–53.

Schmitt, Jean-Claude. *The Holy Greyhound; Guinefort, Healer of Children since the Thirteenth Century.* Translated by M. Thom. Cambridge, 1983.

Stephen of Bourbon. *Anecdotes historiques et apologues tirés du recueil inédit d'Etienne de Bourbon, Dominicain du XIII siècle*, ed. R. Albert Lecoy de la Marche. Paris, 1877.

Tellenbach, Gerd. *The Church in Western Europe from the Tenth to the Early Twelfth Centuries.* Translated by T. Reuter. Cambridge, 1993.

Thomas, Keith. "An Anthropology of Religion and Magic II." *Journal of Interdisciplinary History* 6 (1975): 91–109.

Tubach, Frederic C. *Index Exemplorum: A Handbook Of Medieval Religious Tales.* Folklore Fellows Communications 204. Helsinki, 1969.

Van Engen, J. "The Christian Middle Ages as a Historiographical Problem." *American Historical Review* 91 (1986): 519–52.

Vogel, C. "Pratiques superstitieuses au début de XI siècle d'après le *Corrector sive Medicus de Burchard*, evêque de Worms, 965–1025." In *Etudes de civilisation médievale, IX–XII siècles. Mélanges offerts à Edmond-René Labande.* 751–61. Poitiers, 1974.

Vogel, C. *Les Libri paenitentiales: Typologies des sources du moyen âge occidental.* Turnhout, 1978.

Whitelock, Dorothy, Martin Brett, and Christopher Brooke, eds. *Councils and Synods with Other Documents Relating to the English Church 1, AD 871–1204.* 2 vols. Oxford, 1981.

Wilson, David. *Anglo-Saxon Paganism.* London, 1992.

Chapter 14

Edward P. Thompson

CUSTOM AND CULTURE

ALL THE STUDIES in *Customs in Common* are connected by different paths with the theme of custom as it was expressed within the culture of working people in the eighteenth century and into the nineteenth. It is my thesis that customary consciousness and customary usages were especially robust in the eighteenth century: indeed, some "customs" were of recent invention, and were in truth claims to new "rights". Historians of the sixteenth and seventeenth centuries have tended to see the eighteenth century as a time when these customary usages were in decline, along with magic, witchcraft and kindred superstitions. The people were subject to pressures to "reform" popular culture from above, literacy was displacing oral transmission, and enlightenment (it is supposed) was seeping down from the superior to the subordinate orders.

But the pressures of "reform" were stubbornly resisted, and the eighteenth century saw a profound distance opened, a profound alienation between the culture of patricians and plebs. Peter Burke, in his illuminating study of *Popular Culture in Early Modern Europe* (1978) suggests that this distance was a European-wide phenomenon, and that one consequence was the emergence of folklore, as sensitive (and insensitive) observers in the upper ranks of society sent out exploring parties to inspect the "Little Tradition" of the plebs, and to record their strange observances and rituals. Already, as the study of folklore emerged, these usages were coming to be seen as "antiquities" or survivals, and the great pioneer of folklore, John Brand, thought it necessary to preface his *Observations on Popular Antiquities* with an apology for attending to them at all:

> . . . nothing can be foreign to our enquiry, much less beneath our notice, that concerns the smallest of the Vulgar; of those little Ones who occupy the lowest place, though by no means of the least importance in the political arrangement of human Beings.[1]

Thus folklore at its very origin carried this sense of patronising distance, of subordination (Brand noted that pride and the necessities of civil Polity had "portioned out the human Genus into . . . a variety of different and subordinate Species"), and of customs as survivals. For 150 years the preferred methodology of collectors was to group such survivals as "calendar customs", which found their last refuge in the deepest countryside. As one folklorist wrote at the end of the nineteenth century, his object was to describe:

> The old customs which still linger on in the obscure nooks and corners of our native land, or which have survived the march of progress in our busy city's life.[2]

To such collectors we are indebted for careful descriptions of well-dressings or rush-bearings or harvest homes or, indeed, late examples of skimmington ridings. But what was lost, in considering (plural) customs as discrete survivals, was any strong sense of custom in the singular (although with many forms of expression), custom not as post-anything but as *sui generis* — as ambience, *mentalité*, and as a whole vocabulary of discourse, of legitimation and of expectation.

In earlier centuries the term "custom" was used to carry much of what is now carried by the word "culture". Custom was man's "second nature". Francis Bacon wrote of custom as induced and habitual inertial behaviour: "Men Profess, Protest, Engage, Give Great Words, and then Doe just as they have Done before. As if they were Dead Images, and Engines moved onely by the Wheeles of *Custome*." For Bacon, then, the problem was to induce better habits and as early in life as possible:

> Since Custom is the principal Magistrate of Man's Life, let Men, by all Means, endeavour to obtain good Customs . . . Custom is most perfect when it beginneth in young Years; This we call Education, which is, in Effect, but an early Custom.

Bacon was not thinking of the labouring people, but one hundred years later Bernard Mandeville, who was quite as convinced as was Bacon of the "Tyranny which Custom usurps over us",[3] was a great deal less well-disposed towards any universal provision of education. It was necessary that "great multitudes of People" should "inure their Bodies to Work" both for themselves and to support the more fortunate in Idleness, Ease and Pleasure:

> To make the Society Happy and People Easy under the meanest Circumstances, it is requisite that great numbers of them should be Ignorant as well as Poor. Knowledge both enlarges and multiplies our Desires . . . The Welfare and Felicity therefore of every State and Kingdom require that the Knowledge of the Working Poor should be confin'd within the Verge of their Occupations and never extended (as to things visible) beyond what relates to their Calling. The more a Shepherd, a Plowman or any other Peasant knows of the World, and the things that are Foreign to his Labour or Employment, the less fit he'll be to go through the Fatigues and Hardships of it with Chearfulness and Content.

Hence for Mandeville reading, writing and arithmetic "are very pernicious to the Poor".[4]

If many of the "poor" were denied education, what else did they have to fall back upon but oral transmission with its heavy freight of "custom". If nineteenth-century folklore, by separating survivals from their context, lost awareness of custom as ambience and *mentalité*, so also it lost sight of the rational functions of many customs within the routines of daily and weekly labour. Many customs were endorsed and sometimes enforced by popular pressure and protest. Custom was certainly a "good" word in the eighteenth century: England had long been priding herself on being Good and Old.[5] It was also an operative word. If, along one path, "custom" carried many of the meanings we assign now to "culture", along another path custom had close affinities with the common law. This law was derived from the customs, or habitual usages, of the country: usages which might be reduced to rule and precedents, which in some circumstances were codified and might be enforceable at law.

This was the case, above all, with *lex loci*, the local customs of the manor. These customs, whose record was sometimes only preserved in the memories of the aged, had legal effect, unless directly voided by statute law.[6] . . . There were some industrial groups for whom custom was claimed with equal legal force — the Cornish tinners, with their Stannary Court, the free miners of the Forest of Dean with their "Book of Dennis".[7] The rights claimed by the Dean miners could possibly have descended from the thirteenth century, but the "Laws and Customs of the Miners" were codified in an Inquisition of 1610, when 48 free miners recorded their usages (first printed in 1687). Frequently the invocation of the "custom" of a trade or occupation indicated a usage so long exercised that it had taken on the colour of a privilege or right.[8] Thus in 1718 when clothiers in the South-West attempted to lengthen the cloth piece by half a yard, the weavers complained that they were acting "contrary to law, usage and custom from time immemorial". And in 1805 London printers complained that employers were taking advantage of the ignorance of their journeymen by "disputing or denying custom, and by refusing to acknowledge precedents, which have been hitherto the only reference."[9] Many of the classic struggles at the entry to the industrial revolution turned as much on customs as upon wages or conditions of work.

Most of these customs may be described as "visible": they were codified in some form, or they can be accounted for with exactness. But as the plebeian culture became more opaque to gentry inspection, so other customs became less visible. The ceremonies and processionals of the trades, which had once been built into the calendar of the corporate year — under the patronage of Bishop Blaize for the wool-combers, St. Clement for the blacksmiths, St. Crispin for the shoemakers — might still be celebrated on special occasions, such as coronations or anniversaries, in the eighteenth century. But in the nineteenth century such processionals lost their consensual "trade" endorsement, they were feared by employers and corporations as occasions for high spirits and disorder (as indeed they sometimes were),[10] and St. Clement was honoured, not in the streets, but in the trades' club or friendly society meeting in the tavern.[11]

This is symptomatic of the disassociation between patrician and plebeian cultures in the eighteenth and early nineteenth centuries.[12] It is difficult not to see this division in terms of class. A perceptive folklorist, G. L. Gomme, saw folklore as customs, rites and beliefs belonging to the people —

> And oftentimes in definite antagonism to the accepted customs, rites and beliefs of the State or the nation to which the people and the groups of people belong. These customs, rites and beliefs are mostly kept alive by tradition . . . They owe their preservation partly to the fact that great masses of people do not belong to the civilisation which towers over them and which is never of their own creation.[13]

In the eighteenth century custom was the rhetoric of legitimation for almost any usage, practice, or demanded right. Hence uncodified custom — and even codified — was in continual flux. So far from having the steady permanence suggested by the word "tradition", custom was a field of change and of contest, an arena in which opposing interests made conflicting claims. This is one reason why one must be cautious as to generalisations as to "popular culture". This may suggest, in one anthropological inflexion which has been influential with social historians, an over-consensual view of this culture as "a system of shared meanings, attitudes and values, and the symbolic forms (performances, artifacts) in which they are embodied".[14] But a culture is also a pool of diverse resources, in which traffic passes between the literate and the oral, the superordinate and the subordinate, the village and the metropolis; it is an arena of conflictual elements, which requires some compelling pressure — as, for example, nationalism or prevalent religious orthodoxy or class consciousness — to take form as "system". And, indeed, the very term "culture", with its cosy invocation of consensus, may serve to distract attention from social and cultural contradictions, from the fractures and oppositions within the whole.

At this point generalisations as to the universals of "popular culture" become empty unless they are placed firmly within specific historical contexts. The plebeian culture which clothed itself in the rhetoric of "custom" and which is the central theme of *Customs in Common* was not self-defining or independent of external influences. It had taken form defensively, in opposition to the constraints and controls of the patrician rulers. The confrontations and negotiations between patricians and plebs are explored in a later chapter of *Customs in Common*, and case studies of the conflict between customary and innovative ("market") *mentalités* follow. In these studies I hope that plebeian culture becomes a more concrete and usable concept, no longer situated in the thin air of "meanings, attitudes and values", but located within a particular equilibrium of social relations, a working environment of exploitation and resistance to exploitation, of relations of power which are masked by the rituals of paternalism and deference. In this way (I hope) "popular culture" is situated within its proper material abode.

Let us resume the characteristic features of the eighteenth-century plebeian culture. As a matter of course it exhibits certain features commonly ascribed to "traditional" cultures. In rural society, but also in thickly populated manufacturing and mining areas (the West of England clothing regions, the Cornish tinners, the Black Country) there is a heavy inheritance of customary definitions and expectations. Apprenticeship as an initiation into adult skills is not confined to its formal industrial expression. It is also the mechanism of inter-generational transmission. The child serves her apprenticeship to household duties, first to her mother (or grandmother), then (often) as a domestic or farm servant. As a young mother, in the mysteries of child-rearing, she is apprentice to the matrons of the community. It is the same in the trades without formal apprenticeship. And with the induction into these particular skills comes an induction into the social experience or common wisdom of the community. Although social life is changing, and although there is much mobility, change has not yet reached that point at which it is assumed that the horizons of each successive generation will be different; nor has that engine of cultural acceleration (and estrangement), formal education, yet interpolated itself significantly into this generational transmission.[15]

Both practices and norms are reproduced down the generations within the slowly differentiating ambience of custom. Traditions are perpetuated largely through oral transmission, with its repertoire of anecdote and of narrative example; where oral tradition is supplemented by growing literacy, the most widely circulated printed products, such as chapbooks, almanacs, broadsides, "last dying speeches" and anecdotal accounts of crime, tend to be subdued to the expectations of the oral culture rather than challenging it with alternatives.

This culture transmits vigorously — and perhaps it also generates — ritualized or stylized performances, whether in recreation or in forms of protest. It is even possible that geographic mobility, together with growing literacy, actually extends the range and distributes such forms more widely: "setting the price", as the central action of a food riot, moves across most of the country; the ritual divorce known as a "wife sale" appears to have distributed its incidence throughout the country from some unknown point of origin. The evidence of rough music suggests that in the more traditional communities — and these were by no means always ones with a rural profile — quite powerful self-motivating forces of social and moral regulation were at work. This evidence may show that while deviant behaviour might be tolerated up to a point, beyond that point the community sought to impose upon transgressors its own inherited expectations as to approved marital roles and sexual conduct. Even here, however, we have to proceed with caution: this is not *just* "a traditional culture". The norms so defended are not identical with those proclaimed by Church or authority; they are defined within the plebeian culture itself, and the same shaming rituals which are used against a notorious sexual offender may be used against the blackleg, or against the squire and his gamekeepers, the excise officer, the JP [Justice of the Peace].

This, then, is a conservative culture in its forms, which appeal to and seek to reinforce traditional usages. The forms are also non-rational; they do not appeal to "reason" through the pamphlet, sermon or platform; they impose the sanctions of force, ridicule, shame, intimidation. But the content or meanings of this culture cannot so easily be described as conservative. For in social reality labour is becoming, decade by decade, more "free" of traditional manorial, parochial, corporate and paternal controls, and more distanced from direct client dependence upon the gentry. Hence we have a customary culture which is not subject in its daily operations to the ideological domination of the rulers. The gentry's overarching hegemony may define the limits within which the plebeian culture is free to act and grow, but since this hegemony is secular rather than religious or magical it can do little to determine the character of this plebeian culture. The controlling instruments and images of hegemony are those of the Law and not those of the Church or of monarchical charisma. But the Law does not sow pious sisterhoods in cities nor extract the confessions of sinners; its subjects do not tell their rosaries nor go on pilgrimages to the shrines of saints — instead they read broadsides and carouse in taverns and at least some of the Law's victims are regarded, not with horror, but with an ambiguous admiration. The Law may punctuate the limits tolerated by the rulers; it does not, in eighteenth-century England, enter into the cottages, find mention in the widow's prayers, decorate the wall with icons, or inform a view of life.

Hence one characteristic paradox of the century: we have a *rebellious* traditional culture. The conservative culture of the plebs as often as not resists, in the name of custom, those economic rationalizations and innovations (such as enclosure, work-discipline, unregulated "free" markets in grain) which rulers, dealers, or employers seek to impose. Innovation is more evident at the top of society than below, but since this innovation is not some normless and neutral technological/sociological process ("modernization", "rationalization") but is the innovation of capitalist process, it is most often experienced by the plebs in the form of exploitation, or the expropriation of customary use-rights, or the violent disruption of valued patterns of work and leisure. Hence the plebian culture is rebellious, but rebellious in defence of custom. The customs defended are the people's own, and some of them are in fact based upon rather recent assertions in practice. But when the people search for legitimations for protest, they often turn back to the paternalist regulations of a more authoritarian society, and select from among these those parts most calculated to defend their present interests — food rioters appeal back to the Book of Orders and to legislation against forestallers, etc., artisans appeal back to certain parts (e.g. apprenticeship regulation) of the Tudor labour code.

Nor is the social identity of many working people unambiguous. One can often detect within the same individual alternating identities, one deferential, the other rebellious.[16] This was a problem with which — using different terms — Gramsci concerned himself. He noted the contrast between the "popular morality" of folklore tradition and "official morality". His "man-in-the-mass" might have "two theoretical consciousnesses (or one contradictory consciousness)" — one of praxis, the other "inherited from the past and uncritically absorbed". When discussing ideology in his prison notebooks, Gramsci sees it as resting upon "the spontaneous philosophy which is proper to everybody". This philosophy (he concludes) derives from three sources: first, "language itself, which is a totality of determined notions and concepts, and not just of words, grammatically devoid of content"; second, "common sense"; and, third, popular religion and folklore.[17] Of these three, most Western intellectuals today would unhesitatingly award theoretical primacy to the first (language) as not only the carrier but as the constitutive influence upon consciousness. Indeed, while actual language — for example as dialect — has been little examined,[18] it has become fashionable to assume that the plebs were in a sense "spoken" by their linguistic inheritance, which in turn is seen as a *bricolage* of disparate notions derivative from many sources but held in place by patrician categories. The plebs are even seen as captives within a linguistic prison, compelled even in moments of rebellion to move within the parameters of constitutionalism, of "Old England", of deference to patrician leaders and of patriarchy.

We can follow this argument some way. But what it overlooks are Gramsci's alternative sources of "spontaneous philosophy", and in particular "common sense" or praxis. For Gramsci also insisted that this philosophy was not simply the appropriation of an individual but was derived from shared experiences in labour and in social relations, and is "implicit in his activity and which in reality unites him with all his fellow-workers in the practical transformation of the real world . . ." Thus the "two theoretical consciousnesses" can be seen as derivative from two aspects of the same reality: on the one hand, the necessary conformity with the *status quo* if one is to survive, the need to get by in the world as it is in fact ordered, and to play the game according to the rules imposed by employers, overseers of the poor, etc.;[19] on the other hand the "common sense" derived from shared experience with fellow workers and with neighbours of exploitation, hardship and repression, which continually exposes the text of the paternalist theatre to ironic criticism and (less frequently) to revolt.

Another feature of this culture which is of special interest to me is the priority afforded, in certain areas, to "non-economic" over direct monetary sanctions, exchanges and motivations. This feature is now widely discussed as "the moral economy". Again and again, when examining the behaviour of working people in the eighteenth century one finds it to be necessary to "de-code" this behaviour and its symbolic modes of expression and to disclose invisible rules unlike those which a historian of subsequent working-class movements has come to expect. In attending to the symbolism of protest, or in decoding rough music or the sale of wives, one shares some of the preoccupations of historians of the sixteenth and seventeenth centuries of an anthropological orientation. In another sense the problems are different, and perhaps more acute, for capitalist process and non-economic customary behaviour are in active and conscious conflict, as in resistance to new patterns of consumption ("needs"), or in resistance to technical innovations or work-rationalizations which threaten to disrupt customary usage and, sometimes, the familial organization of productive roles.[20] Hence we can read much eighteenth-century social history as a succession of confrontations between an innovative market economy and the customary moral economy of the plebs.

In these confrontations it is possible to see prefigurements of subsequent class formations and consciousness; and the fragmented débris of older patterns are revivified and reintegrated within this emergent class consciousness. In one sense the plebeian culture is the people's own: it is a defence against the intrusions of gentry or clergy; it consolidates those customs which serve their own interests; the taverns are their own, the fairs are their own, rough music is among their own means of self-regulation. This is not *any* "traditional" culture but a rather peculiar one. It is not, for example, fatalistic, offering consolations and defences in the course of a lifetime which is utterly determined and constrained. It is, rather, picaresque, not only in the obvious sense that more people are mobile, go to sea, are carried off to wars, experience the hazards and adventures of the road.[21] In more settled ambiences — in the growing areas of manufacture and of "free" labour — life itself proceeds along a road whose hazards and accidents cannot be prescribed or avoided by forethought: fluctuations in the incidence of mortality, of prices, of unemployment, are experienced as external accidents beyond any control; in general, the working population has little predictive notation of time — they do not plan "careers", or plan families, or see their lives in a given shape before them, or salt away weeks of high earnings in savings, or plan to buy cottages, or ever in their lives take a "vacation". (A young man, knowing that this will be so, may set off once in a lifetime, upon the road to "see the world".) Hence opportunity is grabbed as occasion arises, with little thought of the consequences, just as the crowd imposes its power in moments of insurgent direct action, knowing that its moment of triumph will last for only a week or a day.

I criticised earlier the term "culture", because of its tendency to nudge us towards over-consensual and holistic notions. And yet I have been driven back to an account of "plebeian culture" which may be open to the same criticisms. This may not much matter if we are using "culture" as a loosely descriptive term. After all, there are other descriptive terms in common currency, such as "society", "politics" and "economy": no doubt these deserve close interrogation from time to time, but if on every occasion that these were employed we had to engage in an exercise of rigorous definition the discourse of knowledge would indeed be cumbersome.

Even so we should not forget that "culture" is a clumpish term, which by gathering up so many activities and attributes into one common bundle may actually confuse or disguise discriminations that should be made between them. We need to take this bundle apart, and examine the components with more care: rites, symbolic modes, the cultural attributes of hegemony, the inter-generational transmission of custom and custom's evolution within historically specific forms of working and social relations. . . .

If I were to nominate those components of the bundle which makes up "popular culture" which most require attention today, these would include "needs" and "expectations". The industrial revolution and accompanying demographic revolution were the backgrounds to the greatest transformation in history, in revolutionising "needs" and in destroying the authority of customary expectations. . . .

Notes

1   John Brand and Henry Ellis, *Observations on Popular Antiquities* (1813), Vol. I, p. xxi. (Brand's Preface is dated 1795.)

2   P. H. Ditchfield, *Old English Customs extant at the Present Time* (1896), Preface.

3   Bernard Mandeville, *The Fable of the Bees* (Harmondsworth, 1970 edn), p. 191: also p. 334.

4   *Ibid.*, p. 294.

5   For an excellent survey of custom, 1700–1880, see Bob Bushaway, *By Rite* (1982). Also R. W. Malcolmson, *Life and Labour in England, 1700–1780* (1981), Chapter 4, "Beliefs, customs and identities".

6   "A custom or prescription against a statute is void": but an exception was made for local corn measures, where "it is said . . . the custom of the place is to be observed, if it be a custom beyond all memory, and used without any visible interruption": Richard Burn, *The Justice of the Peace and Parish Officer* (14th edition, 1780), vol. I, p. 408.

7   For the breakdown of custom in the Forest of Dean, see C. Fisher, *Custom, Work and Market Capitalism* (1981). Is it possible that "Dennis" is a corruption of the Statute of De Donis (1285)?

8   Several of the studies in E. J. Hobsbawm, *Labouring Men* (1964) bear centrally upon custom. See also John Rule, *The Experience of Labour in Eighteenth-Century Industry* (1981), esp. Chapter 8, "Custom, Culture and Consciousness".

9   John Rule, *op. cit.*, pp. 194, 196.

10   In 1837 a Woolwich shopkeeper complained that on St. Clements Day [November 23rd] "a procession got up by the Blacksmiths' apprentices passed through the principal streets of the Town, attended by a large Mob, some carrying Torches, others discharging fireworks in great abundance in the most reckless manner, by which the horses attached to one of Mr Wheatley's Omnibuses . . . were so terrified as to . . . run the Pole of the Omnibus through your Memorialist's shop window". Memorial of Robert Wollett of Woolwich, 27 November 1837, in PRO HO 73.2.

11   William Hone, *Every-Day Book* (1826), vol. I, col. 1499; F. E. Sawyer, "Old Clem Celebrations and Blacksmiths Lore", *Folk Lore Journal*, II, 1884, p. 321; G. P. G. Hills, "Notes on Some Blacksmiths' Legends and the Observance of St. Clement's Day", *Proceedings of the Hampshire Field Club*, vol. VIII, 1917–19, pp. 65–82.

12   For the polarisation of cultures in the seventeenth century, see the editors' introduction to Anthony Fletcher and John Stevenson (eds.), *Order and Disorder in Early Modern England* (Cambridge, 1985); and for the "momentous split" between patrician and plebeian cultures, see Patrick Curry, *Prophecy and Power: Astrology in Early Modern England* (Oxford, 1989), esp. ch. 7.

13   G. L. Gomme, *Encyclopaedia of Religion and Ethics* (Edinburgh, 1913), entry on folklore, pp. 57–9, cited in Bushaway, *op. cit.*, pp. 10–11.

14   P. Burke, *Popular Culture in Early Modern Europe* (1978), Preface, citing A. L. Kroeber and C. Kluckhohn, *Culture: a Critical Review of Concepts and Definitions* (New York, 1952).

15   Two interesting studies of the restraint which custom may impose upon material expectations are: G. M. Foster, "Peasant Society and the Image of Limited Good", *American Anthropologist*, April 1965; Daniel Vickers, "Competency and Competition: Economic Culture in Early America", *William and Mary Quarterly*, 3rd series, vol. xlvii, no. 1, January 1990.

16   See Hans Medick, "Plebeian Culture in the Transition to Capitalism", in R. Samuel and G. Stedman Jones (eds.), *Culture, Ideology and Politics* (1982).

17   See Antonio Gramsci, *Selections from the Prison Notebooks* (1971), pp. 419–25; Bushaway, *op. cit.*, pp. 11–12; T. J. Jackson Lears, "The Concept of Cultural Hegemony: Problems and Possibilities", *American Hist. Rev.*, 90, 1985.

18   Social historians have made too little use of dialect studies, including Joseph Wright's in *English Dialect Dictionary*, 6 volumes (1898–1905), which is full of clues as to working usages.

19   See my "Folklore, Anthropology, and Social History", *Indian Hist. Rev.*, vol. III, no. 2, Jan. 1977, p. 265.

20   See, for example, Adrian J. Randall, "Work, Culture and Resistance to Machinery in the West of England Woollen Industry", in Pat Hudson (ed.), *Regions and Industries: a perspective on the Industrial Revolution in Britain* (Cambridge, 1989).

21   Extreme examples of picaresque livelihoods are in Marcus Rediker, *Between the devil and the deep blue sea* (Cambridge, 1987), and Peter Linebaugh, *The London Hanged* (Harmondsworth, 1991).

Chapter 15

Peter Burke

INTRODUCTION TO THE THIRD EDITION OF *POPULAR CULTURE IN EARLY MODERN EUROPE*

The debate over popular culture

. . . . **THE DEBATE OVER POPULAR CULTURE** has tended to concentrate on two main issues, or two main questions, both of them deceptively simple in formulation. The first question is, What is 'popular'? The second, What is 'culture'?

The problem of the 'popular'

The notion of the 'popular' has long been recognised as problematic. All the same, recent discussions have uncovered even more problems, or brought difficulties more sharply into focus.

An objection that has frequently been made [in comments on the two earlier editions of this book] is that the term 'popular culture' gives a false impression of homogeneity and that it would be better to use the term in the plural, 'popular cultures', or to replace it with an expression such as 'the culture of the popular classes'.[1] The point about the importance of differences, divergences and conflicts is well worth making. I thought that the objection was answered in advance in Chapter 2 of this book, with its discussion of varieties of culture and indeed of the existence of more or less sharply defined 'sub-cultures'. However, some scholars, notably Edward Thompson, have suggested that a 'cosy invocation of consensus' is inseparable from the term 'culture' itself (though Thompson himself continued to use it).[2] Today, following the so-called 'culture wars', the associations of the term are probably less consensual than they were thirty years ago.

Another objection to what is sometimes called the 'two-tier model' of elite and popular culture is as follows. The borderline between the different cultures of the people and the cultures of the elites (which were no less various) is a fuzzy one, so the attention of students of the subject ought to be concentrated on the interaction rather than the division between the two.[3] The increasing interest in the work of the great Russian critic and literary theorist Mikhail Bakhtin, much of which has now been translated into western languages, both reveals and encourages this shift of emphasis. His stress on the importance of the 'transgression' of boundaries is of obvious relevance here. His definition of Carnival and the carnivalesque by its opposition not to elites but to 'official' culture marks an important shift in emphasis which comes close to redefining the popular as the rebel in all of us (as Freud once described it), rather than as the property of any social group.[4]

There are indeed many possible relations between learned culture and popular culture, as I tried to show in a study of four Italian writers – Giovanni Boccaccio, Teofilo Folengo, Ludovico Ariosto and Pietro Aretino – arguing that Boccaccio drew on a popular tradition in which he participated, that Folengo played with the tensions between the two traditions, that Ariosto reappropriated popular themes which had once been borrowed from high culture, while Aretino used popular motifs to subvert high culture, or at least those parts of it which he disliked.[5] It should be added that early modern elites sometimes used popular culture for their own political purposes, for example in the defence of traditional festivals by such English poets as Jonson and Herrick, Milton and Marvell.[6]

Since the notion of the 'popular' leads to such difficulties, historians ought perhaps to attempt to do without it. What might they put in its place? One phrase that has come into regular use since I was writing this book in the 1970s is 'common culture'.[7] It is hardly surprising that this term has been taken up at a time when, as has often been noted, the boundaries between 'high' and 'low' cultural forms have become increasingly porous, when these boundaries are visible at all.[8] Thanks to television and other media, Europeans have acquired something more like a common culture than anything since what I call the great 'withdrawal' of early modern elites from what they came to call 'popular culture'. The 'modernist' condemnation of 'mass culture' has been replaced by the 'postmodernist' interest in popular culture.[9]

The term 'common culture' would have been a useful one to describe the period before the withdrawal, when elites were, as I put it in later chapters, 'bicultural' or 'amphibious'. On the other hand, there is now a danger of underestimating the importance of cultural boundaries in the past. Edward Thompson has been criticised for making too sharp a distinction between two cultures in nineteenth-century England.[10]

Another way of avoiding (if not evading) the difficulty of defining the popular is to talk about history 'from below'; but this notion is more ambiguous than it looks. A history of politics from below might involve a study of the 'subordinate classes', but it might equally well be concerned with what Americans call the 'grass-roots', in other words the provinces. The history of the Church from below might well deal with the laity, whatever their level of culture. The history of education from below might be concerned with the ordinary teacher (as opposed to the ministers or the school inspectors) but it might more reasonably still present the point of view of the pupils. A history of war from below might present the war experienced by common soldiers rather than the generals, but a place ought to be found for the point of view of the civilians caught up in military operations.

A notion that was often employed from the 1960s to the 1980s in analysing the interactions between 'above' and 'below' – by Edward Thompson, for instance is – Gramsci's idea of 'cultural hegemony', with its implication that 'above' should be translated into 'dominant' and 'below' into 'dominated' or 'subordinate'.[11] Discussions with Gramscian historians of popular culture in Britain, France, Italy, Poland, Brazil, India and elsewhere made me realise that my own study did not pay sufficient attention to politics, and could have said more than it did in Chapter 9 about the consequences for popular culture of the process of state-building in early modern Europe. If the sources allow this, it would be good to have a study of the workings of the monarchy and of attitudes to the monarchy at village level, in France for instance, on the analogy of the French historian Maurice Agulhon's *The Republic in the Village*, centred on nineteenth-century Provence.[12]

On the other hand, if a historian is working on any period before (say) 1789, he or she runs the risk of over-estimating the political consciousness of dominated groups, or describing this consciousness in anachronistic terms, or overestimating the power of the state. For example, I still think that Robert Muchembled's *Popular Culture and Elite Culture* (1978) overemphasised the active role of the government in changing popular culture, at the expense of other historical agents such as the small provincial publishers of the *Bibliothèque Bleue*.[13] Again, it is my impression that the historians of India associated with *Subaltern Studies* have assumed rather too easily that the dominated classes with whom they are concerned were conscious of belonging to the dominated classes; that is, that the peasants of certain villages in Bengal, for example, over and above any particular local experience of domination, were aware of what they had in common with peasants from other parts of Bengal and indeed India. It is actually extremely hard to answer the question, in what places and at what times the people (whoever 'they' are) have seen themselves as 'The People'.[14] As for the celebrated studies of popular culture by Christopher Hill, Eric Hobsbawm and Edward Thompson (brilliant, original and influential as they have been), they are all vulnerable to the criticism that these historians tend to equate the 'popular' with the 'radical', ignoring evidence for popular conservatism.

I am indeed still a little uneasy about the constant appeal to the politics of culture and more especially, to 'cultural hegemony' in recent studies, and even more about the way in which a concept used by Gramsci himself to analyse specific problems (such as the influence of the Church in southern Italy), has been taken out of its original context and used more or less indiscriminately to deal with a much wider range of situations. As a corrective to this inflation or dilution of the concept, one might suggest the following three 'directions for use', in the form of questions.[15]

i   Is cultural hegemony to be assumed to be a constant factor, or has it only operated at certain places and times? If the latter, what are the conditions and the indicators of its existence?

ii Is the term descriptive or explanatory? If the latter, does it refer to the conscious strategies of the ruling class (or of groups within it), or to the unconscious or latent rationality of their actions?

iii How are we to account for the achievement of this hegemony? Can it be established without the collusion or connivance of some at least of the dominated? Can it be resisted with success? If so, what are the major 'counter-hegemonic strategies'?[16] Does the ruling class impose its values on the subordinate classes, or is there some kind of compromise, with alternative definitions of the situation? The concept of 'negotiation', as it is currently used by sociologists and social historians, to include the unconscious as well as the conscious adaptation of the attitudes of one group to those of another, might well be of value in this analysis.[17]

The ideas expressed in the last paragraph may help clear up a possible misunderstanding of the process of the 'reform' of popular culture, discussed in Chapter 8 below. Objections have sometimes been raised to the description of this process by myself and others as essentially the work of elites.[18] At one level, the micro-level or level of detail, the objectors have a good case. It is not difficult to find documented examples of godly artisans, whether Protestants, like Nehemiah Wallington in seventeenth-century London, or Catholics, like Pierre-Ignace Chavatte in seventeenth-century Lille. It may well have been the case that the movement of reform would have been unsuccessful without this kind of support.

At the macro-level, on the other hand, and over the long term, it still seems to me that the initiative for reform came originally from elites, especially the upper clergy, before it spread more widely through society. It was part of what is variously called, following the rival social theorists Norbert Elias and Michel Foucault, a process of 'civilising' or 'disciplining', which began as an attempt by elites to control the behaviour of ordinary people but was gradually internalised (up to a point, and among certain groups, at least) and so turned into self-control.[19] The apparent importance of elites in this process may of course be an optical illusion, the result of the relative lack of evidence for popular attitudes, but given the evidence we have, to speak of village Luthers or Loyolas before the time of Martin and Ignatius would be unwarranted speculation.

All the objections to the idea of popular culture discussed so far are relatively mild in the sense that they involve qualifications or shifts of emphasis. Other objections are more radical and involve attempts to replace the concept altogether. Two of these objections remain particularly worth discussing, those of the American anthropologist William Christian and the French historian Roger Chartier.

In his study of vows, relics and shrines in sixteenth-century Spain, Christian argues that the kind of religious practice he is describing 'was as characteristic of the royal family as it was of unlettered peasants', and he therefore refuses to use the term 'popular' at all. In its place he proposes to use the term 'local', on the grounds that 'the vast majority of sacred places and monuments held meaning only for local citizens'.[20] This may well have been the case – though it is surely worth adding that the minority of sacred places remaining (among them Rome, Jerusalem, and Santiago de Compostela in Galicia) held meaning for many European Catholics, as the influx of pilgrims demonstrates.

Christian's discussion of the local features of what is generally called 'popular' religion is important, though new only in its emphasis. What is most original is the suggestion that we scrap one binary model, that of the elite and the people, and replace it by another, that of centre and periphery.

Centre–periphery models of this kind have come increasingly into use by historians, in economic history, political history, religious history and even in the history of art. They certainly have their value, but they are not free from problems and ambiguities. The notion of 'centre', for example, is difficult to define, since spatial centres and power centres do not always coincide (think of London, Paris, Peking . . .). In the case of Catholicism, discussed by Christian, we may reasonably assume Rome to be the centre with which he is contrasting Spanish 'local religion'. It is clear, however, that unofficial devotions were as current in that holy city as they were elsewhere. In the course of smoothing out one conceptual difficulty, another has been created.

The basic problem is that a 'culture' is a system with rather vague boundaries. The great value of Roger Chartier's many essays on 'the cultural uses of print' is that he keeps this vagueness constantly in mind.[21] Chartier argues that it is pointless to try to identify popular culture by some supposedly specific distribution of cultural objects, objects such as books or ex votos, because these objects were in practice used or 'appropriated' for their own purposes by different social groups, noblemen and clerics as well as craftsmen and peasants.

Following the French social theorists Michel De Certeau and Pierre Bourdieu, Chartier suggests that everyday consumption is a kind of production or creation, since it involves people imposing meanings on objects. In that sense we all engage in the *bricolage* that Lévi-Strauss considered part of *la pensée sauvage*. German literary theorists, such as Hans-Robert Jauss and Wolfgang Iser, have reached similar conclusions about the reception of texts and the responses of readers from a different starting-point.[22]

The moral Chartier draws is that historians should not define sets of texts or other objects as 'popular' from the start but study the specific ways in which these objects have been appropriated in particular places and times and by particular groups. In a similar manner, more or less independently, a group of American historians and anthropologists have examined what they call 'the social history of things', emphasising the different uses and meanings of the same object in different contexts.[23]

This analysis of the creative uses of objects is a development from earlier discussions of 'sinking' and 'rising', abandoning the misleading mechanical imagery and emphasising the transformation of cultural items in the course of their reception. It still strikes me as the most important contribution to the popular culture debate since the 1970s. Even today, historians are far from having absorbed all its lessons.

All the same, problems remain. The 'appropriation' model is most useful for the study of material culture and texts. It forces the historian, or anthropologist, to focus on the objects, the 'social life of things' rather than on the life of the social groups who use them. Other concepts will be needed if we wish to focus on these social groups themselves, to try to understand their mentalities, the logic of their different appropriations and adaptations of diverse objects. If what interests us is the manner in which different groups created their particular life-styles, often by means of *bricolage*, in other words 'cobbling together' elements from diverse sources (as the British sociologist Dick Hebdige demonstrated in the case of some post-war British subcultures), we may have to return to some version of the 'two-tier model', modified to allow for the circulation of objects.[24] We also need to be aware of the paradox that while awareness of the interaction between so-called 'high' and 'low' culture has led some scholars to challenge the distinction, the interaction can scarcely be discussed without recourse to the concepts of high and low, viewed as models or 'ideal types' to which actual cultural practices only approximates or as opposite ends of a spectrum rather than two sides of a firm frontier.[25] It may, for example, be unwise to describe public festivals, whether religious or civic, as 'popular', because on such occasions different social groups often walked in procession, or lined the streets to watch the others.

All the same, it may still be useful to describe some festivals in some places and times as more popular than others or to speak of processes of 'popularisation' or 'aristocratisation'. It is hard to deny the fact that lower-status groups often imitated the cultural practices of higher status groups. Explaining the imitation is rather more difficult. The lower groups may have done this because they wanted to rise socially, or to appear to have risen socially, because they accepted the 'cultural hegemony' of the upper classes. On the other hand, they may have imitated the habits of their so-called 'betters' as an affirmation of equality with them.

The implication of this relatively recent historical concern with consumption, 'uses' and 'practices' is that the notion of 'culture', as well as that of 'the people' is in serious need of re-examination and redefinition.

The notion of 'culture'

The problems raised by utilising the concept 'culture' are, if anything, even greater than those raised by the term 'popular'. One reason for these problems is that the concept has widened its meaning in the last generation as scholars have widened their interests. In the age of the so-called 'discovery' of the people, in the early nineteenth century, the term 'culture' tended to refer to art, literature and music, and it would not be unfair to describe the nineteenth-century folklorists as searching for popular equivalents for classical music, academic art, and so on.

Today, however, following the example of the anthropologists, historians and others use the term 'culture' much more widely, to refer to almost everything that can be learned in a given society – how to eat, drink, walk, talk, be silent and so on.[26] Even kinship is now analysed from a cultural rather than or as well as a social point of view.[27] In other words, the history of culture now includes the history of the assumptions underlying everyday life. A concern with the everyday is a striking feature of the history practised in the last few decades, especially in Germany, where *Alltagsgeschichte* has become an influential slogan.[28] The aim is not simply to describe the everyday, but rather, following the lead of social theorists such as Henri Lefebvre, Michel de Certeau or Juri Lotman, to discover its 'poetics', in other words the various rules or principles which underlie everyday life in different places and times.[29] What used to be taken for granted; in other words treated as obvious, normal or 'common sense' is now viewed as part of a cultural system, something which varies from society to society and changes from one century to another, something which is socially 'constructed' and so requires social and historical explanation or interpretation.[30] The concept of time, for example, has been studied in this way.[31] Hence the new cultural history is sometimes called 'socio-cultural' history to distinguish it from the more traditional histories of art, literature and music.

Edward Thompson once accused some historians – including myself – of situating popular culture in what he called 'the thin air of "meanings, attitudes and values"', rather than in 'its proper material abode'.[32] In fact, in the first edition of this book, I did try to take everyday life into account, defining culture in terms of the attitudes and values expressed or embodied in artifacts and performances. The key terms 'artifacts' and 'performances' were intended to be understood in a wide sense; extending the notion of 'artifact' to include such cultural constructs as the categories of sickness, or dirt, or gender or politics, and widening the notion of 'performance' to cover such culturally stereotyped forms of behaviour as feasting and violence.

In general, I have to admit, the book concentrates on a narrower range of objects (notably images, printed matter, and houses), and practices (especially singing, dancing, acting in plays and engaging in rituals), despite the attempt to set these objects and activities in a wider social, economic and political context. Popular revolt was discussed in some detail, but sex, marriage, family life and kinship, for example, were virtually omitted.[33] Occasional references to walking, drinking and making love contrast with a more detailed discussion of less everyday activities. In short, I was working with a more precise and also a narrower concept of popular culture than some later historians.[34]

Was this decision to opt in practice for the narrower definition of culture a wise one? In the early 1970s, when I began research for this study, very few examples of the new type of socio-cultural history had yet been published, so that the time was not ripe for a synthesis. If I were beginning the book now, the idea of writing a general socio-cultural history of early modern Europe would certainly be tempting, difficult as the enterprise would be. On the other hand, I remain convinced that there is room for a book like this one which concentrates on artefacts and performances in the narrower sense, because this more limited subject allows a more rigorous comparative study than the wider subject affords. One advantage of the narrower approach is that it allows one to practise what the French call 'serial history', examining the different series of chap-books, for instance, published in different European countries in the period to see what themes were common or rare, present or absent, in a particular country.

It is impossible to draw any precise boundary between the wider and the narrower sense of 'culture', so it may be useful to end these reconsiderations with a few examples of research that falls between the two. Take, for example, the case of insults, which may be regarded, at least in some cultures, as an art-form or a literary genre as well as an expression of hostility. In seventeenth-century Rome, for example, private insults took written and pictorial as well as oral forms, employed verse as well as prose, and alluded to, or parodied, epitaphs and official notices.[35]

Studies of material culture also fall between the wide and the narrow senses of culture. The German social historian Hans Medick, for instance, has analysed the ways in which conspicuous consumption on food and clothes 'functioned as a vehicle of plebeian self-consciousness' in the eighteenth century.[36] Again, in the case of North America in the middle of the eighteenth century, archaeologists have argued that changes in burial practices, in the mode of food consumption and in the organisation of living space all suggest a shift in values. A rise of individualism and privacy is revealed by the increase in the number of chairs (instead of benches), cups (instead of communal bowls) and bedrooms (instead of beds being placed in living-rooms).[37]

Examples like these suggest that although it is useful to distinguish the concept of 'culture' from that of 'society', rather than using it to refer to almost everything, this distinction should not follow traditional lines. The American historian Keith Baker has suggested that intellectual history should be understood as 'a mode of historical discourse' rather than 'a distinct field of enquiry with a clearly demarcated subject matter'. In similar fashion, cultural historians might usefully define themselves not in terms of a particular area or 'field' such as art, literature or music, but rather by a concern for values and symbols, wherever these are to be found, in the everyday life of ordinary people as well as in special performances for elites.[38]

Notes

1   Ginzburg (1979); Fonquerne and Esteban (1986).
2   Thompson (1991), p. 6.
3   Gurevich (1981); Kaplan (1984).
4   On Bakhtin, G.S. Morson and C. Emerson, *Mikhail Bakhtin: Creation of a Prosaics*, Stanford, 1990. For a survey of some recent work inspired by Bakhtin, Burke (1988b).
5   Burke (1992b).
6   Marcus (1986).
7   P.E. Willis, *Common Culture: Symbolic Work at Play in the Everyday Cultures of the Young*, Milton Keynes, 1990, esp. pp. 1–5; T.E. Crow, *Modern Art in the Common Culture*, New Haven, 1996.
8   On the 'erosion' of the distinction, F. Jameson, *The Political Unconscious: Narrative as a Socially Symbolic Act*, Ithaca, 1983, p. 112; on 'blurring the boundaries'. M. Kammen. *American Culture, American Tastes: Social Change and the 20th Century*, New York, 1999, ch. 5.
9   A point both argued and illustrated by J. Docker, *Postmodernism and Popular Culture: a Cultural History*, Cambridge, 1994.
10   R. Rosaldo, *Culture & Truth: the Remaking of Social Analysis* (1989: 2nd edn, London, 1993), pp. 183–6.
11   Thompson (1991), pp. 76ff; cf. R. Guha, *Elementary Aspects of Peasant Insurgency*, Delhi, 1983, cit., Hall (1981), and P. Bailey, *Leisure and Class in Victorian England*, London, 1987, pp. 9ff.
12   M. Agulhon, *The Republic in the Village: the People of the Var from the French Revolution to the Second Republic* (1970: Engl. Trans., Cambridge, 1982).
13   Muchembled (1978).
14   Burke (1992a).
15   Cf. Lears (1985), which raises questions additional (but complementary) to mine.
16   G. Sider, 'The Ties that Bind', *Social History* 5 (1980), pp. 1–39; J. Scott, *Weapons of the Weak: Everyday Forms of Peasant Resistance* (New Haven, 1987).
17   Burke (1982, 1987, ch. 5).
18   E.g. Mullett (1987), pp. 110, 164.
19   N. Elias, *The Civilizing Process* (1939: Engl. trans., 2 vols, Oxford 1981–2); M. Foucault, *Discipline and Punish* (1975: Engl. trans., London, 1977).
20   Christian (1981b), especially pp. 8, 177.
21   Chartier (1987).
22   H.R. Jauss, *Towards an Aesthetic of Reception* (1974: Engl. trans., Minneapolis, 1982): W. Iser, *The Act of Reading* (1976: Engl. trans., Baltimore, 1978).

23 Appadurai (1986), especially the contributions by Appadurai and Kopytoff. This group has learned from the French social theorists Jean Baudrillard and Pierre Bourdieu.

24 D. Hebdige, *Subculture: the Meaning of Style*, London, 1979.

25 For a defence of the continuing usefulness of the distinction between high and low culture, Gripsrud (1989).

26 An influential (and controversial) explicit discussion in R. Wagner, *The Invention of Culture*, Englewood Cliffs, 1975.

27 D.M. Schneider, *American Kinship: a Cultural Account*, Englewood Cliffs, 1968; cf J. Frykman and O. Löfgren, *Culture Builders: a Historical Anthropology of Middle-Class Life* (1979: Engl. trans., New Brunswick, 1987); Phythian-Adams (1993).

28 E.g. Kuczynski (1980–1); Dinges (1987); Bergsma (1990); Scribner (1990); van Dülmen (1990–4); Mohrmann (1993). Cf. M. Medick, *Weben und Überleben in Laichingen 1650–1900: Lokalgeschichte als allgemeine Geschichte*, Göttingen, 1996.

29 H. Lefebvre, *Critique de la vie quotidienne*, 3 vols, Paris, 1946–81; M. de Certeau, *The Practice of Everyday Life* (1980: Engl. trans., Berkeley 1984); Lotman (1984); S. Greenblatt, *Shakespearean Negotiations: the Circulation of Social Energy in Renaissance England*, Oxford, 1988.

30 C. Geertz, 'Common Sense as a Cultural System', in his *Local Knowledge*, New York, 1983, ch. 4.

31 See, for example, T.C. Smith, 'Peasant Time and Factory Time in Japan', *Past and Present* 111 (1986), pp. 165–97 (modelled on E.P. Thompson's article in the same journal in 1967).

32 Thompson (1991), p. 7.

33 As remarked by M. Ingram in Reay (1985), p. 129.

34 Sabean (1984); Dülmen (1990–4); Cohen and Cohen (1993); Ruggiero (1993).

35 Burke (1987), ch. 8.

36 Medick (1983), p. 94. Cf. Sandgruber (1982).

37 Deetz (1977).

38 K. Baker, 'On the Problem of the Ideological Origins of the French Revolution', in *Modern European Intellectual History*, ed. D. LaCapra and S.L. Kaplan, Ithaca, 1982, p. 197. Cf Peter Burke, *What is Cultural History?* Cambridge, 2004.

Bibliography

A. Appadurai (ed., 1986) *The Social Life of Things*, Cambridge

W. Bergsma (1990) 'Slow to hear God's Holy Word? Religion in Everyday Life in Early Modern Friesland', in L. Laeyendecker *et al.* (eds), *Experiences and Explanations*, Ljouwert (Leeuwarden)

P. Burke (1982) 'A Question of Acculturation', in P. Zambelli (ed., 1982) *Scienze, credenze occulte, livelli di cultura*, Florence

P. Burke (1987) *Historical Anthropology of Early Modern Italy*, Cambridge

P. Burke (1992a) 'We, the People: Popular Culture and Identity in Modern Europe', in S. Lash and J. Friedman (eds) *Modernity and Identity*, Oxford

P. Burke (1992b) 'Learned Culture and Popular Culture in Renaissance Italy', in M. Aymard (eds) *Pauvres et Riches: Mélanges offerts à Bronislaw Geremek*, Warsaw

R. Chartier (1987) *The Cultural Uses of Print in Early Modern France*, Princeton

W.A. Christian (1981) *Local Religion in Sixteenth-Century Spain*, Princeton

T.V. Cohen and E.S. Cohen (1993) *Words and Deeds in Renaissance Rome*, Chicago

J. Deetz (1977) *In Small Things Forgotten*, New York

M. Dinges (1987) 'Materielle Kultur und Alltag – die Unterschichten in Bordeaux im 16./17. Jahrhundert', *Francia* 15

R. van Dülmen (1990–4) *Kultur und Alltag in der Frühen Neuzeit*, 3 vols, Munich

Y.-R. Fonquerne and A. Esteban (eds, 1986) *Culturas populares: differencias, divergencias, conflictos*, Madrid

C. Ginzburg (ed., 1979) *Religione delle classi popolari*, Quaderni Storici 41

J. Gripsrud (1989) 'High Culture Revisited', *Cultural Studies* 3

A.J. Gurevich (1981) *Medieval Popular Culture*, English transl., Cambridge, 1987

S. Hall (1981) 'Notes on Deconstructing the Popular', in R. Samuel (ed.) *People's History and Socialist Theory*, London

S. Kaplan (ed., 1984) *Understanding Popular Culture*, Berlin

Jürgen Kuczynski (1980–1) *Geschichte des Alltags des Deutschen Volkes, 1600–1650, 1650–1810,* 2 vols, Berlin

T.J. Jackson Lears (1985) 'The Concept of Cultural Hegemony: Problems and Possibilities', *American Historical Review* 90

J. Lotman (1984) 'The Poetics of Everyday Behaviour in Russian Eighteenth-Century Culture', in J. Lotman and B.A. Uspenskii (eds) *The Semiotics of Russian Culture*, Ann Arbor

L.S. Marcus (1986) *The Politics of Mirth: Jonson, Herrick, Milton, Marvell, and the Defense of Old Holiday Pastimes*, Chicago

H. Medick (1983) 'Plebeian Culture and the Transition to Capitalism', in R. Samuel and G. Stedman Jones (eds) *Culture, Ideology and Politics*, London

R.-E. Mohrmann (1993) 'Everyday Culture in Early Modern Times, *New Literary History* 24

R. Muchembled (1978) *Popular Culture and Elite Culture in France*, Engl. trans., Baton Rouge, 1985

M. Mullett (1987) *Popular Culture and Popular Protest in Late Medieval and Early Modern Europe*, London

C. Phythian-Adams (ed., 1993) *Societies, Cultures and Kinship, 1580–1850: Cultural Provinces and English Local History*, Leicester

B. Reay (ed., 1985) *Popular Culture in Seventeenth-Century England*, London

G. Ruggiero (1993) *Binding Passions: Tales of Magic, Marriage and Power at the End of the Renaissance*, New York

D. Sabean (1984) *Power in the Blood*, Cambridge

R. Sandgruber (1982) *Die Anfänge der Konsumgesellschaft*, Vienna

R.W. Scribner (1990) 'The Impact of the Reformation on Daily Life', in G. Jarisch (ed.) *Mensch und Objekt im Mittelalter*, Krems

E.P. Thompson (1991), *Customs in Common*, London

PART VI

Religion

Introduction

A S THE STUDY OF PEOPLE'S experiences of life's vicissitudes and of their attempts to find meaning in them, cultural history is particularly well suited to an exploration of religious practice in societies. Of course religion also has a cognitive aspect, interwoven with its daily practice – 'the belief in Spiritual Beings' is how Tylor (1871: 383) pithily defined it. But since cultural history is something more than the history of ideas, we here conceive of religion by reference to rituals and morals, rather than giving priority to beliefs and doctrines.

Applying Geertz's principle (1973: 93) that cultures offer 'models for' as well as 'models of', we might define religion as 'customs and moral expectations that relate to a cosmology'. Geertz himself (1973: 90) gave a lengthier definition of religion as (1) a system of symbols (2) which acts to establish powerful, pervasive and long-lasting moods and motivations in men [sic] (3) by formulating conceptions of a general order of existence and (4) clothing these conceptions with such an aura of factuality that (5) the moods and motivations seem uniquely realistic.

An exploration of historical evidence requires caution about that word 'religion', for it is one that, like 'culture', is notoriously difficult to define (Smith 1998). Its complex connotations and changing meanings over time are liable to make it an obstacle rather than a help in the task of recognising the strangeness of the past. As Greer (2003: 178) puts it: 'the heterogeneous assemblage of phenomena implied by the heading "religion"' needs to be examined 'within a specific social context, rather than as manifestations of a free-floating abstraction'. No single type of religion should be regarded as a yardstick by which to measure another, and any assumption that the world's many families of religious traditions share an underlying similarity is best avoided. Similar caveats apply to particular faiths. It may be better to speak of 'Christianities' than to assume there is an essence of Christianity. Jolly (1997) illustrates through primary sources how diverse Christianity has been.

A simple criterion (not a formal definition) for calling a phenomenon an instance of religion might be that it is a set of routines for expressing a sense of continuity across lifetimes, thus enabling individuals to come to terms with the unpredictability of life and death by relating their own personal experiences and actions to a bigger picture. For most people it has been through customary practices rather than elaborated cosmologies or theologies that this sense of continuity has been nurtured. See Chapter 13 in this Reader (Watkins 2004). Thus it is a mistake to equate religion with any particular type of cognitive framework such as belief in a God or in an afterlife. Likewise it does not necessarily presuppose an organised body of ritual specialists. After all, a core concern of cultural history is with how particular practices and perceptions have enabled ordinary people to make sense of their lives.

To maintain this focus single-mindedly is never straightforward, given that day-to-day practices have so often been embedded in a matrix of power-relationships having their own pragmatic logic. Religious rituals and moral precepts may indeed have been experienced as glimpses of eternal realities, but the forms they have taken may well have reflected an ideological advantage accruing to holders of authority. The historian of religious customs in one period thus finds it necessary to go back to an earlier time for insight into the genesis of later practice, even when change is what is to be explained. Medieval asceticism grew out of responses to the conditions of the later Roman Empire (Dunn 2000; Lawrence 2001). The sixteenth-century upheavals referred to as the Reformation only make sense in the light of religious tensions and compromises in the Middle Ages (Lindberg 2009; Pettegree 2005). More than any other branch of history, religious history presupposes a long time-frame.

A key concept, relevant to many periods, is that of conversion. What attracted inhabitants of the Roman Empire to the new faith? What cultural consequences flowed from the growing power enjoyed by the fourth-century church (Brown 2012)? What kinds of compromise did mass conversion bring, then and later, when peoples in Northern Europe who had never lived under Roman rule obeyed their leaders and accepted baptism (Brown 2013)? In what sense did an individual's entry into a monastic community involve what Benedict called 'moral conversion' (Sheldrake 2013)? What effect did the ninth-century effort at deepening the people's faith have on gender relations (Stone 2011)? The Reformers aspired to convert people from conformism to inward faith – how did they set about doing so? What did Christianity mean to Iroquois converts in the seventeenth century (Greer 2003)? What kind of impact on people's emotional lives was made by the demand of preachers in the eighteenth-century evangelical revival for personal conversion (Mack 2008; Gregory 2009)? In different ways, Mack and Gregory show how greatly the turn to the history of the emotions can enrich the study of religion in the Age of Reason, as do Corrigan (2002) and Karant-Nunn (2010) for other periods.

Our section on 'Others' discusses nineteenth-century interactions between Christians, Buddhists and Theosophists (Gombrich 2006). Here, for reasons of space we focus on forms of Christianity. Both readings deal with extended periods. The first, by Bossy, throws light on changes between the thirteenth and sixteenth centuries in what preachers presented to churchgoers as the basis for Christianity's moral demands. Gradually, he says, an earlier Christian morality concerned with flaws of character to be rectified and with virtues to be striven for was replaced by one centred on obedience to the laws of God as found in the Scriptures. This long-term change outlined by Bossy occurred at different times in different regions. A significant aspect is its link to the ambition increasingly held by political rulers of using religious institutions as a means of instilling in their subjects the moral values considered to be politically expedient.

The reading by Brooke asks how well-founded is the currently widespread view that religious beliefs are or have been inherently inimical to science. This issue needs to be examined over an extended time-span, going back to long before the coining of the word 'scientist' in the 1830s, and even to before the natural sciences came to be separated out from philosophy. As Brooke points out, the thesis that religion is incompatible with science presupposes an ahistorical understanding of the terms 'religion' and 'science', as well as a failure to take into account numerous counter-examples from the early centuries of Islam onwards. On this topic, see also Clayton and Simpson (2006), Haq (2009), Hill (1993) and Saliba (2007).

References

Brown, P.R.L. (2012) *Through the Eye of a Needle: wealth, the fall of Rome, and the making of Christianity in the West, 350–550 AD*, Princeton, NJ: Princeton University Press.

Brown, P.R.L. (2013) *The Rise of Western Christendom: triumph and diversity, AD 200–1000*, Hoboken, NJ: Wiley.

Clayton, P. and Simpson, Z. (eds) (2006) *The Oxford Handbook of Religion and Science*, Oxford: Oxford University Press.

Corrigan, J. (2002) *Business of the Heart: religion and emotion in the nineteenth century*, Berkeley, CA: University of California Press.

Dunn, M. (2000) *The Emergence of Monasticism: from the Desert Fathers to the early Middle Ages*, Oxford: Blackwell.

Geertz, C. (1973) 'Religion as a cultural system', in Geertz, *The Interpretation of Cultures*, New York, NY: Basic Books.

Gombrich, R.F. (2006) *Theravada Buddhism: a social history from ancient Benares to modern Colombo*, second edn, London: Routledge. [This is one of the readings in the section on 'Others' in this volume.]

Greer, A. (2003) 'Conversion and identity: Iroquois Christianity in seventeenth-century New France', in K. Mills and A. Grafton (eds) *Conversion: old worlds and new*, Rochester, NY: Rochester University Press.

Gregory, J. (2009) 'Transforming "the Age of Reason" into "an Age of Faiths": or, putting religions and beliefs (back) into the eighteenth century', *Journal for Eighteenth-Century Studies*, 38: 287–305.

Haq, S.N. (2009) 'Myth 4: that medieval Islamic culture was inhospitable to science', in R.L. Numbers (ed.) *Galileo Goes to Jail and Other Myths about Science and Religion*, Cambridge, MA: Harvard University Press.

Hill, D.R. (1993) *Islamic Science and Engineering*, Edinburgh: Edinburgh University Press.

Jolly, K.L. (compiler) (1997) *Tradition and Diversity: Christianity in a world context to 1500*, Armonk, NY: M.E. Sharpe.

Karant-Nunn, S.C. (2010) *The Reformation of Feeling: shaping the religious emotions in early modern Germany*, Oxford: Oxford University Press.

Lawrence, C. (2001) *Medieval Monasticism*, third edn, Harlow: Longman.

Lindberg, C. (2009) *The European Reformations*, second edn, Hoboken, NJ: Wiley-Blackwell.

Mack, P. (2008) *Heart Religion in the British Enlightenment: gender and emotion in early Methodism*, Cambridge: Cambridge University Press.

Pettegree, A. (2005) *Reformation and the Culture of Persuasion*, Cambridge: Cambridge University Press.

Saliba, G. (2007) *Islamic Science and the Making of the European Renaissance*, Cambridge, MA: MIT Press.

Sheldrake, P. (2013) *Spirituality: a brief history*, Hoboken, NJ: Wiley-Blackwell.

Smith, J.Z. (1998) 'Religion, religions, religious', in M.C. Taylor (ed.) *Critical Terms for Religious Studies*, Chicago, IL: Chicago University Press.

Stone, R. (2011) *Morality and Masculinity in the Carolingian Empire*, Cambridge: Cambridge University Press.

Tylor, E. (1871) *Primitive Culture*, London: John Murray.

Watkins, C. (2004) '"Folklore" and "popular religion" in Britain during the middle ages', *Folklore*, 115: 140-50. [This is one of the readings in the section on 'Popular Culture' in this volume.]

Chapter 16

John Bossy

MORAL ARITHMETIC: SEVEN SINS INTO TEN COMMANDMENTS

AND GOD SPAKE all these words, saying,
I am the Lord thy God, which have brought thee out of the land of Egypt, out of the house of bondage.

Thou shalt have no other gods before me.

Thou shalt not make unto thee any graven image, or any likeness of any thing that is in heaven above, or that is in the earth beneath, or that is in the water under the earth:

Thou shalt not bow down thyself to them, nor serve them: for I the Lord thy God am a jealous God, visiting the iniquity of the fathers upon the children unto the third and fourth generation of them that hate me;

And shewing mercy unto thousands of them that love me, and keep my commandments.

Thou shalt not take the name of the Lord thy God in vain: for the Lord will not hold him guiltless that taketh his name in vain.

Remember the sabbath day, to keep it holy.

Six days shalt thou labour, and do all thy work:

But the seventh day is the sabbath of the Lord thy God: in it thou shalt not do any work, thou nor thy son, nor thy daughter, nor thy manservant, nor thy maidservant, nor thy cattle, nor the stranger that is within thy gates . . .

Honour thy father and thy mother: that thy days may be long upon the land which the Lord thy God giveth thee.

Thou shalt not kill.

Thou shalt not commit adultery.

Thou shalt not steal.

Thou shalt not bear false witness against thy neighbour.

Thou shalt not covet thy neighbour's house, thou shalt not covet thy neighbour's wife, nor his manservant, nor his maidservant, nor his ox, nor his ass, nor any thing that is thy neighbour's.

Exodus 20: 1–17 (Authorized Version)

For most people, for most of the Middle Ages, the moral system which was taught in Western Christianity was constituted by the Seven Deadly or Capital Sins: Pride, Envy,

Wrath, Avarice, Gluttony, Sloth, and Lechery, usually in that order. The list was not Christian, but Greek and possibly astrological in origin. In its medieval form it had been given authority by Pope Gregory the Great, and systematized as part of a larger system of septenary forms of instruction during the twelfth century. It was related to the moral teaching of the New Testament by being treated as a negative exposition of the two commandments of the Gospel, the love of God and the love of one's neighbour. . . .[1] The main advantage of this moral system was that, in an age when the passions of hostility were probably the most vigorous of natural sentiments, it provided a useful set of categories under which people could identify these as un-Christian: it taught fairly effectively a social or community ethics. Its main weaknesses were that it made little of obligations to God, as compared with obligations to one's neighbour; and that it had no scriptural authority. It may be that, directed to the average Christian, it implied that holiness was not his business, but the business of special categories of Christians like 'religious' men and women.

After the sixteenth century, a different moral system was universally taught in the West: the scriptural (though not New Testament) catalogue of the Ten Commandments. . . . From the thirteenth century, as we shall see, the Commandments began to make headway, but it was not until the universal diffusion of the Catechism in the sixteenth century and after that their dominance of the moral scene was established.[2]

Thereafter all mainstream denominations taught the Commandments as the Christian moral code, though there were two schools of thought about what they actually were. Catholics and Lutherans accepted the order adopted by St Augustine, who had included the prohibition of graven images under the first commandment and divided, in the last two, the coveting of wives from the coveting of goods. Calvinists and Anglicans had adopted a numbering which had better authority in Greek and Hebrew tradition and separated the prohibition of graven images as a second commandment, while combining the two forms of coveting in the tenth. . . .

The main substantive difference between the two systems was the greater importance given in the Decalogue to offences against God. True, the first table contained only three commandments (or four in the reformed version), as against the seven (or six) of the second, which concerned one's neighbour; but the first commandment, against worshipping strange gods, was fundamental to the whole system in a way that the equivalent deadly sin, pride, could not be. The rationale of the Decalogue was the prohibition of idolatry, it was a ritual as well as a moral code; its purpose was to keep the people of Israel in holiness, and thereby ensure the perpetuity of their alliance with God; its strategy was the fear of the Lord. Its character could be tempered by Christian expositors, but not radically changed.

The main formal difference was that the Commandments were very much more precise: commands or prohibitions of fairly exactly described actions or, in the case of the last two (or one), dispositions. It is true that the Deadly Sins had been construed, mainly, as implications of the command to love one's neighbour as oneself. But a command to love one's neighbour is not quite the same sort of thing as a command to keep the sabbath holy, or to avoid adultery. What is commanded is a feeling of some generality: to translate it into suitable acts requires interpretation and invites some initiative, either on the part of the recipient or on the part of some authorized interpreter like the church. Even with such an interpreter, the Seven Sins were more a system of indicative moral planning than a code. Of course, the Commandments required some interpretation too, even in the most literally minded Christian traditions: the gravamen of the second (or second part of the first: images) was a matter of intense dispute; everybody interpreted the fourth (fifth), in some degree, as requiring obedience to metaphorical as well as to actual parents; I do not think anyone supposed that the commandment against coveting did not also forbid women to covet their neighbours' husbands. Nevertheless it remained true that, in exchanging the Seven Sins for the Ten Commandments, Christians had acquired a moral code which was stronger on obligations to God, somewhat narrower on obligations to the neighbour, and in both directions more precise, more penetrative, and more binding. The Decalogue was truly a law, in a way that the alternative system had not been.

This was an event in the moral history of Europe, not so far as I know discussed by historians, which nevertheless had important consequences in a number of areas which have traditionally been the subject of historical investigation. Why had it happened? . . .

The story seems to begin with the scholastic theologians of the thirteenth century. Though they admitted the traditional authority of the Seven Sins, they had been sufficiently impressed by the scriptural and patristic evidence to build their treatments of Christian ethics around the Decalogue. In this they were followed by a number of contemporary pastoral authorities. The Franciscan Archbishop of Canterbury, John Pecham, in his Council of Lambeth of 1281, required his clergy to know and teach the Decalogue, after the Creed but before the Seven Sins. He also gave them a hand by providing an exposition of it, which was widely diffused. His scheme was imitated by others, and by the numerous manuals which enlarged on the instructions of thirteenth-century bishops for the benefit of fourteenth-century priests; notably by William of Pagula in his classic *Oculus Sacerdotis*, written in the 1320s.[3] If the clergy had followed these instructions, the average Englishman would by the end of the fourteenth century have been well acquainted with the Commandments and, in so far as he sought to lead a Christian life, would have governed his actions in accordance with them.

It seems reasonably clear that he was not, and did not, though this was not entirely the clergy's fault. If England is a good example, the evidence suggests that they had made an effort to do what was required of them but, faced with alternative moral systems, had found the Seven Sins more manageable for themselves and more persuasive to their hearers. . . . This was still more the case in the writings of secular poets who wrote on or used the themes of the manuals: Langland, Chaucer, and Gower had a great deal to say about the Seven Sins (Chaucer, about 1390, concluded the *Canterbury Tales* with a straightforward exposition of them), but seem scarcely to have heard of the Commandments. It was the same story, we are told, in Germany; in France, the (clumsier) equivalent of Pecham's corpus of Christian knowledge, a vernacular work of the late thirteenth century known as the *Somme-le-Roy*, was a compilation of the second type, where the precedence given to the Commandments was largely honorific. Chaucer's parson seems to have summed up the attitude of the fourteenth-century laity and their teachers when, after his painstaking account of the Seven Sins, he declared himself unable to expound the Commandments. 'So heigh a doctrine I lete to divines.'[4] . . .

Until 1400 the general feeling was that, in communications between the clergy and the laity directly related to confession – that is, in discussion or interrogation between the priest and penitent, and in the Lenten preaching which preceded it, not to mention the Carnival proceedings which often preceded that – the Commandments did not offer a very satisfactory alternative to the Sins.[5] Familiar, flexible, covering remedy as well as disease, the Sins were a more serviceable slate on which, guided by the priest, one might perform an annual calculation of the moral account or annual moral check-up; their prominence in the penitential season cast its shadow over the rest of the year.

Strictly in the field of expository teaching, too, there were difficulties about the Commandments, partly practical and partly theoretical. Even if one omits the elaborations, like those concerning the sabbath, the Commandments are rather a mouthful, and not easy to remember. As the sixteenth-century catechist Robert Bellarmine wisely remarked, it is difficult to remember more than seven of anything; it is particularly difficult, perhaps impossible, when the series is being conveyed by word of mouth.[6] Apart from their brevity, the Sins had the advantage of fitting into, the Commandments the disadvantage of disrupting, a whole string of septenary classifications: the seven Sacraments, the seven works of mercy, the seven petitions of the Paternoster, and so on. Teachers with a knowledge of their flocks were sensibly anxious to integrate their moral teaching as tightly as possible with these other *memoranda*, and though they sometimes overdid it, their concern was realistic. Finally, though it is not actually impossible to represent the Commandments visually, they lack the obvious facility with which the Sins could be represented in visual, symbolic, or allegorical form (for example, as animals).[7] This was an important matter when the visual image was a powerful teaching medium.

On the theoretical side the difficulties seem as follows. Since the Commandments were not, as such, binding upon Christians, it had to be explained why they were being taught. The theological explanation was that they were the elaboration, authorized (more or less) by Christ as recorded by St Matthew, of the two commandments of the Gospel.[8] The first table codified the obligations of the love of God, the second, the obligations of the love of your neighbour. This was Aquinas' view. . . . Aquinas had also held that the Commandments were a compendium of natural law having force prior to their enactment or to Christ's confirmation of them. Although this view was to be confirmed by the *Catechism of the Council of Trent*, it seems both theologically awkward and difficult to teach.[9]

Scholastic authorities after Aquinas found his attempted moral synthesis unconvincing, and were particularly offended by its naturalistic aspect. Scotus with caution, and William of Ockham with perfect confidence, concluded that it was an inadmissible interference with God's sovereignty and freedom to bind his decisions within a normative system of good which would need to be envisaged as somehow outside or apart from himself. If something was good, or conducive to human salvation, it was because God had sovereignly willed it so, not vice versa; he might have willed differently from, or the opposite of, what he actually had willed. Hence there was no method by which Christians could determine what was good or bad, except by discovering what God had actually commanded to be done or avoided. Ethics was a matter of faith, not of reason.[10] This pointed to the Decalogue as the only comprehensive moral code available to or authoritative for Christians, and not as a summary of what was naturally so, but as a free, ungrounded, specific expression of God's legislative will.

Ockham was not always the most acceptable of scholastic authorities, but in this case the genuine force of his argument carried the day, at least for the time being. By the end of the fourteenth century he seems to have convinced most theologians who were not constitutionally required to follow Aquinas (and some who were); in particular he had converted the theology faculty of Paris, whose dominant master towards the close of the century, Cardinal Pierre d'Ailly, gave the doctrine the stamp of his authority, and passed it on to his pupil Jean Gerson.[11]

Gerson, who was no friend to scholastic speculation as such, took the doctrine not as a theoretical statement but as a charter for pastoral activity; and since, at least in northern Europe, he was much the most influential doctor of the Christian life during the century before the Reformation, his was a conversion of importance. He was not the first to write an extended commentary on the Commandments, but the general agreement that he launched a new departure in the teaching of Christianity seems well founded. He did this by treating the Commandments as the rock of Christian ethics, by establishing a tradition of effective vernacular exposition, and by integrating this into a larger theological position and into a general scheme of Catholic piety which included the practice of confession. . . .

One region where Gerson's innovation proved decisive was Germany. Here, in the century between Gerson and Luther, there was a visible shift to the exposition of Christian behaviour through the Commandments. This was particularly true of the innumerable guides to confession which were composed, especially for children, during the period. The invention of the printing-press gave them a considerable boost, and they were perhaps one of the main driving-forces behind its diffusion: they were frequently illustrated. . . .

Outside Germany the innovation met with much inertia and some opposition. . . . The great authority in Italy was St Antonino of Florence, a Thomist whose *Confessionale* and *Summa theologica*, where his moral doctrine was expounded, went through innumerable editions. He gave the Commandments and the Sins equal time, but seems on the whole to have preferred the Sins; this was probably because he was much concerned with business morality, and found it simpler to expound this under Avarice, which he placed first.[12] Artists, who rarely found the Commandments much of an inspiration, depicted the Seven Sins with more vigour than ever before: the genre reached a climax in the early and mid sixteenth century in the Netherlands with Hieronymus Bosch, whose tableau of the Sins was used as a standing *memento* by Philip II of Spain, and the elder Bruegel.[13] In two countries with important unorthodox traditions, Bohemia and England, there was actual opposition to the Commandments, though for opposite reasons. The dissident Czech Unity of Brothers rejected the Old Testament as a moral authority altogether, as they rejected the death penalty in secular law, as breathing a spirit of vengeance incompatible with Christian brotherhood.[14] Their example was to be followed among the English sectarians of the seventeenth century, but at the time the ethical scene in England was dominated by the assertions of John Wycliffe and the Lollards. These affirmed the absolute supremacy of a textually complete version of the Commandments, interpreted with particular reference to the prohibition of idolatry, images, and the veneration of saints. The orthodox reaction of the fifteenth century consequently identified the teaching of the Commandments in English with heretical opinions, and it seems to have remained in bad odour almost until the Reformation. . . . On the eve of the Reformation, the moral universe represented by pillars of orthodoxy like Sir Thomas More and the Scottish poet William Dunbar was still the universe of the Seven Sins, which indeed still had some life in them in the Elizabethan age. The Reformer Hugh Latimer was probably right in suggesting that the average unreformed English layman knew no other system.[15]

Hence it is not quite true that the Reformation introduced the Commandments as the effective moral system of Christianity; what is true is that its insistence on a scriptural ethics caused all resistance to collapse. . . .

Faced by this scriptural onslaught, and already half-converted anyway, the Church of Rome finally went over to its own version of the Commandments as the sole vehicle of its moral teaching. In England, in the reign of Queen Mary, Bishop Bonner even adopted the reformed numbering in his attempt to reconvert the English to Catholicism; though I do not think anyone else went as far as that, the *Catechism of the Council of Trent* (1566) endorsed the view that the Decalogue comprehended the entire moral obligation of Christians. This view governed the structure of Catholic catechisms thereafter: earlier attempts, like those of Peter Canisius in Germany, had kept a place for the Seven Sins, but from now on it became a mere vestige. For Catholics as for Protestants, the age of catechism was an age of the Commandments.[16]

In sketching some historical consequences of this event, we can distinguish between the consequences of adopting as a moral system any particular version of the Commandments, and the consequences of adopting the Commandments in general. Under the first heading we can put the effect of the separation of the ban on images as a second commandment in inspiring in Reformed enthusiasts the iconoclastic passion which, so far as it could, destroyed a whole epoch of European visual culture; and also the interpretation of the third/ fourth commandment as a charter for strict Sabbatarianism, which came to characterize the Calvinist tradition from the close of the sixteenth century. I shall take such particular consequences for granted, as I shall the extremely general consequences of the transition from the Seven Sins which have already been mentioned: the supremacy of the first table over the second, the characterization of Christian behaviour as obedience to the commands of the Divine Legislator, and the primacy of explicitly verbalized over other forms of moral awareness. . . .

Among the consequences of the adoption of an ethics founded on worship was a change in the status of the Devil. Under the old moral regime the Devil had been an anti-type of Christ, teaching universal hatred where Christ taught love: he was the Fiend. Under the new regime he became the anti-type of the Father, the source and object of idolatry and false worship. Norman Cohn has remarked that in the course of the fifteenth century the Devil acquired in the popular mind a grandeur and formidable character which he had not hitherto possessed, and I doubt if we need to look much beyond the Gersonian reform of ethics to explain why this enhancement occurred. The most obvious effect of the new dispensation was a change, universally recognized to have occurred during the fifteenth century, in the character attributed to the offence of witchcraft. Under the regime of the Sins, witchcraft had been the offence of causing by occult means malicious harm to the body or goods of one's neighbour or, in the more sensational cases, of procuring the death of political enemies by such means; in Chaucer's exposition it was dealt with, rather loosely, under Wrath. In the new regime it was an offence against the first commandment, that is, an offence of false worship inferior, in Gerson's *Miroir*, only to heresy and idolatry.[17] The developments which inspired the early-modern witch-craze – the attribution of all occult effects, except those produced by the rituals of the church, to a pact between the offender and the Devil, and the erection of a towering superstructure identifying the witch as a practitioner of Devil-worship – were a lurid elaboration of this original step, the more the Commandments became established as the reigning system of Christian ethics, the more persuasive the spell of the witch-syndrome proved. . . .

Gerson, Luther, and the authors of the Roman Catechism may be thought to be professionals of morality, whose thoughts were of little relevance to the rest of mankind. To suggest that this is not so, I conclude with . . . an example: the Friulian miller Domenico Scandella *alias* Menocchio, burned as a relapsed heretic in 1600, the story of whose encounters with the Roman Inquisition has recently been written by Carlo Ginzburg. In the course of his interrogation in 1584, Menocchio had expressed a number of opinions taken by his inquisitor as contrary to Catholic orthodoxy. Among them was the view that blasphemy was not a serious sin. He defended his opinion on the grounds, in effect, that Christian ethics consisted in the avoidance of the Seven Sins, and that the object of this code was the love of one's neighbour; offences against God were a less serious matter than offences against your neighbour, since they could be forgiven by simple contrition, while offences against your neighbour called for a tiresome process of penance, compensation, or restitution. The inquisitor then asked him whether he knew the Commandments; he said he had never heard of them. Since he had been born in the 1530s, at a time when in Italy the tradition of the Seven Sins was still in possession of the moral field and the catechisms of the Counter-Reformation had not yet been composed, this was quite probably true. On the other hand, he knew very well the two commandments of the Gospel, so it may be that he did know the Decalogue but, with good Christian tradition behind him, rejected its authority.[18] In either case he is a witness to a moral transition of considerable historical significance, and (though he had other difficulties with post-Reformation Catholicism) might even be claimed as a martyr to it.

Notes

1   Morton W. Bloomfield, *The Seven Deadly Sins* (Michigan, 1952).

2   *Dictionnaire de théologie catholique*, ed. A. Vacant, E. Mangenot, E. Amann (15 vols., Parie, 1925–50) (hereafter *D.T.C*), *s.v.* Décalogue, Catéchisme. Though I have not pursued the topic in this paper,

I am very greatly indebted to Margaret Aston's work on the theology of images and iconoclasm, and in particular to chapter vii, 'The sin of idolatry: the teaching of the Decalogue', of her forthcoming book, which the has been kind enough to let me read; for recent writing on the Commandments, see her nn. 78ff. For the moment, see 'Lollards and images', in her *Lollards and Reformers: Images and Literacy in Late Mediaeval Religion* (London, 1984), pp. 135–92.

3   *Councils and Synods [of] the English Church*, ii *(1205–1313)*, ed. F. M. Powicke and C. R. Cheney (2 vols, Oxford, 1964), ii. pp. 900ff.; also pp. 1059ff., and index under *Commandments*. D. L. Douie, *Archbishop Pecham* (Oxford, 1952), pp. 134, 138, 140f., 142; W. A. Pantin, *The English Church in the Fourteenth Century* (Cambridge, 1955), chaps, ix and x, and Appendix II. *The Lay Folks' Catechism*, ed. T. F. Simmons and H. E. Nolloth (Early English Text Society, o.s. vol. cxviii, London, 1901), contains the republication and vernacular translation of Pecham's instructions by Archbishop Thoresby of York in 1357.

4   Pantin, pp. 225f.; note his doubt, concerning Henry of Lancaster, the one contributor to his series of vernacular writers who was neither a priest nor a professional author, 'whether he had ever heard of . . . Pecham's constitutions'. L. W. Spitz, 'Further lines of inquiry for the study of "Reformation and pedagogy"', in H. A. Oberman and C. Trinkaus (eds.), *The Pursuit of Holiness in Late Mediaeval and Renaissance Religion* (Leiden, 1974), pp. 295ff.; citing work by 'Professor Oberlin of Strasburg' which I have not seen. For the *Somme-le-Roy*, see *D. T. C.*, *s.v.* Catéchisme, col. 1900; there is an abstract of it in Ch. V. Langlois (ed.), *La Vie en France au moyen âge: iv, La Vie Spirituelle* (Paris, 1928), pp. 142–98. *The Works of Geoffrey Chaucer*, ed. F.N. Robinson (London, 1957), p. 260.

5   This is my deduction from the discussion of confession manuals in P. Michaud-Quantin, *Sommes de casuistique et manuels de confession au moyen âge* (Louvain, etc., 1962), especially pp. 43, 49f. on the much-used *Confessionale* (c. 1295) of the Dominican John of Freiburg; also p. 66 (Italy); cf. Aston, 'The sin of idolatry', n. 9. For some contrary evidence, see Michaud-Quantin, pp. 54–7; *Councils and Synods*, pp. 1062ff. (Bishop Quivel or Quinel of Exeter, c. 1287). I am extremely grateful to my colleague Peter Bitter for help with the subject of this and the previous note; he is not responsible for my conclusions.

6   J.-C. Dhotel, *Les Origines du catéchisme moderne* (Paris, 1967), p. 37. For two examples of this, consider the 'hash' made by the author of the play of Christ and the Doctors in the Chester cycle (A. C. Cawley, 'Middle English versions of the Decalogue, with reference to the English Corpus Christi cycles', Leeds Studies in English, n.s. viii (1979), 140) when trying to cite the Commandments from memory: and Langland's (Latin) citation of the wrong one in *The Vision of Piers Plowman* (B-text, ed. A. V. C. Schmidt (London, 1978), Passus x, l. 364).

7   Bloomfield, *The Seven Deadly Sins*, pp. 245–9; but cf. Cawley, n. 43, for a spirited set of Commandment windows in Ludlow parish church: 'a thief is quietly cutting the purse-strings of a man who gazes devoutly upon the words "Thou shaft not steal"'; other cases below, nn. 17 and 20.

8   Matthew 19. 16–19, where Christ does not actually recommend the first table; 22. 35–40.

9   *Catechism of the Council of Trent*, chap. 28, sections i–ii (I have used the French version of 1925, repr. Paris, 1969).

10   F. C. Copleston, *A History of Philosophy*, ii (London, 1950), pp. 543–50 (Scotus); iii (1953), pp. 103–10 (Ockham).

11   *D.T.C.*, *s.v.* Gerson, cols. 1322–4, quoting D'Ailly: 'Nullum est ex se peccatum sed praecise quia lege prohibitum.' Gerson, *Liber de vita spirituali animae, De consolatione theologiae,* and *Regulae morales* in *Opera omnia*, ed L. Ellies du Pin (5 vols., Amsterdam, *vere* Antwerp, 1706), cols. 13 (where he states the opinion as only 'probable', but draws d'Ailly's conclusion above), 147; col. 78; cf. T. F. Tentler, *Sin and Confession on the Eve of the Reformation* (Princeton, N.J., 1977), p. 146 (Gerson on mortal sins; and see n. 16 below). Gerson did not identify God's commandments with the Decalogue, but he obviously considered it the handiest compendium of them: cf. the citation in H. A. Oberman, *The Harvest of medieval Theology* (Cambridge, Mass., 1963), p. 337, n. 46: 'Lex Christi sufficienter data est in praeceptis decalogi.'

12   Bloomfield, *The Seven Deadly Sins*, p.91; J. Delumeau, *Le péché et la peur* (Paris, 1983), pp. 246, 260; Ozment, *Reformation in the Cities*, p. 24. I have used the edition of the *Confessionale* (Paris: Jean Petit, n.d.) bound with Nider's *De lepra morali* (? Paris, Raulin Gautier, s.d.) and other works in Bodleian Douce C.76.

13   Delumeau, *Le Péché et la peur*, pp. 265ff.; cf. Spitz, in *The Pursuit of Holiness* (n. 4 above), p. 298, for illustrations of the Commandments by Baldung Grien and Cranach.

14   P. Brock, *The Political and Social Doctrines of the Unity of Czech Brethren* (The Hague, 1957), pp. 86, 89.

15   Aston, *Lollards and Reformers*, especially pp. 147–8, 208, 210; J. A. F. Thomson, *The Later Lollards, 1414–1520* (London, 1965), pp. 74f., 116, 126, 162, 245; *Dives and Pauper*, ed. P. H. Barnum (part 1, Early English Text Society, no. 275, London, 1976), especially pp. 54f., 65f.; Bloomfield,

The Seven Deadly Sins, pp. 224–6 (Pecock) and notes (n. 162 for Latimer), 236, 240; William Dunbar, 'The Dance of the Seven Deadly Sins', in *The Poems of William Dunbar*, ed. W. McKay Mackenzie (Edinburgh, 1932), pp. 120–3, and cf. pp. 163–7.

16   Aston, 'The sin of idolatry', citing Edmund Bonner, *A profitable and necessary doctrine* (1554); *Catechism of the Council of Trent*, part iii; Dhotel, *Les Origines du catéchisme moderne*, pp. 70–3, and cf. pp. 18f.

17   N. Cohn, *Europe's Inner Demons* (London, 1975), pp. 232f.; Gerson, *Oeuvres complètes*, vii, pp. 195, 196.

18   C. Ginzburg, *The Cheese and the Worms* (London, 1980), pp. 37–40, 88f.

Chapter 17

John H. Brooke

SCIENCE AND RELIGION

1. Introduction

IN HIS *SCIENCE and the Modern World* (1925), the philosopher A. N. Whitehead deemed it a matter of urgency that the proper relations between science and religion should be clarified. The models through which the natural world had been analysed and manipulated, and the symbols through which humanity had customarily found meaning and purpose in life were both so powerful that it was essential to determine their relationship.

To achieve a consensus on such an issue has proved highly problematic, for the task presupposes the existence of criteria by which the legitimate domain of the sciences may be differentiated from that of religion. Claims to have established such criteria have generally been controversial, the boundaries have shifted with time and as great a diversity of opinion probably exists today as when Whitehead issued his plea. In certain forms of existentialist theology, for example, scientific and religious discourse are completely isolated, the former referring to I – it relations, the latter to I – thou situations. For as influential a Protestant theologian as Rudolph Bultmann, the Christian doctrine of Creation did not refer to the origins of the physical world, but rather to the creation within the believer of an authentic stance towards his earthly predicament.

By contrast, twentieth-century process theologians such as Charles Hartshorne, taking their inspiration from Whitehead himself, have made scientific knowledge, notably concepts of organic evolution, germane to a religious vision in which God both participates in, and is affected by, events in the material world. By contrast again, there are vociferous minorities who affirm that creationism can be 'scientific' and that neo-Darwinian hypotheses fail to conform to some preconceived standards of verifiable (or falsifiable) science. In contemporary quarrels between creationists and evolutionists, competing concepts both of legitimate science and legitimate religion are brandished in the context of a conflict having educational and political dimensions.

2. The complexity of the relations between science and religion

Since these three broad patterns – of isolation, integration and conflict – have repeatedly occurred in the past, any history of the relations between scientific and religious movements is bound to be complex. Indeed, different models of their 'proper' relationship have served different social, political and religious ends according to time and circumstance. Thus an emphasis on the integration of scientific and religious beliefs often appears in those societies where an emerging scientific community has to make conciliatory gestures towards powerful religious authorities. This may also happen when religious apologists themselves seize a particular scientific innovation as a resource for defending the rationality of their faith, or for legitimating their own religious tradition against others.

An emphasis on the isolation of science and religion has often occurred as a reaction against facile syntheses which have disintegrated as science, or religious sensibilities, have changed. A complete separation has also been attractive as a protective strategy and one which, during the nineteenth century, also reflected the diverging demands of a professional career in both science and academic theology. An emphasis on conflict has appeared either when religious authorities have sensed a challenge to their spiritual values and worldview, or when the scientific community, as in late nineteenth-century Britain, sought to consolidate what it saw as a new set of professional standards and prerogatives which deliberately excluded the clerical amateur. As F. M. Turner has argued, the Victorian conflict between science and religion was, in one sense, a by-product of a profound social shift in which power, authority and prestige were passing from one part of the intellectual nation to another. At the same time, the disintegration of a long tradition of relative harmony was reflecting the growth of scientific specialisms in which a clerical presence all but disappeared. The number of Anglican clergymen presiding over sections of the British Association for the Advancement of Science fell from 41, for the period 1831 to 1865, to three for the period 1866 to 1900.

The rhetoric of T. H. Huxley, to the effect that extinguished theologians lay around the cradle of every new science like snakes around the body of Hercules, was the aggressive manifestation of that shift in the social context and ideology of science. Amid the controversies surrounding Darwin's *Origin of Species* (1859), such rhetoric could appear amply justified. It resulted, however, in historical analyses which reified both science and religion, projected the conflict backwards and even located it in pre-Christian societies. In his *History of the Warfare of Science with Theology* (1896), A. D. White made much of the fact that the Stoic, Cleanthes, had denounced the heliostatic astronomy of Aristarchus as impious, without pausing to consider whether such an occurrence might not have been recorded precisely *because* of its exceptional character. In popular literature on the history of science, the 'conflict' thesis, as enunciated by J. W. Draper, has often been taken as axiomatic: the history of science is 'a narrative of the conflict of two contending powers, the expansive force of the human intellect on one side, and the compression arising from [traditional] faith and human interests on the other'.[1]

This view has been seductive because it chimes with common knowledge about the fate of such innovators as Bruno and Galileo, and with what is known of the religious fury which greeted eighteenth- and nineteenth-century texts in which man was made a product of nature, and in some cases an accidental one. It also chimes with historical models of secularisation which give a prominent place to the manner in which the sciences have transformed our understanding of the natural world, whether by shrinking the domain of the miraculous, or by shrinking the significance of man himself in a universe shown to be overwhelmingly vaster and older than was formerly imagined. It ties in, too, with models of secularisation which stress the role of applied science and technology in transforming societies from a condition in which there is a perceived dependence on Providence to one in which there is greater dependence on the works of man.

Without disputing that scientific and religious interests have not infrequently been locked in confrontation, particularly in the context of educational priorities, scholars have increasingly found the 'warfare' axiom inadequate to cope with the rich tapestry of interaction that has occurred in the past. In the long process of disaggregation, whereby newly-emerging sciences differentiated themselves from what had once been the queen of the sciences, complex patterns of subordination and insubordination arose. In fourteenth-century Paris, for example, Nicole Oresme developed a powerful critique of physical arguments habitually used against the Earth's axial rotation, but his enterprise was subordinate to the theological goal of showing that human reason was impotent to settle the issue. Even at the end of the seventeenth century, it was still possible for Newton to say that part of the business of natural philosophy was to consider the question of God's relation to the physical world. Indeed, one of the defects of the conflict model is that it posits two competing mentalities, disregarding eminent scientific figures who were either clerics or who had a strong religious commitment. Newton himself provides one of the most spectacular examples of the integration of scientific and religious interests in one and the same mind. Not only was he attracted to alchemical texts, with their rich religious symbolism, but he was as much concerned to find the correct rules for interpreting biblical prophecy as for interpreting the planetary orbits.[2]

This is not to imply any correlation between religious orthodoxies and science. With his anti-Trinitarian theology, Newton would be a representative of the many men of science who have deviated from the religious norms of their culture. However, it does acknowledge that scientific and religious interpretations of the natural world have frequently been seen as complementary rather than as mutually exclusive. The many schemes of theistic evolution which flourished in the late nineteenth century would illustrate one form of complementarity. Even Darwin's bulldog, T. H. Huxley, conceded that Darwinism had no more damaged theism (however grave its implications for Christianity) than had the first book of Euclid. The rigid categories of 'science versus religion' have proved inadequate even in those contexts in which they seem most applicable. Immediate responses to Darwin's theory of natural selection included scepticism from notable physicists, but a guarded welcome from certain clergy who, like the Anglicans Frederick Temple and Charles Kingsley, valued the opportunity to divest their Christianity of the demeaning image of God as conjuror.

3. Revisionist historiography

Reacting against the insensitivity of rationalist polemics, historians of science are now more likely to stress that what may look like conflicts between science and religion often turn out to be instances of internecine scientific controversy (in which religious interests may have intruded on either side), or internecine religious controversy (into which concepts of scientific authority are imported). One of the more engaging theses to emerge from such revision states that certain traditions within Christian theology were conclusive to, rather than obstructive of, intellectual changes and the re-evaluation of practice, which allowed a critical, empirical science to displace the natural philosophy of Aristotle.[3]

Rolf Gruner has pointed out that the case has undoubtedly been overstated by religious apologists, tempted to tie the rationality of modern science to a unique metaphysical system, but Marxists and other secular historians have come to recognise that religious beliefs could provide presuppositions, sanctions and even motives for new styles of scientific enquiry.[4] As crucial a conception as that of physical *laws* was regarded by the Marxist, E. Zilsel, as having its origins in the theological conception of a divine legislator who had imposed his will, like an absolute monarch, on the physical world.[5] This interpretation is at least consistent with the pronouncements of such seventeenth-century celebrities as Kepler, Descartes, Boyle and Newton, who variously claimed to be searching out the laws which God had impressed upon His creation.

In the works of Francis Bacon one can perhaps see most clearly how religious beliefs could function as a sanction for science. It was Bacon's contention that scientific activity which promised practical benefits was to be valued because it would help to restore man's dominion over nature, sacrificed when Adam fell from grace. Bacon's advocacy of experimental methods was also justified in theological terms in that a spirit of humility was presented as a prerequisite both of a Christian piety and of a submissive posture before the facts of nature, which only human arrogance would try to determine from *a priori* considerations. Since God had been free to make any world He chose, which world He *had* made could only be discovered by reading the book of His works for one-self, without deference to the pretended authority of earlier commentators. Such a correlation between a voluntarist theology and the justification of empiricism was not uncommon during the seventeenth century and it was not confined to Protestant thinkers. In France, the Minim friar Marin Mersenne (1588–1648) attacked the Aristotelian conception of a central, *natural* place for the Earth by suggesting that there were no natural places in the universe: created objects were where God had freely chosen to put them. Mersenne even attacked Kepler, on similar grounds, for having presumed to space the planetary orbits according to preconceived geometrical criteria.

That religious commitment could provide motivation for scientific activity has been a more controversial claim – not least because motives are notoriously elusive. Where scientific conclusions have assisted the differentiation of one religious position from another, they have, however, often been valued for that reason. According to the controversial thesis of R. K. Merton, the rapid expansion of scientific activity in seventeenth-century England had much to do with the dissemination of Puritan values.[6] Puritan reformers allegedly saw scientific study as an acceptable calling because the injunction to glorify God could be met in at least two ways: by producing knowledge that would alleviate suffering and knowledge which revealed God's power and wisdom. Inquiry into the secondary causes by which natural phenomena were produced was a permissible use of that gift of reason which distinguished man from beast and which, when properly exercised, diverted him from sensuality. Whilst Merton has been justly criticised for an indiscriminate application of the term 'puritan', and for failing to appreciate that the soteriological concerns of puritan divines could result in a low priority being accorded to scientific endeavour, other scholars, notably Charles Webster in *The Great Instauration* (1975) have located a religious motivation for science. This is in the millenarian ideals of those puritan reformers who saw in the restoration of man's dominion over nature a necessary precondition of Christ's earthly rule.

Opinions remain divided, however, as to whether radical puritanism or moderate Anglicanism provided the more auspicious milieu for the advance of scientific understanding (C. Webster (ed.), *The Intellectual Revolution of the Seventeenth Century* (1974).) The question arises because the kind of science advocated by puritan radicals, such as Oliver Cromwell's army chaplain, John Webster, often bore a closer resemblance to the magical philosophies of the Renaissance, with their emphasis on spiritual illumination, than to an emerging mechanical philosophy. The latter, in England, gained ground among those, like Robert Boyle, who had clearly reacted against the extremism of puritan sects, complaining that Christianity was being jeopardised by their proliferation. Presenting himself as a priest in the temple of nature, Boyle, among others, developed a natural theology which capitalised on mechanical images of nature, providing a Christian theism with a rational foundation via the argument from design.

Theses affirming congruence between puritanism and applied science, or between moderate Anglicanism and a more cerebral science, are extremely difficult to test; there is the ulterior problem that even if the correlations were established, they need not imply a direct input from the religion to the science. It is always possible that religious and scientific predilections could independently reflect an underlying social and economic change. Tendentious references to the Anglican *origins* of modern science must also appear parochial when the emerging scientific movement is brought within a wider European focus, and appear positively chauvinistic towards non-Christian civilisations in which, as with Islam in the eleventh and twelfth centuries, analytical tools were forged and significant strides made in such areas as algebraic geometry and physical optics.[7]

Merton's thesis, and the many variants of it, nevertheless continue to attract attention because they constitute a special case for a broader generalization – that, in the Christian West, Protestantism was more conducive to scientific growth than Roman Catholicism. The grounds for such an assertion usually include the absence among the Protestant churches of a strong and centralised system of censorship, the likelihood that a reforming mentality in the religious sphere would create a predisposition towards the reform of natural philosophy (or vice-versa), and that the Roman Church had more vested interests in the philosophy of Aristotle. The trial of Galileo before the Holy Office in 1633 continues to symbolise the contrasts.[8] A generation later, England's foremost Copernican populariser, John Wilkins, ended his days not under house-arrest but as a bishop in the Anglican church and Lent Preacher to the King. Catholic critics of the new cosmology, with one eye on the Netherlands, would even refer to the Calvinist-Copernican theory, suggesting a degree of convergence between the two spheres of reform.

4. The challenge of Copernicanism

The diffusion of Copernican astronomy does indeed throw some light on religious attitudes towards scientific innovation during the first half of the seventeenth century, but closer examination shows the issues to have been extremely complex. First there was the philosophical question of whether a mathematical hypothesis, designed principally to predict the angular position of the planets, need be admitted as a representation of physical reality. Initially, only those scholars such as Rheticus, Kepler, Galileo and Copernicus himself, who took mathematical elegance to be a touchstone of truth, were inclined to give a realist interpretation to the heliostatic model. Second, the theological implications of shifting humanity from the centre of the cosmos were not as clear-cut as is often supposed. There was a profound disorientation, to be sure, but it was still possible for Kepler to argue that mankind retained a privileged position, since the Earth occupied the central orbit around what Kepler believed, in defiance of Bruno, to be the most resplendent sun in the universe. Even within the rubric of Aristotelian cosmology, there was a sense in which man was promoted rather than degraded: he had the exhilaration of whirling in the superlunary region of perfection, transported from that central pit which Galileo dubbed the sink of all refuse in the universe. Indeed, Wilkins reported that a common objection against the Copernican system was that it elevated man above his true station.

A third complication concerns the challenge of Copernicanism to biblical authority. Such difficulties as were posed by Joshua 10 v. 12 and Psalm 93 v. 1 were in principle removable by adopting a principle of biblical accommodation. As formulated by Calvin, the argument was that the Holy Spirit had made due allowance for the frailty of the human intellect when guiding the authors of Scripture, thereby ensuring that spiritual meanings would be clear to all. Accordingly, it was suggested that they had utilised the language of commonsense observation rather than technical astronomy, since the latter would baffle the uninitiated and give them an excuse for disregarding the more urgent matter of their salvation. It was a line of argument which a friendly cardinal, Carlo Conti, mooted to Galileo.

A fourth complication is that Galileo's fate may not be an accurate symbol of the attitude of Roman Catholic authorities towards new learning in general because there were peculiar political dimensions to the case. Not only had Galileo alienated Jesuit philosophers, notably Christopher Scheiner, with whom he had a priority dispute concerning the discovery of sunspots, and Horatio Grassi, with whom he differed on the nature of comets; but he also managed to offend his former ally, now Pope Urban VIII. This he did by including in his *Dialogue Concerning the Two Chief World Systems* (1632) an argument for the Earth's diurnal and orbital motions based on the tides, which violated Urban's injunction to avoid such physical considerations.

Galileo's case was not helped by the fact that most of the evidence he adduced in support of a moving Earth was equally compatible with the alternative cosmology of Tycho Brahe which allowed all the planets, with the exception of the Earth, to revolve around the sun, the latter orbiting the Earth and carrying the planets with it. Furthermore, Galileo's tragedy was not so much the result of inherent animosity between the Catholic Church and scientific enquiry, as a reflection of the political and doctrinal consequences of the ongoing battle *between* Catholicism and Protestantism. Galileo did adopt the principle of biblical accommodation but, by suggesting that the miracle of the long day of Joshua was actually more comprehensible in a Copernican universe, he heightened the suspicion that, like his friend Paolo Sarpi who had led a Venetian revolt against the papacy, he was a crypto-Protestant.

In response to the threat of Protestant expansion, the Council of Trent had earlier decreed that where the Church Fathers had achieved a consensus on the interpretation of a particular biblical text, that consensus was to be respected. As Galileo himself pointed out, this placed him in a bind because the Church Fathers could not be expected to have interpreted Scripture *his* way, given that Copernican astronomy could not have been known to them. Undoubtedly there are layers of political intrigue still to be uncovered. One suggestion is that the real issue behind Galileo's trial was not so much the Copernican system as an atomic theory of matter Galileo had developed which, through its break with Aristotelian conceptions of primary and secondary qualities, posed a direct challenge to the Catholic interpretation of the Eucharist.[9] With Galileo's view of the relationship between matter and form, as with that of Descartes later, it was difficult to see how the bread and wine could change into the body and blood of Christ without visible changes.

5. The mechanical philosophy and Christian theology

The revival of interest in atomic and particulate theories of matter during the early seventeenth century certainly did create difficulties for Christian apologists – and not merely in the context of the Eucharist. As presented in Lucretius's *De Rerum Natura,* the atomic philosophy of antiquity made the world a chance product of atomic collisions, the processes occurring within it needing no deity for their explanation. It was, however, possible to harmonise atomism with a doctrine of Providence by arguing that God was not only responsible for the original organisation and motion of the atoms, but also for sustaining their motion.

By stressing the passivity of the ultimate particles of matter (I know of no man, Boyle was later to say, who has satisfactorily made out how matter can move itself), it was possible to construct a mechanical philosophy of nature which actually had theological advantages. In France, for example, Mersenne was attracted to the mechanical science of

Galileo, in part because a mechanical philosophy could be useful in rebutting the allegation of Protestants that the Catholic Church constantly turned marvels into miracles in order to impress the laity. Wounded by such allegations, Mersenne looked for criteria that would help his Church to discriminate between natural marvels and genuine miracles. A mechanical philosophy could then become attractive because it helped to define the boundaries of a natural order. Another advantage of a mechanical philosophy appealed to Protestants perhaps more than to Catholics: in so far as God was made directly responsible for moving matter, one had the means of emphasising His sovereignty over His creation, whilst at the same time performing the service for the physical sciences of ridding the universe of angels, spirits and demons. These were all intermediate spiritual agencies which, however much they might appeal to platonists, could be seen to detract from God's absolute transcendence and absolute control.

For both Boyle and Newton, there was a fundamental analogy between our ability to move our limbs (showing the power of mind to move matter) and God's activity in the world. Though the mechanical philosophy, as developed by Descartes and Hobbes, was often seen as a danger to Christian belief, it was always possible to argue that, properly understood, it reinforced the rational grounds of belief. A universe that resembled the great clock of Strasbourg rather than a living organism, simply had to have an intelligent Designer.

That there were theological gains as well as losses in a mechanised universe draws attention to one of many ironies in the history of the relations between science and religion in the West. A philosophy of nature which, in the seventeenth century, was often justified in terms of a voluntarist theology, later became the very resource which deists and free-thinkers would use in their attacks on the Christian religion. If there is a sense in which a mechanistic science, grounded in the concept of physical law, was the offspring of a Christian culture, it was an offspring which could easily turn rebellious. The clock-work universe, which for Robert Boyle, pointed to God's continual involvement in the world, was soon to be exploited by the deists of the Enlightenment to transform Him into a benevolent, but absentee, clockmaker.

6. Newton's science

In that historical process, the science of Newton occupied a pivotal place. On the one hand, his laws of motion and gravitation were a gift to deists such as Voltaire who could exploit a mathematically-defined natural order against what they saw as the superstition of Catholic theology and the political repression with which it was allied. On the other hand, there were aspects of Newton's philosophy of nature, formulated in reaction against the mechanical philosophy of Descartes, which enriched rather than depleted the evidence for an active Providence. The gravitational force was invisible, its action inexplicable in mechanistic terms. Leibniz denounced it as unintelligible for that very reason. Moreover, Newton grounded the universality of his law of gravitation in the doctrine that God not only consti-tuted space, but was omnipresent in a universe, the laws of which He had freely chosen. Newton's science also gave fresh impetus to the argument from design in that the planets would not have gone into closed orbits in the first place, had not the deity calculated the correct transverse component of their velocity with which to impel them. Newton's God was a mathematician no less brilliant than Newton himself. But He was also the God of the Bible who had been active in human history. As if to underwrite the doctrine of an active Providence, Newton insisted that the solar system would run down if it were not for the occasional reformation in which God had a hand. The ambivalence in Newton's position is revealed, however, by an ambiguity concerning whether God intervened directly to ensure the stability of the system, or whether He used secondary causes, vested in comets, to achieve the required effect.[10]

Consequently, how Newton's science was interpreted depended on the presuppositions of its interpreters. There were Anglican divines such as Richard Bentley, Samuel Clarke and William Derham who, as popularisers, made the most of its theistic possibilities. By contrast, the free-thinker and political radical, John Toland, found himself obliged to reinterpret Newton's philosophy of matter, insisting that forces which Newton had deemed not to be inherent in matter were precisely that.[11] From William Whiston, in England, who believed Newton's science would reinforce a literal reading of Scripture, to free-thinkers in France, for whom Newton's science was a paradigm of what human reason could achieve, there were almost as many interpretations of the theological significance of Newton's work as there were theological commentators. Opposition to Newton's natural philosophy could also be justified on theological grounds. Thus Leibniz, who may have associated a voluntarist theology with the menace of an absolutist monarchy, resisted Newton's scheme on the grounds, among others, that only a second-rate clockmaker would need to repair His creation.[12]

7. Science and religion in the Enlightenment

Other aspects of the relation between science and religion in the Enlightenment conform to this general point. It was not that a sequence of incontrovertible scientific discoveries drove God out of His world, or even that a unique scientific method had come into being, by the standards of which the claims of established religion could be judged defective. It was rather that the disclosures of the sciences were adopted both by religious protagonists and antagonists according to the exigencies of the moment. More often than not, attacks on the authority of Scripture were based on arguments which emphasised cultural relativism (every religion seemed to have its miracles) or which impugned the rationality and even the morality of traditional Christian doctrines. It is true, however, that powerful images of scientific and technical progress were often invoked, as in the *Encyclopédie* of Diderot and D'Alembert, to enrich an ideology of social reform. And there is no doubt that scientific enquiry, and pre-eminently a science of man, was encouraged by the philosophes, as by Joseph Priestley in England, because it was thought to inculcate modes of thinking which would be destructive of popular superstition and, eventually, of arbitrary political power. Detailed studies nevertheless suggest that even within otherwise coherent groups seeking intellectual liberation and greater religious tolerance, there were often fundamental disagreements, as there were between Diderot and D'Alembert, over what constituted archetypal and authoritative forms of scientific reasoning: the immediate authority of an empirical fact, as in an observational science such as experimental physiology, or the highly formalised deductive authority of a geometrised mechanics.

The ambivalence of 'factual' discoveries, with respect to the significance which could be attached to them, can perhaps best be illustrated by three innovations in the life-sciences which were seized by mid-18th-century French materialists to bolster their position. Reports of the spontaneous generation of micro-organisms, ostensibly achieved by John Needham, were invoked to support the idea that life could emerge from non-life without the aid of gods. The discovery of the property of 'irritability' by Albrecht von Haller, (whereby a muscle fibre would automatically contract when stimulated) could be construed as evidence that matter had the intrinsic power to move itself. And the astonishing discovery of Abraham Trembley that, when a hydra was chopped to pieces, each piece would regenerate into a complete organism, could easily be exploited by those who, in a literally soul-destroying exercise, argued that matter had inherent powers of self-organisation. And yet each of these discoveries could be interpreted quite differently by the non-materialist. Needham himself was a Catholic priest who was accused by Voltaire of having faked a miracle. Haller interpreted his force of irritability as analogous to Newton's force of gravitation, ultimately a manifestation of God's causal agency in the world. And whether the hydra had a soul or not actually had very little bearing on the status of the human soul.

A similarly equivocal pattern obtained in the physical sciences late in the eighteenth century, when Laplace and Lagrange showed that Newton's solar system was self-stabilising and did not require the reformations that Newton had proposed. On one interpretation, God had been further edged out of His world. That may have been the interpretation which Laplace aspired to, for in the 'nebular hypothesis' by which he accounted for the origin of the solar system, teleological considerations were rigorously excluded. However, for natural theologians in Britain and America, a self-stabilising system was evidence of even greater ingenuity on the part of the Creator than one which required a service contract.[13] As the Cambridge mathematician and philosopher William Whewell observed in the 1830s, a savage inspecting a steam-engine would be no less likely to attribute the machinery to intelligence on being shown the self-regulatory part of the mechanism.

8. The place of natural theology

If materialist philosophies were more common in France than in England during the eighteenth century, and if natural theology, with its celebration of the design argument, was more prominent in England, this undoubtedly had much to do with the fact that there were fewer political incentives in England, where a degree of religious toleration had already been achieved, to pit science against religion. In France, and other Roman Catholic countries, there was generally a sharper divide between religious orthodoxy and heterodoxy than in England, where the existence of a spectrum of tolerated opinions had the effect of pointing up the importance of a natural theology which, for the most part, they had in common. As Roy Porter has observed in *The Enlightenment in National Context* (Cambridge, 1981), since there was no Pope, no Jesuits, no comparable grip of the clergy on the family through confession, an integration of science and religion could be sustained in England as part of a wider cultural phenomenon of comprehensiveness which historians have contrasted with the polarities of Enlightenment rhetoric in France.

Despite the well-known critiques of physico-theology advanced by David Hume in Scotland and Immanuel Kant in Germany, the argument from design continued to flourish as part of popular scientific culture in the English-speaking world until well into the nineteenth century. Since references to design in nature were useful in disarming clerical opposition to scientific innovations, they actually fulfilled a more urgent need in Britain in the decades following the French Revolution than before. The conservative backlash, from which Priestley suffered, coupled with a burgeoning evangelical revival, focused attention on scientific concepts which might prove dangerous in the hands of political radicals. The evolutionary speculations of Erasmus Darwin, for example, had been tolerated until the 1790s but, by the first decade of the nineteenth century, they were being treated with abuse. The durability of natural theology in Britain also owed something to the fact that proponents of the design argument were not always so unsophisticated as to expose themselves to the force of Hume's critique. It was sometimes acknowledged, as by Whewell, that claims for design were more a means of corroborating an already existing faith than a pretended *proof* of God's existence or attributes.[14]

Since the literature of natural theology marks the most sustained tradition in which science and religious belief were integrated, it is important to consider what relevance the theologising might have had to scientific practice, and vice versa. Even among those historians who have kept the relevance of the theology to a minimum, there has been an acknowledgement that commitment to a conventional natural theology tended to dispose naturalists towards creationist rather than evolutionary interpretations of the history of living systems (N. C. Gillespie, *Charles Darwin and the Problem of Creation* (1979)). This should not be surprising given that both Hume and Kant showed how the design argument logically presupposed a Creator. From a post-Darwinian perspective, it is therefore easy to regard the preoccupation with design as an obstruction to liberal scientific thinking. The role of teleological considerations in the life-sciences was not, however, a purely negative one. Not only did the study of biological adaptation prosper as evidence was sought for divine contrivance, but in reconstructing past creatures from fossil fragments, the exercise was often regulated by the belief that the organism had been an integrated whole in which each part was functionally correlated with others. It is another of the ironies that, whilst Darwin's theory of natural selection displaced the teleological argument of William Paley, it nevertheless drew on an extensive range of data which had been accumulated under a natural theology paradigm.

On the relevance of science to natural theology, the key question is whether the design argument could survive a series of difficulties which arose in the wake of the historical sciences. That the appearance of design in the organic world was an illusion had been argued from antiquity by sceptics who had observed that living things would never have survived at all had they not been well adapted. The implication was that many non-viable creatures might have come into existence, only to perish as victims of an uncoordinated combination of limbs and organs. During the late eighteenth century evidence for extinct species came to light. Buffon, for example, was deeply impressed by the remains of mammoths in the colder parts of the globe. Since large mammals tended to be found in equatorial regions, Buffon could support his contention that the Earth had cooled from an incandescent state, having had its origins in material ejected when a comet collided with the sun. During the long process of cooling, conditions had so changed on the Earth's surface that many species could well have become extinct. It was Georges Cuvier, however, who did most to establish the fact of extinction by reconstructing fossil species from fragmentary remains in the Paris basin. Whereas his contemporary, Lamarck, by-passed the uncomfortable fact of extinction by suggesting that one form had gradually changed into another, Cuvier insisted that there were fossil forms which had no living analogues. They had been extinguished by local catastrophes, when the inundation of land, for example, might destroy many species simultaneously.

The fact of extinction was a blow to the kind of natural theology that had been erected on a principle of plenitude: that God had created, and cared for, every creature it was possible to create. For many observers, such as the poet Tennyson, the indifference of nature as revealed by the geologists could be emotionally disturbing. Nevertheless, in seeking to quell such disturbance, the defenders of natural theology had little difficulty in making the fossil record an ally rather than a foe. If each species, during the span of its existence, had been well adapted to its environment, one could still argue for design from the manner in which the history of organic forms and the Earth's physical history had been synchronised. Indeed, the Cambridge geologist, Adam Sedgwick, used the fossil record in the 1830s to attack both atheists and deists. Since there was a time when every species in the fossil record had not existed, the atheist was denied the comfort of eternal living forms. The deist, too, had his comeuppance because the progressive creation revealed by the fossil record indicated a Creator involved in, rather than absent from, His Creation.

Under pressure from the historical sciences, natural theology was forced to diversify but it was not immediately destroyed. In the scientific literature of the 1830s, 1840s and 1850s, it is possible to discern at least three quite different versions of the design argument. Some naturalists still stuck to variants of the teleological argument as personified by Paley: each part of an organism had a function for which it was perfectly adapted, or at least as perfectly adapted as correlation with other parts would allow. A more sophisticated argument had, however, taken shape in response to the concept of a unity of structure among vertebrates which Geoffroy Saint-Hilaire had developed in opposition to teleological reasoning. The comparative anatomist, Richard Owen, suggested that all vertebrates were indeed modelled on a skeletal archetype which should, however, be construed as an idea in the mind of the Creator. It was the adaptation of the archetype to the specific needs of each species which, according to Owen, constituted the best argument for design – one which could accommodate features of an organism which did not have an immediate purpose – male nipples for example. But a third version was also taking shape, in the mind of Charles Darwin among others.[15] This was the view, expounded most forcibly by the Oxford mathematician and philosopher, Baden Powell (1796–1860), that the most cogent evidence of design was to be found in the laws of nature, not in the domain of the inexplicable. That so many diverse laws conspired together to produce a viable world had also impressed Whewell, whose statement to the effect that divine wisdom was as discernible in the laws of nature as in presumed instances of intervention was conveniently borrowed by Darwin to legitimate his naturalistic account of speciation.

9. Darwinian evolution

In early drafts of his theory, Darwin had construed the evolutionary process as nature's way of ensuring that species remained in perfect adaptation to their environment. He was also prepared to embrace a broader teleology in that the evolutionary process could be presented as the means to another, foreseeable, end: the production of organisms of increasing complexity. In mature versions of Darwin's theory, however, the concept of perfect adaptation was replaced with concepts of relative and differential adaptation, allowing natural selection to be in constant operation and thereby attenuating the force of references to design. The fact that the process of natural selection could counterfeit design meant that his theory constituted the single most powerful objection that could be levelled at the design argument in its traditional guise. Nevertheless, several Christian commentators, notably Asa Gray in the United States, positively welcomed Darwin's theory for the light it might throw on the classic paradox: why should a beneficent and omnipotent God permit so much suffering in the world? That problem was one of the many sources of Darwin's own agnosticism, but Gray's point was that one could now go some way towards rationalising it if pain and suffering were inevitable concomitants of a struggle for existence which was itself a *sine qua non* of the process of creation. Gray, who did so much to popularise Darwin's theory in the United States, suggested that the problem of suffering was far greater for Paley's creationist theology than for a Darwinian theist who could see its purpose in the creative economy of nature. Darwin's own tentative formula, that the laws of the evolutionary process might have been designed with the details left to chance, also had attractions for rationalist theologians who could exonerate the deity for the more devilish by-products.

The volatility of the public reaction to Darwin's *Origin of Species* was not unrelated to the larger crisis in Christendom provoked by historical criticism of the Bible. In his *Life of Jesus,* made available to the English-speaking world through George Eliot's translation of 1846, D. F. Strauss had insisted that a truly historical approach to the gospels required the recognition that the evangelists had interpreted Christ's life and death through a series of beliefs and expectations peculiar to their own generation and no longer admissible in the modern world. The miracles they ascribed to Christ, in portraying him as the Messiah, had been naturally but retrospectively transferred to him in line with expectations drawn from earlier Messianic prophecy. Scientific and historical criticism were now converging, since both geology and evolutionary biology underlined the mythological elements in the Genesis creation narrative, and since Darwin had effectively removed one of the last great miracles: the origin of species.

Not surprisingly, Darwin's theory continues to be seen as a watershed in the historical relations between science and religion. Recent scholarship, however, has favoured the view that in the ensuing debates concerning human evolution, many issues were brought to the fore which had already been discussed in earlier contexts. These issues were whether mankind was a product of nature or a late addition; whether the process of evolution was, in any sense, goal-directed; whether the workings of the human mind could be construed in exclusively naturalistic terms; whether a naturalistic account could be offered for the emergence of the human conscience and finally, whether religious beliefs were themselves by-products of evolution, socially inculcated and culture-specific. In his *Descent of Man* (1871), Darwin gives a brief sketch of the emergence of religious beliefs, stressing the ease with which belief in one or more gods could arise from a primitive animism. Religious beliefs had even played a role in human evolution by reinforcing particular ethical codes which, in turn, might have been of survival value to the communities which espoused them. Darwin did not intend to undermine the foundations of morals. Quite the reverse: he argued that the golden rule ('as ye would that men should do to you, do ye to them likewise') was the highest but *natural* outcome of the development of social instincts. For many of his contemporaries, however, who were clinging to moral absolutes as the lifeline of a faith that had already been badly shaken, the effect of Darwin's analysis could be desolating. His own wife could not stomach the proposition that all morality had grown up by evolution and excised from his *Autobiography* a passage which compared a child's belief in God with a monkey's fear of a snake.

Both before Darwin and after, the dialogue between transformist and anti-transformist positions was charged with political meanings. In second-Empire France, the transformist Geoffroy Saint-Hilaire perceived himself to be fighting a scientific establishment, dominated by the presuppositions of Cuvier. In Britain, as Adrian Desmond has emphasised, the transformism of Lamarck proved attractive to a counter-culture of materialists and radicals but was generally suppressed by such dignitaries as Charles Lyell and Richard Owen, the latter trampling on the Lamarckian Robert Grant at a critical juncture in his career.[16] The social and political connotations of transformism were such that Darwin was troubled by the thought that to admit the mutability of species was like confessing to a murder. His own theory, however, stood in a somewhat paradoxical relation to the political climate of his time. By adding scientific authority to Herbert Spencer's concept of the survival of the fittest, he seemed to reinforce the values of a *laissez-faire* capitalism, but at the same time undermined the religious foundations on which those values had often been sustained. The rapid dissemination of his theory also had much to do with the fact that it could be invoked to support colonialist and imperialist ideologies in which the racial superiority of white anglo-saxons was commonly taken for granted.

The continuity between humans and animals, which for Darwin was corroborated by a comparable range of emotional expression in both, was also politically attractive to secular thinkers who wished to undermine the credibility of institutional religion. In England, T. H. Huxley showed particular hostility to the Roman Catholic, St George Jackson Mivart, who tried to integrate biological evolution with the teachings of his Church. In so doing,

Mivart attacked Darwin's concept of natural selection, epitomising for Huxley the unacceptable intrusion of religious values into scientific debate. The most aggressive statement of the new naturalism was made by the physicist John Tyndall in his Belfast address to the British Association for the Advancement of Science in 1874: 'We claim and we shall wrest from theology the entire domain of cosmological al theory'.[17] But it was in Germany where the programme was most relentlessly pursued, by materialists such as Ludwig Buchner and Carl Vogt, and by the monist Ernst Haeckel who saw in evolution the basis of a new religion. The fact that Darwinian phylogenies were associated with secularist and materialist propaganda helps to explain why, in France for example, it was not until the 1890s that Catholic commentators began to look at all sympathetically at Darwin's original theory, having at last recognised that it might be disentangled from the rhetoric with which it had been invested. It has been argued by James Moore in his study *of The Post-Darwinian Controversies* (1979) that among Protestants in Europe and America it was actually religious conservatives who had the best resources with which to come to terms with Darwin, in that they were able to resist facile liberal syntheses in which central Darwinian concepts such as natural selection and evolutionary divergence were frequently caricatured. One of the grounds on which Moore affirms his paradoxical thesis is an alleged structural parallel between the reconciliation of natural selection with Providence and the reconciliation, with which Calvinists in particular were only too familiar, between human freedom and divine sovereignty. It is difficult to deny, however, that Darwinian evolution gave the greatest impetus to religious radicalism. Thus David Strauss welcomed Darwin's account of human evolution precisely because it showed that man had risen not fallen. The former view gave hope to the human race, whereas the traditional doctrine of original sin was cause only for despair.

Too sharp a polarity between Darwinian secularism and religious commitment can, nevertheless, conceal many intermediate positions which, during the late nineteenth and early twentieth century, capitalised to a greater or lesser degree on the fact that Darwin's mechanism of natural selection, far from being scientifically sacrosanct, remained highly problematic.[18] Rechristianising the evolutionary philosophy of Herbert Spencer, the Scotsman and liberal evangelical, Henry Drummond, went so far as to claim that Christianity and Evolution were one and the same: each had as its object the making of more perfect living beings. So complete a fusion was only possible, however, if altruism had a higher profile in the evolutionary process than Darwin had indicated. Many other schemes of theistic evolution, notably that of Teilhard de Chardin in the twentieth century, have gained their theological plausibility only in so far as they have departed from neo-Darwinian orthodoxy by importing *a priori* concepts of perfection towards which the evolutionary process is said to be converging. In Teilhard's system, which has been much criticised for its poetic licence in the use of scientific metaphor and for its ascription of incipient forms of life and consciousness to matter itself, the perfection of Christ both symbolises and presages a focal point to which the cosmic process, through the emergence and heightening of human consciousness, is said to be converging.

In the late nineteenth century, many thinkers were just as disenchanted with the ambitious claims of the scientific naturalists as they were with the claims of traditional Christianity (F. M. Turner, *Between Science and Religion* (1974)). The idea that scientific knowledge should be the basis of a new culture, that scientists would be the new arbiters of moral worth, smacked of turning science into a substitute religion which for some, like Darwin's cousin Francis Galton, it almost certainly was – with eugenics as the new creed of human perfectibility. In opposition to such scientism stood some of the leading scientific figures of the nineteenth century: the physicists Clerk Maxwell, William Thomson (Lord Kelvin) and George Stokes, the geologist Charles Lyell (who, whilst a convert to Darwinian evolution, never renounced the view that there were distinct features of the mind which eluded reduction to natural selection) and Alfred Russel Wallace who, as co-founder with Darwin of the theory of natural selection, was nevertheless drawn into spiritualism to account for human creativity and aesthetic appreciation in such spheres as mathematics and music. As he reflected on the religious experience of mankind, the American psychologist William James observed that science would never defeat religion, or entirely usurp its role, because it could not answer the most fundamental human needs which were bound up with the inner world of the psyche. Developing a pragmatic conception of religious truth, he argued that if a religious belief enriched the life of the person who held it, it could be considered true for that person.

10. Science and religion in the twentieth century

The twentieth century has witnessed many 'scientific' critiques of religion. Those deriving from Darwin, Marx and Freud have become almost commonplace. Moreover there has been a powerful philosophical tradition, taking its inspiration from the logical positivism of the Vienna school, which has persisted in affirming a dichotomy between scientific propositions which are in principle falsifiable (even if they are not verifiable) and religious claims which are to be rejected because, as with propositions about the love of God, they conform to neither of those criteria. On the other hand, certain developments within the sciences themselves have created extra space for dialogue between scientists and theologians. Thus the development of quantum mechanics not only created difficulties for a crude scientific determinism, but by drawing attention to the limitations of scientific models, also contributed to a climate in which both scientists and theologians became more prepared to regard their formulations as partial models rather than all-encompassing dogmas. The argument has sometimes been taken to an extreme in which neither scientific theories nor religious doctrines are presumed to represent an external reality, but are assumed to fulfil a purely instrumental role in the two totally different contexts in which they are used. Indeed, a conspicuous feature of twentieth-century literature on the subject has been the prevalence of attempts to insulate theology from any implications which might be drawn from the natural sciences.

One variant of this insularity thesis was mentioned in the introduction: Bultmann's existentialist analysis of the doctrine of Creation. Instrumentalist accounts of both scientific and religious models constitute the grounds of another. A third variant occurs in the work of linguistic philosophers who, claiming a pedigree from Wittgenstein, insist that scientific and religious vocabularies belong to two distinct language games, the one characterised by object detachment, the other by personal commitment. Yet other variants attempt to establish the proposition that scientific and religious language relate to different 'aspects' or 'dimensions' of human experience. Such attempts to protect theology from the relevance of science can, however, seem unduly defensive and, as W. H. Austin has argued in *The Relevance of Natural Science to Theology* (1976), few stand up to vigorous analysis.

In creating space for dialogue, the most significant development has probably been the loss of that faith which, in the Enlightenment, had been placed in science as the key to solving all human problems. Even before the First World War shattered so many illusions, doubts had been expressed about the negative consequences of a technological society, in which unemployment might be increased and the environment rendered more dangerous. It is not merely that atomic bombs and industrial pollution have turned Utopian fantasies into nightmares but, contrary to the triumphalist images of the nineteenth century, science has actually generated problems which it is itself powerless to solve. Many of these are familiar enough in the sphere of medical ethics. Indirectly, as with new penumbras of ignorance created by nuclear technology, they affect us all. The interface between science and moral accountability is one along which religious values can still have relevance as is argued in *The Touch of Midas,* edited by Sardar (1984). There are, however, no neat religious solutions to what are unprecedented moral dilemmas. Many scientists understandably remain suspicious of any attempt to import what can appear simplistic or alien values into policy decisions, especially if they are perceived as harbingers of fanaticism. Nor is there likely to be any consensus achieved on such matters within closed religious communities. There is, for example, considerable disagreement among contemporary Muslim writers as to what a distinctively 'Islamic science' would look like and how a secularised western science can be purged of its materialistic connotations. One conclusion which the history of science has, however, established is that under different value-systems, different priorities are accorded to different subjects of scientific research, and different directions delineated for its practical application. As long as the world's religions continue to stake a claim in the elaboration of those values, the two domains of science and religion are unlikely to be completely severed.

Notes

1   J. W. Draper, *History of the conflict between religion and science* (London, 1875), Preface.
2   F. Manuel, *The religion of Isaac Newton* (Oxford, 1974).
3   R. Hooykaas, *Religion and the rise of modern science* (Edinburgh, 1972).
4   Rolf Gruner, 'Science, nature and christianity', *Journal of theological studies,* 26 (1975), 55–81.
5   E. Zilsel, 'The genesis of the concept of the physical law', *Philosophical review,* 51 (1942), 245–79.
6   R. K. Merton, *Science, technology and society in seventeenth-century England* (New York, 1970).
7   J. and M. Jacob, 'The Anglican origins of modern science', *Isis,* 71 (1980), 251–67.
8   G. De Santillana, *The crime of Galileo* (Chicago, 1955).
9   P. Redondi, *Galileo eretico* (Turin, 1983), English translation: *Galileo heretic,* transl. by Raymond Rosenthal (Allen Lane, 1988).
10   D. Kubrin, 'Newton and the cyclical cosmos: providence and the mechanical philosophy', *Journal of the history of ideas,* 28 (1967), 325–46; also available in C.A. Russel (ed.), *Science and religious belief* (Open University Press, 1973), pp. 147–69.
11   M. C. Jacob, *The Newtonians and the English revolution* (Hassocks, 1976).
12   S. Shapin, 'Of gods and kings: natural philosophy and politics in the Leibniz–Clarke disputes', *Isis* 72 (1981), 187–215.
13   R. L. Numbers, *Creation by natural law: Laplace's nebular hypothesis in American thought* (Seattle, 1977).
14   J. H. Brooke, 'Indications of a creator: Whewell as apologist and priest', in M. Fisch and S. Schaffer (eds.), *William Whewell* (Oxford, forthcoming).
15   J. H. Brooke, 'The relations between Darwin's science and his religion', in J. R. Durant (ed.), *Darwinism and divinity* (Oxford, 1985), chap. 2.
16   A. Desmond, *Archetypes and ancestors* (London, 1982).
      ——— *The politics of evolution* (forthcoming.)
17   J. Tyndall, Presidential Address to the 1874 meeting of the British Association for the Advancement of Science, reproduced in G. Basalla, W. Coleman and R. Kargon (eds.), *Victorian science* (New York, 1970), pp. 441–78, pp. 474–5.
18   P.J. Bowler, *The eclipse of Darwinism* (Baltimore, 1983).

Further reading

I. G. Barbour, *Issues in science and religion* (London, 1966).
J. Dillenberger, *Protestant thought and natural science* (London, 1961).
C. C. Gillispie, *Genesis and geology* (New York, 1959).
N. C. Gillespie, *Charles Darwin and the problem of creation* (Chicago, 1979).

T. Glick (ed.), *The comparative reception of Darwinism* (Austin, 1974).

D. C. Lindberg and R. L. Numbers (eds.), *God and nature: historical essays on the encounter between Christianity and science* (Berkeley, 1986).

D. Ospovat, *The development of Darwin's theory* (Cambridge, 1981).

A. Peacocke (ed.), *The sciences and theology in the twentieth century.*

Z. Sardar (ed.), *The touch of Midas: science, values and environment in Islam and the West* (Manchester, 1984).

S. Schaffer, 'Godly men and mechanical philosophers: souls and spirits in restoration natural philosophy', *Science in context,* 1 (1987), 55–85.

K. Thomas, *Religion and the decline of magic* (Harmondsworth, 1973).

F. M. Turner, 'The Victorian conflict between science and religion: a professional dimension', *Isis* 69 (1978), 356–76.

—— *Between science and religion* (New Haven, 1974).

C. Webster (ed.), *The intellectual revolution of the seventeenth century* (London, 1974).

R. S. Westfall, *Science and religion in seventeenth-century England* (New Haven, 1958).

PART VII

Childhood

Introduction

S EVENTEENTH-CENTURY NEW ENGLANDERS, who set great store by obedience, knew that Native Americans differed from them: in 1689 Roger Williams told how he had chided a Narragansett father for allowing his son to be 'saucy, bold and undutiful' (Davis 1970). But in the United States in the early twentieth century, 'Boys ... who were overly obedient ... became the objects of concern' (Grant 2004). Parents at this later period did want sons to respect their authority – but also to disregard it from time to time. How widespread has this attitude been in different cultural contexts in the past? Is it possible to generalise about childhood in history? A central challenge facing cultural historians is how to reconcile the continuity between one generation and the next with the discontinuity arising when the young strike out in new directions. Without wishing to depict children as cultural clones of those who raised them, a historian is nevertheless likely to find that the influence exerted on someone in their early years sheds light on that person's later actions and beliefs. It is therefore appropriate to analyse the history of relations between children and their elders from the adult perspective.

But besides being interested in the transmission of the older generation's values, cultural historians also look for evidence of children's reaction and resistance, children's experiences and perceptions, and indeed a distinct culture – a children's culture, passed on from older to younger children in play and in other ways. Analysing the meanings of their spontaneous activity raises methodological issues. It requires that differences between boys and girls be taken into account (Fletcher 2008; Formanek-Brunell 1998; Goldberg 2008; Hunter 2003; Popiel 2008). So too must the different influences of males and females in the adult environment, be they parents, grandparents, aunts, uncles, older siblings, foster parents, nannies, teachers, tutors, governesses or clergy. Thinking about children as engaged in their own culture opens up questions concerning cultural forms treated elsewhere in this Reader, including children's reading, religion, commerce and consumerism. (For literature reviews, see Cunningham 1998 and 2004 and King 2007.) Other questions needing to be addressed relate to children's involvement in work (Cunningham 1990, 2005; Humphries 2010) and the experience of abandoned children (Boswell 1989; Gilfoyle 2004).

In a seminal but controversial study by Ariès (1962), childhood was viewed as an invention of the early modern era. Previously, Ariès believed, children were regarded as miniature adults and shared in the lives of adults from a young age. High infant mortality, he wrote, led to a lower level of emotional investment by parents in their offspring. When children became more likely to survive to adulthood, they began to be treated as special. Ariès wrote engagingly, and his ideas rapidly became received wisdom. The strength of his position lay in his appreciation that 'childhood' is a cultural construct, not a direct reflection of the biological immaturity of the human young. But Ariès used pictorial evidence in an impressionistic way (Burton 1989); his use of demographic data did not make enough allowance for regional variations (Woods 2003). Medievalists have rejected the suggestion that parents in the Middle Ages were lacking in affection for their children (Alexandre-Bidon and Lett 1999; Hanawalt 2002; Orme 2001; see also Pollock 1983), and deplored his failure to distinguish different sections of society such as nobles and peasants. In a society with low levels of literacy, most – but by no means all – children were expected to play a part from an early age in the family's economy. Ariès was vague about chronology, being concerned mainly with the contrast between a period when there was little schooling and a period when most children went to school (Wilson 1980).

Fass (2012) suggests an alternative to Ariès, recasting the history of childhood as a narrative in which childhood has been depicted as a privileged status, to which at various times different age-cohorts drawn from different sections of a population were admitted. Her approach provides a flexible framework accommodating evidence about parental aspirations, about the advice of preachers, philosophers, poets and psychologists, about disadvantaged children, about the appeal of consumerism and about contrasts between the treatment of boys and girls. A profound change in attitudes to children has indeed come about since the time of the Puritan insistence on the Christian doctrine of Original Sin. Commerce has expanded, and the Enlightenment and the Romantic movement have brought a more optimistic view of children, founded on a belief in Progress and in childhood innocence. Mass schooling has fundamentally altered the experience of childhood for the majority of young people in the industrialised countries, and has delayed the age of entry into the adult work-sphere (Graff 1995; Hunter 2003).

Many sources refer to children's eagerness to play rather than to work as bidden by adults. Children's own culture may be harder to find recorded than that of their parents, carers and teachers, but it has been typified by its unruliness and earthy humour (Avery 1994; Orme 1995; Thomas 1989). Some orally transmitted rhymes accompanying children's games have been highly durable. Material on 'children's folklore' began to appear in the 1950s, thanks to the Opies (1959, 1969, 1997, see Avery 1999) and subsequently to researchers in the USA (Bronner 1988; Chudacoff 2007; Sutton-Smith *et al.* 1999). Here and in discussion of literature written for children, historians have tried to distinguish between how children chose to play or what they liked to read and the games or reading-matter provided or prescribed by adults, whether teachers or authors. But a presumed capacity to know what children 'really' wanted is perhaps a reflection of historians' presuppositions (Rudd 2010). In the early nineteenth century, a controversy illustrating this danger arose between the advocates of 'improving' literature for children such as Sarah Trimmer, founder of a journal called *The Guardian of Education*, and their Romantic critics such as Wordsworth, for whom her approach represented a utilitarian conception of children's needs. The Romantics, unlike Mrs Trimmer, placed a high value on traditional story-telling (Rowe 2005; Tucker 1997). Though partly to do with views of 'the child', this disagreement reflected a tension in middle-class households between the culture of the parents and the popular culture imbibed by the younger children when servants told them stories (Wroth 2006).

Our first reading, by Mintz, is about how Puritans in seventeenth-century New England brought up their children. Many had left their home country for the sake of freedom to practise their religion and perpetuate it through their offspring. They saw these as the 'children of the Covenant'. God had chosen them to be his people as he had once chosen the Israelites, and had given them this land in fulfilment of his biblical promise. So how successful were the Puritans in imparting this treasured inheritance to their sons and daughters? And how severe was the discipline they imposed? Writing about Puritans in England in the preceding generations, Smucker (1990) sets out to give a sympathetic picture. As Mintz points out, their attitude to childhood is easily caricatured.

In the second piece, Koepp discusses an early children's encyclopedia, produced in France in the mid-eighteenth century by a priest and translated into several languages. Her chapter suggests that many young readers enjoyed this way of learning about the world, and discusses the philosophical ideas about how children learn which guided the encyclopedia's author.

Brewer states in our final reading that it was only in the eighteenth century that children began to be seen as needing toys (but see Jordanova 1990). He sets out to explain this, in a summary reminiscent of Ariès though not uncritical of him, by reference to two processes. One is the increasing sense of the differences between children and adults and a desire to treat children accordingly. The other is the growth of commerce, which makes the material culture of this period especially significant. However, archaeological evidence from the Middle Ages subsequently presented by authors such as Orme (1995, 2001) has shown that toys were made for children long before the eighteenth century.

References

Alexandre-Bidon, D. and Lett, D. (1999) *Children in the Middle Ages,* trans. J. Gladding, Notre Dame, IN: Notre Dame University Press.

Ariès, P. (1962) *Centuries of Childhood,* trans. Robert Baldick, New York, NY: Random House.

Avery, G. (1994) 'The voice of the child, both godly and unregenerate, in early modern England', in E. Goodenough, M.A. Heberle and N. Sokoloff (eds) *Infant Tongues: the voice of the child in literature,* Detroit, MI: Wayne State University Press.

Avery, G. (1999) 'A lifetime's journey: the Opies and the folklore of childhood', *The Lion and the Unicorn,* 23: 286–99.

Boswell, J. (1989) *The Kindness of Strangers: the abandonment of children in Western Europe from late antiquity to the Renaissance,* London: Allen Lane.

Bronner, S.J. (1988) *American Children's Folklore,* Little Rock, AR: August House.

Burton, A. (1989) 'Looking forward from Ariès? Pictorial and material evidence for the history of childhood and family life', *Continuity and Change,* 4: 203–29.

Chudacoff, H.P. (2007) *Children at Play: an American history,* New York, NY: New York University Press.

Cunningham, H. (1990) 'The employment and unemployment of children in England c.1680–1851', *Past & Present,* 126: 115–50.

Cunningham, H. (1998) 'Histories of childhood', *American Historical Review,* 103: 1195–1208.

Cunningham, H. (2004) 'Childhood histories', *Journal of Victorian Culture,* 9: 90–6.

Cunningham, H. (2005) *Children and Childhood in Western Society since 1500,* Harlow: Pearson Longman.

Davis, J.L. (1970) 'Roger Williams among the Narragansett Indians', *New England Quarterly*, 43: 593–604.

Fass, P.S. (2012) 'Is there a story in the history of childhood?', in Fass (ed.) *The Routledge History of Childhood in the Western World*, London: Routledge.

Fletcher, A. (2008) *Growing Up in England: the experience of childhood, 1600–1914*, New Haven, CT: Yale University Press.

Formanek-Brunell, M. (1998) *Made to Play House: dolls and the commercialization of girl culture, 1830–1930*, Baltimore, MD: Johns Hopkins University Press.

Gilfoyle, T.J. (2004) 'Street-rats and gutter-snipes: child pickpockets and street culture in New York City, 1850–1900', *Journal of Social History*, 37: 853–82.

Goldberg, P.J.P. (2008) 'Childhood and gender in later medieval England', *Viator*, 39: 249–62.

Graff, H.J. (1995) *Conflicting Paths: growing up in America*, Cambridge, MA: Harvard University Press.

Grant, J. (2004) 'A "real boy" and not a sissy: gender, childhood, and masculinity, 1890–1940', *Journal of Social History*, 37: 829–51.

Hanawalt, B.A. (2002) 'Medievalists and the study of childhood', *Speculum*, 77: 440–60.

Humphries, J. (2010) *Childhood and Child Labour in the British Industrial Revolution*, Cambridge: Cambridge University Press.

Hunter, J.H. (2003) *How Young Ladies Became Girls: the Victorian origins of American girlhood*, New Haven, CT: Yale University Press.

King, M.L. (2007) 'Concepts of childhood: what we know and where we might go', *Renaissance Quarterly*, 60: 371–407.

Opie, I. and P. (1959) *The Lore and Language of School-Children*, Oxford: Oxford University Press.

Opie, I. and P. (1969) *Children's Games in Street and Playground*, Oxford: Oxford University Press.

Opie, I. and P. (1997) *Children's Games with Things*, Oxford: Oxford University Press.

Orme, N. (1995) 'The culture of children in medieval England', *Past & Present*, 148: 48–88.

Orme, N. (2001) *Medieval Children*, New Haven, CT: Yale University Press.

Pollock, L. (1983) *Forgotten Children: parent-child relations from 1500 to 1900*, Cambridge: Cambridge University Press.

Popiel, J.J. (2008) *Rousseau's Daughters: domesticity, education, and autonomy in modern France*, Hanover, NH: University of New Hampshire Press.

Rowe, K.E. (2005) 'Virtue in the guise of vice: the making and unmaking of morality from fairy tale fantasy', in D. Ruwe (ed.) *Culturing the Child, 1690–1914: essays in memory of Mitzi Myers*, Lanham, MD: Scarecrow Press.

Rudd, D. (2010) 'The development of children's literature', in Rudd (ed.) *The Routledge Companion to Children's Literature*, London: Routledge.

Smucker, R.V. (1990) 'Puritan attitudes toward childhood discipline, 1560–1634', in V. Fildes (ed.) *Women as Mothers in Pre-industrial England*, London: Routledge.

Sutton-Smith, B., Mechling, J., Johnson, T.W. and McMahon, F.R. (eds) (1999) *Children's Lore: a source-book*, Logan, UT: Utah State University Press. Available through Digital Commons: <http://digitalcommons.usu.edu/usupress_pubs>.

Thomas, K. (1989) 'Children in early modern England', in G. Avery and J. Briggs (eds) *Children and Their Books*, Oxford: Oxford University Press.

Tucker, N. (1997) 'Fairy tales and their early opponents. In defence of Mrs Trimmer', in M. Hilton, M. Styles and V. Watson (eds) *Opening the Nursery Door: reading, writing and childhood 1600–1900*, London: Routledge.

Wilson, A. (1980) 'The infancy of the history of childhood: an appraisal of Philippe Ariès', *History and Theory*, 19: 132–53.

Woods, R. (2003) 'Did Montaigne love his children? Demography and the hypothesis of parental indifference', *Journal of Interdisciplinary History*, 33: 421–42.

Wroth, C. (2006) ' "To root the old woman out of our minds": women educationists and plebeian culture in late eighteenth-century Britain', *Eighteenth-Century Studies*, 30: 48–73.

Chapter 18

Steven Mintz

CHILDREN OF THE COVENANT

IN THE PREDAWN DARKNESS of February 29, 1704, 48 French soldiers and 200 of their Abenaki, Huron, and Iroquois allies attacked the frontier settlement of Deerfield, Massachusetts. The attackers burned the village, killing 48 of the 300 inhabitants, and took 111 captives. For the next eight weeks the captives were forced to march northward 300 miles through the snow to Canada.[1]

Among those taken prisoner were seven-year-old Eunice Williams, who lost two brothers in the attack, her clergyman father, her mother, and two surviving siblings. Along the way, Eunice saw at least twenty of her fellow captives executed, including her mother. In Canada the captives were dispersed, some to live with the French, others with the Indians. Eunice, separated from her father and brothers, was taken to a Kahnawake Mohawk mission village, across from Montreal. Two and a half years later, Eunice's father, the Reverend John Williams, was returned to New England as part of a prisoner exchange. In time, her two siblings were also released. But despite Reverend Williams' relentless pleas and protracted negotiations with the French and the Mohawks, Eunice refused to leave the Kahnawake. She had converted to Catholicism, forgotten the English language, adopted Indian clothing and hairstyle, and did not want to return to Puritan New England. At the age of sixteen she married a Kahnawake Mohawk named François Xavier Arosen, with whom she would live for half a century until his death. Reverend Williams in his quest to regain his daughter traveled to Canada and saw her, but she refused to go home with him. "She is obstinately resolved to live and dye here, and will not so much as give me one pleasant look," he wrote in shocked disbelief.[2]

We do not know why Eunice decided to remain with the Kahnawake, separated from her family and friends, but it seems likely that she found life among the Mohawks more attractive than life among the New England Puritans. The Mohawks were much more indulgent of children, and females, far from being regarded as inferior to males, played an integral role in Mohawk society and politics. Nor was Eunice alone in choosing to remain with her captors. A returned captive named Titus King reported that many young captives decided to become members of their Indian captors' tribes. "In Six months time they Forsake Father & mother, Forgit thir own Land, Refuess to Speak there own toungue & Seeminly be Holley Swollowed up with the Indians," he observed.[3]

Eunice Williams was one of many "white Indians," English colonists who ran away from home or were taken captive by and elected to stay with Native Americans. Benjamin Franklin described the phenomenon in 1753:

> When an Indian Child has been brought up among us, taught our language and habituated to our Customs, yet if he goes to see his relations and makes one Indian Ramble there is no perswading him ever to return. When white persons of either sex have been taken prisoners young by the Indians, and lived awhile among them, tho' ransomed by their Friends, and treated with all imaginable tenderness to prevail with them to stay among the English, yet in a Short time they become disgusted with our manner of life, and the care and pains that are necessary to support it, and take the first good Opportunity of escaping again into the woods, from whence there is no reclaiming them.

A fourteen-year-old named James McCullough, who lived with the Indians for "eight years, four months, and sixteen days," had to be brought back in fetters, his legs tied "under his horse's belly," his arms tied behind his back. Still, he succeeded in escaping, returning to his Indian family. When children were "redeemed" by the English, they often "cried as if they should die when they were presented to us." Treated with great kindness by the Indians (the Deerfield children were carried on sleighs and in Indians' arms or on their backs), and freed of the work obligations imposed on colonial children, many young people found life in captivity preferable to that in New England. Boys hunted, caught fish, and gathered nuts, but were not obliged to do any of the farm chores that colonial boys were required to perform. Girls "planted, tended, and harvested corn," but had no master "to oversee or drive us, so that we could work as leisurely as we pleased."[4]

A Puritan childhood is as alien to twenty-first century Americans as an Indian childhood was to seventeenth-century New Englanders. The Puritans did not sentimentalize childhood; they regarded even newborn infants as potential sinners who contained aggressive and willful impulses that needed to be suppressed. Nor did the Puritans consider childhood a period of relative leisure and playfulness, deserving of indulgence. They considered crawling bestial and play as frivolous and trifling, and self-consciously eliminated the revels and sports that fostered passionate peer relationships in England. In the Puritans' eyes, children were adults in training who needed to be prepared for salvation and inducted into the world of work as early as possible. Nevertheless, it would be a mistake to misrepresent the Puritans as unusually harsh or controlling parents, who lacked an awareness of children's special nature. The Puritans were unique in their preoccupation with childrearing, and wrote a disproportionate share of tracts on the subject. As a struggling minority, their survival depended on ensuring that their children retained their values. They were convinced that molding children through proper childrearing and education was the most effective way to shape an orderly and godly society. Their legacy is a fixation on childhood corruption, child nurture, and schooling that remains undiminished in the United States today.[5]

"Why came you unto this land?" Eleazar Mather asked his congregation in 1671; "was it not mainly with respect to the rising Generation? . . . was it to leave them a rich and wealthy people? was it to leave them Houses, Lands, Livings? Oh, No; but to leave God in the midst of them." Mather was not alone in claiming that the Puritans had migrated to promote their children's well-being. Mary Angier declared that her reason for venturing across the Atlantic was "thinking that if her children might get good it would be worthy my journey." Similarly, Ann Ervington decided to migrate because she feared that "children would curse [their] parents for not getting them to means." When English Puritans during the 1620s and 1630s contemplated migrating to the New World, their primary motives were to protect their children from moral corruption and to promote their spiritual and economic well-being.[6]

During the 1620s and 1630s, more than 14,000 English villagers and artisans fled their country to travel to the shores of New England, where they hoped to establish a stable and moral society free from the disruptive demographic and economic transformations that were unsettling England's social order. In the late sixteenth and early seventeenth centuries England experienced mounting inflation, rapid population growth, and a sharp increase in the proportion of children in the population. A 50 percent decline in real wages between 1500 and 1620 prompted a growing number of rural sons and daughters to leave their impoverished families and villages at a very young age to seek apprenticeships or to find employment as live-in servants or independent wage earners. A resulting problem of youthful vagrancy and delinquency led to authorities' ambitious plans to incarcerate idle and disordered youth in workhouses, conscript them into military service, or transport them overseas. Religious reformers, less troubled by youthful vagrancy and crime, focused on childish mischief-making and youthful vice, especially blasphemy, idleness, disobedience, and Sabbath-breaking. This preoccupation with youthful frivolity, religious indifference, and indolence shaped the Puritan outlook, with its emphasis on piety, self-discipline, hard work, and household discipline. When they finally achieved power, the Puritans were eager to suppress England's traditional youthful culture of Maypole dancing, frolicking, sports, and carnival-like "rituals of misrule" in which young people mocked their elders and expressed their antagonisms toward adult authority ritually and symbolically. The Puritans aggressively proselytized among the young, pressed for an expansion of schooling, and sought to strengthen paternal authority.[7]

Against this background of disruptive social change, radically conflicting conceptions of the nature of childhood had emerged in Tudor and Stuart England. Anglican traditionalists regarded childhood as a repository of virtues that were rapidly disappearing from English society. For them, the supposed innocence, playfulness, and obedience of children served as a symbolic link with their highly idealized conception of a past "Merrie England" characterized by parish unity, a stable and hierarchical social order, and communal celebrations. At the same time, humanistic calculators, who invoked the metaphors of "moist wax" and "fair white wool" to describe children, expressed exceptional optimism about children's capacity to learn and adapt. For them, children were malleable, and all depended on the nature of their upbringing and education.[8]

Unlike the early humanists or Anglican traditionalists, who believed that children arrived in the world without personal evil, Puritan sermons and moral tracts portrayed children as riddled by corruption. Even a newborn infant's soul was tainted with original sin—the human waywardness that caused Adam's Fall. In the Reverend Benjamin Wadsworth's words, babies were "filthy, guilty, odious, abominable . . . both by nature and practice." The Puritan minister Cotton Mather described children's innate sinfulness even more bluntly: "Are they *Young?* Yet the *Devil* has been with them already . . . They go astray as soon as they are born. They no longer *step* than they *stray*, they no sooner *lisp* than they *ly*." For Puritans, the moral reformation of childhood offered the key to establishing a godly society.[9]

The New England Puritans are easily caricatured as an emotionally cold and humorless people who terrorized the young with threats of damnation and hellfire and believed that the chief task of parenthood was to break children's sinful will. In fact the Puritans were among the first groups to reflect seriously and systematically on children's nature and the process of childhood development. For a century, their concern with the nurture of the young led them to monopolize writings for and about children, publish many of the earliest works on childrearing and pedagogy, and dominate the field of children's literature.

They were among the first to condemn wetnursing and encourage maternal nursing, and to move beyond literary conceptions that depicted children solely in terms of innocent simplicity or youthful precocity. Perhaps most important, they were the first group to state publicly that entire communities were responsible for children's moral development and to honor that commitment by requiring communities to establish schools and by criminalizing the physical abuse of children.[10]

The Puritan preoccupation with childhood was a product of religious beliefs and social circumstances. As members of a reform movement that sought to purify the Church of England and to elevate English morals and manners, the Puritans were convinced that the key to creating a pious society lay in properly rearing, disciplining, and educating a new generation to higher standards of piety. As a small minority group, the Puritans depended on winning the rising generation's minds and souls in order to prevail in the long term. Migration to New England greatly intensified the Puritans' fixation on childhood as a critical stage for saving souls. Deeply concerned about the survival of the Puritan experiment in a howling wilderness, fearful that their offspring might revert to savagery, the Puritans considered it essential that children retain certain fundamental values, including an awareness of sin.

In New England, the ready availability of land and uniquely healthy living conditions, the product of clean water and a cool climate, resulted in families that were larger, more stable, and more hierarchical than those in England. In rural England, a typical farm had fewer than forty acres, an insufficient amount to divide among a family's children. As a result, children customarily left home in their early teens to work as household servants or agricultural laborers in other households. As the Quaker William Penn observed, English parents "do with their children as they do with their souls, put them out at livery for so much a year." But in New England, distinctive demographic and economic conditions combined with a patriarchal ideology rooted in religion to increase the size of families, intensify paternal controls over the young, and allow parents to keep their children close by. A relatively equal sex ratio and an abundance of land made marriage a virtually universal institution. Because women typically married in their late teens or early twenties, five years earlier than their English counterparts, they bore many more children. On average, women gave birth every two years or so, averaging between seven and nine children, compared with four or five in England. These circumstances allowed the New England Puritans to realize their ideal of a godly family: a patriarchal unit in which a man's authority over his wife, children, and servants was a part of an interlocking chain of authority extending from God to the lowliest creatures.[11]

The patriarchal family was the basic building block of Puritan society, and paternal authority received strong reinforcement from the church and community. Within their households, male household heads exercised unusual authority over family members. They were responsible for leading their household in daily prayers and scripture reading, catechizing their children and servants, and teaching household members to read so that they might study the Bible and learn the "good lawes of the Colony." Childrearing manuals were thus addressed to men, not their wives. They had an obligation to help their sons find a vocation or calling, and a legal right to consent to their children's marriage. Massachusetts Bay Colony and Connecticut underscored the importance of paternal authority by making it a capital offense for youths sixteen or older to curse or strike their father.[12]

The Puritans repudiated many traditional English customs that conflicted with a father's authority, such as godparenthood. The family was a "little commonwealth," the keystone of the social order and a microcosm of the relationships of superiority and subordination that characterized the larger society. Yet even before the first generation of settlers passed away, there was fear that fathers were failing to properly discipline and educate the young. In 1648 the Massachusetts General Court reprimanded fathers for their negligence and ordered that "all masters of families doe once a week (at the least) catechize their children and servants in the grounds and principles of Religion." Connecticut, New Haven, and Plymouth colonies followed suit in 1650, 1655, and 1671 with almost identical injunctions to ensure that "such Children and Servants may [not] be in danger to grow barbarous, rude and stubborn, through ignorance."[13] . . .

The Puritans were set apart from other religious sects by their emphasis on household religion. Although the meetinghouse was the place for public worship (the term *church* referred to the congregation's members, not to the physical structure), the household was the place for young people's initial religious and moral instruction. In 1650 the Connecticut General Court gave "Masters of families" responsibility to "once a week at least catechize their children and servants in the grounds and principles of religion." Bible readings, prayers, self-examination, psalm-singing, and family instruction formed the household curriculum designed to lead children and servants to faith.[14]

During the sixteenth and seventeenth centuries, the Puritans wrote twice as many books in English on proper methods of rearing children as all other groups combined. Precisely because of their belief that children were born in sin, parents had to raise them with great care. Among the Puritans' most important legacies are the beliefs that early childhood is life's formative stage, that children are highly malleable and need careful training, and that parents should be preoccupied with children's spiritual well being. A godly education was to start as early as possible. "Parents," declared one minister, "ought to begin to nurture their children, as soone as they are capable of any instruction." Unlike evangelical Protestants of the eighteenth and nineteenth centuries, the Puritans did not emphasize a sudden, dramatic conversion experience. Rather, children's religious education was a gradual process in which fathers instilled a capacity for grace within their offspring through appeals to their affections and reason. Conceiving of children's socialization in religious terms, Puritan parents surrounded their offspring from birth with prayer and psalm-singing. In devout households, scripture readings took place daily and family prayers were held twice a day. Parents encouraged their children to read "as early as May be" through recitation of catechisms and Bible stories. Even young children were taken to Sabbath observances, where sermons might last six hours.[15]

The emphasis on early moral instruction led the Puritans to view children's play with ambivalence. Puritan children had swings, rode hobbyhorses, and drew on slates. Girls cut out paper dolls with scissors, recited poetry, and played with dollhouses and cradles. Boys flew kites, sailed toy boats, constructed wigwams and played at being Indians, collected rocks and bird eggs, and made pets of squirrels, dogs, and cats. Seventeenth-century records provide a litany of complaints about children playing ball or flying kites in the streets, robbing birds' nests and orchards, and throwing stones and snowballs at passersby. Yet the dominant view was that play was a sinful waste of time, "a snare of the Old Deluder, Satan." Samuel Sewall and Cotton Mather complained about their children's "inordinant love of play" and worried about the energies diverted to it. They especially abhorred game-playing on the Sabbath and any games involving cards and dice.[16]

The Puritans did not mistake children for angels. Unlike the Romantics, who associated childhood with purity and innocence, the Puritans adopted a fairly realistic view, emphasizing children's intransigence, willfulness, and obstinacy. They worried that if indolence, selfishness, and willfulness were not overcome in childhood, these traits would dominate adulthood. The Reverend Thomas Cobbett said that too many insolent and unruly children "carry it proudly, disdainfully, and scornfully toward parents," and that their mother and father should require them to bow before them and stand bareheaded in their presence. Nonetheless, most Puritan authorities were highly critical of harsh physical punishments, convinced that corporal discipline only induced resentfulness and rebelliousness in children.

Parents were told to avoid excessive severity and always to explain the reasons for a punishment. Ministers said that correction of error should never be inflicted arbitrarily or capriciously, and that parents should never discipline a child in anger. Parents were also advised to avoid the indiscriminate use of verbal or physical chastisement and to adapt correction to the child's age, temperament, understanding, and to the nature of the infraction. As the poet Anne Bradstreet explained, "Diverse children have their different natures; some are like flesh which nothing but salt will keep from putrefecation; some again like tender fruits which are best preserved with sugar: those parents are wise that can fit their nurture according to the Nature."[17]

Puritan parents, relatively isolated in a new and difficult land, were in closer and more constant contact with their children for more years than their counterparts in England. Interacting with them more frequently and intensely, they tried to inculcate religious understandings to encourage internal restraints. Joseph Green recalled that when he "was about 4 or 5 years at most," his "father used to tell me I must be a good boy and must service God, and used to ask me whether I went alone and prayed to God to bless me & to pardon my sins." By building up a child's awareness of sin, parents sought to lead children along the path toward salvation. Children's early consciousness of their mortality and of the severity of divine judgment was considered a particularly useful tool for shaping behavior. John Norris' *Spiritual Counsel* advised the young to "be much in contemplation of the last four thyngs, Heaven, Hell, Death and Judgment. Place yourself frequently on your death beds, in your Coffins, and in your Graves. Act over frequently in your Minds, the solemnity of your own funerals; and entertain your Imaginations with all the lively scenes of Mortality."[18]

As early as possible, children were taught to prepare for death. Ministers admonished children to reflect on death, and their sermons contained graphic descriptions of hell and the horrors of eternal damnation. Cotton Mather offered this advice: "Go into Burying-Place, CHILDREN; you will there see *Graves* as short as your selves. Yea, you may be at *Play* one Hour; *Dead, Dead* the next." With his own family, he seized on opportunities to reinforce this lesson. In one incident he explained, "I took my little daughter, Katy, into my study, and there I told my child, that I am to die shortly, and she must, when I am dead, remember every thing, that I said unto her." Awareness of death was inculcated by showing young children corpses and hangings. References to death pervaded children's primers. In illustrating the use of the letter "T," the *New England Primer* noted: "Time cuts down all/ Both great and small." Far from being a sign of parental insensitivity, exposing children to the idea and reality of death was a way to instill in them an awareness of sin and to encourage them to reflect on divine judgment. At least some Puritan children picked up the message that they needed to recognize their sinfulness and strive for repentance and salvation. Samuel Sewall's daughter Betty "burst out" after dinner "into an amazing cry . . . Her Mother ask'd the reason; she gave none; at last said she was afraid she could goe to Hell, her Sins were not pardon'd.[19]

Even sickness offered practical religious lessons. During the seventeenth century, physicians were unable to diagnose or treat scarcely any diseases, and the Puritans regarded illnesses as divinely administered afflictions. "What are sickness," one Puritan divine explained, "but the Rods wherewith GOD counts His own offending Children?" To cope with their children's illnesses, many Puritan parents, like Increase Mather, turned to religious ritual. In 1676, when his son Samuel "was near to death again about a fortnight agoe, I Fasted & prayed for his Life & God hath heard me." Others worried that their unrepented sins caused their children's illnesses. When his eldest son Ebenezer accidentally fell into a fire while napping, Samuel Sewall noted that "for his relief I immediately killed a cat and he washed his hands in the blood." Some children considered illnesses providential signs. Recalling a bout with measles in 1714, when he was eleven, Ebenezer Parkman wrote that his illness "set me upon thinking upon what would be the estate of my soul after my Dissolution, which was apprehended by all to be Nigh, often in my mind repeating the Psalmists words Blessed is he whose Transgression is forgiven whose Sin is Covered."[20]

The Puritan family was not only a little church; it was also a little school. During the early seventeenth century it was within the household that Puritan children gained basic literacy. In general, mothers were responsible for teaching their children to read, while fathers taught writing. Puritans regarded education as critical to salvation, calling education "God's ordinary way for the conveyance of his grace." In teaching children to read, Puritan mothers did not divide reading and religion. Children were expected to learn to read by listening to others read aloud and then by memorizing the Lord's Prayer, psalms, hymns, catechisms, and scripture passages. Nathaniel Eaton explained: "My education was in a religious manner from a cradle that I was trained to read Scripture." After his mother's death, John Paine of Plymouth wrote: "She was unto her children all teaching them God's word to read as they were but Small." As in England, parents bought primers, catechisms, and hornbooks to teach their children to read. Households educated not only children but also servants and apprentices. Contracts between masters and apprentices obliged masters to make sure that servants learned how to read. And all imbibed religion along with literacy. . . .[21]

In 1669, when Richard Mather was on his deathbed, his son asked him if he had any special charge to give to him. The elderly Mather replied: "A special thing which I would commend to you, is care concerning the rising generation in this country, that they be brought under the government of Christ in his church." Early New England was intellectually preoccupied with children and youth because the survival of the community depended upon them. And yet it was hard to keep them within the Puritan fold. Children were ignorant, even animalistic, and easily led astray. Youth was dominated by pride and sensuality, evident in Sabbath-breaking, night revels, blasphemy, fornication, rebellion against family government, and even masturbation. Rising adult concern with youthful sensuality shows up in the court records, especially in prosecutions of fornication and bastardy, which increased dramatically over time.[22]

The Puritan obsession with children and youth was not, however, limited to concern about sin. It also expressed fear for the survival of the Puritan faith. With the death of the first generation of New Englanders, with the rapid decline in conversions relative to population growth, how could the younger generation be nurtured in the faith that had motivated their parents? Freed of the experience of persecution and the struggles of migration, how could the young ensure the survival of the Puritan enterprise? While Puritanism in England originated in part in a generational revolt against the Anglican Church, in New England it seemed necessary to ensure that the younger generation sustained loyalty to their parents' faith. To perpetuate their religion, the Puritans instituted mechanisms for indoctrinating youths, including youth-specific catechisms, covenant-renewal ceremonies in churches and homes, private religious societies, catechetical exercises, lectures, and covenant renewals, in which groups of youths were assembled on the Sabbath to renew their parents' covenants.[23]

No earlier people had ever invested greater responsibilities or higher expectations in their children than did the New England Puritans, but this heavy investment produced intense anxiety. The survival and success of the Puritan enterprise hinged on the willingness of the "rising generation" to maintain their parents' religious beliefs and ideals. The Reverend Eleazer Mather put the point bluntly. "There is no little Expectation concerning you," he declared, "your predecessors . . . [and] all of their expectations under God himself, are in you." Beginning in the 1660s and 1670s, Puritan presses and pulpits produced a stream of jeremiads lamenting the sins of the rising generation and the degeneration of the young from the religion and godliness of their forebears. Young people were made to carry an awesome psychological burden. Morality, religion, indeed the future, depended on them. In secularized form, it is this mixture of hope and fear about the rising generation that remains Puritanism's most lasting legacy.[24]

Notes

1   John Demos, *The Unredeemed Captive: A Family Story from Early America* (New York: Knopf, 1964).

2   Quoted in Rosalie Murphy Baum and Elizabeth Maddock Dillon, "John Williams," in *Heath Anthology of American Literature,* ed. Paul Lauter, 4th ed., vol. 1 (Boston: Houghton Mifflin, 2002), 521–523.

3   Titus King, *Narrative of Titus King* (Hartford: Connecticut Historical Society, 1938), 17.

4   Demos' *Unredeemed Captive,* 144–146; James Axtell, "The White Indians of Colonial America," *William and Mary Quarterly,* 3d ser., 32 (1975), 55–88, 57, 62–63, 68, 85.

5   Anne S. Lombard, *Making Manhood: Growing Up Male in Colonial New England* (Cambridge, Mass.: Harvard University Press, 2003), 43, 52–53, C. John Sommerville, *The Discovery of Childhood in Puritan England* (Athens: University of Georgia Press, 1992).

6   James Axtell, *The School upon a Hill: Education and Society in Colonial New England* (New Haven: Yale University Press, 1974), 4; David Hall, *Worlds of Wonder, Days of Judgment: Popular Religious Belief in Early New England* (New York: Knopf, 1989), 154.

7   Gerald F. Moran and Maris A. Vinovskis, *Religion, Family, and the Life Course: Explorations in the Social History of Early America* (Ann Arbor: University of Michigan Press, 1992), 116, 144, 146–148; Gerald F. Moran, "Adolescence in Colonial America," in *Encyclopedia of Adolescence,* ed. Richard Lerner, Anne C. Petersen, and Jeanne Brooks-Gunn, vol. 1 (New York: Garland, 1991), 157–164.

8   Leah S. Marcus, *Childhood and Cultural Despair: A Theme and Variations in Seventeenth-Century Literature* (Pittsburgh: University of Pittsburgh Press, 1978).

9   Ibid.; Moran and Vinovskis, *Religion, Family, and Life Course,* 116; Sandford Fleming, *Children and Puritanism* (1933; reprint, New York: Arno, 1969), 96; David E. Stannard, *The Puritan Way of Death* (New York: Oxford University Press, 1977), 50.

10   Sommerville, *Discovery of Childhood,* 21–68.

11   Michael Zuckerman, *Friends and Neighbors: Group Life in America's, First Plural Society* (Philadelphia: Temple University Press, 1982), 42; Barry Levy, *Quakers and the American Family: British Settlement in the Delaware Valley, 1650–1765* (New York: Oxford University Press, 1988), 100; Richard Archer, "New England Mosaic: A Demographic Analysis for the Seventeenth Century," *William and Mary Quarterly,* 3d ser., 47 (October 1990), 477–502.

12   Richard L. Bushman, *From Puritan to Yankee: Character and the Social Order in Connecticut, 1690–1765* (Cambridge, Mass.: Harvard University Press, 1967), 14; Roger Thompson, *Sex in Middlesex: Popular Mores in a Massachusetts County, 1649–1699* (Amherst: University of Massachusetts Press, 1986), 34; Lombard, *Making Manhood,* 35.

13   Carole Shammas, "Anglo-American Household Government in Comparative Perspective," *William and Mary Quarterly,* 3d ser., 52 (January 1995), 117. Axtell, *School upon a Hill,* 22–23.

14   Moran and Vinovskis, *Religion, Family, and Life Course,* 121; Colonial Society of New England, ed., *Seventeenth-Century New England* (Charlottesville: University Press of Virginia, 1984), 168; Axtell *School upon a Hill,* 22–23.

15   John Morgan, *Godly Learning: Puritan Attitudes towards Reason, Learning, and Education, 1560–1640* (Cambridge: Cambridge University Press, 1986), 123, 143; Joseph Illick, "Childrearing in Seventeenth-Century England and America," in *The History of Childhood,* ed. Lloyd DeMause (New York: Psychohistory Press, 1974), 316; Moran and Vinovskis, *Religion, Family, and Life Course,* 117, 120.

16   Constance B. Schultz, "Children and Childhood in the Eighteenth Century," in *American Childhood: A Research Guide and Historical Handbook,* ed. Joseph M. Hawes and N. Ray Hiner (Westport, Conn.: Greenwood, 1985), 71; Monica M. Kiefer, *American Children through Their Books* (Philadelphia: University of Pennsylvania Press, 1948), 191.

17   Illick, "Childrearing in Seventeenth-Century England and America," 316, 349 n. 123.

18   John Norris, *Spiritual Counsel, or, The Father's Advice to his Children* (London: S. Manship, 1694).

19   Hall, *Worlds of Wonder,* 230; Moran and Vinovskis, *Religion, Family, and Life Course,* 5, 225; Stannard, *Puritan Way of Death,* 66; Larzer Ziff, *Puritanism in America* (New York: Viking Press, 1973), 278; Lombard, *Making Manhood,* 23.

20   Rose Ann Lockwood, "Birth, Illness, and Death in 18th Century New England," *Journal of Social History* 12 (1978), 118, 119; Charles R. King, *Children's Health in America* (New York: Twayne, 1993) 9–11; Gordon E. Geddes, *Welcome Joy: Death in Puritan New England* (Ann Arbor: UMI Research Press, 1981), 48; Hall, *Worlds of Wonder*, 167.

21   Hall, *Worlds of Wonder*, 34, 35, 37, 47; Axtell, *School upon a Hill*, 12.

22   Fleming, *Children and Puritanism*, 60; Moran and Vinovskis, *Religion, Family, and Life Course*, 152–153.

23   Moran and Vinovskis, *Religion, Family, and Life Course*, 151.

24   Glenn Wallach, *Obedient Sons: The Discourse of Youth and Generations in American Culture* (Amherst: University of Massachusetts Press, 1997) 17; Moran and Vinovskis, *Religion, Family, and Life Course*, 151.

Chapter 19

Cynthia J. Koepp

CURIOSITY, SCIENCE, AND EXPERIENTIAL LEARNING IN THE EIGHTEENTH CENTURY: READING THE *SPECTACLE DE LA NATURE*

I MAGINE A NINE-VOLUME set of small encyclopedias, intended as a compendium of general knowledge, where an amazing array of topics is presented not alphabetically, but in dialogues—between a count, countess, their young visitor, and an extremely knowledgeable local abbot. Imagine further that these little books are exquisitely illustrated with numerous plates by some of the foremost artists and engravers of Paris. Note as well the author's expressed commitment to innovative pedagogy and his desire to captivate and hold his readers' attention by beginning with the most fascinating information he could find (on strange animals, say, or odd geological formations), and then leading them to more serious and abstract kinds of knowledge such as algebra, physics, and law. When I first came across the Abbe Pluche's *Spectacle de la nature* (1732–1751),[1] I sensed that I had found a wonderfully rich set of texts with much to say about life, learning, and attitudes in the eighteenth century. It reminded me of Rousseau's *Émile* and Diderot's great *Encyclopédie*–books that would appear only two decades later.[2] Yet, when I searched for the relevant scholarship, I discovered that most twentieth-century historians typically dismissed Pluche in one sentence: as a mediocre popularizer of science, as a reductionist blinded by his own teleological faith in Divine Providence, as an apologist for the nobility, or as a purveyor or mere "picture books" for children. In any case, scholars early on had determined that Pluche was not an author who deserved serious attention.

Further research confirmed my instincts that he was worth at least another look.[3] For one thing, Pluche's *Spectacle de la nature* was a phenomenal best-seller throughout Europe. In his classic article on the contents of Parisian private libraries (1750–1780), Daniel Mornet found that the *Spectacle de la nature* was the fourth most common book on the shelves.[4] Before 1800 it had already appeared in at least fifty-seven editions in French, twenty-two editions in English, and numerous other versions in Dutch, German, Italian, and Spanish. In 1770 when the famous publishing house at Neuchâtel (that Robert Darnton has studied so thoroughly) needed a quick bit of cash, a book dealer wrote them saying, "Hey, do a pirated version of Pluche—that's one of the surest ways to make money."[5] This is not an insignificant comment, considering that by 1770 the text was already forty years old and existed in dozens of editions. Even if Pluche were a second-rate thinker (and I don't think he was), one might make the case that if we want to know about popular reading habits, the transmission of knowledge and ideas, and the place of the child in the eighteenth century, the *Spectacle de la nature* would be a good place to start. . . .

Curiosity as the key

In the preface to volume one, Pluche spells out in great detail his philosophy of education and simultaneously offers an implicit critique of the status quo: bad pedagogy, boring lessons, too many abstractions, harsh punishments, little fun, and a failure to recognize the unique-ness of each child. He saw all these tendencies as stultifying and counterproductive to the processes of learning. Pluche is not a pioneer in this respect, because Erasmus, Montaigne, John Locke, and Pluche's own mentor Claude Rollin—to mention only a few—had already argued for more interesting and engaging tutors, more useful and practical lessons, more child-friendly teaching strategies, and a gentler hand of discipline. In the *Spectacle de la nature*, however, Pluche brings the many strands of these progressive theories together, articulates them clearly for the lay reader, and then demonstrates how they could work in practice. . . . Like Locke, Pluche hopes that through his method children will develop or "contract" good habits early on that will enable them to become educated, productive, and moral adults.

Nature as the best book

Since, for Pluche, "nature is the best and most complete book," he will first pique his readers' curiosity by going outdoors, in the seemingly familiar world of the backyard garden (1:v). And thanks to new scientific knowledge and inventions—such as the microscope—he can show his readers the amazing characteristics and properties of things when they are observed close at hand. By exposing them to the surprises in nature, Pluche is convinced that young people will be "hooked," their desire to know will be awakened, and real learning will become possible. By beginning with the garden, Pluche also reveals another of his cardinal rules, taken directly from Francis Bacon: never to commence with general axioms and universal ideas, but always to start instead with the particular, concrete, and immediate, "to imitate the order of nature herself, and begin with the first objects that we perceive around us and which are always there" (1:viii). . . .

Evidence suggests that readers were captivated by what they found in his books. Charles Bonnet, the great French entomologist, credited Pluche for initiating his fascination with insects. At age sixteen, he read Pluche's riveting description of the "lion pismer" in battle with an ant, and felt an entirely new sensation: "I did not read the book, I devoured it. It felt as if [the Abbé Pluche] had awakened in me a new sense or new faculties; and I would have willingly said that I was only beginning to live."[6] Louis-François Jauffret (known primarily for his interest in the wild boy of Aveyron) first encountered the *Spectacle de la nature* at age fifteen and seems to have experienced a similar epiphany. Early on, he took Pluche's goals and pedagogy to heart, imitated his tone and style, and by age twenty-five found success publishing children's books of his own.[7]

Many others were clearly seduced as well. For example, the English newspaper, *The Bee, or Universal Weekly*, published excerpts from the *Spectacle de la nature* before the English translations appeared in book form, with notes from the editors claiming that readers wanted more of these "remarkable and entertaining conversations."[8] Some readers vehemently defended the *Spectacle de la nature* by writing letters to journals and newspapers to complain about those critics who had given Pluche unfavorable reviews.[9] Both Pluche's contemporaries and later scholars credited this book with sparking the immense interest in natural history that lasted throughout the eighteenth century. He helped create a public receptive to the works of Buffon and Réaumur, as well as for Diderot's great *Encyclopédie*.[10] . . .

Mothers and young children

In volume six, Pluche addresses the issue of pedagogy and parenting more directly in over 150 pages of advice to mothers and fathers about their involvement in bringing up their children. Here Pluche reasserts the key ideas that childhood has stages and that each child is unique. He stresses the importance of knowing the right moment to introduce certain kinds of knowledge, that the capacity to learn must be encouraged gently in ways appropriate to the individual child's personality, temperament, and interests. In the discourse entitled "The Exercises of Children," he looks closely at the crucial role the mother can play in the early years of development.

Curiosity is again the operative term. He recommends that the mother be very attentive to her children from their earliest moments. She should introduce only activities and information that "would naturally engage their attention." Never pushing too hard, she should instead "regulate the amount of instruction she gives her children by their actual capacity." She should "silently observe the different dispositions of her children in the smallest matters" (by watching them when they are not paying attention to her), so that she might better determine what strategies and games might prove most effective for each (6:61–62).

Drawing a profile of the ideal mother/teacher, Pluche advises: "Instead of frequently repeating tiresome lectures which do but glance upon the mind, or having recourse to threats, which never succeed, our tender mother successively contrives a thousand new and pleasing methods to influence her children." She must find congenial and effective approaches because while her children are young, she is responsible for teaching them morality and "strengthening their weak reason." The solicitous mother should be creative and imaginative, ready to offer "explanations of everything that arises; little surprises, novelties, lots of interesting illustrations; appropriate music; or walks chosen on purpose to introduce new questions"—activities like that walk along the beach. In short, according to Pluche, the mother should create an environment where everything is employed to encourage her children's curiosity and to fill up the "vacuities of their intelligence which only wants more ideas" (6:62–63). And of course, thanks to the wealth of useful and fascinating information these eight volumes contained, adults actually could find answers to many of the questions that those inquiring young minds would be sure to raise once their curiosity was engaged and they began to look more closely at the world around them: Why does the moon wax and wane? Why do bees live in hives? How could one measure the circumference of the earth without leaving home? How does one spin flax into cloth? How does a telescope work? Readers could easily retrieve the answers woven through those leisurely conversations by consulting the indexes in every volume.

Fathers and daughters

In the next section, we find another testimonial, so to speak, entitled "Letter from a Father of a Family, on the First Culture of the Mind." Again Pluche steps back, this time turning over the podium to a fictional father who claims to have had some success in raising his own sons and daughters. This father begins by drawing a damning picture of the education a girl typically received, showing it to be frivolous and harmful with its emphasis on the art of pleasing, etiquette, and mindless pastimes. He notes that many parents of a daughter think she is a tender creature and mistakenly "avoid filling her head with anything that requires the least application or constraint." Girls who endure this type of education, he argues, will end up shallow, void of ideas, lacking discernment except in matters of pleasure and dress, and conversant only in the most superficial aspects of life (6:76–77).

Because he believes that daughters also deserve the chance to develop their reason and acquire a share of useful knowledge, he advocates another approach consistent with Pluche's principles in its avoidance of traditional methods and harsh discipline:

> If you begin by loading young minds with morals, maxims, rules, and what is worse, abstractions and disputes, they will only feel the weight of the words and will be always wishing for the end of an exercise that pains them (6:83).

Here (and many other places throughout the volumes), the father insists that one must avoid overwhelming the child. Strict rules of grammar are especially suspect and he instead embraces a sort of "whole language method," when he proposes a number of alternative activities that might appeal to a girl's imagination. His ultimate goal is to help children find their own voices in natural, conversational prose. For example, he talks about various ways a father might help teach a daughter of ten or eleven years to write—first by encouraging her to pen imaginary letters to cousins, merchants, or even a great prince. . . .

Liberty and learning

Near the end of this letter, the fictional father expresses his distress about how wrongheaded teaching methods for very young boys frequently destroy their love of the classics and literature forever: "The mistakes committed [at the rudimentary level] are of such a nature that our most ingenious professors and our best books are often so many treasures lost, even to those of our children most able to benefit from them." Frustration with the typical ineffectiveness (and worse) of early language instruction leads him to reflect on the "pleasures of childhood." Here he offers a more philosophical discussion about the nature of children, in hopes that these insights might serve as the foundation for new approaches to teaching. He asserts that young children are most passionate about two things: amusing objects they can see and physical play. Hence, he argues, effective instruction should incorporate sights to attract the eye and opportunities to move about.

Accompanying these recommendations, however, is a more important and fundamental message: to learn, children need liberty because their feelings of pleasure are based partly on the perception of having the freedom to follow their curiosity, freedom to move their bodies, and freedom to play at will. Thus, when designing amusing play to facilitate learning, he advises adults to conceal their aims, while neither confining nor subjecting the children to regular classroom discipline: "When children are to be diverted in this way, they must perceive nothing but their own pleasure and liberty" (6:141). Following his own advice, he suggests using lots of pictures and engravings to delight the eye. To give them that sense of freedom of movement, he suggests particular kinds of toys, especially those with many moving parts or many pieces designed to be assembled in different ways. What children need are

> objects that belong to them, and instruments which they may dispose of as their own property. Give them an old-fashioned clock, a small timber-framed house put together with removable pegs, a jack, a small crane, rammers, and all the engines for driving piles into the ground to be taken apart, with each piece numbered in order to put the whole thing together again . . . add a box of blocks shaped like bricks as well. Soon you will see them practicing masonry of all kinds, and raising complete edifices. You will see industry and prudence shining through every operation (6:141–142).

Here Pluche reveals his great trust in children's ability to learn through the initiation of free play—entertaining themselves with toys like these will help them gain practical and useful knowledge, prudence, industry, and judgment. And note too that these toys would also introduce basic skills necessary for carpentry or masonry, artisanal work that Pluche prefers to trifling diversions or metaphysical speculations.

Hands-on science

Thus far, I have tried to stress the ways that the *Spectacle de la nature* explains and justifies its pedagogy's fundamental principles, while simultaneously demonstrating how it can be implemented in the classroom with carefully designed diversions to enhance many aspects of teaching. The sections on science and crafts offer Pluche's readers yet another kind of activity intended to engage children's curiosity, those we now characterize as opportunities for hands-on learning.

Like Mr. Wizard of 1950s television, the Abbé is very good at describing how to carry out experiments that demonstrate various scientific principles that on the printed page may be rather more difficult to grasp. In volume one, for example, he described an experiment that requires a trip to the butcher. In order to disprove the concept of spontaneous generation, Pluche recommends comparing the outcomes of two pieces of fresh raw meat allowed to go rotten in different circumstances. His plan: place one piece of meat in a jar with a lid tightly closed and the other in an open pan, and see which generates maggots (1:26–27). In a section on rivers and oceans, he suggests making various tests on pans of water under different conditions to demonstrate the processes of evaporation (3:137–138). In the entry on microscopes, Pluche offers extensive comparisons of different types, and then describes how to put together the simplest makeshift microscope at home:

> You may procure a microscope by piercing a very small piece of lead with a pin, and by filling the aperture with a very little drop of water, that you put over the orifice with the beak of a clean pen. If that drop remains round like a bubble over the pinhole, it becomes a lens . . . that will prodigiously magnify any small object you shall present to it. And the loss of that excellent microscope may be repaired at a very small expense, by one that is equivalent, or perhaps superior to it in goodness (4:316).

On the next page, in case a reader needs ideas or encouragement, he describes all kinds of things one could look at under a microscope: the scales of various fish, types of wood pulp, fibers, a variety of plants and seeds, pollen, bird feathers, and the flesh of animals (4:317). . . .

Experiential learning and work

Throughout the *Spectacle de la nature*, then, Pluche offers his readers a wealth of entertaining activities that describe new pedagogies and incorporate those teaching methods as they explain the workings of nature. However, Pluche's emphasis on experiential "hands-on" learning is symptomatic of a much larger project that carries with it a social critique. . . .

Thus, from the very first pages of volume one, the Abbé Pluche vigorously challenges the attitudes underlying the traditional social hierarchy where mechanical labor stands at the bottom, by showing that acquiring an understanding of manufacturing processes can be quite compelling. Dialogue Three, for example, lays out the life cycle of silkworms, but also includes the countess's descriptions of how to raise silk worms (another activity one could do at home) with more details on silk weaving to come in volume seven. In the dialogue discussing the apple tree's particular characteristics, conversation eventually touches upon the maintenance of orchards, and offers plates of the cider mill and wine press, the text's first technical illustrations (2:365, 385).[11] In Dialogue Four, a scientific exposition on the spider takes an unexpected turn when it describes how the student and the prior visit a local weaver, learn all the parts of the loom, and try their hands at the machine (both student and prior break many threads in their efforts to understand the process of weaving). The young man responds to this "hands-on experience" at the weaver's with the comment: "Nothing ever amused me better, and I am very desirous of seeing all of the implements of each Artisan one after another. I cannot understand why they should be concealed from us" (1:90). Here Pluche's student voices a protest against the traditional attitudes that keep him aloof from the artisan and discourage upper-class men from witnessing his skills and techniques firsthand. Eventually, the prior will take his charge (and Pluche's readers) to workshop after workshop in Paris, "not in a superficial manner, but by making it his serious endeavor to get a competent idea of the real object and most valuable methods of each particular trade" (1:90). As Pluche will admonish his readers, the only way to understand the craft well is to visit the workshop, talk to the artisan, and try to practice the craft under helpful eyes of skilled practitioners. Parents could initiate similar visits to workshops themselves.

While the Abbé blames noble prejudice for disdainful attitudes toward mechanical skills, he also faults traditional education, with its emphasis on abstract speculation. Pluche deplores that students

> never hear one word of the perfection and usefulness of the arts, or the industry of people whose work supports our lives. . . . Everyone of us has seen the sails of a windmill and the wheel of a watermill in action. . . . But we know nothing of the structure of them, and can hardly avoid confusing a carpenter with a wood cutter. We all carry watches in our pockets. But do we understand the mechanism? . . . It is the same with most common trades: We know the names of them, and no more (1:91).

. . . . It is only the search for applied knowledge through an experimental process of trial and error, Pluche contends, that will lead to necessary new knowledge which in turn will allow men to make discoveries in the sciences and in the arts and crafts beneficial to society as a whole. He frequently points to the serious consequences of the harmful divides between theory and practice, the high and the low. For example, to improve agriculture, he writes, we really need serious study of soils, "but our great naturalists are not willing to get down on their knees and crawl on the earth" (1:279). Elsewhere he complains that "There's not yet a decent book on animal husbandry in French, because none of our bright minds will deign to study in the barnyard" (6:280).[12] In these discourses Pluche emerges not as a traditional apologist but an enlightenment reformer, determined to highlight the many ways that the prejudices against manual or mechanical work cost society. He fears that without cooperation between philosophy and the crafts, between theory and practice, between the learned and workers, much valuable knowledge will be lost or left undiscovered. . . .

Dialogues and debates

In my attempt to rehabilitate Pluche, I also want to argue that his pedagogy, especially his extensive footnotes and use of dialogue, makes the *Spectacle de la nature* a much less dogmatic or teleologically blind work than its critics have suggested—indeed, I would say that its very format alone could encourage reason and reflection. In the *Spectacle*'s later volumes, we can find debates over whether a mother should breast feed or not, competing arguments about the causes of poverty, beggary, and unemployment, or diverse opinions about the mechanics of Newton and Descartes. Pluche is very careful to present every argument faithfully—even those with which he disagrees. Moreover, one could always go back to his original sources and compare, because he provides exact citations. We always know what his sources were and hence can determine for ourselves how often he got it right.

Openness and developing a reliance on one's own reason, however, seem even more served by the dialogic format itself.[13] Whatever his intent, Pluche's dialogues give time to competing voices: to opinions that occasionally challenge and undercut each other. At certain moments, the dialogues bring to the surface many of the deep tensions in the society; they have the capacity to make the reader (at least some readers at some moments) acutely aware of social realities and inequities.

In a discussion of ornamental gardens, for example, we see the young chevalier asking the hard questions when he is embarrassed by taking his leisure in front of the hard-working peasants (2:266). At another point, he wonders why hunting is solely a right of the nobility (2:470). And what looks to be an innocuous discussion of sugar cane and sugar production soon leads to conversations about the plantation and slavery. Our young student ends that dialogue with the following words: "I think the Europeans involved in transporting the poor slaves to the Caribbean are as guilty as the plantation owners" (1:395). This statement from 1732 is decades before any serious abolition movement. I know at least one young reader in the eighteenth century, a fifteen-year-old from Louvain, who noticed that line because he copied it into his notebook.[14]

Finally, I would like to briefly mention gender. As we saw earlier, in volume six, the section on education for girls urged some improvements, such as adding history and geography to the standard curriculum or encouraging them to write in order to develop the imagination and strengthen her reason. However, the dialogues themselves in the *Spectacle de la nature* implicitly underscore an even stronger message: they show us an active and knowledgeable woman participating in the conversations, a countess who can hold forth on many topics. Interestingly, at one moment during a discussion about the attributes of various birds, she actually changes the topic, lamenting her lack of a formal education and expressing her sadness about never having received the same opportunities as her brother, husband, and sons (1:299–302). Whether readers noticed these little eruptions I am still trying to sort out.

A forgotten and influential best-seller

I would argue that the publishing success alone indicates that the *Spectacle de la nature* clearly touched a nerve, filled a need—and I think it had a great deal to do with new thinking about children and their education that coincided with a burgeoning excitement about discoveries in natural history. New knowledge about bees, wasps, spiders, and silkworms, about science, technology, and the crafts would be presented in ways that would help make a child receptive to looking at work, the social order, and the acquisition of knowledge in a different light—with the help of their parents, tutors, and the Abbé Pluche. The Abbé must have been offering many readers something they wanted or were at least willing to take the trouble to consider.

What is equally important, I think, is Pluche's confidence in the innate abilities of children. He believed that their curiosity could guide them without the threat of harsh discipline; be argued that they could learn to reason if given engaging activities, familiar tools, and the liberty to explore from the very beginning; he trusted their capacity to consider increasingly difficult matters as their abilities to reflect matured; and he hoped many could reevaluate the efficacy of a social system that favored noble leisure while denigrating the work of artisans, peasants, servants, and slaves that made that leisure possible. . . .

Notes

I am grateful to the Society for Eighteenth-Century Studies, the Lewis Walpole Library, the Friends of the Princeton Library, and the Bibliographical Society of America for providing funds for this research. I wish to thank Dennis Trinkle for his kindness in sharing with me the Pluche materials that he had collected. I also want to thank Michael Witmore and Andrea Immel for organizing the stimulating conference "Seen and Heard: The Place of the Child in Early Modern Europe," for editing this volume, and for their immense patience.

1   Noël-Antoinc Pluche, *Le Spectacle de la nature, ou Entretiens sur les particularités de l'histoire naturelle, qui ont paru les plus propres á rendre les Jeunes-Gens curieux, & à leur former l'esprit*, eight volumes in nine books (Paris: Les Frères Estienne, 1732–51). Henceforth all references to the *Spectacle* will appear in the text.

2   Recently I learned that Jean-Jacques Rousseau used Pluche's *Spectacle de la nature* when he was the tutor for Mably's nephews, which confirmed for me that there might be a relationship here. I hope eventually to write an essay exploring the sources of Rousseau's pedagogy, especially the possible role of the Abbé Pluche. For more on the connections between Pluche's text and Diderot's *Encyclopédie*, see below.

3   In a recent article, Dennis Trinkle points out there have been no books and almost no articles devoted to the Abbé Pluche published in either French or English, and argues that Pluche and the *Spectacle de la nature* definitely deserve further study. See Trinkle, "Noël-Antoine Pluche's *Spectacle de la nature*: an encyclopaedic best-seller," in *Studies on Voltaire and the Eighteenth Century* 358 (1997): 93–114. The only full length work is an unpublished thesis by Caroline V. Doane, "Un succès littéraire du XVIIIe siècle: *Le Spectacle de la nature* de l'abbé Pluche," (thèse dactylographiée, Paris: Sorbonne, 1957).

4   Daniel Mornet, "Les enseignements des bibliothèques privées (1750–80)," *Revue d'historie littéraire de la France* 17 (1910): 460–477.

5   Quoted in Robert Darnton, *Edition et sédition: L'univers de la littérature clandestine au xviiie siécle* (Paris: Gallimard, 1991), 52. My translation.

6   Charles Bonnet, *Mémoires autobiographiques*, ed. Raymond Savioz (Paris: J. Vrin, 1948), 46.

7   See Robert-Marie Reboul, *Louis-François Jauffret: Sa vie et ses oeuvres* (Paris, 1869), 23. Like Pluche, Jauffret wanted learning to be fun and wanted to celebrate the wonders of the natural world. So, just as the *Spectacle de la nature* begins with a promenade in the garden, Jauffret first conducted a series of actual promenades and staged festivals in the woods where children could celebrate the likes of Pluche and other famous writers in natural history. Then he published accounts of these events, as well as many other books and magazines. Later Jauffret also became an expert on deaf mute children.

As the founder of the *Société des observateurs de l'homme* (the first scholarly organization to practice anthropology), Jauffret became extremely interested in the scientific study of children, their socialization, and the connections between childhood and adult identity.

8   *The Bee, or Universal Weekly Pamphlet*, containing something to hit every man's taste and principles 6 (March-July, 1733): 247–250, 342, 1020.

9   See the *Mercure de France*, January 1733, 530, where a young writer offers an ardent defense of the *Spectacle de la nature*, refuting last month's review point by point. See also L'Abbé Desfontaines, *Observations sur les écrits modernes* 2 (Paris, 1736), 225–238.

10   See Frédéric Godefroy, *Histoire de la littérature française*, 2nd ed (Paris, 1877, 232). See also Jacques Proust, *Encyclopédie* (Paris: Armand Colin, 1965), 12–14.

11   Volumes five, six, and seven of the *Spectacle de la nature* are primarily devoted to the arts and crafts, with countless plates illustrating workshops and work techniques.

12   True to his goals, in another dialogue about which is the most useful animal, Pluche chooses the ass whom he compares to a peasant—a category he also sees as grossly undervalued and yet absolutely essential to society. See *Spectacle*, 1:352–356.

13   See Mikhail Bahktin, *Dostoevsky's Poetics* (Ann Arbor: Ardis, 1974), 3–37, for a discussion of the "side-glancing" polyphonic voices in dialogues that can challenge and undercut a dominant perspective.

14   Bibliothéque Nationale, Fonds Français, MS, 15326. Prince d'Elbeuf, "Analyse du *Spectacle de la nature* de M. Pluche."

Chapter 20

John Brewer

CHILDHOOD REVISITED: THE GENESIS
OF THE MODERN TOY

IT IS A COMMONPLACE that a culture can be understood by an examination of its artifacts. Yet the history of 'material culture', as opposed to a history of a society's finest works of sculpture, is still an embryonic science. Costume, the tools of a man's (or woman's) trade, household utensils, furnishings, playthings – all of these, especially those that did not belong to the elite or leaders of a society, have not received the attention devoted to 'high' culture. Yet many aspects of everyday life exhibit the beliefs and social experience of the bulk of a nation's people. Costume can tell us how the members of a society are ranked and ordered, how sexes are differentiated (if at all), and what qualities are least or most admired. Toys are equally revealing, for they almost always contain statements made by adults (often though not invariably parents) either about the culture in which they live and/ or the values that they think desirable. Toys mirror a culture – or at least, aspects of it; conversely, if we wish to understand the significance of an individual toy or game, we must set it within a broad context, looking at it in the light of prevailing attitudes towards work and play, the psychology of man, the nature of learning and the place of the child in both family and society. Toys are cultural messages – sometimes simple, occasionally complex and ambiguous, but invariably revealing.

Yet the idea of the 'educational toy' – indeed, even the concept of the toy as a plaything peculiar to children – is a relatively recent one. Before the eighteenth century there were virtually no toy manufacturers nor toyshops in Europe and America; equally, there were almost no books written or produced especially for children, who shared most games and recreations with adults. The world of the child was not precisely separated from the realm of the adult; no special sector or segment of the culture was devoted exclusively to children. Thus Dr. Johnson defined 'toy' in his famous *Dictionary* as 'a petty commodity; a trifle; a thing of no value; a plaything or bauble'. There was absolutely no mention of children. The term 'toy' meant any small inexpensive object or trinket sold to young and old alike. The travelling pedlar or chapman, the town's 'toyman', offered cheap jewellery, buckles, bangles and hairpins; his wares were those of the modern Woolworth's. Even 'dolls' were not intended for children but were in fact miniature mannequins clothed to display the latest fashion, fad or frippery. There were therefore almost no toys in the modern sense. This did not, of course, mean that children had no playthings; it simply meant that they had to fall back on the things that they shared with their elders. They improvised and invented toys and games. Domestic utensils, the resources of field and forest, the debris of the urban environment: all of these contributed towards imaginative and open-ended play.

How do we explain this almost total absence of toys in the sixteenth and seventeenth-century English and colonial American household? Historians have advanced several explanations, nearly all of which attribute the lack of toys to parental attitudes towards children and social attitudes towards play. Judged by modern standards, it is argued, parents treated their children either with an indifference that verged on callousness or were actively brutal towards them, beating them with monotonous frequency. The world of the Anglo-American child before the modern era is therefore often portrayed as cruel, cold, unemotional and lacking in the sort of family affection that might encourage play. These attitudes are usually explained as a reaction to the horrifying rates of infant and child mortality which militated against a close parent-child bond, and by the prevailing contemporary view that when children came into the world they were, like all human creatures, tainted with original sin against which a constant and brutal war had to be waged.

Those historians who look on the history of childhood as the gradual emancipation of the child from this callous and cruel régime have used several types of evidence to demonstrate the harshness of seventeenth-century childhood. English infants, they point out, were swaddled, bound so tightly that they could not move their legs and arms. This does not, however, seem to have been the practice in the thirteen colonies of America where babes wore loose-fitting garments. Nevertheless in both cultures parental breast-feeding was far from universal, and the infant was often packed off to a wet-nurse, where quite commonly neglect and ill-treatment resulted in the child's death. From the age of two corporal punishment seems to have been the staple of the child's educational diet. School-masters ('my system is to whip, and to have done with it') as well as parents and tutors rarely spared the rod to spoil the child. Punishment, corporal or otherwise, was generally severe: one unfortunate colonial child who wet his bed was forced 'to drink a pint of piss'. The time between infancy and gainful employment was mercilessly brief: service, apprenticeship or labour in the family began as early as seven, and all children were put to work before they were twelve or thirteen. Children died in such numbers that they left very little trace of their lives behind them. Even in the communities on the colonial frontier, where infant mortality rates were lower than in the coastal towns or back in Europe, the death of a child – your child – was a frequent occurrence.

This picture of the heartless and cruel world inhabited by children needs some qualification. Nearly all of the evidence that appears to demonstrate parental indifference towards the child in fact shows simply that his *individuality* was not strongly recognised. We tend to assume that parental affection cannot flourish unless children are regarded as individuals. But this is essentially a modern (and Western) assumption that in part stems from our elevation of the bond between the parent (or, at least, the mother) and the individual child above almost all other forms of attachment. The chief affective bonds of the pre-modern American and English parent were probably to the family as a whole rather than to its individual members; this does not mean that they never showed affection to their children, only that they cared for them as a 'brood'.

Other evidence of lack of affection is either ambiguous or can be matched by examples of affection. The pervasive presence of infant and child mortality undoubtedly helped generate psychological mechanisms for parents to cope with and distance themselves from the inescapability of deaths within the family. But many of the statements made by the bereaved parents speak more of an attempt to flee from and suppress grief than of a genuine indifference. Moreover parental attitudes towards children began to change even though a dreadfully high rate of infant mortality persisted. There is therefore some reason to doubt that its effect on parent–child relations was quite as strong as some historians have suggested.

But what are we to make of the frequent beatings and floggings of young colonial children? Some of the parents who appear to have been the most brutal certainly thought of themselves as being cruel in order to be kind. Brought up as (usually Calvinist) Protestants, their fierce religiosity required them to curb their children. Since the human (and therefore children's) proclivity for wickedness, sloth and indolence was known to be extraordinarily strong, and because sin constantly threatened to engulf a child, the caring, attentive and loving parent was obliged – almost compelled – to impose a harsh, punitive régime of the strictest discipline to keep children on the straight and narrow. The terrors of corporal punishment were necessary to produce a good citizen and Godly person who was industrious and virtuous. Paradoxically, therefore, and because nearly all parents assumed that the only way to socialise and educate their children was by overpowering and overcoming their inherent propensity for sin and sloth, the harshest parents were often the most caring. It is a tribute to many parents' remarkable sense of religious duty that they persisted in being cruel to be kind, despite the considerable psychological toll – the extraordinary domestic tension – which emanated from the conflict between parental desire and parental obligation.

This is not to condone the systematic physical punishment of children, nor is it to deny that in the sixteenth and seventeenth centuries children, as weak and subordinate members of society, were sometimes the victims of capricious and senseless violence, but it is to emphasise that this 'no toy' culture was radically different from our own, and cannot be understood by the application of modern social and moral standards.

The play of both adults and children in the seventeenth-century American colonies was almost never regarded as being instructive, purposeful or educationally useful. Rather it was condemned by puritans and zealots as a sinful and idle pursuit, or justified as a catharsis – a periodic and exuberant release from the rigours of work that refreshed body and soul. Most communities had a calendar of recreations tied to important local events, the seasonal rhythms of work or, in western Europe, to saints' days. In colonial Williamsburg, for example, recreations were concentrated in April and in autumn, when the town was crowded because the courts and assemblies were sitting. Such occasions verged on the Brueghelesque. They were often boisterous and sometimes violent – cockfighting and wrestling (which, with its eye-gouging, horrified English visitors to the colonies) accompanied cudgelling and boxing. The audiences for these 'rude' recreations were often as violent as the sports themselves. The pattern of these celebrations varied from colony to colony in format and degree of restraint, but most of them, if their critics are to be believed, involved gargantuan feasting, prodigious drinking and sexual licence. Instructive play was almost entirely absent; games of chance – dice and cards – and gambling (in the South particularly on horse-racing) were extremely popular. Nevertheless such recreations did serve important functions: old and young, rich and poor were all expected to participate in events that gave symbolic expression to the ideal of community and solidarity. The customary distinctions of age, wealth and power were briefly swept aside in the maelstrom of egalitarian celebration. As one fastidious observer of a Virginia cockfight disapprovingly observed, the cockpit was 'surrounded by many genteel people, promiscuously mingled with the vulgar and debased'. Children were also present. It was thought neither necessary nor desirable to distinguish 'child's play' from the recreations of others.

Play occurred publicly, often out-of-doors and usually with other members of the community. It was therefore not especially associated with the domestic environment, except in the most prosperous households. Rather the household was associated with work: there was a 'family economy' to which all of its members, of every age, were expected to contribute. The family that worked together in the home also played together, but they did so not within the confines of the household but in the community at large.

The 'no toy' culture, which scarcely seems to have recognised the special state of childhood, was gradually but radically transformed between the late seventeenth and early nineteenth centuries. The most significant changes were the development of a new conception of man, and a parallel recognition of new processes of human learning. Man came to be seen as a malleable and manipulable creature who entered the world with a mind that was not primed with evil but was a *tabula rasa*, like a blank sheet of paper, on which appropriate sense impressions could imprint knowledge and learning. Man, in other words, was capable of moral improvement provided that he was nurtured in the right environment. This view was accompanied by the relatively novel theory of the human psyche that emphasised man's innate tendency to eschew pain and pursue pleasure. From this perspective the widespread use of brutal corporal punishment was clearly counter-productive: by associating learning and pain it was more likely to discourage an interest in learning than to teach or socialise. Such crude practices, it was argued, should be replaced by a much more subtle psychological manipulation of the child, one that used the propensity for play to make learning stimulating and pleasurable.

These educational theories are traditionally associated with the English philosopher, John Locke, whose *Some Thoughts concerning Education* (1693), which went through numerous editions in several languages and on both sides of the Atlantic, made him the Dr. Benjamin Spock of his age. Locke was not the first philosopher to realise that play could be used didactically, nor was his psychology unique but, as an intellectual of prodigious repute in both North America and Europe, he lent considerable weight to the 'environmentalist' theory of learning. Moreover the book was timely. Like childcare manuals such as Dr. William Cadogen's *Essay on the Nursing and Management of Children* and Dr. William Buchan's *Domestic Medicine* (twenty editions between 1769 and 1819), Locke's *Thoughts* was read chiefly by the affluent and middling classes of America and England who had the time, the leisure, the money and the social predisposition to lavish attention on their children.

We should not, of course, assume that these ideas swept all before them. Their acceptance varied from place to place and class to class. They were taken up predominantly by middle-class parents eager to 'improve' their children. But the old attitudes and practices continued: many children were still whipped and flogged, and imaginative learning rarely ousted the more traditional method of rote memorisation. Indeed, for many children the situation deteriorated at the end of the eighteenth century, when evangelicals on both sides of the Atlantic returned to the older view of infant depravity and renewed the practice of wholesale flogging.

Nevertheless Lockean theory marks the growing acceptance in North America of the idea that education was a matter of carrot rather than stick. It also heralds the genesis of the toy both as a plaything peculiar to children and as an educational device. Locke and his eighteenth-century followers were adamant that play was the key to successful learning: 'the chief Art is to make all that they have to do, Sport and Play too . . . Learning anything, they should be taught, might be made as much a Recreation as their Play, as their Play is to their learning'. Both play and playthings, which had previously been regarded either as an obstruction to learning or as matters of no didactic consequence, became crucial to the educational process. As Locke remarked about playthings (in sentiments remarkably similar to those of Froebel over 100 years later), 'nothing that may form adult's minds, is to be overlook'd and neglected, and whatsoever introduces Habits, and settles Customs in them, deserves the Care and Attention of their Governors, and is not a small thing in its Consequences'. Toys and games were recognised as being very important. Indeed Locke was responsible for popularising one of the earliest 'educational' toys, the so-called 'Locke blocks', whose role in teaching the alphabet he lovingly describes in his *Thoughts on Education*.

Locke's theories seem remarkably modern, and certainly they approximate much more closely to present-day views of learning than to the régime of flogging that he so vehemently opposed. Nevertheless his concept of play and of the role of toys and games was remarkably circumscribed. In his desire to establish a controlled environment for the child, he recommended education at home under a private tutor; schools and schoolboys, he believed, conveyed 'the contagion of Rudeness and Vice' which threatened a young man's 'Innocence and Vertue'. By seeking to locate education primarily in the home, Locke contributed towards the concern with domesticity that was such a marked feature of genteel and bourgeois life in the eighteenth and nineteenth centuries. The idea of the home as a sanctum, a haven in a heartless world, developed largely through the dissociation of the dwelling-place from the place of work, and because of the transformation of the middle-class woman from an important figure in the family economy to the mother and guardian of children kept in the home. Prosperity and the desire for gentility produced a growing leisured class of women whose chief tasks were to adorn themselves and their homes and to superintend the moral welfare of their progeny. For the middle classes of America 'work', which had once been associated both with the home and with the entire family, became a predominantly masculine activity conducted beyond the domestic horizon. Play, especially children's play, became restricted to the domestic environment in which parental (especially maternal) control could be most successfully exercised. On those occasions when bourgeois children went out to visit the circus, the theatre or some improving public exhibit, they went *en famille* to an occasion attended by other families. There was no question of children venturing forth, even in the cause of self-improvement, without a nurse or parent in tow.

This desire to control the play of children stemmed from notions of play itself. Neither Locke nor the aspiring middle-class parent thought of play as a means by which children could learn from *each other;* nor, though they saw play as a means of teaching individuals social and moral precepts, did they envisage play itself as a form of socialisation. Rather they regarded it as a tool of the tutor or parent, a *means* by which children could be educated. Play, therefore, was looked on as an individualistic endeavour, even when it involved other children, and as being didactic in a rather narrow sense.

Judged by these criteria a great many traditional forms of recreation were found wanting. It is not surprising, therefore, that the very classes which encouraged child's play and bought their children educational toys simultaneously attacked both the traditional conception of play and the recreations themselves. During the course of the eighteenth century rumbustious community events were increasingly criticised for their barbarity, their indiscriminate intermingling of classes and ages (now regarded as a reprehensible rather than desirable aspect of leisure), and their encouragement of depravity. Community festivals and popular 'rough' sports were either domesticated, controlled or actively suppressed. Thus Christmas was transformed into the family festival *par excellence*, admission to sports events was regulated by admission charges, and 'cruel' or 'rude' recreations were attacked by reform groups and through legislation. Games of chance were flatly condemned as 'incroaching Wasters of useful Time'. Play and recreation, both for adult and child, now either had to be 'profitable' and productive, a workhorse harnessed to the load of earning, or to be suppressed as a nuisance.

These attitudes and values were clearly expressed in the earliest toys and games for children. Marketed in North America in the last quarter of the eighteenth century, they were almost all remorselessly didactic: they taught skills, they moralised, they imparted knowledge. The old and well-loved games of chance – cards, dice and a board game known as the Game of Goose (the precursor of snakes and ladders) – were transformed into educational aids. Card packs, for instance, were designed to teach geography, history, spelling and astronomy; board games with such titles as 'The Cottage of Content; or, Right roads and Wrong ways', 'The New Game of Human Life' and 'Virtue rewarded and Vice punished' combined a quite extraordinary unctuousness with competitive play. Packets of puzzles and riddles, the Chinese tangram (a figure of seven pieces), the rebus, where images and pictures were substituted for words, and the jigsaw (invented in the 1760s by an Englishman named Spillsbury) all demanded calculation, patience, application, skill, ingenuity and a modicum of imagination. Such toys, together with a burgeoning children's literature, were advertised, bought and sold for their 'Lockean' qualities. Liza Lucas Pinckney asked a friend in England to help her young son by buying him 'the new toy, the description of which I enclose, to teach him according to Mr Locke's methods – which I have carefully studied – to play himself into learning'. The early toy manufacturers and entrepreneurs were fully aware of the marketability of this concept: their advertising emphasised 'improving toys' that inextricably combined 'entertainment, amusement and instruction'. Educational games, however tedious and demanding, were packaged in bright boxes and decorated in gay colours to catch the youthful eye.

In certain respects the lot of children – especially of the middle-class child whose parents could afford the new toys and games – seems to have improved. Parents were encouraged to take their children to the circus, pantomime and theatre, and to visit museums. There were brightly coloured and sensibly worded spelling, reading and elementary science books. Toyshops bulged not only with strictly didactic playthings, but with mechanical devices (of varying degrees of delicacy and complexity) for young boys, and with the inevitable dolls and dolls' houses, complete with fashionable furniture, for the female child whose future, as far as her parents were concerned, could be summarised in one word – motherhood. 'Role-model' toys, with their mimetic preparation for adult life, even toys intended simply to entertain were developed and marketed by the same manufacturers who had seen the commercial advantage of linking play and learning. By the early nineteenth century there was an international toy market, centred primarily on England and Germany which, for the first time, made widely available the sort of playthings that we take for granted today.

But the purveyors of such toys were selling much more than attractive objects; they were marketing a particular social morality – one that emphasised competitiveness, industry, probity and *individual* endeavour. Nearly all of the toys that countenanced interaction between children emphasised competitiveness to the exclusion of other types of social intercourse. And most of the games, with their emphasis on general progressive accumulation of either 'points' or an equivalent of money, could hardly have been more appropriately designed to teach delayed gratification. Several others stressed respectability, placing emphasis on 'appearances', 'making a good impression', as the key to success: 'Habit', as one game succinctly put it, 'makes the Man'. These toys and games – educational or otherwise – also helped children develop a sense of private property. Previously most children's playthings had not belonged to them; they had been everyday objects whose use was often shared with the rest of the family. Toys – objects given by parents or adults to children to play with – were for a child's exclusive use. He or she *owned* toys, whereas they had formerly *shared* playthings. In sum, play had been transformed from the imaginative and unstructured pursuit of the 'no toy' culture into a rigorous training in social duties and family obligations. The new toys and games, which left so little to the imagination, epitomised the bourgeois attributes necessary for commercial, industrial and social success in adult life. They were not only puzzles and problems but the concrete expression of a strict morality.

The birth of toys – and of the educational toy in particular – therefore marks an important moment in our cultural history. It commemorates the recognition that both social behaviour and scholarly learning are best assimilated by the judicious use of encouragement, praise, shame and blame, rather than by the indiscriminate use of the rod, and marks the point at which an individualistic, competitive ethic came to dominate the social thinking of the middle and upper classes of American society. This development, as I have tried to emphasise, was a mixed blessing. Certainly it did not, as some historians have assumed, constitute a 'liberation' for children; rather it involved the exchange of one set of parental and social controls for another – less brutal, no doubt, but more successful in bridling the child. Toys were the frosting on a cake that was designed to look delicious but which might well prove unpalatable.

The subsequent history of the educational toy after its period of gestation in the eighteenth and its birth in the early nineteenth century was marked by two developments: the escape of the toy out of the household and, via the kindergarten, into the school; and the progressive liberalisation of the concept of play. Both of these changes stemmed largely from the adoption in the second half of the nineteenth century of the educational ideas of the German, Friedrich Froebel. Like many of his predecessors Froebel saw play and the creation of an appropriate environment as the keys to learning. His approach, however, was more 'permissive' than almost all of his precursors: parents and teachers were not to determine or interfere with children's play, but gently to guide the child on a voyage of self-discovery which would simultaneously reveal the richness of his environment. Imagination, exploration, self-development, all of these were emphasised as never before: child-centred education became acceptable. And Froebel and his followers, most notably Elizabeth Peabody, created a new controlled environment, neither home nor school, in the form of the kindergarten where children could learn by playing with Froebel's specially designed (and highly abstract) toys – the sphere, the cube and coloured rods. These simple playthings, almost devoid of a local cultural context, were the symbols of a highly integrated system of learning that saw self-development, socialisation and the exploration of the environment as complementary facets of the growth of human knowledge.

It is difficult to overestimate the influence of Froebel. His ideas were assimilated in the United States and Britain and even became institutionalised parts of the school system. His methods and his toys were used to teach both rich and poor; and it is very largely as a result of his followers that almost every modern daycare centre, nursery-school, kindergarten and primary school has its building blocks and modular toys. Certainly by the late nineteenth century the conception of play and of its role in education was altogether more flexible than it had been at the end of the eighteenth century, and was more readily accepted as a didactic tool outside the home. Today the belief that children can 'play themselves into learning' is tantamount to an unquestioned orthodoxy.

The history of the educational toy (as of toys in general) can therefore be seen as going through three stages: the first, to which most of my discussion has been devoted, saw the gradual emergence in the eighteenth century of the toy as we know it today; the second phase, between c. 1760 and 1840, witnessed the widespread marketing of such playthings, and was also characterised by a rather narrow definition of both play and learning. The final phase, which began in the mid-nineteenth century, has seen the gradual liberalisation of play and an enormous diversification of playthings.

A society with many different (sometimes conflicting) values will produce many different kinds of toys. But when we look at the modern Cindy-doll[1], at the spin-off playthings from the successful cinema or television series, we should ask ourselves exactly the same questions that we ask of the earliest toys: What does this aspect of our material culture tell us about our society? What values do the toys seek to sustain? What do they reveal of the world of parents and children, and of the world of work and play? If we can go some way towards answering these questions we may well learn not only about 'child's play' but also uncover many of our own assumptions which are at once a part of our modern culture and a comment upon it.

Note

1   A doll that can be dressed up, known in America as a barbie-doll.

PART VIII

Individualism

Introduction

'INDIVIDUALISM' AS A WAY of relating to others has been associated with independent thinking, self-reliance, a desire for autonomy and a willingness to challenge authority. Individualism as a shared set of values has been linked with egalitarianism (Béteille 1986), rights-based morality and regard for human dignity and privacy. Has there been any underlying semantic unity in the way cultural historians have used the word 'individualism'? How consistent have they been in applying criteria for its presence or absence in a particular historical milieu? What connections have they believed to exist between individualism in face-to-face relationships and individualism as an ethos or a value-system?

Writing about the theme of individualism in cultural history poses a semantic challenge: the concept is ill-defined. It is a 'convenient but insecure concept on which to base an analysis' (Verderber 2013). Ever since the word was coined in the early nineteenth century it has been a focus of contention. The term was used by de Tocqueville (1840) in a widely read analysis of social and political relationships in the United States. Burckhardt in his study of the Italian Renaissance (1860, trans. 1878) used it 'as a blanket term to cover a wide variety of phenomena which his synthetic mind moulded into an apparently homogeneous whole' (Nelson 1933). However, in later life Burckhardt came to doubt its value (Burke 1995). But imprecise though it may be, the word 'individualism' has been used as a way of pointing to a cluster of important ideas. The vagueness has derived partly from a lack of agreement about how the elements in that cluster fit together, and about which should be considered central. As Lukes (1973) points out, its meaning varies with context. For instance, in religion it has implied rejection of intermediaries between the believer and God (Dülmen 1999), whereas in economics it has postulated self-interested motivation in those taking part in market transactions (Myers 1983; Persky 1995). French writers place more emphasis on rights, and German authors on creativity. Rather than attempting a single definition, we here consider issues of chronology: which periods have authors considered crucial for the history of individualism in its diverse forms?

Writing in an ironic style, Porter (1997) presents 'the authorized version', as he calls it – a 'narrative purporting to trace the rise over time of true individuality'. It is a story of progress, listing a succession of milestones in the liberation of humanity from tutelage to mere custom and conformity and the achievement of ever greater authenticity. Porter's sceptical introduction to an edited volume on the history of the self serves to distance him and his contributors from this presentist approach. Instead each innovation is seen as a separate episode rather than as one more step in the march towards a predestined outcome.

Burckhardt's claim that individualism in the sense of self-confidence first appeared in the Italian Renaissance was rejected by medievalists such as Hanning (1977), Morris (1972) and Ullmann (1966), who argued for a 'discovery of the individual' in the twelfth century. (For assessments of this issue, see Bagge 1993, Bynum 1980, Clanchy 2003 and Gurevich 1995.) Yet a change in Romanesque sculpture from stylised faces to the portrayal of distinctive features (Duby 1988) is historically noteworthy, regardless of whether it is construed as a specifically twelfth-century artistic innovation or as an anticipation of Renaissance individualism.

The preaching of salvation by personal faith was seen by a nineteenth-century Reformed church historian like d'Aubigné (1843) as a watershed between an oppressive collectivist medieval Catholic epoch and the freedom brought by Calvin's Protestant theological revolution. That kind of interpretation is called in question by Ocker (2012) and Marshall (2009). Change there certainly was in the sixteenth century, but continuity too. Significant, but diverse, changes in later periods include the proliferation of spiritual journal-writing (Booy 2007; Cambers 2007; Jacob and Kadane 2003; Webster 2006), the rise of the novel and autobiography as a means of exploring the emotions (McKeon 1987; Mullan 1997; Spacks 1976) and the Romantic emphasis on aesthetic experience (Cardinal 1997; Steinberg 2006). Clearly these were not coordinated rungs on a single ladder whereby Westerners climbed to higher levels of self-awareness.

Such examples illustrate people's subjective ways of experiencing personal identity – or of representing such experience. But 'individualism' also touches on social morality and on individual pursuit of economic and political advantage. For instance, in the early eighteenth century Mandeville's *Fable of the Bees* proposed that a community thrives when each member acts out of pure self-interest: 'private vices, publick benefits' (Hundert 1994, 1997; Mandeville 1997). Though contemporaries found the idea shocking, it became influential. A century later de Maistre (quoted in Lukes 1971) responded that the French Revolution had been the deplorable outcome of 'political protestantism carried to the most absolute individualism' – the first recorded use of this ambiguous word. This was a rhetorical flourish by a proponent of papal theocracy. Yet how much sense does it make to lump together in one word Reformation theology and the atomistic theory of human relationships here being denounced?

'Individualism', then, has meant different things to different historians, but there is no need to abandon the concept altogether. The 'family likeness' model of how words acquire multiple meanings enables us to distinguish between different (but related) types of individualism. Muldrew (2000) calls in question any radical contrast between cultural patterns based on community and those where the interests of individuals have priority. Instead, Muldrew distinguishes two forms of community. That which prevailed in medieval and early modern Britain he calls 'negotiated' community, as opposed to the 'architectural', formally structured types of relationship that took shape with increasing urbanisation and commercialisation in the eighteenth and nineteenth centuries. Distinguishing liberal, market-oriented individualism from other types means the term can be applied in a wider range of contexts than allowed in Porter's caricature of an 'authorised version'. There can be a gendered approach to the concept (Brown 1992; Smith and Watson 1998), and a specifically Japanese type of individualism (Ikegami 1995).

If Burckhardt's Renaissance individualist turns out to be a mythological character, as Martin argues in our first reading, there is scope for a nuanced appreciation of different ways in which people in this period could conceive of who they were. The first is a communally oriented or 'civic' self, as against the second, a more reflective self with an awareness of playing a variety of roles – what Martin calls a 'performative' self. Nor do these exhaust the possibilities.

In the second reading, Mascuch analyses the significance of spiritual notebooks (he is reluctant to call them diaries) kept by a few pious individuals in seventeenth-century England. He also traces the ways in which the motives for this kind of self-scrutiny altered in the course of that period. The extract illustrates the value, and potential pitfalls, of Presser's concept of 'ego-documents' (Greyerz 2010).

Our third reading tells how *Self-Help*, a book from Victorian Britain extolling self-reliance, became an instant best-seller in Japan just after the Meiji Restoration of 1868 which marked the start of that country's rapid industrialisation. Kinmonth's study of the author Smiles and the translator Nakamura reveals the inadequacy of the stereotype (discussed in Rosenberger 1992) depicting Japanese culture as inherently collectivist by contrast with the 'Western sense of self' and the sturdy variety of individualism advocated by Smiles. Whatever validity may be credited to such stereotypes on the basis of psychological research (e.g. Nisbett 2005), this reading shows that the message of *Self-Help* spoke equally to the Victorians and contemporary samurai.

References

Bagge, S. (1993) 'The autobiography of Abelard and medieval individualism', *Journal of Medieval History,* 19: 327–50.

Béteille, A. (1986) 'Individualism and equality', *Current Anthropology*, 27: 121–34.

Booy, D. (ed.) (2007) *The Notebooks of Nehemiah Wallington, 1618–1654: a selection*, Farnham: Ashgate.

Brown, G. (1992) *Domestic Individualism: imagining self in nineteenth-century America*, Berkeley, CA: University of California Press.

Burckhardt, J. (1878) *The Civilization of the Renaissance in Italy*, trans. S.G.C. Middlemore (1990), Harmondsworth: Penguin.

Burke, P. (1995) 'The Renaissance, individualism and the portrait', *History of European Ideas*, 21: 393–400.

Bynum, C.W. (1980) 'Did the twelfth century discover the individual?', *Journal of Ecclesiastical History,* 31: 1–17.

Cambers, A. (2007) 'Reading, the godly, and self-writing in England, circa 1580–1720', *Journal of British Studies*, 46: 796–825.

Cardinal, R. (1997) 'Romantic travel', in R. Porter (ed.) *Rewriting the Self: histories from the Renaissance to the present*, London: Routledge.

Clanchy, M.T. (2003) 'Documenting the self: Abelard and the individual in history', *Historical Research*, 76: 293–309.

d'Aubigné, J.H.M. (1843) *The History of the Reformation in Europe in the Time of Calvin*, trans. H. White, London: Longman, Green, Longman, Roberts, & Green.

Duby, G. (1988) 'Solitude: eleventh to thirteenth century', in Duby (ed.) *A History of Private Life – Vol. II: Revelations of the Medieval World*, trans. A. Goldhammer, Cambridge, MA: Harvard University Press.

Dülmen, R. van (1999) 'The Reformation and the modern age', in C.S. Dixon (ed.) *The German Reformation: the essential readings*, Malden, MA: Blackwell.

Greyerz, K. von (2010) 'Ego-documents: the last word?', *German History*, 28: 273–82.

Gurevich, A. (1995) *The Origins of European Individualism*, Oxford: Blackwell.

Hanning, R.W. (1977) *The Individual in Twelfth-Century Romance*, New Haven, CT: Yale University Press.

Hundert, E.J. (1994) *The Enlightenment's Fable: Bernard Mandeville and the discovery of society*, Cambridge: Cambridge University Press.

Hundert, E.J. (1997) 'The European Enlightenment and the history of the self', in R. Porter (ed.) *Rewriting the Self: histories from the Renaissance to the present*, London: Routledge.

Ikegami, E. (1995) *The Taming of the Samurai: honorific individualism and the making of modern Japan*, Cambridge, MA: Harvard University Press.

Jacob, M.C. and Kadane, M. (2003) 'Missing, now found in the eighteenth century: Weber's Protestant capitalist', *American Historical Review*, 108: 20–49.

Lukes, S. (1971) 'The meanings of "individualism"', *Journal of the History of Ideas*, 32: 45–66.

Lukes, S. (1973) *Individualism*, Oxford: Blackwell.

Mandeville, B. (1997) *The Fable of the Bees and Other Writings*, ed. E.J. Hundert, Indianapolis, IN: Hackett.

Marshall, P. (2009) *The Reformation: a very short introduction*, Oxford: Oxford University Press.

McKeon, M. (1987) *The Origins of the English Novel 1600–1740*, Baltimore, MD: Johns Hopkins University Press.

Morris, C. (1972) *The Discovery of the Individual 1050–1200*, London: SPCK.

Muldrew, C. (2000) 'From a "light cloak" to an "iron cage": historical changes in the relation between community and individualism', in A. Shepard and P. Withington (eds) *Communities in Early Modern England*, Manchester: Manchester University Press.

Mullan, J. (1997) 'Feelings and novels', in R. Porter (ed.) *Rewriting the Self: histories from the Renaissance to the present*, London: Routledge.

Myers, M.L. (1983) *The Soul of Modern Economic Man: ideas of self-interest, Thomas Hobbes to Adam Smith*, Chicago, IL: University of Chicago Press.

Nelson, N. (1933) 'Individualism as a criterion of the Renaissance', *Journal of English and Germanic Philology*, 32: 316–34.

Nisbett, R.F. (2005) *The Geography of Thought: how Asians and Westerners think differently – and why*, London: Nicholas Brealey.

Ocker, C. (2012) 'The German Reformation and medieval thought and culture', *History Compass*, 10: 13–46.

Persky, J. (1995) 'The ethology of *homo economicus*', *Journal of Economic Perspectives*, 9: 221–31.

Porter, R. (1997) 'Introduction', in R. Porter (ed.) *Rewriting the Self: histories from the Renaissance to the present*, London: Routledge.

Rosenberger, N.R. (1992) 'Introduction', in Rosenberger (ed.) *Japanese Sense of Self*, Cambridge: Cambridge University Press.

Smith, S. and Watson, J. (1998) 'Introduction: situating subjectivity in women's autobiographical practices', in Smith and Watson (eds) *Women, Autobiography, Theory: a reader*, Madison, WI: University of Wisconsin Press.

Spacks, P.M. (1976) *Imagining a Self: autobiography and novel in eighteenth-century England*, Cambridge, MA: Harvard University Press.

Steinberg, M.P. (2006) *Listening to Reason: culture, subjectivity, and nineteenth-century music*, Princeton, NJ: Princeton University Press.

Tocqueville, A. de (1840) *Democracy in America*, vol. 2, trans. H. Reeve, London: Saunders & Otley.

Ullmann, W. (1966) *The Individual and Society in the Middle Ages*, Baltimore, MD: Johns Hopkins University Press.

Verderber, S. (2013) *The Medieval Fold: power, repression, and the emergence of the individual*, Basingstoke: Palgrave Macmillan.

Webster, T. (1996) 'Writing to redundancy: approaches to spiritual journals and early modern spirituality', *Historical Journal*, 39: 33–56.

Chapter 21

John Jeffries Martin

THE MYTH OF RENAISSANCE INDIVIDUALISM

I MAGES OF RENAISSANCE individuals – their portraits, their biographies, their letters, even their signatures – seem to us, now half a millennium later, importantly familiar. From the age of Petrarch and Giotto until that of Montaigne, Shakespeare, and Rembrandt (from about 1350 until about 1650), the individual appears to have emerged as a salient, well-defined force in western culture. Unlike their medieval ancestors, Renaissance men and women seem to have placed new value on the will and on agency, on expressiveness, prudence, and choice – and to have done so self-consciously and self-reflectively. Inevitably we feel that we recognize such individuals (or their robust, three-dimensional representations) as autonomous, self-contained, psychologically complex persons much like ourselves. They make a powerful impression, especially when the Renaissance is viewed (as it used to be) as the inauguration of modern western culture.

The "discovery of the individual" is such a central dimension of the popular understanding of the Renaissance that it would seem virtually heretical to challenge the notion that it was in Europe in this period that modern notions of personal identity first emerged. Yet no other single aspect of the Renaissance has been subject to attacks from so many different quarters. Medievalists have pointed to evidence for an interest in the individual in the eleventh and twelfth centuries, well before the age of Petrarch (1304–74). Cultural historians have attacked the elitism of the view that the Renaissance "discovered the individual," demonstrating quite clearly that claims about individualism have been based on a limited sampling of works drawn from high culture. Social historians have made compelling arguments for the decisiveness of communal, civic, and family structures in shaping notions of identity that they see as rooted in collective rather than individualistic contexts. Theorists have underscored the degree to which the very notion of the "individual" is suspect, viewing it as a cultural construction in the service of larger political and ideological interests that often had the paradoxical effect of hemming in individual autonomy through such factors as codes of civility or religious prohibitions and the increasing power of the state. Similarly, comparativists have questioned the notion of the individual as a uniquely western ideal.

But perhaps most devastating of all have been critiques that have argued that the very idea of the "discovery of the individual" is merely one component of a larger myth that portrayed the Renaissance as a major act in the drama of what we comfortably used to call the "history of western civilization."[1] Along with other major elements that make up the traditional stories we tell about the Renaissance – from the claim that it was this period that witnessed the emergence of capitalism and republicanism as well as realism, humanism, and secularism – the idea that the Renaissance was the period in which individualism first emerged from its previously dormant state and became a defining aspect of the modern western world is dubious at best. Historians are simply no longer able to offer such a neatly packaged history of the self, without recognizing that such a story, in the final analysis, itself served as a myth that both bolstered and explained a broad array of assumptions about individualism and identity throughout most of the nineteenth and twentieth centuries.

The rejection of liberal and teleological narratives of the self has not, however, resulted in a lessening of interest in this theme in Renaissance studies. If anything, the focus on this topic has expanded, and the perspectives on it have multiplied at an almost dizzying rate. Traditionally, historians and others had approached this theme from the vantage point of a few canonical autobiographies (those of Benvenuto Cellini, St. Teresa of Avila, Michel de Montaigne) or a few celebrated self-portraits (Albrecht Dürer, Raphael, Maarten van Heemskerck) that seemed to provide evidence for the development of modern forms of introspection, reflection, and individual expression. There was, furthermore, a corollary assumption that this development was related primarily to the emergence of humanism, a set of scholarly practices that – in their varied and often passionate efforts to interpret ancient and early Christian ideas and values – placed a new emphasis on context, contingency, and ultimately authorship in the explanation of texts and their meanings.

Today scholars are skeptical of this interpretative framework. On the one hand, it is no longer possible to view a few autobiographies as representative of a general trend. It is true that there was a veritable explosion of letter collections, diaries, memoirs, journals, *ricordanze*, *livres de famille*, *Hauschroniken* (many of which contain significant autobiographical elements) in late medieval and early modern Europe – as many as five hundred such texts in fifteenth-century Florence alone; and recent work has identified a plethora of autobiographies and other forms of personal documents or "ego-documents" in the sixteenth and early seventeenth centuries.[2] But regional variations render almost all generalizations suspect. While it was fashionable to keep *ricordanze* or *libri di famiglia* in fifteenth-century Florence, such works were rare in fifteenth-century Venice.[3] Ego-documents abounded in early modern England but were unusual across the North Sea in Holland. Even within the Netherlands, there were curious variations, with the inhabitants of the maritime provinces (Friesland, Zeeland, Holland) more likely to record aspects of their lives in journals and house-books than their inland contemporaries. . . . .[4]

On the other hand, humanism played a less determining role in the development of such representations than has been generally assumed. This does not mean that humanists did not foster new perspectives that reinforced an interest in autobiography or self-portraiture. Rather it means that it is now possible to discern certain larger social, cultural, and political forces in the making of Renaissance identities. . . .

In the wake of the collapse of traditional paradigms, scholars have begun to take a more particularistic approach, examining the diverse functions of a broad array of representations of the individual. What precise functions, for example, did portraits and self-portraits serve? What about humanist biographies and autobiographies, on the one hand, and spiritual biographies and autobiographies, on the other? Or how should we understand the relation of philosophical and theological discussions of the will to changing notions of the individual? Similarly how should we approach the relation of lay confession and other devotional practices to new notions of the self? What about the diaries, journals, and housebooks of Renaissance merchants and artisans? What about printing privileges and copyrights? Or contracts and changes in property law, inheritance laws, and marriage? Finally, what are we to make of the great silence that enshrouds most late medieval and early modern men and women? Should we assume that the absence of individualized representations for this great majority indicates an indifference to questions of identity? This last question is perhaps the most intractable, but nonetheless it is plain that it is no longer possible to tell the story of the Renaissance discovery of the self as a straightforward and heroic narrative that lays the foundations for the more "modern" forms of individualism seen as characteristic of the Enlightenment, the Romantic period, or even modern life generally.

Nevertheless, it is possible to distinguish three basic types of selfhood in Renaissance Europe. The first, which was the dominant type of the entire period, was what we might call the "communal" or "civic" self. In this context, group or collective identity was the defining characteristic of an individual's sense of his or her place in society, with the individual's family or lineage often serving as his or her primary point of reference. The second type, by contrast, which came to the fore quite suddenly in the early sixteenth century (though we find adumbrations of it in the late Middle Ages) was characterized by novel notions of the individual as an expressive, self-reflective subject, increasingly conscious about the need to assume different roles in different contexts – a notion that we might best describe as the "performative" or "prudential" self. But, in addition to these two fundamental types, scholars have in recent years begun to discover considerable evidence that points to a third species of selfhood, one that we might best call the "porous" or "open" self. Late medieval and early modern identities, that is, were often not constituted, as we might expect, of one soul contained or neatly enclosed in one body. To the contrary, considerable evidence – particularly though not exclusively at the level of popular culture – suggests that the body was itself imagined as porous, open to strong influences from "spiritual" forces (through witchcraft or possession) from the outside: a far cry, in short, from the autonomous and self-contained individualist that is often assumed to have been a defining characteristic of the self in this era. The typology I offer here makes no claim that these species of selfhood were ever pure or exclusive; the "types" are offered rather as a way of pointing to certain tendencies or tensions in Renaissance culture. In fact, most individuals would have combined elements of all three types, though frequently only one would be dominant. The goldsmith Benvenuto Cellini (1500–71) certainly showed traits of each of these forms of selfhood. An incorrigible braggart, he was an indefatigable performer in his friendships, his craft, and his writing. At the same time he also celebrated his family, his guild, and his state. But he also had a brush with demonic magic – during two heart-stopping necromancy sessions led by a Sicilian priest in the Colosseum in Rome.[5] A student of the Renaissance, therefore, should not expect to find clearly defined notions of individualism. Rather he or she should enter the study of the period recognizing that even such a basic concept as the "category of the person" itself has a complex history, with multiple possible representations, in an era that too often has born the burden of serving as a precursor to our own.[6]

The communal self

Fifteenth-century Italian artists frequently portrayed individuals in their works. Nonetheless, their tendency was to offer such portraits in paintings that celebrated a communal event, such as the consecration of a new parish, or made a didactic point about the importance of faith, such as Masaccio's paintings in the Brancacci Chapel in Florence. Even when individual portraits were produced in this period, they were generally grouped with others from the same family, guild, or magistracy. Moreover, at times little emphasis was placed on a likeness, with attention given to the type or the social station of the person depicted crowding out attention to what we might call "individuality." In fact, in the early age of printing, printers would often use the same block or image of a human figure over and over again, now as a representation of one personage, now as the representation of another – in one case actually representing the German artist Albrecht Dürer (1471–1528) and the Flemish mathematician Gemma Frisius (1508–55) with precisely the same features. And Dürer also, in perhaps his most famous self-portrait, depicted himself not only as Dürer but also as Christ – a decision that suggests his own notions of individual identity did not always differentiate the self from the larger religious culture in which he was still absorbed and out of which he drew his own power of expression and creativity. In such contexts, there is little evidence that such portrayals were individualistic in the sense of either pointing to psychological complexity or staking out claims to uniqueness. What mattered was the collectivity or the station, with individual identity articulated in the context of something larger – one's family, one's faith, one's city.[7] . . .

Although scholars in recent years have emphasized the cultural construction of the self in different historical periods, social and economic forces too deserve emphasis. In a famous essay, the French historian Marc Bloch drew a connection between individualism and agrarian regimes, noting that agricultural technologies and practices played a key role in shaping more collectivist outlooks among peasants in certain parts of Europe (those in which the long-furlong open field and the wheeled plough were the norm) and more "individualistic" outlooks in others (those where the irregular open field and the scratch plough dominated).[8] And it is undoubtedly the case that the commercial revolution of the eleventh and twelfth centuries, which initiated a process of urban growth and the gradual penetration of market forces into the countryside, encouraged a more individualist outlook. Largely because of their favored location, the cities and towns of the Italian peninsula played a precocious role in this economic revival. Yet even in England where urbanization was far less intense in the late Middle Ages than in Italy, agricultural practices combined with "a highly flexible social structure," may have led to certain forms of economic individualism as early as the twelfth and thirteenth centuries. Land, for example, was often held or alienated or inherited by individuals rather than the family or the group; and certain villagers, at least, showed remarkable independence in relation to their lords.[9]

By the thirteenth and fourteenth centuries these shifts had made an imprint on European culture. In the sphere of religion, for example, the stipulation by the Church that every Christian make his or her confession at least once a year (*omnis utriusque sexus* [1215]) undoubtedly fostered a sense of individuality. The growth of the mendicant orders, along with the rise of popular heresies, also contributed to and reflected this leavening of individualism. The ideas were equally felt in intellectual currents in both scholasticism (especially among the nominalists) and in humanism. Both offered a new vocabulary that laid particular emphasis on the will, a theme that was perhaps most forcefully expressed in Pico della Mirandola's *Oration on the Dignity of Man* (1486) and that was reinforced both by humanist biography, especially in its emphasis on the exemplary life, and by the ideals of the civic life.[10] . . . .

In certain contexts, especially in Florence and Tuscany where painted or sculpted portraits were increasingly concerned with conveying a recognizable likeness of the individual so memorialized, scholars have often found evidence for the birth of individualism. Yet the evidence equally supports the notion that what was really decisive to such men and women was the commemoration through an individual memorial of the entire lineage.[11] Again, in the late medieval as well as in the early modern period, the tendency was for the individual to be depicted as part of a greater whole, and in Italy, as a kind of communal or civic self, tied together with kinfolk and townsfolk in a web of interdependencies that make it difficult to speak of the Renaissance as an age of the "discovery of the individual."

The performative self

"Homines non nascuntur, sed finguntur – men are not born, but fashioned," the Dutch humanist Erasmus wrote in 1513 in his influential book of manners. In the same year, Machiavelli offered a similar argument in *The Prince,* a treatise that radically severed the ruler from a prescribed social role and stressed the importance of fictions in the shaping of a political power. It was no longer virtue but the appearance of virtue that mattered. Painted self-portraits in this decade (by Dürer, Raphael, Parmigianino) were equally self-reflective, underscoring the diversity of roles an individual might assume. In these works, the individual was represented not as a member of a larger group but as isolated, self-reflective, preoccupied with roles and decorum.[12] As Stephen Greenblatt has written, this was an age of "self-fashioning," adding that "perhaps the simplest observation we can make is that in the sixteenth century there appears to be an increased self-consciousness about the fashioning of the human identity as a manipulable, artful process.[13] . . . Their readers were invited to reinvent themselves, play the proper role at the proper time. Portraiture seemed to dig deeper into the self than ever before. Lorenzo Lotto's many early sixteenth-century portraits give evidence of a psychological depth rare in the later Middle Ages. Self-reflection seemed to reach a new level of intensity in autobiographical writing also. Montaigne's *Essays* struggled self-consciously with issues of self-presentation. In the next century the Venetian rabbi Leone Modena (1571–1648) showed similar preoccupations in his autobiographical *Life of Judah.*[14] Women too articulated new roles for themselves, as works by such feminist authors as Lucrezia Marinella and Moderata Fonte make clear.[15] An individual's social role seemed less significant than the particular role he or she assumed. . . . At roughly the same time, the English poet John Donne (1572–1631), writing in the wake of the astronomical discoveries of Copernicus (1473–1543) and Galileo (1564–1642), captured something of the new individualism in his poetry:

> And new philosophy calls all in doubt
> . . . all coherence gone;
> All just supply, and all relation:
> Prince, subject, father, son, are things forgot
> For every man alone thinks he hath got
> To be a phoenix, and that then can be
> None of that kind, of which he is, but he.
> (*The First Anniversary*, ll. 205–18)

None of this is to claim that notions of the communal self vanished. What we find in the early modern period is a set of fundamental tensions between the communal self – still probably the fundamental type for most Europeans – and the ideal of the performative or prudential self that seems to have become increasingly diffused in this age. The perdurance of the former type is clear in many forms: in the continuation of the practice of collective biographies, most famously perhaps in Giorgio Vasari's *Lives of the Artists* (1550; 2nd edn. 1568) and Karel van Mander's *Book of Painters* (1604); in the *ricordanze* tradition, with French and German merchants now keeping *livres de raison* or *Hauschroniken* that had much the same communal function that the housebooks of their Florentine counterparts did a century or two earlier; and in portrait collections. . . .

The communal self was clearly the norm for most European peasants as well. There, even such basic categories as emotions (hate, envy, guilt) and memory appear to have played themselves out largely as functions of one's position in the social and power relations of village culture rather than as internal matters of conscience.[16]

Nonetheless, certain forms of individuality do appear to have marked late medieval and early modern peasant culture. At least when an occasional source such as an inquisitorial register records the voices and identities of peasants in this era, individualizing traits can be quite striking, as in the case of the libidinous inhabitants of the southern French village of Montaillou in the early fourteenth century or the sixteenth-century case of the northern Italian miller Domenico Scandella, whose readings and opinionated harangues made him stand out as something of an eccentric among his fellow villagers in the Friuli.[17]

On the other hand, the performative or prudential self was not entirely new. In fifteenth-century Florence, for example, overlapping social networks had often led to the cultivation of what Ronald F. E. Weissman has called "the importance of being ambiguous." As Leon Battista Alberti put it in his famous treatise on the family – in language that is a striking anticipation of Machiavelli's – "How can anyone dream that mere simplicity and goodness will get him friends? . . . The world is amply supplied with fraudulent, false, perfidious, bold, audacious, and rapacious men. Everything in the world is profoundly unsure. One has to be far-seeing in the face of frauds, traps and betrayals."[18] Other contemporary texts (memoirs, books of etiquette, and sermons) show how widespread the pressure to perform or "to manage impressions" had become. . . .

Nonetheless, strategies of self-presentation reached a new level of intensity in the early sixteenth century. Once again, social and economic factors played a key role. For the first time, Europe saw the development of many large cities – Paris, London, Antwerp, Amsterdam – north of the Alps, with London's population, for example, racing from some 50,000 in the early 1500s to nearly 200,000 a century later. International commerce also intensified. Urbanization and trade clearly had the effect of bringing men and women into new forms of social relationships in which more traditional forms of identity based on familial or village life were less viable. New technologies played contributing roles. Some scholars have speculated, for example, that the development of the flat mirror in this period enabled a new sense of self, encouraging a kind of self-reflection and self-portraiture that had little precedent before the 1500s. One of Dürer's many self-portraits, in which he portrayed himself as a full-length nude, is one of the most striking artifacts of this new technology and constitutes on the visual plane something approaching the level of naturalism and honesty that Montaigne would attempt in his *Essays*. The introduction of the fork also shaped new sensitivities, at the very least facilitating the gradual shift from the medieval meal, at which men and women often ate from a common plate and used their hands, to the more individualized place settings of the early modern world and the use of utensils for the manipulation of many foods (viands in particular). But, in relation to new notions of the self, the new technology with the most far-reaching consequences was undoubtedly the printing press.

Introduced in Germany in the mid-fifteenth century, printing had become widely diffused throughout western Europe by the early sixteenth century. Books, which until then had to be copied out by hand and had circulated primarily among clerical elites, became accessible to a significant portion of the population. Literacy rates rose markedly, especially in the cities. In this context the diffusion of biographical writings, ancient and modern, provided new models for self-expression. And, indeed, this was the age not only of learned but also of popular autobiography – one historian has compiled a preliminary checklist of nearly one hundred artisan biographies from this period.[19] Printing also problematized the relationship of author to their texts. To be sure, there had been arguments about plagiarism in the late medieval period, but the question of printing privileges came to the fore in the sixteenth century, eventually resulting in the invention of copyright – laws that reinforced humanist notions of authorship. . . . .

Yet two factors, in particular, were especially decisive in the development of the performative or prudential conception of the self: the rise of the court as a center of monarchial power and the religious turmoil of the Reformation, which now made religious identity an increasingly complex component of public and private life in the late Renaissance.

Courts had been important in the Middle Ages, but the early modern court was a new creature, with carefully scripted rituals and increasingly large gathering of courtiers and other hangers-on. In a Europe that was still largely a patchwork of independent principalities, duchies, and bishoprics, there were hundreds of such courts on the continent, from the enormous Papal Curia in Rome to the much more modest, though nonetheless influential court of the Dukes of Urbino. In such contexts men and women came to find that the arts of prudence and self-reflection were necessary for survival. . . . Courtiers grappled constantly with the questions of language, silence, decorum, and dissimulation. Life at court was studied and self-examined. One was expected to give the appearance of spontaneity but, in fact, be calculating at all times. . . .

Religious factors were also crucial. The rise of Protestantism itself brought with it new conceptions of the individual. In particular, reformers such as Martin Luther (1483–1546) and John Calvin (1509–64) portrayed the human subject as fallen, as corrupted and sinful. There was also a new emphasis, especially among Calvinists, on sincerity – an ideal that clashed with courtly counsels of prudence. It is likely that the tensions between counsels of prudence and sincerity, moreover, played some role in the shaping of new notions of individual identity in the early modern period.[20] Such tensions were by no means exclusively Protestant. . . . Protestants residing in Catholic lands both dissimulated their beliefs and simulated those of their Catholic neighbors—in a practice that has come to be known as *Nicodemismo* after the Gospel figure of Nicodemus, who had gone to Jesus "by night" to conceal his beliefs from his neighbors (John 3: 1–3). Catholics in Protestant lands did the same. Jews also often found it necessary to assume a Christian identity in one place and a Jewish identity in another, living life, like a "ship with two rudders," as Enriques Nuñes, a Portuguese Jew living in Venice, put it during his interrogation by the Inquisition in 1580. . . .[21]

The porous self

Finally, recent studies, especially those concerned with the histories of *mentalités*, popular religion, magic, and folk culture, have unearthed curious fragments of a Renaissance culture defined in part at least by a view of the self that was anything but autonomous or self-contained – for a self, in short, that had little psychic or psychological integrity. . . . In the sixteenth century Cornelius Agrippa (1486–1535) in Germany, John Dee (1527–1608) in England, and Tommaso Campanella (1568–1639) in Italy were exponents of Hermeticism – a corpus of late antique magical doctrines that Ficino had done much to popularize – and their ideas did much to propagate the view that the self was in the grip of larger, cosmic forces.[22] There was also a widespread belief in the conjuring of spirits and the invocation of angels, practices that betrayed an underlying assumption that psychic forces were not to be understood on purely individualized grounds. . . .

It is, however, on the level of popular culture that the self appears to have been most porous, most labile. As Natalie Zemon Davis has pointed out, in the sixteenth century, "the line drawn around the self was not firmly closed," and she points to such widespread instances of possession by another's soul or subjection to the curse of a witch to underscore the porous or permeable nature of identity in this period. . . . [23] We must understand Renaissance notions of identity on their own terms. Some Renaissance writers, artists, courtiers, and religious and political leaders may well have had a fairly well-articulated notion of an "individualist" self, but in many other respects, identity appears to have been fluid, protean, without the sharp lineaments of a centered, unitary self that we associate with Descartes's mid-seventeenth-century description of the self as an internal *res cogitans* — an internal thing doubting or thinking. Even if the anthropologist Clifford Geertz were correct in his observation that the "western" view of the individual privileges the "person as a bounded, unique, more or less integrated motivational and cognitive universe, a dynamic center of awareness, emotion, judgment, and action, organized into a distinctive whole," we would be hard put to find such "individuals" as the norm in the late medieval or early modern Europe.[24]

Conclusion

A narrative of an emerging individualism has given way, therefore, to a far more variegated history of the self in the late medieval and early modern periods. In the late Middle Ages and in much of the Renaissance, representations of individuals (biographies, *libri di famiglia*, portraits, and so on) were rarely expressions or celebrations of individuality. To the contrary, more often than not, they served to articulate something about one's group identity. With few exceptions, it is only in about 1500 that we begin to find the kind of self-consciousness and self-reflection that approximate what modern thinkers mean by "individualism." But even here we must exercise caution about generalizing this category. Such expressions were the exception, not the rule. Moreover, as many scholars have argued, even the most individualistic self was often more a function of social, cultural, and political factors than of will, choice, or agency. What is striking about this period is the perdurance of the communal self on the one hand and the fact that many Renaissance selves were not demarcated or neatly bounded in one clearly individuated body. To the contrary, the Renaissance body was often porous or permeable, at times under the influence of dual or multiple spirits or souls, at other times without a spirit at all – and yet somehow still vital, capable of animation.

In his celebrated book *The Civilization of the Renaissance in Italy* (1860), the Swiss historian Jacob Burckhardt argued that the "development of the individual" was a defining attribute of the period. The claim is tantalizing; late medieval Italy does indeed appear, as Burckhardt put it, "to swarm with individuality; the ban laid upon human personality was dissolved; and a thousand figures meet us each in its own special shape and dress."[25] But we must take great care here in assessing this argument. Only four years before Burckhardt published his now classic work, Alexis de Tocqueville made the opposite point. "That word 'individualism' which we have coined for our own requirements," Tocqueville wrote, "was unknown to our ancestors, for the good reason that in those days every individual necessarily belonged to a group and no one could regard himself as an isolated unit."[26] Increasingly, scholars are likely to side with Tocqueville. Burckhardt – it now seems clear – read nineteenth-century notions of individuality back into fourteenth- and fifteenth-century Italy. The Renaissance "discovery of the individual" turns out to be mostly myth.

Notes

1   Bouwsma, "The Renaissance," along with Bouwsma's *aggiornamento*, *American Historical Review* 103 (1998), p. 115.
2   Cicchetti and Mordenti, *I libri di famiglia*; Pandimiglio, "Ricordanze"; Amelang, *Flight of Icarus*; and Dekker, "Egodocuments."

3   Grubb, "Memory and Identity."
4   Dekker, "Egodocuments," p. 64. For England, Mascuch, *Origins*.
5   Cellini, *Autobiography*, pp. 120–4.
6   Mauss, "Category."
7   Burke, "Renaissance, Individualism."
8   Bloch, *French Rural History,* pp. 48–56.
9   Macfarlane, *Origins of English Individualism,* p. 197 especially.
10   Trinkaus, *In Our Image.*
11   Cohn, "Burckhardt Revisited."
12   Woods-Marsden, *Renaissance Self-Portraiture.*
13   Greenblatt, *Renaissance Self-Fashioning*, p. 2.
14   Modena, *Life of Judah.*
15   Cox, "Single Self."
16   Sabean, *Power in the Blood,* pp. 30–6.
17   Le Roy Ladurie, *Montaillou* and Ginzburg, *Cheese and the Worms.*
18   Cited in Weissman, "Being Ambiguous," p. 272.
19   Amelang, "Checklist," in *Flight of Icarus*, pp. 253–350.
20   Martin, "Inventing Sincerity."
21   Pullan, "Ship," p. 37.
22   Walker, *Spiritual and Demonic Magic.*
23   Davis, "Boundaries."
24   Geertz, "Native's Point of View," p. 126.
25   Burckhardt, *Civilization of the Renaissance,* vol. I, p. 143.
26   de Tocqueville, *Old Regime*, p. 96.

References

Amelang, James, *The Flight of Icarus: Artisan Autobiography in Early Modern Europe* (Stanford: Stanford University Press, 1998).

Bloch, Marc, *French Rural History: An Essay on its Basic Characteristics*, trans. Janet Sondheimer (Berkeley: University of California Press, 1966).

Bouwsma, William J., "The Renaissance and the Drama of Western History," *American Historical Review* 84 (1979), pp. 1–15.

Burckhardt, Jacob, *The Civilization of the Renaissance in Italy*, 2 vols., trans. S. G. C. Middlemore (New York: Harper, 1958).

Burke, Peter, "The Renaissance, Individualism, and the Portrait," *History of European Ideas* 21 (1995), pp. 393–400.

Cellini, Benvenuto, *The Autobiography*, trans. George Bull (Harmondsworth and New York: Penguin, 1985).

Cicchetti, Angelo and Mordenti, Raul, *I libri di famiglia in Italia* (Rome: Edizioni di storia e letteratura, 1985).

Cohn, Samuel K., "Burckhardt Revisited from Social History," in *Language and Images of Renaissance Italy*, ed. Alison Brown (Oxford: Clarendon, 1995), pp. 217–34.

Cox, Virginia, "The Single Self: Feminist Thought and the Marriage Market in Early Modern Venice," *Renaissance Quarterly* 48 (1995), pp. 513–81.

Davis, Natalie Zemon, "Boundaries and the Sense of Self in Sixteenth-Century France," in Thomas C. Heller et al., eds., *Reconstructing Individualism: Autonomy, Individuality, and the Self in Western Thought*, ed. Thomas C. Heller, Morton Sosna, and David E. Wellbery (Stanford: Stanford University Press, 1986), pp. 53–63.

Dekker, Rudolf, "Egodocuments (Autobiographies, Diaries, Travel Journals) in the Netherlands, 1500–1814," *Dutch Crossing* 39 (1989), pp. 61–72.

de Tocqueville, Alexis, *The Old Regime and the French Revolution,* trans. Stuart Gilbert (Garden City, NY: Doubleday, 1955).

Gardner, Victoria C., "*Homines non nascuntur, sed finguntur*. Benvenuto Cellini's *Vita* and Self-Presentation of the Renaissance Artist," *Sixteenth Century Journal* 28 (1997), pp. 447–65.

Geertz, Clifford, "'From the Native's Point of View': On the Nature of Anthropological Understanding," in *Culture Theory: Essays on Mind, Self, and Emotion,* ed. Richard Shweder and Robert Levine (Cambridge: Cambridge University Press, 1984).

Ginzburg, Carlo, *The Cheese and the Worms: The Cosmos of a Sixteenth-Century Miller* (Baltimore: Johns Hopkins University Press, 1980).

Greenblatt, Stephen, *Renaissance Self-Fashioning: From More to Shakespeare* (Chicago: University of Chicago Press, 1980).

Grubb, James S., "Memory and Identity: Why Venetians Did Not Keep *Ricordanze,*" *Renaissance Studies* 8 (1994), pp. 375–87.

Le Roy Ladurie, Emmanuel, *Montaillou: village occitan de 1294 à 1324* (Paris: Gallimard, 1975).

Macfarlane, Alan, *The Origins of English Individualism: The Family, Property and Social Transition* (Cambridge: Cambridge University Press, 1978).

Martin, John Jeffries, "Inventing Sincerity, Refashioning Prudence: The Discovery of the Individual in Renaissance Europe," *American Historical Review* 102 (1997), pp. 1309–42.

Mascuch, Michael, *The Origins of the Individualist Self: Autobiography and Self-Identity in England* (Stanford: Stanford University Press, 1996).

Mauss, Marcel, "The Category of the Person," in *The Category of the Person*, ed. Michael Carrithers (Cambridge: Cambridge University Press, 1985).

Modena, Leone, *Life of Judah: The Autobiography of a Seventeenth-Century Venetian Rabbi*, ed. and trans. Mark R. Cohen (Princeton: Princeton University Press, 1988).

Montaigne, Michel de, *The Complete Essays* (Stanford: Stanford University Press, 1958).

Pandimiglio, Leonida, "Ricordanze e libro di famiglia: il manifestarsi di una nuova fonte," *Lettere italiane* 39 (1987), pp. 3–19.

Pullan, Brian, "'A Ship with Two Rudders': 'Righetto Marrano' and the Inquisition in Venice," *The Historical Journal* 20 (1977), pp. 25–58.

Sabean, David, *Power in the Blood: Popular Culture and Village Discourse in Early Modern Germany* (Cambridge: Cambridge University Press, 1984).

Trinkaus, Charles, *In Our Image and likeness: Humanity and Divinity in Italian Renaissance Thought,* 2 vols. (Chicago: University of Chicago Press, 1970).

Walker, D. P., *Spiritual and Demonic Magic from Ficino to Campanella* (London: Warburg Institute, 1958).

Weissman, Ronald F. E., "The Importance of Being Ambiguous: Social Relations, Individualism, and Identity in Renaissance Florence," in *Urban Life in the Renaissance*, ed. Susan Zimmerman and Ronald F. E. Weissman (Newark: University of Delaware Press, 1989), pp. 269–80.

Woods-Marsden, Joanna, *Renaissance Self-Portraiture: The Visual Construction of Identity and the Social Status of the Artist* (New Haven: Yale University Press, 1998).

Chapter 22

Michael Mascuch

WRITING ON THE HEART:
PRESERVING EXPERIENCE
IN FIRST-PERSON DISCOURSE
IN SEVENTEENTH-CENTURY
ENGLAND

Not long before he fell sick, he said to one that lay with him, that he slept very little in the nights; adding, when I lye waking in my Bed, I sometimes run through the course of my whole life; and if a pen-man were ready by me, I could relate many observable passages of Gods Providence about me: his friend said, Sir, you may do well to write them down as they come into your thoughts: he made no answer to that.

The Holy Life and Happy Death of Mr. John Angier (1684)

Do you not know who hath said to you so often, *Remember me?* How often have you heard that sweet Word since you came hither? What? Do you think it is enough to remember Him for an Hour? No, but let it be a Living, and Lasting remembrance. Do not you write that Name of his in the Dust, that hath written your Names upon his Heart. Your High Priest hath your Names upon his Heart, and therewith is entered into the Holy Place, and keeps them there for a Memorial before the Lord continually. O that his remembrance might be ever written upon your Hearts, as with a Pen of Diamond, upon Tables of Marble, that might never be worn out!

The Life and Death of Mr. Joseph Alleine (1672)

I N THE EARLY MODERN PERIOD England witnessed the growth of the habit of keeping separate notebooks relating to personal experience. These texts represent the primitive form of a practice which would, by the nineteenth century, produce the narrativized autobiography and the concept of the individualist self. Though it may seem so to us, this development was not inevitable. Writing, personal experience, and self-identity have no intrinsic affiliation; their merging and maturation together depended upon a relationship being created, codified, and acculturated. The process of the invention and rationalization of what we inelegantly call "self-writing" began in the late sixteenth century and accelerated during the seventeenth century.

Though ship's logs, business ledgers, corporate chronicles, and family estate and household account books had been utilized since medieval times at least, the use of private notebooks by individual persons to record matter pertaining to their own experience was something new in 1600. The advent of the interleaved pocket almanac book certainly contributed to this novelty. The first English printed almanac intended for use as a diary or memorandum book seems to have appeared in 1565; it contained a blank page facing the calendar for each month. A year later was published *A Blancke and Perpetuall Almanack*, designed for the user to note financial matters and, it said, "things that passeth from time to time (worthy of memory to be registered)." An edition of 1571 described itself as "a book of memory, necessary for all such, as have occasion daily to note sundry affairs."[1] Such diaries became common in the seventeenth century, and a number containing MS notes have survived.[2] However, the types of memoranda these tiny books allowed – the average dimensions of a pocket-sized bound "blank" almanac were about two inches by four – were hardly the means by which an individualized narrative identity could be realized. More pertinent to the development we are tracing are the more discursive personal notebooks, sometimes composed with the aid of memoranda contained in pocket almanacs, kept mostly by persons of intense Protestant piety. It is a commonplace of European cultural history that these so-called private spiritual confessionals were largely responsible for the emergence of a so-called autonomous, interiorized self-identity in the early modern period. Yet little has been done in the way of empirical research to document the circumstances directly contributing to this new mode of self-configuration.

In his classic account of the rise of Puritanism in England, William Haller wrote that "The usual practice of the saint was to begin his new life by setting down on paper an account of his spiritual rebirth, which account also he frequently continued in the form of a daily written record of his subsequent spiritual struggles."[3] This is a sweeping generalization crying out for qualification, but we have taken it as given for quite some time. Yet we now know that at least two persons of exceptional piety, the Mistresses Stubbes and Brettergh, failed to produce writings of their Christian experiences for their biographers to draw upon. It is likely that many others whose faith was no less intense also neglected to write anything about themselves. In fact, such documentation was not a necessary passport into heaven. A seventeenth-century sermon assured its illiterate hearers that "Though you cannot read a letter in the book, yet if you can, by true assurance, read your name in the *Book of Life,* your scholarship will serve. . . . If you cannot write a word, yet see you transcribe a fair copy of a godly, righteous, and sober life, and you have done well."[4] Historical research into literacy suggests that throughout the early modern period the habit of writing may have been the exception, rather than the norm, of "Puritan" piety. Unfortunately, we have only written records to draw upon for knowledge, which tell us little about the "usual" practice of pious illiterates. Still, through written texts we can interpret the nature of the practice of recording personal experience, at least for those saints and others who could and did write.

According to the literary scholar Brian Vickers, "the Renaissance was – to an extent which never ceases to surprise one – a notebook culture."[5] This statement makes sense only if we recall that but a tiny proportion of the total population actually participated in such culture. To use a notebook, a person had to be capable of taking and reading manual notes. The distribution of literacy within the British population in the early modern period is nearly impossible to know accurately. As the historian Margaret Spufford has convincingly argued, probably more people could read than could write, because many children were removed from school after the teaching of reading, but before they had completed lessons in writing, which commenced only after pupils had obtained basic reading skills.[6] However, most studies of literacy in the early modern period are based upon evidence of the ability to write. The historian David Cressy's analysis, for example, uses signatures to depositions taken in eccle- siastical courts in the south-east of England. Though they probably underestimate the number of readers in the population, Cressy's conclusions are meaningful to us because our notebook culture was composed exclusively of writers. Cressy determines that writing skills were limited to 30 per cent of the total male population and only 10 per cent of the female popula- tion by 1640, reaching 45 per cent and 25 per cent respectively by the accession of George I.[7] Thus we can see that, even as late as the end the seventeenth century, the number of potential participants in the notebook culture comprised a minority of the total population.

In the lifetimes of Katherine Stubbes [c. 1570–1590] and Katherin Brettergh [1579–1601], however, writers were probably even scarcer than they were in the Stuart period. Outside the monasteries, writing skills were indispensable only to persons engaged in trade. With the dissolution of the monasteries in the mid-sixteenth century the general demand for writers increased, but the ability to write was not absolutely required of entrants to the grammar schools until about 1570, the same time at which Roger Ascham, in his *Scholemaster*, first proposed the method of written rather than oral exercises in the teaching of Latin.[8] A consensus about the utility and necessity of writing skills for those obtaining a classical education – typically young men intending to pursue careers in the church or the professions, such as law – seems therefore not to have been reached by educators until about the time of Mistress Stubbes's birth. It is not surprising that she left no writings despite her extensive study of scripture: she probably was not taught to write, as in her youth there was undoubtedly a dearth of qualified writing tutors available to parents wishing to expose their children, male or female, to this new technology. The wealthier young gentlemen stood at the head of the line for writing instruction; their sisters were probably fit in as opportunities arose. The first English self-education manual to include lessons on learning how to write appeared in 1596. Books on domestic duties in pious households did not begin to hint at the necessity of writing instruction until about 1620.[9] Reading remained the dominant and only really necessary skill to the practice of piety recommended by such manuals until the mid- seventeenth century.

Moreover, even when instruction was available, the apparatus of writing itself was for many prohibitively expensive. To write required, in addition to time to practice it, the purchase of pens, ink (or the ingredients to concoct it), and paper. Before the advent of print- ing in the late fifteenth century, most texts were written on parchment, which did not readily lend itself to recreational composition.[10] Though paper was in use alongside parch- ment from the fourteenth century, it did not gain ascendancy as a vehicle for writing until Tudor times. Even then, most of the paper used in England had to be imported from the Continent, which added to its cost. Until about the second decade of the seventeenth century, a quire (24 sheets) of small folio-size white writing-paper cost retail purchasers between 4*d.* and 5*d.* – about as much as a laborer's daily wage.[11] A blank notebook of several quires bound and covered either in vellum (recycled) or calf was not cheap; even as late as 1647, a diarist noted paying 11*d.* for "inkle and a dyurnall."[12] The cost was enough to preclude a habit of writing for purely personal purposes. After paper manufacture in Britain began in earnest toward the end of the seventeenth century its price became less prohibitive. But before then ordinary people probably found little cause to consume paper in any quantity, and even those who could write likely used what they could afford sparingly. Last, we should also consider the prohibitions on writing imposed by the need for space in which to do so, especially for writers of personal notebooks. Such work would have to take place at home, as the manipula- tion of pen and ink made difficult all but the rudest shorthand note-taking away from a proper writing-desk, and the one public location in which extensive composition might be feasible, the alehouse, would not normally allow sufficient privacy for writing of a personal nature. The coffee-houses of the late seventeenth century were hospitable to readers, but less so to writers. Even at home, privacy was scarce. In most houses, solitude was obtainable only late at night or in the early morning, when the rest of the household was asleep. Few but the very wealthy had access to private studies, or "closets," as they were called; but these do not seem to have been commonly fitted for writing before the mid-sixteenth century, and not purpose-built for it until the seventeenth.[13] In short, before the mid-seventeenth century at the very earliest, a person wanting to pursue "the usual practice of the saint" by writing a personal record of any kind, let alone a daily one, had to be both unusually wealthy and determined.

But even more than this, a person possessing the means to render his spiritual experience in writing had also to have a motive for doing so. Reasons to write about oneself in any manner are hard to come by before the mid-seventeenth century. The earliest mention of a personal spiritual diary in a printed book appeared in 1641, in *The Holy Life and Happy Death of John Bruen* [1560–1625] which, in a side-note, identified a paper of Bruen's entitled "declaration of some of the works of the Lord," as "A book of Rememb." However, neither the extracts quoted from it nor the surrounding narration offered an explanation of why Bruen produced this book, or what part it played in his spiritual practice.[14] The first manual of piety to advocate diary-keeping explicitly, Isaac Ambrose's *Media: The Middle Things, in Reference to the First and Last Things,* was printed in London in 1652. This work, treating "the Means, Duties, Ordinances, Both Secret, Private, and Publike, for continuance and increase of a Godly life," recommended the use of a diary especially as an aid to the exercise of "Self-Tryal," or "a Discussion of a man's life, that his thoughts, Words and Deeds may be seen, and censured according to the Rule of God's Law," "besides many other uses" unnamed. In the diary of self-trial, Ambrose explained, the Christian does the following:

> 1. Hereby he observes something of God to his soul, and of his soul to God. 2. Upon occasion he pours out his soul to God in prayer accordingly, and either is humbled or thankful. 3. He considers how it is with him in respect of time past, and if he have profited in grace, to find out the means whereby he hath profited, that he may make more constant use of such means; or wherein he hath decayed, to observe by what temptation he was overcome, that his former errors may make him more wary for the future.

Ambrose also supplied extracts from his own personal diary, to suggest appropriate types of entries for the reader.[15] Though *Media's* title-page claimed that Ambrose compiled his treatise "for the most part, out of the most eminently Pious, and learned writings of our Native Practical Divines," the addition of diary-keeping to the Christian exercise regime appears to have been Ambrose's own innovation. No prior text in the canon of printed handbooks of Christian duty, either in English or in any other language, made explicit mention of making accounts or keeping diurnal records of personal experience in writing.[16]

In the sixteenth and early seventeenth centuries, treatises on the forms of Christian devotion and directions to Christian practice published in English were typically translations of Jesuit works from the Continent. These texts recommended routines of daily prayer and meditation as a means to ensure personal salvation.[17] For example, the *Institutio Spiritualis* of 1551 explained that

> If the spiritual beginner is careful to exercise his soul daily in the manner laid down, and thus to unite himself to God; if, through internal conversations and loving desires, he strives without ceasing to join himself to God; if he takes care

to persevere constantly in self-denial and mortification and never gives up his holy purpose, either on account of his frequent falls or because he becomes discouraged by the innumerable distractions of his mind, he will certainly arrive at perfection and mystical union, if not in this life at least in death.[18]

In adapting such practices for their own purposes, English Protestants advocated regular performance of meditation and prayer as a sign of the practitioner's election.[19] In one of the first treatises on meditation originally written in English, the Church of England bishop Joseph Hall explained that its practice was "the pastime of saints, the ladder of heaven and . . . the best improvement of Christianity. Learne it who can, and neglect it who list; hee shall neuer find ioy, neither in God nor in himselfe, which doeth not both knowe and practice it."[20] But for both Catholics and Protestants, meditation was an exercise of the imagination, rather than of the hand. It began in oral prayer and then turned steeply inward, toward the mental image of God. In Hall's words, it was "a bending of the mind vpon some spirituall obiect, through diuers formes of discourse, vntill our thoughts come to an issue."[21] Richard Rogers, in another early Protestant guidebook, called meditation a "practice of musing;" it was the Christian's "secret talking with God, and with [his] own heart."[22] Self-examination played a supporting role in such musing. According to Hall, "the soule must . . . bee purged, ere it can profitably meditate"; hence self-examination was promoted as a mandatory preparation for prayer and meditation.[23] And, like meditation, it was also to be performed as a purely mental exercise.

Although the technology of script is absent from English devotional guides of the Tudor and early Stuart period, almost from their inception such works employed the script-related metaphors of print and engraving to illustrate aspects of Christian practice. The anonymous *A Dyurnall for deuoute soules to ordre them selfe thereafter*, printed by Robert Wyer in London sometime before 1533, for example, instructed the reader at night to "imprynte . . . in your mynde with purpose to confesse them to your ghostly father" both the benefits of the Lord and his own negligence in word, deed, and thought occurring in the course of the day. Making reference to "our frayle and oblyuyous memory," it recommended that "by often rehersynge," Christians could cause such instructions to "be depely wryten and grauen in oure stony hertes."[24] But the use of paper evidently was not an option, either for recording such instructions or for carrying them out: "heart" was a metonym for soul, whose repository was the unaided memory. This relation of heart-soul-memory made sense, since "writing on the heart" was more feasible for most would-be practitioners of piety than writing in notebooks. However, a puzzle still remains for us. Haller's "usual practice" cannot be found inscribed in the letter of Christian duty before the mid-seventeenth century, yet spiritual diaries survive from the late sixteenth century. Ambrose actually merely reflected rather than inaugurated the notebook tradition. How then did the practice originate? Let us search the diaries themselves for clues.

One of the earliest spiritual diaries to have survived from the sixteenth century belonged to Richard Rogers, the "Puritan" lecturer and acting curate of the parish of Wethersfield, Essex, and the author of *Seven Treatises*, probably the first book of Christian direction by an English Protestant to be printed in England, in 1603. . . . . Rogers kept a personal record on paper at least for a portion of his lifetime. The text we have, written in his hand, consists of an unbound paper book measuring approximately six by eight inches, now in the possession of Dr Williams's Library in London, where it arrived as part of the manuscript papers of the seventeenth-century Presbyterian divine Richard Baxter.[25] . . . What we have today consists or entries beginning 28 February 1587 and ending 25 July 1590, when Rogers was in his late thirties (he died in 1618, at age 67). Thus his work is the product of a practice conducted during the prime of his life.[26] . . .

The notebook exercise functioned for Rogers as an instrument for self-examination. It was a personal speculum through which he saw the condition of his own heart. It exhibited plainly his need for the grace of God, and thereby helped to focus his attention in professing his faith and asking for mercy. Had Katherine Stubbes kept such a book, she would have turned to it during the moment at which instead she concentrated her attention upon her dog. As Rogers's notebook did for him, Mistress Stubbes's puppy served to remind its owner of her sinful and corrupt nature, and so became the catalyst for her repentance and her meditative soliloquy. Some mnemonic device, be it a dog or a notebook, seems to have been indispensable to practitioners of meditation. . . .

Rather than a diary in the modern sense, Rogers's notebook was a book of commonplaces taken from personal experience. It served him as a sourcebook for the invention of personal meditations and prayers . . . . In this scheme the diary was the medium, but not the message: a means to the end, not the object of the exercise. . . . Its model or prototype can be found in the reading notebook Rogers was no doubt instructed to keep as a student, both in grammar school and at the university.

Although humanist educators never explicitly urged personal journal- or diary-keeping *per se*, commonplacing, the practice of . . . recording on paper pithy matter for personal use out of the various texts one read, was central to the method of study they advocated. . . . Though this method of reading was originally advocated for the study of pagan texts, it proved equally applicable to religious matter, both written and spoken. . . .

[Thus] the records of personal experience generated by Protestant saints were originally embedded in a context quite different from that of modern self-representation. The usual practice of saints, at least in the early stages of English Protestantism, was to keep a personal notebook of miscellaneous experiences and other writings, some original but many gleaned from sermons and printed books, as a useful (though not essential) aid to the daily ritual of devotion. Thus, to segregate the purely self-reflexive parts of it in order to isolate an individual and self-authorizing "life" controlling the text, as modern scholarship has displayed a propensity to do, is to distort the original design and function of such works. The great gulf of meaning standing between the original texts and their modern misconstrual can be observed in the case of the "diary" of Samuel Ward, Master of Sidney Sussex College in Cambridge from 1610 to his death in 1643, printed along with Richard Rogers's diary in *Two Elizabethan Puritan Diaries*. . . . Ward's notebook was not devoted exclusively to self-representation or even to self-examination; instead, it was merely a component of a larger experiment in the practice of religious study and worship – a means to an end, but hardly an end in itself. Accordingly, it had no intrinsic structure or design. It remained open, permeable, amorphous. . . . Instead of just a diary, Ward produced a pile of papers representing his practice of piety, throughout which his self-identity is distributed and, it appears, disintegrated and therefore appropriately mortified.[27] Moreover, he was not alone in producing such a heterogeneous mass. Besides the books of sermon notes, commonplaces, self-examination, and meditation already mentioned, several other sets of diverse and extensive quasi-autobiographical personal religious papers survive from the early modern period.[28] In preparing such materials for later audiences, modern editors have tended to boil these complex soups down to a simple residue, the autonomous "diary" or "autobiography" text representing an individual "life." Such fare would have been unpalatable to early modern men and women without at least the broth of religious worship to dissolve the substance of individual personality and self-reflexivity in it. The point of such writings was to reduce the self-identity of the individual voice, rather than to help it to coagulate.

On the other hand, the precedent for the modern predilections clearly lies in the early modern period. By the mid-seventeenth century, the personal diary text had already achieved a special kind of aura in the contemporary imagination, arguably because of its latent self-reflexive quality rather than its exemplary self-mortification: . . . some of these supposedly private documents generated a public notoriety either through direct exposure or hearsay.[29] Without anyone's deliberate advocacy, it seems, toward the end of the seventeenth century the balance was beginning to tip toward an entirely different conception of personal religious papers. Some ministers articulated what others grasped unconsciously, that the spiritual notebook was losing its status as instrument, and acquiring a new status as an object created by a subject; that is, as an autonomous text deliberately wrought by an individual intending it to represent some aspect of his personality. . . .

Many ejected ministers in the mid-1660s drew up memorials from the raw material of their diaries, intended to represent their nonconformity as both conscionable and consistent with their personal sense of piety and honor. About this time Robert Blair, the deposed minister of St Andrews, began a long personal memoir from his many "short notes," a project he justified as follows: "I think myself obliged to leave some notes concerning the chief passages that have occurred to me in my pilgrimage, that my wife and children, at least, might have these to be a memorial of the way that I kept in the world, and that they may be the better furnished to answer the calumnies and reproaches that have been, and possibly may be cast upon me."[30] Blair was 70 when he began his work; his revision had progressed to the year 1636 before he fell ill and died, in 1666. . . . [T]he implicit intention of such personal memorials [was]: to teach and to incite, as well as to vindicate, conscientious religious nonconformity.

In these texts we finally recognize examples of the "usual practice of saints" described by Haller: that is, the production of a seamless narrative account of one's spiritual growth, continued in the form of a serial record of trials and tribulations in and for the faith. In making this discovery we must note, in addition to the number of qualifications already registered in the course of our enquiry thus far, two further particulars. First, that instead of being written at the start of a "new birth," such accounts were typically made toward the end or at the middle of the saint's life, long after his spiritual awakening. Furthermore, despite their retrospective perspective, the texts fail to conform to the classic "conversion narrative" pattern – of the conviction of sin, the conversion through grace, and consequential harmony with Christ – typically ascribed to them.[31] The presence of this plot, or, for that matter, of any other story-like structure, working to integrate and totalize these discourses, is a fiction projected onto them by the modern critical imagination.[32] . . .

The second and more significant deviation from received wisdom about these works worth noting here concerns their motivation, of which we have already seen some hint in the quotations taken from the texts themselves. They were not the pure products of a "private self." Despite their largely personal and spiritual focus, public pressures informed the memorials as much as, and perhaps even more than, private desire did. At the very least, we must say that the texts were products of interaction between private and public relations. The saint who transcribed his diary into a record "at large" was more conscious of writing to defend himself from the hostile accusations (both real and imagined) of neighbors and others than he was of an urge to represent the spontaneous expression of piety in his soul. The works do not constitute a retreat into the interior recesses of the mind, but instead an advance from those recesses into the realm of publicity, and (modest) self-promotion. . . .

To conclude this chapter, we should now acknowledge that the usual practice of saints was, in the first place, not usual at all. It depended upon the acquisition of writing skills, and the possession of sufficient leisure time and a situation in which it was possible to write. Moreover, it developed in two distinct phases. The first phase was that of commonplacing from experience, of compiling lists of personal matter pertinent to religious meditation. In the second phase, which began with the Restoration, the lists began to be enlarged, and treated as historical source materials. Some notebooks were written over into personal memorials intended to be preserved for the family, to vindicate writers vilified for their piety. It is these later books that Haller likely had in mind when he described the usual practice. Finally, in this practice we can observe the stirrings of a personal voice and an individual self-identity structured in written narrative discourse. This concept of personality is still latent, and altogether pious. But a tendency to place the person before the piety had begun to emerge, and would be made more palpable by the advent of print.

Notes

1   Bernard Capp, *English Almanacs 1500–1800: Astrology and the Popular Press* (Ithaca: Cornell University Press, 1979), p. 30.
2   For a list of examples, see ibid., p. 61.
3   William Haller, *The Rise of Puritanism,* Harper Torchbook edn (New York: Harper & Row, 1957), p. 94.
4   Quoted by David Cressy, "Levels of Illiteracy in England, 1530–1750," in Harvey J. Graff, ed., *Literacy and Social Development in the West: A Reader* (Cambridge: Cambridge University Press, 1981), p. 111.
5   Brian Vickers, *Francis Bacon and Renaissance Prose* (Cambridge: Cambridge University Press, 1968), pp. 76–7.
6   Margaret Spufford, "First Steps in Literacy: The Reading and Writing Experiences of the Humblest Seventeenth-Century Spiritual Autobiographers," *Social History* 4 (1979), pp. 407–35.
7   David Cressy, *Literacy and the Social Order: Reading and Writing in Tudor and Stuart England* (Cambridge: Cambridge University Press, 1980), tables 6.1–6.5. It should be noted that Cressy's evidence is drawn from a region exceptional in commercial activity and militant Protestantism, two factors linked by historians to high levels of literacy.
8   Foster Watson, *The English Grammar Schools to 1660: Their Curriculum and Practice* (Cambridge: Cambridge University Press, 1908), pp. 186–7.
9   John Morgan, *Godly Learning: Puritan Attitudes Towards Reason, Learning and Education, 1560–1640* (Cambridge: Cambridge University Press, 1986), pp. 165–6.
10   At least one London stationer sold blank membrane books, used for keeping the accounts of the royal wardrobe, in 1313. But this use of a parchment notebook was unusual. See G. S. Ivy, "The Bibliography of the Manuscript-Book," in Francis Wormald and C. E. Wright, eds, *The English Library Before 1700* (London: Athlone Press, 1958), p. 50.
11   D. C. Coleman, *The British Paper Industry 1495–1860: A Study in Industrial Growth* (Oxford: Clarendon Press, 1958), p. 11.
12   H. J. Morehouse, ed., "A Dyurnall, or Catalogue of All My Accions and Expences from the 1st of January, 1646[/7] – Adam Eyre," in Charles Jackson, ed., *Yorkshire Diaries and Autobiographies in the Seventeenth and Eighteenth Centuries,* vol. 1, Surtees Society Publications LXV (Durham, 1877), p. 36.
13   Mark Girouard, *Life in the English Country House: A Social and Architectural History* (Harmondsworth: Penguin, 1980), p. 166.
14   Hinde, *John Bruen,* p. 146, misprinted as "142."
15   Isaac Ambrose, *Media: The Middle Things, in Reference to the First and Last Things . . .*, 2nd edn (London, 1652), pp. 58, 72, 73–5.
16   Joseph Hall alludes to the practice in the proem to his *Occasional Meditations*, first published in 1620, where he begins, "I have heedlessly lost (I confesse) many good thoughts, these few my Paper hath preserued from vanishing; The example whereof may perhaps be more usefull then the matter" (Joseph Hall, *Occasional Meditations,* 3rd edn [London, 1633], sig. A7).
17   See Helen C. White, *The Tudor Books of Private Devotion* (Madison: University of Wisconsin Press, 1951).
18   Louis de Blois, *A Book of Spiritual Instruction: Institutio Spiritualis,* trans. Bernard A. Wilberforce (2nd edn, London: Art and Book Co., 1901), p. 95, quoted in Louis B. Martz, *The Poetry of Meditation: A Study in English Religious Literature of the Seventeenth Century,* revised edn (New Haven and London: Yale University Press, 1962), p. 19.
19   For an overview, see Helen C. White, *English Devotional Literature [Prose] 1600–1640,* University of Wisconsin Studies in Language and Literature, no. 29 (Madison, 1931).
20   Joseph Hall, *The Arte of Divine Meditation: Profitable for all Christians to knowe and practise* (London, 1606), p. 4.

21   Ibid., p. 7.

22   Richard Rogers, *Seven Treatises* . . . (London, 1603), pp. 239, 238.

23   Hall, *Arte of Divine Meditation,* p. 25; see also Martz, *Poetry of Meditation,* pp. 118ff.

24   *A Dyurnall for deuoute soules to ordre them selfe thereafter* ([London] n.d., sig. c.i, sig. a.ii).

25   Dr Williams's Library, Baxter MS 61.13.

26   M. M. Knappen, *Two Elizabethan Puritan Diaries by Richard Rogers and Samuel Ward* (Chicago: American Society of Church History, 1933).

27   This point is also made, with a somewhat different emphasis, by Margo Todd in her "Puritan Self-Fashioning: The Diary of Samuel Ward," *Journal of British Studies* 31 (1992), pp. 236–64. I endorse Todd's attempt to rescue the historical Ward and his text from what she calls the "unabashed condescension of modern scholarship," though I differ from her in seeking to reunite Ward's practice with the contemporary tradition of meditation. Todd instead considers the influence of individual teachers and books on Ward's diary; among the books, she identifies the Bible and St Augustine's *Confessions* as being especially important. Her case for the latter text strikes me as rather tenuous. Though she cites numerous references to Augustine's works in works by Ward, Todd can only describe aspects of Ward's diary as being "reminiscent" of the *Confessions.* Superficial comparisons may be made, but the argument for influence requires more direct evidence if it is to be convincing. Despite our different emphases, however, the general thrusts of Todd's and my interpretation run, I think, together.

28   For a sense of the contents of a few of these, see Heywood, *Life and Death of John Angier,* esp. pp. 82–127; J. H. Turner, ed., *The Autobiography, Diaries, Anecdote and Event Books of the Rev. Oliver Heywood,* 4 vols (Brighouse, 1882–5), esp. vol. III, pp. 9–16; Linda Pollock, *With Faith and Physic: The Life of a Tudor Gentlewoman Lady Grace Mildmay 1552–1620* (London: Collins & Brown, 1993); *The Life and Death of Mr. Vavasor Powell;* Charles Jackson, ed., *The Autobiography of Alice Thornton,* Surtees Society Publications LXII (Durham, 1875); Paul S. Seaver, *Wallington's World: A Puritan Artisan in Seventeenth-Century London* (Stanford: Stanford University Press, 1985). esp. pp. 199–208.

29   In his diary, Richard Rogers mentioned "reading the writings of an other brother about his estate an houre and longuer" (fo. 27); the Scottish nonconforming minister Robert Blair wrote that he began a diary in 1622, at age 29, because he "heard of the practice of some diligent Christians, who daily took brief notes of the condition of their souls"; in Thomas M'Crie, ed., *The Life of Mr. Robert Blair* (Edinburgh: Wodrow Society, 1848), p. 31; Vavasor Powell complained that, at a moment of spiritual crisis early in his life, he went to take up his "little Diary" for help, "but having lent it to a Christian Friend that was far distant, could not" – which may be read as a warning to others doing the same with their books; see *The Life and Death of Mr. Vavasor Powell,* p. 12. Somewhat later, the Essex vicar and diarist Ralph Josselin wrote in 1657 that he "saw part of Mrs. Mabel Elliston's diurnal of her life, full of spiritual observation and sweetness"; see Alan Macfarlane, ed., *The Diary of Ralph Josselin, 1616–1683,* British Academy Records of Social and Economic History, new ser., III (London, 1976), p. 396.

30   M'Crie, *Life of Robert Blair*, p. 3.

31   For example by Watkins, *Puritan Experience*, p. 37.

32   For a particularly inspired exercise in this mode of reading, see Patricia Caldwell, *The Puritan Conversion Narrative: The Beginnings of an American Expression* (Cambridge: Cambridge University Press, 1983).

Chapter 23

Earl H. Kinmonth

NAKAMURA KEIU AND SAMUEL SMILES: A VICTORIAN CONFUCIAN AND A CONFUCIAN VICTORIAN

IN EARLY 1868, shortly after toppling the Tokugawa house, the leaders of the new Meiji government issued a proclamation known as the "Charter Oath." "The common people, no less than the civil and military officials," it declared, "shall be allowed to pursue [their] own calling[s] so that there shall be no discontent."[1] This statement implied that the new government was dedicated to dismantling the social structure of the previous regime, a structure based largely on hereditary succession. That regime had been bolstered by legal restraints on social mobility and supported by ideologues who advised that, since wealth and honor were determined only by heaven, the individual ought not to seek to alter his status.[2] Despite its implied commitment to reform, the new Meiji government maintained the restrictions on personal activities, especially as they applied to members of the samurai class, with little change. Samurai continued to receive their hereditary stipends and to move about, wearing the two swords that were the symbols of their membership in a hereditary ruling class. And, on all levels of society, the distribution of wealth and rank remained essentially what it had been during the last days of the Tokugawa house.

In the face of this apparent continuity, there was one early indication that Meiji Japan would not simply be Tokugawa Japan with a new set of rulers. In early 1871, members of the samurai class,[3] especially government officials and educators, were lining up—even camping out overnight—to buy copies of a work that attacked hereditary wealth and power from its very first line, "Heaven helps those who help themselves."[4] The book with the famous opening sentence was *Saikoku risshi hen*, a rendering by Nakamura Keiu (Masanao) of *Self-Help* by the English author, Samuel Smiles.

This initial popularity was only the beginning. Reprints of *Saikoku risshi hen* were still commercially viable as late as 1921, and new translations of *Self-Help* were produced as late as 1938.[5] Nevertheless, the works are most intimately associated with the first decades of the Meiji era. Meiji writers who had grown up with *Saikoku risshi hen* declared that its impact on early Meiji youth was "almost beyond imagination" and that it and *Seiyō hinkō ron*, Nakamura's translation of Samuel Smiles's *Character*, "had a greater influence over young men in the early [1870s] than any other book of the day."[6] Enumerating those Meiji figures who used *Saikoku risshi hen* in their own writings, praised it, or cited its influence on their lives amounts to listing the Meiji intellectual, academic, and journalistic worlds.[7] Early Meiji

Japanese not only read *Saikoku risshi hen* but also attended plays based on its stories, studied it as a textbook, and were treated to a variety of imitations and derivative works.[8] Commonly and quite correctly, *Saikoku risshi hen* is described as one of the "holy books" (*seisho*) of the Meiji era.

The first step in analyzing the popularity of *Self-Help* must be an explication of its ideas and the motivation behind them. . . . The Victorian tradition of writing on self-culture contains more than one genre, each of which preaches somewhat different values. *Self-Help* belongs to the "character-ethic" genre,[9] in which accomplishments and advancement derive primarily from an individual's virtues: hard work, diligence, frugality, perseverance, attention to detail, and the like. The task for the individual is to develop these virtues, upon which achievement depends. Chance has no place in this ethic. As Asa Briggs, a noted scholar of Victorian England, has observed, "There [are] no fairy god mothers or fairy god fathers in Smiles assisting the thrifty hero to find money and success. . . ."[10] Smiles's character ethic is not immediately concerned with making money or with personal success.[11] In *Self-Help* Smiles defined individual accomplishment not as a publicly recognized increase in rank and wealth but as the achievement of something that advanced civilization in either its material or its cultural aspects. . . . The character ethic emphasizes—rather than minimizes—the difficulties, especially the hard labor, involved in any type of accomplishment.

Although ultimate responsibility lies with the individual, the character ethic does not preclude mutual aid or cooperation. Nothing demonstrates this better than the genesis of *Self-Help*, which began as a series of lectures that Smiles gave in 1845 to a mutual study group organized by young workmen in Leeds. Smiles had lived in the city for a number of years, practicing medicine and editing a Radical newspaper. When these young workmen asked him "to talk to them a bit," he responded with a series of lectures entitled "The Education of the Working Classes." During a subsequent career as a secretary for several railroad companies operating in the vicinity of Leeds, Smiles continued to lecture on the subject of self-help for the working class and to embroider those lectures with more examples. In 1857, at a low point in his railroad career, Smiles assembled his notes and pieces of his lectures into the manuscript of *Self-Help*. Initially, no publisher would accept it, and Smiles was forced to subsidize its publication.[12] His risk was well rewarded, for, beginning in 1859, *Self-Help* started on its course, and in the next thirty years more than one hundred and sixty thousand copies were sold in England alone.[13] *Self-Help* was translated into several languages, including Japanese, and in later years Smiles traveled to a number of countries (though not to Japan) where his work had been popular and received awards and acclaim. In England, W. E. Gladstone, George Eliot, and even Queen Victoria acknowledged Smiles and praised his works.[14] After *Self-Help*, Smiles wrote four other didactic works of similar style, of which three were published: *Character* (1871), *Thrift* (1871), and *Duty* (1880). All three were translated into Japanese but only *Self-Help* through *Saikoku risshi hen* was so widely popular as to be counted as one of the holy books of the Meiji era.

Smiles's literary method was to illustrate his lessons with anecdotes. . . . Many names merely appeared in lists. . . . In other instances, however, Smiles devoted several pages to each model. Those to whom he gave the greatest attention were scientists, engineers, and particularly technologically innovative manufacturers. In describing such manufacturers, Smiles became most enthusiastic, styling them "Industrialized Heroes of the Civilized World."[15] As a trained though seldom practicing physician, Smiles had a personal and professional interest in science. He first achieved fame as an author with his biography of George Stephenson in 1857, beginning a series, *Lives of the Engineers*. Smiles took considerable pains with these biographies, doing substantial research, making extensive interviews, and giving attention to both technical accomplishments and personal attributes. These works still have value for scholars.[16]

Despite his veneration of technologically and scientifically creative men, Smiles did not give them extraordinary attributes, least of all genius. Instead, he claimed that "the men who have most moved the world have not been so much men of genius, strictly so called, as men of intense mediocre abilities and untiring perseverance.[17] Genius as it appeared in *Self-Help* was not raw intelligence but the ability to work diligently toward a single goal, to combine simple principles and common knowledge, and to turn them to new ends—that is, to put together what many had seen but no one had been able to use before.[18] According to Smiles, those of even mediocre ability could achieve by intense application and perseverance, although he did not deny talent entirely. He merely argued that talent without hard work and similar virtues would come to nothing. . . .[19]

Inventors and innovative industrialists embodied the virtues that Smiles admired, but he claimed that the origin of those virtues was social circumstance rather than middle-class values. Over and over again *Self-Help* documents accomplishments that were achieved only after difficulties during formative years were surmounted. Smiles denied that poverty was a misfortune and claimed instead that "it may, by vigorous self-help, be converted into a blessing," for it roused "a man to that struggle with the world in which, though some may purchase ease by degradation, the right-minded and the true-hearted find strength, confidence, and triumph."[20] . . .

While championing those of humble origins, Smiles did not celebrate uncritically all who had risen. The mere acquisition of fortune by a man born in poverty had no intrinsic value. "Riches," he declared, "are no proof whatever of moral worth; and their glitter often serves only to draw attention to the worthlessness of their possessor, as the light of the glow-worm reveals the grub." Disturbed that the original edition of *Self-Help* had been misinterpreted as a "eulogy of selfishness," Smiles reworked it in an attempt to clarify his position. "It will also be found, from the examples of literary, scientific men, artists, inventors, educators, philanthropists, missionaries, and martyrs," he wrote in the preface to this revised edition of 1867, "that the duty of helping one's self in the highest sense involves the helping of one's neighbors." To support this assertion, he extensively treated a number of social activists, including such men as Jonas Hanway and Granville Sharp.[21]

In attacking wealth, Smiles paid more attention to inherited than to first-generation fortunes. As Reinhard Bendix has aptly noted, much in Smiles's celebration of lowly origins and his condemnation of the rich supported the claims of new wealth against established power and privilege.[22] His treatment of the English peerage explicitly demonstrates this distinction. Smiles observed that the English nobility, unlike Continental aristocracies, had been enriched by new blood, by men who had moved up by "the diligent exercise of qualities in many respects of an ordinary character, but potent by force of application and industry." Men with only inherited, unearned wealth, he believed, were likely to lose their privileged positions.[23] Only those who resisted the corrupting effects of unearned wealth could expect to retain their social status. . . .

When the Japanese edition of *Self-Help, Saikoku risshi hen*, first appeared as a runaway best-seller in 1871, neither the political issues nor the social classes to which *Self-Help* had been addressed existed in Japan. There was no industrial bourgeoisie to use the antiaristocratic rhetoric of Smiles and assert its own claims against established hereditary privilege. The issue of state aid and the extension of the franchise versus self-help as alternate means of aiding the working class had no meaning in Japan, which had no industrial labor force, no franchise, and no legislature. What, then, was the appeal of *Self-Help* and *Saikoku risshi hen*? For the translator, Nakamura Keiu, the chief attraction of *Self-Help* was Smiles's assertion, "National progress is the sum of individual industry, energy, and uprightness, as national decay is of individual idleness, selfishness, and vice.[24] For Smiles this statement was an injunction against tampering with the free play of natural forces in the market place and an argument against state aid to the working class, but for Nakamura it was a formula for achieving national prosperity and security and world peace. Thus, *Saikoku risshi hen* provides a prime example of what can happen to the meaning of ideas in their transition from one culture to another.

In his preface to the first chapter of *Saikoku risshi hen,* Nakamura noted that he had been asked why he did not translate a work on military affairs. Explaining that it was a mistake to believe that the strength of the West lay in military might alone, he argued that Western nations were strong because their people followed the way of heaven (*tendō*), because they had the right of autonomy (*jishu no ken*), and because they enjoyed benevolent government. As for war, no less a military figure than Napoleon, whom Smiles had cited, had declared that moral conduct (*tokkō*) was ten times more important than military might, and Smiles himself had explained that a country was weak or strong according to the character of its people. To emphasize martial virtues and military affairs would be to invite war and killing, to go against the way of heaven, which sought to have all men enjoy tranquility and happiness. The way to national strength and social benefit was, therefore, through the cultivation of peaceful virtues, respecting the will of heaven and doing good on the basis of a true heart. This was the way for the individual, the family, the nation, and the world. If men cultivated such virtues, the light of love and the wind of benevolence would spread to the four seas, and clouds of affection and the spirit of harmony would envelop the universe.[25]

These Confucian-sounding expectations that Nakamura Keiu tacked onto *Self-Help* did not just reflect the intellectual background that all educated Japanese of the period shared. Nakamura had been and, for all practical purposes, still was a Confucian scholar in the employ of the Tokugawa house. Born in 1832 into an ambitious peasant family that had purchased samurai status, Nakamura had early shown intellectual brilliance. At the age of ten he won a scholarship to the Shōheikō ("School of Prosperous Peace"), the official Confucian academy of the Tokugawa operated by the Hayashi family. He studied at the Shōheikō between 1848 and 1853 and, upon graduation, served the Tokugawa in various educational posts. In 1862, at the unusually young age of twenty-nine he was appointed as a full-fledged Confucian scholar at the Shōheikō. Although educated and employed within one of the more conservative academies of the period, Nakamura had early tempered his Confucian learning with a secret study of Western works that he had hidden inside Confucian texts. When the Tokugawa policy on foreign studies changed, this surreptitiously acquired knowledge served him well. In 1866, he was chosen to go to London to study English and to chaperon younger students sent abroad by the Tokugawa government.[26]

The England that Nakamura confronted was virtually at the height of its power, and it was more than enough to overawe him. He later remarked that the Chinese text[27] he had read before leaving Japan had not prepared him to understand how such a tiny nation, let alone one ruled by a woman, could have humbled the Middle Kingdom in war. In contrast to the Chinese view of the English as fond of liquor, extravagant, and only clever with gadgets, Nakamura came to see them as exceptional. The English were ruled by a Parliament, whose members were learned; they loved heaven and revered mankind; and the workers were prudent and exercised self-restraint.[28] Less than a year after Nakamura had arrived in England, the Tokugawa regime was overthrown, and, after some debate, he and his charges decided to return to Japan. Before leaving, Nakamura sought advice on how he might transmit to the Japanese people the spirit he had discovered in England. In answer, one of his English friends, H. U. Freeland, presented Nakamura with a copy of the revised edition (1867) of *Self-Help*. On the way back to Japan, Nakamura—in good Confucian fashion—set out to memorize the book. Still a loyal retainer of the Tokugawa, he dutifully followed the former ruling house into exile in Shizuoka. There he returned to his profession of educator, operating the local domain school and translating *Self-Help*. The translation was a major undertaking given the brevity of his training in the English language and the difficulties of rendering the ideas of a work aimed at the British working class into terms comprehensible to Japanese, for whom many features of feudalism were more than just a memory. The first, hand-printed copies of *Saikoku risshi hen* were ready for sale early in 1871,[29] a remarkable achievement under the circumstances. . . .

On its title page, Nakamura styled *Saikoku risshi hen* in English a "translation of *Self-Help*.[30] By modern standards, however, it is a paraphrase, and an incomplete one at that. Nakamura frequently cut and occasionally expanded sections of *Self-Help* with the net result that *Saikoku risshi hen* is at least 20 percent shorter than a full rendering would have been. His cutting and compression is most noticeable in those chapters dealing with industrial and artistic activities. And his fullest renderings, in contrast, cover the ethical and moral portions of the text. . . .

The interest in national prosperity and social progress expressed in Nakamura's preface to *Saikoku risshi hen* is much in evidence in the text itself. Over and over again, Nakamura inserted references to national prosperity in passages that he otherwise translated more or less literally. When Smiles declared that "the world" was indebted to those from "humbler ranks," Nakamura wrote of those who "profit the world and benefit the country." When Smiles argued that not "a single step in civilisation has been made without labour," Nakamura added "in our country." . . . Smiles was intensely interested in the prosperity of England.[31] But, whereas Smiles was content to mention the nation once at the beginning of a paragraph or chapter and thereafter to refer to society, civilization, the world, or some other transnational beneficiary, Nakamura could never let the reader forget that the country (*hōkoku*) benefited from the virtues or actions under consideration.

A potentially more serious problem for Nakamura involved the lack of Japanese equivalents for many English terms, especially those that pertained to relations between individuals and the state or between individuals and society. Nakamura's Confucian vocabulary was not well prepared to deal with such terms as "rights," "liberty," and "freedom," and at some points he resorted to parenthetical explanations and English glosses; for example, he glossed *jishu jiyū* ("autonomy" and "freedom") as "independence."[32] Nevertheless, he did not avoid introducing such concepts, even though they conflicted with both Confucian and samurai values. On the contrary, Nakamura went out of his way to translate and explain these terms, which he could just as well have left out of *Saikoku risshi hen*. Nakamura ascribed importance to what he called "the right of autonomy" (*jishu no ken*) held by the English people, and he stressed the role of Parliament in both his preface to and his afterword for *Saikoku risshi hen*.[33] These emphases were unusual; such issues did not become matters of wide intellectual debate until the so-called *Jiyū minken undō* ("Movement for Liberty and People's Rights") of the 1870s and early 1880s.

Individualism and individuality were two important concepts in *Self-Help* that were not well articulated in either the Confucian or the samurai traditions. Thus, Nakamura's translation had to be free, not literal. When Smiles quoted John Stuart Mill from *On Liberty*, for example, to the effect that despotism is never complete as long as individuality exists and that whatever stamps out individuality is despotism, regardless of the name attached, Nakamura wrote, "Whatever form of government destroys a people's self-reliance ["jiritsu"] must be called a tyrannical government ["kyakusei"]."[34] . . . Nakamura's translation (again really a paraphrase) of *On Liberty*, which was published in 1872 as *jiyū no ri* ("Principle of Freedom"), shows just how interested Nakamura was in the concept of individuality.[35] Having no equivalent for the term, he used a circumlocution—"that which makes each one distinct" (*dokuji ikko naru mono*)—or equated individuality with "character" (*hinkō*), something Mill himself did. Although he abridged *On Liberty* to a much greater degree than he did *Self-Help*, Nakamura struggled to render the full range of meanings Mill attached to individuality, including "eccentricity," which became "character that is out of the ordinary, disobedient, and evil" (*kaiheki hijō no hinkō*).[36] That he sought to introduce these concepts is more significant than the difficulties he experienced. He was taken by Mill's justification of individualism in terms of national and social progress, especially Mill's explanation of European progress (in contrast to Chinese stagnation) as the consequence of the "remarkable diversity of character and culture" existing in European countries. . . . [37]

Contrary to what might be assumed, the absence of an articulated concept of individualism and individuality in *Self-Help* did not represent a significant problem for its Japanese translation. Smiles's definition of individualism was narrower than that of Mill. . . . When Smiles used the term "individualism," he meant individual initiative or self-reliance, nothing more. Expressions like "energetic individualism" or "strenuous individual application" had nothing to do with either philosophical or romantic individualism and were easily translatable with conventional Japanese or Chinese terms.[38] Nakamura had little difficulty in rendering literally a statement such as "steady application to work is the healthiest training for every individual ["jinmin no tenten hitori"], so it is the best discipline of the state."[39] While emphasizing social obligations, Confucianism required the individual to perfect his own conduct and did not allow blaming society for failure. Since no traditional word for "self-help" existed, Nakamura had to coin one (*jijo*),[40] but its constituent traits all had equivalents: "self-culture" became *mizukara mi o osamuru*; "self-control," *mizukara onore ni katsu*; "self-development," *jiko no chikara ni yorite shitaru*; and so on. Emphasis on individual effort in such a context was quite traditional, part of popular Confucianism in Japan and China.[41] . . .

The samurai ethos was centered on the performance of individuals, not groups. As Ronald P. Dore has pointed out, the traditional popular literature of the warrior class celebrated the exploits of individual heroes, and pre-Tokugawa samurai had been notorious for their individual search for glory and their unwillingness to work in disciplined units. The comments of Europeans who sought to train samurai in Western military techniques indicate little change in the samurai ethos by the end of the period. Peasants were much easier to train in close order drill and disciplined group action than were the samurai. Similarly, the late Tokugawa idea of patriotism, as developed by Yoshida Shōin, among others, championed unaffiliated patriots acting independently according to each individual's sense of right and wrong.[42] Because they insisted on their own selflessness in their service to the nation, they cannot be said to have advocated individualism. They did not, nevertheless, think of themselves as cooperating for some collective goal.

Smiles, Nakamura, and late Tokugawa activists all regarded the individual as the unit of performance. Group action versus individual action was not an issue. The men who benefited society acted independently, not collectively. . . . Nakamura was content with Smiles's statements on the subject because they fit Japanese patterns. Smiles wrote, "No individual in the universe stands alone. . . . No man's acts die utterly; and, though his body may resolve into dust and air, his good and bad deeds will still be bringing forth fruit after their kind, and influencing generations for all time to come." "Every act" performed and every word uttered, he stressed, influence "not only the whole" of one's "future life" but also "the whole frame of society."[43] . . .

As this analysis shows, any characterization of Western thought as individualistic and of Eastern, specifically Japanese, thought as collectivistic would overstate the differences between the two traditions. Certainly, within Western thought there is a tradition of absolute individualism, which celebrates all individual activity—good and evil, social and antisocial—and which has no analog in Japanese thought. But, to find such absolute formulations of individualism totally divorced from social utility, one must look beyond popular moralists like Smiles and even beyond major intellectuals like Mill. Especially at the level of popular morality, the cross-cultural comparison yields not the black and white contrast of an individualistic tradition versus a collectivistic tradition but, rather, many shades of gray. . . .

The translation of *Self-Help* and its reception in Japan illustrates a number of principles that should be common in the writing of bicultural history. . . . Ideas are shaped by the social and economic milieu in which they appear and serve the interests of the class or group that produces them. But ideas may also have an existence of their own. A work and the ideas it espouses that were constructed to serve one segment of society under one social structure may serve a very different segment of society under a very different social structure. A work that is part of the "popular culture" in one country may become part of the elite, intellectual culture in another. And the materials included in the purview of intellectual history need not be limited to those that present-day scholars consider valuable and original. The preferences and priorities of historical actors must be respected, even if their taste in reading matter seems questionable by contemporary standards. Works that seem trite and cliché-ridden today may well have been exciting, even revolutionary, to an earlier audience or to one facing a different set of socioeconomic and political problems.

The original text and the translation must be compared, for at the opening point of contact between two cultures ideas cannot be transmitted totally unaltered from one to the other. The translator may not even try such a transmission but may use the translation as a form of disguise for his own thoughts or seek to wrap his own ideas in the aura and prestige of a foreign work. . . . Finally, . . . actual interpretations of the translation must be documented. Readers often do more to make a work historically significant than does its author. No analysis of *Saikoku risshi hen* itself could explain how it became a political tract for disgruntled samurai. But that was precisely what it did become. . . .

Notes

The author gratefully acknowledges the assistance of K. C. Liu of the history department at the University of California, Davis, for his help in Chinese language usage and sources in Nakamura Keiu's works.

1   Ryusaku Tsunoda *et al.*, eds., *Sources of Japanese Tradition*, 2 vols. (New York, 1964), 2: 137.

2   The theme that heaven assigns wealth and honor—rank—at birth and that they cannot be changed by human effort is found throughout Tokugawa writing. For examples that had wide circulation, see "Rikuyu engi tai-i," in *Kyōjun,* vol. 5 of *Nihon kyōkasho taikei* (Tokyo, 1969), 421; and Kaibara Ekiken, "Rakujun," in *Kaibara Ekiken,* ed. Matsuda Michio, vol. 14 of *Nihon no meicho* (Tokyo, 1969), 251, and "Yamato zokujun," in *Kaibara Ekiken,* 123.

3   I am using "samurai" here with full knowledge that the term was not commonly used during the period under discussion, and it did not stand for a precisely definable social category. For a cogent discussion of the problems in defining the limits of the samurai class, see W. G. Beasley, *The Meiji Restoration* (Stanford, 1972), 22–34.

4   That the readership was largely samurai is suggested both by contemporary recollections and by the language and style of *Saikoku risshi hen*; for the latter, see pages 549–54, below. For example, Ishii Tamaji has claimed that the initial readers of *Saikoku risshi hen* were largely officials and educators, and in the early Meiji period these were primarily samurai occupations; Ishii, *Nakamura Masao den* (Tokyo, 1907), 10–11. One G. Takeda reported to Samuel Smiles that "almost all the high class of our fellow countrymen know what *Self-Help* is"; Smiles, *The Autobiography of Samuel Smiles, LL.D.*, ed. Thomas Mackay (New York, 1906), 230.

5   For the publication history of *Saikoku risshi hen* and its derivatives, see Sangu Makoto, " 'Saikoku risshi hen' oyobi sono ruisho ni tsuite," *Gakutō,* 43 (February 1939): 20–25, (March 1939): 15–16.

6   Yone Noguchi, "A True Founder of Empire," *Japan Times,* March 9, 1907, as reprinted in Ishii, *Nakamura Masao den,* unpaginated foldout; and Ukita Kazutami, "Educationalists of the Past and Their Share in the Modernization of Japan," in Okuma Shigenobu, ed., *Fifty Years of New Japan,* 2 (New York, 1910): 156.

7   For an example of such a listing, see Mitsuhashi Takeo, *Meiji zenki shisō shi bunken* (Tokyo, 1976), 80–86.

8   For a list of various editions of *Saikoku risshi hen* as an ethics text, see Torii Miwako, *Meiji ikō kyōkasho sōgō mokuroku-I: Shōgakkō hen* (Tokyo, 1967), 18. Concerning plays based on *Saikoku risshi hen*, see Yanagita Izumi, *Meiji shaki honyaku bungaku*, vol. 5 of his *Meiji bungaku kenkyū* (Tokyo, 1961), 169.

9   For a comparison of the "character ethic" and later American writing focused on personality, see Richard M. Huber, *The American Idea of Success* (New York, 1971), 160–63. Note that even within the "character ethic" there is considerable variation; the explanation that appears below is most applicable to Smiles.

10   Briggs, *Victorian People: Some Reassessments of People, Institutions, Events, and Ideas, 1851–1867* (London, 1965), 126.

11   For the difference between "success" and "achievement," see Karl Mannheim, *Essays on the Sociology of Knowledge,* ed. Paul Kecskemeti (London, 1952), 236–37.

12   Smiles, *Autobiography,* 131–34, 221–23.

13   Timothy H. E. Travers, "Samuel Smiles and the Victorian Work Ethic" (Ph.D. dissertation, Yale University, 1970), 333.

14   Smiles, *Autobiography,* 224–31.

15   Smiles, *Self-Help, with Illustrations of Conduct and Perseverance* (2nd ed., London, 1876), 93. This version, published by John Murray, is a slightly later printing of the revised edition of 1867, which Nakamura used for *Saikoku risshi hen*.

16   Interest in these biographies is indicated by their continued republication. See, for example, Samuel Smiles, *Selections from Lives of the Engineers*, ed. Thomas Parke Hughes (Cambridge, Mass., 1966).

17   Smiles, *Self-Help,* 96–97.

18   *Ibid.*, chap. 5: "Helps and Opportunities—Scientific Pursuits."

19   *Ibid.*, chap. 6: "Workers in Art."

20   *Ibid.*, 19.

21   Smiles, *Self-Help,* 330, iv, 245–57.

22   Bendix, *Work and Authority in Industry* (New York, 1963), 112.

23   Smiles, *Self-Help,* 222, 203.

24   Smiles, *Self-Help,* 3.

25   Nakamura Keiu, "Jijoron dai-ichi hen jo," in Ōkubo Toshiaki, ed., *Meiji keimō shisō shū*, vol. 3 of *Meiji bungaku zenshū* (Tokyo, 1967), 283–84. For an alternative source for this and the other prefaces, see *Meiji shisōka shū*, vol. 13 of Itō Sei *et al.*, eds., *Nihon gendai bungaku zenshū* (Tokyo, 1968), 89–110.

26   Biographical details for Nakamura's career are largely taken from Takahashi Masao's *Nakamura Keiu* (Tokyo, 1966). In addition, the following are useful: "Nakamura Masanao," in *Kindai bungaku sōshō*, 1 (Tokyo, 1956): 406–58; Maeda Ai, "Nakamura Keiu," *Bungaku*, 33 (October 1965): 61–71; Yanagita Izumi, *Meiji shoki no bungaku shisō-I*, vol. 4 of *Meiji bungaku kenkyū* (Tokyo, 1965), 250–61; and Jerry K. Fisher, "The Meirokusha" (Ph.D. dissertation, University of Virginia, 1974).

27   Nakamura specifically referred to Wei Yuan's *Hai-kuo t'u-chih,* a geography written between 1844 and 1852.

28   These comments were originally contained in an afterword appended to the first book (chapter) of *Saikoku risshi hen*; "Sho Saikoku risshi hen go," in *Meiji keimō shisō shū,* 286. In 1876, they became the preface to a revised edition of the translation; see Takahashi, *Nakamura Keiu,* 47–49.

29   For a detailed discussion of the printing and financing of *Saikoku risshi hen,* see Ōkubo Toshiaki, "Nakamura Keiu no shoki yōgaku shisō to 'Saikoku risshi hen' no yakujitsu oyobi kankō," *Shien,* 26 (January 1966): 67–92.

30   *Saikoku risshi hen* exists in numerous editions. Throughout I have used Nakamura Masanao, *Saikoku risshi hen* (Tokyo, 1888). This text is based on the original 1871 version. A portion of the original (the first three chapters) is available in modern printed form: Nakamura, "Saikoku risshi hen," in Ishikawa Ken, ed., *Nihon kyōkasho taikei,* 1 (Tokyo, 1961): 8–77. Because the pagination in the early editions is unreliable, citations here take the form "chapter (book)": arbitrary section number (a number that Nakamura gave to the subdivisions of each chapter). Corresponding material from the original work follows in parentheses, where appropriate.

31   Travers, "Samuel Smiles and the Victorian Work Ethic," 144.

32   Nakamura, *Saikoku risshi hen,* 1: 6.

33   This emphasis appears in both the preface and afterword of *Saikoku risshi hen.* See Nakamura, "Jijoron dai-ichi hen jo," in *Meiji keimō shisō shū,* 283–84; and "Sho Saikoku risshi hen go," in *ibid.*, 286. In addition, he endorsed the idea of a representative assembly in a speech printed in the journal of the Meirokusha; see Nakamura, "Jinmin no seishitsu o kaizō suru setsu," in *ibid.*, 300.

34   Nakamura, *Saikoku risshi hen*, 1: 4 (Smiles, *Self-Help*, 3).

35   I have used David Spirtz's edition of Mill, *On Liberty* (New York, 1975). For the translation, see Nakamura Keiu, *Jiyū no ri*, in *Jiyū minken hen*, vol. 2 of *Meiji bunka zenshū* (Tokyo, 1969), 1–84.

36   Nakamura, *Jiyū no ri*, 52 (Mill, *On Liberty*, 63). In this passage Mill stated, "That so few dare to be eccentric marks the chief danger of the time." Nakamura translated faithfully and thus endorsed the statement.

37   Nakamura, *Jiyū no ri*, 55–57 (Mill, *On Liberty*, 66–68).

38   Nakamura, *Saikoku risshi hen*, 1: 9, 1: 24 (Smiles, *Self-Help*, 6, 18).

39   Nakamura, *Saikoku risshi hen*, 2: 2 (Smiles, *Self-Help*, 27).

40   The lack of a vocabulary word or phrase does not in itself point to the lack of a concept. The term *onore* ("self") occurs very frequently in Confucian writing. Although the context in which *onore* is used often involves the suppression of the self, the continual repetition of such injunctions could not fail to call attention to the concept. Moreover, "self-help" is not an especially old English word. The earliest example given in the *Oxford English Dictionary* is 1831, used by Thomas Carlyle. Smiles could easily have borrowed the word from Carlyle. Travers has suggested, however, that the term came to Smiles from Emerson; "Samuel Smiles and the Victorian Work Ethic," 187.

41   For an exceptionally interesting account of this aspect of popular Confucianism, see Tadao Sakai, "Confucianism and Popular Educational Works," in William Theodore de Bary, ed., *Self and Society in Ming Thought* (New York, 1970), 331–67. For examples of this score-keeping in samurai writing, see Udono Chōkai, "Kanyō kōfu," in Inoue Tetsujirō, ed., *Bushidō sōsho,* 3 (Tokyo, 1905): 263; Yoshida Shōin, "Bukyō zensho kōroku," in *Yoshida Shōin,* ed. Matsumoto San'nosuke, vol. 31 of *Nihon no meicho* (Tokyo, 1973), 131; and Kaibara Ekiken, "Yamato zokujun," 74.

42   Dore, "The Legacy of Tokugawa Education," in Marius B. Jansen, ed., *Changing Japanese Attitudes toward Modernization* (Princeton, 1965), 126; Ienaga Saburō, *Nihon dōtoku shisō shi* (Tokyo, 1955), 80; Marius B. Jansen, *Japan and China from War to Peace* (Chicago, 1974), 62; and Harry D. Harootunian, *Toward Restoration: The Growth of Political Consciousness in Tokugawa Japan* (Berkeley and Los Angeles, 1970), 219–45.

43   Smiles, *Self-Help*, 363–64.

PART IX

Literacy and Orality

Introduction

THIS SECTION OF THE READER is concerned with the spoken word, the written word and the printed word. Cultural history focuses on the processes through which people's lives are given meaning. That involves reflection on changing ways of using language. Here we consider critically the concepts of 'oral culture' and 'literate culture' and the relations between them, and also the difference it made when texts could be reproduced mechanically. A past society where writing was unknown might be called an 'oral culture'; but the phrase also captures the situation in which people relate to each other in terms of what is said and done rather than what is written. Here we are concerned with orality in the latter sense.

Preserving stories and wisdom from oblivion, irrespective of the method employed, has been a shared endeavour to keep alive significant patterns of cultural life. In cultural contexts where memory was the only means of holding on to cherished narratives, declaiming them to an audience has been a valued skill. Twentieth-century research on the techniques involved (Lord 1991) brought to light affinities between Balkan folklore and Homeric epic, and has stimulated global comparisons of orally transmitted poetry (Foley 2002). But what kind of difference did it make to people's ways of perceiving, thinking and acting when they made a transition from orality to using written forms?

Havelock (1986) suggested that phonetic writing based on letters representing spoken sounds was a causal factor in the emergence of intellectual enquiry in ancient Greece. The thesis that being able to write could alter consciousness and culture was developed by several authors (Finnegan 1973; Goody and Watt 1963; Goody 1977, 1986; Olson 1994; Ong and Hartley 2012). Ong's aphorism (1986) that 'writing is a technology that restructures thought' touches on a wider issue in the cultural history of technology as a whole: do culture and technology in fact mutually shape each other? Critics (Graff 2007; Stock 1983) have pointed to the apparently deterministic implications of saying that literacy in and of itself causes people to experience the world differently. This seems to imply a condescending attitude to oral cultures – reminiscent of Gibbon's remark (1776) that 'the use of letters is the principal circumstance that distinguishes a civilised people from a herd of savages incapable of knowledge or reflection.' The alternative is exploring why people sought a way to store words and later retrieve them, and investigating in detail the circumstances in which reading and writing were being used – which, to do them justice, was the aim of historians like Goody, Olson and Ong.

Cultural historians of technology have broadened out from a focus on invention to an interest in the user's perspective: how cultural influences were appropriated matters as much as how they were generated. Chartier (1984, 1999) and others have studied the meaning of the act of reading as well as the significance of what was written. For example, girls often learned only to read (Monaghan 2005), writing being seen as an additional skill they would not require as adults. Saenger (1982, 1997) has pointed out that reading aloud to others (whether to a largely illiterate congregation, to a group of friends, or as a help in committing a text to memory) was only gradually displaced by the practice of individuals reading silently to themselves. Camille (1985) quotes the saying attributed to Pope Gregory I (Chazelle 1990) that pictures are the books of the illiterate – a reminder that oral and visual culture can interact with the culture of the written word. After printing had made books more accessible, there were still numerous ways in which 'orality suffused the world of print' (Reay 1998, and see Fox 2000).

The advent of print with movable type has often been depicted as a breakthrough which fundamentally altered Western culture (Eisenstein 2005). That printing, as part of a complex of changes occurring after the mid-fifteenth century, facilitated the more rapid circulation of ideas is undeniable. But it should not be isolated as a force in its own right, for the new practices that it made possible depended on many other factors. For instance, the new availability of cheaply reproduced texts required paper-making technology. Western historians, unlike their Chinese counterparts (Barrett 2011) pay surprisingly little attention to this pre-condition. Another factor, simultaneously economic and cultural, is the demand for books. As Green (1990) puts it: 'Only the winning of laymen for reading in the late Middle Ages made the invention of printing a paying proposition.' Clanchy (1983) argues that it was thanks to medieval cultural developments that printing caught on rapidly, just as it was partly thanks to printing that early modern Europe changed so fast. Johns (1998) criticises Eisenstein's way of reifying 'the printing press' as if it were a single entity, rather than an ever-changing set of devices, skilled operators (authors, printers, compositors) and commercial developments. Scribner (1984) questions whether the rapid spread of Reformation ideas in Germany depended on this new technology.

The first reading below, by Clanchy, discusses the transition in medieval England from a legal system based on oral testimony to one based on written depositions. Those who had been accustomed to assessing the reliability of a person as a witness were wary of the scope for forgery that was opened up by the new arrangements. The extract comes from the second half of a book rich in detailed accounts of cases where written evidence was accepted 'cautiously – and perhaps reluctantly'.

The reading by Franklin sets the scene for a study of a similar transition occurring on the Eastern edge of Europe (in medieval Rus, centred on Kiev). These introductory pages presuppose no prior knowledge about Rus. They outline some central conceptual issues raised by any systematic study of literacy.

Hudson is concerned in the third of these readings with the eighteenth century. He deals with a transitional phase in attitudes prevalent among English-speaking authors at this time, from a mentality that took the inferiority of oral culture for granted to a recognition that the spoken word and the written word served different purposes. Moreover the spontaneity of speech could now be seen as giving a freshness and vitality to cultures based on face-to-face relationships which might be lacking in more elaborately organised societies.

References

Barrett, T.H. (2011) 'The woman who invented notepaper: towards a comparative histori-ography of paper and print', *Journal of the Royal Asiatic Society,* 21: 199–210.

Camille, M. (1985) 'Seeing and reading: some visual implications of medieval literacy and illiteracy', *Art History,* 8: 26–49.

Chartier, R. (1984) 'Culture as appropriation', in S.L. Kaplan (ed.) *Understanding Popular Culture,* Berlin and New York: Mouton.

Chartier, R. (1999) 'Reading matter and "popular" reading: from the Renaissance to the seventeenth century', in G. Cavallo and R. Chartier (eds) *A History of Reading in the West,* trans. L.G. Cochrane, Amherst: University of Massachusetts Press.

Chazelle, C.M. (1990) 'Pictures, books, and the illiterate: Pope Gregory I's letters to Serenus of Marseilles', *Word & Image,* 6: 138–53.

Clanchy, M.T. (1983) 'Looking back from the invention of printing', in D.P. Resnick (ed.) *Literacy in Historical Perspective,* Washington, DC: Library of Congress.

Eisenstein, E. (2005) *The Printing Revolution in Early Modern Europe,* 2nd edition, Cambridge: Cambridge University Press.

Finnegan, R.H. (1973) 'Literacy versus non-literacy: the great divide?', in R. Horton and R.H. Finnegan (eds) *Modes of Thought: essays on thinking in Western and non-Western societies,* London: Faber.

Foley, J.M. (2002) *How to 'Read' an 'Oral' Poem,* Urbana: University of Illinois Press. See <http://www.oraltradition.org/hrop/>.

Fox, A. (2000) *Oral and Literate Culture in England 1500–1700,* Oxford: Oxford University Press.

Gibbon, E. (1776) *The Decline and Fall of the Roman Empire,* H.H. Milman (ed.) (1899), New York, NY: P.F. Collier, vol. 1, ch. 9, p. 257, <http://babel.hathitrust.org/cgi/pt?id=nyp.33433081571147;view=1up;seq=8>.

Goody, J. (1977) *The Domestication of the Savage Mind,* Cambridge: Cambridge University Press.

Goody, J. (1986) *The Logic of Writing and the Organization of Society,* Cambridge: Cambridge University Press.

Goody, J. and Watt, I.P. (1963) 'The consequences of literacy', *Comparative Studies in Society and History,* 5: 304–45.

Graff, H.J. (2007) 'Introduction' and 'Literacy, myths, and legacies: lessons from the history of literacy', in Graff (ed.) *Literacy and Historical Development: a reader,* Carbondale, IL: Southern Illinois University Press.

Green, D.H. (1990) 'Orality and reading: the state of research in medieval studies', *Speculum,* 65: 267–80.

Havelock, E.A. (1986) 'The alphabetic mind: a gift of Greece to the modern world', *Oral Tradition,* 1: 134–50.

Johns, A. (1998) *The Nature of the Book: print and knowledge in the making,* Chicago: University of Chicago Press.

Lord, A.B. (1991) *Epic Singers and Oral Tradition,* Ithaca, NY: Cornell University Press.

Monaghan, E.J. (2005) *Learning to Read and Write in Colonial America,* Amherst: University of Massachusetts Press.

Olson, D.R. (1994) *The World on Paper: the conceptual and cognitive implications of writing and reading,* Cambridge: Cambridge University Press.

Ong, W. (1986) 'Writing is a technology that restructures thought', in G. Baumann (ed.) *The Written Word: literacy in transition,* Oxford: Oxford University Press.

Ong, W. and Hartley, J. (2012) *Orality and Literacy: the technologizing of the word,* 3rd edition, London: Routledge.

Reay, B. (1998) *Popular Cultures in England 1550–1750,* London and New York: Longman.

Saenger, P. (1982) 'Silent reading: its impact on late medieval script and society', *Viator,* 13: 367–414.

Saenger, P. (1997) *Space Between Words: the origins of silent reading,* Stanford, CA: Stanford University Press.

Scribner, R. (1984) 'Oral culture and the diffusion of reformation ideas', *History of European Ideas,* 5: 237–56.

Stock, B. (1983) *The Implications of Literacy: written language and models of interpretation in the eleventh and twelfth centuries,* Princeton: Princeton University Press.

Chapter 24

Michael T. Clanchy

THE LITERATE MENTALITY:
TRUSTING WRITING

LITERACY IS UNIQUE among technologies in penetrating and structuring the intellect itself, which makes it hard for scholars, whose own skills are shaped by literacy, to reconstruct the mental changes which it brings about. This difficulty has often been noticed and is most clearly put, with reference to medieval England in particular, by Maitland:

> The habit of preserving some written record of all affairs of importance is a modern one in the north and west of Europe. But it is so prevalent and so much bound up with our daily habits that we have almost forgotten how much of the world's business, even in communities by no means barbarous, has been carried on without it.[1]

Having described in the first part of this book how and when 'the habit of preserving some written record of all affairs of importance' grew up, the chapters which follow analyse developments in literate ways of thought. Because the formation of literate habits was relatively slow in England, documents from different dates can be used to pinpoint various aspects of the development. Some of these aspects are peculiar to medieval England, whereas others are common to all societies which have experienced the transition from memory to written record. Although it is difficult to reconstruct pre-literate ways of thought from historical documents, there is sufficient evidence over the two-and-a-half centuries 1066–1307 to discern the main outlines. What is most evident is that literate habits and assumptions, comprising a literate mentality, had to take root in diverse social groups and areas of activity before literacy could grow or spread beyond a small class of clerical writers.

In medieval England all kinds of problems and prejudices had to be overcome before literate modes became acceptable to the rulers, and particularly to the knights in the counties upon whose lead further change depended. It was not, for example, a simple matter of writing down the language which was spoken, as a variety of languages and dialects were used, and Latin had a special status as the traditional language of literacy. To be *litteratus* meant to know Latin and not specifically to have the ability to read and write. The literacy of the laity is the most frequently discussed aspect of medieval literacy, yet that cannot be understood until the terms are defined in their medieval contexts.

The problems just described are peculiarly medieval. Added to them are the psychological differences between learning by ear and learning by looking at script. Medieval writing was mediated to the non-literate by the persistence of the habit of reading aloud and by the preference, even among the educated, for listening to a statement rather than scrutinizing it in script. Writing had the profoundest effects on the nature of proof, as it seemed to be more durable and reliable than the spoken word. On the other hand, those who valued the traditional wisdom of remembrancers within their communities had reason to distrust it. In England at least, in matters of legal proof, compromises were made which helped written modes to become more acceptable. The growth of literacy was not a simple matter of providing more clerks and better schooling, as it penetrated the mind and demanded changes in the way people articulated their thoughts, both individually and collectively in society.

Giving prominence to the term 'the literate mentality' is not intended to prejudge the question of whether literacy really does restructure thought in psychological terms, or whether a 'mentality' can exist as a separate entity in philosophical terms.[2] In order to avoid a technical language of their own, historians use common general terms as convenient descriptive labels. The records of the medieval past are cluttered with abstruse terminology, without historians adding another layer of their own. In what follows, 'the literate mentality' is used simplistically to describe the cluster of attitudes which literates in medieval England shared, and expressed in all sorts of ways in surviving records. . . .

To compensate for the imprecision of the term 'the literate mentality', part II of this book, like part I, proceeds by specific – and even anecdotal – examples in order to show what the shift from memory to written record involved. This was a cultural shift, taking place in the imaginations and assumptions of numerous individuals. . . .

The spoken versus the written word

The increasing use of documents created tension between the old methods and the new. Which was the better evidence, for example, seeing a parchment or hearing a man's word? How was the one to be evaluated if it conflicted with the other? A good illustration of this particular dilemma is Eadmer's account of the investiture controversy between St Anselm, archbishop of Canterbury, and Henry I.[3] Both Anselm and the king had sent envoys to Pope Paschal II; Anselm sent two monks of Canterbury, while the king sent the archbishop of York and two other bishops.

The envoys returned to England in September 1101 with papal letters addressed to the king and to Anselm, prohibiting royal investiture of churches and exhorting resistance to them. When the pope's letter to Anselm had been publicly read out, Henry's envoys objected. They claimed that Paschal had given them a purely verbal message that he would treat the king leniently on the investiture question and would not excommunicate him; the pope had added that he did not wish this concession to be put in written form (*per carte inscriptionem*) because other rulers would use it as a precedent. Anselm's envoys replied that the pope had given no verbal message which conflicted in any way with his letters. To this Henry's bishops answered that Paschal had acted in one way in secret and another in public. Baldwin of Bec, Anselm's chief envoy, was outraged at this allegation and said that it was a calumny on the Holy See.

Dissension then arose in the audience. Those favouring Anselm maintained that credence should be given to 'documents signed with the pope's seal' (*scriptis sigillo pape signatis*) and not to 'the uncertainty of mere words'. The king's side replied that they preferred to rely on the word of three bishops than on 'the skins of wethers blackened with ink and weighted with a little lump of lead'. They added further venom to the argument by alleging that monks were unreliable anyway, as they should not be engaged in worldly business. Eadmer puts the controversy into dialogue form:

Anselm's monks: 'But what about the evidence of the letters?'
Henry's bishops: 'As we don't accept the evidence of monks against bishops, why should we accept that of a sheepskin?'
Anselm's monks: 'Shame on you! Are not the Gospels written down on sheepskins?'

Obviously the conflict could not be quickly resolved. In Lent 1102 Anselm set out for Rome and opened on his way another letter from the pope, in which Paschal denied that he had ever given contradictory verbal instructions to the bishops or said that he was reluctant to set a precedent in writing.[4] Who was telling the truth is of course impossible to resolve. Paschal was attempting to make peace and settle the investiture controversy by diplomacy. He may well therefore have said something off the record to the bishops which they had possibly exaggerated. Like all statesmen, the pope obviously had to make a formal denial of such secret negotiations once they became public.

The substance of the story is not our concern here, but the attitudes it reveals towards documentary evidence. Papal letters, sealed with the leaden bull and bearing the symbols and monograms of curial officials, were the most impressive documents produced in medieval Europe, their only rival being Byzantine imperial letters. Yet in Eadmer's story the papal bull is disparagingly described as a sheepskin blackened with ink with a bit of lead attached to it, an extreme example of a document being treated simply as a physical object rather than for its contents. Anselm's supporters were entitled to riposte that the Gospels too were written on parchment – in other words, that Christianity was essentially the religion of a book. At Orléans in 1022 a group of heretics had been burned for disparaging the book learning of the clergy cross-examining them, which they had called human fabrications 'written on the skins of animals', whereas the heretics claimed to believe 'in the law written in the inner man by the Holy Spirit'.[5] The heretics had therefore been arguing that the true written law *(lex scripta)* was not canon law nor Justinian's code, but inspiration retained in the mind alone; real writing was not man-made script on animal parchment. Such an idea may well have derived from the Scripture itself, most probably from St Paul's Second Epistle to the Corinthians, 'written not with ink, but with the spirit of the living God . . . for the letter killeth, but the spirit giveth life'.[6] Early in the thirteenth century St Francis was to take up this theme as part of his revolt against the spiritually empty book learning of some monks: 'Those religious have been killed by the letter who are not willing to follow the spirit of the divine letter, but only desire to know words and interpret them for other men.'[7] As so often in his work, Francis blended orthodox and heretical viewpoints in an insight of his own. Literacy was not a virtue in itself. Emphasis on the word inscribed spiritually on the minds of men, as contrasted with letters written on parchment, retained its strength in the Christian message as it did in secular conveyancing ceremonies.

The argument of Henry I's envoys, that their word was better evidence than a papal bull, would not in fact have appeared as outrageous or surprising to contemporaries as Eadmer suggests in his account of the controversy with Anselm. The principle that 'oral witness deserves more credence than written evidence' was a legal commonplace. It was cited, for example, by Hubert Walter, archbishop of Canterbury, in a letter to Innocent III in 1200 controverting Gerald of Wales's well-documented claim to be bishop-elect of St David's.[8] Gerald conceded the point in his reply to the pope, but added that he had brought both documents and witnesses. Behind this principle lay the correct assumption that numerous documents used in legal claims, from the Donation of Constantine downwards, were forgeries. Not all those who relied on the traditional use of the spoken word, rather than parchments, were necessarily therefore obscurantist conservatives. The technology of written record was insufficiently advanced to be efficient or reliable. . . .

Trusting writing

Documents did not immediately inspire trust. As with other innovations in technology, there was a long and complex period of evolution, particularly in the twelfth century in England, before methods of production were developed which proved acceptable both to traditionalists and to experts in literacy. There was no straight and simple line of progress from memory to written record. People had to be persuaded – and it was difficult to do – that documentary proof was a sufficient improvement on existing methods to merit the extra expense and mastery of novel techniques which it demanded.

A modern literate tends to assume that statements in writing, especially if they are in print, are more reliable than spoken words. This assumption is the result of schooling in reading and writing from an early age and the constant use of documents, such as bills, for even the smallest transactions. The obvious advantage to a modern literate of documentary proof is that it cannot be as easily or as readily changed as a person's word. But this advantage of writing was less obvious in medieval England, since even literates did not use documents in ways which assured their effectiveness as proof. Most charters of the twelfth century were neither dated nor autographed, nor were they copied into registers for future reference. In the earliest private charters draftsmen and scribes give the impression that, instead of sharing a common training in the drawing up of instruments, they are each making a personal and individual but necessarily amateur effort to master the complexities of documentary proof for the first time. . . .

At first, each charter tended to differ in its phraseology, because every document was felt to be an individual affirmation fixing human relationships at a certain point in time and space. Doubts about whether such stability was possible or appropriate may explain why early drafters of charters are often reluctant to state the time and place of writing and why they invoke the aid of God and his saints so frequently. The advantage to the historian today, though not to the property-owner at the time, of this diversity of practice is that it provides a record, like an archaeological stratification, of how a literate mentality developed over generations. Information, which students of diplomatics have accumulated in order to date charters and identify forgeries, can be used to illustrate how attitudes to writing changed over the twelfth and thirteenth centuries. The evolution of common form is not commonplace, as it marks the stages in the gradual acceptance of literate ways of doing business.

Memory and writing

Before documents were used, the truth of an event or transaction had been established by personal statements, often made on oath, by the principals or witnesses. If the event were too far in the past for that, the oldest and wisest men were asked what they could remember about it. Numerous examples could be cited of collective oral testimony being given from memory, particularly in cases involving the proof of age of feudal heirs. The example which follows illustrates the method in answer to a less routine question. In 1127 a writ of Henry I ordered a jury to be chosen of twelve men from Dover and twelve from Sandwich to settle a dispute between St Augustine's abbey at Canterbury and Christ Church about customs dues at the port of Sandwich. The jurors were described as 'twenty-four mature, wise seniors of many years, having good testimony'.[9] Each in turn then swore on a Gospel book in public that the tolls belonged to Christ Church, saying: 'this I have received from my ancestors, and I have seen and heard from my youth up until now, so help me God and these Holy Gospels.'

Whether in circumstances like these the jurors really told the historical truth is impossible to establish, since the past events in question were recorded only in people's living memories. As the jurors had publicly sworn on the Gospels that they were telling the truth, no more could be said, unless their Christian principles were to be impugned. Thus, without documents, the establishment of what passed for truth was simple and personal, since it depended on the good word of one's fellows. Remembered truth was also flexible and up to date, because no ancient custom could be proved to be older than the memory of the oldest living wise man. There was no conflict between past and present, between ancient precedents and present practice. Customary law 'quietly passes over obsolete laws, which sink into oblivion, and die peacefully, but the law itself remains young, always in the belief that it is old.'[10] Written records, on the other hand, do not die peacefully, as they retain a half-life in archives and can be resurrected to inform, impress, or mystify future generations.

Those who objected in the Middle Ages to the literate preference for the artificial memory of written record, instead of the living memory voiced by wise men of age and experience, were in a long tradition – had they known it – which extended back to myths about the invention of writing. According to Socrates, the god who invented writing had been rebuked by the king of Egypt, Thamuzz, who said:

> If men learn this, it will implant forgetfulness in their souls: they will cease to exercise memory because they rely on that which is written, calling things to remembrance no longer from within themselves, but by means of external marks; what you have discovered is a recipe not for memory, but for reminder.[11]

Both to ignorant illiterates and to sophisticated Platonists written record was a dubious gift, because it seemed to kill living eloquence and trust and substitute for them a mummified semblance in the form of a piece of parchment. Henry I's partisans in the dispute with Anselm, who had called a papal bull a sheepskin 'blackened with ink and weighted with a little lump of lead', were arguing for the priority of the personal testimony of the three bishops who exercised memory over the mere 'external marks' of a writing.[12] Those medieval Christians who recalled St Paul's warning, 'the letter killeth, but the spirit giveth life', were in a similar long tradition.[13] . . .

Objectors to written record had a case which was strong in substance as well as in sentiment, since numerous medieval charters were forged and the authenticity of the genuine ones was difficult to prove. Such a bewildering variety of 'external marks' had been used in idiosyncratic attempts to demonstrate the authenticity of charters that written record was highly suspicious. . . .

In these circumstances, where practice was so varied and even eccentric, both literate and illiterate were entitled to distrust charters. Authentic-looking documents might well be forged, or conversely amateur scrawls might turn out to be genuine. In addition to inconsistencies and lack of uniform scribal training, the principal difficulty was that monks, who were the traditional experts in writing, were also the greatest forgers. The more powerful and ancient the house, the more likely it was that its documents would be forged in a professional manner. Of the seals used by Christ Church Canterbury, Archdeacon Simon Langton wrote to Gregory IX in 1238: 'Holy Father, there is not a single sort of forgery that is not perpetrated in the church of Canterbury. For they have forged in gold, in lead, in wax, and in every kind of metal.'[14] Much the same, of course, could be said of the papal *curia* in an earlier period, when it had used the Donation of Constantíne and other forged decretals.

Yet in theory at least it would have been relatively easy for English medieval writers to make documents whose authenticity could normally have been proved. Although no system of safeguards could cover all cases, the great majority could certainly be guaranteed. All that was required was to follow elementary principles of Roman legal practice, which were familiar in twelfth-century Italy and throughout the *pays du droit écrit* [the lands of written law] bordering on the Mediterranean, and ensure that each document was precisely dated and written by an authorized scribe or notary. Ideally, in addition, the notary needed to register a copy of the document in a record kept by a public authority. As is well known, these elementary principles were not followed in medieval England, nor elsewhere at first in northern Europe. Although some notaries practised in England in the thirteenth century, their activities were normally restricted to a few types of ecclesiastical business. . . . Sometimes the king's government could not trace its own documents, let alone other people's.

The reason why England did not develop a notarial system on the Roman model is generally thought to be simple and obvious: 'customary law prevailed.'[15] Although correct, this explanation is inadequate, as customary law did not prevail in other areas of bureaucratic activity because twelfth-century England had been opened to Italian and other European influences, first by the Norman Conquest and then by the Angevins. . . . Why England remained largely unaffected by the Roman notarial system, while being influenced by other continental bureaucratic procedures, is therefore a question worth pursuing further, as it goes to the roots of the non-literate's lack of understanding and consequent distrust of written modes of proof. . . .

The Roman system of authorizing notaries was a relatively simple and normally effective way of coping with the problems of authenticating documents in the Middle Ages. Not every party to a document, even if he were able to read, could be expected to sign personally with a distinctively penned signature of his own, as in modern western culture, because writing on parchment was a business for specialists. Confining signing to professional scribes had other advantages. It imposed uniform standards on the production of documents and it restricted writers to a manageable number, whose credentials could be checked. A notary signed documents with his *signum* in much the same way as a master mason marked the stones he cut before they were built into a permanent fabric. Despite these advantages, qualified notaries were not much used in England. . . .

The symbolism of seals and crosses

The reasons why England did not develop a uniform scribal system for authenticating documents seem to centre on the use of seals. Although medieval seals varied considerably in size, materials, and design, they had two typical elements – a device or pictorial symbol in the centre, such as a knight on horseback . . . and a legend or inscription around the circumference bearing the sealer's name.[16]. . . The typical seal, combining a device or *signum* with the signatory's name, functioned in much the same way as a notarial form of authentication. Moreover, in one way a seal was more efficient than a notary's manual *signum,* as every seal in wax from the same matrix was identical. Because seals reproduced script, they enabled people to sign their names in an acceptable form without labour or skill. In effect every possessor of a seal could be his own notary, as he could authenticate documents with his individual *signum* and name, even if he were unable to manipulate a pen. Like the practice of reading documents aloud, seals helped to bridge the gap between the literate and the non-literate. For the possessor of a seal, the scribe who wrote the document, like the clerk who read it aloud, was a mere intermediary, an artisan of script. Perhaps English scribes were not required to identify themselves, nor to put their *signa* on the documents they wrote, because writers were of little significance. Instead, the donor and witnesses themselves authenticated the documents with their own *signa* in the ready-made form of seals.

> Not only by intent but also in practice a seal does exactly the same as the printing press: it reliably copies and multiplies information by mechanical means – in this case information of ownership. This information can consist of a picture (illustration), one single sign (movable type), or a short text (block print). We have here in embryo all the basic elements of printing. The reason for the long hiatus between the first Mesopotamian seal, the first Far Eastern block print and the Gutenberg Bible must not be sought in a lack of creative ability.[17]

The European type of printing invented by Gutenberg in the fifteenth century depended on technologies of metallurgy – in engraving, punching, casting, and compressing – which had been developed for coins and seals centuries earlier. For example, a screw-press similar in form to the earliest printing-press was made for Canterbury cathedral in c. 1232, where it was used to fix the church's double-sided seal to documents.[18] Every possessor of a large double-sided seal (which was the form favoured by the royal Chancery and great churches) required a press of this sort. . . . Seal impressions could be produced in malleable metals, like gold and silver, which are more durable than wax. An old practice, exemplified by the papacy, was to use a seal of lead – the *bulla*. But . . . sealing wax . . . could be stuck on to the document itself, whereas the papal *bulla* had to be attached with string. . . . [However,] for seals to stand permanently 'as testimony of the truth' necessitated devising a method of preserving the wax impression on the charter, instead of destroying it as happened when a letter close was opened. This is why . . . Edward the Confessor, or rather the official who later became known as the spigurnel, 'appended' the wax to the charter. The seal hung ('appended') from a tongue of parchment or on strings, instead of being stuck tightly to the document. Instead of using the adhesive quality of the wax to show the recipient that the document had reached him unopened, Edward the Confessor's innovation made the hardened adhesive itself a symbol of the royal will. The seal was intended to stick to the charter in perpetuity in validation of the grant. Henceforward a charter without a seal was not acceptable as evidence in the king's court.

The new seal of Edward the Confessor was much larger and heavier than ordinary seals and it was also double-sided, in imitation of papal and imperial seals; this was made possible by its hanging freely, instead of sticking to the body of the document. The apparatus like a printing press for producing these double-sided seals was not easily portable as the seal-press (judging by the one at Canterbury) required two people to lift it. . . . The 'great seal' of Edward the Confessor was a portentous object which gave weight, physically and symbolically, to the king's most solemn grants. . . . Its wax impression was a visible sign of the king's will, which could be transferred from hand to hand at the charter conveyancing ceremony like a symbolic knife or rod. It had the advantage over other symbolic objects that it was harder to forge and easier to fix securely to the charter because it adhered to the parchment. Another advantage was that it printed out the king's name, titles, and icons of authority automatically. . . . The great seal also automated and depersonalized the signing process, as it had a little cross at its head which made the king's sign of the cross on his behalf and even in his absence. The seal's icon of the king enthroned in majesty made his authority present wherever his image was present, like Christ in Majesty. . . . A great seal was a desirable object in its own right, however, irrespective of whether it was useful, because it was a symbol of status and power. This is precisely what the seals of Edward the Confessor and William the Conqueror had been. . . .

The seal was indeed a 'two-faced image', as the Ramsey chronicler had called it, though not because it was specially deceptive; indeed seals were harder to forge than the signs of the cross penned on charters. Metaphorically it was two-faced. In the formation of a literate mentality the seal looked back over centuries – or even millennia – to message sticks, charms, and traditional symbols of conveyance like knives and rods. At the same time it looked forward to the automation of writing and government. The mass-production of the king's image on sealed writs was the basis of the English Exchequer and common law system of bureaucracy from the twelfth century onwards. Although the writing process itself was not automated until the invention of printing, sealing resolved the problem which was prior to that of reproducing books for the literate public. Before being offered printed books, the public had to be persuaded of the value of writing itself. Sealing resolved this problem in terms which were acceptable both to chanceries and to non-literates. The seal was the harbinger of literacy, as it was the device which brought literate modes even into remote villages, particularly in the form of taxation demands from the Exchequer sealed with the hated green wax. Sealing was a labour-saving technology, both at the exalted level of the royal Chancery and at the humble level of the peasant who could sign his name with his seal without being able to write.

Notes

1   F. Pollock and F.W. Maitland, *The History of English Law before the Time of Edward I*, Cambridge University Press, 2nd edition (1898), p 25.

2   G. E. R. Lloyd, *Demystifying Mentalities* (1990); D. R. Olson, *The World on Paper: the Conceptual and Cognitive Implications of Writing and Reading* (1994). Both books published by Cambridge University Press.

3   Eadmer, ed. M. Rule, *Eadmeri Historia Novorum in Anglia,* Rolls Series LXXXI (1884), pp. 132–40.

4   Eadmer, *Historia,* pp. 149–51. R. W. Southern, *Saint Anselm*, Cambridge University Press (1990), p. 295, n. 17.

5   *Recueil des historiens des Gaules* ed. L. Delisle (1869–94), x, p. 539; R. I. Moore, *The Birth of Popular Heresy*, Edward Arnold (1975), pp. 10–15. The author of this account is discussed by B. Stock, *The Implications of Literacy*, Princeton University Press (1983), pp. 107–15.

6   *2 Corinthians*, III, 3: 6. Cf. B. Smalley, *The Study of the Bible in the Middle Ages*, Blackwell (1952), ch. 1 ('The Letter and the Spirit').

7   R. B. Brooke, *The Coming of the Friars*, George Allen & Unwin (1975), p. 126.

8   'testibus et non testimoniis credi oportet,' Giraldus III, pp. 14, 21, H. E. Butler, *The Autobiography of Giraldus Cambrensis,* Jonathan Cape (1937), pp. 168, 175–6.

9   D.M. Stenton, *English Justice between the Norman Conquest and the Great Charter*, George Allen & Unwin for the American Philosophical Society (1965), p. 118. B. O'Brien shows that both sides in this dispute also possessed Anglo-Saxon charters concerning these rights, 'Forgery and the Literacy of the Early Common Law', *Albion* xxvii (1995), pp. 5–6.

10 F. Kern, *Kingship and Law in the Middle Ages* trans. S. B. Chrimes, Blackwell (1939), p. 179; M. T. Clanchy, 'Remembering the Past and the Good Old Law', *History* LV (1970), pp. 165–76, at p. 172.

11 Plato, *Phaedrus*, pp. 274–5, trans. R. Hackforth (1952). Cf. E. R. Curtius, *European Literature and the Latin Middle Ages,* Routledge & Kegan Paul (1953, trans. W.R. Trask), p. 304; J. Goody and I. Watt, 'The consequences of literacy', in J. Goody (ed.), *Literacy in Traditional Societies,* Cambridge University Press (1968), pp. 27–68, at p. 50; M. J. Carruthers, *The Book of Memory*, Cambridge University Press (1990), pp. 30–1, 296–7.

12 See n.4 above.

13 See nn.5–7 above.

14   C. R. Cheney, *Medieval Text & Studies*, Oxford University Press (1973), p. 104.
15   C. R. Cheney, *Notaries Public in England,* Oxford University Press (1972), p. 6.
16   In general see P. D. A. Harvey and A. McGuiness, *A Guide to British Medieval Seals* (1996).
17   A. Gaur, *A History of Writing* (1984), p. 194.
18   Illustrated in Alexander, J. J. G. and Binski, P. (1987) (eds), *Age of Chivalry: Art in Plantagenet England, 1200–1400,* Exhibition Catalogue, pp. 399–400, no. 460. Cf. the printing press of 1499 illustrated by V. Scholderer, *Johann Gutenberg* (1963), plate xiv.

Chapter 25

Simon Franklin

INTRODUCTION TO *WRITING, SOCIETY AND CULTURE IN EARLY MODERN RUS, C. 950–1300*

AT THE RISK OF LABOURING what may be obvious, it would be as well to outline in advance some of the main elements of my approach to the theme of writing in cultural history: first, in general; then, in relation to Rus.

In the very broadest definition, *any* graphic sign or set of signs can be labelled 'writing'. All visual representation is a form of 'text', which can be 'read'. Writing is a form of depiction; or, more simply, depiction is writing. Indeed, some languages (including, for the present context, Greek and Church Slavonic) use the same word for 'to write' as for 'to depict'. More narrowly, writing is a system of graphic signs, the primary use of which, in combination with one another, is to indicate the sound-, word- or thought-sequences of language. 'Thought-writing' (pictograms, ideograms) is not necessarily tied to a specific language; hence identical signs – such as mathematical symbols, or road signs, or manufacturers' logos, or Chinese characters – can 'mean' roughly the same thing, yet are decoded through entirely different sets of sounds. 'Sound-writing' (syllabic, consonantal or alphabetic script) is a system of graphic signs which, when combined, are designed to be decoded as specified words of a particular language.[1] In the present book 'writing' for the most part implies alphabetic script. In principle, alphabetic script is generally understood to represent graphically the sounds of speech. In practice, the functions of real alphabets in real use are not so straightforward, either in relation to the sounds of speech or in relation to other graphic devices.

On the one hand, even in their main function as signifiers of utterances through their constituent sounds, alphabets depend on cultural collusion among their users more than on the transparent 'logic' implied in the alphabetic principle. Except in the early stages of learning, the act of reading – the act of decoding the graphic sign – tends to be by word-recognition rather than by the sequential reconstitution of sounds. Modern reading is mostly silent, so that the 'sound' is in any case notional. The same alphabet can be used in different languages, such that the same graphic signs (letters) are decoded as different sounds. Within a language, alphabets tend to be normative and conservative, taking little account of variation in speech-sounds over time or region (nor do we fully abolish the problem by speaking of 'phonemes' instead of 'sounds'). In other words, real alphabetic writing should not be confused with phonetic transcription, its more pliant derivative.

On the other hand, what alphabetic writing 'says' is not always directly retrievable as speech. Though the basic job of an alphabet is to serve as a form of notation for words, those who use alphabetic script are also free to exploit other dimensions of its semantic potential as a graphic medium. A piece of writing is a made object, with visual and perhaps even tangible properties. Variables in the way writing is presented – in its materials, or its design, size, context, colours or techniques – can be used to convey non-verbal messages: messages about status and authority, for example, or about wealth, or taste. In some situations the non-linguistic (or non-glottal) messages even constitute the main 'text' to be read, more important than the bare words. Although alphabetic script does have its own distinct functions, it can also share the semantic functions of other graphic devices, and on this non-linguistic level the boundary between writing in the narrow sense and writing in the broad sense (where any depiction is a 'text') is far from clear. For example, the ability to 'sign' one's name is commonly taken as a measure of the ability to write alphabetic script; yet the point of a modern 'signature' is not to convey a word through correct spelling (modern signatures are often strictly indecipherable as alphabetic script), but to form a unique and identifiable shape, a personal graphic 'sign', to function as an ideogram. The writing of meaning is only a part of the meaning of writing. In this respect, alphabetic writing should be seen as only a part of what might be called the total *graphic environment*. I shall be concerned not only with who wrote or read what kinds of articulated words, but also with the semantic implications of writing in the wider graphic environment.

Writing is a technique, as is reading. Those who acquire the technical skills tend to be labelled 'literate', and the study of the uses of reading and writing is generally associated with the study *of literacy*. With reference to individuals, 'literacy' has two meanings, one technical, the other cultural. In the technical sense it implies some level of ability in reading and/or writing. In the cultural sense it implies some level of familiarity with, and mastery of, cultural activities in which reading and writing are used. In both cases the criteria for what constitutes literacy, in an individual, vary from society to society, and there is no point in setting a universal standard. Nowadays, in order to be functionally literate, an individual needs to be able to perform quite complex tasks fluently. At other times, for technical literacy, it may have been sufficient to be able to write one's name or to struggle through a document with guidance. The two skills can even be separated. Just as it is possible to read a language without being able to speak it, so it is possible to write without being able to read (i.e. merely to reproduce letter-forms from an exemplar, such as when a monoglot typesetter sets a text in foreign script) or to read without being able to write. What matters is what matters in context, what one needs to be literate *for*. With reference to the individual, the notional opposite of 'literacy' is 'illiteracy'. The opposition is notional, because the boundary is socially constructed. A person considered literate in one society may be considered illiterate in another; or, more confusingly, a person obviously literate in the technical sense may nevertheless be branded – or confess to being – illiterate in the cultural sense. In this book I try to avoid any general measure of individual literacy, reserving the word instead for the technical skills required in specific contexts, or for occasions when the term is specifically justified by an equivalent expression in the sources.[2]

In cultural history 'literacy' has acquired a third meaning: it denotes the sum of social and cultural phenomena associated with the uses of writing (here the notional opposite of 'literacy' is 'orality').[3] 'Literacy studies', in this sense, flourish. However, if one accepts this use of the term, one must be wary of implicit contamination with the technical meanings of the word with regard to individuals. In industrial or post-industrial societies it is reasonable to link the study of the uses of writing with the study of the individual technical skills, since mastery of the technical skills is a prerequisite for any form of significant involvement in the uses of writing. Not so in a pre-industrial age, or for a different type of cultural 'literacy'.[4]

Of course it is interesting, and relevant, to know who could read and/or write, and to what level and for what purposes, but an individual or social literacy-index is not at all the same thing as a survey of those who were, to varying degrees and in various ways, involved in the *culture of the written word*. Participation in, or access to, the culture of the written word was far from being the exclusive preserve of technically literate people. The written word reaches and may affect anybody who can listen to it being read (or even recited from third-hand memory), or anybody who sees written objects in their graphic environment. The culture of the written word may even be partly shaped by people who do not themselves apply the technical skills: 'writers' need not write, if they can dictate, and texts are produced by those who commission them as much as by those who copy them out. 'To read' may mean 'to hear', and 'to write' may mean 'to cause to be written'. No points are being stretched here. Nowadays 'to build' can mean 'to cause to be built', as in 'we built an extension to our house last year'. Or, perhaps a closer analogy: computer culture is a far larger and more complex phenomenon than the culture of computer programmers. This book is about the culture of the written word, of which individual, technical literacy is a necessary component, but not necessarily a major component, and certainly not the only component.

Writing is also a technology. The invention of writing, and its acquisition in successive societies, is one of the great leaps in *information technology*, along with the emergence of speech itself, the invention of printing and the development of electronic media (hence such metaphorical usages as 'computer literacy').[5] In a period of unprecedentedly rapid global change in information technology, the historical study of the uses of writing can become an oblique form of self-exploration: what are the implications of technological change? How profound or predictable or controllable are its consequences in which areas of social and personal life? This is a fertile environment for interdisciplinary and cross-cultural study, where the theoretical and the practical, the past and the present, the remote and the immediate, mingle to mutual advantage. The study of the sociocultural ramifications of writing fits into no single academic niche. It is nobody's property. Insights derived from case-studies of ancient Mesopotamia, or of classical Greece, or of medieval England, or of twentieth-century West Africa, are exchanged in productive dialogue across chronological, geographical, institutional and disciplinary boundaries.

Writing is a technology which turns words into objects. It gives them form, or signifies them by means of form. It makes words visible, tangible, portable. It separates speech from speaker, message from messenger, known from knower. It resituates the word in time and space. It enables words to be preserved, verified and copied, rearranged and revised, contemplated and analysed at leisure. Such, in principle, are some of its properties. The contentious issue is how, in general and in particular cases, the properties of the technology relate to social and cultural change. Answers can be arranged on a scale running from an extreme 'technocentric' approach at one end to an extreme 'anthropocentric' approach at the other.

According to the 'technocentric' approach, technology causes change, and the spread of writing has profound *consequences* both for individuals and for societies. In the individual the acquisition of the technical skills changes not only the scope of activities and social opportunities but also structures and habits of thought. Since writing can be preserved and perused, its messages can be analysed and criticised. Writing engenders habits of abstract argument, formal logic, critical thought. In society the ability to make and keep written records of transactions encourages the emergence of new institutions, new forms of social control. Written procedures allow the standardisation of administrative norms across vast areas. Record-keeping swells the power of the record-keeper, or the record-validator. The spread of writing enables – hastens, even causes – the growth of centralised bureaucracies. And then there is 'culture': religion, ideology, literature. Writing enables the dissemination of authoritative texts which cut across social, communal and geographic divisions. It allows the words of authority to extend beyond their immediate audience. It creates, in effect, new communities, 'textual' communities,[6] those who share a written language, or who acknowledge the authority of a particular body of writings. In all these capacities writing not merely enables its users to perform certain tasks more effectively; it alters the very nature of the tasks which they are able to perform, and it alters their perception of such tasks. Writing changes the world. When fully exploited, the technology of writing, whether it functions as a means of information storage or as a means of expression or as a means of communication, fundamentally affects the way societies are organised, the hierarchies of power, the criteria of authority, the forms of cultural activity, the structures of thought,[7] even the very workings of the human brain.[8]

The grand technocentric vision has opened broad avenues of speculation and inquiry, but in its pure form (which, to be fair, few of its proponents would advocate) it is easier to knock than to defend.[9] Above all, a normative scheme of technologically determined cultural evolution stumbles against the diversity of actual case-studies. If technology is the cause, why do not all societies show the same effects? Writing has existed for millennia, most societies have had opportunities to acquire and exploit the technology, but why have not all of them produced Greek philosophers, Hebrew scribes, Arab calligraphers, Roman lawyers, or Soviet bureaucrats? Demonstrably, 'the mere availability of writing does not transform a society'.[10] The anthropocentric response is to assert that the agent of change is not the technology but the user: people, society. People choose, or do not choose, to adopt writing or to explore its potential according to their perception of their own needs. There is resistance to writing in those societies, or in those activities within a society, which are perceived to function adequately without it. Writing is accepted or rejected, expanded or contracted, according to need. If it ain't broke, don't fix it. Societies do not change because they introduce writing; they introduce writing because they change.

The anthropocentric riposte sounds eminently reasonable, but this plain reversal of causation is no less crude; as if 'needs' are consistently identified independently of the means available to meet them. People may indeed exploit writing according to their needs, but people's perception of their needs can be affected by their experience of writing. Writing is not literally an agent, and it does not bring inevitable consequences, but through the use of writing and through reflecting on writing, people can develop habits of thought and behaviour which they would not otherwise have suspected in themselves; they can develop new needs. There is an interaction, a dynamic relationship. The contrastive approaches can be recast as an inclusive approach: societies exploit writing because they change, *and* societies change because they exploit writing. We may well distrust technological determinism and prefer human agency, but we can still accept, if not that the technology changes people, then at least that people's own experience of the technology can induce them (individually and collectively, as societies) to change themselves.

The uses of writing must therefore be considered not just in themselves, but in their dynamic relationship with, on the one hand, the *non*-uses of writing and, on the other hand, social perceptions of what writing is, of its nature, status, authority and functions.

Writing and non-writing, the sphere of the written and the sphere of the spoken ('literacy' and 'orality') have often been presented as polar opposites, or – in the technocentric scheme – as ideally distinct stages in sociocultural evolution.[11] This is misleading. The written mode and the spoken mode are neither discrete stages on an evolutionary journey nor entirely interchangeable options at any given time. The notion of a distinct 'orality' is properly tenable only with regard to societies where writing is wholly unknown. Otherwise the culture of the written word and the culture of the spoken word overlap, interact, modify and modulate each other. Writing does not obliterate speech and memory, but rather the functions of each are affected by the presence of the other. The ways in which they do so are not simply predictable, but are specific to the sociocultural dynamics of a given society. To risk some analogies: contrary to prediction, computerisation has not led to mass bankruptcies among paper manufacturers, though the functions and status of print-copy are affected (in some areas reduced, in other areas enhanced) by the existence of electronic storage. Contrary to some predictions (and to early trends), television and video have not rendered cinemas redundant; instead cinemas have adapted in response to television and video, and film-production has adapted to explore the differential qualities of the large and the small screen, of public and domestic display. Contrary to what might seem practical logic, telephone and e-mail have not led to a decline in academic and business travel. Words delivered in a face-to-face meeting, by telephone, by e-mail, in a hand-written letter, or in a computer-generated letter may carry an identical verbal meaning, but the choice of modes may convey different cultural messages. In none of these cases should one speak of either 'residual' survivals of the older technology or of straightforward alternatives. In all cases the functions of one mode are adapted through the presence of the other. The uses of writing have a bearing on the cultural semantics of non-writing, and vice versa.[12]

Writing is a cultural phenomenon. Its meanings are not implicit. As a set of signs, it has the significance and functions ascribed to it by those who use it or who come into contact with it. Its *status and authority* (and hence its non-verbal meaning) reflect cultural values. The value attributed to writing is rarely constant in all its contexts, and it is rarely appropriate to speak of 'the' status of writing throughout a given society. On the contrary, the sociocultural dynamics of writing in a society may be characterised by the patterns of variation in the status and authority of types of writing within that society. Variables include the social or occupational status of the producers of writing (author, scribe, editor, individual or institutional patron), the verbal contents, the social or transactional context, the consumer (individual reader, recipient, communal addressee), as well as the forms of presentation of the medium itself. In their fluctuating combinations, such variables produce quite complex patterns of differentiation within and between the linked communities of a given society. Before seeking a unifying theory, or perhaps instead of seeking a unifying theory, one needs to map the patterns of differentiation which, taken together, characterise the culture (or cultures) of the written word in Rus.

Such patterns are not rigidly predictable, and to that extent the adoption and spread of writing does not have a fixed set of consequences, or even of implications. But neither are the patterns completely random. Although few if any societies reproduce the totality of each other's uses and perceptions of writing precisely in every detail, few if any societies develop features in their uses and perceptions of writing which are wholly unparalleled elsewhere. Hence, however fragile any unified theory, the cultural history of writing remains a unified field of study in which each case history has a bearing on our understanding of the field as a whole. . . .

Notes

1   Here I fall into the 'scriptist' heresy excoriated by Roy Harris, *The Origin of Writing* (London, 1986), pp. 29–56, although Harris's theory of writing, which stresses its nature as graphic sign, is a stimulating corrective to complacent identification between writing and language; see his later book, *Signs of Language* (London, 1996). For the convenient distinction between 'thought-writing' and 'sound-writing' see Albertino· Gaur, *A History of Writing,* revised edn (London, 1992), pp. 14–15.

2   See e.g. below, pp. 223–4, on the *knizhnik* (bookman, man of letters, *litteratus).*

3   Compare the sharply contrastive approach of Walter J. Ong, *Orality and Literacy. The Technologizing of the Word* (London, 1982), with the more nuanced essays in David R. Olson and Nancy Torrance (eds.), *Literacy and Orality* (Cambridge, 1991).

4   See esp. Michael Clanchy, *From Memory to Written Record: England 1066–1307* (London, 1979); Franz H. Baüml, 'Varieties and Consequences of Medieval Literacy and Illiteracy', *Speculum* 55 (1980), 237–65; D. H. Green, 'Orality and Reading: The State of Research in Medieval Studies', *Speculum* 65 (1990), 267–80; Charles F. Briggs, 'Literacy, Reading and Writing in the Medieval West', *Journal of Medieval History* 26 (2000), 397–420.

5   For an overview see e.g. Michael E. Hobart and Zachary S. Schiffman, *Information Ages. Literacy, Numeracy, and the Computer Revolution* (Baltimore and London, 1998), although here the authors argue that 'information' as such is first made possible through writing, not through speech alone: see *ibid.*, pp. 27–30.

6   A term usefully developed by Brian Stock, *The Implications of Literacy: Written Language and Modes of Interpretation in the Eleventh and Twelfth Centuries* (Princeton, 1983).

7   See, especially, the influential 'trilogy' by Jack Goody: *The Domestication of the Savage Mind* (Cambridge, 1977); *The Logic of Writing and the Organization of Society* (Cambridge, 1986), and *The Interface Between the Written and the Oral* (Cambridge, 1987).

8   Leonard Schlain, *The Alphabet Versus the Goddess: the Conflict Between Word and Image* (London, 1999) has argued with considerable verve that writing brings about the dominance of 'left-brain' capabilities over 'right-brain' capabilities, and hence leads to the triumph of militant rationalism and the destruction of matriarchy; cf. Richard Hellie, 'Late Medieval and Early Modern Russian Civilization and Modern Neuroscience', in A. M. Kleimola and G. D. Lenhoff (eds.), *Culture and Identity in Muscovy, 1359–1584* (UCLA Slavic Studies, New Series, vol. III; Moscow, 1997), pp. 146–65, who speculates that traditional low levels of literacy were responsible for Muscovy being a 'right-brained civilization'.

9   See, for example, the critiques by Carol Fleischer Feldman, 'Oral Metalanguage', in Olson and Torrance, *Literacy and Orality*, pp. 47–65; and J. Peter Denny, 'Rational Thought and Literate Decontextualization', *ibid.*, pp. 66–89.

10   Gaur, *A History of Writing*, p. 15.

11   Hence, for example, the persistent retention of oral methods, where writing is available, can be classified as merely 'residual': sec Ong, *Orality and Literacy*, pp. 99, 109, 115–16.

12   See the 'ecological' metaphor applied by David Barton, *Literacy. An Introduction to the Ecology of the Written Word* (Oxford, 1994).

Chapter 26

Nicholas Hudson

CONSTRUCTING ORAL TRADITION: THE ORIGINS OF THE CONCEPT IN ENLIGHTENMENT INTELLECTUAL CULTURE

[M]any circumstances of those times we call barbarous are favourable to the poetical spirit. That state, in which human nature shoots wild and free, though unfit for other improvements, certainly encourages the high exertions of fancy and passion . . . An American chief, at this day, harangues at the head of his tribe, in a more bold and metaphorical style, than a modern European would adventure to use in an epic poem.[1]

THIS STATEMENT FROM HUGH BLAIR'S *A Critical Dissertation on the Poems of Ossian* (1763) reflects an important reassessment of oral tradition among scholars during the middle decades of the eighteenth century. It was during this period that scholars began to acknowledge that a society without writing could, as Blair indicates, function as an organized political culture with a tradition of common values and practices. Such a culture, it was thought, could also nourish a 'poetical spirit' that equalled and even excelled the literary resources of European nations in their modern, developed state. These views marked a radical departure from the generally negative opinion of pre-literate cultures that prevailed in the Renaissance and the seventeenth century. In *Purchas his Pilgrimes* (1625), a major source of information about non-European peoples in the early century, Samuel Purchas echoed the conventional view that alphabetical writing marked the main distinction between civilized peopled and 'barbarians': 'amongst Men, some are accounted Ciuill, and more both Sociable and Religious, by the Vse of *letters* and Writing, which others wanting are esteemed Brutish, Sauage, Barbarous.'[2] According to Purchas and his contemporaries, illiterate 'savages' lacked history, government, poetry or really 'society' of any kind.

Between the Renaissance and the Enlightenment, in short, Western attitudes to non-literate cultures transformed fundamentally, paving the way for our modern appreciation of oral tradition as a legitimate basis for poetical expression and social organization. What were the historical factors that instigated this change? Elsewhere, I have traced the concept of oral tradition to theological debates between Catholics and Protestants concerning the authority of customary or 'unwritten' practices and doctrines.[3] In this chapter, I will argue that the emergence of this concept in the Enlightenment was linked to a much wider revolution of ideas about language, history and culture. Increasingly, scholars began to recognize the predominant and, in some respects, damaging influence of writing over their conceptions of language and society. They began to recognize more clearly the special powers of speech not possessed by written language, a development that led to a deeper appreciation of so-called 'primitive' language in non-literate societies.

Readers will recognize the irony of this development: as European society became *more* literate, it gained an ever sharper awareness of oral cultures and their special characteristics. Despite being surrounded by a predominantly oral culture, medieval authors were virtually unconscious of 'orality' as a special state of either language or society. They failed to distinguish between oral and literate societies, for they did not conceive of speech and writing as inherently dissimilar forms of language. Relying on Aristotle's *De interpretatione* (largely as explained in the late Roman tradition of Porphyry and Boethius), they regarded writing as an 'image' of spoken language, which in turn was an 'image' of 'mental experience'. Aristotle's definition implied no deficiency in the power of writing to convey either words or thoughts. Consider, for example, the following paraphrase of Aristotle's model (as presented by Boethius) by William of Ockham, the great nominalist philosopher of the early fourteenth century:

> According to Boethius in the first book of *De interpretatione*, language is threefold: written, spoken and conceptual . . . A written term [*terminus scriptus*] is part of a proposition written on some material, and is or can be seen with the bodily eye. A spoken term is part of a proposition uttered with the mouth and able to be heard with the bodily ear. A conceptual term is a mental content or impression which naturally possesses signification or consignification, and which is suited to be part of a mental proposition and to stand for what it signifies.[4]

According to Ockham, the difference between mental, verbal and written discourse consisted merely in the *medium* of transmission. This understanding of language justified the medieval practice of treating the propositions of written logic as the key to understanding the structure of reality itself. They assumed that language, written or spoken, mirrored the world, and that the syntax of written Latin revealed mysteries of predication immanent in the very things of nature.

Hence, contrary to what might be assumed, the failure to distinguish clearly between oral and written language is especially characteristic of European scholarship *before* the advent of print culture. It was, indeed, only after Gutenberg that scholars gained a strong awareness of the special characteristics of oral and written language. With the new humanist concern for popular education (leading, as Lawrence Stone argued, to an educational 'revolution'), scholars began to worry about the predominance of illiteracy and the alleged deficiency of oral language and its associated habits of thought.[5] For example, the Spanish humanist Juan Luis Vives lamented the wandering of minds undisciplined by the practice of writing:

> [T]here are some people who do not understand how to write down what they would be well able to speak; this happens, as far as I can discover, because a wandering and unsettled mind is capable of sufficient attention for speech, but not for understanding what is written; it cannot support the strain of collecting and, as it were, compelling itself.[6]

Vives's conviction in the value of literacy, highly typical of humanist educators,[7] was further promoted in Northern Europe by Protestantism, with its demand for the individual reading of Scripture and its decreased value for the oral transmission of Christian practice. The steep, even meteoric, rise in literacy in Britain and other parts of Northern Europe during the sixteenth century arose from both these sources.[8] The expanding middle-classes sent their boys to new grammar schools; universities entered an era of flourishing expansion. Everywhere educated people began to associate illiteracy with ignorance, superstition and social inferiority.

Influenced by the same movement of ideas, Renaissance authors began to differentiate more clearly between societies with writing and those without. Their conception of language gained a temporal dimension virtually absent from medieval thought: because humanists thought that the invention of writing had inaugurated progress towards reason, civil order and religious enlightenment, they characterized non-literate people as embodying an *original* state of pre-literate barbarity. Accounts of the New World often included references to the childish amazement of native peoples at the writing of the Europeans, for the alphabet seemed to exemplify, more than other inventions, the technical superiority of the conquering culture. As Roger Williams wrote in his *Key into the Language of America* (1643), 'when they talke amongst themselves of the *English* ships, and great buildings, of the plowing of their Fields, and especially of Bookes and Letters, they will end thus: *Manittôwock*. They are Gods.'[9] The ignorance of oral people with writing was a source of self-congratulatory humour: in a popular story, rehearsed by several authors, an 'Indian slave' steals a gift of figs that he is carrying to a neighbour, along with a letter explaining the gift. When his theft is exposed by the letter, the lesson is not lost on the slave. The next time, he is careful to hide his master's 'talking paper' under a rock so that it will not see him eating the figs.[10]

Yet neither Williams nor the authors who told this story had a full or sophisticated concept of an 'oral tradition': they viewed non-literate peoples simply in contrast to the rationality and order that they closely associated with literacy. . . .

Influenced by humanism, with its profound reverence for the *written* traditions of language, authors of the Renaissance regarded poetical language as the last product of linguistic refinement, the highest achievement of an advanced and literate culture. As Walter J. Ong observed, humanists set out 'to make the measure of all speech a fixed *written* tradition'.[11] . . . These attitudes continued to shape perceptions of non-literate peoples and cultures in the early eighteenth century. As Jean Terrasson wrote in 1715, 'Language never improves among a savage and barbarous people, who make no other use of it but only to express the Necessities of the Animal Life.'[12] In 1741, John Oldmixon was still referring to the American languages as 'dreadful' and 'barbarous'.[13] Even authors who studied and understood native tongues, like Roger Williams, had nothing complimentary to say about native poetry or oratory. While acknowledging that native oratory was 'copious and patheticall',[14] Williams regarded books and letters as an important sign of European superiority to Americans in all areas of life.

Obviously, such an understanding of language differed profoundly from the praise of native oratory found in the work of Enlightenment authors like Hugh Blair. During the late eighteenth century, authors increasingly departed in significant ways from a humanist tradition that regarded written tradition as the foundation of literary excellence. But how and when did new ways of conceiving language emerge?

A major development in linguistic thought from the Renaissance to the Enlightenment was increasing awareness of the differing natures and functions of writing and speech. This is a historical development that I have described in detail elsewhere:[15] for my purposes here, I will review some of the main features of the scholarly process that led to a clearer recognition of the special features of spoken language. As I have contended, grammarians and other scholars before the eighteenth century made no clear distinction between the nature of writing and speech. They tended, indeed, to understand language largely as it was *written*, and placed little significance on those features of language exclusive to speech. This tendency to imagine language entirely through the medium of writing was exemplified by two major branches of sixteenth- and seventeenth-century linguistics. The first was the vigorous campaign to rationalize the orthography of vernacular languages to make writing a more faithful 'copy' of speech. In the works of Sir Thomas Smith, James Hart, Charles Butler, Robert Robinson and others, discrepancies between writing and speech were decried as failures correctable by the reform of spelling. The aim of these authors was to create a script in which 'each simple sound hauing a proper mark appointed to it selfe, may by the same be as apparently seene to the eye, as the sound it selfe is sensibly discerned by the eares'.[16] A second branch of early modern linguistics was the invention of a 'real character' or written language to replace speech for the purposes of international communication and science. The many projects of seventeenth-century scholars – including Francis Lodwick, Cave Beck, George Dalgarno and John Wilkins – envisioned a visual language that mirrored the nature of things more accurately than any existing form of speech.[17]

Common among these trends was the assumption that writing can replace speech, for the two media differ essentially in their *means of transmission*, not in their natures. It is significant, therefore, that both these areas of linguistic study became more-or-less defunct after 1700, particularly in Britain. Even some earlier authors had strongly questioned the capacity of any writing to replace speech entirely. The sixteenth-century grammarian Richard Mulcaster, for example, denied that orthography could mirror speech in the way envisaged by contemporaries like Smith and Hart. These objections became more common towards the end of the seventeenth century: in *A Dissertation on Speech* (1700), Johann Conrad Amman elucidated some of the objections to the wide-spread belief in the adequacy of writing to duplicate the nature and function of spoken language. Amman was a teacher of deaf-mute people, and this experience convinced him that any purely visual form of communication was inherently inadequate. First, the sound of speech was far richer and more various than any alphabet: 'many letters have their own compass and peculiar modifications; and the same character, even the same language, is not always pronounced in one and the same manner'.[18] Second, speech is the only 'natural' way for human beings to express their thoughts. 'Besides that certain signs, not uttered by the living voice, are liable to deceive', wrote Amman, 'every sincere mind, giving attention to itself when about to converse with another on a serious subject, feels a desire to declare the hidden thoughts of his heart . . . by the use of Speech'.[19] . . .

Amman was challenging a very general confidence in written language exhibited, as we have considered, by projects for orthographic reform and a 'real character'. But these attitudes were also in the process of change. By the middle of the eighteenth century, Samuel Johnson both ignored projects for a 'real character' to replace speech and declared that projects to reform alphabetical writing were the defunct preoccupation of a previous age.[20] Johnson complained in the Preface to his *Dictionary* (1754) that 'penmen' had vitiated language by attempting to duplicate 'the boundless chaos of living speech' in their spellings. These reformers, he argued, forgot that all pronunciations reflect only the temporary habits of a particular time and place, and cannot be preserved as an absolute standard.[21] Hence, Johnson's own modest reforms of spelling in his *Dictionary* attempted to strengthen the internal analogies of written English rather than mirror speech. He viewed writing not as a 'copy' of speech, but rather as essentially distinct form of discourse with its own rules and standards.

What Johnson exemplified, in short, was a heightened appreciation that writing and speech were inherently *distinct* modes of communication. Writing and speech certainly influenced each other: indeed, Johnson was among the first to consider how literacy changes and (he believed) improves spoken language, making it available for study and improvement by 'poets', grammarians and lexicographers.[22] Such a position is correctly seen as reflecting Johnson's personal linguistic preference for print over the 'boundless chaos of living speech'.[23] Yet Johnson was saying something more interesting: he was challenging the ancient Aristotelian model of writing as an 'image' of speech – a challenge undertaken by many other writers of his generation. Even an author who did not, on the whole, agree with Johnson on linguistic issues, the elocutionist Thomas Sheridan, stressed the essential difference of writing and speech:

> These two kinds of language [writing and speech] are so early in life associated, that it is difficult ever after to separate them: or not to suppose that there is some kind of natural connection between them. And yet it is a matter of importance to us, always to bear in mind, that there is no sort of affinity between them, but what arises from habitual association of ideas. Tho' we cannot so easily separate them in our own minds, yet when we come to separate them in relation to others, we see clearly enough their utter independence of each other.[24]

The point made by Johnson and Sheridan was [that] . . . writing cannot even potentially duplicate the functions of speech, for the two media operate according to different principles. Johnson stressed the inherently fluid and adaptable nature of speech, as opposed to the relative fixity of writing; Sheridan found a major deficiency in the incapacity of writing to express the passions through the oral resources of intonation and gesture. Johnson and Sheridan reflect an important shift in the understanding of the writing and speech: in an age increasingly dominated by writing and print, European scholars were beginning to acknowledge the inherent limitations of what could be achieved by visual language.

This is the crux of my thesis. With this separation of writing and speech in theories of language, European scholars also began to imagine oral and literate cultures as quite separate and dissimilar. Societies without writing, it was thought, retained a language that exhibited all the special powers of speech in their purest form, unchanged by writing. It was even proposed that the language of oral cultures might be *better* for lacking the pervasive influence of writing. This was a controversial point. Many scholars of language, such as Samuel Johnson, stressed that only writing and print could give language stability, coherence and elegance: the speech of oral cultures was unstable, vague and indistinct. But another school of thought contended that the propagation of literacy and print culture had destroyed the expressive force of speech, rendering it toneless and cold. This critique was made in France by Rousseau and in Britain, within a different context, by Thomas Sheridan. In his influential *Course of Lectures on Elocution* (1762), Sheridan complained that 'some of our greatest men have been trying to do that with the pen, which can only be performed by the tongue; to produce effects by the dead letter, which can never be produced but by the living voice, with its accompaniments'.[25] Sheridan's goal was to promote a more passionate oratory – the kind of persuasive elocution needed to promote Christianity and political freedom. This kind of oratory could only be achieved if speakers cultivated 'tones' and 'accents'. These qualities were the very 'life, blood, and soul' of language, yet they were 'utterly unnoticed in writing'.[26]

It was this general disdain for the stultifying influence of literacy, as exemplified by Sheridan, that led to the important reassessment of native oratory that we have already noted in Hugh Blair. Blair's tendency to 'classicize' native Americans, whose style of oratory he compared with the epic, echoed the view of previous authors like Cadwallader Colden, surveyor-general of New York. In *The History of the Five Indian Nations of Canada* (1747), Colden portrayed a chief named 'Decanesora' who 'had a great Fluency in speaking, and a graceful Elocution, that would have pleased in any Part of the World'.[27] Decanesora reminded Colden of Cicero: with his noble nose and patrician bearing, he even 'looked' like that Roman orator. Another historian of the Scottish Enlightenment, Adam Ferguson, shared Blair's opinion on the 'magnificent beauty' of Indian speech which 'no change of language can improve, and no refinements of the critics reform'.[28]

These passages reflect an important re-evaluation of oral language and culture in the mid-eighteenth century – a re-evaluation connected with the increasing tendency of linguists and grammarians to separate the functions of writing and speech. Enlightenment authors were contending, in particular, that writing lacked the resources of intonation that gave speech its special passionate force. But this new attention to intonation was not the only factor leading to a new interest in oral language and culture. A greater appreciation for oral cultures was connected as well with the critique of European society that was, indeed, a major characteristic of Enlightenment ideology. In the work of Adam Ferguson and Jean-Jacques Rousseau, the willingness to acknowledge the advantages of oral societies formed part of a challenge to the injustice and inequality of modern civilization, which both authors regarded as overrun with books and bookish speculation. . . .

Sentimentalized Indians, almost invariably lamenting or dying, became stock figures in poetry. This poetry reflected the supposed virtues of native oratory, simple and passionate, yet filled with bold metaphors redolent of pagan myth and the natural world. Here was how Joseph Warton imagined the language of a native chief in *The Dying Indian* (1747):

> The dart of Izdabel prevails! 'twas dipt
> In double poison. – I shall soon arrive
> At the blest island, where no tygers spring
> On heedless hunters; where ananas bloom
> Thrice in each moon; where rivers smootly glide,
> Nor thund'ring torrents whirl the light canoe
> Down to the sea.[29]

Warton's poem reflects two significant trends in eighteenth-century poetics. The first was a heightened emphasis on the powerful expression of passion as the major characteristic of poetry. In contrast with neo-classical poets like Boileau or Pope, who described poetry as the 'painting' or 'dress' of thought, the English critic John Dennis maintained that the primary characteristic of poetry was the expression of strong emotions. 'Poetry is Poetry', he wrote, 'because it is more passionate and sensual than Prose.'[30] This heightened passion inspired the 'bold and figurative' language of poetry: Dennis and other authors of the 'Age of Sensibility' anticipated Wordsworth and the romantics in regarding metaphor as a natural response to states of heightened passion. In this way, we will note, new fashions in poetry and poetics dovetailed with trends in linguistics during the same period: non-literate language was deemed more 'poetic' because, as the grammarians were insisting, only speech could express the sentiments with full force.

A further, closely related, trend exemplified by Warton's poem was 'primitivism' – for 'primitive' people, in the supposed 'childhood' of human development, were surely more inclined to strong passions than civilized people. As Enlightenment philosophers were concluding, these strong passions, and not reason, inspired the first languages.[31] 'Primitive' language was therefore inherently more 'poetic' than modern European languages, which had lost in passion what they had gained in clarity and logic.[32] This way of understanding the history of language inspired works such as Robert Lowth's *Lectures on the Sacred Poetry of the*

Hebrews (1753), which re-interpreted the Psalms and other lyrical parts of the Old Testament as the impassioned and spontaneous effusions of a primitive people. Moreover, the bold metaphorical style of the Old Testament reflected an essentially *oral* culture where poetic declamation, not writing, was the primary vehicle for cultural authority and memory. As Lowth wrote, 'Poetry was of singular utility, since before any characters expressive of words were invented, at least before they were commonly received, and applied to general use, it seems to have afforded the only means of preserving the rude experience of early times.'[33]

The significance of Lowth's comments is clear. Most obviously, he was beginning to identify a specifically oral kind of poetry, which he connected with a particularly passionate and metaphorical kind of language. More daringly, he was claiming that one of the central texts of the Western tradition, the Old Testament, emerged from this very well of oral eloquence. The Enlightenment had opened the door to a reinterpretation of even sacred texts in the light of contemporary developments in linguistics, philosophy and poetics. And if the Bible could be interpreted as exhibiting traits of oral tradition, it was a short step to re-evaluating the great pagan texts of classical literature in the same way.

At the fountainhead of this pagan tradition was, of course, Homer. Ancient critics of Greek culture, such as the Jewish historian Josephus, had raised the heretical possibility that Homer was illiterate.[34] This possibility was revived during . . . the late seventeenth and early eighteenth centuries. Scholars who advocated the claims for modern literature over ancient literature – Claude Perrault, Jean Terrasson, Richard Bentley and others – portrayed Homer as an early and therefore primitive poet in a literary tradition that was essentially progressive. Paradoxically, this originally critical view of Homer as 'primitive' (and therefore inferior to modern authors) later became the inspiration for praising the peculiar beauties of ancient epic poetry. A key work in this re-evaluation was Thomas Blackwell's *An Enquiry into the Life and Writings of Homer* (1735), which rehearsed many of the new ideas about the history of language. The first languages, Blackwell conjectured, were emitted in states of strong passion typical of primitive people. They were therefore highly intoned, song-like and figurative, for Homer belonged to an age still influenced by the first verse. He was not utterly barbaric, for his work shows the literary polish gained only by some degree of civilization or 'policy'. Nevertheless, the special power of the Homeric epic, its '*Original*, amazing, *metaphorical* Tincture', reflects the unique energy of language in its earliest state.[35]

Significantly, Blackwell did not try to argue that Homer was illiterate or belonged to an entirely oral culture: such a proposal still strained the credulity of scholars raised on the belief that only writing could preserve a substantial body of knowledge with any fidelity. Even in Blackwell's Scotland, where new ideas of the Enlightenment were accepted more readily than in England, scholars developed the concept of oral tradition with slowness and caution. An important text in this development was *The Poems of Ossian* (1762–63) by the Highland scholar James Macpherson, who may well have trained under Blackwell at Marischal College in Aberdeen. Macpherson claimed that he had reconstructed the work of a great Highland bard, Ossian, from fragments preserved in the memories of ordinary people around Scotland. That such a substantial body of poetry – including two epics and other poems – could survive merely by oral transmission was indeed a claim of arresting novelty and interest. Influenced by prevailing notions of 'primitive' verse, Macpherson attempted to capture the flavour of oral recitation, its vivid metaphors, epithets and song-like cadences. Anticipating the modern discoveries of Milman Parry, Macpherson maintained that the very form of Ossianic verse had a mnemonic function that aided its survival in unwritten tradition.[36] . . .

As this survey suggests, many of the authors who led the way in theorizing on the poetic potential of oral and 'primitive' cultures came from the periphery of English civilization –

Scotland (Blair, Blackwell, Macpherson). Ireland (Swift, Sheridan), America (Colden). It was, that is, at the *periphery* that disillusionment with modern, literate culture was felt most keenly. Mostly here, it seems, authors were willing to experiment with the idea that non-literate peoples could be, in certain respects, superior. Nevertheless, as I have also considered, 'oral traditions' do not readily recognize their own predominant orality: it is a society emerging from orality into literacy which is positioned to perceive this difference most distinctly, for such a society has experienced this transition within living memory and will still retain a large body of oral culture in its midst. In mid-century England, we might note, about half the adult population remained so illiterate that they could not sign a marriage register (though, somewhat more probably, they read a little, a skill that usually precedes writing). Yet literacy had been the norm for generations in the gentry and upper-merchant classes, and had made important inroads into the class of small merchants and tradespeople.[37] The difference between orality and literacy, that is, was visible (and audible) all around, and this experience shaped the understanding of literate people towards non-alphabetic societies elsewhere in the world. Orality and literacy, moreover, became temporalized: histories of language, such as Warburton's influential history of scripts in *The Divine Legation of Moses* (1738), strengthened the assumption that writing developed long after speech, and that this event represented a pivotal stage in the progress towards modern civilization.[38] In looking to their own past, therefore, Europeans increasingly expected to find evidence of 'oral' culture.

That eighteenth-century England was precisely at that point of emerging as a 'literate' society perhaps explains why an Englishman advanced the first sustained argument that Homer belonged to an 'oral tradition'. Almost unnoticed amid the noise of the Ossian controversy, Robert Wood made this case in *An Essay on the Original Genius and Writings of Homer*, written in 1767 and published in 1769. Wood represents a crescendo in the intellectual developments that I have traced from the Renaissance. For he had absorbed the intellectual conditions of his time – a time of increased interest in the sound of language, along with a new interest in 'primitive' speech and culture. His case for the oral sources of Homeric verse was grounded not in historical evidence, but rather in the conjecture that only a tradition without letters could have produced poetry of this kind. The very 'genius' of Homer, the 'musical' quality of his language and his direct knowledge of nature, derived from a primitive age when speech, unrestrained by writing, was passionate and spontaneous. In contrast with the 'cold and languid circumlocution' of modern 'artificial language', the language of Homer exemplifies the 'passionate expression of Nature, which, incapable of misrepresentation, appeals directly to our feelings, and finds the shortest road to the heart'.[39] The faithful *mimesis* that Wood found in Homeric verse showed the advantages of an 'unlettered' time when nature was known through direct experience rather than books. In contrast with scholars of the Renaissance and the seventeenth century, therefore, Wood portrayed the peculiar beauties of Homer not as the fruits of literate refinement but of untrammelled nature. He suggested that Homer exemplified the same virtues found in the orators of the New World. If scholars like Blair and Ferguson were classicizing the American native, Wood and others compared Homer to the 'primitive' peoples of the New World. . . . The general thesis nonetheless stands: as society grows in literacy, it also becomes more aware of 'orality' as a separate mode of expression and being. Orality is a fundamentally *literate* concept.

Yet the groundwork for these developments had already been laid in the Enlightenment. During that age, intellectual culture nourished a new understanding of non-literate language and culture. The old view that both literature and society had benefited from literacy was challenged by a more complicated view celebrating the supposed beauties of 'primitive' speech. Authors of this era increasingly acknowledged that pre-literate peoples could have a continuous tradition of history, government and poetry. This acknowledgment arose from a number of interrelated intellectual factors – doubts concerning the adequacy of writing, a connected revival of prosody, satire of European manners and society, a new aesthetic and moral taste for sentiment. . . . These factors led scholars to reassess not only non-European cultures but *themselves*. The 'Other' of oral culture became ambivalent and complicated. For a new generation, the Other was no longer just a negative, a mere absence of all order and knowledge, as it was for authors of the Renaissance and the seventeenth century. When Enlightenment scholars measured Europe against the pre-literate cultures of the New World, they generally found both gain and loss – a gain of clarity, sophistication and reason, but also a loss of passion and the expressive energy. In these ways, the difference between orality and literacy became a site for exploring a range of philosophical, linguistic and historical divisions at the centre of Europe's perception of itself and the world.

Notes

1   Hugh Blair, *A Critical Dissertation on the Poems of Ossian* (London, 1763), 2.
2   Samuel Purchas, *Purchas his Pilgrimes*, 4 vols (London, 1625), 1. 176.
3   See Nicholas Hudson, '"Oral Tradition": the Evolution of an Eighteenth-century Concept', in Alvaro Ribeiro, S. J., and James G. Basker (eds), *Tradition in Transition: Woman Writers, Marginal Texts, and the Eighteenth-century Canon* (Oxford: Clarendon Press, 1996), 161–76.
4   William of Ockham, *Philosophical Writings,* trans. Philotheus Boehner. rev. Stephen F. Brown (Indianapolis, IN and Cambridge: Hackett Publishing Co., 1990), 47.
5   See Lawrence Stone, 'The Educational Revolution in England, 1560–1640', *Past and Present* 28 (1964), 41–80. Stone's views are expanded and refined in Rosemary O'Day's *Education and Society 1500–1800: the Social Foundations of Education in Early Modern Britain* (London and New York: Longman, 1982).
6   Juan Luis Vives, *Vives: On Education. A Translation of the 'De Tradendis Disciplinis'*, trans. Foster Watson (Cambridge: Cambridge University Press, 1913), 114.
7   See Richard Mulcaster, *The First Part of the Elementarie* (London, 1582: facsimile reprint, Menston: Scolar Press, 1970), 24–5. See also Lawrence Stone, 'Literacy and Education in England 1640–1900', *Past and Present* 42 (1969): 69–139; Joan Simon, *Education and Society in Tudor England* (Cambridge: Cambridge University Press, 1966).
8   See David Cressy, *Literacy and the Social Order: Reading and Writing in Tudor and Stuart England* (Cambridge: Cambridge University Press, 1980).
9   Roger Williams, *A Key into the Language of America* (London, 1643), 118.
10 See Francisco Lopez de Gómara, *Histoire géneralle des indes occidentales & terres neuues* (1554), trans. M. Fumée (Paris, 1569), ch. 28, sig. D5v; Gerardus Vossius, *De quatuor artibus popularibus* (Amsterdam, 1650), 14–15; John Wilkins, *Mercury: or the secret and swift messenger* (1641), 3rd edn (London, 1707; facsimile reprint, Amsterdam and Philadelphia: John Benjamins, 1984), 3–4.
11 Walter J. Ong, *Ramus, Method, and the Decay of Dialogue* (Cambridge, MA: Harvard University Press, 1958), 122.
12 Jean Terrrasson, *A Critical Dissertation upon Homer's Iliad* (1715), 2 vols (London, 1722), 2, 526.
13 John Oldmixon, *The British Empire in America*, 2 vols, 2nd edn (London, 1741), 1. 276.
14 Williams, *A Key into the Language of America*, 177.
15 See Nicholas Hudson, *Writing and European Thought, 1600–1830* (Cambridge: Cambridge University Press, 1994).
16 Robert Robinson, 'The Art of Pronunciation' in E. J. Dobson (ed.), *Phonetic Writings* (London, New York and Toronto: Oxford University Press, 1957), 19–20. On the rationalization of orthography in the Renaissance, see D. G. Scragg, *A History of English Spelling* (Manchester: Manchester University Press; New York: Barnes & Noble, 1974); F. H. Brengelman, 'Orthoepists, Printers, and the Rationalization of English Spelling', *Journal of English and Germanic Philology,* 79 (1980), 332–54; Hudson, *Writing and European Thought,* 92–9.
17 There are now numerous good discussions of the projects for a new universal or philosophical script that proliferated in the seventeenth century. Especially useful studies include Vivian Salmon's Introduction to *The Works of Francis Lodwick* (London: Longman's, 1972), James Knowlson's *Universal Language Schemes in England and France 1600–1800* (Toronto and Buffalo, NJ: University of Toronto

Press, 1975), and M. M. Slaughter's *Universal Languages and Scientific Taxonomy in the Seventeenth Century* (Cambridge: Cambridge University Press, 1982).

18   Johann Conrad Amman, *A Dissertation on Speech* (London: Sampson Low, Marston Low & Searle, 1873), 60.

19   Amman, *A Dissertation on Speech*, 8.

20   Samuel Johnson, *Grammar of the English Tongue*, in *A Dictionary of the English Language* (London, 1755: facsimile reprint, New York: AMS, 1967), sig. a2v.

21   Johnson, Preface to *Dictionary*, sig. a2r.

22   See Samuel Johnson, *A Journey to the Western Isles of Scotland,* ed. Mary Lascelles, vol. 9 of *The Yale Edition of the Works of Samuel Johnson* (New Haven, CT: Yale University Press, 1971), 114–15. This discussion of the influence of literate culture on language occurs as part of Johnson's case against the authenticity of Macpherson's *Poems of Ossian*, discussed below.

23   Johnson, Preface to *Dictionary*, sig. a2r.

24   Thomas Sheridan, *A Course of Lectures on Elocution, Together with Two Dissertations on Language* (London, 1762), P 7. On Sheridan's views concerning writing and speech, see Michael Shortland, 'Moving Speeches: Language and Elocution in Eighteenth-century Britain', *History of European Ideas,* 8 (1987), 639–53: Peter de Bolla, *The Discourse of the Sublime: Readings in History, Aesthetics and the Subject* (Oxford and New York: Blackwell, 1989), 163–82.

25   Sheridan, *Course of Lectures*, xii.

26   Ibid., 71.

27   Cadwallader Colden, *The History of the Five Indian Nations of Canada* (London, 1747), 156.

28   Adam Ferguson, *A History of Civil Society* (Edinburgh, 1767), p. 265.

29   In *The Three Wartons: a Choice of Their Verse*, ed. Eric Partridge (London: Scholartis Press, 1927), 92.

30   John Dennis, *The Advancement and Reformation of Modern Poetry* (London, 1721), 24.

31   The thesis that language began with 'cries of passion' derives from classical philosophy, particularly Lucretius's discussion of primitive speech in Book 5 of *De rerum natura*. This argument was widely revived in the 'conjectural histories' of language by Enlightenment philosophers such as Bernard Mandeville and Etienne Bonnot, Abbé de Condillac. For a good discussion of Mandeville's theories on the origin of language, see E. J. Hundert, 'The Thread of Language and the Web of Dominion: Mandeville to Rousseau and Back', *Eighteenth-century Studies,* 21 (1987), 169–91. The major modern scholar on the linguistic thought of Condillac is Hans Aarsleff. See Aarsleff's 'The Tradition of Condillac: the Problem of the Origin of Language in the Eighteenth Century and the Debate in the Berlin Academy Before Herder', in *From Locke to Saussure: Essays on the Study of Language and intellectual History* (Minneapolis: University of Minnesota Press, 1983), 149–209.

32   For discussion of this theory on how languages develop, see Nicholas Hudson, 'Theories of Language', in H. B. Nisbet and Claude Rawson (eds), *The Cambridge History of Literary Criticism* (Cambridge: Cambridge University Press, 1997), 4. 335–47. 'Primitivism' is discussed in the same volume by Maximilian E. Novak, 456–69.

33   Robert Lowth, *Lectures on the Sacred Poetry of the Hebrews*, trans G. Gregory (London, 1787).

34   Flavius Josephus, 'Against Apion', in *Works*, trans. William Whiston (Baltimore, MD: Armstrong & Berry, 1839), part 1, section 2. 580.

35   Thomas Blackwell, *An inquiry into the Life and Time of Homer* (London, 1735), 46.

36   James Macpherson, *Fingal, an Ancient Epic Poem in Six Books: together with several Other Poems, composed by Ossian the Son of Fingal* (London, 1762). See Hudson, 'Oral Tradition'.

37   On rates of literacy in eighteenth-century England, see Roger S. Schofield, 'Dimensions of Illiteracy in England, 1750–1850', in Harvey Graff (ed.), *Literacy and Social Development in the West* (Cambridge: Cambridge University Press, 1981), 201–13; idem, *The Legacies of Literacy* (Bloomington and Indianapolis: University of Indiana Press, 1987), 230–3.

38   Warburton's dissertation on writing comprises book 4, section 4, of the second volume of *The Divine Legation of Moses* (London, 1738–41). It was later translated into French and published separately by Marc-Antoine Léonard des Malpeines as *Essai sur les hiéroglyphes des égyptiens* (Paris, 1744), a version that became the basis for the French Enlightenment's understanding of the history of writing, including the article 'Écriture' in the *Encyclopédie*.

39   Robert Wood, *An Essay on the Original Genius and Writings of Homer* (London: John Richardson, 1824), 176.

PART X

Technology

Introduction

TECHNOLOGY IS AN ASPECT of material culture which is best understood in the context of users' experiences. The word itself was coined in the nineteenth century to mean a systematic study of practical 'art' and, only later, tools and artefacts. To talk of 'technology' in earlier periods is convenient if, strictly speaking, anachronistic. It covers devices of many different kinds, from prehistoric hand-axes to space-rockets and from the specialised to those in everyday use. Humans have developed technologies to achieve three broad purposes: investigating and exploiting natural processes (e.g. in agriculture, astronomy and healing), transport and communication (moving goods and conveying messages), and making the tools or devices themselves (e.g. in the 'mechanization' associated with the Industrial Revolution). The analysis below focuses on the second category but we begin by considering the relationship between 'technology', religion and narratives of 'progress' which since the thirteenth century have resonated strongly in Western culture, notably in North America in the nineteenth and twentieth centuries (Nye 2003, 2006).

At one time historians drew a contrast between religious concerns with an afterlife and the practical drive to improve human material conditions in this life. During the French Enlightenment, Condorcet (1795) developed this theme. But we should not assume a simplistic opposition between religion and respect for technical achievements. Technologies were many and varied in the medieval period (Gies and Gies 1994 survey them), in the twelfth century they were explicitly linked to theology (Ovitt 1987), and White (1962, 1978) even argued that a propensity for technical invention characterised medieval Western Christianity (see also Hall 1996). An example White uses is a sermon preached in Florence in 1306 which praised inventiveness and referred to the skill of making eyeglasses, discovered 'not twenty years ago' (Ilardi 2007). Mechanical clocks were another new device of this time (Scattergood 2003), appearing c.1300 in abbeys, where they marked the monastic hours.

A counterpart to the critiques levelled against binary histories contrasting technology with religion can be seen in the rejection by Blaut (1993, 2000) of narratives attributing 'the rise of the West' to an inventiveness not found elsewhere. As Adas (1989) points out, during the

eighteenth century the theme of the backwardness of the Other, coupled later with that of despotism as a hindrance to progress, had gradually replaced the earlier tendency for alleged
Western superiority to be attributed to Christianity. Blaut accepts that new machinery multiplied in the Western world from the seventeenth century but he criticises those who explain it
in terms of long-term cultural developments uniquely conducive to experimentation. He attaches
more weight to the increase in commerce ensuing from the discovery and exploitation of the
Americas, followed by imperial conquests elsewhere. The demanding task of comparing China
and the West with respect to the interplay of culture and technology has been undertaken by
Davids (2012) among others. Pacey (1990) attempts a global history of technology, and elsewhere offers a cultural analysis (Pacey 1992) that goes beyond questions of pure utility to
consider 'meaning'.

The danger in accounting teleologically for how technologies 'evolve' (Basalla 1988) is
that they seem to take on a life of their own, determining how people use them. While the
choices available to individuals at any given moment are limited, a historical perspective makes
it possible to appreciate the complex socio-economic processes that construct and also narrow
possibilities. Cultural historians seek to understand human beings not as determined by outside
forces but as active agents making technological choices and assigning meanings. Accordingly,
as well as studying producers' invention and dissemination of technologies they emphasise the
contingent fashioning of inventions by users for specific purposes (Bijker, Hughes and Pinch
1987).

Examples illustrating that principle can be seen in the histories of transport and of communication. As Freeman (1999) shows, the Victorians greeted the railways enthusiastically. For
its advocates the new 'system' epitomised people's freedom from the limitations of previous
generations. In city centres, grandiose architectural designs were adopted for stations, some of
them like cathedrals. Railways were useful and they were good to think with, transforming
experiences of space, time and vision (Kern 1983; Schivelbusch 1986). The electric telegraph,
which spread just after the railways and spanned oceans as a 'tool of empire', attracted talk of
universal peace, a single common language, and the annihilation of space and time (Morus
2000; Headrick 2000). New transport and communication systems, like other technologies,
may have met pre-existing needs in new ways but they also generated novel demands, and
users often developed and fulfilled desires unexpressed in inventors' manifestos (Marsden and
Smith 2005). Culture is not simply shaped by technology, but can also shape it (Hughes 1994,
2004). Technology and culture are not separate entities (Staudenmaier 1985). As Edgerton
(2007) points out, much of what can be classified as 'technology' rapidly loses its novelty
and its association with inspired inventors, and becomes part of life's everyday routines,
used by the many and not the few. That said, creative users have ensured that the standardiza-
tion underpinning the global dissemination of technologies has not led to cultural homogeneity
(Nye 2006).

The reading by Otto Mayr shows how in early modern Europe the rhetoric deployed in
support of authoritarian political regimes included use of clockwork as a source of metaphors
recommending obedience to rulers, on the grounds that otherwise the machinery of State would
malfunction. Mayr's evidence takes the discussion of technology's meaning to a different level
than that of practical utility, by highlighting the role of symbols in the communication of ideas
and feelings.

Our second reading, by Christine MacLeod, focuses on the widespread celebration of
inventors in eighteenth- and nineteenth-century Britain. Here the theme of progress is being
symbolised. But in addition, the cult of the individual genius is a way of understanding and
representing how processes of technological change work. It is an unsatisfactory type of history
as it distracts attention from the influence of cultural context, an understanding of which is
crucial to explaining success in innovation.

Just as the word 'culture' has a history that merits study, so too does the word 'technology', which is of even more recent vintage. Our third reading in this section, by Leo Marx, is about that history. The author suggests that sometimes a neologism enters people's vocabulary because it fills what he calls a 'semantic void' – that is to say, because no existing term quite captures what they want to say. In the case of 'technology', he suggests that the attraction of the new term may derive from its ideological overtones rather than from any power to pinpoint a clearly definable content.

References

Adas, M. (1989) *Machines as the Measure of Men: science, technology and ideologies of Western dominance*, Ithaca, NJ: Cornell University Press.

Basalla, G. (1988) *The Evolution of Technology*, Cambridge: Cambridge University Press.

Bijker, W., Hughes, T.P. and Pinch, T. (eds) (1987) *The Social Construction of Technological Systems*, Cambridge, MA: MIT Press.

Blaut, J.M. (1993) *The Colonizer's Model of the World: geographical diffusionism and Eurocentric history*, New York, NY: Guilford Press.

Blaut, J.M. (2000) *Eight Eurocentric Historians*, New York, NY: Guilford Press.

Condorcet, Marquis de (1795) *Sketch for a Historical Picture of the Progress of the Human Mind*, trans. J.M. Barraclough (1955) London: Weidenfeld and Nicolson. The anonymous 1796 Philadelphia translation is available online at http://oll.libertyfund.org/.

Davids, K. (2012) *Religion, Technology and the Great and Little Divergences: China and Europe compared, c.700–1800*, Leiden: Brill.

Edgerton, D. (2007) *The Shock of the Old: technology and global history since 1900*, Oxford: Oxford University Press.

Freeman, M. (1999) *Railways and the Victorian Imagination*, New Haven, CT: Yale University Press.

Gies, F. and Gies, J. (1994) *Cathedral, Forge, and Waterwheel: technology and invention in the Middle Ages*, New York, NY: HarperCollins.

Hall, B. (1996) 'Lynn White's *Medieval Technology and Social Change* after thirty years', in R. Fox (ed.) *Technological Change: methods and themes in the history of technology*, Amsterdam: Harwood Academic.

Headrick, D.R. (2000) *When Information Came of Age: technologies of knowledge in the Age of Reason and Revolution*, Oxford: Oxford University Press.

Hughes, T.P. (1994) 'Technological momentum', in M. Roe Smith and L. Marx (eds) *Does Technology Drive History? The dilemma of technological determinism*, Cambridge, MA: MIT Press.

Hughes, T.P. (2004) *The Human-Built World: how to think about technology and culture*, Chicago, IL: University of Chicago Press.

Ilardi, V. (2007) *Renaissance Vision from Spectacles to Telescopes*, Philadelphia, PA: American Philosophical Society.

Kern, S. (1983) *The Culture of Time and Space 1880–1918*, Cambridge, MA: Harvard University Press.

Marsden, B. and Smith, C. (2005) *Engineering Empires: a cultural history of technology in nineteenth-century Britain*, Basingstoke: Palgrave Macmillan.

Morus, I.R. (2000) '"The nervous system of Britain": space, time and the electric telegraph in the Victorian age', *British Journal for the History of Science*, 33: 455–75.

Nye, D.E. (2003) *America as Second Creation: technology and narratives of new beginnings*, Cambridge, MA: MIT Press.

Nye, D.E. (2006) *Technology Matters: questions to live with*, Cambridge, MA: MIT Press.

Ovitt, G., Jr. (1987) *The Restoration of Perfection: labor and technology in medieval culture*, New Brunswick, NJ: Rutgers University Press.

Pacey, A. (1990) *Technology in World Civilization: a thousand-year history*, Cambridge, MA: MIT Press.

Pacey, A. (1992) *The Maze of Ingenuity: ideas and idealism in the development of technology*, Cambridge, MA: MIT Press.

Scattergood, J. (2003) 'Writing the clock: the reconstruction of time in the later Middle Ages', *European Review*, 11: 453–74.

Schivelbusch, W. (1986) *The Railway Journey: the industrialization of time and space in the 19th century*, Berkeley, CA: University of California Press.

Staudenmaier, J.M. (1985) *Technology's Storytellers: reweaving the human fabric*, ch. 4, Cambridge, MA: MIT Press.

White, L. (1962) *Medieval Technology and Social Change*, Oxford: Oxford University Press.

White, L. (1978) *Medieval Religion and Technology*, Berkeley, CA: University of California Press.

Chapter 27

Otto Mayr

THE AUTHORITARIAN CONCEPTION
OF ORDER

NOW THAT A TENTATIVE RECONSTRUCTION, in an empirical, quasi-archaeological manner, of the career of the clock metaphor has been completed, it demands interpretation. What did those metaphors say? What do they mean? For whom did they speak? How is the history of the metaphor related to that of the mechanism itself? And what, finally, does the mechanical clock have to do with the original problem, the disregard for feedback mechanisms in Europe before 1700?

Metaphors and kindred devices of figurative expression are comparisons: some notion in need of illustration is compared with a different notion that must be familiar. The metaphor can be effective only if the two notions, the actual and the figurative, have some similarity despite their differences, some common characteristic, a *tertium comparationis*. A basic question is: within each individual clock metaphor, what is this common characteristic shared by the two notions under comparison? Which leads to a broader question: what do all the clock metaphors, despite their evident diversity, have in common?

Common characteristics do indeed emerge. The most important one is elementary. From the beginning, the image of the clock was linked with concepts that people held in high regard: the clock was called upon to illustrate the attributes of God; the harmony of the universe; the joys of paradise; temperance, the highest of the seven virtues; the truth of the new science; and the effectiveness of absolute monarchy. A machine that was not only popularly regarded as akin to such subjects but that was also invoked purposely to add to their praise clearly enjoyed the public's approval to an extraordinary degree. But such universal public approval, although an important fact, tells us little. We need to know more precisely in what way the clock was linked with the chief values of early modern European society.

A characteristic of the mechanical clock that seems to have aroused admiration from the start was the regularity of its running. Seeing a clock run, early viewers who, of course, had never known anything like it were enchanted by its harmony and orderliness, otherworldly qualities normally associated with things eternal and divine.

This connection between the clock and the Divine received added authority from having first been pointed out by a poet of the stature of Dante and by a widely read theologian like Suso. The perceived regularity of the clock's running (all-too-frequent breakdowns, it seems, were charitably overlooked) was also the basis for its identification with the recognized chief virtue of the age, temperance, an identification that became conventional both in literature and in art. And regularity became the basis for many other comparisons on less lofty levels, down to jibes for excessive punctuality.

An idealized clock, running for weeks and months with a constancy of pace that seemed unaffected by worldly troubles and that seemed to rival in regularity and dependability the eternal cycles of day and night and the motions of the stars, such a clock invited comparison with the world itself, and the comparison pointed to God as the divine clockmaker. From the late fourteenth to the late eighteenth centuries, this resemblance was observed innumerable times. It was made the basis of a formal proof of the existence of God, the "argument from design," which concluded that a divine creator must exist because the world has all the characteristics of a clockwork-like artifact. This analogy of clock and world, which was deeply and widely believed for centuries, came to play the role of a master metaphor from which most of the other clock metaphors were derived.

From the conviction that the world had the character of clockwork followed the belief that nature obeyed the laws of mechanics. This belief became one of the constituting elements of the new science and found expression in the often-repeated call that philosophers should approach the secrets of nature in the manner of the clockmaker who uncovers the causes of trouble by taking the malfunctioning mechanism apart.

The new science insisted that all of nature was subject to the same laws. The clockwork character of the Creation was not confined to celestial events but applied just as well to the phenomena on earth, notably, living organisms. The laws of mechanics, then, were valid also in the fields of medicine and biology. This belief received support from specific similarities between animal bodies and clocks and from spectacular achievements in the construction of automata.

The clock image called forth a number of related meanings. One sequence of associations, as just demonstrated, led from the clock's qualities of regularity, order, and harmony to the universe as a whole, to the Creation and the heavenly clockmaker, and to the mechanical character of all nature. Viewed from another angle, the clock image served to illustrate quite different notions.

Some viewers were not content to admire the clock's excellent qualities but were more interested in the machinery that had brought these qualities about. In comparing the clock with the planetary system, the living body, or the well-governed state, their focus was not on the order and harmony of these mechanisms' functioning but on the similarities in their structures. The purpose of such comparisons was to express approval and sometimes explicit delight over the thoughtfulness of the design, the perfect coordination of so many moving parts, and the astonishing efficiency of the total mechanism. Clockwork became a metaphor for the flawless working together of a complex combination of parts. It became one of the first concrete illustrations of a new abstraction that was in the process of formulation, namely, the concept *system*. Eventually the kinship was explicitly acknowledged. The article on system in Diderot's *Encyclopédie* adduced only one physical example: the mechanical clock.

The word *system* did not often appear explicitly in connection with clock metaphors. More commonly, when the meaning *system* was intended, that is, when the discourse was about a complex but well-integrated entity composed of many parts, the clock analogy was introduced directly. Systems illustrated by the image of the clock usually displayed certain common characteristics.

The actions of the various parts of a system always originated in the same way: they were initiated by a single central cause. The entire system was organized around a central authority that was directly linked to the multitude of organs or elements carrying out the system's various functions. The relationship between central authority and operating organ was conceived in principle as a cause-and-effect relationship, but it was usually described in terms of mechanical linkages. The custom of envisioning the system as ordered around a central authority led to certain rather obvious comparisons. God, the sun, the king, the brain (or the heart), and similar agents seen as central authorities were likened to the escapement, the program drum, the spring, or the weight of a clock. That the clock functioned by means of a central command structure was widely enough perceived, but there was no agreement as to which element in it was most analogous to the central authority. Was it its source of energy, its regulating element, or its memory device?

The relationship between the single central authority and the multitude of operating elements within the system had something hierarchical about it. Doubtless the system's organization was deeply shaped by the old and powerful intellectual tradition of arranging systems in hierarchies, many-layered and pyramid-shaped. But there were differences from the medieval concept of hierarchy: in the new clocklike systems there was much emphasis on the two ranks of the central authority and the operating elements; intermediate ranks between the highest and lowest, although not actually denied, received little attention. Emphasis was on the directness of the connection between these two ranks and on the indispensability for the whole of every single element of the system.

Indispensability of all parts did not imply equality in rank. Differences between the elements of the system were necessary because they were shaped and equipped differently according to their specialized tasks. Rigorous division of labor of the various parts gave the system efficiency. The specialties of the central authority were information, memory, judgment, and decision. The other elements of the system carried out their divers functions only as instructed by the central authority. No need was perceived, and no provision made, for return communication from the operatives to the center. No dialogue was possible between the center and the lower branches; the flow of communication was one-way—downward.

The similarity between the structure underlying this centralist and authoritarian conception of system and the structure of clocks and automata was acknowledged in numerous metaphors. This form of organization had its characteristic strengths and weaknesses and developed characteristic forms of behavior. A system that insisted on dealing with all problems centrally and that left its local operatives no discretion to act upon their own judgment was not well equipped to act spontaneously in the face of the unexpected. Its best hope for success was in the anticipation of all eventualities, in meeting them with plans and programs developed in advance, and in its dealings with the outside world, in always keeping the initiative. This was precisely how automata functioned; their mechanical programs—often interchangeable—enabled them to perform amazing feats, but they were incapable of making spontaneous responses to unforeseen challenges of even the simplest kind.

This preference for organizing complex systems around central authorities, for acting according to carefully laid plans, and for acting on one's own initiative was closely related to a deep-seated and widely shared belief in determinism. This was the belief that the world, once created by a maker of absolute and perfect wisdom, now proceeded along a course that was wholly predetermined by the choices made at the moment of creation. Such determinism was accurately illustrated in the way clocks functioned, be it in the automaton's preprogrammed feats or in the clock's basic function as timekeeper, where it duplicated the heavenly phenomena. Fittingly, the clock served as the conventional literary illustration of determinism.

These, then, were the principal implications of the clock metaphor. Recalling the original question, What were the metaphors actually saying? it is clear now that there is no single answer. Clock metaphors were saying several, albeit similar, things:

— They idealized the qualities of regularity, order, and harmony.
— They insisted on the clock as the prototype for the world, with regard to both its creation and its normal functioning.
— By pleading the mechanical character of the physical world, they sought to discredit magic; they sought to advance rationality both in the selection of evidence and in the analysis of causal connections.
— They promoted the mechanical clock as a physical illustration of the hitherto amorphous notion of *system,* that is, of an integrated assembly of numerous, dynamically interacting parts.
— They advertised the advantages of authoritarian, centralist command structures, be they in the body, in society, or in the universe.
— They illustrated and thus reinforced the general world view of determinism.

These statements summarize in condensed form but with all required fidelity to the original text the varying meanings of the vast majority of clock metaphors examined in the previous chapters. This is as far, however, as testimony of that time will take us. In any efforts to identify the single common denominator that unites all clock metaphors, the original sources will offer no further help. That question would not have been asked at the time. If all the clock metaphors had anything in common it would not have been anything explicit and distinct but something unexpressed and unacknowledged that existed only in the un- and subconscious minds of those who wrote clock metaphors and of those who applauded them.

Among the themes of the various groups of clock metaphors listed above, a certain basic affinity, some general connecting theme, is readily apparent. Together they outline a specific approach to the problems of establishing order among a mass of related, interacting parts and of organizing, maintaining, and controlling complex dynamic systems. The clock metaphor thus becomes an illustration of a general conception of order that is applicable to the most diverse areas of experience, from the living body to the state to the universe. The principal features of this authoritarian conception of order are its insistence upon control by one authority and a centralist command structure. The central authority communicates with the subordinate members of the system through rigid cause-and-effect relationships that are unidirectional and do not provide for or appreciate return signals ("back talk" in authoritarian usage, "feedback" in modern systems technology).

It is revealing to consider how the authoritarian conception of order envisions the maintenance of stability in its systems. The answer is contained in the image of the clock: an ideal clock is expected to run forever and function perfectly, entirely by virtue of its construction. A skillful designer knows the causes of all possible troubles; with such knowledge, he will fortify the mechanism against all dangers in advance and will program into it the appropriate responses to all foreseeable disturbances. In the face of unforeseen problems, however, the mechanism is helpless; the only salvation is with the intervention of its maker. The consequences of this approach to maintaining stability in the system are a pervasive dependence on central control and on decision making based on careful planning and forecasting and an abhorrence of on-the-spot decision making and of ad hoc problem solving, that is, of "muddling through."

What the clock metaphors meant but what they did not explicitly say can now be stated simply: they expressed, proudly and confidently, a peculiar conception of order that is perhaps best described as authoritarian and that was shared, if only unconsciously and in implicit form, by a significant part of the societies of early modern Europe.

Recognizing that the authoritarian conception of order was inseparably connected with the mechanical clock, one wonders how the emergence of the one was related to the invention and development of the other. This relationship, it seems, was one of intimate interaction and mutual reinforcement over three or four centuries.

When the mechanical clock was first invented, it was greeted—if writers like Dante and Suso are reliable witnesses—with almost religious veneration. Its immediate acceptance, rapid spreading, and quick technical maturing indicate how congenial and fascinating the clock seemed to the public. Demonstrating, in an impressively concrete manner, a particular kind of rationality and logic and a distinctive method of achieving desired results, it appealed to unexpressed desires and latent inclinations. For several centuries, the clock's most important function was perhaps to serve as an instrument of popular education and, indeed, indoctrination. To progress-minded Europeans of the Renaissance, the clock embodied the best things the future could bring: an end to magic and superstition, rationality in thought, and order in public life. No wonder that they pointed to this symbol of their aspirations at every opportunity.

While the authoritarian conception of order took shape in the minds of the literate upper classes, the clock also had its effect, partly in a nonverbal manner, upon the thinking and feeling of the unlettered rural majorities. They were not likely to get clocks into their hands, but they would see them in the village church, on the towers of the town, or at regional fairs. In both its roles, as a timekeeper and as a demonstration model of rational, purposeful action, the clock served as an important and purposely used instrument in preparing the masses for the ways of modern industrial society. This latter role of the clock—as an instrument for changing popular mentalities, attitudes, and behaviors—would warrant more detailed investigation.

The relationship between the technological advance of the mechanical clock and the formation and rise of the authoritarian conception of order was one of continuous interaction and mutual reinforcement. At first, as evidence of the public's general predisposition and sympathy for the new invention, the best minds and great material resources were committed to the development of the mechanism. In time the clock became more perfect and more widely accessible, and the more it affected public mentalities and attitudes, the more it generated support for itself. Thus a particular technology and a distinctive set of social ideals, values, and attitudes promoted each other in spiraling manner until the great climax in the seventeenth century with its extraordinary production of clocks and the conspicuous flourishing of the authoritarian conception of order.

We have perhaps finally arrived at an answer for our original question: Why the disregard for feedback before 1700? Was the public mind too fascinated with clockwork-like mechanisms, too full of the authoritarian conception of order, to be capable of any sympathy for another type of mechanism which, inconspicuous in appearance and subtle in functioning, represented a radically different and, indeed, rather anti-authoritarian conception of order?

Chapter 28

Christine MacLeod

INVENTORS AND OTHER HEROES

THE INVENTOR WAS AN IMPROBABLE HERO. Neither his conceptual pedigree nor his personal attributes marked him out as a transparently heroic figure. Long distrusted as a monopolist and 'projector', he toiled in an anonymous workshop, far from the glorious field of battle, or the terrors of the ice floes, the desert, or the jungle. Yet, in a century remarkable for its celebration of heroes, the inventor too had his pedestal and his laurel wreath. Notoriously, in the essays of Samuel Smiles, he took centre stage, the epitome of 'self help', but this was only one facet of a cult whose origins preceded Smiles' worthy gospel by several decades and whose significance ran much deeper. The intrusion of inventors amidst the warriors, monarchs and statesmen who dominated the pantheon of early nineteenth-century Britain represented a challenge to aristocratic society. As astute observers recognized, the 'colossal' statue of James Watt, installed in Westminster Abbey in 1834, was the harbinger of a new age; it was the cultural counterpart of the Reform Act of 1832.[1]

The politics of invention

James Watt was posthumously fashioned into the standard-bearer of the rising industrial classes. He personified their claim that it was not military prowess that made Great Britain great, but the ingenuity and enterprise of its 'industrious' citizens: the country's strength and global influence rested on the prosperity generated by manufacturing and trade; peaceful competition was a more secure route than war to individual happiness and national supremacy. Never was this claim in greater jeopardy than during the Napoleonic wars and their aftermath: Nelson's victory at Trafalgar in 1805 and Wellington's at Waterloo, ten years later, appeared to confirm the fitness of an aristocratic military caste for government. It fed a swelling tide of nationalism and triggered a cult of hero worship, which found its most visible expression in the erection of large-scale public monuments to the victors of the battlefield.[2] It threatened to suppress the demands for political representation and fiscal justice that the excluded classes had been advancing for over half a century – with mounting confidence since the American and French revolutions. In this bellicose climate, it became necessary to advance that campaign by redefining the nation and the nation's heroes: they would be men of peaceful conquest. The death of James Watt in 1819 provided the reformers' first opportunity to subvert the dominant heroic image.

Eulogistic obituaries lauded Watt's inventive genius and exaggerated the role of his improved steam engine in creating Britain's wealth and defeating Napoleon. The efforts of influential friends to commemorate his memory culminated in a grandiose public meeting at Westminster in 1824, chaired by the prime minister, Lord Liverpool, which launched the national appeal for his monument. There, a glittering array of leading politicians, men of science, literary figures and manufacturers promoted Watt's reputation as a saviour of his country and a benefactor of humanity: thanks to him, they proclaimed, steam power promised a future of peace and prosperity, British naval supremacy, and the extension of Christian civilization around the globe. In effect, a significant element of the governing class was endorsing the growth of industry and opening a dialogue with the men whose business ventures had promoted it. Across the country, manufacturers and their workers responded enthusiastically to the opportunity to install 'one of their own' in the national pantheon. Alarmed by this new alliance, however, radical politicians sought to reclaim Watt for their own cause; simultaneously they opened a debate about the nature of invention. The press started to show a new respect for inventors, and cartoonists lampooned the prospect of a steam-powered future, paying tribute thereby to the new-found significance of technology.

Gradually, during the 1830s and 40s, this new regard for technical achievements expanded, fuelled by the daring feats of the civil engineers, as they propelled railways across the landscape, bridged estuaries and gorges, and tunnelled (not without terrifying mishaps) beneath the River Thames. In a highly visible way they were taming nature. The leading civil engineers – George and Robert Stephenson, Marc and Isambard Kingdom Brunel, in particular – became celebrities in their lifetimes. Explanations of Britain's extraordinary growth in prosperity since the eighteenth century were increasingly couched in terms of technological change, often by reference to particular inventors. Historians and social commentators began to chronicle the rise of manufacturing industry (not always favourably): authors as disparate as Lord Macaulay and Friedrich Engels credited the importance of Watt, Richard Arkwright and other industrial pioneers. Inventors received sympathetic treatment from Charles Dickens and Mrs Gaskell, not to mention the mixed attentions of a bevy of minor novelists, poetasters and *Mr Punch;* their lives were sanctioned by obituaries in *The Times.*

The popular celebration of inventors reached its zenith in the third quarter of the nineteenth century. The Great Exhibition of 1851 played a pivotal role, orchestrating a sense of national pride in British manufacturing supremacy and an ethos of peaceful international competitiveness. From the revolutionary design of the Crystal Palace, to the power and ingenuity on display in the machinery hall, everything put new technology in a positive light and excited curiosity about its creators. Less ostentatiously, the Patent Law Amendment Act of 1852, the first major reform of the patent system in over 200 years, stirred up a ferment of controversy. Not only did its passage through Parliament stimulate debate over the inventor's role in the creation of national wealth, but it also sparked the 'patent controversy', which threatened the patent system with abolition and kept the issue in the public eye for another three decades. Prompted perhaps by this threat, Bennet Woodcroft, at the head of the new Patent Office, made enormous efforts to preserve and publicize the achievements of inventive men, both living and dead. He supplied Samuel Smiles and other biographers with information, and began to rescue machinery that marked 'the great steps in every invention' for the new Patent Office Museum at South Kensington.

Controversy of a different kind was provoked in 1854 by the outbreak of war in the Crimea and, a few years later, in India. Pacifists and others who had believed that war was an anachronism, doomed to extinction as modern nations engaged in mutually beneficial free trade, were shocked to find inventors supplying the state with new technologies of destruction. In more conservative eyes, however, this was further cause to celebrate the contribution that inventors and manufacturing industry made to Britain's international predominance: the heroes of the battlefield were impotent without the support of ingenious men on the home front, both directly in the production of weapons and indirectly in filling the nation's coffers, thanks to its booming industries. Few were prouder of their place in 'the workshop of the world' than the skilled men whose trades were at the forefront of industrialization, and many of them identified with the inventors who had been instrumental in their success. In the heavy industries and mechanized textile trades, in particular, they drank toasts to the memory of their heroes and celebrated them on their trade-union insignia. Just as in 1832 the manufacturers had staked their claim to enfranchisement under the banner of Watt and steam-powered industry, so at mid-century skilled working man campaigned for equal political rights by reference to the ingenious artisans' role in the nation's greatness.

As hero-worshipping Britain went 'statue mad' during Victoria's reign and embellished the country's squares, parks and buildings with the images of great men (only rarely women), inventors too were ostentatiously commemorated.[3] Towns and cities, universities and professional bodies paid public tribute to men with whose inventive achievements they wished to be identified. They launched public subscriptions in order to honour, in bronze or marble, both those recently deceased and others long dead. While the contributors of guineas headed the lists of subscribers, often the most striking feature was the preponderance of working men who donated their shillings and pence. Occasionally, it was skilled workers who took the initiative, as they did in Bolton (Lancs.) and Penzance (Cornwall), where the statues of Samuel Crompton and Sir Humphry Davy, respectively, still bear testimony to their campaigns. These were bold, symbolic, statements about the contribution of working people to Britain's industrial supremacy. Soon, the most prominent inventors could expect official recognition in their lifetimes, as the state became more liberal in its award of honours to professional men and industrialists. A few inventors were even elevated to the peerage: by 1900, engineering, physics and surgery were all represented in the House of Lords, as was the textile industry.[4]

It was a dizzy ascent, from 'projector' to peer, in scarcely a century. But it proved to be a brief interlude of glory: the inventor would soon return to the obscurity from which he had emerged. The twentieth century's energies were turned inevitably to honouring the dead of the Great War, and simultaneously public art ceased to favour the individual statue.[5] Already, however, the independent inventor's star was dimming, as more powerful groups became attuned to the value of commemorative activity and laid claim to his glory. Professional scientists, campaigning for the public funding of research, were redefining invention as 'applied science': the hard intellectual work, they often implied, lay in the discovery of natural phenomena; the application of such new knowledge to practical ends was a straightforward, virtually automatic procedure that scarcely merited notice, let alone reward. Better organized, in the Royal Society, new university laboratories, and specialist institutions, they reclaimed the space around the monument to Sir Isaac Newton in Westminster Abbey, establishing there a 'scientists' corner' – its most triumphant (and ironic) moment being the burial in 1882 of that ultimate threat to Christianity, Charles Darwin.[6] At considerable expense, the engineers' equally assertive professional bodies maintained their presence close to the same site, with a series of commemorative windows. Devoid of such support in death as in life, the heterogeneous ranks of 'mere' inventors faded from public view.[7] Simultaneously, the publishing industry was redirecting its focus from the biographies of inventors towards the technologies themselves, while academics in the new social sciences elaborated deterministic theories of invention at the expense of the heroic inventor.[8] In a grand final flourish, the showmanship of Thomas Edison and Gulielmo Marconi and the daring feats of the Wright Brothers made them transatlantic household names, the epitome of inventive modernism at the dawn of the twentieth century – none of them available, however, to become British heroes. The inventor, increasingly taken for granted by the British public, came to be seen as an eccentric individualist: he reverted into a benign version of the 'projector', not least in the cartoons of William Heath Robinson and films such as *The Man in the White Suit* (1951).[9]

As the tide of celebration ebbed, it stranded the reputations of a famous few above the high-water mark. Watt, Stephenson, Trevithick, Arkwright, Crompton and Davy headed the list of names secured in the grand narrative of Britain's Industrial Revolution (Brunel's is a later revival); those of Lords Armstrong, Kelvin and Lister remain familiar to people with a specialist interest in the history of engineering, science and medicine. They all lived at the right time to be swept up into the Victorian hero-worshippers' net and preserved for posterity. If we recognize the names of their inventive predecessors (Thomas Newcomen, William Lee, John Kay, for example), it is also largely thanks to the historical and commemorative efforts of the Victorians. Their twentieth-century successors, lacking such champions, have fared relatively badly. Securing a place in another grand narrative – that of British victory in the Second World War – appears to provide their strongest suit. The names, for example, of Sir Barnes Wallis and Sir Frank Whittle are remembered (and celebrated on film) thanks to the former's invention of the dam-busting 'bouncing bomb' and the latter's struggle to convince the Air Ministry of the strategic value of his jet engine. Belatedly, Alan Turing's vital contribution to wartime code breaking is receiving public recognition. Other twentieth-century inventors, such as Laszlo Biro, Henry Ford and Sir James Dyson have succeeded in branding their names on the consumer goods that they invented or redesigned, because they became manufacturers.[10] Name recognition, however, is not the same as popular celebration: the hero-worship of inventors is one nineteenth-century 'tradition' that has not survived. [11]

Inventing culture

This book explores the inventor's rise and fall, from several perspectives. At one level, it can be read as a study in 'the social history of remembering'.[12] Peter Burke recommends close scrutiny of 'the process by which the remembered past turns into myth', here using the term 'myth' to mean 'a story with a symbolic meaning, made up of stereotyped incidents and involving characters who are larger than life, whether they are heroes or villains'. Why, he ponders, do only a few monarchs 'become heroes in popular memory', only a few pious individuals become saints?[13] Similarly, I wish to know why so few British inventors are famous today, and why those particular ones (mostly males, born in the eighteenth and early nineteenth centuries)? This is not, however, a systematic analysis of the myths or stories that are woven around many inventors, though such an undertaking could prove very fruitful: as Carolyn Cooper has suggested, they 'may be able to tell us truths about basic human experience, such as "how inventive minds work".'[14] Nonetheless, as Cooper and others appreciate, historians of technology put considerable effort into exposing the inaccuracies in popular myths surrounding inventors – often to little avail.[15] If the mythologizing of inventors has hitherto attracted little attention, scientists have fared better.[16] Not only have historians of science problematized the notion of the scientific hero and offered valuable insights into the making of individual and collective reputations, but they have pursued the philosophical implications of celebrity and myth for the way that scientists see themselves and science itself is understood.[17] In particular, the strategic process by which the credit for scientific 'discoveries' is attributed to particular individuals has become an important field of study and prompted debate about the very concept of 'discovery' itself.[18]

My interest in the popular memory of the inventor was sparked by astonishment at the turn-round in his reputation. Having begun my research in the seventeenth century, when the 'patentee' was frequently viewed as the comrade-in-arms of the pickpocket and fraudster, it intrigued me that his descendants should be offered to Victorian working men as models of good character. Even more startling was the discovery that, not only had Westminster Abbey opened its doors to Watt's monument, but the king, at the instigation of his prime minister, had headed the list of subscribers. In parallel, the research of Harry Dutton was revealing a growing regard for patentees during the second quarter of the nineteenth century: judges and juries were becoming more sympathetic and finding more often in their favour; Parliament held its first enquiry into the operation of the patent system and, in 1852, finally legislated to make it more transparent and accessible to inventors.[19] Given that it is generally much easier to lose a good reputation than to overcome a bad one, how, against the odds, had the nineteenth-century inventor become a reformed character, even a hero?

Furthermore, what part had this cultural development played in the history of the patent system – in its modernization in 1852 and its subsequent survival through three decades of sustained campaigning for its abolition? How did it affect the conception of invention and technological change? Did those who wished to abolish the patent system conceive of invention and the role played by the individual inventor differently from its supporters? Clearly, the providential theory of invention current before 1800 offered neither scope for heroic action, nor justification for the rewarding of individuals with patents, so what had replaced it?[20] How invention was understood had important ramifications for the nascent 'invention industry' and its clients, prompting both the elaboration of heroic notions of 'genius' and also a reaction against them, which elicited more deterministic and democratic explanations. These competing accounts of invention provide a theoretical framework to the politics of reputation.

The significance of the inventor's construction as a hero extends much further than the development of the patent system and nineteenth-century philosophies of invention. It offers a novel perspective on nineteenth-century British culture more generally, one that chimes with recent challenges by historians to the discourses of 'decline' and aristocratic hegemony. Quantitative demonstrations of Britain's economic robustness in the twentieth century tend to be vitiated by a national myth that its industry, in tandem with its science and technology, has been in decline for over a century. As one of this myth's most cogent critics, David Edgerton, remarks, 'this declinist historiography of British science and technology has been primarily cultural'.[21] In the late nineteenth century, profound anxieties about the loss of international leadership, as other countries began to industrialize energetically, coalesced with the opportunistic propaganda of scientists and engineers campaigning for state sponsorship. Together they launched an influential discourse of 'decline'. This has obscured the evidence of positive attitudes towards innovation and the burgeoning provision of scientific and technical education in late-Victorian and Edwardian Britain.[22]

As for inventors, the discourse of 'decline' has ignored the Victorians' fervent celebration of them as heroes. Instead, it has privileged the complaints of campaigners for reform of the patent system, who portrayed inventors as the pitiable victims of ruthless capitalists unrestrained by a negligent state, and later of scientists, who argued that only well-funded laboratory research could save the nation from foreign competition. It is such cultural shifts, rather than an actual change in the nature of invention and innovation, that accounts for the inventor's eclipse at the start of the twentieth century. Present-day ignorance of the names and achievements of the successors of the industrial revolution's 'heroes' should not be excused – as it regularly is – by reference to their absorption into the anonymous routine of corporate research laboratories, which, in any case, remained scarce before 1914.[23] We have been culturally programmed simultaneously to underrate the one and overrate the other, and seem unable to strike an accurate balance that values creativity without putting it on a false pedestal.[24]

This study is also intended, therefore, as a corrective to the common misconception that, beyond Samuel Smiles' now unfashionable pages, British inventors and engineers have always suffered from opprobrium or neglect – the victims of Luddite mobs, grasping capitalists, cynical politicians and high-minded critics of industrial society. Their nineteenth-century interlude of glory casts a relatively unfamiliar gleam on the cultural history of the period. Although the precise term 'the Industrial Revolution' was not in common usage until the 1880s, the preceding century witnessed a growing awareness and analysis of the revolutionary developments that were transforming the British economy. We are more familiar with the voices of those who deplored industrialization's harmful effects than of those who welcomed its benefits and hymned its achievements. By no means is it my intention to silence the former, but lack of attention to the latter has produced an unbalanced picture of nineteenth-century popular culture, which is only starting to be remedied. This is especially true of the century's second half, as the visible excitement of early railway construction and the triumphalism of the Great Exhibition in 1851 appear to fade, submerged beneath the anxieties generated by Britain's supposedly faltering international competitiveness.

In part, this simply reflects the focus of much historical literature. As its title indicates, *Iron Bridge to Crystal Palace,* Asa Briggs' anthology of visual sources – many of them celebrating heroic technical achievements – terminates in 1851; Klingender's *Art and the industrial revolution* covers a similar period.[25] The familiar names of the early canal and railway engineers present publishers and television producers with easier options than their less well-known successors.[26] To a certain degree, it also results from reading a late twentieth-century preoccupation with decline back into the second half of the nineteenth. To suggest, for example, that the deaths, in 1859, of Robert Stephenson and Isambard Kingdom Brunel marked the end of an era, such that 'the public began to lose confidence in the engineer so that he began to lose confidence in himself', is to ignore the evidence of advancing status to which the engineering professions laid claim during the subsequent half century.[27] Loss of confidence was not on the agenda of men who, as we shall see, adorned Westminster Abbey with monuments to eminent colleagues and increasingly expected high honours to reward their successful completion of a major project.

Stefan Collini contends that our very concept of 'culture' has been shaped, as a distinct and separate phenomenon, through the critique of industrial society advanced by literary historians, such as Raymond Williams, who adopted the 'catastrophist' view of the industrial revolution that the Hammonds and other first-generation economic historians popularized.[28] From 1882, when Arnold Toynbee vilified what he was the first to term (in English) 'the Industrial Revolution', to study British industrialization was normally to study the evils of capitalism and the degradation of working people.[29] 'Culture' represented the humane, ethical alternative to one-dimensional economic rationality, the bulwark against a new, debased civilization founded solely on the profit motive.[30] Williams explained that his book, *Culture and society,* rested on 'the discovery that the idea of culture, and the word itself in its general modern uses, came into English thinking in the period . . . of the Industrial Revolution'.[31] He structured it around the responses to 'the new industrial system' of major literary and philosophical figures, who lived through its first century. Thomas Carlyle, that arch-critic of 'industrialism' (a word he coined), looms large. 'It is here', says Williams of Carlyle's thought, 'that the idea of culture as the body of arts and learning, and the idea of culture as a body of values superior to the ordinary progress of society, meet and combine'.[32]

Nothing celebratory of 'the new industrial society' emerges from beneath this condemnatory weight: it is crushed out of the record.[33]

Notes

1   Christine MacLeod, 'James Watt, heroic invention, and the idea of the industrial revolution', in Maxine Berg and Kristine Bruland (eds.), *Technological revolutions in Europe: historical perspectives* (Cheltenham and Northampton, MA: Edward Elgar, 1998), pp. 96–7; James Fentress and Chris Wickham, *Social memory* (Oxford: Blackwell, 1992), p. 127.

2   Linda Colley, *Britons: forging the nation, 1707–1837* (New Haven and London: Yale University Press, 1992); Alison W. Yarrington, *The commemoration of the hero, 1800–1864: monuments to the British victors of the Napoleonic wars* (New York and London: Garland, 1988).

3   Benedict Read, *Victorian sculpture* (New York and London: Yale University Press, 1982), pp. 3–24, 67; Ludmilla Jordanova, *Defining features: scientific and medical portraits, 1660–2000* (London: Reaktion Books, with the National Portrait Gallery, 2000), pp. 86–137.

4   F. M. L. Thompson, *Gentrification and the enterprise culture, Britain 1780–1980* (Oxford: Oxford University Press, 2001), pp. 45–74; R. Angus Buchanan, *The engineers: a history of the engineering profession in Britain, 1750–1914* (London: Jessica Kingsley, 1989), pp. 192–3.

5   Thomas W. Laqueur, 'Memory and naming in the Great War', in John R. Gillis (ed.), *Commemorations: the politics of national identity* (Princeton, NJ: Princeton University Press, 1994), pp. 150–67; Rosalind Krauss, 'Sculpture in the expanded field', in Hal Foster (ed.), *Postmodern culture* (London: Pluto Press, 1985), pp. 33–4; Read, *Victorian sculpture,* pp. 3–4.

6   James Moore, 'Charles Darwin lies in Westminster Abbey', *Biological Journal of the Linnean Society* 17 (1982), 97–113.

7   Buchanan, *Engineers,* pp. 194–5.

8   David McGee, 'Making up mind: the early sociology of invention', *T&C* 36 (1995), 773–801.

9   Simon Heneage, 'Robinson, William Heath (1872–1944)', *Oxford Dictionary of National Biography,* Oxford University Press, 2004, www.oxforddnb.com/view/article/35803, accessed 12 September 2006; Jon Agar, 'Technology and British cartoonists in the twentieth century', *Transactions of the Newcomen Society* (henceforth *TNS*) 74 (2004), 191–3; www.screenonline.org.uk/film/id/441408/index.html, accessed 12 September 2006.

10   See Sir James Dyson's profile on his company's web site: www.dyson.co.uk/jd/profile/default.asp?sinavtype=pagelink, accessed 12 September 2006.

11   Eric Hobsbawm, 'Introduction: inventing traditions', in Eric Hobsbawm and Terence Ranger (eds.), *The invention of tradition* (Cambridge: Cambridge University Press, 1983), pp. 1–14.

12   Peter Burke, 'History as social memory', in Thomas Butler (ed.), *Memory: history, culture and the mind* (Oxford: Basil Blackwell, 1989), p. 100. For an extended study of heroic myth-making, see Graeme Morton, *William Wallace, man and myth* (Stroud: Sutton Publishing, 2001).

13   Burke, 'History as social memory', pp. 103–4; Fentress and Wickham, *Social memory,* pp. x–xii, 73–4, 88.

14   Carolyn C. Cooper, 'Myth, rumor, and history: the Yankee whittling boy as hero and villain', *Technology & Culture* (henceforth *T&C*) 44 (2003), 85; also 94–6.

15   Ibid., 82–4, 90–4. See also Eric Robinson, 'James Watt and the tea kettle: a myth justified', *History Today* (April 1956), 261–5; David Philip Miller, 'True myths: James Watt's kettle, his condenser, and his chemistry', *History of Science* 42 (2004), 333–60; D.A. Farnie, 'Kay, John (1704–1780/81)', *ODNB,* www.oxforddnb.com/view/article/15194, accessed 27 October 2006.

16   See, however, Patrick O'Brien, 'The micro foundations of macro invention: the case of the Reverend Edmund Cartwright', *Textile History* 28 (1997), 201–33; MacLeod, 'James Watt'; Christine MacLeod and Alessandro Nuvolari, 'The pitfalls of prosopography: inventors in the *Dictionary of National Biography*', *T&C* 48 (2006), 757–76; Christine MacLeod and Jennifer Tann, 'From engineer to scientist: re-inventing invention in the Watt and Faraday centenaries, 1919–1931', *BJHS* 40 (2007), 389–411.

17   Pnina G. Abir-Am, 'Essay review: how scientists view their heroes: some remarks on the mechanism of myth construction', *Journal of the History of Biology* 15 (1982), 281–315; Pnina G. Abir-Am, 'Introduction', in Pnina G. Abir-Am and C.A. Eliot (eds.), *Commemorative practices in science, Osiris* 14 (2000), 1–14; Alan J. Friedman and Carol C. Donley, *Einstein as myth and muse* (Cambridge: Cambridge University Press, 1985); Ludmilla Jordanova, 'Presidential address: remembrance of

science past', *BJHS* 33 (2000), 387–406; Patricia Fara, 'Isaac Newton lived here: sites of memory and scientific heritage', ibid., 407–26; Patricia Fara, *Newton: The making of genius* (Basingstoke: Macmillan, 2002); Steven Shapin, 'The image of the man of science', in Roy Porter (ed.), *The Cambridge history of science, Volume 4: eighteenth century science* (Cambridge: Cambridge University Press, 2003), pp. 159–83; Janet Browne 'Presidential address: commemorating Darwin', *BJHS* 38 (2005), 251–74.

18   Augustine Brannigan, *The social basis of scientific discoveries* (Cambridge: Cambridge University Press, 1981); Barry Barnes, T.S. *Kuhn and social science* (London: Macmillan, 1982); Simon Schaffer, 'Scientific discoveries and the end of natural philosophy', *Social Studies of Science* 16 (1986), 387–420; Robert Bud, 'Penicillin and the new Elizabethans', *BJHS* 31 (1998), 305–33; Thomas Nickles, 'Discovery', in R.C. Olby *et al.* (eds.), *Companion to the history of modern science* (London: Routledge, 1990), pp. 148–65; Richard Yeo, *Defining science: William Whewell, natural knowledge, and public debate in early Victorian Britain* (Cambridge: Cambridge University Press, 1993); Simon Schaffer, 'Making up discovery', in Margaret A. Boden (ed.), *Dimensions of creativity* (Cambridge, MA, and London: MIT Press, 1994), pp. 13–51; Michael Shortland and Richard Yeo, 'Introduction' to Michael Shortland and Richard Yeo (eds.), *Telling lives in science: essays on scientific biography* (Cambridge: Cambridge University Press, 1996), pp. 1–44; Geoffrey Cantor, 'The scientist as hero: public images of Michael Faraday', in ibid., pp. 171–94; Thomas F. Gieryn, *Cultural boundaries of science: credibility on the line* (Chicago: Chicago University Press, 1999); David Philip Miller, *Discovering Water: James Watt, Henry Cavendish and the nineteenth-century 'water controversy'* (Aldershot: Ashgate, 2004), esp. pp. 11–26; Marsha L. Richmond, 'The 1909 Darwin celebration: re-examining evolution in the light of Mendel, mutation, and meiosis', *Isis* 97 (2006), 447–84.

19   H.I. Dutton, *The patent system and inventive activity during the industrial revolution, 1750–1852* (Manchester: Manchester University Press, 1984), pp. 42–6, 59–64,76–81.

20   Christine Macleod, *Inventing the industrial revolution: the English patent system, 1660–1800* (Cambridge: Cambridge University Press, 1988), pp. 202–4.

21   David Edgerton, *Science, technology and the British industrial 'decline', 1870–1970* (Cambridge: Cambridge University Press for the Economic History Society, 1996), p. 68.

22   Ibid., pp. 5–29, and passim; David Edgerton, 'The prophet militant and industrial: the peculiarities of Correlli Barnett', *Twentieth Century British History* 2 (1991), 360–79; Frank Turner, 'Public science in Britain', *Isis* 71 (1980), 360–79; David Cannadine, 'Engineering history, or the history of engineering? Re-writing the technological past', *TNS* 74 (2004), 174–5.

23   Edgerton, *Science,* pp. 31–2.

24   For a critique of today's 'ideology of creativity', see Thomas Osborne, 'Against "creativity": a philistine rant', *Economy and Society* 32 (2003), 507–25.

25   Asa Briggs, *Iron Bridge to Crystal Palace: impact and images of the industrial revolution* (London: Thames & Hudson, 1979); Francis D. Klingender, *Art and the industrial revolution,* ed. Arthur Elton (London: Evelyn, Adams & Mackay, 1968).

26   R. A. Buchanan, 'The Rolt Memorial Lecture 1987: the lives of the engineers', *Industrial Archaeology Review* 11 (1988–9), 5.

27   L. T. C. Rolt, *Victorian engineering* (Harmondsworth: Penguin Books, 1974), p. 163. Cf. Buchanan, *Engineers,* and W.J. Reader, '"At the head of all the new professions": the engineer in Victorian society', in Neil McKendrick and R. B. Outhwaite (eds.), *Business life and public policy: essays in honour of D. C. Coleman* (Cambridge: Cambridge University Press, 1986), pp. 173–84.

28   Stefan Collini, 'The literary critic and the village labourer: "culture" in twentieth-century Britain', *Transactions of the Royal Historical Society,* 6th series, 14 (2004), 93–116.

29   D C. Coleman, *Myth, history and the industrial revolution* (London and Rio Grande: Hambledon Press, 1992), pp. 16–30; David Cannadine, 'The present and the past in the English industrial revolution', *Past & Present* 103 (1984), 133–8; Timothy Boon, 'Industrialisation and catastrophe: the Victorian economy in British film documentary, 1930–50', in Miles Taylor and Michael Wolff (eds.), *The Victorians since 1901: histories, representations and revisions* (Manchester: Manchester University Press, 2004), pp. 111–14.

30   Collini, 'Literary critic', passim.

31   Raymond Williams, *Culture and society, 1780–1950* (London: Chatto & Windus, 1958), p. vii.

32   Ibid., p. 84.

33   For a similar emphasis, see the anthology of literary extracts compiled by Williams' contemporary, Humphrey Jennings, who commented 'that he found a theme emerging from the collection almost spontaneously – that the coming of the Machine was destroying something in our life': *Pandaemonium: the coming of the machine as seen by contemporary observers* (London: Deutsch, 1985), p. xvi.

Chapter 29

Leo Marx

TECHNOLOGY: THE EMERGENCE OF A HAZARDOUS CONCEPT

". . . the essence of technology is by no means anything technological."
—Martin Heidegger[1]

New concepts as historical markers

THE HISTORY OF TECHNOLOGY is one of those subjects that most people know more about than they realize. Long before the academy recognized it as a specialized field of scholarly inquiry, American schools were routinely disseminating a sketchy outline of that history to millions of pupils. We learned about James Watt and the steam engine, Eli Whitney and the cotton gin, and about other great inventors and their inventions. Even more important, we were led to assume that innovation in the mechanic arts is a—perhaps *the*—driving force of human history. The theme was omnipresent in my childhood experience. I met it in the graphic charts and illustrations in my copy of *The Book of Knowledge,* a popular children's encyclopedia, and in the alluring dioramas of Early Man in the New York Museum of Natural History. These exhibits represented the advance of civilization as a sequence of the inventions in the mechanic arts with which Homo sapiens gained a unique power over nature. This comforting theme remains popular today and is insinuated by all kinds of historical narrative. Here, for example, is a passage from an anthropological study of apes and the origins of human violence:

> Our own ancestors from this line [of woodland apes] began shaping stone tools and relying much more consistently on meat around 2 million years ago. They tamed fire perhaps 1.5 million years ago. They developed human language at some unknown later time, perhaps 150,000 years ago. They invented agriculture 10,000 years ago. They made gunpowder around 1,000 years ago, and motor vehicles a century ago.[2]

This typical summary of human history from stone age tools to Ford cars illustrates the shared "scientific" understanding, circa 2010, of the history of technology. But one arresting if scarcely noted aspect of the story is the belated emergence of the word used to name the very rubric—the kind of thing—that allegedly drives our history. The word is *technology*. The fact is that during all but the very last few seconds, as it were, of the ten millennia of recorded human history encapsulated in this account, the concept of technology—as we know it today—did not exist. The word *technology,* which joined the Greek root, *techne* (an art or craft) with the suffix *ology* (a branch of learning), first entered the English language in the seventeenth century. At that time, in keeping with its etymology, a *technology* was a branch of learning, or discourse, or treatise concerned with the mechanic arts. As Eric Schatzberg has demonstrated in a seminal essay, the word then referred to a field of study, not an object of study.[3] But the word, even in that now archaic sense, was a rarity in nineteenth-century America. By 1861, to be sure, it was accorded a somewhat greater prominence by the founders of the Massachusetts Institute of Technology, but they also were invoking the limited sense of the term to mean higher technical education. As for *technology* in the now familiar sense of the word—the mechanic arts collectively—it did not catch on in America until around 1900, when a few influential writers, notably Thorstein Veblen and Charles Beard, responding to German usage in the social sciences, accorded *technology* a pivotal role in shaping modern industrial society. But even then, the use of the word remained largely confined to academic and intellectual circles; it did not gain truly popular currency until the 1930s.

But why, one might ask, is the history of this word important? The answer, from the viewpoint of a cultural historian, is that the emergence of a keyword in public discourse—whether a newly coined word or an old word invested with new meaning—may prove to be an illuminating historical event. Such keywords often serve as markers, or chronological signposts, of subtle, virtually unremarked, yet ultimately far-reaching changes in culture and society. Recall, for example, Tocqueville's tacit admission, in *Democracy in America,* that in order to do his subject justice he was compelled to coin the (French) word *individualisme,* "a novel expression to which a novel idea has given birth"; or Raymond Williams's famous discovery, in writing *Culture and Society,* of the striking interdependence (or reflexivity) in the relations between certain keywords and fundamental changes in society and culture. Williams had set out to examine the transformation of culture coincident with the advent of industrial capitalism in Britain, but he found that the concept of *culture* itself, along with such other pivotal concepts of the era as *class, industry, democracy,* and *art*, was a product of—indeed had been invested with its new meaning by—the very changes he proposed to analyze. Not only had those changes lent currency to the concept of *culture,* but they had simultaneously changed its meaning. I believe that a similar process marked the emergence of *technology* as a keyword in the lexicon we rely on to chart the changing character of contemporary society and culture.[4]

But how, then, are we to identify the specific changes that prompted the emergence of *technology*—the concept, the word, the purported thing itself? My assumption is that those changes, whatever they were, created a semantic—indeed, a conceptual—void, which is to say, an awareness of certain novel developments in society and culture for which no adequate name had yet become available. It was this void, presumably, that the word *technology,* in its new and extended meaning, eventually would fill. It would prove to be preferable—a more apt signifier—for the new agents of change than any of its precursors, received terms such as the *mechanic* (or *useful* or *practical* or *industrial*) *arts,* or *invention, improvement, machine, machinery,* or *mechanism.* In a seminal essay of 1829, Thomas Carlyle had posed a variant of my question: if one had to sum up the oncoming age in a word, he asked, what might it be? His unequivocal answer was: *machinery.* "It is the Age of Machinery," he wrote, "in every outward and inward sense of that word."[5] During the next half century, however, *machinery*—like the alternatives just mentioned—turned out to be unsuitable. But why? Why did *technology* prove to be preferable? To answer the question, we need to identify the specific character of the concurrent changes in the mechanic arts—not only the changes within those arts, but also the changes in the interrelations between them and the rest of society and culture.

As for the hazardous character of the concept of technology, here I need only say that I am not thinking about weaponry or the physical damage wrought by the use of any particular technologies. The hazards I have in mind are conceptual, not physical. They stem from the meanings conveyed by the concept *technology* itself, and from the peculiar role it enables us to confer on the mechanic arts as an ostensibly discrete entity—one capable of becoming a virtually autonomous, all-encompassing agent of change.

The mechanic arts and the changing conception of progress

By the 1840s, several of the developments that contributed to the emergence of the concept of *technology* had become apparent in America. They fall into two categories, ideological and substantive: first, changes in the prevailing conception of the mechanic arts, and second, the material development of the machinery itself, and of the institutional setting from which it emerged. As a reference point for both kinds of change, and for early traces of the semantic void that eventually was to be filled by the concept of *technology,* here is the peroration of a ceremonial speech delivered by Senator Daniel Webster at the dedication of a new section of the Northern Railroad in Lebanon, New Hampshire, on 17 November 1847:

> It is an extraordinary era in which we live. It is altogether new. The world has seen nothing like it before. I will not pretend, no one can pretend, to discern the end; but every body knows that the age is remarkable for scientific research into the heavens, the earth, and what is beneath the earth; and perhaps more remarkable still for the application of this scientific research to the pursuits of life. The ancients saw nothing like it. The moderns have seen nothing like it till the present generation. . . . We see the ocean navigated and the solid land traversed by steam power, and intelligence communicated by electricity. Truly this is almost a miraculous era. What is before us no one can say, what is upon us no one can hardly realize. The progress of the age has almost outstripped human belief; the future is known only to Omniscience.[6]

Perhaps the most significant ideological development that the emergence of *technology* eventually would ratify, as implied by Webster's grandiloquent tribute to the progress of the age, is a new respect for the power of innovations in the useful arts to transform prevailing ideas about the world. When he singles out the railroad and the telegraph as embodiments of the progress of the age, he in effect confirms a subtle but important modification of the received Enlightenment view of progress. To be sure, the idea of progress had been closely bound up, from its inception, with the accelerating rate of scientific and mechanical innovation. By the time of Webster's speech, however, the idea of *progress* had become the fulcrum of a comprehensive worldview effecting the sacralization of science and the mechanic arts, and creating a modern equivalent of the creation myths of premodern cultures. Two centuries earlier, the concept of progress had served, in a common place, literal sense, to describe incremental advances in explicitly bounded enterprises like the development of new scientific instruments—say, for example, the microscope or telescope. But as more and more specific instances of progress of that sort occurred—progress in that particularized, circumscribed sense of the word—the reach of the idea gradually was extended to encompass the entire, all-encompassing course of human events. By the time of the French and American revolutions, in other words, history itself was conceived as a record of the steady, cumulative, continuous expansion of human knowledge of—and power over—nature. Thus the future course of history might be expected to culminate in a more or less universal improvement in the conditions of human existence.

But the radical thinkers who led the way in framing this master narrative of progress—Condorcet and Turgot, Paine and Priestley, Franklin and Jefferson—did not, like Webster, unreservedly equate human progress with the advance of the mechanic arts. They were committed republicans, political revolutionists, and although they celebrated mechanical innovation, they celebrated it only as the means of achieving progress; the true and only reliable measure of progress, as they saw it, was humanity's step-by-step liberation from aristocratic, ecclesiastical, and monarchic oppression, and the institution of more just, peaceful societies based on the consent of the governed. What requires emphasis is the republican thinkers' uncompromising insistence that advances in science and the mechanic arts are valuable chiefly as a *means* of arriving at social and political ends.[7]

By Webster's time, however, that distinction already was losing much of its force. This was partly due to the presumed success of the republican revolutions, hence to a certain political complacency reinforced by the rapid growth of the immensely productive and lucrative capitalist system of manufactures. Thus, for example, Senator Webster, whose most influential constituents were factory owners, merchants, and financiers, did not regard innovations in the mechanic arts as merely instrumental—a technical means of arriving at social and political goals. He identified his interests with those of the company's directors and stockholders, and as he saw it, therefore, wealth-producing innovations like the railroad represented a socially transformative power of such immense scope and promise as to be a virtual embodiment—a perfect icon—of human progress.

Thus the new entrepreneurial elite for whom Webster spoke was to a large extent relieved of its tacit obligation to carry out the republican political mandate. Consider, for example, the Boston Associates—the merchants who launched the Lowell textile industry. They, to be sure, were concerned about the inhumane conditions created by the factory system—and they surely wanted to be good stewards of their wealth—but they assumed that they could fulfill their republican obligations by acts of private philanthropy.[8] They believed that innovations in the mechanic arts could be relied upon, in the long run, to result in progress and prosperity for all. Their confidence in the inherently progressive influence of the new machines was reinforced, in their view, by the distinctive material tangibility of the machines—their omnipresence as physical, visible, sensibly accessible objects. In the ordinary course of their operations, accordingly, the new factories and machines unavoidably disseminated the ideology of social progress to all who saw and heard them. As John Stuart Mill acutely observed, the mere sight of a potent machine like the steam locomotive in the landscape wordlessly inculcated the notion that the present was an improvement on the past, and that the future promised to be so wondrous as to be "known," in Webster's high-flown idiom, "only to Omniscience."[9]

But in the 1840s the blurring of the distinction between mechanical means and political ends also provoked an ideological backlash. To a vocal minority of dissident artists and intellectuals, the worshipful view of material progress was symptomatic of moral negligence and political regression. Thus Henry Thoreau, who was conducting his experiment at the pond in 1847, the year Webster gave his speech, writes in *Walden*:

> There is an illusion about . . . [modern improvements]; there is not always a positive advance. . . . Our inventions are wont to be pretty toys, which distract our attention from serious things. *They are but improved means to an unimproved end.*[10]

And in *Moby Dick* (1851), Melville, after having Ishmael, his narrator, pay tribute to Captain Ahab's preternatural intellect and his mastery of the complex business of whaling, has the crazy captain acknowledge the hazards he courts by placing his technical proficiency in the service of his irrational purpose: "Now, in his heart, Ahab had some glimpse of this, namely, all my means are sane, my motive and my object mad."[11]. . .

The construction of complex sociotechnical systems

Turning now to the substantive or material changes in the character and organizational matrix of the mechanic arts in nineteenth-century America, it is evident that they too helped to create the semantic void that the concept of *technology* eventually would fill. In his 1847 speech, Webster depicted the railroad and the telegraph as wondrous mechanical innovations with a far-reaching capacity to alter prevailing ways of life. During the early phase of industrialization, innovations in the mechanic arts typically had been represented as single, free-standing, more or less self-contained mechanical devices: the spinning jenny, the power loom, the steam engine, the steamboat, the locomotive, the dynamo, or, in a word, machines. By Webster's time, however, the discrete machine was being replaced, as the typical embodiment of the new power, by a new kind of sociotechnological system. The railroad was one of the earliest and most visible of the large-scale, complex systems of the modern era.[12] A novel feature of these elaborate systems is that the single, typifying, tangible, physical-artifactual, or mechanical component—the steam locomotive, for example, despite its commanding symbolic stature—constitutes a relatively small but crucially definitive part of the whole.

Thus, in addition to the crucially important engine itself, the operation of the railroad required: (1) several kinds of ancillary equipment (rolling stock, stations, yards, bridges, tunnels, viaducts, signal systems, and a huge network of tracks); (2) a corporate business organization with a large capital investment; (3) specialized forms of technical knowledge (railroad engineering, telegraphy); (4) a specially trained workforce with unique railroading skills, including civil and locomotive engineers, firemen, telegraphers, brakemen, conductors—a workforce large and resourceful enough to keep the system functioning day and night, in all kinds of weather, 365 days a year; and (5) various facilitating institutional changes, such as regulations establishing standardized track gauges and a national system of standardized time zones.

With the formation of these large, sociotechnical systems—the telegraph and wireless systems, the electric power and use system, the urban water and waste disposal systems—the private family (father & sons) firm was supplanted by the anonymous, public corporation as the typical form of American business organization, and a new kind of professional or (as it later would be called) "scientific" management.[13] A prominent feature of these complex, ad hoc systems is the blurring of the borderlines between their constituent elements—notably the boundary separating the artifactual equipment (the machinery or hardware) and all the rest: the reservoir of technical—scientific—knowledge; the specially trained workforce; the financial apparatus; and the means of acquiring raw materials.

The complexity and scale of these systems were augmented by the increasingly systematic application of science to the improvement of the mechanic arts. In 1847 Webster, referring to the railroad and the telegraph, had ascribed the singularity of the age to scientific research, and indeed the building of the railroads marked a new departure in that respect. Unlike the innovations associated with the eighteenth-century Industrial Revolution, which often had been introduced by practical, rule-of-thumb mechanics with relatively little formal scientific training, many of the engineers who worked on the railroads had been educated at West Point, where the curriculum bore the imprint of the scientifically advanced École Polytechnique. That French influence, incidentally, led to the establishment of *civil* engineering, thereby institutionalizing the distinction between the civilian and military branches of the ancient, but newly professionalized vocation.[14] Although the confluence of the sciences and the practical arts was well under way by 1847, it was not until the final quarter of the century, with the rise of the electrical and chemical industries, that the large-scale amalgamation of science and industry helped to create the semantic void that would eventually call forth the new concept—*technology*.[15]. . .

In fact the latter-day meaning of *technology* did not gain wide currency for almost a century. The new sense of the word was rarely invoked before 1900. As late as 1880–81, for example, Arnold Toynbee delivered his influential lectures on the Industrial Revolution—a topic that would seem in retrospect to have made references to *technology* unavoidable—yet he relied exclusively on the long-established lexicon featuring such terms as *mechanical discoveries, improvements,* and *inventions*.[16] As late as 1911, the *Encyclopaedia Britannica* contained no entry on *technology,* whereas the entry on "Technical Education" noted that the word technology might be an acceptable alternative to *technical.*[17] An important exception, however, is the erratic practice of Karl Marx, who formulated a sophisticated, historically precocious concept of technology as early as the 1860s but for some reason failed to use it consistently. In the body of the long, detailed, painstakingly documented chapter of *Capital* devoted to "Machinery and Modern Industry," he chiefly relies on the old lexicon—*machine, machinery, mechanism*—along with such awkward relics of the James Watt era as *factory mechanism, implements of a mechanism,* and *mechanical implements*. But then he inexplicably tucks away his striking ideas about the significance of *technology* in a long footnote—one that contains tantalizing allusions to Darwin's work in "the history of Nature's technology," and to the need for "a critical history of technology," along with this cogent summary of what that history might be expected to reveal:

> Technology discloses man's mode of dealing with Nature, the process of production by which he sustains his life, and thereby also lays bare the mode of formation of his social relations, and of the mental conceptions that flow from them.[18]

Even more puzzling is the fact that Marx, after having developed this sophisticated conception of *technology* and its pivotal role in human history, repeatedly avoided using the word where it patently was apposite—a conundrum to which I will return.

Early in the twentieth century the avant-garde of the modernist movement in the graphic arts and architecture, along with a variety of technologically oriented offshoots—such as the vogue of "Machine Art," the geometric styles in the graphic arts associated with Futurism, Precisionism, Constructivism, and Cubism, and, most conspicuously, the International Style in architecture—all helped to invest incidental mechanistic motifs with the aura of intrinsic aesthetic value. In the Bauhaus aesthetic, moreover, design was married to industrial production. In 1923 Walter Gropius, the group's founder, coined the slogan, "Art and Technology: A New Unity."[19] Indeed, the sudden modernist turn toward Mondrian-like abstraction—the new respect accorded to novel geometric, rectilinear, non-representational subject matter—comported with the markedly abstract, mathematical, cerebral, practical, and artificial (as distinct from "organic" or "natural") connotations of the emerging conception of *technology*.

And yet, to repeat, this expanded sense of *technology* did not gain wide currency until after the eruption of mechanical inventions, sometimes called the "Second Industrial

Revolution" (c. 1880–1910), that gave us the electric light, the phonograph, the radio, the telephone, the X-ray, the airplane, the moving picture, and—arguably—the automobile. In contrast with the typical breakthroughs of *the* Industrial Revolution, these innovations stemmed more directly from advances in science, and several of them, notably the lightbulb and the telephone, became the artifactual fulcrum of these large, complex socio-technological systems. Henry Adams gives a particularly vivid, telling account of this sudden, unprecedented acceleration of the rate of change—and its consequences—in *The Education of Henry Adams* (which he first published privately in 1907). Here he announces the appearance of what he takes to be a uniquely empowered human being, an American "born since 1900":

> the child of incalculable coal-power, chemical power, electric power, and radiating energy, as well as new forces yet undetermined—[and who] must be a sort of God compared with any other former creation of nature. At the rate of progress since 1800, every American who lived to the year 2000 would know how to control unlimited power. He would think in complexities unimaginable to an earlier mind.[20]

And yet Adams never—so far as I know—adopted the concept of *technology,* and indeed the language he preferred—*energy, power, forces*—seems more descriptive, accurate, evocative, and telling. But most American social scientists felt differently. In spite of— or perhaps because of—its abstract, inert, general character, its very lack of denotative specificity—the word *technology* attracted their attention soon after the turn of the century. By 1906 Thorstein Veblen, who was familiar with the German literature on *Technik* and who probably did more than any of his Anglophone contemporaries to disseminate the concept, asserted that "the machine technology has become a cultural force of wide-reaching consequence," and, indeed, *the* "factor in the modern situation that is alien to the ancient regime." He predicted that the introduction of the new technology would—in addition to its far-reaching material and economic consequences—transform the mental habits and, most importantly, the moral and metaphysical assumptions of those who worked with it.

> The machine compels a more or less unremitting attention to phenomena of an impersonal character and to sequences and correlations not dependent for their force upon human predilection nor created by habit or custom. The machine throws out anthropomorphic habits of thought. It compels the adaptation of the workman to his work, rather than the adaptation of the work to the workman. . . . [It] gives no insight into questions of good and evil, merit and demerit. . . . The machine technology takes no cognizance of . . . rules of precedence; . . . it can make no use of any of the attributes of worth. Its scheme of knowledge . . . is based on the laws of material causation, not on those of immemorial custom, authenticity, or authoritative enactment. Its metaphysical basis is the law of cause and effect, which in the thinking of its adepts has displaced even the law of sufficient reason.[21]

And later, in the 1930s, when Veblen (like Howard Scott and Frederick Winslow Taylor) was associated with the Technocracy Movement, he helped to disseminate the seductive notion that the engineers, with their pragmatic, matter-of-fact outlook, might replace politicians as the specialists entrusted with making social policies. . . .

Technology fills the void

These radical turn-of-the-century developments in the mechanic arts mark the final stage in the formation of the semantic void that soon would be filled by the concept of *technology*. On close inspection, in fact, an inchoate, anticipatory sense of the void already was discernible in the peroration of Daniel Webster's 1847 speech. . . .

What Webster was striving to express . . . was the need to replace the language associated with the mechanic arts, and to identify—literally to name—a wholly new form of human power that the abstract, intangible, neutral, and fittingly synthetic idea of *technology* was destined to fulfill. Whereas the term *mechanic* (or *industrial*, or *practical*) *arts* calls to mind men with soiled hands tinkering at workbenches, *technology* conjures clean, well-educated, white male technicians in control booths watching dials, instrument panels, or computer monitors. Whereas the *mechanic arts* belong to the mundane world of work, physicality, and practicality—of humdrum handicrafts and artisanal skills—*technology* belongs on the higher social and intellectual plane of book learning, scientific research, and the university. This dispassionate word, with its synthetic patina, its lack of a physical or sensory referent, its aura of sanitized, bloodless—indeed, disembodied—cerebration and precision, has eased the induction of what had been the *mechanic arts*—now practiced by engineers—into the precincts of the finer arts and higher learning.

Turning to the other, organizational and material aspect of the semantic void, what was needed, by way of modernizing the outmoded lexicon of the *mechanic arts,* was a concept capable of representing the novel formations which historians of technology describe as "large-scale, complex technological systems." . . .

In common parlance, nonetheless, when we refer to one of these complex systems as a *technology,* the material component more often than not serves as the tacit referent. But that restricted sense of the word, as in the case of the railroad, can be ambiguous and misleading. It is ambiguous because the whole system, apart from the hardware, is so inclusive, so various—its boundaries so vague as to defy exact representation. This ambiguity evidently is what Heidegger had in mind by his paradoxical if telling assertion that "the essence of technology is by no means anything technological."[22] . . . It is noteworthy that the concept of *technology* gained currency during the "incorporation of America," as Alan Trachtenberg persuasively describes the era during which "machines became working parts of a dynamic system, and the motives for change, the source of industrial dynamism, lay not in the inanimate machine but in the economic necessities perceived by its owners."[23]

There is a compelling logic in the retrospective application of the nebulous adjective *technological* to these hybrid, dynamic, expansionary profit-making enterprises. It exemplifies the congruence of *technology* and corporate capitalism, recalling Raymond Williams's observations about the circularity, or reflexivity, involved in the social construction of keywords—words like *culture, industry, democracy*—which came to serve as historical markers for the periods when they acquired new, fundamentally altered, meanings. So with *technology*. It is now customary to single out the transformative power of *technology* as the defining characteristic of the era when, in response to remarkable advances in the mechanic arts, the meaning of the word *technology* underwent a radical change. The term that formerly had named a field of study now referred to the society's entire stock of technical knowledge and equipment. Williams's analysis is borne out, in the case of *technology,* by the blurring of the boundary between the material (physical, or artifactual) components of these large socio-technological systems and the other, bureaucratic and ideological components. . . .

Why the concept of *technology* is hazardous

The hazardous character of *technology*—the word, the concept—is a consequence of the history just outlined. As I have argued, the generality of, the word—its lack of specificity, the very aspect which evidently enabled it to supplant its more explicit and substantial precursors—also made it peculiarly susceptible to reification. Reification, as the philosopher George Lukacs famously explained, is what occurs when we endow a human activity with the characteristics of a thing or things. It thereby acquires, as he put it, "a 'phantom-objectivity,' an autonomy that seems so strictly rational and all-embracing as to conceal every trace of its fundamental nature: the relation between people."[24] In contemporary discourse, private and public, technologies are habitually represented by "things"—by their most conspicuous artifactual embodiments: transportation technology by automobiles, airplanes, and railroads; nuclear technology by reactors, power plants, and bombs; information technology by computers, mobile telephones, and television; and so on. By consigning technologies to the realm of things, this well-established iconography distracts attention from the human—socio-economic and political—relations which largely determine who uses them and for what purposes . . .

We amplify the hazardous character of the concept by investing it with agency—by using the word *technology* as the subject of active verbs. . . . [This] is particularly hazardous when referring to technology in general—not to a particular technology, but rather to our entire stock of technologies. . . . To expose the hazards embodied in this pivotal concept is a vital responsibility of historians of technology.

Notes

1   Martin Heidegger, *The Question Concerning Technology and Other Essays,* trans. William Lovett (New York, 1977), 4.

2   Richard Wrangham and Dale Peterson, *Demonic Males: Apes and the Origins of Human Violence* (New York, 1996), 61.

3   Erik Schatzberg, "*Technik* Comes to America: Changing Meanings of *Technology* before 1930," *Technology and Culture* 47 (2006): 486–512. The first use of the amplified sense of the word, referring to the mechanic arts themselves, according to the *Oxford English Dictionary* (*OED*), was in 1859; variants of the older meaning of *technology*—e.g., *technik, technique,* etc.—also had appeared in German, Swedish, French, and Spanish in the late eighteenth century.

4   Alexis de Tocqueville, *Democracy in America,* trans. Phillips Bradley (New York, 1946), 11:98 (the *OED* credits the Henry Reeve translation of 1835 with the first use of the word in English); Raymond Williams, *Culture and Society, 1780–1950* (New York: 1983), xiii–xviii; *Keywords: A Vocabulary of Culture and Society* (New York, 1985), 11–26 and 315–16.

5   Thomas Carlyle, "Signs of the Times," *Edinburgh Review* (1829), reprinted in *Selected Writings,* ed. Alan Shelston (New York, 1971), 64. Carlyle, incidentally, is credited with the first use of the word *industrialism,* in *Sartor Resartus* (1831).

6   Daniel Webster, *Writing and Speeches of Daniel Webster* (Boston, 1903), IV:105–7. For a more detailed analysis of the speech in the context of American pastoralism, see Leo Marx, *The Machine in the Garden: Technology and the Pastoral Ideal in America* (New York, 1964), 209–14.

7   Thus when Benjamin Franklin was offered a potentially lucrative patent for his ingenious new stove, he explained his refusal to accept the patent by invoking the communitarian republican notion that inventions are valued for their contribution to the polity: "I declined it from a principle which has ever weighed with me on such occasions, that as we enjoy great advantages from the inventions of others, we should be glad of an opportunity to serve others by any invention of ours" (*The Autobiography of Benjamin Franklin* [New York, 1950], 132). For other discussions of this topic, see Leo Marx, "Does Improved Technology Mean Progress?" *Technology Review* (January 1987): 32–41, and Leo Marx and Bruce Mazlish, eds., *Progress: Fact or illusion?* (Ann Arbor, Mich., 1996).

8   Robert F. Dalzell Jr., *Enterprising Elite: The Boston Associates and the World They Made* (Cambridge, Mass., 1987).

9   John Stuart Mill, "M. de Tocqueville on Democracy in America," *Edinburgh Review* (October 1840), reprinted in John Stuart Mill, *Dissertations and Discussions . . .* (Boston, 1865), 11:148.

10   Henry Thoreau, *Walden and Other Writings* (New York, 1950), 46 (my emphasis).

11   Herman Melville, *Moby Dick* (New York, 1967 [1851]), 161.

12   I add the qualification, "the modern era," to acknowledge the provocative theory, advanced by Lewis Mumford, to the effect that the first "machine" was in fact such a system, the systematic organization of work contrived by the Egyptians to build the pyramids. A fatal shortcoming of Mumford's theory is that it omits the indispensable artifactual component of both the *machine* and also, when it later emerges, the concept of *technology*. Lewis Mumford, *The Myth of the Machine: Technics and Human Development* (New York, 1966); for a more extended critical analysis of Mumford's theory, see Leo Marx, "Lewis Mumford, Prophet of Organicism," in *Lewis Mumford, Public Intellectual,* ed. Thomas P. Hughes and Agatha C. Hughes (New York, 1990), 164–80.

13   Wiebe E. Bijker, Thomas P. Hughes, and Trevor J. Pinch, eds., *The Social Construction of Technological Systems: New Directions in the Sociology and History of Technology* (Cambridge, Mass., 1987), 51–82; Alfred D. Chandler Jr., *The Visible Hand: The Managerial Revolution in American Business* (Cambridge, Mass., 1977), 79–120.

14   Colleen Dunlavy, *Politics and Industrialization: Early Railroads in the United States and Prussia* (Princeton, N.J., 1994); Forest G. Hill, *Roads, Rails, and Waterways: The Army Engineers and Early Transportation* (Tulsa, Okla., 1957). At West Point, the military engineers, trained in the tradition of the École Polytechnique, acquired a more sophisticated knowledge of geometry, physics, and of science generally than most American engineers of that era. A number of them left the army to became "civil" engineers and worked on the railroad. I am grateful to Merritt Roe Smith for calling my attention to this development.

15   David Noble, *America by Design: Science, Technology, and the Rise of Corporate Capitalism* (New York, 1977).

16   Arnold Toynbee, *The Industrial Revolution* (Boston, 1960).

17   *Encyclopaedia Britannica,* 11th ed., XXVI:487.

18   Karl Marx, *Capital A Critique of Political Economy,* ed. Friedrich Engels (New York, 1906), 406n2. The text is that of the first American edition of the initial (1867) English translation.

19   Cited by Peter Schjeldahl, "Bauhaus Rules: The Making of a Modern Aesthetic," *The New Yorker,* 16 November 2009, 82.

20   Henry Adams, *The Education of Henry Adams,* ed. Ernest Samuels (Boston, 1973), 496–97.

21   Thorstein Veblen, "The Place of Science in Modern Civilization," in *What Veblen Taught,* ed. Wesley C. Mitchell (New York, 1945), 20; Thorstein Veblen, *The Theory of Business Enterprise* (New York, 1932), 303 and 310–11. For a detailed analysis of Veblen's pivotal role in introducing the concept of technology in America, see Schatzberg (n. 3 above).

22   Heidegger (n. 1 above), 4. For my criticism of Heidegger's argument, see "On Heidegger's Conception of 'Technology' and Its Historical Validity," *The Massachusetts Review* 25 (winter 1984): 638–52.

23   Alan Trachtenberg, *The Incorporation of America* (New York, 1982), 55.

24   George Lukacs, *History and Class Consciousness: Studies in Marxist Dialectics,* trans. R. Livingstone (Cambridge, 1971), 83–87. See also Langdon Winner, *Autonomous Technology: Technology-out-of-Control as a Theme of Political Thought* (Cambridge, 1977).

PART XI

War

Introduction

WARS HAVE OFTEN EVOKED the rhetoric of sacrifice (Gregory 2008; Kaeuper 2009). Soldiers have been invited to accept the prospect of their death as a price worth paying for the safety and well-being of their families and communities. The experience of danger, especially when shared with comrades, has thus been given a meaning (Madigan 2013; Watson 2008). Yet the psychological breakdown suffered by some who fought in twentieth-century wars implies that war experiences could be so traumatic as to overwhelm a person's capacity to attribute meaning to them (Shephard 2000; Winter 2000). This paradox of the simultaneously meaningful and meaningless aspects of war has been manifest at the level of individual psychology and also of culture. Actual and hypothetical situations of armed conflict have elicited a wide range of cultural responses, including martial discourse, music and art (Foucault 2003; Hichberger 1988), rituals of remembrance (Porter 2005; Winter 1995) – and cynicism, too (Fussell 1989; Shimazu 2009). These responses and reflections may be assigned schematically to four phases: worldview, challenge, hostilities and memories.

Even when future armed conflict has been just an abstract possibility, cultural factors such as the status of soldiering as an occupation have reflected widely shared visions of an overall pattern to human affairs. A religion promising divine assistance to a chosen people (Garrison 2000; Hutchison and Lehmann 1994) would be one instance. Another would be a sense of the world as a scene of perpetual struggle, wherein the strong inevitably dominate (Hawkins 1997; Treitschke 1916).

In a second phase, the breakdown of specific negotiations over a dispute has come to appear imminent. 'Hawks' argue that the only alternatives are humiliation or taking up arms. The gender stereotype of submission as feminine leads men to feel their mettle is being tested and that their masculinity requires them not to shrink from a fight (Hoganson 1998). This sense of honour being at stake can be seen in the context of leadership choices between peace and war and in the recruitment of men to the armed forces (Hughes 2012; Meyer 2009). Unique features affect the calculus in particular processes, but intransigence leading to an outbreak of hostilities also reflects background cultural tendencies.

The conduct of hostilities has involved many sorts of cultural influence. Military historians refer to 'strategic culture' (Black 2012) when they analyse presuppositions affecting how campaigns have been planned. The demonisation of adversaries has helped people to make sense of war's destructiveness and the loss of life. Relationships between officers and their subordinates have long reflected cultural attitudes towards social hierarchy (Rhoden 2012), but also the degree to which the dangers being confronted were felt by the troops themselves to be commensurate with the values at stake (Smith 2007a). Where civilian support was vital, cultural factors have shaped the methods deployed in the attempt to render the contest meaningful to those at home (Balfour 1979; Mackenzie 2001; Verhey 2000) and the extent to which they have had access to detailed information about the fighting (Markovits 2009). What sort of restraint has been exercised in the treatment of prisoners and non-combatants has also reflected cultural pressures (Dower 1986; Lee 2007).

Cultural historians have explored the theme of history as memory. When patriotism has been at a premium, narratives of a country's formative years have often depicted warfare as the crucible wherein the shared identity of its people was forged (Brewer 2009; Gildea 1994). An instance of a tendency to reach out to the distant past for inspiration can be seen in the enthusiasm, discussed by Goebel (2006), for comparing modern soldiering with medieval knighthood. The ideals of crusading chivalry could thus be invoked, bestowing on the impersonality of industrial warfare a romantic kinship with hand-to-hand combat in a cause considered noble.

Lee (2011) provides a useful overview of some central themes in the cultural history of war. As Citino (2007) remarks, the 'cultural turn' had been manifest in the historiography of medieval war (e.g. Keen 1984) before its influence spread into academic studies of more recent warfare. Military history long shared with the history of technology a tendency to be written with a 'whiggish' emphasis on themes of progress and an assumption of Western superiority. Black (2004) and Porter (2009) argue for a less Eurocentric approach and a greater appreciation of war's cultural dimensions.

In our first reading, Hirsch discusses the contrast between what armed conflict meant to the New England Puritans, with their conviction of being governed by divine providence, and to their Pequot neighbours. The two groups had radically different conceptions of war. In Hirsch's view this helps explain the escalation of violence. Not all subsequent analyses of this episode (which include Cave 1996, Karr 1998, Katz 1991 and Lipman 2008) coincide with his interpretation.

The reading by Smith on debates over the First World War among French historians nearly a century after its outbreak highlights two issues: first, what kind of evidence entitles historians to conclude that the war-effort elicited support from the mass of the French population? Second, what accounts for the ferocity with which the war was fought? In addressing these questions, Smith underlines the importance of asking what the war meant to the participants.

References

Balfour, M. (1979) *Propaganda in War 1939–1945: organisations, policies and publics in Britain and Germany*, London: Routledge.

Black, J. (2004) *Rethinking Military History*, London: Routledge.

Black, J. (2012) *War and the Cultural Turn*, Cambridge: Polity.

Brewer, S.A. (2009) *Why America Fights: patriotism and war propaganda from the Philippines to Iraq*, Oxford: Oxford University Press.

Cave, A.A. (1996) *The Pequot War*, Amherst, MA: University of Massachusetts Press.

Citino, R.M. (2007) 'Military histories, old and new: a reintroduction', *American Historical Review*, 112: 1070–90.

Dower, J.W. (1986) *War without Mercy: race and power in the Pacific war*, New York, NY: Pantheon.

Foucault, M. (2003) *"Society Must Be Defended": lectures at the Collège de France 1975–1976*, London: Allen Lane.

Fussell, P. (1989) *Wartime: understanding and behavior in the Second World War*, Oxford: Oxford University Press.

Garrison, M. (2000) 'The Franks as the New Israel? Education for an identity from Pippin to Charlemagne', in Y. Hen and M. Innes (eds) *The Uses of the Past in the Early Middle Ages*, Cambridge: Cambridge University Press.

Gildea, R. (1994) *The Past in French History*, New Haven, CT: Yale University Press.

Goebel, S. (2006) *The Great War and Medieval Memory: war, remembrance and medievalism in Britain and Germany 1914–1940*, Cambridge: Cambridge University Press.

Gregory, A. (2008) *The Last Great War: British society and the First World War*, Cambridge: Cambridge University Press.

Hawkins, M. (1997) *Social Darwinism in European and American Thought, 1860–1945: nature as model and nature as threat*, Cambridge: Cambridge University Press.

Hichberger, J.W.M. (1988) *Images of the Army: the military in British art, 1815–1914*, Manchester: Manchester University Press.

Hoganson, K.L. (1998) *Fighting for American Manhood: how gender politics provoked the Spanish-American and Philippine-American wars*, New Haven, CT: Yale University Press.

Hughes, M.J. (2012) *Forging Napoleon's Grande Armée: motivation, military culture, and masculinity in the French Army, 1800–1808*, New York, NY: New York University Press.

Hutchison, W.R. and Lehmann, H. (eds) (1994) *Many Are Chosen: divine election and Western nationalism*, Minneapolis, MN: Fortress Press.

Kaeuper, R.W. (2009) *Holy Warriors: the religious ideology of chivalry*, Philadelphia, PA: Pennsylvania University Press.

Karr, R.D. (1998) '"Why should you be so furious?" The violence of the Pequot War', *Journal of American History*, 85: 876–909.

Katz, S.T. (1991) 'The Pequot War reconsidered', *New England Quarterly*, 64: 206–24.

Keen, M. (1984) *Chivalry*, New Haven, CT: Yale University Press.

Lee, W.E. (2007) 'Peace chiefs and blood revenge: patterns of restraint in Native American warfare, 1500–1800', *Journal of Military History*, 71: 701–41.

Lee, W.E. (ed.) (2011) *Warfare and Culture in World History*, New York, NY: New York University Press.

Lipman, A. (2008) '"A meanes to knitt them togeather": the exchange of body parts in the Pequot War', *William and Mary Quarterly*, 65: 3–28.

Mackenzie, S.P. (2001) *British War Films 1939–1945: the cinema and the services*, London: Hambledon.

Madigan, E. (2013) '"Sticking to a hateful task": resilience, humour, and British understandings of combatant courage, 1914–1918', *War in History*, 20: 76–98.

Markovits, S. (2009) *The Crimean War in the British Imagination*, Cambridge: Cambridge University Press.

Meyer, J. (2009) *Men of War: masculinity and the First World War in Britain*, Basingstoke: Palgrave Macmillan.

Porter, P. (2005) 'Beyond comfort: German and English military chaplains and the memory of the Great War, 1919–1929', *Journal of Religious History*, 29: 258–89.

Porter, P. (2009) *Military Orientalism: Eastern war through Western eyes*, New York, NY: Columbia University Press.

Rhoden, C. (2012) 'Another perspective on Australian discipline in the Great War: the egalitarian bargain', *War in History*, 19: 445–63.

Shephard, B. (2000) *A War of Nerves: soldiers and psychiatrists 1914–94*, London: Jonathan Cape.

Shimazu, N. (2009) *Japanese Society at War: death, memory and the Russo-Japanese War*, Cambridge: Cambridge University Press.

Smith, L.V. (2007a) *The Embattled Self: French soldiers' testimony of the Great War*, Ithaca, NY: Cornell University Press.

Treitschke, H. von (1916) *Politics*, trans. B. Dugdale and T. de Bille, 2 vols, London: Constable.

Verhey, J. (2000) *The Spirit of 1914: militarism, myth and mobilization in Germany*, Cambridge: Cambridge University Press.

Watson, A. (2008) *Enduring the Great War: combat, morale and collapse in the German and British Armies, 1914–1918*, Cambridge: Cambridge University Press.

Winter, J.M. (1995) *Sites of Memory, Sites of Mourning: the Great War in European cultural history*, Cambridge: Cambridge University Press.

Winter, J.M. (2000) 'Shell-shock and the cultural history of the Great War', *Journal of Contemporary History*, 35: 7–11.

Chapter 30

Adam J. Hirsch

THE COLLISION OF MILITARY CULTURES IN SEVENTEENTH-CENTURY NEW ENGLAND

HISTORIANS OF THE AMERICAN FRONTIER have come to appreciate the relativity of their subject. Gone are the days when scholars portrayed the expansion of the colonial pale as a simple diffusion of European civilization into the vacuum of savage anarchy. Contemporary scholars view the frontier as a permeable barrier between two sophisticated, dynamic societies. In their model, both Indians and Europeans encountered pressure for cultural change, and both peoples underwent the process of interaction, exchange, and adjustment that anthropologists term acculturation.

Within the resulting cultural maelstrom, the role of warfare has not been clear. Many historians have treated Anglo-Indian warfare as a manifestation of cultural incompatibility between peoples, and as a principal means whereby one people was able to enforce its physical and cultural supremacy over the other. Fewer scholars have addressed warfare as a *part*, rather than a *product*, of the acculturation process.[1]

In fact, the ways of war constituted distinct elements of the cultures colliding in the New World. European colonists and native Indians alike devoted much attention to the practice of war, and each brought to the battlefield an elaborate code of martial conduct. Those codes expressed the "military culture" of each people, encompassing all attitudes, institutions, procedures, and implements of organized violence against external enemies. The interaction of military cultures (that is, military acculturation) shaped the history of conflict between colonists and Indians in early America. Only by examining warfare as one pattern in the mosaic of cultural contact can that history be understood. This study endeavors to analyze military conflict in seventeenth-century New England from that perspective.

The colonists who ventured to New England in the 1620s and 1630s fully appreciated the physical dangers awaiting them there. European rivals had already established several settlements within striking distance of Massachusetts, and the local Indian tribes would verge on the newcomers' very doorsteps. William Bradford fretted that his Pilgrim community at Plymouth would be "in continual danger of the savage people," and the Puritan leaders at Massachusetts Bay soon echoed his fears.[2] New England, then, promised to be a spiritual haven, not a terrestrial one. To survive and prosper in a hostile wilderness, the "Citty upon a Hill" had to be fortified with ugly parapets and ramparts.

To ensure their physical security in America, the New England colonists relied on experts. Miles Standish, John Underhill, and other professional soldiers accompanied the settlers to supervise the defense of their plantations. Those veterans carried with them a set of rules and customs governing every detail of the practice of war. To be sure, the Puritans insisted on a number of administrative reforms, over protests from the professionals who opposed any deviation from the orthodox "Schoole of warre."[3] For the most part, however, the Puritans deferred to the experts and installed a military system rooted in European tradition.

Conceptions of the overall nature and purpose of war are fundamental to any military culture. In seventeenth-century European practice, armed conflict remained a ritualized activity, regulated by a code of honor and fought between armies, not entire populations. Yet, with the rise of the nation state, warfare had developed into a massive undertaking. Waged to settle economic and religious disputes of national significance, warfare came to entail substantial expense and bloodshed. Accordingly, the New England settlers did not rejoice at the prospect of war. But if events demanded it, the settlers were determined, in Underhill's words, to "conquer and subdue enemies."[4] . . .

The Indians of New England, meanwhile, had different notions about the theory and practice of war. Though as steeped in ritual as its European analogue, Indian military culture had evolved to accommodate the separate needs of aboriginal society.[5]

Central to Indian military culture was a distinctive conception of the purposes and objectives of armed conflict. Given ample land and a system of values by and large indifferent to material accumulation, the New England tribes rarely harbored the economic and political ambitions that fueled European warfare. Roger Williams, who knew the natives of New England better than most of his English contemporaries, traced Indian wars instead to "mocking between their great ones" or "the lusts of pride and passion." Other observers cited retaliation for isolated acts of violence as the most common *casus belli*.[6] If waged in the name of retaliation, an Indian war ostensibly ceased when the aggrieved had inflicted retribution. Otherwise, native hostilities generally aimed at symbolic ascendancy, a status conveyed by small payments of tribute to the victors, rather than the dominion normally associated with European-style conquest.[7]

The organization and execution of native warfare reflected its objectives. Often the demand to take up arms came from solitary tribesmen rather than their leaders. Hostilities frequently pitted kin group against kin group rather than tribe against tribe. Summoned to the call of battle, potential combatants "gather[ed] together without presse or pay" and agreed to fight only after weighing the instigators' "very copious and pathetical . . . Orations." On the march, an Indian war party might melt away as individual warriors had second thoughts and returned home.[8] The contrast to colonial conscription speaks in part to the limits of tribal authority, but also to the characteristics of native warfare as such: voluntary participation in hostilities followed naturally from the Indians' individualistic motivations.

The most notable feature of Indian warfare was its relative innocuity. Williams observed of intertribal conflict:

> Their Warres are farre lesse bloudy, and devouring then the cruell Warres of *Europe;* and seldome twenty slain in a pitcht field: partly because when they fight in a wood every Tree is a Bucklar. When they fight in a plaine, they fight with leaping and dancing, that seldome an Arrow hits, and when a man is wounded, unlesse he that shot followes upon the wounded, they soone retire and save the wounded.

Treated to a demonstration of traditional Indian battle in 1637, Captain John Mason scoffed that "their feeble Manner . . . did hardly deserve the name of fighting." New England's native warriors apparently saw little logic in spilling oceans of blood over matters of largely symbolic importance. Their restrained efforts reflected equally restrained objectives.[9]

Indian battle array also contrasted sharply with European practice. Though Indians did occasionally assemble, as Williams noted, on a "pitched field," native warfare more frequently consisted of guerrilla raids and ambushments conducted in forested regions by small companies.[10] That style of combat took maximum advantage of the natives' renowned wilderness savvy, while also minimizing casualties.

In other respects, the Indians' martial temperance drew their military culture into line with that of the colonists, whose traditions included vestiges of medieval chivalry, ingrained when the aims of Old World warfare resembled those of native conflicts. Evidence indicates native adherence to a code of honor remarkably similar to the one governing European battlegrounds. Thus, native combatants ordinarily spared the women and children of their adversaries. Tribes typically opened hostilities with a formal declaration of war rather than an unannounced assault. And on at least one occasion, sources tell of a challenge to single combat between leading sachems to settle an intertribal quarrel.[11]

Only in one particular was native warfare arguably more brutal than that of Europeans. Male prisoners of war frequently suffered ritual torture at the hands of their captors. Such isolated acts of cruelty did not add substantially to the death toll of native conflict and in fact may have served as emotional compensation for the participants' prescribed restraint in combat. But while torture remained an accepted element of European jurisprudence, martial tradition held it dishonorable in the nobler trial of arms.[12] . . .

Physical contact between Englishmen and Indians during the early years of peaceful coexistence thus engendered substantial mutual adjustments in the material implementation of war. Yet, the deeper behavioral characteristics of the two military cultures appear to have changed little during that initial phase of acculturation. Even while the colonists took pains to protect themselves against flying arrows, they took pride in traditional drill, seemingly oblivious to the demands of combat in the wilderness. And even while the Indians gradually gave up their bows for guns, they gave vent to traditional emotions in frequent small-scale conflicts, seemingly oblivious to the colonists' tougher conception of war.

Military acculturation remained limited during the peaceful years before 1636 precisely because Englishmen and Indians were at peace. Absent a full-blown war between them, the two peoples never felt the need to make wrenching adjustments in their traditional modes of warcraft. But more than a want of necessity was involved: So long as peace prevailed, settlers and natives also lacked the knowledge required to reorient their military cultures. Though isolated engagements and skirmishes might have taught each people something about the motives and methods of the other, those had all been minor episodes. Even the "battle" of Wessagusett, in which nine Pilgrim militiamen attacked a party of Massachusetts tribesmen, resulted in but seven native casualties. Before 1636 Indians had never witnessed a sizable colonial army take to the field. And while vague reports of aboriginal struggles filtered into the settlements, Williams did not publish his discerning observations on the subject until 1643. Small wonder that Captain Underhill, though professionally responsible for colonial defense, confessed his own ignorance of "the nature of the Indian war." The differences between musket balls and arrowheads were plain to see, but the disparities between colonial and Indian military strategy would not come to light until they were directly experienced.[13] Indeed, the very possibility that such disparities existed may have been difficult for ethnocentric Englishmen — and Indians — to imagine.

In sum, on the eve of New England's first Anglo-Indian war, each of the two contending peoples had made strides in adjusting to the material, but not to the conceptual, aspects of the other's military culture. The material aspects were conspicuous even in peacetime; only in wartime would the deeper conceptual foundations be exposed and reconciled. Thus in the Pequot War of 1636–1637 military acculturation in New England entered a new and more active phase.

The story of the Pequot War has often been told; and though conflicting interpretations still abound, the basic sequence of events is clear and amply documented.[14] The Pequot Indians inhabited a stretch of land along the Pequot River (now the Thames) in southeastern Connecticut. By most accounts they were an aggressive people, feuding periodically with the powerful Narragansett Indians to the east and exacting tribute from the smaller "river tribes" that skirted the banks of the Connecticut River to the west. In 1634 Pequot emissaries signed a treaty of friendship with Massachusetts Bay, whereby the tribe quitted its claims to the Connecticut River valley. Shortly thereafter, migrant Puritans erected Fort Saybrook at the mouth of the Connecticut River and established three plantations (Hartford, Windsor, and Wethersfield) upstream.

Relations between the Pequots and their colonial neighbors deteriorated rapidly. In August 1636 Massachusetts Bay dispatched a military expedition under John Endicott to bring the Pequots and a smaller tribe on Block Island to account for a string of alleged transgressions. Endicott landed his forces on Block Island but was unable to engage the natives, who fled to the swamps. Frustrated, Endicott proceeded to Pequot Harbor where he launched another attack. Again the Indians fled, leaving the militiamen free to do as they would with the natives' plantation. Endicott's army spent the next twenty-four hours "burning and spoiling the country," but the Pequots kept their distance. Having demolished everything in sight, the troopers returned to Boston. As Lion Gardiner, commander of Fort Saybrook, reported ironically, "the Baymen killed not a man, save that one Kichomiquim, an Indian Sachem of the Bay, killed a Pequit; and thus began the war between the Indians and us in these parts."[15]

Throughout the fall of 1636, the Pequots harassed Fort Saybrook, assaulting isolated patrols and any harvesters who dared to stir beyond its ramparts. When reinforcements arrived in the spring, the Pequots shifted their energies to another target, staging a hit-and-run raid against Wethersfield in which a number of settlers, including one woman, perished. In May 1637 the Connecticut colonists delivered their counterthrust. A force of ninety militiamen under the command of John Mason sailed to Rhode Island and linked up with the Narragansett Indians, with whom the settlers had concluded an alliance. From there Mason plodded overland, accompanied by Indian guides and warriors, to meet the unsuspecting Pequots.

On the morning of May 26, Mason reached his primary objective: a Pequot village situated off Mystic River, where several hundred members of the tribe were known to be congregated. Mounting his assault as the inhabitants slept, Mason penetrated the village and set it afire. Falling back, the troopers encircled the village, and as the flames spread, they slew every Indian who sought to escape, with no allowance for age or sex. "And thus in little more than one Hour's space was their impregnable Fort with themselves utterly Destroyed," Mason exulted. Its mission accomplished, the army marched home to a triumphal welcome.[16]

The surviving Pequots promptly gave the colonists cause for further rejoicing. Stunned by Mason's victory, the tribe began to flee the country in a myriad of small bands. "[N]ot a Pequt is to be found," proclaimed Williams, "it is said . . . they are gone farr and finally." Even in the face of this new providence, colonial authorities mobilized fresh levies "to chase the barbarians, and utterly root them out." Of the Pequots subsequently captured, some went to Indian allies of the settlers and "(as they say is their general Custome) [were] used kindly, ha[ving] howses and goods and fields given them."[17] The remainder, kept for colonial disposition, suffered crueler fates: Most of the men were executed summarily, many of the women and children became slaves, while some others appear to have languished in colonial prisons. To starve out those Pequots still at large, advancing troopers spoiled all the corn they came upon.[18] A witness tersely summarized the outcome of the conflict: "The Pequetans now seem[ed] nothing but a name."[19]

So runs a chronicle of New England's first Anglo-Indian war. From the standpoint of military acculturation, however, a number of issues remain. Having remarked the initial disparity of military cultures in New England, we must first inquire into how that disparity affected events in 1636–1637. Analysis suggests a dramatic impact: Not only did discrepancies in military culture help ignite hostilities, they also influenced the outcome of the ensuing struggle.

The causes of the Pequot War remain mired in scholarly controversy. Alden Vaughan, taking the Puritans at their word, contends that the settlers' determination to enforce their own conception of law and order throughout New England, regardless of the beliefs and desires of the Pequot tribe, underlay the conflict of 1636–1637. Francis Jennings, reviewing the evidence with a more skeptical eye, perceives beneath the Puritans' veil of justice a covert desire to exploit and subjugate the Pequots. Without question, there had developed by 1636 substantial tensions in the region, of whatever origin.[20] Those tensions lay at the root of the conflict that followed. Yet scholars have overlooked the rather startling fact that the action that directly precipitated hostilities — Endicott's expedition to Pequot country — was not intended or expected to do anything of the sort.

"We went not to make war upon [the Pequots]," John Winthrop (then deputy governor of Massachusetts Bay) protested in his *Journal*, "but to do justice." However candid the latter portion of that statement may have been, the first clause need not be doubted. Endicott's instructions stipulated that he assert the demands of Massachusetts "by force" should diplomacy fail, but he had no authorization to declare open war against the Pequot tribe. Nor was the decision to launch the expedition accompanied by perceptible debate, preparations, or warning to the Connecticut plantations.[21] To be sure, the Massachusetts magistrates did not send all those heavily armed men to accompany Endicott merely as an escort. "Justice" he would obtain, if necessary, at the point of a sword. But the magistrates do seem to have believed that the expedition could secure the Pequots' immediate submission to their demands, if not by verbal threats, then through a swift demonstration of European arms. That such a demonstration might, on the contrary, occasion a protracted conflict appears never to have crossed their minds. The melancholy truth is that New England's first Anglo-Indian war owed its inception to a ghastly mistake.

At the heart of the magistrates' miscalculation was the presumption that Indians would conduct themselves like Englishmen under the same circumstances. The settlers therefore anticipated no difficulty in engaging their adversaries in open combat, where European firearms would prove immediately decisive. When Endicott's troopers "beat up the drum and bid [the Indians] battle," they expected the Pequots to respond in similar fashion, when "[m]arching into a champaign field we displayed our colors." One can imagine the soldiers' surprise and chagrin upon discovering that "none would come near us, but standing remotely off did laugh at us." Only after the mass of Endicott's army had withdrawn did the Pequots emerge from the woods to fight an Indian-style skirmish with the Puritans' rear guard.[22]

When he heard the news, Winthrop was indignant. "[We] suppos[ed] they would have stood to it awhile," he complained. Underhill, who accompanied the expedition, voiced similar sentiments. But if that development irritated and puzzled the Puritan leadership, the Pequots' decision to continue hostilities left them angry and thoroughly bewildered. "When they saw that they could not save themselves nor their houses and corn from so few of ours," Winthrop penned, ". . . it was very likely they would have taken notice of our advantage against them, and would have sitten still, or have sought peace, if God had not deprived them of common reason."[23] As if that were not enough, the other settlements showered Massachusetts Bay with recriminations, blaming her government for embroiling New England in an unwanted war.[24] Yet according to Winthrop's "English" calculations, he had been treading on firm ice; only in terms of Indian psychology did that ice prove to be razor-thin.

Why did the Pequots take up the gauntlet in 1636 despite their technological disadvantage? In part, the answer probably lies in the traditional character of native warfare. Custom compelled retribution for all offenses against a kin group or tribe, and here the offense had been substantial. What is more, the Pequots were a powerful tribe, "puffed up with many victories," and they doubtless placed great value on the maintenance of that stature.[25] Had the Pequots submitted to the colonists, they would have lost face, both in their own eyes and in the eyes of their neighbors. Winthrop's ignorance of those cultural imperatives contributed to his indiscretion.

More fundamentally, however, the Pequots do not appear to have realized what they were risking by challenging the settlers in 1636. In all likelihood, they expected the struggle to resemble their previous conflicts with native enemies, in which a tribe lost little even when it faced defeat. Until colonial militiamen demonstrated that they marched to a different tune, that was a natural assumption for the Pequots to make — indeed, it was equivalent, *mutatis mutandis*, to Winthrop's assumption concerning the Indians' response.[26]

The Endicott expedition, resulting in the depredation of Indian fields and wigwams, might have offered a clue to the settlers' intentions. Still, that initial attack drew little blood. In framing their response, the Pequots manifested no awareness that the future of their tribe hung in the balance. Throughout, Pequot warriors stuck to the letter of customary restraints, though they certainly commanded the military skills, and had a thousand opportunities, to do far more. Lieutenant Gardiner at Fort Saybrook reported that his antagonists for the most part lay idle over the winter of 1636–1637. And even in the spring, Edward Winslow marveled, "the Pecoats follow their fishing and planting as if they had no enemies." Though Connecticut's upriver plantations lay virtually defenseless for months on end, the Pequots never undertook more than a single, hit-and-run raid against any of them. And even that incident — at Wethersfield — was prompted by special considerations. The Pequots acted at the behest of a tribe of tributary river Indians who, the Connecticut magistrates later conceded, had been wronged by the Wethersfield settlers in an episode unrelated to the Pequot War.[27]

The colonial death toll in the Pequot War further attests to the Indians' martial temperance. By the time of the Mystic attack, approximately thirty settlers had lost their lives to Indian assaults — minute losses by European standards, but wholly in conformity with native mores. Nor can the low toll be attributed to the antagonists' technological disparities. Though munitions would have served at one time to terrorize New England's Indians, years of experience with such ordnance had gradually transformed irrational fear into healthy respect. By 1636, Indians no longer cringed at the sight of one or two guns. And while their paucity of munitions probably put the Pequots at a tactical disadvantage, the destructiveness of warfare in New England hinged on the combatants' willingness to use a weapon of universal access: *fire*. Forty years later, in King Philip's War, native warriors put countless colonial settlements to the torch. By contrast, the Pequots refrained from using fire against either Fort Saybrook or the settlements upriver, where it could have been employed to murderous effect.[28]

As the Pequots went through the motions of a traditional Indian war, the settlers viewed the conflict through European eyes. John Mason never doubted that the Indians "resolv[ed] the utter Ruin and Destruction of all the English," and he anticipated an "Invasion" of Puritan

Connecticut. John Higginson, a witness to the siege of Fort Saybrook, more accurately gauged the guerrilla nature of native warfare, but he hopelessly exaggerated its magnitude. For Higginson, the crisis became "an universal deluge creeping and encroaching on all the English in the land."[29] Especially after the Wethersfield raid, every Connecticut settlement girded for Armageddon. Practice alarums were held daily, agriculture was restricted, and an apprehensive Connecticut Council decreed that "none should go to work, nor travel, no, not so much as to church, without arms." For someone with access to both societies, it would have made for a jarring, even farcical, contrast: on the one hand the colonists, grimly drilling and toting their muskets about; on the other hand the Pequots, calmly tending to their everyday fishing and planting — and only occasionally sending out a small war party to harry their enemies.[30]

The humor of this incongruous situation dissolves when one contemplates the next stage of events. As dawn broke on May 26, 1637, Mason burst into Mystic village and brought its inhabitants squarely into contact with the settlers' conception of war.

For the Pequots it was, in more ways than one, a rude awakening. Roused to the living nightmare of enemy militiamen in their midst, the Indians discovered what sort of havoc those militiamen meant to wreak upon them. Almost surely, New England had never before witnessed such a slaughter, and for once Mason's bombast rings true: The native defenders, he reported, "ran as Men most dreadfully Amazed." When a company of Pequot braves encountered the ruins of Mystic village, their incredulity was equally palpable. Mason recorded:

> Beholding what was done, [the Indians] stamped and tore the Hair from their Heads: And after a little space, came mounting down the Hill upon us, in a full career, as if they would over run us; But when they came within Shot, the Rear faced about, giving Fire upon them: Some of them being Shot, made the rest more wary: Yet they held on running to and fro, and shooting their Arrows at Random.[31]

Underhill agreed that the Pequots were "much affrighted with the destruction of so many." Indeed, even the Indians who fought alongside the colonists took exception to Mason's brand of warfare. "Our Indians came to us, and much rejoiced at our victories," Underhill noted, "but cried Mach it, mach it; that is, it is naught, it is naught, because it is too furious, and slays too many men."[32] Meanwhile, the surviving Pequots, at last perceiving that the colonists' "advantage against them" translated into imminent annihilation, did not let pride, the thirst for retribution, or any other principle impede their abandonment of a futile struggle. They immediately sought to evacuate Connecticut.

Years later, Gardiner captured the tragedy of the Pequot War when he averred that his memoir should serve to let "all men and posterity . . . know how and why so many honest men had their blood shed, yea, and some flayed alive, others cut in pieces, and some roasted alive, only because Kitchamokin, a Bay Indian, killed one Pequit." Gardiner intuitively grasped the senselessness of the conflict. But it was a special sort of senselessness, grounded in ignorance more than irrationality.[33] Puritans and Pequots labored under the reciprocal misconception that each would behave in familiar ways. When confronted with their error, each in turn was equally surprised, and equally regretful, but by then it was too late to stanch the flow of events. Sensitive to the protagonists' failure of judgment, historians have often characterized their policies as "impulsive" and "thought[less]."[34] Yet, given the state of each people's knowledge of the other, it remains problematic whether additional reflection would have made much difference. Anthropologists have long reasoned that cultural disparities between peoples may lead to tension, misunderstanding, and ultimately war. That disparities in *military* culture can have the same effect is demonstrated by the Pequot War.

Cultural disparity between settlers and natives also speaks directly to the outcome of the Pequot War. Although traditional explanations of the settlers' victory stress the superiority of colonial weaponry, the foregoing analysis would suggest that more basic incongruities of strategy and decorum also helped decide the struggle.[35] To Underhill, it seemed as if the Indians had prosecuted their warfare for "pasttime" — a description that, for all its ethnocentricity, cast the two cultures' differing levels of violence into sharp relief. Given their grimmer outlook on war, the Puritans would probably have prevailed over the Pequots whatever the quality of their respective arsenals. And by the time the Puritans made their intentions clear at Mystic village, it was too late for the Pequots to make the necessary strategic adjustments. Just as Indians reacted initially to colonial weaponry with panic, so now they panicked when confronted for the first time with colonial strategy; they fled in disarray.

The initial disparities of military culture shaped events in 1636–1637. But as a cultural interpretation of the Pequot War, that account is only half the story. So long as colonists and Indians remained at peace, their military cultures held fast, responding only to such glaring discrepancies as prevailed in material weaponry. But once the conflict of 1636–1637 set the two military cultures against each other, their deeper principles and standards — theretofore obscure and irrelevant — became suddenly appreciable and a matter of life and death. Cultural interaction occurred in earnest, and the stalled process of military acculturation abruptly accelerated. How, then, were disparate military practices reconciled in the Pequot War? In what ways did each culture adjust to the compelling presence of the other — and why?

In some respects, the Puritans responded to native military culture by emulating it. Faced with an enemy who refused all invitations to the open field, colonial strategists presently realized that they had little choice but to match his stealth. When Mason prepared to set out against the Pequots in 1637, he therefore rejected the orthodox plan of attack mandated in his commission. Instead, Mason plotted a circuitous route to Pequot country, up the coast to Rhode Island and then back across Connecticut, so that his party "should come upon their Backs, and possibly might surprize them unawares." During King Philip's War in 1675, the colonists continued to adapt to native tactics, borrowing and honing the Indians' own guerrilla methods, without which they could never have engaged their adversaries.[36]

Yet, even as colonial military culture fell into step with its native analogue, it also struck out in new and ominous directions. Certainly the most startling characteristic of colonial operations during the Pequot War was their sheer wantonness. The slaughter of noncombatants at Mystic village, the ruthless pursuit of the vanquished tribe, the enslavement or execution of prisoners, all represented an approach to warfare more suggestive of the twentieth century than the seventeenth. The battlefields of the Old World had been sanguinary, but honor-bound. In the New World, honor was tossed aside — and once the colonists set the precedent, the surrounding Indians followed suit. Out of the turmoil of New England's first Anglo-Indian conflict, an antecedent of total war had somehow emerged.[37]

That the interaction of military cultures in New England should have produced a compound more toxic than *either* of its elements seems paradoxical. More plausible, surely, would have been a compromise between the two systems or, at most, the supersession of one by the other. To understand what went wrong in 1637, we must explore further the tangle of circumstances and beliefs that weighed on colonial military policy. . . .

One explanation for colonial wantonness in the Pequot War was the settlers' conception of Indians as savage beasts or evil instruments of the devil. Underhill typically super-imposed the two images when he denounced his adversaries as "wicked imps. . . . Like the devil, their commander, they run up and down as roaring lions, compassing all corners of the country for their prey." Having metaphorically deprived the Pequots of their humanity, settlers could easily deem them undeserving of humane treatment; and as an enemy of God as well as men, they surely merited a terrible fate. Underhill and other contemporaries interpreted the colonial victory as a divine judgment against the Pequot tribe.[38] What needs emphasis, however, is the extent to which those formulae developed during wartime, *in reaction* to cultural contact, rather than apart from it.

Colonial literature antedating 1636 made occasional reference to diabolical religious practices among the natives, but there was no early consensus that the Indians lay in the clutches of Satan. Colonists also acknowledged the Indians to be men, primitive to be sure, but nonetheless exhibiting many human virtues. Only with the advent of the Pequot War did Underhill's darker image of the Indians spring into focus.[39]

In part, the change in outlook may have flowed naturally from the onset of conflict with Indians. All peoples vilify their military rivals, and having already judged Indians to be primitive and heathen, the settlers stood only a small step away from the conceptions that took root during wartime. What is more, Puritan theology provided an ideological foun-dation for the settlers' perception of enemies as minions of the devil. But it is likely that contact with unfamiliar elements of native warcraft also contributed to the formation of such attitudes. Never did the Indian appear so "savage" as when he took to the warpath. Indian braves advancing into battle sported war paint "to make them more terrible to their foes" and howled war cries alternately described as "dreadful" and "horrid." Even hardened Indian fighters of later generations conceded that native warriors thus adorned and demeaned "made a formidable appearance." Settlers treated to the display for the first time must have been petrified.[40]

Various formalities of native warcraft served to reinforce the settlers' visual impres-sions. During the Pequot War the settlers received their first taste of ceremonial torture, and tales of native cruelty circulated widely. Pequot warriors also boasted of their power, in words that the Puritans interpreted as blasphemous. Such brash assurances, flung across the battlefield like so many gauntlets, constituted merely another ritual of native warfare. Unacquainted with the ritual, Puritans read them as literal pledges of allegiance to the devil. The Reverend Edward Johnson drew a direct connection between Pequot boasting and Puritan ruthlessness. After recording the Indians' taunt that "Englishmans God was all one Flye," he continued, "The English hearing this report were now full assured the Lord would deliver them into their hands to execute his righteous judgment against these blasphemous murderers."[41] In short, colonial images of the Pequots grew at least in part out of the settlers' misinterpretation of certain features of native military culture. Those features did not have to be *quantitatively* sanguinary to make the Indians appear demoniacal.

As Johnson suggested, the settlers' impressions of Indians were closely tied to another sentiment: their sense of injured righteousness. Colonists believed that the Indians, and not themselves, had been first to defy the laws of martial decorum by failing to observe Old World traditions. Settlers subsequently justified their own departures from tradition as acts of retaliation. Years after the Pequot War, the Reverend Solomon Stoddard put the case bluntly. "If the Indians were as other people are, and did manage their warr fairly after the manner of other nations, it might be looked upon as inhumane to persue them" in a manner contrary to "Christian practice," Stoddard allowed. "But they are to be looked upon as thieves and murderers, . . . they don't appeare openly in the field to bid us battle, they use those cruelly that fall into their hands." Stoddard closed with the familiar imagery that followed from and reinforced his analysis: "They act like wolves," he concluded, "and are to be dealt withall as wolves."[42]

There remains a puzzling aspect to that line of reasoning. It was one thing for the settlers to torture captured Pequots in retaliation for native treatment of colonial prisoners.[43] But how could settlers rationalize wholesale slaughter as a righteous response to isolated atrocities or to a mere unwillingness to fight in the open field? Part of the answer is that by participating in torture ceremonies, Indian noncombatants came to be seen as "confederates in the action," and thereby a just object of vengeance. Yet the crux of the matter appears to lie elsewhere: By taunting the settlers, by leaving them to stand quite alone on the champion field, the Pequots had done more than inflict physical harm — they had humiliated them. The settlers did not suffer humiliation gladly. When Endicott's troopers realized that the Indians would not engage them, they vented their fury by "destroy[ing] some of their dogs instead of men, which they left in their wigwams." To be taken lightly by peers would have been frustrating; to be so treated by persons deemed primitive was insufferable. Colonial contact with native military culture thus unleashed strong emotions. And emotion in turn played upon logic: Settlers frequently cited the Pequots' "insolency" as a grievance and as an excuse for military harshness.[44]

In assessing the influences on colonial military policy, it may be pertinent that the settlers turned to ruthless measures only after they had offered the Indians "civilized" battle. Whatever the temptations, fears, misconceptions, and emotions weighing on their minds, Endicott's troopers still bade the Pequots assemble on the champion field. Even after the Indians spurned the invitation, the colonists remained willing to return to accustomed practices, where everyone's integrity might be preserved, if only the Indians would acquiesce. Mason, who had pioneered in improvising the settlers' new strategies, continued to declare himself "loth to destroy Women and Children." After the war, Mason set off to dislodge Indian squatters from newly claimed territory in Pequot country. When the Indians informed Mason of their determination to fight, the captain reported, "we were somewhat moved, and told them, It was not far to the Head of the Creek where we would meet them, and then they might try what they could do in that Respect." Only after the Indians balked did Mason relinquish his visions of genteel combat and fall back on "burning Wigwams, and carrying Corn aboard [ship] all that Day."[45]

Here lies the irony of the debacle: It was largely the Indians' disapproval and avoidance of the debilitating modes of Old World warfare that led the settlers to employ new strategies and tactics even more murderous than the original ones. The paradox of a meeting of disparate military cultures ringing in a new variety of combat more baneful than either forebear dissolves with the realization that inhibition in war is not unlike a house of cards. Inherently unstable due to the relentless pressure for greater violence, its perpetuation depends on a precarious equilibrium of values, gradually evolved. Drastic cultural imbalances, latent in the prewar period and suddenly exposed in 1636–1637, razed the fragile edifice in one quick motion. . . .

Notes

Adam J. Hirsch is William & Catherine VanDercreek Professor of Law at Florida State University. He was educated at Yale University and Yale Law School. The author wishes to thank Edmund S. Morgan and Alden T. Vaughan for their many helpful criticisms and suggestions.

1   Three limited attempts are James Axtell, "The Scholastic Philosophy of the Wilderness," *William and Mary Quarterly*, 29 (July 1972), esp. 340–52; Patrick Malone, "Changing Military Technology among the Indians of Southern New England, 1600–1677," *American Quarterly*, 25 (March 1973), 48–63; and Louis Morton, "The End of Formalized Warfare," *American Heritage*, 6 (Aug. 1955), 13–19, 95.

2   William Bradford, *Of Plymouth Plantation, 1620–1647*, ed. Samuel Eliot Morison (New York, 1952), 25–26, esp. 26; Nathaniel B. Shurtleff, ed., *Records of the Governor and Company of the Massachusetts Bay in New England* (5 vols., Boston, 1853–1854), I, 26, 85, 392. For references to the danger posed by Old World enemies see, for example, *ibid.*, 392; William Bradford to the Council of New England, June 15, 1637, in "Governour Bradford's Letter Book," *Massachusetts Historical Society Collections*, 3 (1794), 56; John Winthrop, *Winthrop's Journal "History of New England," 1630–1649*, ed. James Kendall Hosmer (2 vols., New York, 1908), I, 212.

3   John Underhill to the governor and assistants of Massachusetts, c. Nov. 1637, in *Winthrop Papers*, ed. Massachusetts Historical Society (5 vols., Boston, 1929–1947), III, 503. Puritan administrative reforms, such as democratization of officer selection, are examined in T. H. Breen, "The Covenanted Militia of Massachusetts Bay: English Background and New World Development," in *Puritans and Adventurers: Change and Persistence in Early America* (New York, 1980), 24–45.

4   See George N. Clark, *War and Society in the Seventeenth Century* (Cambridge, Eng., 1958); Maurice P. Ashley, *The Golden Century: Europe, 1598–1715* (London, 1969), 187–97; Richard A. Preston and Sydney F. Wise, *Men in Arms: A History of Warfare and Its Interrelationships with Western Society* (New York, 1970), 98–118, 138; and S. H. Steinberg, *The Thirty Years War and the Conflict for European Hegemony, 1600–1660* (London, 1966), 91–122. On New England attitudes to war, see Governor Lovelace to Governor Arnold, Aug. 24, 1669, in *A Narrative of the Causes which Led to Philip's Indian War of 1675 and 1676, by John Easton of Rhode Island*, ed. Franklin B. Hough (Albany, 1858), 36; Nathaniel Shurtleff and David Pulsifer, eds., *Records of the Colony of New Plymouth* (12 vols., Boston, 1855–1861), X, 428. John Underhill, "News from America," [1638], *History of the Pequot War*, ed. Charles Orr (Cleveland, 1897), 82.

5   Any treatment of native warfare must be tentative, given the unavoidable reliance on European sources. The instant discussion is indebted to Alden T. Vaughan, *New England Frontier: Puritans and Indians, 1620–1675* (New York, 1979), xix–xxii, 37–41; and Francis Jennings, *The Invasion of America: Indians, Colonialism, and the Cant of Conquest* (Chapel Hill, 1975), 146–70.

6   Roger Williams, "A Key into the Language of America" [1643], ed. James Hammond Trumbull, in *The Complete Writings of Roger Williams* (7 vols., New York, 1963), I, 200, 202 (parentheses omitted); Trumbull, ed., *Public Records of the Colony of Connecticut*, III, 479–80; J. Franklin Jameson, ed., *Narratives of New Netherland* (New York, 1909), 50, 58, 80, 213, 301; John Josselyn, *An Account of Two Voyages to New England* [1675] (Boston, 1865), 98; Benjamin Church, "Entertaining Passages Relating to Philip's War" [1716], in *Diary of King Philip's War*, ed. Alan Simpson and Mary Simpson (Chester, Conn., 1975), 133, 143, 150.

7   Winthrop, *Winthrop's Journal "History of New England,"* ed. Hosmer, I, 140. Daniel Richter finds that among the Iroquois warfare also served to gain captives for adoption into the tribe to replace deceased members. It is unclear whether, or to what extent, New England tribes practiced prisoner adoption. Daniel Richter, "War and Culture: The Iroquois Experience," *William and Mary Quarterly*, 40 (Oct. 1983), 529–37; Jennings, *Invasion of America*, 152.

8   William Hubbard, *The History of the Indian Wars in New England from the First Settlement to the Termination of the War with King Philip in 1677*, ed. Samuel G. Drake (2 vols., Roxbury, Mass., 1865), I, 98; Daniel Gookin, *Historical Collections of the Indians in New England; of their Several Nations, Numbers, Customs, Manners, Religion and Government, Before the English Planted There* [1674], ed. Jeffrey H. Fiske (Towtaid, 1970), 13–14; Edward Johnson, *Johnson's Wonder-Working Providence* [1654], ed. J. Franklin Jameson (New York, 1910), 148; Williams, "Key into the Language of America," ed. Trumbull, 164, 201; Thomas Morton, "New English Canaan," in *Tracts and Other Papers Relating Principally to the Origin, Settlement and Progress of the Colonies of North America*, ed. Peter Force (4 vols., Washington, 1836–1846), II, 72–73; John Mason, "A Brief History of the Pequot War" [c. 1656], in *History of the Pequot War*, ed. Orr, 25–27.

9   Williams, "Key into the Language of America," ed. Trumbull, 204; Mason, "Brief History of the Pequot War," 41. See also Underhill, "News from America," 82. In one typical clash in 1631, seven Indians were reported slain, and several others wounded. Winthrop, *Winthrop's Journal "History of New England,"* ed. Hosmer, I, 66–67. The limited intensity of native combat, as reported by seventeenth-century sources, may have stemmed in part from earlier (nonmilitary) contact with Europeans. Exposure to European diseases, dating from the early sixteenth century, caused a sharp drop in the size of the Indian population of New England before the settlers arrived. See Jennings, *Invasion of America*, 15–31; and Neal Salisbury, *Manitou and Providence: Indians, Europeans, and the Making of New England, 1500–1643* (New York, 1982), 22–30, 101–5. This demographic transition may have drastically reduced the pressure for land in the region and impressed on the survivors the folly of unnecessary bloodshed.

10   Underhill, "News from America," 51; Josselyn, *Account of Two Voyages to New England*, 114; "The Representation of New Netherland" [1650], in *Narratives of New Netherland*, ed. Jameson, 300–301; William Wood, *New England's Prospect* [1634], ed. Alden T. Vaughan (Amherst, 1977), 78.

11   Roger Williams to Sir Henry Vane and John Winthrop, May 15, 1637, in *Winthrop Papers*, ed. Massachusetts Historical Society, III, 414; Jennings, *Invasion of America*, 151n. Note the sparing of "two English boys" when John Oldham's ship was attacked by Indians in 1636, Winthrop, *Winthrop's Journal "History of New England,"* ed. Hosmer, I, 183, 185. On tribes' declaration of war, see Bradford, *Of Plymouth Plantation*, ed. Morison, 96; E[dward] W[inslow], "Good News from New England" [1624], in *The Story of the Pilgrim Fathers, 1606–1623*, ed. Edward Arber (London, 1897), 518–19; Williams to the General Court of Massachusetts Bay, Oct. 5, 1654, in "The Letters of Roger Williams," ed. John Bartlett, *Complete Writings of Roger Williams*, VI, 275. For challenges to single combat, see also Shurtleff and Pulsifer, eds., *Records of the Colony of New Plymouth*, IX, 11; Gardiner, "Relation of the Pequot Warres," 138–39; and Morton, "New English Canaan," 27.

12   Indians wove torture *into* their code of honor: the victims earned posthumous esteem by bearing themselves stoically under the ordeal. "Representation of New Netherland," 301; Winthrop, *Winthrop's Journal "History of New England,"* ed. Hosmer, I, 194; Josselyn, *Account of Two Voyages to New England*, 114–15. On the treatment of prisoners in the Old World, see Steinberg, *The Thirty Years War and the Conflict for European Hegemony*, 102; Raimondo Montecuccoli, "Concerning Battle" [c. 1639], in Thomas M. Barker, *The Military Intellectual and Battle* (Albany, 1975), 165.

13   The introduction of munitions into native military culture probably reinforced the Indians' preference for guerrilla tactics over increasingly suicidal pitched battles. Jennings, *Invasion of America*, 166; James Axtell, *The European and the Indian: Essays in the Ethnohistory of Colonial North America* (New York, 1981), 262. Cultural inertia among the colonists is illustrated by the persistence of the essentially useless pike until King Philip's War. Shurtleff, ed., *Records of the Governor and Company of the Massachusetts Bay*, I, 26, II, 43, 119, IV, part 2, 319, V, 47; Underhill's observation appears in Underhill, "News from America," 82. For an early colonial adjustment in troop organization in recognition of the native preference for guerrilla formation, see *ibid.*, 51.

14   For detailed narratives of the struggle and its background, *cf.* Alden T. Vaughan, "Pequots and Puritans: The Causes of the War of 1637," *William and Mary Quarterly*, 21 (April 1964), 256–69; Vaughan, *New England Frontier*, 93–154; Jennings, *Invasion of America*, 186–227; Salisbury, *Manitou and Providence*, 203–35.

15   Underhill, "News from America," 51–60; Gardiner, "Relation of the Pequot Warres," 127–28. On casualty figures (all in rough agreement), see also Mason, "Brief History of the Pequot War," 18; Winthrop, *Winthrop's Journal "History of New England,"* ed. Hosmer, I, 189–90.

16   Mason, "Brief History of the Pequot War," 30–31. On the death toll at Mystic village, see Sherburne Cook, "Interracial Warfare and Population Decline among the New England Indians," *Ethnohistory*, 20 (Winter 1973), 6–8.

17   Williams to Winthrop, c. June 2, c. June 21, 1637, in *Winthrop Papers*, ed. Massachusetts Historical Society, III, 427, 434; Vincent, "True Relation of the Late Battell Fought in New England," 106; Williams to Winthrop, June 21, July 10, 1637, in *Winthrop Papers*, ed. Massachusetts Historical Society, III, 434, 447.

18   On executions, see Winthrop, *Winthrop's Journal "History of New England,"* ed. Hosmer, I, 225, 230; Hubbard, *History of the Indian Wars in New England*, II, 30, 36–37; Johnson, *Johnson's Wonder-Working Providence*, 170. For the capital trial of one native combatant, see Charles Hoadley, ed., *Records of the Colony and Plantation of New Haven, from 1638–1649* (Hartford, 1857), 22–24. On slavery, see Winthrop, *Winthrop's Journal "History of New England,"* ed. Hosmer, I, 225–28; Mason, "Brief History of the Pequot War," 39; *Winthrop Papers*, ed. Massachusetts Historical Society, III, 435, 436, 450, 457, 459, 508–9. One Indian captured on Block Island by the Endicott expedition had already been sentenced to slavery for life, Shurtleff, ed., *Records of the Governor and Company of the Massachusetts Bay*, I, 181. On colonial prisons and starvation tactics, see Mason, "Brief History of the Pequot War," 42; *Winthrop Papers*, ed. Massachusetts Historical Society, III, 453, 481, 482, 491.

19   Vincent, "True Relation of the Late Battell Fought in New England," 107.

20   Compare the sources cited in note 14. An attempt to reconstruct the historical background of the Pequot War is beyond the scope of the instant study. While Jennings brilliantly reveals the significance of intercolonial rivalries that Vaughan ignores, my own assessment is that Jennings oversimplifies colonial attitudes and intentions toward the Pequots.

21   Winthrop, *Winthrop's Journal "History of New England,"* ed. Hosmer, I, 194. For Endicott's instructions, see *ibid.*, 186. On the absence of warning, see *ibid.*, 186, 214, II, 115–16; Gardiner, "Relation of the Pequot Warres," 126. The neglect of long-term preparations is evidenced by the failure of Massachusetts to participate again in the war effort until fully seven months had passed.

22   Underhill, "News from America," 60; Gardiner, "Relation of the Pequot Warres," 127. Likewise, Winthrop had expected the assault against the Indians of Block Island to be "of small difficultie." Winthrop to Bradford, May 20, 1637, in *Winthrop Papers*, ed. Massachusetts Historical Society, III, 417–18.

23   Winthrop, *Winthrop's Journal "History of New England,"* ed. Hosmer, I, 189, 194; Underhill, "News from America," 53.

24   Winthrop, *Winthrop's Journal "History of New England,"* ed. Hosmer, I, 194, 212, II, 115; Gardiner, "Relation of the Pequot Warres," 126; Gardiner to John Winthrop, Jr., Nov. 6, 1636, in *Winthrop Papers*, ed. Massachusetts Historical Society, III, 319–20; Winthrop to Bradford, May 20, 1637, *ibid.*, 417–18; John Mason to commissioners of the United Colonies, Sept. 1659, in Shurtleff and Pulsifer, eds., *Records of the Colony of New Plymouth*, X, 229. That the Pequots' reaction was unforeseen is further evidenced by the ensuing debate over what to do next. Edward Winslow was apparently not belaboring the obvious when he suggested that "concerning your present business we conceive it will be simply necessary for you to proceed in the war begun with the Pequots." Winslow to Winthrop, April 17, 1637, in *Winthrop Papers*, ed. Massachusetts Historical Society, III, 391.

25   Bradford, *Of Plymouth Plantation*, ed. Morison, 290; Winthrop, *Winthrop's Journal "History of New England,"* ed. Hosmer, I, 140; Johnson, *Johnson's Wonder-Working Providence*, 148.

26   Williams observed the phenomenon in another context: "This question they [the Indians] oft put to me: Why come the *Englishmen* hither? and measuring others by themselves; they say, It is because you want *firing*: for they, having burnt up the *wood* in one place . . . they are faine to follow the *wood;* and so to remove to a fresh new place for the *woods* sake." Williams, "Key into the Language of America" ed. Trumbull, 87.

27   Gardiner to John Winthrop, Jr., March 23, 1637, in *Winthrop Papers*, ed. Massachusetts Historical Society, III, 381; Winslow to Winthrop, May 22, 1637, *ibid.*, 420. On the Wethersfield attack, see Jennings, *Invasion of America*, 217; Trumbull, ed., *Public Records of the Colony of Connecticut*, I, 19–20. The one woman who perished at Wethersfield had "stoutly" resisted abduction. *Cf.* the benign treatment of two young "maids" who submitted to abduction. Johnson, *Johnson's Wonder-Working Providence*, 149–50; Winthrop, *Winthrop's Journal "History of New England,"* ed. Hosmer, I, 319.

28   Vaughan, *New England Frontier*, 133 (the Wethersfield attack accounted for nine of the casualties). The English population of Connecticut at that time was approximately 600; the total colonial population of New England about 21,200. Evarts Greene and Virginia Harrington, *American Population before the Federal Census of 1790* (New York, 1932), 473; John Josselyn, "Chronological Observations of America," in *Massachusetts Historical Society Collections*, 3 (1833), 381. On Indians' reaction to guns, see Higginson to Winthrop, c. May 1637, in *Winthrop Papers*, ed. Massachusetts Historical Society, III, 404; Winthrop, *Winthrop's Journal "History of New England,"* ed. Hosmer, I, 208; Bradford, *Of Plymouth Plantation*, ed. Morison, 70, 204, 294; [Morton?], *Mourt's Relation*, 96–97, 106, 122; Francis Higginson, "New England's Plantation" [1629], in *Chronicles of the First Planters of the Colony of Massachusetts Bay*, ed. Alexander Young (Boston, 1846), 258; Van Wassenaer, "Historisch Verhael," 73. On Pequots' lack of munitions, *cf.* Underhill, "News from America," 53, 80, 81, 85; Mason, "Brief History of the Pequot War," 45–46; Gardiner, "Relation of the Pequot Warres," 130, 132; Winthrop, *Winthrop's Journal "History of New England,"* ed. Hosmer, I, 191–92. For modern assessments, *cf.* Malone, "Changing Military Technology," 50–51; Karen Ordahl Kupperman, "English Perceptions of Treachery," *Historical Journal*, 20 (June 1977), 271–72; Axtell, *The European and the Indian*, 259–62. On King Philip's War, see Leach, *Flintlock and Tomahawk*, 243. The Pequots' use of fire was restricted to the burning of several empty storehouses outside Saybrook Fort. Gardiner, "Relation of the Pequot Warres," 128, 134–35.

29   Mason, "Brief History of the Pequot War," 30, 34, 35. Higginson to Winthrop, c. May 1637, in *Winthrop Papers*, ed. Massachusetts Historical Society, III, 405; see also Winthrop to Bradford, May 20, 1637, *ibid.*, 417.

30   Roger Ludlowe to William Pincheon, [May 17?] 1637, *Massachusetts Historical Society Collections*, 8 (1826), 235; Vincent, "True Relation of the Late Battell Fought in New England," 101; Bradford, *Of Plymouth Plantation*, ed. Morison, 294; Underhill, "News from America," 66. Despite its remoteness from the scene of conflict, Massachusetts Bay took similar precautions. Shurtleff, ed., *Records of the Governor and Company of the Massachusetts Bay*, I, 190. For a different interpretation, see Jennings, *Invasion of America*, 211–17, who infers Pequot cognizance that the war would be fought by the settlers' rules (even while expressing puzzlement at the Pequots' military restraint). Jennings had a bone to pick with historians who denied Indians' capacity for rational action; I assert only that on this occasion they lacked the information to make *informed* policy judgments.

31   Mason, "Brief History of the Pequot War," 29, 32.

32   Underhill, "News from America," 85, 84. On the Indian allies' surprise, see also Bradford, *Of Plymouth Plantation*, ed. Morison, 297; Mason, "Brief History of the Pequot War," 7; Williams to Vane and Winthrop, May 15, 1637, in *Winthrop Papers*, ed. Massachusetts Historical Society, III, 413.

33   Gardiner, "Relation of the Pequot Warres," 139. Ignorance of another sort — Indians' inability to distinguish Europeans of various nationalities — may have contributed to animosity between the Massachusetts settlers and Pequots prior to the Pequot War. See Underhill, "News from America," 56–58. Compare the settlers' analogous inability to distinguish Indians of different tribes: Israel Stoughton to the governor and Council of Massachusetts, Aug. 14, 1637, in *Winthrop Papers*, ed. Massachusetts Historical Society, III, 481; Williams to Winthrop, c. June 2, 1637, *ibid.*, 427; Gardiner, "Relation of the Pequot Warres," 132.

34   Vaughan, *New England Frontier*, 137; Douglas Edward Leach, *Arms for Empire: A Military History of the British Colonies in North America* (New York, 1973), 45; Darrett B. Rutman, *A Militant New World: 1607–1640* (New York, 1979), 654.

35   Vaughan, *New England Frontier*, 154; Charles M. Segal and David C. Stineback, *Puritans, Indians, and Manifest Destiny* (New York, 1977), 106. *Cf.* note 28 above.

36   Mason, "Brief History of the Pequot War," 21; see also Gardiner, "Relation of the Pequot Warres," 136; Underhill, "News from America," 77. A second assault on Block Island in August 1637 was carried out at night in an effort to evade detection. Winthrop, *Winthrop's Journal "History of New England,"* ed. Hosmer, I, 228. On colonial adoption of Indian tactics, see Axtell, "Scholastic Philosophy of the Wilderness," 342–52.

37   The aggravation of colonial warfare has been recognized; see John E. Ferling, *A Wilderness of Miseries: War and Warriors in Early America* (Westport, 1980), 29–56. For the view that colonial warfare "had changed not a whit from the European style" see Axtell, "Scholastic Philosophy of the Wilderness," 341–42, esp. 341. See also Vaughan, *New England Frontier*, xix–xxii, 19; and Jennings, *Invasion of America*, 169, 212. Whereas isolated atrocities committed during the Thirty Years War were attributable to troops out of control and elicited universal condemnation, attacks on noncombatants during the Pequot War occurred at officers' direction and were condoned by the colonial leadership. Mason, "Brief History of the Pequot War," 28–29; Winthrop, *Winthrop's Journal "History of New England,"* ed. Hosmer, I, 218; *cf.* Underhill, "News from America," 81; Williams to Winthrop, c. June 30, 1637, in *Winthrop Papers*, ed. Massachusetts Historical Society, III, 437. The decision to pursue the Pequots following the victory at Mystic drew virtually unanimous support, see Winthrop, *Winthrop's Journal "History of New England,"* ed. Hosmer, I, 221–22; *Winthrop Papers*, ed. Massachusetts Historical Society, III, 428, 434–37, 452, 479; *cf. ibid.*, 429–32, 440–41. On the Thirty Years War, see Steinberg, *Thirty Years War and the Conflict for European Hegemony*, 56–57, 102. On Old World battlefield honor, see note 4 above.

38   On bestial imagery, see Underhill, "News from America," 57, 60, 66; Johnson, *Johnson's Wonder-Working Providence*, 148, 165, 168; Williams to Winthrop, July 10, 1637, July 3, 1637, in *Winthrop Papers*, ed. Massachusetts Historical Society, III, 445, 438. That theme attained symphonic proportions during King Philip's War, both in regard to the enemy Indians of that crisis, and retroactively in regard to the Pequots. Roger Clap, "Captain Roger Clap's Memoirs" [c. 1676], in *Chronicles of the First Planters of the Colony of Massachusetts Bay*, ed. Young, 363–64; Hubbard, *History of the Indian Wars in New England*, I, 52–53, 123, 213, II, 29, 36, 178; Mather, "Relation of the Troubles which have Hapned in New England by Reason of the Indians There," 169, 180, 183, 190; Increase Mather, "A Brief History of the War with the Indians in New-England" [1676], in *The History of King Philip's War*, ed. Samuel Drake (Boston, 1862), 138, 190, 197, 208, 212; Benjamin Tompson, *New Englands Crisis* (Boston, 1676), 19. On the theme of divine judgments see, Underhill, "News from America," 78, 81; Mason, "Brief History of the Pequot War," 30, 44–46; Bradford, *Of Plymouth Plantation*, ed. Morison, 296; Johnson, *Johnson's Wonder-Working Providence*, 164–65, 169; Williams to Winthrop, July 31, 1637, in *Winthrop Papers*, ed. Massachusetts Historical Society, III, 459. For scholarly discussions, see Jennings, *Invasion of America*, 212–13; Reginald Stuart, *War and American Thought* (Kent, 1982), 7–9; Ferling, *Wilderness of Miseries*, 44; G. E. Thomas, "Puritans, Indians, and the Concept of Race," *New England Quarterly*, 48 (March 1975), 23–26; and Nicholas Canny, "The Ideology of English Colonization: From Ireland to America," *William and Mary Quarterly*, 30 (Oct. 1973), 575–98; Salisbury, *Manitou and Providence*, 221; Karen Ordahl Kupperman, *Settling with the Indians: The Meeting of English and Indian Cultures in America, 1580–1640* (Totowa, 1980), 185–86; William Simmons, "Cultural Bias in the New England Puritans' Perception of Indians," *William and Mary Quarterly*, 38 (Jan. 1981), 67–68; Roy Harvey Pearce, *The Savages of America* (Baltimore, 1965), 19–24; *cf.* Vaughan, *New England Frontier*, xix–xxii, 19.

39   On Indians and Satan, cf. Bradford, Of Plymouth Plantation, ed. Morison, 84; Wood, New England's Prospect, 101–2; Higginson, "New England's Plantation," 257; W[inslow], "Good News from New England," 582–83. On Puritan perceptions, see Frank Shuffelton, "Indian Devils and Pilgrim Fathers: Squanto, Hobomok, and the English Conception of Indian Religion," New England Quarterly, 49 (March 1976), 108–16; Simmons, "Cultural Bias," 56–72; Kupperman, Settling with the Indians, 64–79. On Indians as men, see ibid., 107–40. There are scattered analogies of Indians to beasts in the early literature. See Wood, New England's Prospect, 101. Some scholars have noticed that colonial perceptions changed, but they have not endeavored to explain the evolution; see Vaughan, New England Frontier, 19–21; Pearce, Savages of America, 22; Simmons, "Cultural Bias," 71–72. On the evolution of colonial conceptions of Indians as a separate race, see Alden T. Vaughan, "From White Man to Redskin: Changing Anglo-American Perceptions of the American Indian," American Historical Review, 87 (Oct. 1982), 917.

40   For a theological interpretation of the Puritans' Indian policy, see David C. Stineback, "The Status of Puritan-Indian Scholarship," New England Quarterly, 51 (March 1978), 80–87; David C. Stineback, "White Nationalism and Native Cultures," American Indian Culture and Research Journal, 2 (1978), 19–22. For descriptions of Indian war paint and war cries, see Wood, New England's Prospect, 103; Josselyn, Account of Two Voyages to New England, 114; [George Morton?], Mourt's Relation [1622], ed. Henry Dexter (Boston, 1865), 53; Williams "Key into the Language of America," ed. Trumbull, 199, 87; Increase Mather, "A Relation of the Troubles which have Hapned in New England By Reason of the Indians There," in Early History of New England, ed. Samuel Drake (Boston, 1864), 65; Church, "Entertaining Passages Relating to Philip's War," 70; Mason, "Brief History of the Pequot War," 21, 27; Winthrop, Winthrop's Journal "History of New England," ed. Hosmer, I, 228; Underhill, "News from America," 56. See also George Percy, "Observations Gathered Out of a Discource of the Plantation of the Southern Colonie in Virginia by the English," in Narratives of Early Virginia, 1606–1625, ed. Lyon Tyler (New York, 1930), 10.

41   On Pequot torture, see Winthrop, Winthrop's Journal "History of New England," ed. Hosmer, I, 194; John Hull, "Memoir and Diary of John Hull," Transactions and Collections of the American Antiquarian Society, 3 (1857), 171; Underhill, "News from America," 66–67; Hubbard, History of the Indian Wars in New England, II, 12–13; Gardiner, "Relation of the Pequot Warres," 128–29. Occasional references to native torture appeared before the Pequot War, Bradford, Of Plymouth Plantation, ed. Morison, 26. On native boasting, see Mason, "Brief History of the Pequot War," 25, 43; Underhill, "News from America," 60–63; Gardiner, "Relation of the Pequot Warres," 132; Hubbard, History of the Indian Wars in New England, II, 13; Williams to Winthrop, c. Sept. 1636, in Winthrop Papers, ed. Massachusetts Historical Society, III, 298; Hull, "Memoir," 171–72; Mather, "Relation of the Troubles which have Hapned in New England by Reason of the Indians There," 181–82, 184; Johnson, Johnson's Working-Wonder Providence, 164.

42   Solomon Stoddard to Joseph Dudley, Oct. 22, 1703, in Axtell, The European and the Indian, 142. See also "The Present State of New-England with Respect to the Indian War" [1675], in Narratives of the Indian Wars, 1675–1699, ed. Charles Lincoln (New York, 1913), 33; Williams to Leverett, Oct. 11, 1675, in "The Letters of Roger Williams," ed. Bartlett, 375; N[athaniel] S[altonstall], "A New and Further Narrative of the State of New England" [1676], in Narratives of the Indian Wars, ed. Lincoln, 89; Hubbard, History of the Indian Wars in New England, I, 114–15. For earlier examples of this rationale (justifying colonial action during the Pequot War), see Underhill, "News from America," 66–67, 78, 81; Vincent, "True Relation of the Late Battell Fought in New England," 103; Winthrop, Winthrop's Journal "History of New England," ed. Hosmer, I, 219.

43   Winthrop, Winthrop's Journal "History of New England," ed. Hosmer, I, 219.

44   Underhill, "News from America," 54, 81. For references to Pequot insolence, see Vincent, "True Relation of the Late Battell Fought in New England," 103; Underhill, "News from America," 60–63, 66–67; Johnson, Johnson's Wonder-Working Providence, 164; and Bradford, Of Plymouth Plantation, ed. Morison, 296. For a psychoanalytical, instead of a cultural, explanation of this grievance, see Salisbury, Manitou and Providence, 224–25.

45   Underhill, "News from America" 60; Mason, "Brief History of the Pequot War," 38, 43. Note the pre-1637 emphasis on military legalism in W[inslow], "Good News from New England," 519.

Chapter 31

Leonard V. Smith

THE "*CULTURE DE GUERRE*" AND FRENCH HISTORIOGRAPHY OF THE GREAT WAR OF 1914–1918

IN **THE PREFACE** to a collection of papers presented at a colloquium at the Université de Paris X-Nanterre on December 8–11, 1988, Professor Jean-Jacques Becker observed that seventy years after the Armistice of 1918, the time had come to direct attention toward

> the attitude and the comportment of people, their mentalities and their sentiments, thereby permitting us to go beyond the old opposition between military history and civilian history, to arrive at the following idea – if it is possible to plagiarize a famous expression of one of the central participants of the first world conflict – that the war of 1914–1918 is a bloc.[1]

Becker referred to the famous statement by wartime premier Georges Clemenceau that the French Revolution had to be seen as a bloc. Clemenceau meant that posterity had to take the bad with the good, the Terror with the Declaration of the Rights of Man. Likewise, Becker argued, historians would have to take the civilians with the soldiers, the hatreds with the patriotism and the brutality with the noble sacrifice.

The term *culture de guerre* (literally 'war culture') emerged to summarize just how historians ought to think about the Great War as a bloc. In a 1997 article, Stéphane Audoin-Rouzeau and Annette Becker provided a definition of breathtaking scope:

> the field of all the representations of the war forged by contemporaries; of all the representations that they construed for themselves of this immense trial, first during the war, then after it.[2]

For good or for ill, historians of the *culture de guerre* engaged only to a limited degree with the thorny epistemological issues that so preoccupied Anglophone practitioners of cultural history, and so more or less avoided historians' 'culture wars' in the 1980s and 1990s. Ironically, given the impact of French theorists such as Michel Foucault and Jacques Derrida on the 'culture wars', French historians in general tended to debate the epistemology of history less vigorously than their colleagues in North America or the United Kingdom.[3]

Yet the particulars of the *culture de guerre* remain controversial in some historiographical quarters, for reasons explained below. Not all scholars concerned with the subject are French nationals, and as a group they proclaim firmly and often their attachment to comparative rather than national history. Yet there remains something 'French' about scholars of the *culture de guerre*, in their links to a specific institution located in France, and the influence in their work of well-established French historiographical traditions. This article will focus on two central aspects of the *culture de guerre* – *consentement* (consent) and *brutalisation* (brutalization).

Consentement and its implications

'*Consentement*', translated literally as 'consent', evolved as an answer to the problem of total war in the trenches.[4] In material terms, the problem of fighting the Great War on the Western Front constituted the irresistible force of the will to win on the part of all the protagonists pushing against the immoveable object of a front that almost everywhere strongly favored the defense. Consent became a way to articulate this will to win – as a form of commitment that deepened rather than lessened with adversity. Consent had various components, including political loyalties, affective attachments to national, religious, and racial and ethnic communities, loyalty to comrades, and hatred of the enemy.

While historians have taken consent in many different national and transnational directions, the concept itself has clear roots in French historical traditions. Nothing cast a longer shadow over French historiography in the twentieth century than the Annales School, with its attention to the *longue durée* (long-run) of slow-changing structures and societies beneath the *événements* (particular events, especially political) that characterize the turbulent narrative of modern French history. In this context, an 'Eternal France' endured beneath the successive traumas of the Great War, the Depression, the Defeat of 1940, Vichy, and the Algerian War. One of the fathers of the Annales school, Marc Bloch, was himself a veteran of the Great War. But Bloch grew increasingly skeptical about his own ability to comment on the war and upon resuming his career after the Armistice turned his attention to the distant temporal structures of the Middle Ages.[5] The great political and diplomatic historian of the 1914–1918 war, Pierre Renouvin (who lost an arm at the Chemin des Dames in 1917), was not himself an Annaliste.[6] But he had three students whose path-breaking work clearly situated the Great War in the *longue durée* of a resilient, republican France. In a monumental study of French public opinion in 1914, Jean-Jacques Becker described a national community motivated by grim determination rather than atavistic nationalist fury.[7] Guy Pedroncini wrote the first history of the 1917 French army mutinies based on archival sources.[8] He concluded that collective disobedience had not been 'political', but rather constituted a sophisticated protest against the existing strategy for carrying out the war. In other words, ever-patriotic French soldiers simply sought proper leadership on the battlefield. In a similar vein, Antoine Prost argued that trench experience did not serve as a conduit to fascism through veterans' organizations, which in France remained characterized by consistent loyalty to the Third Republic.[9]

The opening in 1992 of the Historial de la Grande Guerre in Péronne, in the battlefields of the Somme, provided an institutional locus for the continued articulation of consent. The whole intellectual project of the Historial revolved around thinking about the Great War differently. As one piece of promotional literature put it:

> As up to date as the architecture, the 'scenography' (that is, the staging of the objects) favors understanding and emotion. . . . The Historial de la Grande

Guerre seeks, along with its visitors, to grasp what were the lives of everyone in
and around the conflict; it does not limit itself to a single point of view.[10]

But the pedagogy of what became known as 'Péronne' historians proved more focused than
the elegant yet detached ambiance of the museum suggested. To mark its opening, the
Historial held a large international conference in July 1992 the proceedings of which were
published in 1994. The organizers and the papers clearly articulated the close relationship
between *culture de guerre* and consent:

What is striking about this term [*culture de guerre*] is the sense of homogeneity
that it carries with it, linked to the crushing weight of this culture on the societies
that took part in the conflict.[11]

The homogeneity of war culture was both cause and effect, as the protagonists fought the
stalemated war with ever-greater ferocity. Commitment on both sides of the conflict
deepened with adversity.[12]

Péronne historians over the course of the 1990s produced a broad array of studies
that examined the particulars of consent. In the published version of his doctoral dissertation, Audoin-Rouzeau affirmed the deep, consensual patriotism of French soldiers as
conveyed in trench newspapers.[13] He argued that censorship mattered, both official censorship and 'self'-censorship [not bothering to write things soldiers knew would cause them
trouble with the authorities]. But the boundaries enforced by censorship did not mean that
soldiers lacked means of articulating their relationship to the war in surprisingly nuanced
terms. Soldiers wrote for each other, and rarely spared themselves the ghastly details of
service in the trenches. It is thus necessary to take seriously their self-construction of
their experience. I revisited the French army mutinies of 1917, in a study of one infantry
division from 1914 to 1918 that both drew from and contested Pedroncini's conclusions.[14]
I agreed with him that the mutinies constituted an agonized recommitment to the war
rather than a refutation of it. But as an overt challenge to the army, most fundamental institution of the French state, the mutinies were inherently 'political'. Consequently, historians'
attention ought to shift to the soldiers themselves, and how they reconfigured their relationship to the war in a situation in which formal command authority had temporarily vanished.
Because of a deeply internalized sense of themselves as citizens of the French Republic,
I concluded, the discontented soldiers decided to return to repression and the trenches rather
than lose the war. Paradoxically, the mutinies are thus best understood as an articulation of
consent.

Other scholars focused on consent in civilian society, or how consent at the front
and in the interior evolved in tandem. Annette Becker showed how religion informed
consent, both in the front lines and behind them. Her analysis drew from a trenchant observation written by Jacques Rivière from a prisoner-of-war camp in Germany in 1915: 'One
makes war for a certain way of seeing the world. Every war is a war of religion'.[15] Europeans
by the millions flocked to houses of worship as war broke out in August 1914. Catholicism,
Protestantism, and Judaism all provided ways for soldiers and civilians to understand death,
and to convey meaning on a desperate and ever more totalized struggle. Individual soldiers
and the families they left behind could imagine themselves as martyrs, whose agonies
imitated those of Jesus Christ. Countless postcards, stained-glass windows, and stone monuments portrayed soldiers in what Catholics call the *imitatio Christi*, the imitation of Christ.
Soldiers seized upon religious imagery as avidly as civilians, whether in carving graffiti or
whole altars dug into exposed rock at the front, or in fashioning elaborate crucifixes carved
out of shell casings. Many believers were convinced that the most horrible of wars had to

have eschatological implications. The Almighty Himself must have designed the conflict as a final showdown between good and evil. Some conceived the war as a Crusade, a global struggle to rid the world of sin and disbelief. Utopians such as Woodrow Wilson, and strident critics of organized religion such as Henri Barbusse, were profoundly influenced by religions notions of apocalyptic time.[16]

Other historians of consent drew from well-established practices of social history, and situated France in a transnational history of the Great War. A collection of essays edited by John Horne explored a 'second mobilization', as societies shifted in from the expectations of a short war in 1914 to a long war after 1915.[17] Coming out of the tradition of demographic history at Cambridge University, Jay Winter arrived at some surprising conclusions about the effects of war on public health.[18] Using data for the British case, he argued that apart from those age cohorts actually at the front, life expectancy actually improved between 1914 and 1918. A broader comparative study of wartime Paris, London, and Berlin carried out by Winter and a team of historians yielded similar results in a more nuanced form.[19] As Winter later put it, 'in France and Britain, in contrast to Germany, the war was not waged at the expense of the health of the civilian population'.[20] In other words, the consent of civilians to continuing the war had material foundations.

Labor and gender historians also articulated consent, generally without expressly intending to do so. Their work stressed the continuities that underpinned the resilience of societies at war, and hinted at the more ruthless characteristics of consent. Jean-Louis Robert examined the evolution of the militant worker during the Great War, as the exception that proved the rule. As the war dragged on, a minority of French workers denounced the war as the distillation of the iniquities of capitalism. But these just warriors of Socialism simply threw into relief the cooperation of the millions of other workers who toiled night and day for years on end, at wages that never really kept up with wartime inflation, to keep the war going.[21]

Indirectly, the work of gender historians also revealed the ideological underpinnings of consent. They showed how constructed roles of male and female bent but never broke under the stresses of war. Indeed, the flexibility of gender roles, paradoxically, contributed to the resilience of gender hierarchies. In turn, these hierarchies contributed to the resilience of the societies that fought so desperate a struggle for so long. While they seldom addressed the issue of consent directly, gender historians showed how the effects of consent need not be admirable. Laura Lee Downs showed how employers in the metallurgical and armaments industries proved endlessly inventive at recasting and exploiting gender differences in order to keep weapons and profits flowing.[22] Mary Louise Roberts showed how images of gender disorder caused by the Great War helped mobilize political conservatism, both during the war and after.[23]

By the late 1990s, the renaissance in French historiography of the Great War had not yet given rise to any unusual amount of controversy. Apart from a handful of very elderly exceptions, the remaining veterans had all died, sparing scholars of the Great War the kinds of reproaches that still sometime render fraught the study of World War II. But the study of the *culture de guerre* had within it implications that would lead to controversy. Before the late 1990s, Péronne scholars had not particularly concerned themselves with the violence that, after all, had made the Great War the bloodiest conflict in all of European history up to that time. In the *culture de guerre*, societies mobilized, died, mourned, and remembered, all rather bloodlessly. But the further interrogation of consent eventually had to pose the question of violence. For what exactly was it that societies in the war of 1914–1918 needed to consent to?

Brutalisation, consent, and coercion

> Death, the ultimate violence, lay at the heart of the totalization of the conflict.
> But paradoxically, first soldiers' testimony, and then the historiography, long
> made death 'aseptic' [«aseptisé» la mort], at the risk of making partly
> incomprehensible the history of the Great War. A great deal of what lies at
> the heart of the worst experiences of the century lay hidden and await
> exploration.[24]

In their 1997 article on the *culture de guerre*, Audoin-Rouzeau and Annette Becker laid down a gauntlet; the time had come for historians to delve into the darker side of consent. While perhaps they pushed it further than necessary, they had a point about the historiography. One could dispute whether soldiers' testimony in fact spared readers many gory details, above all in testimony published in close proximity to the conflict.[25] Certainly the contents of the most famous literary accounts, such as Barbusse's *Le Feu* (1916) or Erich Marie Remarque's *All Quiet on the Western Front* (1929), were drenched in blood. Perhaps there seemed little left to add. Military historians traditionally were interested in military outcomes more than in the details of the carnage producing them. My own first book explored limiting and regulating violence, and largely avoided detailed descriptions of its effects.

But the scholarly ground around the violence of war was clearly shifting by the late 1990s, for a variety of reasons. Here too, historians of France and the Great War followed more general shifts in the study of the history of war. The century and the millennium were coming to an end. The wars of ex-Yugoslavia grimly reminded the inhabitants of a uniting European continent of the hatreds and the brutality they wanted to forget in their rather recent past. Historians more generally continued to restore violence to the history of modern warfare. As long ago as 1986, John Dower argued that the Pacific War could only be thought of as a race war, on both sides.[26] Niall Ferguson dared suggest in 1998 that some enjoyed killing in the Great War, while Joanna Bourke in a book published in 1999 believed that personal killing in the twentieth century deserved an 'intimate' history.[27] Omer Bartov examined the 'barbarization' of warfare on the Eastern Front during World War II.[28] Most famously, Christopher Browning and Daniel J. Goldhagen debated whether perpetrators of the Final Solution were 'ordinary men' or 'ordinary Germans'.[29]

More specifically, many Péronne historians saw themselves following in the footsteps of George Mosse, who had shown how the cultural processes of memory of Europe's wars could trivialize and instrumentalize the violence to which whole societies had consented in waging them.[30] They sought to show that the Great War had done the 'cultural work' of breaking down nineteenth-century boundaries of appropriate violence in warfare and the distinction between combatants and civilians. In short, the carnage of the war of 1939–1945 in Europe had been made thinkable in the war of 1914–1918.[31]

Some of the reasons for the unprecedented ferocity of combat in the Great War were technological. The macabre possibilities of nineteenth-century innovations such as refined rifles, smokeless powder, machine guns, and large-caliber artillery were fully realized in 1914, with the outbreak of the first general European war since Napoleon. Poison gas, while responsible for only a tiny proportion of casualties in the Great War, offered a new and uniquely terrifying way to maim and kill.[32]

Yet some of the reasons for the specific frightfulness of the Great War battlefield were social and cultural. In a painstaking study that disentangled fact from fiction in the German atrocities of 1914, John Horne and Alan Kramer concluded a form of battlefield panic coupled with a fear of guerrilla warfare behind the rapidly advancing German lines led the invaders to kill at least 5500 Belgian civilians and 500 French.[33] Audoin-Rouzeau continued to elaborate the rather bloodthirsty ways in which the French mobilized for total war. Numberless stories of the *enfant héroique* (heroic child) told of miniature guerrilla warriors who killed and died with a child's dedication and innocence.[34] Women could achieve acquittal for the serious crimes of abortion and infanticide by claiming that they had been raped by the invaders in 1914, and had killed the flesh of their flesh only to preserve the purity of the French race.[35] Annette Becker and Helen McPhail explored the chilling severity, not to say the brutality, of the German occupation of Belgium and Northern France.[36] An argument has begun to emerge that the 'civilized boundaries' of warfare in the nineteenth century were largely shattered in the first year of the war, culminating in an episode historians still barely broached, the Turkish massacres of the Armenians.[37] Nor did the *culture de guerre* easily become a culture of peace, as Bruno Cabanes showed in a study of the demobilization of the French army after the Armistice.[38]

Major anniversaries can both bring history abruptly into the public sphere and create or at least expose fault lines in historical inquiry. In November 1998, the eightieth anniversary of the end of the Great War, French Prime Minister Lionel Jospin made a speech in which he stated that those soldiers executed in the wake of the 1917 mutinies ought to be 'reintegrated, completely, into our national memory'.[39] The claim was somewhat disingenuous, given that some 49 soldiers executed as a result of the mutinies had never left national memory, as indicated by their sporadic but continued appearance in books and films.[40] In retrospect, the speech looked like an ill-fated jockeying for position in an unhappy political cohabitation between Jospin and President Jacques Chirac. An unseemly polemic followed, as politicians on the Right took the bait offered by Jospin, and railed against those who would honor soldiers who defied military authority. Neither side consulted historians until the dispute was in full flower.

The affair helped crystallize what could be called a counter-*culture de guerre* at the dawn of the new millennium, among scholars who disagreed with the arguments made by Péronne historians. To be sure, there remained something to discuss. Péronne historians' preoccupation with consent and brutalization had at the very least marginalized the voices of those who in one way or another opposed the war at the time. Contrary currents of opinion had long been in the mix, notably in Rémy Cazal's persistent advocacy of the antiwar diary of Louis Barthas, and in Frédéric Rousssseau's survey of European combatants' experience, which emphasized coercion.[41]

Yet the year 2000 proved a turning point, with the publication by Audoin-Rouzeau and Annette Becker of *14–18: Retrouver la guerre* (literally '14–18: To Find Again the War') in a high-profile series, published by Gallimard and overseen by Pierre Nora.[42] In itself, the book did not seek to break new ground so much as to synthesize a decade of research by an international group of scholars. Some read it, perhaps unfairly, as a manifesto of a dogmatic historiographical school. Several critics found the book too categorical and overstated in its argument, as indicated in some of the titles of review essays such as 'The War of 1914 is Not Lost' (and hence not in need of finding again) and '1914–1918: Keep Looking'.[43]

The notion of consent proved particularly divisive. Rémy Cazals and Frédéric Rousseau argued that consent amounted to little more than nationalist coercion under another name. They contended instead that the whole foucauldian array of disciplinary institutions inculcated in the soldier what they call a 'culture of obedience', the prelude to victimization at the front. They wrote,

> Education and instruction did not just make patriots, they made obedient patriots. Whether they came from the countryside or the workers' cities, all soldiers interiorized at the most profound level this culture of obedience.[44]

Likewise, such critics rejected brutalization as an extreme manifestation of consent. They pointed out, correctly, that artillery did most of the killing in the Great War, under conditions not much less anonymous than those of war from the air today. The few who killed individuated enemy soldiers they saw, and the fewer still who enjoyed it, could safely be considered the exceptions that proved the rule.[45]

Of the controversy over consent versus constraint, and perhaps letting himself get a bit carried away by military language, journalist Jean Birnbaum wrote of 'fortified conferences, editorial ambushes, academic assassinations, and targeted reviews' to describe the resulting war-within-the-war over consent.[46] In a survey of the controversy in English, Jay Winter agreed: 'when you touch the First World War in France, you are playing with fire'.[47] Although he was himself a participant in the debate, Antoine Prost concluded that 'the polemic between the school of constraint and the school of consent is largely artificial.'[48] I had argued some years previously that republican political identity constituted a critical source of internalized suasion in the mutinies, and none of the historians of consent argued that it presumed an utterly free human will. Nevertheless, criticism of consent continued for a time with undiminished vigor.[49]

Historiographical controversies, of course, do not last forever. Differences often turn out to be epistemological or political in nature, and controversies that go on too long can simply deteriorate into restatements of these differences. Some Péronne historians (myself among them) have begun to move away from the Great War per se. The counter-*culture de guerre* historians have established their own organization, the Collectif de Recherche International et de Débat sur la Guerre de 1914–1918 (CRID 14–18), with its own sophisticated Web site.[50] Wisely moving beyond simply critiquing Péronne historians, the CRID group seeks to contribute to 'social history in understanding the war, and to a social history renewed by contributions from the other social sciences over the last twenty years'.[51] Péronne historians' fixation on 'culture', it seems, had fostered an 'exoticism that too often contributed to the event studied for itself alone and from the perspective of the exception'. Yet CRID seems to wear the theory of social history as lightly as Péronne historians have worn the theory of cultural history. The end of the first decade of the new millennium will bring with it the 90th anniversaries of the 1917 mutinies, the Armistice of 1918, and the Paris Peace Conference of 1919. We should not be surprised if controversy in some form about the legacy of the Great War reappears.

Notes

1   J. J. Becker, 'Présentation', in J. J. Becker and S. Audoin-Rouzeau (eds.), *Les sociétés européennes et la guerre de 1914–18* (Nanterre: Publications de l'Université de Nanterre, 1990), 11–12. Unless otherwise indicated, all translations are my own.

2   S. Audoin-Rouzeau and A. Becker, 'Violence et consentement: la «culture de guerre» du premier conflit mondial', in J-P. Rioux and J-F. Sirinelli (eds.), *Pour une histoire culturelle* (Paris: Éditions du Seuil, 1997), 252.

3   For a work on the Great War that operates squarely in debates over cultural history, see D. Sherman, *The Construction of Memory in Interwar France* (Chicago, IL: University of Chicago Press, 1999).

4   Overviews of consent include J. Winter and A. Prost, *The Great War in History* (Cambridge: Cambridge University Press, 2005), esp. ch. 4, 7; S. Audoin-Rouzeau and A. Becker, *14–18: Understanding the Great War* (New York, NY: Hill and Wang, 2002).

5   See L. Smith, 'Le récit du témoin: Formes et pratiques d'écriture dans les témoignages sur la Grande Guerre', in C. Prochasson and A. Rasmussen (eds.), *Vrai et Faux dans la Grande Guerre* (Paris: La Découverte, 2004), esp. 295–300.

6   Renouvin remained a towering presence in French historiography of the Great War through the 1960s. Among his famous general works see *La Crise européenne et la grande guerre: 1914–1918*

(Paris: Félix Alcan, 1934); *Histoire des relations internationales* (Paris: Hachette, 1955–57); *La première guerre mondiale* (Paris: Presses Universitaires de France, 1965).

7   J. J. Becker, *1914: Comment les français sont entrés dans la guerre* (Paris: Presses de la Fondation des Sciences Politiques, 1977). On civilian society, see Becker, *The Great War and the French People* (New York, NY: St. Martin's Press, 1986).

8   Guy Pedroncini, *Les Mutineries de 1917* (Paris: Presses Universitaires de France, 1967).

9   A. Prost, *Les Anciens Combattants et la société française*, 3 vols. (Paris: Presses de la Fondation des Sciences Politiques, 1977).

10   T. Compère-Morel, *L'Historial de la Grande Guerre et le Circuit de Souvenir* (Tournai: La Renaissance du Livre, 2000), 7.

11   J. J. Becker, et al. (eds.), 'Introduction', *Guerres et cultures, 1914–1918* (Paris: Armand Colin, 1994), 8.

12   This aspect of consent is further explored in L. Smith, *The Embattled Self: French Soldiers' Testimony of the Great War* (Ithaca, NY: Cornell University Press, 2007), ch. 3. I suggest further that there may be something uniquely 'French' about consent as presently construed, as a form of commitment derived from a particular form of republican citizenship.

13   S. Audoin-Rouzeau, *Men at War, 1914–1918: National Sentiment and Trench Journalism in France during the First World War*, trans. Helen McPhail (Providence: Berg, 1992).

14   *Between Mutiny and Obedience: The Case of the French Fifth Infantry Division during World War I* (Princeton: Princeton University Press, 1994). See also L. Smith, S. Audoin-Rouzeau, and A. Becker, *France and the Great War, 1914–1918* (Cambridge: Cambridge University Press, 2003).

15   A. Becker, *La Guerre et la foi: de la mort à la mémoire, 1914–1930* (Paris: Armand Colin, 1994), 15. Also published in English as *War and Faith* (Oxford: Berg, 1998).

16   See also Audoin-Rouzeau and Becker, *Understanding the Great War*, ch. 6, 'Great Expectations, Eschatology, Demobilization'. Barbusse was the author of *Under Fire* (1916), to this day the best-selling French novel of the Great War.

17   J. Horne, *State, Society and Mobilization in Europe during the First World War* (Cambridge: Cambridge University Press, 1997).

18   J. Winter, *The Great War and the British People* (Cambridge: Harvard University Press, 1986).

19   J. Winter and J. Louis Robert (eds.), *Capital Cities at War: London, Paris, Berlin 1914–1919* (Cambridge: Cambridge University Press, 1997). The contributors continued their work in the direction of cultural history in *Capital Cities at War: London, Paris, Berlin 1914–1919, Vol. 2, A Cultural History* (Cambridge: Cambridge University Press, 2007).

20   Winter and Prost, *Great War in History*, 161.

21   J. L. Robert, *Les Ouvriers, la Patrie et la Révolution: Paris, 1914–1919*, Les Annales littéraires de l'Université de Besançon, No. 592 (Besançon: l'Université de Besançon, 1995).

22   L. L. Downs, *Manufacturing Inequality: Gender Division in the French and British Metalworking Industries, 1914–1939* (Ithaca, NY: Cornell University Press, 1995). See also S. Grayzel, *Women's Identities at War: Gender, Motherhood, and Politics in Britain and France during the First World War* (Chapel Hill, NC: University of North Carolina Press, 1999).

23   M. L. Roberts, *Civilization without Sexes: Reconstructing Gender in Postwar France, 1917–1927* (Chicago, IL: University of Chicago Press, 1994). See also M. Darrow, *French Women and the First World War: War Stories of the Home Front* (Oxford: Berg, 2000).

24   Audoin-Rouzeau and Becker, 'Violence et consentement', 257.

25   I suggest otherwise in *Embattled Self*.

26   J. Dower, *War without Mercy: Race and Power in the Pacific War* (New York, NY: Pantheon Books, 1986).

27   N. Ferguson, *The Pity of War: Explaining World War I* (London: Allen Lane, 1998); J. Bourke, *An Intimate History of Killing: Face to Face Killing in Twentieth Century Warfare* (London: Granta Books, 1999).

28   O. Bartov, *The Eastern Front, 1941–45: German Troops and the Barbarization of Warfare* (New York, NY: St. Martins, 1986); Bartov, *Hitler's Army: Soldiers, Nazis, and War in the Third Reich* (New York, NY: Oxford University Press, 1991).

29   C. Browning: *Ordinary Men: Reserve Police Battalion 101 and the Final Solution in Poland* (New York, NY: Harper Collins, 1992); D. Goldhagen, *Hitler's Willing Executioners: Ordinary Germans and the Holocaust* (New York, NY: Alfred A. Knopf, 1996).

30   G. Mosse, *Fallen Soldiers: Shaping the Memory of the World Wars* (New York, NY: Oxford University Press, 1990).

31   See particularly the essays in S. Audoin-Rouzeau, A. Becker, C. Ingrao, and H. Rousso (eds.), *La Violence de guerre, 1914–1945: Approches comparées des deux conflits mondiaux* (Brussels: Éditions Complexe, 2002).

32   O. Lepick, *La Grande Guerre chimique, 1914–1918* (Paris: Presses Universitaires de France, 1998).

33   J. Horne and A. Kramer, *German Atrocities, 1914: A History of Denial* (New Haven, CT: Yale University Press, 2001).

34   S. Audoin-Rouzeau, *La Guerre des enfants, 1914–1918* (Paris: Armand Colin, 2004 [1996]), especially ch. 3.

35   S. Audoin-Rouzeau, *L'Enfant de l'ennemi, 1914–1918* (Paris: Aubier, 1995).

36   A. Becker, *Oubliés de la grande guerre: humanitaire et culture de guerre, populations occupées, déportés civils, prisonniers de guerre* (Paris: Noêsis, 1998); H. McPhail, *The Long Silence: Civilian Life under the German Occupation of Northern France, 1914–1918* (London: I. B. Tauris, 1999).

37   See J. Horne (ed.), *Vers la guerre totale: le tournant de 1914–1915* (Paris: Tallandier, forthcoming).

38   B. Cabanes, *La Victoire endeuillée: la sortie de guerre des soldats français (1918–1920)* (Paris: Seuil, 2004).

39   N. Offenstadt, *Les Fusillés de la grande guerre et la mémoire collective (1914–1999)* (Paris: Odile Jacob, 1999). A short summary of the polemic around Jospin's speech appears in Smith, Audoin-Rouzeau, and Becker, *France and the Great War*, 186–8.

40   These 49 constituted only a tiny percentage of some 147,000 casualties resulting from the Chemin des Dames offensive precipitating the mutinies.

41   R. Cazals (ed.), *Les Carnets de guerre de Louis Barthas, tonnelier, 1914–1918* (Paris: Librairie François Maspero, 1978); Cazals and S. Caucanas (eds.), *Traces de 14–18: Actes du colloque de Carcassonne* (Carcassonne: Éditions 'Les Audois', 1997); F. Rousseau, *La Guerre censurée: une histoire des combattants européens de 14–18* (Paris: Éditions Seuil, 1999).

42   'Bibliothèque des Histoires' Series (Paris, Gallimard, 2000). This is the French version of *14–18: Understanding the Great War*.

43   Antoine Prost, 'La Guerre de 1914 n'est pas perdue', *Le Mouvement Social*, 199 (2002): 95–102; Rémy Cazals, '1914–1918: Chercher Encore', op cit., 107–13.

44   Rémy Cazals and Frédéric Rousseau, *14–18: le cri d'une génération* (Toulouse: Éditions Privat, 2001), 145. See also Rousseau, *L'Affaire Norton Cru* (Paris: Seuil, 2003). The most relevant work by Michel Foucault is *Discipline and Punish: The Birth of the Prison*, trans. Alan Sheridan (New York, NY: Vintage Books, 1979).

45   See Rémy Cazals, '1914–1918, Oser penser, oser écrire', *Genèses*, 46 (2002): 26–43; Nicolas Mariot, 'Faut-il être motivé pour tuer?: sur quelques explications aux violences de guerre', *Genèses*, 53 (2003): 154–77; Antoine Prost, 'Les limites de la brutalisation: tuer sur le front occidental, 1914–1918', *Vingtième Siècle*, 81 (2004): 5–20.

46   Jean Birnbaum, '1914–1918, guerre de tranchées entre historiens', *Le Monde*, March 11, 2006, http://www.lemonde.fr/web/article/0,1-0@2-3230,36-749539,0.html, accessed on 26 July 2006.

47   Jay Winter, 'P vs C: The Still Burning Anger when the French Talk of the First World War', *Times Literary Supplement*, June 16, 2006.

48   Prost, 'La Guerre de 1914 n'est pas perdue', 98.

49   See also Nicolas Offenstadt (ed.), *Le Chemin des Dames: de l'événement à la mémoire* (Paris: Stock, 2004); Rémy Cazals, Emmanuelle Picard, and Denis Rolland (eds.), *La Grande Guerre: pratiques et experiences* (Toulouse: Éditions Privat, 2005); Denis Rolland, *La Grève des tranchées: les mutineries de 1917* (Paris: Imago, 2005).

50   http://www.crid1418.org.

51   'Charte scientifique du CRID 14–18', http://www.crid1418.org/a_propos/charte)_ini.html, accessed on 26 July 2006.

Index

acculturation *see* anthropology

adolescence: nineteenth-century conceptions 32; in Puritan New England 193; and value formation 20; *see also* childhood

advertising: and consumer economy 62–3; of 'improving' toys 214

agency: attributed to 'technology' 306; divine 177; in history xxx, xlvii; human, versus technological determinism 267; individual, in shaping culture xix, xxi, xli, li; in the Renaissance 223; women's 2; women's consumption as a declaration of 66; *see also* appropriation; creativity; reception; socialization

almanac *see* print

anatomy: and Christian Platonism 179; and race 104

ancient world: and biographies 228; and geography 79; Israel's history xix; rediscovery of classics 72; and time 72; and writing 251, 274–6

Annales school xxxvi, xxxvii, xl, xli, xlii, xliii, xliv, xlvii, 329; *see also* Ariès; Bloch; Braudel; Febvre; Le Goff

anthropology: and acculturation 11, 313–20; Barzun on xxxviii; and cultural history xix, xxvii, xxxiii, xlv, xlvi, xlix; and 'culture' xliii, 152; and Darnton xlv, xlvi; and Davis xlvi, 127; and economic history 40; and Geertz xlv; and history xxii, xxxviii, xlv; and medieval history 46–7; and military culture 313–20; and 'new cultural history'

xlvii–xlviii; and *nouvelle histoire* xliv; and the 'Other' 104; and 'popular culture' 127–8, 151–2; and 'social life of things' 152; and technological 'progress' 298; and Thomas xlv; and Tylor xxxiii; and Ware xli; *see also* Douglas

antisemitism 104–5, 107

apprentice: early modern 193, 197, 210; and initiation into adult skills 143–4; nineteenth-century professional 32, 35

appropriation (cultural) xli, xlvi, 152; and Chartier xlvii, xlviii, l, li, 60, 64, 127, 129, 151; collective (Gramsci) 145; and cultural encounter 104; of historical writing 19; and popular culture 127; *see also* bricolage; creativity; reading

archaeology: and cultural history xix; and material culture xxviii, xxxiii, xl, 154, 187

Ariès, Philippe: on death xliii; discovery of childhood xliii, 186–7

Arnold, Matthew: and Burckhardt xxxv, xl; on 'culture' xxi, xxxii–xxxiii; *Culture and Anarchy* xxxii; and literature xliii

art (fine): as culture xxi, xxviii, xxix, xxx, xl, xlii, xlix, 152, 299; Cubism 72; and cultural history xxviii, xxxi–xxxv, xxxix; and perspective 71; portraits and the self 224–8, 230; twentieth-century and technology 303; and war 309

artifact: and consumption 61; as cultural construct 143, 153; material xix, xxviii, xxxiii, 209; technological 281, 306

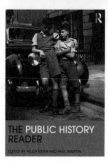

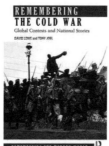

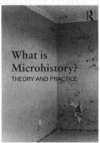